THE
STUART CONSTITUTION
1603-1688

FOR
JACK PLUMB

THE
STUART CONSTITUTION
1603-1688

DOCUMENTS AND COMMENTARY

EDITED AND INTRODUCED BY

J. P. KENYON

G. F. GRANT PROFESSOR OF HISTORY
IN THE UNIVERSITY OF HULL
SOMETIME FELLOW OF CHRIST'S COLLEGE, CAMBRIDGE

CAMBRIDGE
AT THE UNIVERSITY PRESS
1969

Published by the Syndics of the Cambridge University Press
Bentley House, 200 Euston Road, London N.W.1
American Branch: 32 East 57th Street, New York, N.Y. 10022

Standard Book Numbers:
521 05884 8 clothbound
521 09370 8 paperback

First Published 1966
Reprinted 1969

Printed in Great Britain
at the University Printing House, Cambridge
(Brooke Crutchley, University Printer)

PREFACE

This volume is intended to provide a representative and easily accessible selection of documents concerned with, and often in themselves comprising, the political and constitutional history of the seventeenth century in England. It overlaps two older collections, J. R. Tanner's *Constitutional Documents of the Reign of James I* and S. R. Gardiner's *Constitutional Documents of the Puritan Revolution.* Since they were published in a less affluent society each is comparable in size with the present volume, and they retain their value as source books, as a glance at my footnotes will show. But Tanner's commentary is in many respects out of date, while Gardiner offered none at all, apart from a short introduction, and his choice of documents was geared to the requirements of the Oxford Schools in the closing years of the nineteenth century.

The Civil Wars and the Interregnum make it impossible to submit the seventeenth century to a static analysis, which is why this volume falls into three books, divided at 1640 and 1660, with a fourth book dealing with certain themes that persisted throughout the period. Moreover, the immense volume of printed material produced in an age of almost continuous crisis in Church and State has obliged me to omit a great deal which I regard as desirable and some will think essential.

I have been fortunate in coming after Dr G. R. Elton, whose *Tudor Constitution* not only provided me with a model but also treated of some organs common to the Tudor and Stuart state so fully and admirably that I have been able to omit them altogether or mention them only briefly. My book, therefore, should be read in conjunction with his, even though it must be to my disadvantage. I might add that without Dr Elton's firm encouragement at every stage I doubt whether I would ever have completed this book. He also gave me the benefit of his advice on several specific points, read the whole of the first draft in typescript and helped me to reduce it by one third to its present size. That is not to say that he, or anyone else mentioned in this preface, is responsible for errors of fact or judgement remaining.

I am also grateful to Professor William Haller, for answering questions on specific points, and to Professor G. E. Aylmer, who discussed the project with me at an early stage, to my great advantage.

Mr J. Anthony Williams placed at my disposal his specialised knowledge of seventeenth-century recusancy, and thereby contributed a great deal to chapter 13. I also owe much to the staff of the University Library, Hull, and particularly Mr Peter Sheldon. My wife and my secretary, Mrs Kay Austin, between them typed the final draft of the book; a thankless task performed with great patience and accuracy.

Finally, I must acknowledge the patience and consideration of two successive secretaries to the Syndics, who have waited five years for this book and never doubted that it would be completed.

West Ella,   J.P.K.
East Yorks
April 1965

CONTENTS

vii

CONTENTS

TABLE OF DOCUMENTS

In chronological order
References are to the numbers of the documents

TABLE OF DOCUMENTS

TABLE OF DOCUMENTS

Throughout the book figures in heavy type refer to documents

ACKNOWLEDGEMENTS

Thanks are due to the following for permission to reprint the documents indicated: The University of Minnesota (**10a, b, c, d**); Messrs Jackson Son & Co. Ltd (**138**), (**139**); Harvard University Press (**95**); Chetham Society (**131**); Yale University Press (**10d, e**), (**30**), (**54**), (**63**); Suffolk Records Society (**82**); Columbia University Press (**89**); Manchester University Press (**81**); J. M. Dent & Sons Ltd and The University of Chicago Press (**87**); and also to the Public Record Office and Dr Williams' Library for their assistance. Particulars of sources are given at the end of each extract.

ABBREVIATIONS

APC	*Acts of the Privy Council.*
CJ	*Commons Journals.*
CSPD	*Calendars of State Papers Domestic.*
EHR	*English Historical Review.*
GCD	S. R. Gardiner (ed.), *Constitutional Documents of the Puritan Revolution*, 3rd ed. Oxford, 1906.
HMC	*Historical Manuscripts Commission.*
LJ	*Lords Journals.*
PCD	G. W. Prothero (ed.), *Select Statutes and Other Constitutional Documents Illustrative of the Reigns of Elizabeth and James I*, 4th ed. Oxford, 1913.
PH	William Cobbett (ed.), *The Parliamentary History of England*, 36 vols. London, 1806–20.
P.R.O.	Public Record Office, London.
SR	*Statutes of the Realm.*
ST	W. Cobbett and T. B. Howell (eds.), *State Trials*, 33 vols. London, 1809–26.
TCD	J. R. Tanner (ed.), *Constitutional Documents of the Reign of James I.* Cambridge, 1930.

The full titles of all other books cited will be found in the bibliography. The spelling and punctuation in documents have been modernised wherever it is possible to do so without altering the sense or the emphasis. All dates are in the old style, with the year beginning on 1 January.

INTRODUCTION

The study of the seventeenth-century constitution is dominated by the work of the great Victorians, Gardiner and Macaulay, interpreted and to a limited extent amplified by Sir Charles Firth and J. R. Tanner. Both Gardiner and Macaulay were often extremely acute, realistic and, of course, well-informed, and they still have a great deal to offer the student;[1] but their whig interpretation of the seventeenth century in general—of an aggressive but incompetent dynasty, whose attempts to suppress the rights of the subject to free speech, property and due process of law were resisted in manly fashion by a representative assembly which mirrored all that was best or most important in the nation—is long out of date.

Today we believe that there was no right or wrong solution to the problems of the seventeenth century. The Revolution of 1688 stamped England as a wildly eccentric country outside the mainstream of European political development; indeed, it is doubtful if more than half the governing classes accepted it, and if they could have foreseen its consequences, or even if they had realised clearly what they were doing at the time, that proportion would have sunk to five per cent or less. The natural bent of European government was towards enlightened despotism and centralisation, which involved the sacrifice of the medieval estates or representative assemblies; England in the 1630's and to some extent in the 1680's was moving along these lines. The Diet of Brandenburg was soon to follow the Cortes of Castile and Aragon and the States General of France into obscurity, and the Parliament at Westminster might well be next. Its counterparts at Dublin and Edinburgh were already the obedient tools of king and Council.

But to emulate their European colleagues the Stuarts needed two things they did not possess: a paid bureaucracy in the provinces, and a standing army. (It would be advantageous also to be able to secure a steady supply of money, but this was not essential; most European monarchs were chronically short of money, and periodically went bankrupt altogether, without endangering their regimes.) So, despite

---

[1] For an example of Gardiner's disconcerting modernity, see Hill, *Society and Puritanism*, pp. 221–2.

I

a background of contestation over forms of worship, taxation and the administration of justice, which was merely a continuation of similar squabbles under Elizabeth, in the foreground of the disputes between the Stuart kings and their Parliaments lay foreign policy and the army. All these kings hoped to fight a successful war, which had always eluded their predecessors, and at the end of that war establish a permanent army. Thus Charles I, Charles II, even James I, spent the greater part of their time and energy—more than is commonly supposed—in fashioning their foreign policy. It was their misfortune that these policies were not only unsuccessful but bitterly unpopular. Up to 1618 James I's attempts at a *rapprochement* with Spain were regarded with indulgence, but the outbreak of the Thirty Years War brought an immediate revulsion of feeling. From then on Parliament was obsessed with the danger of the Counter Reformation, and despite the war with Spain from 1625 to 1630 the policy of Charles I was so ambiguous that in 1640 it was easy for his opponents in Parliament to associate him in the public mind with the great European conspiracy for the suppression of Protestantism. It was this suspicion that led to the outbreak of the Civil Wars. Of course, Charles I's fiscal and ecclesiastical policies were a source of irritation, and made accommodation much more difficult, but in the summer of 1641 he and the Long Parliament reached agreement on a series of reforms which satisfied all the demands they had put forward, except one. And Charles went to war in 1642, not in defence of his right to levy taxation at will (he had abandoned that), nor in defence of his right to control the Church (he might have done, but Parliament had not yet seriously challenged that control), but in defence of his right to command the army and to choose his own advisers. Contemporaries, at any rate, were quite clear on this point.[1]

The Civil Wars broke down temporarily the exceedingly strong and well-organised assumptions that maintained the pre-war social structure, and the subsequent inability of Parliament to reach agreement with the defeated king or deal effectively with its own captains left the way open for some of the most daring experiments that have ever been made with the English constitution. For a few wild months in 1647 and 1648 it seemed that England might even topple into democracy.

[1] Though the claim of some of the spokesmen of the New Model Army to be fighting for religious freedom later obscured the point. (See, for instance, no. 91, p. 325 below). Edmund Ludlow said bluntly in 1659: 'The great quarrel between the king and us was the militia. Either he or we were guilty' (Burton, *Diary*, III, 145).

But the massive inertia of the class structure was far too strong. The king was executed, but only to make way for a narrow, oligarchic republic on the Dutch or Venetian model. Cromwell overthrew the republic, but by then the messianic radicalism of his fighting years was fast sloughing away, and his consolidation or consummation of the 'Revolution' was only superficially experimental. By 1657 the retreat on monarchy had begun, and on Cromwell's death it became a rout, which ended in the confusion of the Restoration.

The *status quo ante bellum* restored, the situation of 1642 soon recurred. Charles I had tried to rule without Parliament, his son kept his parliaments too long; and in 1678 the Popish Plot of 1640 returned in a more virulent and hysterical form. Probably only the cult of the martyred Charles I and visceral fear of another civil war saved the monarchy. James II's remedy, naturally, was to raise an army, which he found it remarkably easy to do, and if he had not at the same time played on his subjects' nerves by attempting to secure complete toleration for his co-religionists, and if he had not quarrelled with the ruling classes in the process, he might well have succeeded.

But even in 1689 the measures taken to deal with the central problem of the seventeenth-century constitution, military power, were feeble and hesitant. It was solved indirectly, even furtively, by Parliament's refusal to vote William III a regular income. Because 1689 saw the inauguration of 'parliamentary monarchy' it is too easily assumed that the opposition programme triumphed. In fact, it is difficult to see that the opposition to the Stuarts had any programme, except the preservation of what they conceived to be the 'ancient constitution' and the maintenance of their own class power. The years 1640 to 1645 were the great years of the parliamentary gentry, but then they were swept aside; and they were swept aside not only because there were no leaders to replace Pym and Hampden, but because neither Pym nor Hampden nor their successors had any viable programme for the future. They were 'conservationists' just as much as Charles I or Strafford. And subsequently the quality of the Commons gentry shows a remarkable decline; from Pym's Middle Party to the Exclusionists, and from the Exclusionists to the October Club of 1710. What these groups had in common was a dislike of efficient, centralised government, extreme gullibility and a poor tactical sense. They produced plenty of demagogues and incendiaries, like Eliot, Russell and St John, but only one statesman, John Pym—and even he would have lost his opportunity but for the intervention of the Scots. [1] Pym and his immediate associates were selfish, narrow minded and class-orientated, but they had a sense of public and national responsibility lacking in their sons and grand-sons. An opposition that became increasingly reactionary and irrespon-sible won the plaudits of posterity but lost the day, and the broad stream of statesmanship that stemmed from Pym, Hampden, Brooke and Holles petered out in the eighteenth-century inanities of Sir John Hinde Cotton and Sir Watkyn Williams-Wynn. Who gained by the revolution of 1688 has yet to be decided, but it was not the House of Commons.

[1] It is often forgotten that Charles I's defeat was precipitated by his failure to control Scotland and Ireland, not England. The role of Scotland was particularly important, and Professor Burrell's detailed study of Scotland 1630–41 is eagerly awaited. In the meantime see H. R. Trevor-Roper, 'Scotland and the Puritan Revolution', in *Historical Essays 1600–1750*, p. 78, and Sidney A. Burrell, 'The Covenant Idea as a Revolutionary Symbol', *Church History*, XXVII (1958), 3, 'The Apocalyptic Vision of the Early Covenanters', *Scottish Historical Review*, XLIII (1964), 1.

BOOK I

THE ANCIENT CONSTITUTION
1603–1640

He that goeth about to persuade a multitude that they are not so well governed as they ought to be shall never want attentive and favourable hearers; because they know the manifold defects whereunto every kind of regiment is subject, but the secret lets and difficulties, which in public proceedings are innumerable and inevitable, they have not ordinarily the judgement to consider. And because such as openly reprove supposed disorders of state are taken for principal friends to the common benefit of all and for men that carry singular freedom of mind, under this fair and plausible colour whatsoever they utter passeth for good and current. That which wanteth in the weight of their speech is supplied by the aptness of men's minds to accept and believe it.

RICHARD HOOKER

CHAPTER I

THE MONARCHY

Samuel Rawson Gardiner's services to scholarship were many and great: his greatest disservice was his persistent description of the Great Rebellion as 'the Puritan Revolution', implying first that all Charles I's opponents shared a certain attitude towards the Church, and second, that they were bent on changing the nature of the State. In fact, the opponents of the monarchy were for the most part sturdy reactionaries who wanted nothing more than to restore the 'ancient constitution' of a century, perhaps even two or three centuries before. One of the most radical men in the Long Parliament was Sir Arthur Haslerigg; yet in 1659, when he reviewed the events of 1642, he was sure 'there was at this time no thought to alter government', and all he and his kind had wanted was 'our ancient liberties with our ancient government'.[1] Perhaps this does not need restating; but Gardiner is not dead when a professional historian can publish a book in 1957 entitled *The Rise of the Revolutionary Party in the English House of Commons, 1603–1629*.[2]

Political theory in the early seventeenth century was simple, patriarchal and authoritative, virtually untouched in terms of practical politics by continental writers like Bodin. From Adam descended the heads of families, from heads of families chiefs of tribes, and from chiefs of tribes, kings. To this extent the patriarchal theories of Sir Robert Filmer were a commonplace (1, 4). The opposing theory, of elective kingship and government by the people, was familiar enough, too, but sturdily rejected (2).

England had the additional complication of a native system of law that appeared to have grown up with the monarchy. The king enjoyed many privileges at Common Law,[3] but whether he was outside or above it or not was a question that had never been settled, largely because it had so very rarely been raised. It was raised often in the reigns of James I and Charles I, for three reasons. First, the steady fall in the value of money made it impossible for the king to live on his hereditary revenues, even in peace-time, though Elizabeth's financial skill and the long war against Spain had disguised the fact. Secondly, James I and Charles I showed no tactical skill in dealing with the House of Commons, a proud and sensitive body whose members were subject to the same economic pressures as the Crown. The Commons were reluctant to authorise additional taxation which might become permanent, so in the intervals of Parliament the king tried various ways of supple-

[1] Burton, *Diary*, III, 87 ff. (7 February 1659).   [2] Williams B. Mitchell.
[3] For a summary of the position, see Holdsworth, *History of English Law*, X, 340 ff.

menting his income, including devices like impositions and ship-money, which had never been specifically declared illegal, but which depended on the assumption that the king—in certain matters at least—had absolute power. The next parliament felt obliged to debate these illicit methods of supply before it even thought of voting any itself, and a vicious circle was established. At the same time the king's position as supreme governor of the Church was continually under review in the Commons, who always insisted that since their predecessors had passed the legislation establishing the English Church in 1559 they were free to amend that establishment. Finally, the king, with the support of certain clerics and lawyers, publicly laid claim to powers as full and complete as those of any monarch in Europe, including the Ottoman Sultan.

Some of James's pronouncements are notorious. In *The Trew Law of Free Monarchies* he asserted that kings were God's vice-regents on earth, that there were no legal limits to their power, and that the sole function of elected assemblies was to give advice.[1] But such pronouncements give a wrong impression of James I. His absolutism was confined to the realm of theory, and though he always believed that he stood in a special relationship with God, in an important and carefully argued speech to Parliament on 21 March 1610 (4) he distinguished between kings in their first creation, whose powers knew no limit, and kings of settled states, who were not obliged to respect the rights and customs of their subjects, but if they did not would answer for it to God. He himself regarded his coronation oath with great seriousness, and by that oath he had promised to respect the laws and customs of England.[2] Thus he was careful always to operate within the framework of the Common Law; he never imprisoned anyone without trial, he never levied money from his subjects without authorisation from Parliament or the courts of Common Law, he never promulgated law of his own accord, even if he believed he could, and he was certainly more moderate and 'constitutional' than Queen Elizabeth.[3] Particularly significant was his reaction in 1610 when the Commons complained that he was abusing proclamations, creating new crimes not recognised by Common Law, and transferring established crimes from one jurisdiction to another. He consulted the two chief justices, Coke and Altham, and meekly accepted their decision against him, though in *The Trew Law of Free Monarchies* he had declared, 'The king makes daily statutes and ordinances, enjoining such pains thereto as he thinks meet, without any advice of Parliament or Estates'.[4] In the same year Dr John Cowell was bitterly criticised for defining the powers of the Crown in terms similar to those used by James in *The Trew Law*.[5] James ordered his book, the *Interpreter*, to be withdrawn, and authorised Salisbury to inform Parliament that he regarded himself as 'king by the Common Law of the land' (3).

---

[1] *TCD*, pp. 9–10.   [2] See *PCD*, pp. 391–2.   [3] Wormuth, *Royal Prerogative*, p. 93.
[4] Coke, *Reports*, pt. XII, §§ 75–6 (vi, 297–9); *TCD*, p. 9.   [5] *Ibid.* pp. 12–14.

James was sensible enough to realise that the practical attributes of a despotic monarchy were an efficient standing army and a paid local bureaucracy, the latter to levy taxes, the former to enforce their collection. Without these, it was best to accept with grace what could not be amended, and in his later parliaments he even abandoned his theoretical position. His opening speech to the Parliament of 1624 is particularly significant in this respect.[1]

Charles I never wrote any books, and he was much more pragmatical than his father. For instance, the long *apologia* he published after the dissolution of Parliament in 1629 reviews recent events in considerable detail, and asserts his right to levy tunnage and poundage and to summon and dismiss Parliament at will, but it does not expound any general theory of kingship. Clearly he tended to regard his duties as supreme governor of the Church more emotionally than his predecessors, perhaps because he was the first king to be raised from birth in the Anglican Church. But he did not necessarily agree with the advanced theologians of his reign, like Sibthorpe, Manwaring and Montague, who asserted the royal supremacy in the State as well as the Church—no doubt he would have liked to do so, but it is not clear that he regarded it as practical politics. There was a strong element of benevolent patriarchalism in the political thinking of the time; it is well expressed in Laud's sermon before Parliament in 1625,[2] and it appears to have caused neither comment nor surprise. From this it is not a long step to Roger Manwaring's sermons on *Religion and Allegiance*, delivered before the king in 1627 and later published (5).[3] No doubt Charles listened complacently enough to Manwaring's absolutist theories, and it is natural that he should offer him promotion in the Church; but when the House of Commons protested he agreed to suppress the sermons without entering upon a discussion of their contents.

Like his father, he was careful not to stray outside the pale of the Common Law as he understood it, and though it is dangerous to lay too much stress on disconnected utterances, his political thought appears to have been entirely conventional, and essentially the same as that voiced by the opposition to his regime. With remarkable unanimity early seventeenth-century Englishmen believed that they were bound to abide by the ancient constitution, which had existed without change time out of mind. By that constitution the monarch had certain prerogatives, the subjects certain rights—particularly rights of property—and neither could be infringed without a dangerous imbalance resulting.[4] Both sides were aware that an imbalance existed by the 1620's, and this was a decade of tension, tension evident, for instance, in the clashing

[1] No. **16**, p. 48 below. [2] No. **42a**, p. 152 below.
[3] Wormuth, *op. cit.* pp. 93–8, makes claims for Manwaring's originality which he cannot sustain. On the other hand, Perry Miller goes too far when he dismisses his central thesis as a 'Reformation platitude' (*Orthodoxy in Massachusetts*, p. 46).
[4] The whole theory is discussed by Pocock, *The Ancient Constitution and the Feudal Law*.

phrases of Thomas Wentworth's famous speech to the Council of the North in December 1628 (7). Similar tension lay behind Charles's denunciation in 1626 of those 'unquiet and restless spirits' whose sole aim was to 'break that circle of order which without apparent danger to Church and State may not be broken'.[1]

But if Charles I and Strafford were obsessed with the maintenance of the 'circle of order', 'the arch of government', so was their enemy, John Pym. In June 1628, in the magnificent speech he made at Manwaring's impeachment, he produced one of the best examinations in this era of the classic contemporary view of the constitution (6). One of the main burdens of his discourse was that it was perilous to alter the ancient constitution so as to exalt the power of either the king or the people, but in January 1641 Charles announced, too, that his policy was 'to reduce all matters of religion and government to what they were in the purest times of Queen Elizabeth's days', and he sternly warned the Commons of the danger of innovation or change: 'I make a great difference between reformation and alteration of government' (8).

Everyone spoke the same language. When Pym opened his case against the Earl of Strafford on 25 November 1640 his words echoed Strafford's own speech to the Council of the North twelve years before—'A king and his people make one body; the inferior parts confer nourishment and strength, the superior sense and motion.' Strafford in his turn echoed Pym in his last speech in his own defence, in April 1641.[2]

King Charles produced the most elaborate and reasoned exposition of the classic theory of the constitution, in his Answer to the Nineteen Propositions of the Long Parliament in June 1642 (9).[3] He insisted that as king he was given certain powers, to defend the people against their social superiors, and the law against the encroachment of Parliament; he also foretold with remarkable accuracy the social upheaval that was to follow the civil wars. The 'class' bias thus introduced into the theory of the constitution was again stressed by the king at his trial in 1649, when he once more insisted that he was the only upholder of law and order ('order' meaning the right order of society).[4] Yet in the main he was enunciating principles laid down by Pym

[1] A Proclamation for the establishing of the Peace and Quiet of the Church of England, 16 June 1626, no. **43**, p. 154 below.
[2] No. **55c**, p. 211 below.
[3] It was written by Culpepper and Falkland. Edward Hyde objected most strongly to their admission that the king was merely one of the Three Estates (Clarendon, *Life* (1759), I, 130–2.) See Wormuth, *op. cit.*, and Corinne C. Weston, 'The Theory of Mixed Monarchy under Charles I and after', *EHR*, LXXV (1960), 426. Clarendon's suspicions were confirmed when Sir Henry Vane used it in his defence to a charge of treason in 1662 (*ST*, VI, 158). It was also pressed into service by the Exclusionists in 1680 (*State Tracts*, I, 477 ff.).
[4] See especially his 'Reasons Against the Pretended Jurisdiction of the High Court of Justice', printed in J. G. Muddiman, *Trial of King Charles I* (1928), pp. 231–2.

and Strafford from opposite sides of the gulf that had opened beneath men's feet in 1629.

Wild claims were made on both sides, by Eliot as well as Manwaring, but these were ignored, just as the theories of political philosophers like Hobbes were rejected. In the sphere of practical politics the disagreement essentially lay in how to operate a constitution of whose nature few had any doubts.

1. Introduction to the Commons Journals, 19 March 1604

Liceat Praefari

The first frame of this earthly body of a Chaos became a distinct essence of Creatures. Man, the most noble by Nature, born to a Law, out of that gave law to others, and to himself. Hence Order, the lustre of Nature, guided by a First Essence, put all government into form: First, in two, who, by procreation, according to the rule of power (increase and multiply) made a Family, with one Head; by propagation, a Tribe, or Kindred, with one Elder, or Chief; by multiplication, a Society, a Province, a Country, a Kingdom, with one or more Guides or Leaders, of spirit aptest, or of choice fittest, to govern.

This division, sorting itself into proprieties, fell in parts of right, greater or smaller, to some Tribe, Kindred, or elective change of Person. *Vicissitudo rerum*, the herald of time, doth warrant this to be the true original pedigree of Government; and by a present change, in our own eyes, hath made the demonstration more subject to our sense, by our loss of an excellent Princess, by our gain of a successor, for eminent virtue and experience in government famous and peerless, leading us, by a momentary fear, to a better sight of a permanent happiness....

CJ, I, 139

2. The Canons of 1606[1]

* * * * * *

II. If any man shall affirm that men at the first, without all good education and civility, ran up and down in woods and fields, as wild

[1] James I declined to license these canons, chiefly because of no. xxviii, which stated, 'If any man shall affirm...that when any such new forms of government, begun by rebellion, are after thoroughly settled, the authority in them is not of God, or that any who live within the territories of such new governments are not bound to be subject to God's authority which is there executed, but may rebel against the same..., he doth greatly err'. The king was posthumously justified when the canons were at last published in 1689, under the title of 'Bishop Overall's Convocation Book', and promptly used by divines like William Sherlock to justify their support for William III. See Charles F. Mullett, 'William Sherlock and the Revolution of 1688', *Huntington Library Quarterly*, x (1946), 83.

creatures, resting themselves in caves and dens, and acknowledging no superiority one over another, until they were taught by experience the necessity of government; and that thereupon they chose some among themselves to order and rule the rest, giving them power and authority so to do; and that consequently all civil power, jurisdiction and authority was first derived from the people, and disordered multitude; or either is originally still in them, or else is deduced by their consents naturally from them, and is not God's ordinance originally descending from him and depending upon him; he doth greatly err.

* * * * * *

Cardwell, Synodalia, I, 331–2

3. The earl of Salisbury, 8 March 1610

His Majesty said further that for his kingdom he was beholden to no elective power, neither doth he depend upon any popular applause; and yet he doth acknowledge that, though he did derive his title from the loins of his ancestors, yet the law did set the crown upon his head, and he is a king by the common law of the land. Which as it is most proper and natural for this nation, so it is the most equal and just law in any kingdom in the world. He said further that it was dangerous to submit the power of a king to definition. But withal he did acknowledge that he had no power to make laws of himself, or to exact any subsidies *de jure* without the consent of his three Estates; and therefore he was so far from approving the opinion as he did hate those that believed it; and lastly he said that there was such a marriage and union between the prerogative and the law as they cannot possibly be severed. . . .   Gardiner, Parliamentary Debates in 1610, p. 24

4. James I on monarchy: speech to Parliament, 21 March 1610

The state of monarchy is the supremest thing upon earth; for kings are not only God's lieutenants upon earth, and sit upon God's throne, but even by God himself they are called gods. There be three principal similitudes that illustrate the state of monarchy: one taken out of the word of God, and the two other out of the grounds of policy and philosophy. In the Scriptures kings are called gods, and so their powers after a certain relation compared to the divine power. Kings are also compared to fathers of families, for the king is truly *parens patriae*, the politic father of his people. And lastly, kings are compared to the head of this microcosm of the body of man.

Kings are justly called gods for that they exercise a manner or resemblance of divine power upon earth, for if you will consider the attributes to God you shall see how they agree in the person of a king. God hath power to create or destroy, make or unmake, at his pleasure; to give life or send death, to judge all and to be judged not accountable to none; to raise low things and to make high things low at his pleasure; and to God are both soul and body due. And the like power have kings: they make and unmake their subjects; they have power of raising, and casting down; of life, and of death, judges over all their subjects, and in all causes, and yet accountable to none but God only. They have power to exalt low things, and abase high things, and make of their subjects like men at the chess—a pawn to take a bishop or a knight—and cry up or down any of their subjects, as they do their money. And to the king is due both the affection of the soul and the service of the body of his subjects....

But yet is all this power ordained by God, *ad aedificationem, non ad destructionem*. For although God hath power as well of destruction, as of creation or maintenance, yet will it not agree with the wisdom of God to exercise his power in the destruction of nature, and overturning the whole frame of things, since his creatures were made, that his glory might thereby be the better expressed. So were he a foolish father that would disinherit or destroy his children without a cause, or leave off the careful education of them; and it were an idle head that would in place of physic so poison or phlebotomise the body as might breed a dangerous distemper or destruction thereof.

But now in these our times we are to distinguish between the state of kings in their first original, and between the state of settled kings and monarchies that do at this time govern in civil kingdoms; for even as God, during the time of the Old Testament, spake by oracles and wrought by miracles, yet how soon it pleased him to settle a Church, which was bought and redeemed by the blood of his only son Christ, then was there a cessation of both, he ever after governing his people and Church within the limits of his revealed will; so in the first original of kings, whereof some had their beginning by conquest, and some by election of the people, their wills at that time served for law, yet how soon kingdoms began to be settled in civility and policy, then did kings set down their minds by laws, which are properly made by the king only, but at the rogation of the people, the king's grant being obtained thereunto. And so the king became to be *lex loquens*, after a sort, binding himself by a double oath to the observation of the fundamental laws of the kingdom: tacitly, as by being a king, and so bound to protect as well the people as the laws of his kingdom; and expressly, by his oath at his coronation. So, as every just king in a settled kingdom is bound to observe that paction made to his people by his laws, in framing his government agreeable thereto, according to that paction which God made with Noah after the deluge, 'Hereafter seed time and harvest, cold and heat, summer and winter, and day and night shall not cease, so long as the earth remains'; and therefore a king governing in a settled kingdom leaves to be a king, and degenerates into a tyrant, as soon as he leaves off to rule according to his laws.... As for my part, I thank God I have ever given good proof that I never had intention to the contrary, and I am sure to go to my grave with that reputation and comfort, that never king was in all his time more careful to have his laws duly observed, and himself to govern thereafter, than I.

I conclude then this point touching the power of kings with this axiom of Divinity, that as to dispute what God may do is blasphemy, but *quid vult Deus*, that divines may lawfully and do ordinarily dispute and discuss, for to dispute *a posse ad esse* is both against logic and divinity; so is it sedition in subjects to dispute what a king may do in the height of his power, but just kings will ever be willing to declare what they will do, if they will not incur the curse of God. I will not be content that my power be disputed upon, but I shall ever be willing to make the reason appear of all my doings, and rule my actions according to my laws. *Works*, pp. 529–31

5. Roger Manwaring: a sermon preached before the king at Oatlands, 4 July 1627

I counsel thee to keep the King's commandment, and that in regard of the oath of God. *Ecclesiastes* viii. 2.

. . . All powers created are of God; no power, unless it be given from above (St John xix. 11); and all powers that are of this sort are ordained of God (Rom. xiii. 1). Among all the powers that be ordained of God the regal is most high, strong and large: kings [are] above all, inferior to none, to no multitudes of men, to no Angels, to no order of Angels. For though in nature, order and place the Angels be superior to men, yet to powers and persons royal they are not, in regard of any dependence that princes have of them. Their power [is] then the highest. No power in the world or in the hierarchy of the Church can lay restraint upon these supremes; therefore theirs [is] the strongest. And the largest it is, for that no parts within their dominions, no person under their jurisdictions (be they never so great) can be privileged from their power, nor be exempted from their care, be they never so mean. To this power, the highest and greatest peer must stoop, and cast down his coronet at the footstool of his sovereign....

...All the significations of a royal pleasure are, and ought to be to all loyal subjects in the nature and force of a command; as well for that none may nor can search into the high discourse and deep counsels of kings, seeing their hearts are so deep, by reason of their distance from common men, even as the heavens are in respect of the earth. Therefore said he who was wise in heart and deep in counsel, 'The heavens for height, and the earth for depth, and the heart of a king is unsearchable' (Prov. xxv. 3)....Who then may question that which God doth proclaim from heaven to be in his hands, and at his guidance?

Nay, though any king in the world should command flatly against the law of God, yet were his power no otherwise at all to be resisted but for the not doing of his will, in that which is clearly unlawful, [and] to endure with patience, whatsoever penalty his pleasure should inflict upon them, who in this case would desire rather to obey God than Man. By which patient and meek suffering of their sovereign's pleasure they should become glorious martyrs, whereas by resisting of his will they should for ever endure the pain and stain of odious traitors and impious malefactors.

But on the other side, if any king shall command that which stands not in any opposition to the original laws of God, Nature, Nations and the Gospel (though it be not correspondent in every circumstance to laws national and municipal), no subject may, without hazard of his own damnation, in rebelling against God, question or disobey the will and pleasure of his sovereign. For, as a father of the country he commands what his pleasure is, out of counsel and judgement; as a king of subjects, he enjoins it; as a lord over God's inheritance he exacts it; as a supreme head of the body he adviseth it; as a Defender of the Faith he requires it as their homage; as a protector of their persons, lives and estates he deserves it; and as the sovereign, procurer of all the happiness, peace and welfare which they enjoy who are under him he doth most justly claim it at their hands. To kings therefore in all these respects nothing can be denied (without manifest and sinful violation of law and conscience) that may answer their royal estate and excellency, that may further the supply of their urgent necessities, that may be for the security of their royal persons (whose lives are worth millions of others), that may serve for the protection of their kingdoms, territories and dominions, that may enable them to yield relief, aid and succour to their dear and royal confederates and allies, or that may be for the defence and propagation of that sacred and precious truth, the public protection whereof they do maintain by their laws, and prerogatives royal....

[As for Parliament], though such assemblies as are the highest and greatest representatives of a kingdom be most sacred and honourable, and necessary also for those ends to which they were first instituted, yet know we must that ordained they were not to this end, to contribute any right to kings, whereby to challenge tributary aids and subsidiary helps, but for the more equal imposing, and more easy exacting of that which unto kings doth appertain by natural and original law and justice, as their proper inheritance annexed to their imperial crowns from their very births. And therefore if, by a magistrate that is supreme, if upon necessity, extreme and urgent, such subsidiary helps be required, a proportion being held respectively to the abilities of the persons charged, and the sum, or quantity so required surmount not (too remarkably) the use and charge for which it was levied, very hard would it be for any man in the world that should not accordingly satisfy such demands to defend his conscience from that heavy prejudice of resisting the ordinance of God and receiving to himself damnation, though every of those circumstances be not observed which by the municipal laws is required.   *Religion and Allegiance* (1627)

6. Pym's speech at Manwaring's impeachment, 4 June 1628

...He said there did result three positions, which he was to maintain as the groundwork and foundation of the whole cause.

The first, that the form of government in any state could not be altered without apparent danger of ruin to that state. The second, [that] the law of England, whereby the subject was exempted from taxes and loans not granted by common consent of Parliament, was not introduced by any statute, or by any charter or sanction of princes, but was the ancient and fundamental law, issuing from the first frame and constitution of the kingdom. The third, that this liberty of the subject is not only most convenient and profitable for the people, but most honourable, most necessary for the King—yea, in that point of supply for which it was endeavoured to be broken.

The form of government is that which doth actuate and dispose every part and member of a state to the common good; and as those parts give strength and ornament to the whole, so they receive from it again strength and protection in their several stations and degrees. If this mutual relation and intercourse be broken, the whole frame will quickly be dissolved, and fall in pieces, and instead of this concord and interchange of support, whilst one part seeks to uphold the old form of government, and the other part to introduce a new, they will miserably consume and devour one another. Histories are full of the calamities of whole states and nations in such cases. It is true that time must needs bring some alterations, and every alteration is a step and degree towards a dissolution; those things only are eternal which are constant and uniform. Therefore it is observed by the best writers upon this subject that those commonwealths have been most durable and perpetual which have often reformed and recomposed themselves according to their first institution and ordinance; for by this means they repair the breaches and counterwork the ordinary and natural effects of time.

The second question is as manifest. There are plain footsteps of those laws in the government of the Saxons; they were of that vigour and force as to overlive the Conquest, nay, to give bounds and limits to the Conqueror, whose victory gave him first hope. But the assurance and possession of the Crown be obtained by composition, in which he bound himself to observe these and the other ancient laws and liberties of the kingdom, which afterwards he likewise confirmed by oath at his coronation. From him the said obligation descended to his successors. It is true they have been often broken, they have been often confirmed by charters of kings, by acts of parliaments, but the petitions of the subjects upon which those charters and acts were founded were ever petitions of right, demanding their ancient and due liberties, not suing for any new.

To clear the third position (he said) may seem to some men more a paradox: that those liberties of the subject should be so honourable, so profitable for the King, and most necessary for the supply of his Majesty.

It hath been upon another occasion declared that if those liberties were taken away there should remain no more industry, no more justice, no more courage; for who will contend, who will endanger himself for that which is not his own? But (he said) he would not insist upon any of those points, nor yet upon others very important. He said, that if those liberties were taken away there would remain no means for the subjects, by any act of bounty or benevolence, to ingratiate themselves to their sovereign.... The hearts of the people, and their bounty in Parliament, is the only constant treasure and revenue of the Crown, which cannot be exhausted, alienated, anticipated, or otherwise charged and encumbered.... *ST*, III, 341–3

7. Thomas Lord Viscount Wentworth's speech when he first sate Lord President of the North, December 1628

...To the joint individual well being of sovereignty and subjection do I here vow all my cares and diligences through the whole course of this my ministry. I confess I am not ignorant how some distempered minds have of late very far endeavoured to divide the considerations of the two, as if their ends were distinct, not the same, nay in opposition; a monstrous, a prodigious birth of a licentious conception, for so we should become all head or all members. But, God be praised, human wisdom, common experience, Christian religion teach us far otherwise.

Princes are to be indulgent, nursing fathers to their people; their modest liberties, their sober rights, ought to be precious in their eyes; the branches of their government be for shadow, for habitation, the comfort of life, repose, safe and still under the protection of their sceptres. Subjects on the other side ought with solicitous eyes of jealousy to watch over the prerogatives of a crown; the authority of a king is the keystone which closeth up the arch of order and government, which contains each part in due relation to the whole, and which once shaken, infirmed, all the frame falls together into a confused heap of foundation and battlement, of strength and beauty....

Verily, these are those mutual intelligences of love and protection descending, and loyalty ascending, which should pass, be the entertainments, between a king and his people. Their faithful servants must look equally on both, weave, twist these two together in all their counsels, study, labour to preserve each without diminishing or enlarging either, and by running in the worn, wonted channels, treading the ancient bounds, cut off early all disputes from between them. For whatever he be which ravels forth into questions the right of a king and of a people, [he] shall never be able to wrap them up again into the comeliness and order he found them....

The Academy, VII (1875), 582–3

8. King's Speech, 25 January 1641

My Lords and Gentlemen,

A principal cause of my coming here now is, that I foresee the great inconveniences that may daily arise by the slow pace of this Parliament in those businesses that most import the welfare of this kingdom....

I must lay before you the present distractions of government, occasioned partly because of the Parliament, not by it; for some men, taking occasion now by the sitting thereof (more maliciously than ignorantly) will put no alteration betwixt reformation and alteration of Government. Hence it seems that divine service is irreverently interrupted, petitions tumultuously given, and much of my revenue detained or disputed.

More particulars I will not mention, because I will hasten to put you in a way of remedy, which I will do, first, by showing you my clear intentions; then by warning you to eschew those rocks that may hinder this good work.

First then know, that I shall willingly concur with you to find out and reform all innovations in Church and Commonwealth; and consequently, that all courts of justice shall be regulated according to law, my intention being to reduce all matters of religion and government to what they were in the purest times of Queen Elizabeth's days.

Moreover, what parts of my revenue that shall be found illegal or grievous to the public, I shall willingly lay down, relying entirely upon the affections of my people.

Having thus clearly shown you my intentions, I will now tell you what you are to eschew; to which purpose I cannot but take notice of those petitions (I cannot tell how to call them) given in the name of several counties, against the present established government of the Church, and of the greater threats that are given out, that bishops shall be no better than ciphers, if not clean done away.

Now I must clearly tell you, that I make a great difference between reformation and alteration of government; though I am for the first, I cannot give way to the latter. I will not say but that bishops may have overstretched their power, or encroached upon the temporal; which if you find, correct and reform the above, according to the wisdom of former times, so far I am with you.

Nay further, if, upon serious debate, you shall show me that bishops have some temporal authority inconvenient to the state, and not so necessary to the Church for the support of the episcopacy, I shall not be unwilling to persuade them to lay it down; yet, by this, you must not understand that I can consent for the taking away of their voice in parliament, which they have so anciently enjoyed, under so many of my predecessors, even before the Conquest, and ever since; and which I conceive I am bound to maintain, as one of the fundamental institutions of this kingdom.

There is but one other rock, and that not in substance, but in form; yet that form is so essential that, except it be reformed, it will mar the substance. There is a bill given in for frequent parliaments. The thing I like; that is to say, to have often parliaments; but to give power to sheriffs and constables, and I know not whom, to do my office, that I cannot yield unto. But, to show you that I am desirous to please you in forms (which destroy not the substance), I am content you shall have an act for this purpose, but so reformed, it neither trench on mine honour, nor on that inseparable right of my crown concerning parliaments. To which purpose I have commanded my learned counsel to wait on you, my Lords, with such propositions as I hope will give contentment, for I ingenuously confess that frequent parliaments is the best means to preserve that right understanding betwixt me and my subjects which I so heartily desire.

To conclude all, I have now showed you the state of my affairs, my own clear intentions, and the rocks I wish you to eschew; in all which you may perceive the desire I have to give you contentment, as you shall likewise find by those ministers I have and intend to employ in my affairs, for the pursuance of my good intentions, which I doubt not but will bring peace and happiness to my subjects, to the contentment of us all....

LJ, IV, 142

9. The king's answer to the Nineteen Propositions,[1] 18 June 1642

* * * * * *

There being three kinds of government among men, absolute monarchy, aristocracy and democracy, and all these having their particular conveniences and inconveniences, the experience and wisdom of your ancestors hath so moulded this out of a mixture of these as to give to this kingdom (as far as human prudence can provide) the conveniences of all three, without the inconveniences of any one, as long as the balance hangs even between the three estates, and they run jointly on in their proper channel (begetting verdure and fertility in the meadows on both sides) and the overflowing of either on either side raise no deluge or inundation. The ill of absolute monarchy is tyranny, the ill of aristocracy is faction and division, the ills of democracy are tumults, violence and licentiousness. The good of monarchy is the uniting a nation under one head to resist invasion from abroad and insurrection at home; the good of aristocracy is the conjunction of counsel in the ablest persons of a state for the public benefit; the good of democracy is liberty, and the courage and industry which liberty begets.

In this kingdom the laws are jointly made by a king, by a house of peers, and by a House of Commons chosen by the people, all having free votes and particular privileges. The government, according to these laws, is [en]trusted to the King; power of treaties of war and peace, of making peers, of choosing officers and councillors for state, judges for law, commanders for forts and castles, giving commissions for raising men, to make war abroad, or to prevent or provide against invasions or insurrections at home, benefit of confiscations, power of pardoning, and some more of the like kind are placed in the King. And this kind of regulated monarchy, having this power to preserve that authority without which it would be disabled to preserve the laws in their force and the subjects in their liberties and properties, is intended to draw to him such a respect and relation from the great ones, as may hinder the ills of division and faction, and such a fear and reverence from the people as may hinder tumults, violence and licentiousness.

Again, that the prince may not make use of this high and perpetual power to the hurt of those for whose good he hath it, and make use of the name of public necessity for the gain of his private favourites and

---

[1] No. 67, p. 244 below.

followers, to the detriment of his people, the House of Commons (an excellent convener of liberty, but never intended for any share in government, or the choosing of them that govern) is solely entrusted with the first propositions concerning the levy of money (which is the sinews as well of peace as of war), and the impeaching of those who for their own ends, though countenanced by any surreptitiously gotten command of the King, have violated the law, which he is bound (when he knows it) to protect; and to the prosecution of which they are bound to advise him, at least not to serve him to the contrary. And the Lords, being trusted with a judicatory power, are an excellent screen and bank between the prince and people, to assist each against any encroachments of the other, and by just judgements to preserve that law which ought to be the rule of every one of the three....

Since therefore the power, legally placed in both houses, is more than sufficient to prevent and restrain the power of tyranny, and without the power which is now asked from us we shall not be able to discharge that trust which is the end of monarchy, since this would be a total subversion of the fundamental laws, and that excellent constitution of this kingdom which hath made this nation so many years both famous and happy to a great degree of envy, since to the power of punishing (which is already in your hands according to law) if the power of preferring be added, we shall have nothing left for us but to look on, since the encroaching of one of these estates upon the power of the other is unhappy in the effects, both to them and all the rest, since this power of at most a joint government in us with our councillors (or rather, our guardians) will return us to the worst kind of minority, and make us despicable both at home and abroad, and beget eternal factions and dissensions (as destructive to public happiness as war) both in the chosen, and in the houses that chose them, and the people who chose the choosers, since so new a power will undoubtedly intoxicate persons who were not born to it, and beget not only divisions among them as equals, but in them contempt of us, as become an equal to them, and insolence and injustice toward our people, as now so much their inferiors, which will be the more grievous unto them, as suffering from those who were so lately of a nearer degree to themselves, and being to have redress only from those that placed them, and fearing they may be inclined to preserve what they have made, both out of kindness and policy, since all great changes are extremely inconvenient, and almost infallibly beget yet greater changes, which beget yet greater inconveniences.

Since as great a one in the Church must follow this of the Kingdom, since the second estate would in all probability follow the fate of the first, and by some of the turbulent spirits jealousies would soon be raised against them, and the like propositions for reconciliation of differences would then be sent to them as they now have joined to send to us till (all power being vested in the House of Commons, and their number making them incapable of transacting affairs of state with the necessary service and expedition, these being retrusted to some close committee) at last the common people (who in the meantime must be flattered, and to whom licence must be given in all their wild humours, how contrary soever to established law, or their own real good) discover this *arcanum imperii*, that all this was done by them, but not for them, and grow weary of journey-work, and set up for themselves, call parity and independence liberty, devour that estate which had devoured the rest, destroy all rights and proprieties, all distinctions of families and merit, and by this means this splendid and excellently distinguished form of government end in a dark, equal chaos of confusion, and the long line of our many noble ancestors in a Jack Cade or a Wat Tyler.

*   *   *   *   *   *

Rushworth, v, 728, 730–32

CHAPTER 2

PARLIAMENT

I. STATUS AND PRIVILEGE

The pretensions of Parliament in the seventeenth century rested on the theory that it was the representative element in the constitution. In the first statute passed in James I's reign it described itself as:

> This High Court of Parliament, where all the whole body of the realm, and every particular member thereof, either in person or by representation (upon their own free elections), are by the laws of this realm deemed to be personally present.[1]

This principle was never denied, least of all by the Crown, and in his first speech to the Commons, in March 1604, James addressed them as 'you who are here presently assembled to represent the body of this whole kingdom and all sorts of people within the same'.[2]

The practice by which boroughs paid their Members' wages was dying out, and so was the concept that a knight of the shire must be a native of that county, but in some senses the Members of the Commons were still regarded as delegates. It was still common for the session to begin with each Member stepping forward to present the grievances of his own county (**11**); in fact this was done as late as 1640. Yet it was never explicitly stated whom the Commons were representing, apart from the taxpayers. In fact apart from landowners the only sizeable elements in the Commons were the professional lawyers, who in 1614 numbered 48 in a House of 475, and in 1640 75 in a House of 507, and the merchants, who numbered 42 and 45 respectively.[3] It is significant that in a period when taxation on trade was increasing by leaps and bounds the number of merchants in the Commons remained static. The divine right of landowners to govern the nation was duly accepted by contemporaries; what is surprising is that it should have been accepted so complacently by historians. The fact is that seventeenth-century parliaments were not always representative of the wealthiest and most advanced elements in the nation, who did not have the leisure and the local connections which were essential to successful electioneering.

---

[1] The Succession Act, 1 Jac. I, c. 1., printed *TCD*, pp. 10–12.
[2] *Ibid.* p. 24. See, however, no. **12**, p. 40 below.
[3] Mary F. Keeler, *The Long Parliament 1640–41*, and Thomas L. Moir, *The Addled Parliament*, from which these figures are taken, are the most exhaustive examinations of particular parliaments. See also Brunton and Pennington, *Members of the Long Parliament*.

Yet the House of Commons had grown steadily in size during the sixteenth century, partly because of the incorporation of Wales and the county palatine of Chester, but mainly because of the free use of the Crown's right to confer parliamentary representation on new boroughs by letters patent. From 350 Members in 1509 it had grown to 467 in 1601. It could expel Members, and in the Buckinghamshire Election Case in 1604 it established its right to scrutinise election returns and determine which candidate should sit. By a strained construction on this case it began in 1621 to award representation to many boroughs which had allowed their rights to lapse in the later Middle Ages.

In contrast, the House of Lords had remained static during the sixteenth century, and on Elizabeth's death its numbers stood at fifty-five, not including the bishops. James I increased their numbers to eighty by 1610, and was proud of it,[1] but the House of Lords was still hampered by the bishops, whose vote was almost always at the government's disposal, and by the fact that under the first two Stuarts some of the government's most able ministers were peers. But Buckingham's policy of selling peerages on a large scale, raising the numbers in the House to 126 by 1628, was a disaster. The older peers were enraged with the king and his advisers, and the loyalty of the new peers could not be relied on, with the result that in 1621, 1626 and 1628 the Lords joined the Commons to inflict heavy defeats on James I and Charles I. In the crisis of 1629 many peers returned to their traditional allegiance, encouraged, too, by Charles's ostentatious abandonment of Buckingham's policy, but the government's unprecedented weakness in the House of Lords was still evident in 1640 and 1641.[2]

All Members of Parliament, in Lords or Commons, enjoyed important personal privileges. For instance, they and their servants were immune from arrest during a session except on a charge of treason, felony, or breach of the peace; in 1604 this principle was resoundingly confirmed, and embodied in a statute.[3] However, Parliament had not yet established its complete freedom of speech. Elizabeth had always maintained that the Commons could speak as they wished to the business before them, but—apart from a reserve right to raise 'commonwealth matters' in which the public safety was involved—only the Crown could decide what that business should be. James I and Charles I never surrendered this point, though they came perilously near it at times. Moreover, though it was a bold king who proceeded against Members during a session, he need have no qualms about falling on them when Parliament rose, no more than their creditors; as James said in 1604, 'The

---

[1] He told a deputation from the Commons on 26 April 1604 that since his accession 'the Church was decided, the nobility increased, the burden of the people eased' (CJ, I, 192).
[2] See Stone's Crisis of the Aristocracy, the most detailed examination we have of any social class, and the most important.
[3] Shirley's Case, TCD, pp. 302–17.

parliament not sitting the liberties are not sitting' (12). In 1621 he went further, saying, 'We think ourself very free and able to punish any man's misdemeanours in Parliament, as well during their sitting as after'. Immediately after the dissolution of the Addled Parliament in 1614 nine Members who had conferred with the Lords on impositions were brought before the Council, and their notes of the conference were confiscated and burnt on the spot. Four of them were sent to the Tower, where one stayed a year, and four others were ordered not to leave town for the time being.[1] When the Commons showed a disposition to investigate these events in 1621 they were warned off by Sir Edward Coke, who pointed out that to apply to the king was to put their privileges in jeopardy whether he granted them satisfaction or not.[2] However, Sir Edwin Sandys spent a month in the Tower during the summer recess later that year, ostensibly because he had corresponded with the king's daughter without his permission, and the following January, on the dissolution, Coke himself and two other M.P.s were haled before the Council and sent to the Tower, where they remained until August, this time without any pretence that the offences for which they were being punished had been committed outside Parliament.[3] Eliot tried to make a stand on this question in 1624, but he received little support, and two years later Charles I took the dangerous step of imprisoning him and Dudley Digges in the middle of a session. But as his relations with Parliament deteriorated Charles grew less, not more, restrained in the use of his authority, and in 1629, and even 1640, Members were imprisoned after Parliament rose.[4]

But James I was not disposed to treat Parliament lightly, and his angry remark to Gondomar in 1614, just after the debacle of the Addled Parliament, has been given too much publicity.[5] He was equally hysterical on 9 November 1605, just after the discovery of the Gunpowder Plot, when he told Parliament:

> One thing, for my own part, have I to thank God in; that if God for our sins had suffered their wicked intents to have prevailed, it should never have been spoken or written in ages succeeding that I had died ingloriously in an alehouse, or stew, or such vile place, but mine end should have been with the most honourable and best company, and in that most honourable and fittest place for a king to be in, for doing the turns most proper to his office.[6]

[1] Gardiner, *History of England*, II, 249–50; Mitchell, *Revolutionary Party*, pp. 77–8, 147.
[2] *Commons Debates 1621*, II, 57–8 (12 February).
[3] Gardiner, *op. cit.* IV, 133, 267. John Pym was also confined to his London house for three months. [4] See p. 32 below.
[5] 'The House of Commons is a body without a head. The Members give their opinion in a disorderly manner. At their meetings nothing is heard but cries, shouts and confusion. I am surprised that my ancestors should ever have allowed such an institution to come into existence' (Gardiner, *op. cit.* II, 251). [6] *LJ*, II, 359.

Unfortunately, the first session of his first parliament, in 1604, set the pattern. On the first day there was a series of unfortunate accidents; the Commons were not summoned to the Lords' House to hear the king's speech, and some who went up on their own initiative were insulted by a yeoman of the guard, and so on. Everyone seemed full of grievances, and determined to air them (11). The tremendous row which followed over the Buckinghamshire election showed the king at his worst: almost at once he drifted from the strict legal point at issue (on which he had a good case) and settled on the vague and dangerous question of parliamentary privilege. As a result he sustained a heavy defeat, though to save his face the immediate issue of the election was compromised.[1] So irritated were the Commons that at the end of the session they drew up a *Form of Apology and Satisfaction* which was couched in such strong language that the majority recommitted it.[2] James prorogued them on 7 July with a thoroughly bad-tempered speech (12). He was probably right when he described the Opposition as being a small minority, but his clumsiness and lack of tact had given them their chance.

The Commons' freedom of speech was on the anvil again in 1610. Late in April, with the king away at Newmarket, they set about investigating the legality of the new impositions on trade lately imposed by the government.[3] James sent the Council word that he could not allow Parliament to debate any aspect of his prerogative without leave, especially after it had been confirmed in a court of law, and on 21 May the king returned to London and made a speech to both Houses in which he repeated his prohibition.[4] When the Committee of Grievances discussed this speech, Francis Bacon brought forward a whole series of awkward precedents from Elizabeth's reign, demonstrating that she had often stopped a debate when she considered that it touched on her prerogative (13), but what the House could not deny it was prepared to ignore, and on 23 May it submitted a petition claiming the right to debate any aspect of the royal prerogative which encroached on the subject's liberties.[5] James's answer, though it was remarkably conciliatory, was very far from settling the question, which was abandoned for the moment.[6] However, the House did debate impositions.

The Commons' handling of James and his ministers was not unskilful, considering the large and heterogeneous nature of the assembly. This owed a great deal to skilful committee work. The great standing committees (or

[1] *TCD*, pp. 201–71.
[2] Extracts are printed in *TCD*, pp. 217–30. In 'A High Road to Civil War', shortly to be published in a memorial volume to Garrett Mattingly, G. R. Elton shows that it was not acceptable to the House as a whole. I am very grateful to Dr Elton for showing me a typescript of this paper.
[3] See p. 55 below.
[4] *House of Lords Manuscripts*, XI, 3314; Gardiner, *Parliamentary Debates in 1610*, p. 34 n.
[5] *TCD*, pp. 245–7.
[6] Gardiner, *Parliamentary Debates in 1610*, pp. 41–2.

general committees) elected at the beginning of each Parliament to deal with Privileges, Grievances, Elections and Religion naturally contained the leaders of Opposition.[1] Moreover, from 1606 the use of the Committee of the Whole House (10c) enabled Members to speak more than once to the same motion, and also enabled them to replace the Speaker by an elected chairman. The Speaker was one of the most important ministers in the House, and in the Parliament of 1604–10 he and the Opposition leaders were engaged in constant guerrilla warfare (10a). The majority of the House were still unsure of themselves, and many points of procedure were still not covered by rules; it is astonishing how often the whole House sat dumb for minutes on end (10b). But in 1614, with procedure hardening, measures were taken to stop the Speaker stampeding the House, and in 1621 he was forbidden to bring on bills before nine o'clock in the morning, or introduce a third reading without adequate warning the day before (10a). In 1621 Speaker Richardson was rebuked three times in the course of one debate, on monopolies, for 'intricating and deferring' the question, and for trying to close a debate without leave of the House. It was asserted, 'Mr Speaker [is] but a servant to the House, and not a master, nor a master's mate'.[2] But he remained a key figure in the government management of Parliament, and Charles I's failure to secure a suitable Speaker for the Long Parliament was decisive.[3]

Also in the first parliament of James I there was a sharp decline in the numbers of the government servants in the Commons.[4] This was not entirely accidental or inevitable. Salisbury preferred to control the Commons from the Lords by the use of conferences between the two Houses (10d); he disliked and distrusted Francis Bacon, yet there was no one else of any ability whom he could use as government spokesman in the lower House. Unfortunately by 1610 the Commons were no longer prepared to surrender the initiative to a small committee in negotiations with the Lords, and the conference 'system' collapsed, bringing on the failure of the Great Contract and Salisbury's fall from favour. The king now took over the direction of Parliament, and the disastrous failure of his preparations in 1614 did not deter him from trying to negotiate once more with the Commons leaders in 1621. He was also remarkably complacent. After Bacon's impeachment in 1621 he could still remark, with probable sincerity: 'The House of Commons at this time have showed greater love, and used me with more respect in all their proceedings than ever any House of Commons have heretofore done to

---

[1] Mitchell, *Revolutionary Party*, passim. Cf. Mary F. Keeler, 'Some Opposition Committees, 1640', in *Conflict in Stuart England*, ed. W. A. Aiken and B. D. Henning (1960).

[2] *CJ*, I, 546–7 (9 March 1621).

[3] H. R. Trevor-Roper, 'Oliver Cromwell and his Parliaments', in *Essays Presented to Sir Lewis Namier*, pp. 12–13.

[4] See, in general, Wallace Notestein, 'The Winning of the Initiative by the House of Commons', *Proc. British Academy*, 1924, and D. H. Willson, *The Privy Councillors in the House of Commons*.

me.'[1] In 1621 and again in 1628 special efforts at the elections produced a large number of Privy Councillors and other dependants in the House, but royal policy was by now so erratic and unpredictable, and above all so unpopular, that their efforts to pacify or control the Commons were quite ineffective.

By 1621 the outbreak of the Thirty Years War in Germany had drawn the attention of Parliament to foreign affairs. The renewed war between Spain and the Dutch and the initial victories of the Counter Reformation—particularly the expulsion of James's son-in-law Frederick from Bohemia and the Palatinate—filled the Commons with alarm, and with the survival of European Protestantism in jeopardy they demanded that James abandon the plan with which he had been flirting for nearly ten years, of marrying the Prince of Wales to the Spanish Infanta. Drawing entirely false conclusions from the financial success of privateers like Drake in the great days of Elizabeth, the Opposition had also convinced themselves that maritime war was self-supporting or even profitable, and a means of resolving the current economic crisis. (This delusion was to persist into the reign of Charles II, and may have been one result of the poor representation of merchants in the House.) When James ignored them they sent up a petition on 3 December 1621 which implied that they were ready to withhold supply until their advice was accepted (14). James, at Newmarket again, wrote the same day forbidding them to 'meddle with anything concerning our government or deep matters of state', and tactlessly referring to the King of Spain as a 'friend and confederate'.[2] The Commons at once withdrew their petition and redrafted it in a more tactful form, and a deputation took it to the king at Newmarket on 11 December. He ordered 'stools for the ambassadors', and dictated a long and learned reply. He told them he was 'an old and experienced king, needing no such lessons', and in any case the House of Commons was not equipped to discuss foreign relations. As for their privilege of freedom of speech, he told them:

> We cannot allow of the style, calling it your 'ancient and undoubted right and inheritance', but could rather have wished that you had said that your privileges were derived from the grace and permission of our ancestors and us.

This roused a veritable storm in the Commons, and it was useless for James to send another letter on 16 December, expanding his remarks and to some extent modifying them. All other business was dropped for a week, and on the 18th they produced a Protestation in which they claimed the right to debate any matter of state whatsoever (15). The king ordered them to adjourn at once, and on 30 December he presided over a meeting of the Privy Council

---

[1] 26 March 1621 (*LJ*, III, 69).   [2] For full documentation, see *TCD*, pp. 279–88.

at which the Protestation was formally torn out of the Journals of the House.[1] He then took the unprecedented step, followed by his son in 1629 and his grandson in 1681, of issuing a public declaration reviewing the events of the last session at some length and justifying his conduct in dissolving parliament forthwith.[2]

It was unfortunate that in the next parliament his son and his favourite should force him to eat his words. Charles and Buckingham sustained a humiliating personal defeat at Madrid in 1623, and they came back determined to provoke war with Spain. Buckingham persuaded him to call another parliament, came to terms with the Opposition behind his back, and forced him in his speech opening parliament on 19 February 1624 to request its advice on foreign policy. He carried off the humiliation as best he could, in one of his last appearances. James's abilities as a speech-maker are usually judged unfairly by the long, florid orations he chose to publish in a collected edition in 1616. Now, it is true he was involved, repetitious, and somewhat homely, but he displayed considerable courage and a very real humanity, which was always absent from his son's pronouncements on similar occasions. Even his self-conceit was magnificent rather than threatening; as when he remarked, 'Of all the kings that ever were, I dare say, never king was better beloved of his people than I am', or when he casually referred to Jesus Christ, 'in whose throne I sit in this part of the earth' (16). But it was a heavy defeat, and an awkward precedent; Parliament was not being asked to rubber-stamp an arrangement agreed upon by the king and his advisers, they were being asked, in effect, to arbitrate in a matter on which the Privy Council and the royal family itself were deeply divided. Parliament, full of courtesy and self-importance, advised him to break off all negotiations with Spain. James tried to hedge, but a Joint Address from both Houses, on 22 March, kept him in line. When it was all over he had to endure the congratulations of Parliament for abandoning a policy to which he had devoted a large part of his energies for many years, and in which (there can be little doubt) he still sincerely believed.[3]

This was Prince Charles's doing. But even when he ascended the throne the following year he showed little disposition to quibble over Parliament's conduct provided they granted him money and did not argue about his efforts to obtain more from other sources. He was much brisker than his father, and much less disposed to indulge in theoretical arguments.

Nevertheless, though he discussed his rights much less, he was willing to go farther and strike harder in their defence, as he showed in May 1626, when he committed Sir John Eliot and Sir Dudley Digges to the Tower in the middle of the session for what he regarded as seditious, if not treasonable words used in the management of Buckingham's impeachment. Moreover,

[1] *APC 1621–1623*, pp. 108–10.   [2] *TCD*, pp. 289–95.   [3] *Ibid.* pp. 296–302.

he authorised Sir Dudley Carleton to warn the Commons that he might, like other European monarchs, decide to dispense with elected assemblies altogether (**17**). Digges was released after five days, but the king held on to Eliot another three, arguing that his actions outside the House revealed a conspiracy to wreck the session—an argument he was to use again in 1629. He was forced to give way when the Commons suspended their sittings *sine die*.

But in 1629 Eliot and his supporters overreached themselves, when they delayed the adjournment of the House on 2 March by physical coercion of the Speaker.[1] Next day he and eight other Members[2] were arrested by order of the Council. Parliament was dissolved on the 10th, and on the 27th Charles issued a proclamation in which he referred to Eliot as 'an outlawed man, desperate in mind and fortune'.[3] Indeed, Charles held Eliot responsible for the public outcry which had led to Buckingham's assassination the previous summer, and he was determined to punish him despite a division of opinion in the Council, which was reflected in Star Chamber. Informations were laid before Star Chamber in May, but the Court was obviously unwilling to rule that it had jurisdiction, and over the Long Vacation the case was allowed to lapse. When the prisoners sued out a writ of *habeas corpus* Charles complied with the Petition of Right by specifying the cause of their imprisonment as sedition, and King's Bench decided that this was not bailable. Further pressure was brought to bear on the judges, and at last, on 25 January 1630, proceedings were opened in King's Bench against Eliot, Holles and Valentine.

The indictment was for seditious words spoken during the actual session, as well as violence to the Speaker. It was open to Charles to argue that from the moment Black Rod knocked on the door of the Commons' House the session stood adjourned, and that anything said or done after that was said or done outside Parliament. But he spurned this evasion, and the attorney general was briefed to argue that parliamentary privilege did not extend to seditious words, and that Strode's Act of 1512,[4] pleaded by the defence, was a private act, having no general application. On the question of jurisdiction Heath argued that though King's Bench could certainly not reverse judgements of the High Court of Parliament it could take notice of events happening therein. The judges agreed, and gave judgement for the Crown accordingly (**18**). The three men refused to pay their fines and were imprisoned indefinitely. Holles escaped and went into hiding, and Eliot died in 1632. Apart from Valentine, the others were given the opportunity of making their submission and going free. All of them took it except Strode, and he and Valentine were not released until February 1640, when the writs were going

[1] See p. 61 below.
[2] Denzil Holles, Benjamin Valentine, John Selden, Sir Miles Hobart, William Strode, Sir Peter Heyman, Walter Long and William Coryton.
[3] No. 28, p. 85 below.   [4] Elton, *Tudor Constitution*, pp. 254–5.

out for the Short Parliament. The Short Parliament took up their case, but this did not deter Charles. Immediately after the dissolution, in May 1640, John Crew, the chairman of the Committee on Religion, was sent to the Tower for refusing to surrender his papers to the Clerk of the Parliaments (19), and Sir John Hotham and Henry Bellasis followed him there, while the houses of Pym, Hampden and Sir Walter Erle were searched for incriminating documents.[1]

So, on the very eve of the final crisis the Commons were still unable to defend their privilege of free speech, though the more general privilege of discussing any matter they chose, in any order, had been virtually conceded in practice, Charles I's only counter being prorogation or dissolution. The Long Parliament was obsessed with the question of privilege to an unhealthy degree, but it did remarkably little to put the matter on a firm legal footing. In July 1641 it was resolved that the proceedings against Eliot, Holles and Valentine had been a gross breach of privilege, but not until 1668, on the motion of Holles himself—now Lord Holles of Ifield—was the judgement of 1630 reversed on a writ of error.[2]

10. Procedure in the Commons

(a) The Speaker

(i) [25 February 1606]

Much debate was whether the House in the case of purveyance should proceed with the bill, which had been twice read and committed, and now with some amendments was to be delivered in, or by way of composition....[3] [The House voting in favour of the bill,] it was required that the amendments should be read, but because Mr Hare, being demanded by the Speaker whether the said amendments were long, answered, yea, therefore the time being spent the reading thereof was deferred until the next day.

[The Speaker wrote to warn Salisbury that night:]

This last day Monday [24 February] they grew in hot resolution to proceed with their bill, but being by me remembered that the first motion of conference grew from his [Majesty's] gracious message to the House, and secondly from the honourable offer of you my Lord [to] the Committees, I drew them to a Committee to advise what was fit in their next conference to your lordships to be propounded, and till

[1] Gardiner, *History of England*, IX, 129–30.　　　[2] *ST*, III, 310–15, 332–3.

[3] The bill was to abolish purveyance outright, instead of pursuing negotiations with the Lords for the voluntary abandonment of this right in return for a financial consideration. See the Speaker's letter below.

then the bill to stay. Which the Committees this day reporting what they had concluded of, the House in the end were inflamed to call for their proceeding in the bill, and much pressed me also to make a question whether they would compound or no. To satisfy their importunity, which I could not avoid, I made the question whether they would proceed with the bill, but took occasion to forbear the second question concerning the composition, for that I found as the state of the House then stood it would be rejected. They then would have pressed me to have made a question upon the engrossing of the bill, which by some means I delayed to do, not without the distaste of some, as I understand. Which their humour in putting it to the question to engross the bill no doubt they will eagerly tomorrow pursue, and all message or honourable offers made before will be to them distasteful (as I fear). Notwithstanding I will follow the direction I received, except otherwise I shall be by your Lordship commanded.

[26 February]

The Speaker wrote unto the Clerk, being in the House, that he should excuse him to the company, for that having taken pills overnight which did not work as expected he had not been well all night, but would attend between 9 and 10, at which time he came accordingly. In the meantime the opinion of the House and the ordinary speech was that he had taken a pill from the purveyors.

[As soon as the Speaker had taken his seat the bill was brought in, and Mr Hare, the chairman of the committee, explained the amendments. The amendments were being read when messengers arrived from the Lords.]

Sir John Crooke, one of his Majesty's Serjeants-at-Law, and Sir George Coppin, Clerk of the Crown in Chancery, came from the Lords, whose message was in effect that their Lordships since the last conference touching the purveyors have expected a second meeting concerning that business, and that now they are desirous of a conference to consider what course may be taken not only to reform abuses but to abolish the very name of purveyors, and how in lieu thereof to yield the King some amends in regard of his great charge, and the Judges to be called to be present....This conference was entertained, and the Judges' presence allowed, and the next day after dinner in the Painted Chamber the conference appointed.

[For the moment the bill was dropped.]   Bowyer, *Diary*, pp. 53–5

(ii) [11 April 1614]

Sir Edwin Sandys moveth, that no bill may be read the second time until half an hour past eight, and the third time, till past nine [in the morning]. And ordered accordingly.

He moveth again, for avoiding precipitation, and prevention of division, that in all such motions as shall not come in by bill, and shall concern the general, no resolution may be that day, but it may be committed and reported, the rather because here one may speak but once in one day, where[as] at the Committee two or three times, whereupon often the committees, first disagreeing, afterwards agree.

CJ, 1, 458

[7 February 1621]

Sir Thomas Trevor—To have no bill read the second reading till nine of the clock.

Mr Alford—No bill to be put to pass till past nine of the clock, and notice to be given, a day before, that bills shall be passed the next day. And both ordered. *CJ*, 1, 511

(b) *Voting*

[22 November 1606]

Hereupon the question was made and propounded by Mr Speaker, viz., as many as think fit and convenient that a new Member be chosen in place of Mr Attorney, may it please you to say, yea, and e *converso*.[1] But the voices by the noise being doubtful, and neither side yielding, a second doubt arose, viz., whether the yea[s] or the no[es] should go forth. Mr Speaker moved that the yea[s] should go forth, giving this reason, [that] that party which seeketh a new thing is to go forth. Then, quoth Sir Herbert Croft, the no[es] must go forth, for they would have the King's Attorney to remain a Member here, which was never seen, and is without precedent.

Herein the House would not agree, and so without concluding anything in the point a silence followed. Then Sir William Morrice made an idle speech touching a bill by himself preferred the last session, for to enact the King to be Emperor of Great Britain, which moved laughter in the House; to which mirth silence for half an hour succeeded. And so the House arose, Mr Speaker saying it was almost eleven of the clock.

Bowyer, *Diary*, pp. 188–9

[1] The issue was whether the attorney general could be a Member, and it was not settled until 1614. See Willson, *Privy Councillors*, pp. 215–17.

(c) Committee of the Whole House

[24 April 1606]

The committees for the matter of Grievances, or so many of them as were present, and such as offered and arose voluntarily to accompany them, went up into the Committee Chamber to marshal these grievances, during which time, being a full hour, the House did sit idle without doing anything. After which long pausing, the committees sent word that they would come down into the House (if so it pleased the House) and confer with the company, not as in the House, but by way of Committee. This the Speaker having received from them by the Sergeant, did deliver to the House, and the House allowing thereof the Speaker added that himself in this case was to depart the place, which with allowance he did, and the most of the company departed with him. A few stayed until after eleven of the clock expecting the coming down of the committees, and then likewise departed, and after them the committees followed.

Bowyer, *Diary*, p. 136

(d) Conferences between the Houses

(i) [4 February 1606]

Sir Francis Bacon moved, touching the conference to be had on Thursday with the Lords, that the committees may first meet and confer; also, forasmuch as in his opinion the conference is not to rest merely upon propositions of the Lords, but the committees appointed to confer do likewise propose to their Lordships, there[fore] he wished that some might be sent to their Lordships to signify so much, and to desire that their committees may come authorised accordingly, and that this House would be pleased to authorise the committees for the conference to propose as well as to hear, and to direct them what and how to propose, for, said he, otherwise if they shall only hear what the Lords will say this is no conference. [The Speaker supported him, but]...*Sir Edward Montague* thought that we ought not to show our proceedings, but to hear only what the Lords will propose.

Doctor Perkins thought that we ought also to propound, otherwise it were no conference but a reference.

Sir Francis Hastings thought that we ought not to propound until we had a conference; in the meantime we are only to talk with the Lords of that which was yesterday referred to the subcommittees, viz., touching the laws now in force against recusants, but not to declare our articles now in hand and treaty here in this House.

Bowyer, Diary, pp. 24–5

(ii) [27 November 1640]

The Lords desire a conference (by a committee of thirty of their House with a proportionable number of this House) concerning the Message that was brought unto them by Mr Pym, touching the examination of their members in the accusation of the earl of Strafford; and desire a free conference touching the last point of that message, 'that some of the Members of this House should be present at the examination'.

[This occasioned a long debate as to whether the conference should be 'free' or not:]

Mr Pym. There is a difference between a conference and a free conference. In a conference we only carry our ears; in a free conference we carry not only our ears but all must go prepared to maintain what we have delivered up upon the Message to the Lords.

CJ, II, 38; D'Ewes Journal, ed. Notestein, p. 543

(e) *Elections*

[22 March 1621]

Sir George Moore made a report concerning returns and privileges. Touching the election of Sandwich, a question was betwixt Mr Barrowes and Sir Richard Hatton. By a late Order of the Council Table, the election was appointed to be made by the Mayor, the Jurats and Common Council.[1] But it appears that anciently the commonalty did join and never were debarred, and now likewise gave their consent to the election of Sir Edwin Sandys. But Sir Richard Hatton was chosen the other way, which election the Committee had judged to be void, and that no other election was perfected on the behalf of Mr Barrowes.

This sentence was confirmed by the House.

Commons Debates 1621, IV, 181

---

[1] Sandwich was one of the Cinque Ports, and therefore in theory particularly amenable to government pressure. In fact it harboured Sandys, one of the leaders of the Opposition.

11. The opening of a new Parliament, 1604 (Sir Edward Montague's Journal)

The first day, being Monday, 19 of March, after the King was gone to church, the Lord High Steward, which was the Earl of Nottingham, came into the usual place in Westminster, and after he had called all the knights, citizens and burgesses, and sworn some to the Supremacy, the rest went into the rooms next the Parliament House, and there were sworn by certain of the House appointed commissioners by the Lord Steward. And there most of them remained, expecting to be sent for into the higher House.

The King's Majesty, after he was set and all the Lords placed, and the King demanding once or twice whether the lower House was come, and answer being made they were (though indeed the tenth were not there), his Majesty, putting off his cap and crown and putting it on again, made a most excellent speech....

This done, all those that were in the higher House...returning into the lower, which was almost full, and staying till Mr Vice Chamberlain [Sir John Stanhope] and Sir John Herbert [Secretary of State], the only Privy Councillors then returned of the House, were come, an ancient parliament man made complaint unto them of the wrong that they were not sent for into the higher House. Sir John Herbert stood up, and showed how sorry he was for it, and...repeated shortly the heads of his Majesty's speech....

On Thursday, 22, the Speaker was presented. The King, most graciously, to satisfy the grief of the House, repeated his speech unto them; and then as many as could possibly stand were let in, and the doors set open; nay, when the King was ready he sent a sergeant-at-arms to call up the lower House, that so they might come in. This did notably please the House.

The Speaker returned and sat in his place, and going according to the custom to read a bill, Sir William Fleetwood, knight, returned for one of the knights of Buckinghamshire, made known a grievance of Sir Francis Goodwin, who, though he were elected by the voice of the county, and as he thought returned, yet he was not called and admitted; and going to the Clerk of the Crown [in Chancery] to know the reason, he refused to show him the return, or the file; whereupon [he] desired the Clerk might be sent for, to know the cause, which being put to the House, command was given that he should be sent for....

Then motion was made for committees to be nominated for the examining of the privileges of the House. Some stick there was at first, but, put to the question, it was agreed there should be a committee, which accordingly were [*sic*] named.

Then Sir Herbert Croft made complaint of Brian Tash, one of the guard, for that the first day of the parliament, some burgesses pressing to go into the higher house, he thrust them out, [saying:] 'Nay, good-man burgess, you must stay a while.' Some debate there was upon this, but at last ordered that he should be sent for by the Sergeant....

Friday, 23. After prayers read, Sir Robert Wroth stepped up and made this motion: first, the confirmation of the Book of Common Prayer lately set up by his Majesty's authority, and that consideration might be had of these grievances following: first, for wardship, that the King might have a composition, and the subjects freed of that tenure; secondly, against purveyors; 3, against monopolies; 4, against licences of alienation; 5, against transporting of iron ordnance; 6, against abuses of the Exchequer; and 7, against dispensation of [penal] statutes.

The motion was well liked of, and committed to have bills drawn, and to be sat on that afternoon.

Myself next to him delivered further griefs enjoined me by the county [Northamptonshire] to make known to the House. First, the intolerable burden, vexation, travail and charge of the Commissaries' Courts, as now they are used; 2, the suspension of grave, learned and sober-minded Ministers for not observing certain ceremonies long time by many disused; [3,] the depopulation and daily excessive conversion of tillage into pasture.[1]

This motion it pleased the House to commit likewise as the former, and to be sat on on Monday.

One Mr Wentworth, a lawyer, he moved two points to the House: one, for the infirmities of it, in lacking some of the Members; another for the deformity, having more than it ought to have, viz., certain burgesses newly appointed for the universities.

After some debate about the former matter, especially concerning Sir Francis Goodwin's case, the Clerk of the Crown was sent for in, who brought two returns and delivered them into the House. The former writ bare *teste* 30 Jan.; the election was 22 Feb., and Sir Francis Goodwin

---

[1] Northamptonshire was a centre of Puritanism, and Montague was one of the signatories of the notorious petition the following year (p. 127 below). It was also the centre of the Midlands Revolt of 1607 against enclosures and rack-renting.

and Sir William Fleetwood were returned; but on the return the sheriff had certified that Sir Francis stood outlawed, and therefore not fit, whereupon another writ was sent out, the *teste* 16 March, and the election of 21 March, and Sir John Fortescue returned.

This matter was long debated, with divers arguments pro and con, especially by the lawyers, and at length determined by the House that the first return was good, and that the sheriff had inserted more than he ought to do; and so Sir Francis was sworn and admitted into the House.

Then was called in Brian Tash, the Yeoman of [the] Guard, who confessed that he called one 'Goodman Burgess', and confessed his fault, and because of his Majesty's former grace to us the day before was pardoned and released without fees.

In the afternoon the committee met to consider of those things propounded by Sir Robert Wroth.

For the confirmation of the Book of Common Prayer lately set forth it was ordered that some few of the committee should look into the old and this new, and report the alterations and explanations, and what else was thought fit in the Book to receive examination, and to bring it in upon Wednesday to receive further debate.

For the matter of wardship, it was ordered to be moved to the House that a conference might be had with the Lords, to see if they would join with us in making a petition to the King to give us leave to treat of those matters and to offer him a project.

For purveyors, it was ordered that some few lawyers should draw a bill, and bring it in upon Wednesday, to be further considered of.

The rest of the matters, the day being spent, were referred to Tuesday next....   *HMC*, Buccleuch, III, 78–81

12. James I: speech at the prorogation of Parliament, 7 July 1604

My Lords, and you the knights and burgesses of the lower House: Though in the true nature of a Parliament you are but one body, yet because you are not conjoined as in Scotland, but divided into two houses, I must speak unto you distinctly.

With you (my Lords) I will not be long. I will not flatter, nor by God's grace speak an untruth publicly or privately; less than this I cannot afford you, and give you your due, that you have carried yourselves with discretion, modesty, judgement, care and fidelity. Never king had better subject to praise good subjects than I you. In fine, you have done that both in circumstance and effect that became you.

I have more to say to you, my Masters of the lower House, both in regard of former occasions, and now of your Speaker's speech. It hath been the form of most kings to give thanks to their people however their deserts were; of some, to use sharp admonishment and reproof. Now if you expect either great praises, or reproofs out of custom, I will deceive you in both. I will not thank where I think no thanks due; you would think me base if I should; it were not Christian, it were not kingly. I do not think you, as the body of the realm, undutiful. There is an old rule, *qui bene distinguit, bene docet*. This house doth not so represent the whole commons of the realm as the shadow doth the body, but only representatively. Impossible it was for them to know all that would be propounded here; much more all those answers that you would make to all propositions. So, as I account not all that to be done by the commons of the land which hath been done by you, I will not thank them for what you have well done, nor blame them for what you have done ill. I must say this for you, that I never heard nor read that there were so many wise, and so many judicious men of that house generally. But where many are some must needs be idle heads, some rash, some curious, some busy informers. The greatest part of you were well affected, but where there is a like liberty the worst likely carries away the best. The reason is the corruption of our nature. The pertness and boldness of some cries all modest men down. You see I am not such a stock as to praise fools. I cannot say you all did well, or all ill; and whether well or ill you must not expect I will give you the same answer. There were wise men amongst you; so was there a roll of knavery. I do not think that any of you had seditious minds to overthrow and confound this monarchy, but out of divers humours and respects you were moved to curiosities.

    1. Some out of boldness to press upon my lenity, and likewise on the thanks I gave you at the beginning of the parliament. They thought they would put me to it; and now it was time to be done or never.

    2. Some wanted fame, and rather than they would not win fame, would do as he that burnt the temple of Ephesus.

    3. Some had an itching humour ever to be talking, and this common saying is proper to common babblers, *in multiloquis non deest peccatum*.

    4. Some were great populars, that did not cut even way betwixt their duty to their king and love to the country.

5. And some of a new religion, framed to their own appetite, who in all haste would build new Jerusalem, and had not patience to stay for their fellows till Doomsday.

No marvel if such concurrence bred perturbation. Too curious you were, and (God forgive you) too jealous of me. In my government by-past of Scotland (where I ruled amongst men not of the best temper) I was heard not only as a king, but, suppose I say it, as a counsellor. Contrary, here nothing but curiosity from morning to evening to find faults with my propositions. There, all things warranted that come from me; here all things suspected....

You had great business amongst yourselves about religion. I can not enough wonder that in three days after the beginning of the parliament men should go contrary to their oaths of Supremacy. In my first speech I did lightly note those of that novelty; I did not think they had been so great, so proud, or so dominant in your House. This I say of it. It is the most dangerous sect that claims to novelty. Advise unto it. In things that are against the word of God I will with as great humility as any slave fall upon my knees or face; but in things indifferent they are seditious which obey not the magistrate. There is no man half so dangerous as he that repugns against order, yet some which make scruple I would use with clemency; but let them meet me with obedience. To discreet men I say, they shall obtain their desires by grace, but to all I profess, they shall extort nothing by violence.

Touching the Purveyors (who have much busied you this parliament), you have good laws already; see them executed in God's name. Punish them, but wrong not their Master. I were a tyrant if I should uphold those scribes and publicans. I will punish the great officers if they punish not the less. And now you are going into your several countries I would have you advise of the fittest means to ease yourselves of that burden, but so that you lay not a greater burden upon me.

You see how in many things you did not well. The best apology-maker of you all, for all his eloquence, cannot make all good. Forsooth, a goodly matter to make apologies when no man is by to answer. You have done many things rashly. I say not you meant disloyally. I receive better comfort in you, and account better to be king of such subjects than of so many kingdoms. Only I wish you had kept a better form. I like form as much as matter. It shows respect, and I expect it, being a king well born (suppose I say it) as any of my progenitors. I wish you would use your liberty with more modesty in time to come.

You must know that the Parliament not sitting the liberties are not sitting. My justice shall always sit in the same seat. Justice I will give to all, and favour to such as deserve it. In cases of justice, if I should do you wrong I were no just king; but in cases of equity, if I should show favour except there be obedience I were no wise man.

Take this with you for a conclusion, and believe it. That never king was more loving or thankful to a people, or more careful than I am, to ease their burdens. P.R.O., S.P. 14/8, 93

13. Debate in committee, 22 May 1610, on the Commons' Petition of Right

Mr Fuller[1] repeated part of a speech that was formerly spoken by Mr Whitelock,[2] which was that the English nation was accompted in times past by all others in three special respects:

1. That that which is the subjects' cannot be taken from them without their consent, but by due course of law.

2. That laws cannot be made without the consent of the three estates.

3. That the Parliament, consisting of these three estates, was the armamentary or storehouse wherein these things were safely reposed and preserved, as well the laws of the land as the rights and proprieties of the subjects to their lands and goods. And that the special privilege of parliament is to debate freely of all things that shall concern any of the subjects in particular, or the commonwealth in general, without any restraint or inhibition.

Secondly, it was said[3] that in all ages the King's prerogative...hath been examined and debated in Parliament....Also it was said that in all the Courts of Justice at Westminster the King's prerogative is there ordinarily disputed, and therefore may much more be debated in Parliament, being the highest court of justice in the realm.

But Sir Francis Bacon took upon him to answer these reasons, and said...that he had been a Parliament man ever since he was seventeen years old, within which time he did observe that the Parliament had received divers inhibitions from the Queen to restrain them from debating the matter then in question; wherein he took this difference,

---

[1] Nicholas Fuller, M.P. for the City of London.
[2] James Whitelock, M.P. for Woodstock. The speech that Fuller summarises had actually been delivered that morning in the House.
[3] By Thomas Wentworth, M.P. for Oxford City.

that if the matter debated concerned the right or interest of any subject or the commonwealth, if in that case an inhibition came, he for his part would not advise the House to desist, but to inform the King of the liberty of the House, and so to proceed. But if the matter in question were an essential thing which concerned the prerogative and power of the Crown, then the House did always desist from proceeding any further upon such inhibitions received. He gave instance[s] of divers in his time....

In answer to this speech divers stood up, by whom it was answered that, as we *ambulare in via recta* so it is an express text also not to remove the ancient landmarks, and therefore we must be careful to follow the steps of our ancestors, but [also] to preserve and maintain the liberties and privileges of our House....

[After further speeches] it was moved therefore, that as the King had granted us freedom of speech at the beginning of the parliament concerning all matters of the commonwealth (which could not well be taken from us without shaking the foundations of the liberties of Parliament), so we should by a Petition of Right make known our liberties to his Majesty, and desire him to remove the impediment, for though it is Solomon's counsel not to move the King, yet it is counsel also, that if his spirit be moved yet leave not thy place.

Gardiner, Parliamentary Debates in 1610, pp. 37–9

14. Commons Petition, 3 December 1621

Most gracious and dread sovereign: We, your Majesty's most humble and loyal subjects, the knights, citizens and burgesses now assembled in Parliament, who represent the commons of your realm, full of hearty sorrow to be deprived of the comfort of your royal presence, the rather for that it proceeds from the want of your health, wherein we all unfeignedly do suffer; in all humble manner calling to mind your gracious answer to our former petition concerning religion, which, notwithstanding your Majesty's pious and princely intentions, hath not produced that good effect which the danger of these times doth seem to us to require; and finding how ill your Majesty's goodness hath been requited by princes of different religion, who even in time of treaty have taken [the] opportunity to advance their own ends, tending to the subversion of religion and disadvantage of your affairs and estate of your children; by reason whereof your ill-affected subjects at home, the Popish recusants, have taken too much encouragement and are dangerously increased in their number and in their insolencies; we cannot but be sensible thereof, and therefore humbly represent what we conceive to be the causes of so great and growing mischiefs, and what be the remedies.

I. The vigilancy and ambition of the Pope of Rome and his dearest son; the one aiming at as large a temporal monarchy as the other at a spiritual supremacy.

II. The devilish positions and doctrines whereon Popery is built, and taught with authority to their followers for advancement of their temporal ends.

III. The distressed and miserable estate of the professors of true religion in foreign parts.

IV. The disastrous accidents to your Majesty's children abroad, expressed with rejoicing, and even with contempt of their persons.

V. The strange confederacy of the princes of the Popish religion, aiming mainly at the advancement of theirs and subverting of ours, and taking the advantages conducing to that end upon all occasions.

VI. The great and many armies raised and maintained at the charge of the King of Spain, the chief of that league.

VII. The expectation of the Popish recusants of the match with Spain, and feeding themselves with great hopes of the consequences thereof.

VIII. The interposing of foreign princes and their agents in the behalf of Popish recusants for connivance and favour unto them.

IX. Their open and usual resort to the houses and, which is worse, the chapels of foreign ambassadors.

X. Their more than usual concourse to the City, and their frequent conventicles and conferences there.

XI. The education of their children in many several seminaries and houses of their religion in foreign parts appropriated to the English fugitives.

XII. The grants of their just forfeitures intended by your Majesty as a reward of service to the grantees but, beyond your Majesty's intention, transferred or compounded for at such mean rates as will amount to little less than a toleration.

XIII. The licentious printing and dispersing of Popish and seditious books, even in the time of Parliament.

XIV. The swarms of priests and Jesuits, the common incendiaries of all Christendom, dispersed in all parts of your kingdom.

And from these causes, as bitter roots, we humbly offer to your Majesty that we foresee and fear there will necessarily follow very dangerous effects both to Church and State. For,

I. The Popish religion is incompatible with ours in respect of their positions.

II. It draweth with it an unavoidable dependency on foreign princes.

III. It openeth too wide a gap for popularity to any who shall draw too great a party.

IV. It hath a restless spirit, and will strive by these gradations: if it once but get a connivancy, it will press for a toleration; if that should be obtained, they must have an equality; from thence they will aspire to superiority, and will never rest till they get a subversion of the true religion.

The remedies against these growing evils, which in all humility we offer unto your most excellent Majesty, are these:

I. That seeing this inevitable necessity is fallen upon your Majesty which no wisdom or providence of a peaceable and pious king can avoid, your Majesty would not omit this just occasion speedily and effectually to take the sword into your hand.

II. That once undertaken upon so honourable and just grounds, your Majesty would resolve to pursue and more publicly avow the aiding of those of our religion in foreign parts; which doubtless would reunite the Princes and states of the Union, by these disasters disheartened and disbanded.[1]

III. That your Majesty would propose to yourself to manage this war with the best advantage, by a diversion or otherwise, as in your deep judgement shall be found fittest, and not to rest upon a war in these parts only, which will consume your treasure and discourage your people.

IV. That the bent of this war and point of your sword may be against that prince (whatsoever opinion of potency he hath) whose armies and treasures have first diverted and since maintained the war in the Palatinate.

V. That for securing of our peace at home, your Majesty would be pleased...to put in execution, by the care of choice commissioners to be thereunto specially appointed, the laws already and hereafter to be made for preventing of dangers by Popish recusants and their wonted evasions.

---

[1] The Union of Protestant Princes was dissolved in April 1621.

VI. That to frustrate their hopes for a future age, our most noble Prince may be timely and happily married to one of our own religion.

VII. That the children of the nobility and gentry of this kingdom, and of others ill-affected and suspected in their religion, now beyond the seas, may be forthwith called home by your means and at the charge of their parents or governors.

VIII. That the children of Popish recusants, or such whose wives are Popish recusants, be brought up during their minority with Protestant schoolmasters and teachers, who may sow in their tender years the seeds of true religion.

IX. That your Majesty will be pleased speedily to revoke all former licences for such children and youth to travel beyond the seas, and not grant any such licence hereafter.

X. That your Majesty's learned counsel may receive commandment from your Highness carefully to look into former grants of recusants' lands, and to avoid [sc. cancel] them if by law they can; and that your Majesty will stay your hand from passing any such grants hereafter.

This is the sum and effect of our humble declaration, which we (no ways intending to press upon your Majesty's undoubted and regal prerogative) do with the fullness of our duty and obedience humbly submit to your most princely consideration: the glory of God, whose cause it is; the zeal of our true religion, in which we have been born and wherein (by God's grace) we are resolved to die; the safety of your Majesty's person, who is the very life of your people; the happiness of your children and posterity; the honour and good of the Church and State, dearer unto us than our own lives, having kindled these affections truly devoted to your Majesty.

And seeing out of our duty to your Majesty we have already resolved to give at the end of this session one entire subsidy, for the present relief of the Palatinate only, to be paid in the end of February next, which cannot well be effected but by passing a bill in parliamentary course before Christmas, we most humbly beseech your Majesty (as our assured hope is) that you will then also vouchsafe to give life by your royal assent to such bills as before that time shall be prepared for your Majesty's honour and the general good of your people; and that such bills may also be accompanied (as hath been accustomed) with your Majesty's gracious pardon (which proceeding from your own mere grace, may by your Highness's direction be drawn to that latitude and extent as may best sort with your Majesty's bounty and goodness).

And that not only felons and criminal offenders may take benefit thereof, but that your good subjects may receive ease thereby. And if it shall so stand [with] your good pleasure, that it may extend to the relief of old debts and duties to the Crown before the first year of your Majesty's reign, to the discharge of alienations without licence, and misusing of liveries, and *ouster le mains* before the first summons of this Parliament, and of concealed wardships, and not suing of liveries, and *ouster le mains* before the twelfth year of your Majesty's reign. Which gracious favour would much comfort your good subjects, and ease them from vexation, with little loss or prejudice to your own profit.

And we by our daily and devout prayers to the Almighty, the great King of Kings, shall contend for a blessing upon our endeavours, and for your Majesty's long and happy reign over us, and for your children's children after you for many and many generations.   Rushworth, I, 40–43

15. The Commons' Protestation, 18 December 1621

The Commons now assembled in Parliament, being justly occasioned thereunto concerning sundry liberties, franchises and privileges of Parliament, amongst others here mentioned, do make this Protestation following.

That the liberties, franchises, privileges and jurisdictions of Parliament are the ancient and undoubted birthright and inheritance of the subjects of England; and that the arduous and urgent affairs concerning the King, state and defence of the realm, and of the Church of England, and the maintenance and making of laws, and redress of mischiefs and grievances which daily happen within this realm, are proper subjects and matters of counsel and debate in Parliament; and that in the handling and proceeding of those businesses every Member of the House of Commons hath, and of right ought to have, freedom of speech to propound, treat, reason and bring to conclusion the same; and that the Commons in Parliament have like liberty and freedom to treat of these matters in such order as in their judgements shall seem fittest; and that every Member of the said House hath like freedom from all impeachment, imprisonment and molestation (other than by censure of the House itself) for or concerning any speaking, reasoning or declaring of any matter or matters touching the Parliament or Parliament business; and that if any of the said members be complained of and questioned for anything done or said in Parliament, the same is to be showed to the King by the advice and assent of all the Commons assembled in Parliament before the King give credence to any private information.

Rushworth, I, 53

16. The King's Speech at the opening of Parliament, 19 February 1624

It is a true saying and uttered by the spirit of God, that the glory of a king stands in the multitude of his people. And I am sure it is as true, that the strength of a kingdom stands next, and immediately after God's protection, in the hearts of the people. That you may see, and have a proof, that I have not this only in my tongue but have it likewise settled in my heart (as God can bear me record), and that every way, I have therefore called you at this time to speak freely my mind unto you; for remembering many misunderstandings between me and you before, I am now brought hither with an earnest desire to do my duty that God hath called me unto, by declaring unto you the verity of this, that God hath put in my heart, and to manifest my actions to be true by my words. I remember very well, it is a very fit similitude for a king and his people to be like to a husband and wife, for even as Christ, in whose throne I sit in this part of the earth, is husband to the Church, and the Church is his spouse, so I likewise desire to be your husband, and ye should be my spouse; and therefore, as it is the husband's part to cherish his wife, to entreat her kindly, and reconcile himself towards her, and procure her love by all means, so it is my part to do the like to my people. . . .

The properties and causes of calling a parliament (and so go the writs) are to confer with the king and give him their advice in matters of greatest weight and importance. For this cause have I now called you together, that ye may have proof of my love, and of my trust; I have now called you to give me your advice in the greatest matters that ever could concern any king; a greater declaration of my confidence in you I cannot give.

I have been these many years upon treaties;[1] but so far as I thought (and, God is my witness, I never had any other intention) for settling a peace in Christendom, and settling of peace at home. And in these treaties I went long on, but finding in them a slower success than I expected, or had reason to do, I was willing, and especially in one thing

---

[1] Meaning 'negotiations' throughout.

concerning the estate of my grandchildren, to see a good and speedy end. And in this finding as great promises as I could wish, and yet finding their actions clean contrary, it stirred up my son to offer himself to make that journey, and I thank God, having him here now, I have no cause to repent it; for, being of fit age and ripeness for marriage, he urged me to know the certainty in a matter of so great weight, that he might not be put off with long delays, for delay in such a case is more dangerous than denial. In it I was content, as a rare example, to grant his desire, and with him I only sent the man whom I most trusted, Buckingham, commanding him never to leave him, nor to return home without him; and I thank God for it, for it hath learned me a wisdom, for *in generalibus versatur dolus*. I had general hopes before, but particulars will resolve matters, generals will not, and before this journey things came to me as raw, as if I had never treated of them before; and I was as far disappointed of my ends as if I had been wakened out of a dream. Now I have put it into a certainty, and whereas I walked in a mist before I have now brought it to particulars.... And, when you have heard all *super totam materiam*, I shall then entreat your good and sound advice, for the glory of God, the peace of the kingdom, and the weal of my children. Never king gave more trust to his subjects than to desire their advice in matters of this weight, for I assure you ye may freely advise me, seeing, of my princely fidelity, ye are entreated thereunto. And never subjects had better hearts and experience to give me good advice than you, of which I make no doubt, for if you love yourselves you will give me good advice, your own felicity depending upon it.

One particular I must remember of you, because it hath been much talked of in the country, that I should be slack in my care of religion for other occasions.

My Lords, and you Gentlemen all, I pray you judge me charitably, as you would have me to judge you; for I never made public nor private treaties but I always made a direct reservation for the weal public and [the] cause of religion, for the glory of God [and] the good of my subjects. I only thought good sometimes to wink and connive at the execution of some penal statutes, and not to go on so rigorously as at other times, but to dispense with any, to forbid or alter any that concern religion, I never promised or yielded; I never did think it with my heart, nor speak it with my mouth...

* * * * * *

God judge me, I speak as a Christian prince, never man in a dry and sandy wilderness, where no water is, did thirst more in hot weather for drink, than I do now for a happy conclusion of this parliament. And now I hope, after the miscarriage of three, this may prove happy. I am neither curious nor captious. Eschew all occasions of curious questions, that may hinder you in this great cause for which I have called you; and remember that spending of time is spoiling of business. And this I hope in God, and that by a faith in God, that by your actions this parliament I shall clearly see your hearts, and that you are the true representative body of my subjects. For you know in your consciences that of all the kings that ever were, I dare say, never king was better beloved of his people than I am. Therefore be ye true glasses and mirrors of their faces, and be sure you yield true reflections and representations, as you ought to do. And this doing I hope you shall not only find the blessing of God, but also by these actions procure the thanks and love of the whole people for being so true and faithful glasses. And you shall never find me desire any thing of you, but what shall tend to the common good and weal of the kingdom.

LJ, III, 209–10

17. Speech by Sir Dudley Carleton, House of Commons, 12 May 1626

...I beseech you, gentlemen, move not his Majesty with trenching upon his prerogatives, lest you bring him out of love with parliaments. You have heard his Majesty's often messages to you, to put you forward in a course that will be most convenient. In those messages he told you, that if there were not correspondency between him and you, he should be enforced to use new counsels. Now, I pray you consider what these new counsels are, and may be; I fear to declare those that I conceive. In all Christian kingdoms you know that parliaments were in use anciently, by which their kingdoms were governed in a most flourishing manner, until the monarchs began to know their own strength, and, seeing the turbulent spirit of their parliaments, at length they little by little began to stand upon their prerogatives, and at last overthrew the parliaments throughout Christendom, except here only with us.

And indeed, you would count it a great misery if you knew the subjects in foreign countries as well as myself, to see them look not like our nation, with store of flesh on their backs, but like so many ghosts, and not men, being nothing but skin and bones, with some thin cover to their nakedness, and wearing only wooden shoes on their feet, so that they cannot eat meat or wear good clothes, but they must pay and be taxed unto the King for it. There is a misery beyond expression, and that which yet we are free from. Let us be careful then to preserve the King's good opinion of parliaments, which bringeth this happiness to this nation, and makes us envied of all others, while there is this sweetness between his Majesty and his Commons, lest we lose the repute of a free-born nation by turbulency in Parliament. For in my opinion the greatest and wisest part of a parliament are those that use the greatest silence, so as it be not opiniative, or sullen, as now we are by the loss of these our members that are committed.

This good correspondency being kept between the King and his people will so join their love and favour to his Majesty with liking of parliaments, that his prerogative shall be preserved entire to himself, without our touching upon it, and also the privilege of the subject (which is our happiness) inviolated, and both be maintained to the support of each other. *PH*, II, 120–21

18. Proceedings in King's Bench, 25 January–12 February 1630

Sir Robert Heath, the King's attorney-general, exhibited informations in this court against Sir John Eliot, knight, Denzil Holles and Benjamin Valentine, esquires, the effect of which was,...that the said Eliot publicly and maliciously in the House of Commons, to raise sedition between the King, his nobles and people, uttered these words: 'That the Council and the judges had all conspired to trample under foot the liberties of the subject.' He further showed...that the King, for divers reasons, had a purpose to have the House of Commons adjourned, and gave direction to Sir John Finch, then the Speaker, to move an adjournment; and if it should not be obeyed, that he should forthwith come from the House to the King. And that the defendants, by confederacy beforehand, spake a long and continued speech, which was recited *verbatim*, in which were divers malicious and seditious words, of dangerous consequence.[1] And to the intent that they might not be prevented of uttering their premeditate speeches, their intention was, that the

---

[1] The speech quoted in the indictment is by Eliot (*ST*, III, 322–3; Forster, *Sir John Eliot*, II, 449–52). It is perhaps unnecessary to add that Heath's account of the events of 2 March 1629 is decidedly partial; for what really happened, see Hulme, *Sir John Eliot*, pp. 307–15.

Speaker should not go out of the Chair till they had spoken them, [and] the defendants Holles and Valentine laid violent hands upon the Speaker, to the great affrightment and disturbance of the House. And the Speaker being got out of the Chair, they by violence set him in the Chair again; so there was a great tumult in the House....

And to this Information the defendants put in a plea to the jurisdiction of the court, because 'these offences are supposed to be done in Parliament, and ought not to be punished in this court, or in any other but in Parliament....'.

[12 February 1630]

...Inasmuch as the Defendants would not put in any other plea, the last day of the Term judgement was given against them upon a *nihil dicit*, which judgement was pronounced by [Mr Justice William] Jones to this effect:

The matter of the information now, by the confession of the defendants, is admitted to be true, and we think their plea to the jurisdiction insufficient for the matter and manner of it. And we hereby will not draw the true liberties of Parliament-men into question; to wit, for such matters which they do or speak in a parliamentary manner. But in this case there was a conspiracy between the defendants to slander the State, and to raise sedition and discord between the King, his peers and people, and this was not a parliamentary course. All the judges of England, except one, have resolved the statute of 4 H. 8 to be a private act, and to extend to Strode only. But every Member of Parliament shall have such privileges as are there mentioned; but they have no privilege to speak at their pleasure. The Parliament is a high court, therefore it ought not to be disorderly, but ought to give good example to other courts. If a judge of our court should rail upon the State, or clergy, he is punishable for it. A Member of Parliament may charge any great officer of state with any particular offence, but this was a malevolous accusation in the generality of all the officers of state, therefore the matter contained within the information is a great offence, and punishable in this court.

For the punishment, although the offence be great, yet that shall be with a light hand, and shall be in this manner.

1. That every of the defendants shall be imprisoned during the King's pleasure: Sir John Eliot to be imprisoned in the Tower of London, and the other defendants in other prisons.

2. That none of them shall be delivered out of prison until he give security to this court for his good behaviour, and have [*sic*] made submission and acknowledgement of his offence.

3. Sir John Eliot inasmuch as we think him the greatest offender, and the ringleader, shall pay to the King a fine of 2000*l.* and Mr Holles a fine of 1000 marks; and Mr Valentine, because he is of less ability[1] than the rest, shall pay a fine of 500*l.*

And to all this all the other justices with one voice accorded.

ST, III, 293–4, 309–10

19. Parliamentary privilege

[10 May 1640,] Order of Council, the King present.

This day John Crew, Esq., being convented before the board and required by his Majesty to deliver up to [the] Clerk of the House of Commons all such petitions, papers and complaints as he received, being in the chair at the Committee for Religion, refused to obey his Majesty's and the Lords of the Council's command therein, albeit it was declared to him to be agreeable to the practice and course of all others who had served in the like employment at committees appointed by that House of Parliament, for which his obstinate refusal he was by his Majesty's command committed close prisoner in the Tower of London. *And the said Mr Crew being further required by one of the Clerks of the Council to tell where these petitions and papers were, said he had delivered the same into the hands of other persons, whose names he refused to tell.*[2]

CSPD 1640, pp. 141–2

II. FINANCE

The parliaments of the first two Stuarts, like the later parliaments of Elizabeth, were mainly preoccupied with questions of finance, or direct and indirect taxation. The general rise in prices had depressed the real income of the Crown, and at the same time made the land-owning classes unwilling or unable to supplement that income. In the closing years of the sixteenth century Elizabeth had begun to exploit with greater vigour certain ancient rights which could be made to yield an income to the Crown. The feudal incidents of wardship and marriage were unashamedly exploited, especially after Robert Cecil succeeded his father, Lord Burleigh, as Master of the Court

[1] Meaning 'property' or 'wealth'.
[2] The sentence in italics is crossed out in the original.

of Wards in 1598.[1] Purveyance was levied as a nation-wide tax, and even more galling was the queen's insistance on her right to buy provisions in the open market at prices fixed by her purveyors; but the attempt of Parliament to abolish it in 1589 was unsuccessful.[2] Finally, the queen's reckless grant or sale of monopolies on the manufacture, or even the import, of specific products produced in 1601 a full-scale parliamentary revolt.[3]

These grievances were at once raised in 1604. By 26 March the situation in the Commons was so alarming that Robert Cecil decided to take the initiative in arranging conferences between the two Houses on wardship and purveyance.[4] To a Commons petition on purveyance James replied, with unconscious cynicism, that all his most eminent predecessors had legislated against abuses of this right, and he was prepared to follow suit. The officers of the household had a brush with the Commons' spokesman at the same time:

That they had these things only by relation [sc. hearsay].
Answer. They would be verified.
They did according to ancient usage.
Usage or prescription contrary to a positive statute void.
Not possible the king should otherwise be served.
Quia mirium, magnum mysterium, that the king could not be served if his laws observed.[5]

But the end was stalemate. The Commons declined to recognise that the Crown had any right to purveyance at all, and therefore rejected the Lords' proposals for an annual tax in lieu of it. On the other hand the Lords rejected the Commons' proposals on wardship, which did offer financial compensation, on the grounds that it would be 'inconvenient and unseasonable' to press such demands in the first Parliament of a new reign.[6]

The chance of initiating serious negotiations on taxation was thrown away. Elizabeth's debts, the rising expenditure of the government (despite the end of the Spanish War),[7] made further exploitation of extra-parliamentary methods of taxation inevitable, and only the wave of enthusiastic loyalty following the discovery of the Gunpowder Plot prevented a crisis in the session of 1606. Even then, in March 1606 the Commons submitted a list of grievances which included monopolies, purveyance, the recent rise in customs

---

[1] Hurstfield, *The Queen's Wards,* and 'The profits of fiscal feudalism', *Economic History Review,* VIII (1955), 53.
[2] Allegra Woodworth, 'Purveyance for the Royal Household in the Reign of Queen Elizabeth', *Transactions American Philosophical Society,* N.S., xxxv (1945); G. E. Aylmer, 'The Last Years of Purveyance, 1610–1660', *Economic History Review,* x (1957), 81.
[3] J. E. Neale, *Elizabeth I and Her Parliaments, 1584–1601* (London, 1957), pp. 384–5.
[4] *CJ,* I, 153–4.   [5] *Ibid.* 190–3.
[6] *Ibid.* 204, 207–8; *LJ,* II, 294, 309.
[7] Dietz, *English Public Finance,* pp. 110–14.

duties, and the new import duties, or 'impositions'.[1] It was useless for James to inquire 'whether these began not in the Queen's time, yet [she] a just, a glorious queen?';[2] though he gave a full answer in November (21), the same grievances came up in 1610, much to his irritation.[3]

By 1610 the attention of the Commons was focused on impositions. The Crown had always possessed the right to levy import duties for the regulation of trade and the protection of English manufactures.[4] In 1601, when the Levant Company surrendered the charter which gave it exclusive rights of trade with Venice, Elizabeth recouped herself for the loss of the annual rent paid by the company by levying a duty of 5s. 6d. a cwt. on imported currants, and later on tobacco. In 1606 the merchant John Bate refused to pay and was committed to prison; his action was probably inspired by the Levant Company's desire to regain their monopoly, but the merchants summoned to give evidence before the Commons prophesied the utter ruin of trade if impositions continued,[5] and the House was sufficiently impressed to include them in their petition of grievances, in March 1606.

James promptly sued Bate in the exchequer to test his rights, and in July he predictably won his case. Indeed, Chief Baron Fleming's judgement appeared to give the king the power to levy duties on any commodity at any time (20). It is difficult to know what weight to attach to this; as Tanner remarks, 'It was very usual in this period for judges whose real conclusions were based on the narrowest and most technical grounds to embellish their judgements with vague philosophy'.[6] Coke later claimed that he and the other Chief Justice, Popham of King's Bench, had privately dissented from Fleming's judgement,[7] but William Hakewill and other radical barristers found it perfectly convincing. Moreover, the House of Commons would find it difficult to defend men whose sole preoccupation was obviously money, and Fleming's gibe—'It is well known that the end of every private merchant is not the common good but his particular profit'—struck home. The topic was not raised again in the session of 1606–7.

[1] The original petition does not appear to survive, but those who still believe that parliaments of this era were concerned exclusively, or even preponderantly, with questions of religion or right, should study James's answer to it (21). Compare a similar petition presented in 1624 (PH, I, 1489–92), which descended to such trivia as the lighthouse at Winterton, Norfolk, and the scandalous conduct of the President of Corpus Christi College, Oxford.

[2] CJ, I, 309 (15 May).

[3] He accused the Commons of taking up grievances 'in the streets', to 'have a show made', and ordered them to confine themselves to grievances originating in their constituencies, of which they had personal knowledge (Works, p. 356, 21 March 1610).

[4] G. D. G. Hall, 'Impositions and the Courts, 1554–1606', Law Quarterly Review, LXIX (1953), 200.

[5] 'The merchants offer to leave all rather than this shall stand, go beyond seas' (CJ, I, 297 (11 April 1606)).

[6] TCD, p. 338.

[7] Coke, Reports, pt. XII, §§ 33–5 (VI, 237–40).

But in July 1608 Robert Cecil, now Earl of Salisbury, extended impositions to almost every imported commodity except basic foodstuffs, munitions and ships' stores,[1] and as soon as Parliament reassembled for its fourth session in February 1610 the Commons called for an inquiry.[2] The whole topic was ventilated on 23, 28 and 29 June, but without much result. The incorrigible antiquarianism of the Commons, and their belief that precedents of the Hundred Years War were immediately applicable to modern conditions, sterilised the debate, and James Whitelocke was the only man to rise above it (22). His argument that in England taxation was vested in the sovereign authority, and this was neither King nor Parliament alone but King-in-Parliament, was probably above the heads of most of his hearers, but in the circumstances a resounding victory for the Opposition was inevitable, and impositions were placed at the head of a new Petition of Grievances, covering the whole field of Church and State, which was presented to the king on 7 July (23).

In these unpromising conditions Salisbury had been trying to negotiate a new basis for taxation and persuade the Commons to recognise that the king's real income had fallen disastrously and must be supplemented by regular taxation in return for the abandonment of such ancient rights as wardship and purveyance. As part of this 'Great Contract' James reluctantly agreed to abandon his right to levy new impositions in the future.[3] But the failure of the Contract was not caused by impositions. The king was profoundly reluctant to bargain over his prerogative, and the Commons could see no way of raising the extra money needed except by a permanent land-tax or an excise, both equally deplorable in their eyes. The House was adjourned in disorder on 24 November and dissolved the following January. The attempt to revise the English fiscal system was postponed until 1660.

Impositions, in fact, continued, in the face of diminishing opposition. They were levied on a wide variety of imports until 1641, when they were retrospectively legalised by the Tunnage and Poundage Act, and after a typically confused and acrimonious debate in 1614[4] Parliament took little notice of them. James fulfilled his promise to review impositions with the aim of moderating them and overhauling their distribution. A new commission issued on 5 September 1610 answered many of the specific complaints against the new tax, and by carefully weighting it against alien merchants the government pacified the City. Some merchants renewed their opposition on Charles I's accession, perhaps simply because James had so often stated in

[1] Dietz, *English Public Finance*, pp. 369–71.
[2] Gardiner, *Parliamentary Debates in 1610*, pp. 58 ff., and *ST*, II, 407–520; partly printed in *TCD*, pp. 247–63.
[3] Gardiner, *op. cit.* pp. 162–3. See also *TCD* pp. 345–7.
[4] *TCD*, pp. 267–8.

1610 that he claimed the right only for his own lifetime. A small minority of merchants carried their protests to extreme lengths in 1627 and 1628, but their efforts were swallowed up in the more general resistance to tunnage and poundage.[1]

In 1614 there were elaborate plans for renewed negotiations with Parliament, along the lines drawn up in 1610, but less coherently expressed.[2] Unfortunately the tactical incompetence of the King and the ministers who had succeeded Salisbury, and the intractability of the Commons, wrecked the whole project at the outset. In the ensuing seven years James found an able financial adviser in Lionel Cranfield, but he also found a new and more expensive favourite in George Villiers, earl, marquess and finally duke of Buckingham. So pressing were his commitments that he was soon obliged to issue patents of monopoly again on an unprecedented scale. On his accession he had cancelled all existing patents and renewed very few of them, but after 1612 their numbers steadily increased. The insensate fury with which Parliament fell upon the monopolists in the first session of 1621 was roused by the economic crisis which began to develop in 1620, and the shortage of bullion, which was blamed on the monopolies in the manufacture of gold and silver thread awarded to Buckingham's brothers. Indeed, the attack on Mitchell and Mompesson was the first round in the attack on Buckingham himself, and the House of Lords turned on the Crown for the first time for a century. James wisely decided that he could not defend Mitchell and Mompesson, and he surrendered to the demand of the Commons that he put his own household in order; he allowed them to proceed by impeachment, and he even allowed this weapon to be turned against the lord chancellor, Francis Bacon.[3] When Parliament adjourned on 4 June it had been discussing grievances for more than sixteen weeks; it had unseated the lord chancellor, and it had forced James to cancel all outstanding patents of monopoly, but it had only punished three out of a whole host of guilty men, and Coke's attempt to make monopolies illegal by statute failed. Whether intentionally or not, James and his advisers had conducted their retreat with success. In the second session the Opposition was off on another tack, foreign policy, and early in 1622 Parliament was again dissolved without any constructive accomplishments to its name.[4] But James had been voted two subsidies in the first session, which was more than he got in 1610 or 1614.

In 1624 all was changed. Buckingham and the Prince of Wales, anxious to reverse England's foreign policy, did a deal with the Opposition. Parliament was allowed to debate foreign relations; the lord treasurer, Lionel Cranfield, earl of Middlesex, was impeached and ruined; and the Commons

---

[1] Dietz, *English Public Finance*, pp. 371–5.
[2] Moir, *The Addled Parliament*, ch. VI, and app. VII, and Willson, *Privy Councillors*, ch. v.
[3] See p. 93 below.
[4] See p. 29 above.

secured a Monopolies Act, which confined their use to new inventions.[1] In return the Commons only offered three subsidies and three fifteenths and tenths, and the preamble to the Subsidy Act declared that the money was to be expended only on the defence of England and Ireland, the navy and aid to the Dutch (24). Furthermore, the act provided that the money collected should be paid to treasurers strictly accountable to Parliament, and should be paid by them to the Council of War only for the purposes specified. This device of 'appropriation' was premature, and does not seem to have been followed up. The Lords were disturbed, and entered a protest, and James threatened to alter the preamble to include 'the recovery of the Palatinate', the ostensible cause of the war, but it is not clear that this was done.[2]

Parliament was prorogued at the end of May, and by the autumn war had broken out with Spain, though it was not officially declared until September 1625. Unfortunately, it proved difficult to mount an attack on Spain at any vulnerable point, and the decision to hire the German freebooter Mansfeld to lead an English expedition into central Europe was most unpopular. The public, and especially the landed classes, were resolute in their determination to restore the Palatinate to the king's son-in-law, but equally determined not to provide the money for such an operation. Buckingham's attempts to involve Sweden were unsuccessful, and though he did succeed in securing for the Prince of Wales the hand of Henrietta Maria of France he could obtain no aid from that quarter either. Indeed, the French government weakened James's position by insisting in December 1624 that he suspend the recusancy laws and release all Roman Catholics then in custody; and in the same month, when the Huguenots rose in revolt, he even agreed to aid in their suppression. When he died on 27 March 1625 the military and diplomatic policy of Buckingham and the Prince was already exposed as a complete failure.

* * * * * *

There is no greater contrast between James I and his son than in their handling of Parliament. At the beginning of almost every session James treated both Houses to an extensive speech in which he outlined his views on kingship, his policy in general, and went into great detail on any topic which had happened to catch his interest. He often intervened in the course of the session to make further speeches, almost as long; he sent long letters to the Speaker, he sent impromptu messages by Privy Councillors almost every week, and he positively encouraged deputations from the Commons to wait on him. Charles's conduct was in marked contrast. His speeches were clipped and curt; Wentworth told the Dublin Parliament in 1634, 'I shall, as near as I can, speak in the style of my royal master, which is to be with brevity

[1] TCD, p. 269.
[2] Gardiner, History of England, v, 234–5. The Lords' protest is in PH, I, 1586–7.

and clarity'.[1] He regarded the Commons with apparent scorn, and though he would occasionally send down a brief message by one of his servants in the House he made little effort to prompt debate or even explain his wishes.

These defects were patently obvious in his first Parliament, which assembled in June 1625 in a mood of grudging goodwill, despite the difficult economic situation, and was abruptly dissolved in mid-August in a mood of resentful bewilderment. Starved of information, even the secretaries of state could not explain the decision to employ Mansfeld, to send aid against the Huguenot city of La Rochelle, and to relax the persecution of Roman Catholics under the terms of the French marriage treaty. Anger which had no other outlet was focused on Buckingham, and the failure of his expedition against Cadiz in the late autumn left him exposed to the vicious attack which came in the Parliament of 1626. The king compounded his favourite's difficulties by taking steps to bar from the Commons the leaders of the Opposition, like Wentworth and Coke, forgetting that these same men were also the spokesmen of the 'war party'. This left the field open for personal enemies of Buckingham like Sir John Eliot, who wanted nothing better than to head a crusade against him. The impeachment of his friend roused Charles to bitter anger, and he warned the Commons: 'Parliaments are altogether in my power for their calling, sitting and dissolution; therefore as I find the fruits of them good or evil, they are to continue, or not to be[2].'

He believed it was possible for him to rule without Parliament, and he authorised his servants to publish his views without reserve.[3] When he was obliged to order another dissolution in June 1626, without a penny voted for the war, he at once put these threats into execution. The successful levy of forced loans on a large scale, and the decision of King's Bench in 1627 that men imprisoned for refusing such loans were not bailable, filled the parliamentary classes with alarm.[4] Like King John, King Charles was probing the wall of law and custom which protected his subjects' money in the hope of finding the odd gap through which he could press. The gap he had found was not wide—the prisons were not large enough for him to coerce large numbers of taxpayers—but his success had serious theoretical implications. When further disasters in war and diplomacy forced him to summon a third parliament for 17 March 1628 the Opposition abandoned their attack on Buckingham and proceeded to examine the Five Knights' Case as well as the king's recent practice of billeting troops on civilians and subjecting whole areas to martial law.[5]

[1] W. Knowler (ed.), *The Earl of Strafforde's Letters and Despatches* (2 vols., 1739), I, 287. See p. 9 above.
[2] *PH*, II, 56 (29 March 1626).   [3] See Carleton's speech, no. **17**, p. 50 above.
[4] For the Five Knights' Case, see no. **33**, p. 106 below.
[5] See Lindsay Boynton, 'Billeting, the example of the Isle of Wight', *EHR*, LXXIV (1959), 23, and 'Martial Law and the Petition of Right', *ibid*. LXXIX (1964), 255.

The tortured manœuvres which followed cannot be traced in detail here.[1] Charles's opening speech was typically brief and curt, to the point of rudeness; he was always to confuse bravery and courage (25). He only succeeded in incensing a strong Opposition, and though he fought every inch of the way, for ten weeks, the impossibility of continuing the war at all without a parliamentary grant, and the importunity of Buckingham, who never looked beyond the next campaigning season, forced him to give way, and on 7 June he gave his assent to the Petition of Right (26). There was some doubt at the time, and there is still doubt, precisely what the Petition was, and whether it was equivalent to a statute or superior to it.[2] However this may be, Parliament petitioned the king not to levy taxation without consent of Parliament, not to imprison his subjects without cause shown, not to billet soldiers on civilians without their consent, and not to subject civilians to martial law, and the king agreed. Less than a week later disputes as to its interpretation broke out, but there was no doubt as to its binding force.

Tunnage and poundage, the customs duties on wine and wool, had been granted to each of the Tudors and to James I for life by their first parliament. But in 1625 the Commons decided to review the whole field of the customs, and apparently without malicious intent they only granted tunnage and poundage to Charles I for one year, pending further discussions. However, their bill for this purpose was lost in the Lords, so Charles never received any authorisation at all; nevertheless, he proceeded to collect the duties. The parliament of 1626 declared that he was acting illegally, and brought in a bill to indemnify him, but this never passed, and on 8 July, after the dissolution, the Privy Council declared that tunnage and poundage was an inseparable part of the king's revenue, which he had enjoyed ever since Henry VI's reign, and which he enjoyed now independent of any parliamentary grant. In 1628 the Opposition were prepared to be reasonable; they agreed that Charles ought to have these duties, and they discussed ways and means, but unfortunately nothing was done until after the passing of the Petition of Right, and then the situation suddenly got out of control.

As soon as the petition was passed Wentworth and Coke relinquished their grip on the House—whether voluntarily or not it is difficult to say. Pym initiated an attack on the royalist divine Roger Manwaring, and Eliot resumed his campaign against Buckingham; this led to a remonstrance on 17 June severely critical of the conduct of the war.[3] In this unpromising atmosphere discussion of tunnage and poundage was resumed, and the Commons proposed once again to review the whole field of import and export duties. They suggested that this might be left until next session; in the

---

[1] Consult Francis H. Relf, *Petition of Right.*

[2] Relf, *op. cit.* and E. R. Adair, 'The Petition of Right', *History*, v (1921), 99. Also Hulme, *Sir John Eliot*, ch. x–xi, and Judson, *Crisis of the Constitution*, pp. 240–69.

[3] Rushworth, I, 631–8.

meanwhile they would pass a simple enabling bill. But Charles now insisted that Parliament had no control over tunnage and poundage, and the Commons, with equal folly, tabled a remonstrance on 25 June which ended with a 'humble declaration',

> That the receiving of tunnage and poundage, and other impositions not granted by parliament, is a breach of the fundamental liberties of this kingdom, and contrary to your Majesty's royal answer to the said Petition of Right; and therefore they do most humbly beseech your majesty to forbear any further receiving of the same, and not to take it in ill part from those of your Majesty's loving subjects who shall refuse to make payment of any such charges.[1]

When he prorogued Parliament next day Charles made a moderate speech, in which he reaffirmed his intention of abiding by the Petition of Right, but insisted that no one regarded tunnage and poundage as included in it.[2]

He was probably right. In any case, the action of the Commons in virtually appealing to the people not to pay a tax was unprecedented and indefensible, and the decision of a group of merchants, led by John Rolles, to take them at their word only brought them into further disrepute. The Council ordered the merchants' goods to be confiscated, the Court of Exchequer ratified their action, and the responsible public agreed that the Commons were encouraging self-interested men to break the law. Since 1621 the House of Lords had been in sympathy with the Commons, and had often worked in concert with them, but the Remonstrance of 25 June alienated them completely. The assassination of Buckingham in August removed one of the principal threats to domestic peace, and leaders of opposition like the earl of Bristol at once rejoined the king, on a platform that included the strengthening of the Church and the purification of the government. When Parliament re-assembled in January 1629 the House of Commons found itself isolated; it intensified its isolation by at once espousing the cause of the delinquent merchants and declining to offer the compromise on tunnage and poundage that common sense dictated. It secured no support from the Lords in this, nor in its exaggerated and intemperate attack on Charles's ecclesiastical policy.[3] Eliot, who had framed this policy of disaster, brought the session to a disgraceful close on 2 March, when he and his supporters held the Speaker down in the Chair to prevent an adjournment, and pushed through three resolutions, on the Church and tunnage and poundage, which were yet another attempt to impose the will of the Commons, as distinct from Parliament, on the nation (27).

So, Parliament's financial policy, in so far as it had one at all, was crude and unconstructive. From 1604 to 1610 it had attacked wardship, purvey-

---

[1] GCD, p. 73.   [2] Ibid. pp. 73–4.   [3] See p. 149 below.

ance and impositions; all three continued, wardship with renewed vigour, and after 1614 they met with little criticism. It was the same with monopolies; savagely criticised in 1621, firmly legislated against in 1624, yet they continued. It was almost impossible to prevent the king using such extra-parliamentary means of financing his regime while his legitimate financial needs were unsatisfied and parliament's meetings were intermittent. There was a chance to remedy the situation in 1610, but the king's ministers and the Commons between them let the chance slip and none of Charles I's finance ministers was able enough or daring enough to devise a second Great Contract. Yet the final assault on tunnage and poundage showed the dangers of a merely negative approach, and the attempt of the London merchants to organise a stop in trade, which brought the nation to the verge of economic disaster in 1630, only alienated public opinion further. On 10 March 1629 the king issued a lengthy 'Declaration to all his loving subjects of the causes which moved him to dissolve the last parliament',[1] but he was more his usual self in a proclamation issued a fortnight later, in which he announced that he would continue to levy tunnage and poundage as long as he pleased, and he would call another parliament when he saw fit, and not before (28).

20. Bate's case, 1606

[Chief Baron Fleming]

...To the King is committed the government of the realm and his people; and Bracton saith that for his discharge of his office God has given to him power, the act of government and the power to govern. The King's power is double, ordinary and absolute, and they have several laws and ends. That of the ordinary is for the profit of particular subjects, for the execution of civil justice, the determining of *meum*; and this is exercised by equity and justice in ordinary courts, and by the Civilians is nominated *jus privatum*, and with us Common Law: and these laws cannot be changed without Parliament, and although that their form and course may be changed and interrupted, yet they can never be changed in substance. The absolute power of the King is not that which is converted or executed to private use, to the benefit of any particular person, but is only that which is applied to the general benefit of the people and is *salus populi*; as the people is the body and the King the head; and this power is [not] guided by the rules which direct only at the Common Law, and is most properly named policy and govern-

---

[1] *GCD*, pp. 83–99.

ment; and as the constitution of this body varieth with the time, so varieth this absolute law according to the wisdom of the King for the common good; and these being general rules and true as they are, all things done within these rules are lawful. The matter in question is material matter of State, and ought to be ruled by the rules of policy; and if it be so, the King hath done well to execute his extraordinary power. All customs, be they old or new, are no other but the effects and issues of trade and commerce with foreign nations; but all commerce and affairs with foreigners, all wars and peace, all acceptance and admitting for current, foreign coin, all parties and treaties whatsoever, are made by the absolute power of the King; and he who hath power of causes hath power also of effects. No exportation or importation can be but at the King's ports, they are the gates of the King, and he hath absolute power by them to include or exclude whom he shall please; and ports to merchants are their harbours and repose, and for their better security he is compelled to provide bulwarks and fortresses, and to maintain for the collection of his customs and duties collectors and customers; and for that charge it is reason that he should have this benefit. He is also to defend the merchants from pirates at sea in their passage. Also by the power of the King they are to be relieved if they are oppressed by foreign princes... [etc.].

It is said that an imposition may not be upon a subject without Parliament. That the King may impose upon a subject I omit; for it is not here the question if the King may impose upon the subject or his goods, but the impost here is not upon a subject, but here it is upon Bates, as upon a merchant who imports goods within this land charged before by the King; and at the time the impost was imposed upon them they were the goods of the Venetians and not the goods of a subject, nor within the land, but only upon those which shall after be imported; and so all the arguments which were made for the subject fail. And where it is said that he is a merchant, and that he ought to have the sea open and free for him, and that trades of merchants and merchandise are necessary to export the surplus of our commodities and then to import other necessities, and so is favourably to be respected; as to that, it is well known that the end of every private merchant is not the common good but his particular profit, which is only the means which induceth him to trade and traffic. And the impost to him is nothing, for he rateth his merchandise according to that....

The commodity of currants is no commodity of this land, but foreign. And whereas it is said that it is victual and necessary food, it is no more necessary than wine, and impost for that hath been always paid without contradiction; and without doubt there are many drinkers of wine who are also eaters of currants. That which should be said [to be] victual for the commonwealth is that which ariseth from agriculture and of the earth within this land, and not nice and delicate things imported by merchants, such as these currants are....

And whereas it is said that if the King may impose, he may impose any quantity what he pleases, true it is that this is to be referred to the wisdom of the King, who guideth all under God by his wisdom, and this is not to be disputed by a subject; and many things are left to his wisdom for the ordering of his power, rather than his power shall be restrained. The King may pardon any felon; but it may be objected that if he pardon one felon he may pardon all, to the damage of the commonwealth, and yet none will doubt but that is left in his wisdom.... And the wisdom and providence of the King is not to be disputed by the subject; for by intendment they cannot be severed from his person, and to argue *a posse ad actum* to restrain the King and his power because that by his power he may do ill is no argument for a subject. To prove the power of the King by precedents of antiquity in a case of this nature may easily be done, and if it were lawful in ancient times it is lawful now, for the authority of the King is not diminished and the Crown hath the same attributes that then it had....

Now for restraint of commodities many precedents are to prove it.

[After reviewing the precedents he concluded:]

...All these statutes prove expressly, that the King had power to increase the impost, and that upon commodities of the land, and that he continually used this power notwithstanding all acts of Parliament against it.... Wherefore I think, that the King ought to have judgement....   *ST*, II, 387–94

21. Grievances, 1606

[19 November 1606]

Mr Speaker publisheth, that the Clerk of the higher House, by his Majesty's commandment, had delivered unto him a roll of parchment, written and entitled:

A Memorial of such Resolutions as his Majesty hath taken, with the advice of his Privy Council, assisted with the two Chief Justices, the Lord Chief Baron, and his Majesty's Counsel at Law, upon examination of those Grievances which were presented to his Majesty by the lower House of Parliament at the last Session.[1] . . .

1. *Lord Danvers' Suit.* First, whereas his Majesty hath granted to the Lord Danvers and Sir John Gilbert three parts in four of all such benefit as should arise to his Majesty by fines, issues, amercements, forfeitures, &c., over and above the sum of 2,800*l.*, which sum is supposed to be the medium of those profits accruing in former years; although their profit was only to arise by such augmentation as should appear to be made in the Court of Exchequer, upon order given by his Majesty to the barons, and all other officers, for reformation of the great frauds and abuses committed in the levying of the fines and amercements; nevertheless, because the said grant appeareth to be subject to inconvenience in the execution, his Majesty hath been contented to revoke the said Patent. . . .

2. *Green Wax.* To the second, which is concerning a patent granted to Sir Roger Aston for all fines, amercements and other penalties and forfeitures known under the name of Green Wax, growing from the tenants of the Duchy of Lancaster, it is resolved by the judges that they be things grantable by the King, and are enjoyed by a patent of the late Queen's. Nevertheless, because this grant...dependeth upon some recitals which the judges have not examined, and therefore cannot now determine of it, in point of law, and because there may be some inconvenience to the subject in the execution, except some things may be reformed, his Majesty hath taken order with the patentee for surrender of his patent, and to grant him a new patent upon these conditions: First, that the patentee dispense not aforehand with offences or default of jurors...; the second, that upon every General Pardon the subject may enjoy the benefit thereof, as though the things pardoned were not granted, but still in the King's hands. . . .

3. *Issues of Jurors.* To the third, which is touching a patent made to Sir Henry Brouncker of the issues of jurors not appearing, throughout England, forasmuch as there are in this patent some such inconveniences as in the former of Sir Roger Aston's, it is also resolved to resume the

[1] *CJ*, I, 309.

old patent, which the judges already have determined to be void in law, and to grant a new, with the like provisions as are appointed for ...Sir Roger Aston.

4. *Licence to sell Wines.* To the fourth, concerning the Lord Admiral, for the licences to sell wines by retail, at a greater price than the laws now in force do allow, the judges resolve the grant to be good in law; and touching the supposed abuses complained of, such are the answers which have been given by the patentees after due examination, as it seemeth that the informers have abused the lower House with many untruths.

5. *Logwood.* To the fifth, concerning a patent which doth permit the use of a stuff for dyeing made of a mixture of logwood, or block-wood, with other things...; although both sides have been heard before his Majesty's council, and there received the opinion of the judges that his Majesty's grant is justifiable by the law; and some suggestions made by the dyers, as well concerning the price supposed to be demanded for every ton as touching some other abuses in the execution, proved false upon the hearing; nevertheless, such is and ever shall be his Majesty's precious care to prevent all colour of vexation to his subjects in general, and in this particular, more than in any other, [it] tending to discredit the making of cloth (which is one of the greatest and richest commodities of the kingdom), as he hath been pleased to resume into his hands this grant....

6. *Raising of Customs.* To the sixth, concerning the raising of the customs, it is apparent that his Majesty may by the laws of this realm require 12*d.* in the pound, according to the very value of most merchandises, nevertheless the King hath not done this, neither (according to some use of former times) were these new rates set by oath; but his Majesty, by his commissioners calling to them principal merchants of all sorts, and using their opinion and advice, caused the old rates to be changed according to the change of times, abating the former customs of divers commodities that are fallen, or too hardly rated, and so likewise advancing some others; and yet with great moderation, far under the due in commodities that are much risen. Which course, as it hath been used by former kings of this realm from age to age, applying themselves to the times, so is it necessary now in point of state, seeing all the neighbour princes and states have divers times of late mounted their customs; otherwise, if they shall increase theirs, and by consequence raise the price of their commodities, and his Majesty by the contrary

course undervalue his, the stranger merchants shall sell dear to his Majesty's subjects and buy cheap of them, whereby the importation shall exceed the exportation, to the exhausting of treasure, and undoing of the State. And therefore the complaint appears to be without cause, and might well have been forborne.

7. *Imposition upon Currants.* To the seventh, which is touching the imposition upon currants, forasmuch as that complaint carried with it among other things a suggestion that this imposition would not be found warrantable by the law, in case the complainants might be permitted to try the right in course of justice, his Majesty, for satisfaction of all parties interested therein, hath remitted the determination thereof to such proceedings in law as is usual in like cases and standeth with the common justice of the realm. Which hath already proceeded so far as it hath been pleaded largely and often against the King, as well as for him, upon his Majesty's special directions to afford the plaintiff free and favourable hearing; and thereupon being publicly argued by all the Barons of the Exchequer, without contradiction it hath received there a final judgement for the King. In the carriage whereof, as his Majesty assureth himself, that those who preferred those complaints unto him have cause to remain satisfied, considering his Majesty's extraordinary and gracious dealing herein, in suffering a case which so nearly toucheth his ancient prerogative in this nature to be disputed in the common form of law. So if any other persons, either out of unquietness or partiality to their own gain, shall further importune them to deal with his Majesty in cases so greatly concerning him, he expecteth they shall be rejected, as persons worthy rather of reproof than to find any favour in that place.

8. *Imposition upon Tobacco.* To the eighth, concerning the imposition set upon tobacco, his Majesty is pleased to leave it to the same course, as a thing depending upon the same reasons.

9. *Sealing of New Draperies.* To the ninth, touching a patent granted to the duke of Lennox for the searching and sealing of divers stuffs by the name of 'new draperies', it is thought fit that the validity thereof be left to be judged by the law, and whensoever any abuse arising in the execution thereof shall appear it is intended that the same shall be severely punished.[1]

10. *Sheriffs' Accounts.* To the tenth, which is the great charge that sheriffs of counties are put to by the clerks and officers in the Exchequer,

[1] See Stone, *Crisis of the Aristocracy*, p. 437.

upon their accounts, which are made merely for the King's service; forasmuch as those things are to be redressed, upon complaint and proof in the Court of Exchequer, his Majesty hath commanded the Lord Treasurer and that Court to examine the particularities thereof, and to give order for reformation.

11. *Muster Masters*. To the eleventh, concerning muster masters;[1] as his Majesty persuadeth himself that there is no meaning in this complaint, to take exception to those courses which his predecessors have used for the orderly and necessary training up of his subjects, wherein consisteth a great part of the strength of this realm, so whensoever it appears that any [lord] lieutenant, by virtue of his commission, hath taken or shall take any indirect course for the execution of that service, his Majesty is determined, upon proof, to see the same redressed.

12. *Pre-emption of Tin*. To the twelfth, concerning the pre-emption of tin, it is a right of inheritance so anciently and justly appertaining to his Majesty as none can or ought to impugn the same; to which being added, that in the execution thereof it is apparent that a number of his Majesty's good subjects in those parts of Cornwall that live by the labour of their hands receive great relief by receiving reasonable payments, where the merchants used in former times to make what payment they list for that which they bought of them. The exception to this appeareth not to be worthy the name of a grievance, unless some abuses be committed, which shall be reformed upon complaint whensoever any cause shall appear.

13. *Blue Starch*. To the thirteenth, which is concerning the making of smalt, or blue starch; it was granted upon suggestion that it would be a means to set many poor people a-work, which if it shall be found unwarranted by the law it is left free to be called in question, and there determined.

14. *Purveyance*. To the fourteenth, concerning purveyance; his Majesty hath already declared his pleasure, by proclamation, for reformation of any abuses to be offered to his subjects by continuing the ancient use of his prerogative of the same, whereof there is, and hath been always, so great necessity for him and his predecessors as there needs no further answer to that complaint than that his Majesty is

---

[1] Muster masters were veteran N.C.O.s appointed by the government to drill and train the local militia in each county. It is not clear whether the Commons were complaining, as they often did, of having to pay these men, or whether some lord-lieutenants were employing their own servants in this duty.

graciously pleased to continue the course he hath done, in punishing all that shall abuse the meanest of his subjects in execution thereof.

15. *Iron Ordnance.* To the fifteenth, concerning licence for transportation of iron ordnance and bullets; although his Majesty assureth himself that no man will presume to call in question his power to grant them at his pleasure, yet he is well content to make it known, that as there hath not been of late any grants passed of such nature, so his Majesty will then be sparing; except it be when he shall find it fit in his great judgement and consideration.

16. *Saltpetre.* To the sixteenth, concerning those grievances which his Majesty's subjects have suffered in the execution of a commission granted to certain persons for getting saltpetre; his Majesty granted no other commission than such as was drawn by his learned counsel, and more restrained than the former in the late Queen's time. Wherein, as his Majesty had never an intention to make any application of his prerogative further than may stand with the lawful and necessary use thereof, so his Majesty was never minded to show himself so improvident as to suffer his crown and people to depend upon the uncertainty of foreign supply for [gun]powder, which is made of the saltpetre within this realm, the provision and proportion whereof doth so highly concern the defence and safety of the same. Nevertheless, because there never was anything in like cases so well devised and perfected by the wisdom and providence of man which hath not been in time by inferior ministers, deputies and servants corrupted, and diverted from the true and original institution (as hath appeared in this particular, wherein divers injuries and grievances have been offered by some of the meanest persons used therein, not only repugnant to the authority of the commission, rightly examined, but merely contrary to his Majesty's meaning...), his Majesty, upon consideration of the matter contained in this complaint concerning that particular, and in regard of the reverent form which hath been used in presenting all your petitions, hath been pleased out of his gracious care and goodness to revoke and anull all commissions or grants made to any person or persons for and concerning digging and working for saltpetre, intending to consider of some such course hereafter, as the same may be made without any just cause of complaint. ....   *CJ,* I, 316–18

22. James Whitlocke's speech on Impositions[1] (House of Commons, 29 June 1610)

...It will be admitted for a rule and ground of state that in every commonwealth and government there be some rights of sovereignty, *jura majestatis*, which regularly and of common right do belong to the sovereign power of that state, unless custom or the provisional ordinance of that State do otherwise dispose of them; which sovereign power is *potestas suprema*, a power that can control all other powers and cannot be controlled but by itself. It will not be denied that the power of imposing hath so great a trust in it, by reason of the mischiefs [that] may grow to the commonwealth by the abuses of it, that it hath ever been ranked among those rights of sovereign power. Then is there no further question to be made but to examine where the sovereign power is in this kingdom, for there is the right of imposition. The sovereign power is agreed to be in the King: but in the King is a twofold power—the one in Parliament, as he is assisted with the consent of the whole State; the other out of Parliament, as he is sole and singular, guided merely by his own will. And if of these two powers in the King, one is greater than the other and can direct and control the other, that is *suprema potestas*, the sovereign power, and the other is *subordinata*. It will then be easily proved that the power of the King in Parliament is greater than his power out of Parliament, and doth rule and control it; for if the King make a grant by his letters patent out of Parliament, it bindeth him and his successors; but by his power in Parliament he may defeat and avoid it; and therefore that is the greater power. If a judgement be given in the King's Bench by the King himself, as may be and by the law is intended, a writ of error to reverse this judgement may be sued before the King in Parliament.... So you see the appeal is from the King out of the Parliament to the King in Parliament; the writ is in his name; the rectifying and correcting the errors is by him, but with the assent of the Lords and Commons, than which there can be no stronger evidence to prove that his power out of Parliament is subordinate to his power in Parliament; for in Acts of Parliament, be they laws, grounds, or whatsoever else, the act and power is the King's but with the assent of the Lords and Commons, which maketh it the most sovereign and supreme power above all and controllable by none. Besides this right of imposing, there be others in the kingdom of the

---

[1] Incorrectly ascribed to Henry Yelverton in *ST*.

same nature: as the power to make laws, the power of naturalisation, the power of erection of arbitrary government, the power to judge without appeal, the power to legitimate; all which do belong to the King only in Parliament. Others there be of the same nature that the King may exercise out of Parliament, which right is grown unto him in them more in those others by the use and practice of the commonwealth, as denization, coinage, making war; which power the King hath time out of mind practised without the gainsaying and murmuring of his subjects. But these other powers before mentioned have ever been executed by him in Parliament, and not otherwise but with the reluctation [*sc.* opposition] of the whole kingdom....

It hath been alleged that those which in this cause have enforced their reasons from this maxim of ours, that the King cannot alter the law, have diverted from the question. I say under favour, they have not, for that in effect is the very question now in hand; for if he alone out of Parliament may impose, he altereth the law of England in one of these two main fundamental points. He must either take his subjects' goods from them without assent of the party, which is against the law; or else he must give his own letters patent the force of a law to alter the property of his subjects' goods, which is also against the law....

ST, II, 481–3

23. Commons' Petition of Grievances, 7 July 1610

Most Gracious Sovereign,

Your Majesty's most humble Commons assembled in Parliament, being moved as well out of their duty and zeal to your Majesty, as out of the sense of just grief wherewith your loving subjects are generally through the whole realm at this time possessed, because they perceive their common and ancient right and liberty to be much declined and infringed in these late years, do with all duty and humility present these their just complaints thereof to your gracious view, most instantly craving justice therein, and due redress.

And although it be true that many of the particulars whereof we now complain were of some use in the late Queen's time, and then not much impugned, because the usage of them being then more moderate gave not so great occasion of offence, and consequently not so much cause to inquire into the rights and validity of them; yet the right being now more thoroughly scanned, by reason of the great mischiefs and inconveniencies which the subjects have thereby sustained, we are confident that your Majesty will be so far from thinking it a point of honour or greatness to continue any grievance upon your people, because you found them begun in your predecessor's times, as you will rather hold it a work of great glory to reform them, since your Majesty knoweth well, that neither continuance of time, nor errors of men, can or ought to prejudice truth or justice....In this confidence, dread sovereign, we offer these grievances...to your gracious consideration....

[1. *Impositions.*] The policy and constitution of this your kingdom appropriates unto the kings of this realm, with the assent of parliament, as well the sovereign power of making laws, as that of taxing or imposing upon their subjects' goods or merchandises, wherein they have justly such a propriety as may not without their consent be altered or changed. This is the cause that the people of this kingdom, as they ever showed themselves faithful and loving to their kings, and ready to aid them in all their just occasions with voluntary contributions, so have they been ever careful to preserve their own liberties and rights, when anything hath been done to prejudice or impeach the same.

And therefore when their princes, occasioned either by their wars, or their over-great bounty, or by any other necessity, have without consent of parliament set impositions either within the land or upon commodities either exported or imported by the merchants, they have in open parliament complained of it, in that it was done without their consents, and thereupon never failed to obtain a speedy and full redress, without any claim made by the kings of any power or prerogative in that point.

And though the Law of Property be originally and carefully preserved by the common laws of this realm, which are as ancient as the kingdom itself, yet these famous kings, for the better contentment and assurance of their loving subjects, agreed that this old fundamental right should be further declared and established by Act of Parliament; wherein it is provided that no such charges should ever be laid upon the people without their common consent, as may appear by sundry records of former times.

We therefore, your Majesty's most humble Commons assembled in Parliament, following the example of this worthy care of our ancestors, and out of a duty to those for whom we serve, finding that your Majesty, without advice or consent of parliament, hath lately in time of peace set both greater impositions, and far more in number, than any of your noble ancestors did ever in time of war, have with all humility presumed to present this most just and necessary petition unto your Majesty: that all impositions set without the assent of parliament may be quite abolished and taken away, and that your Majesty, in imitation likewise of your noble progenitors, will be pleased that a law may be made during this session of Parliament, to declare that all impositions set or to be set upon your people, their goods or merchandises, save only by common assent in parliament, are and shall be void. Wherein your Majesty shall not only give your subjects good satisfaction in point of their right, but also bring exceeding joy and comfort to them which now suffer, partly through abating the price of native commodities, and partly through the raising of all foreign, to the overthrow of merchants and shipping, [and] the causing of a general dearth and decay of wealth among your people, who will be hereby no less discouraged than disabled to supply your Majesty when occasion shall require it.

[2. *High Commission.*] Whereas by...[the Act of Supremacy, 1559] power was given to the Queen and her successors to constitute and make a Commission in Causes Ecclesiastical, the said Act is found to be inconvenient and of dangerous extent in divers respects:

First, for that it enableth the making of such a Commission as well to any one subject born as to more.

Secondly, for that, whereas by the intention and words of the statute ecclesiastical jurisdiction is restored to the Crown, and your Highness by that statute enabled to give only such power ecclesiastical to the said Commissioners, yet under colour of some words in that statute, where the Commissioners are authorised to execute their Commission according to the tenor and effect of your Highness's Letters Patent, and by Letters Patent grounded thereupon, the said Commissioners do fine and imprison, and exercise other authority not belonging to the ecclesiastical jurisdiction restored by that statute, which we conceive to be a great wrong to the subject; and that those Commissioners might as well, by colour of those words, if they were so authorised by your Highness's Letters Patent, fine without stint and imprison without limitation of time; as also, according to will and discretion, without any rules of law, spiritual or temporal, adjudge and impose utter confiscation of goods, forfeiture of lands, yea, and the taking away of a limb, and of life itself; and this for any matter whatsoever pertaining to the spiritual jurisdiction, which never was nor could be meant by the makers of that law.

Thirdly, for that by the statute the King and his successors (however your Majesty hath been pleased out of your gracious disposition otherwise to order) make and direct such Commission into all the counties and dioceses, yea, into every parish of England; and thereby all causes may be taken from jurisdiction of bishops, chancellors and archdeacons, and laymen solely to be enabled to excommunicate and exercise all other censures spiritual.

Fourthly, that every petty offence pertaining to the spiritual jurisdiction is by colour of the said words and Letters Patent grounded thereupon made subject to excommunication and punishment by that strange and exorbitant power and Commission, whereby the least offenders, not committing anything of any enormous or high nature, may be drawn from the most remote places of the kingdom to London or York, which is very grievous and inconvenient.

Fifthly, for that limit touching causes subject to this Commission, being only with these words, viz., 'Such as pertain to spiritual or ecclesiastical jurisdiction', it is very hard to know what matters or offences are included in that number, and the rather because it is unknown what ancient canons or laws spiritual are in force and what not. From hence ariseth great inconveniency, and occasion of contention.

*   *   *   *   *   *

And touching the execution of the Commission, it is found grievous these ways among other:

First, for that laymen are by the Commissioners punished for speaking (otherwise than in judicial places and courses) of the simony and other misdemeanours of the spiritual men, though the thing spoken be true, and the speech tending to the inducing of some condign punishment.

Secondly, in that these Commissioners usually appoint and allot to women discontented at and unwilling to live with their husbands such portion and allowance for present maintenance as to them shall seem meet, to the great encouragement to wives to be disobedient and contemptuous against their husbands.

Thirdly, in that their pursuivants and other ministers employed in the apprehension of suspected offenders in any thing spiritual, and in the searching for any supposed scandalous books, use to break open men's houses, closets and desks, rifling all corners and secret custodies, as in cases of high treason or suspicion thereof.

All which premises, amongst other things considered, your Majesty's most loyal and dutiful Commons in all humbleness beseech you that for the easing of them as well from the present grievance as from the fear and possibility of greater in times future, your Highness would vouchsafe your royal assent and allowance to and for the ratifying of the said statute, and the reducing thereof, and consequently of the said Commission, to reasonable and convenient limits, by some act to be passed in the present session of Parliament.

[§ 3 complained of the excessive use of proclamations, in a manner not supported by custom,[1] and § 4 of the delay in issuing certain remedial writs, particularly writs of prohibition and *habeas corpus*; § 5 dealt with the vexed question as to whether the marcher counties of Gloucester, Hereford, Worcester and Shropshire were subject to the Council of Wales, and § 6 again called attention to a complaint made in 1606, against the Duke of Lennox and his New Draperies.[2] § 7 was about wine licences, and § 8 revealed a new abuse, the lease to private individuals of the right to grant alehouse licences. In the final section the Commons typically used a very mundane grievance, the price of sea coal, as a peg on which to hang some profound observations on the function and duties of government.]

[9. *Sea Coal.*] Among many resemblances which are observed to be between natural and politic bodies, there is none more apt and natural than this, that the disease of both do not at one instance commonly seize upon all parts, but beginning in some one part do by tract of time and by degrees get possession of the whole, unless by applying of wholesome and proper remedies in due time they may be prevented, which, as it is in many things very visible, so it is in nothing more apparent than in this matter of Impositions; which beginning at first either with foreign commodities brought in or such of your own as were transported, is now extended to those commodities which, growing in this kingdom, are not transported, but uttered to the subjects of the same.

For proof whereof, we do in all humility present unto your Majesty's view the late imposition of one shilling the chaldron of sea coals, rising in Blyth and Sunderland not by virtue of any contract or grant (as in the coals of Newcastle) but under a mere pretext of your Majesty's most royal prerogative, which imposition is not only grievous for the present...but dangerous also for the future, considering that the reason

---

[1] See p. 8 above. [2] See p. 67 above.

of this precedent may be extended to all the commodities of this kingdom. May it therefore please your most excellent Majesty, which is the great and sovereign Physician of the Estate, to apply such a remedy as this disease may be presently cured, and all diseases for time to come of like nature prevented. *Petyt, Jus Parliamentarium, pp. 321–36*

24. Subsidy Act, 1624

21 Jac. I, c. 33: *An Act for payment of Three Subsidies and Three Fifteenths by the Temporalty.*

Most Gracious sovereign, we your Majesty's most faithful and loving subjects, by your royal authority now assembled in your High Court of Parliament, having entered into serious and due consideration of the weighty and most important causes which at this time more than at any other time heretofore do press your Majesty to a much greater expense and charge than your own treasure alone can at this present support and maintain, and likewise of the injuries and indignities which have been lately offered to your Majesty and your children, under colour and during the time of the treaties for the marriage with Spain and the restitution of the Palatinate, which in this Parliament have been clearly discovered and laid open unto us; and withal what humble advice with one consent and voice we have given unto your Majesty to dissolve those treaties, which your Majesty hath been graciously pleased to our exceeding joy and comfort fully to yield unto, and accordingly have made your public declaration for the real and utter dissolution of them, by means whereof your Majesty may haply be engaged in a sudden war: we in all humbleness, most ready and willing to give unto your Majesty and the whole world an ample testimony of our dutiful affections and sincere intentions to assist you therein, for the maintenance of that war that may hereupon ensue, and more particularly for the defence of this your realm of England, the securing of your kingdom of Ireland, the assistance of your neighbours the States of the United Provinces and other your Majesty's friends and allies, and for the setting forth of your Royal Navy, we have resolved to give for the present the greatest aid which ever was granted in Parliament, to be levied in so short a time. And therefore we do humbly beseech your Majesty that it may be declared and enacted, and be it declared by the authority of this present Parliament, that the said two treaties are by your Majesty utterly dissolved, and for the maintenance of the war which may ensue thereupon, and for the causes aforesaid, be it enacted that three whole fifteenths and tenths shall be paid, taken and levied of the moveable goods, chattels and other things usual to such fifteenths and tenths, to be contributory and chargeable within the shires, cities, boroughs, towns and other places of this your Majesty's realm, in manner and form aforetime used...to be paid in manner and form following: that is to say, the whole entire payment of the first of the said whole fifteenths and tenths...to be paid into the hands of Sir Thomas Middleton knight and alderman of London, Sir Edward Barkham knight and alderman of London, Sir Paul Baning knight and baronet, Sir Richard Grubham knight, James Campbell, George Whitmore and Ralph Freeman, aldermen of London, and Martin Bond, citizen and haberdasher of London, Treasurers especially appointed in and by this Act to receive and issue the same..., on or before the 10th of July next coming.... [The second by December 10, and the third by May 10, 1625.]

II. [Collectors are to be appointed in each shire by the Members of Parliament for that shire; their qualifications, duties, etc.]

III. [Such Collectors must enter into recognisances for the due payment.]

IV. And furthermore, for the great and weighty considerations aforesaid, we the Lords Spiritual and Temporal and the Commons in this present Parliament assembled, do by our like assent and authority of this Parliament give and grant to your Highness our said sovereign lord the King's Majesty, your heirs and successors, three entire subsidies, to be rated, taxed, levied and paid at three several payments, of every person spiritual and temporal, of what estate or degree soever he or they be of, according to the tenor of this Act, in manner and form following, that is to say: as well that every person born within this realm of England, Wales or other the King's dominions, as all and every fraternity, guild, corporation, mystery, brotherhood and commonalty, corporated or not corporated, within this realm of England, Wales or other the King's dominions, being worth three pounds, for every pound as well in coin and the value of every pound that every such person, fraternity...[etc.] hath of his or their own or any other to his or their use, as also plate, stock of merchandise, all manner of corn and grain, household stuff, and of all other goods moveable, as well within this realm as without and of all such sums of money as to him or them is or shall be owing, whereof he or they trust in his or their conscience surely to be paid, except and out of the said premises deducted such sums of money as he or they owe, and in his or their consciences intendeth truly to pay, and except also the apparel of every such person, their wives and children, belonging to their own bodies, saving jewels, gold, silver, stone and pearl, shall pay to and for the first subsidy, at one entire payment, two shillings and eight pence of every pound.... [And the same for each of the other two subsidies. Aliens are to pay 5s. 4d. in the £.]

V. And be it further enacted by the authority aforesaid, that every person born under the King's obeisance, and every corporation, fraternity, guild, mystery, brotherhood and commonalty, corporate or not corporate, for every pound that every of the same persons, and every corporation...[etc.], or any other to his or their use, hath in fee simple or fee tail, for term of life, term of years, by execution, wardship or by copy of court roll, of and in any honours, castles, manors, lands, tenements, rents, services, hereditaments, annuities, fees, corrodies or other yearly profits of the yearly value of twenty shillings, as well within ancient demesne and other places privileged as elsewhere, and so upward, shall pay to and for the said first subsidy, in one entire payment, four shillings of and for every pound...[and the same for each of the other two subsidies.]

VI. And the payment of the first subsidy shall be, by authority aforesaid, taxed, assessed and rated according to this Act, in every shire, riding, lathe, wapentake, rape, city, borough, town and every other place within this realm before the 20th day of June now next coming... [the second subsidy before October 10, and the third before March 10 next]. And the particular sums of every shire, riding, town or other places aforesaid, with the particular names of such as are chargeable for and to the payment of the said first subsidy, to be taxed and set by the Commissioners..., and in the same form shall be certified into the King's Exchequer before the 30th day of June now next ensuing...[for the second subsidy by October 30, for the third by March 30 next]. And the said sums in form aforesaid to be taxed to and for the payment of the said first subsidy, shall be paid on one entire sum to the uses before by this present Act appointed into the hands of the said Treasurers before named for the receiving of the said fifteenths and tenths, at or before the said 10th day of July following...[December 10 for the second subsidy, May 10 for the third].

VII. [Rating for absentees.]

VIII. And be it further enacted by the authority aforesaid, that for the assessing and ordering of the said three subsidies to be duly had, the Lord Chancellor of England or the Lord Keeper of the Great Seal, the Lord Treasurer of England, the Lord President of the King's Council, the Lord Privy Seal, the Lord Steward of the King's Majesties Household, the Lord Admiral of England, the Lord Chamberlain of his Majesty's most honourable Household for the time being, or two of them at the least, whereof the Lord Chancellor...be one, shall and may name and appoint of and for every shire, riding and other places, ...as also of and for every city and town being a county of itself..., such number of persons of every of the same shires...[etc.] as they shall think convenient, to be commissioners of and within the same place whereof they be inhabitants...

[Similar provisions for boroughs follow; they are dealt with separately because the powers of their commissioners are limited.]
[IX–XV deal in detail with the functions and powers of these commissioners.]

XVI. And that all persons of the estate of baron or baroness, and every estate above, shall be charged with their freehold and value as is aforesaid by the Chancellor or Lord Keeper of the Great Seal of England, the High Treasurer for the time being, or one of them, together with other such persons as by the King's Majesty's authority or commandment shall be named or appointed...

[XVII–XXXVI deal mainly with the High Collectors, appointed by the Commissioners, and the actual collection of the tax.]

XXXVII. And to the end that all and every the sums of money by this present Act granted as aforesaid, and also to be collected and expended as aforesaid, may be truly expended for and towards the uses aforesaid and not otherwise, according to your Majesty's own gracious desire, be it further enacted, that the monies to be received by the said Treasurers by virtue of this Act shall be issued out and expended for or towards the uses aforesaid to such person and persons, and in such manner and form as by the warrant of George Lord Carew, Fulke Lord Brooke, Oliver Lord Viscount Grandison of Limerick within the realm of Ireland, Arthur Lord Chichester, Sir Edward Cecil, knight, Sir Edward Conway, knight, one of the principal Secretaries to his Majesty, Sir Horace Vere, knight, Sir Robert Mansell, knight, Sir John

Ogle, knight, and Sir Thomas Button, knight, which ten persons before mentioned his Majesty hath already nominated and hath made choice of to be his Council for the War, or any five or more of them, whereof two to be of his Majesty's most honourable Privy Council, under their hands and seals shall be directed and not otherwise. And such warrant or warrants of the said Councillors of War or of any five of them, whereof two to be of the Privy Council as aforesaid, together with the acquittances of those persons who shall receive those monies according to those warrants or the enrollment thereof to be for that purpose likewise kept by his Majesty's remembrancer of the said Court of Exchequer, shall be unto the said Treasurers and every one of them, their heirs, executors and administrators, a full and sufficient discharge.

XXXVIII. [Expense allowance for Treasurers.]

XXXIX. And be it further enacted, that as well the said Treasurers as the said persons appointed for the Council of War as aforesaid, and all other persons who shall be trusted with the receiving, issuing, bestowing and employing of these monies or any part thereof, their heirs, executors and administrators, shall be answerable and accountable for their doings or proceedings herein to the Commons in Parliament when they shall be hereunto required by warrant under the hand of the Speaker of the House of Commons for the time being, and there they and every one of them, according to their several places and employments, shall give a true and real declaration and account of their several and respective doings and proceedings therein, and that the said Commons in Parliament shall have power by this Act to hear and determine the said account and all things thereunto appertaining.

[XL–XLIII provide for the keeping of accounts and the punishment of offenders.]

SR, IV, 1247–62

25. King's Speech, 17 March 1628

My Lords and Gentlemen,

These times are for action; wherefore, for example's sake, I mean not to spend much time in words, expecting accordingly, that your (as I hope) good resolutions will be speedy, not spending time unnecessarily, or (that I may better say) dangerously, for tedious consultations at this conjuncture of time is [*sic*] as hurtful as ill resolutions.

I am sure you now expect from me both to know the cause of your meeting, and what to resolve on; yet I think there is none here but knows what common danger is the cause of this parliament, and that supply at this time is the chief end of it; so that I need but to point to you what to do. I will use but few persuasions, for if to maintain your own advices and (as now the case stands by the following thereof) the true religion, the laws, liberties of this State, and the just defence of our true friends and allies, be not sufficient, no eloquence of men or angels will prevail.

Only let me remember you, that my duty most of all, and every one of yours according to his degree, is to seek the maintenance of this Church and Commonwealth; and certainly there was never a time in which this duty was more necessarily required than now.

I, therefore, judging a Parliament to be the ancient, speediest and best way, in this time of common danger, to give such supply as to secure ourselves and to save our friends from imminent ruin, have called you together. Every man now must do according to his conscience, wherefore if you (which God forbid) should not do your duties in contributing what this State at this time needs I must in discharge of my conscience use those other means which God hath put into my hands to save that that the follies of particular men may otherwise hazard to lose.

Take not this as a threatening (for I scorn to threaten any but my equals), but an admonition from him that, both out of nature and duty, hath most care of your preservations and prosperities, and hopes (though I thus speak) that your demeanours at this time will be such as shall not only approve your former counsels but lay on me such obligations as shall tie me by way of thankfulness to meet often with you, for be assured that nothing can be more pleasing unto me than to keep a good correspondency with you.

I will only add one thing more, and then leave the Keeper to make a short paraphrase upon the text I have delivered you; which is, to remember a thing to the end we may forget it. You may imagine I came here with a doubt of good success of what I desire, remembering the distractions at the last meeting; but I shall assure you, that I shall very easily and gladly forget and forgive what's past, so that you will at this time leave the former ways of distractions and follow the counsel lately given you, 'To maintain the Unity of the Spirit in the Bond of Peace'.[1]

LJ, III, 687

---

[1] Presumably the text of the pre-session sermon.

26. The Petition of Right, 1628

The Petition exhibited to his Majesty by the Lords Spiritual and Temporal and Commons in this present Parliament assembled concerning divers rights and liberties of the subject.

To the King's Most Excellent Majesty

Humbly show unto our Sovereign Lord the King the Lords Spiritual and Temporal and Commons in Parliament assembled, that whereas it is declared and enacted by a statute made in the time of the reign of King Edward the First commonly called Statutum de Tallagio non Concedendo, that no tallage or aid should be laid or levied by the King or his heirs in this realm without the good will and assent of the archbishops, bishops, earls, barons, knights, burgesses and other the freemen of the commonalty of this realm; and by authority of Parliament holden in the five and twentieth year of the reign of King Edward the Third it is declared and enacted, that from henceforth no person should be compelled to make any loans to the King against his will because such loans were against reason and the franchise of the land, and by other laws of this realm it is provided that none should be charged by any charge or imposition called a benevolence nor by such like charge, by which the statutes before mentioned and other the good laws and statutes of this realm your subjects have inherited this freedom, that they should not be compelled to contribute to any tax, tallage, aid or other like charge not set by common consent in Parliament.

II. Yet, nevertheless of late divers commissions directed to sundry commissioners in several counties with instructions have issued, by means whereof your people have been in divers places assembled and required to lend certain sums of money unto your Majesty, and many of them upon their refusal so to do have had an oath administered unto them not warrantable by the laws or statutes of this realm, and have been constrained to become bound to make appearance and give attendance before your Privy Council and in other places; and others of them have been therefore imprisoned, confined, and sundry other ways molested and disquieted, and divers other charges have been laid and levied upon your people in several counties by Lord Lieutenants, Deputy Lieutenants, Commissioners for Musters, Justices of Peace and others by command or direction from your Majesty or your Privy Council against the laws and free customs of the realm.

III. And where also by the statute called the Great Charter of the Liberties of England it is declared and enacted, that no freeman may be taken or imprisoned or be disseised of his freehold or liberties or his free customs or be outlawed or exiled or in any manner destroyed, but by the lawful judgement of his peers or by the law of the land.

IV. And in the eight and twentieth year of the reign of King Edward the Third it was declared and enacted by authority of Parliament, that no man, of what estate or condition that he be, should be put out of his land or tenement, nor taken, nor imprisoned, nor disherited, nor put to death without being brought to answer by due process of law.

V. Nevertheless against the tenor of the said statutes and other the good laws and statutes of your realm to that end provided, divers of your subjects have of late been imprisoned without any cause shown; and when for their deliverance they were brought before your justices by your Majesty's writ of habeas corpus there to undergo and receive as the Court should order, and their Keepers commanded to certify the causes of their detainer, no cause was certified, but that they were detained by your Majesty's special command signified by the Lords of your Privy Council, and yet were returned back to several prisons without being charged with any thing to which they might make answer according to the law.

VI. And whereas of late great companies of soldiers and mariners have been dispersed into divers counties of the realm, and the inhabitants against their will have been compelled to receive them into their houses, and there to suffer them to sojourn against the laws and customs of this realm and to the great grievance and vexation of the people.

VII. And whereas also by authority of Parliament in the five and twentieth year of the reign of King Edward the Third it is declared and enacted that no man should be forejudged of life and limb against the form of the Great Charter and the law of the land; and by the said Great Charter, and other the laws and statutes of this your realm, no man ought to be adjudged to death but by the laws established in this your realm, either by the customs of the same realm or by Act of Parliament, and whereas no offender of what kind soever is exempted from the proceedings to be used and punishments to be inflicted by the laws and statutes of this your realm; nevertheless of late time divers commissions under your Majesty's great seal have issued forth, by which certain persons have been assigned and appointed commissioners with power and authority to proceed within the land according to the justice of martial law against such soldiers or mariners or other dissolute persons joining with them as should commit any murder, robbery, felony, mutiny or other outrage or misdemeanour whatsoever, and by such summary course and order as is agreeable to martial law and as is used in armies in time of war to proceed to the trial and condemnation of such offenders, and them to cause to be executed and put to death according to the law martial.

By pretext whereof some of your Majesty's subjects have been by some of the said commissioners put to death, when and where, if by the laws and statutes of the land they had deserved death, by the same laws and statutes also they might and by no other ought to have been judged and executed.

And also sundry grievous offenders by colour thereof claiming an exemption have escaped the punishments due to them by the laws and statutes of this your realm, by reason that divers of your officers and ministers of justice have unjustly refused or forborne to proceed against such offenders according to the same laws and statutes upon pretence that the said offenders were punishable only by martial law and by authority of such commissions as aforesaid. Which commissions and all others of like nature are wholly and directly contrary to the said laws and statutes of this your realm.

VIII. They do therefore humbly pray your most excellent Majesty that no man hereafter be compelled to make or yield any gift, loan, benevolence, tax or such like charge without common consent by Act of Parliament, and that none be called to make answer or take such oath or to give attendance or be confined or otherwise molested or disquieted concerning the same or for refusal thereof. And that no freeman in any such manner as is before mentioned be imprisoned or detained. And that your Majesty would be pleased to remove the said soldiers and mariners, and that your people may not be so burdened in time to come. And that the aforesaid commissions for proceeding by martial law may be revoked and annulled. And that hereafter no commissions of like nature may issue forth to any person or persons whatsoever to be executed as aforesaid, lest by colour of them any of your Majesty's subjects be destroyed or put to death contrary to the laws and franchises of the land.

All which they most humbly pray of your most excellent Majesty as their rights and liberties according to the laws and statutes of this realm, and that your Majesty would also vouchsafe to declare that the awards, doings, and proceedings to the prejudice of your people in any of the premises shall not be drawn hereafter into consequence or example. And that your Majesty would be also graciously pleased for the further comfort and safety of your people to declare your royal will and pleasure, that in the thing aforesaid all your officers and ministers shall serve you according to the laws and statutes of this realm as they tender the honour of your Majesty and the prosperity of this kingdom.

SR, v, 23–4

27. Protestation of the Commons, 2 March 1629

1. Whosoever shall bring in innovation of religion, or by favour or countenance seek to extend or introduce Popery or Arminianism, or other opinion disagreeing from the true and orthodox Church, shall be reputed a capital enemy to this Kingdom and Commonwealth.

2. Whosoever shall counsel or advise the taking and levying of the subsidies of tonnage and poundage, not being granted by Parliament, or shall be an actor or instrument therein, shall be likewise reputed an innovator in the Government, and a capital enemy to the Kingdom and Commonwealth.

3. If any merchant or person whatsoever shall voluntarily yield, or pay the said subsidies of tonnage and poundage, not being granted by Parliament, he shall likewise be reputed a betrayer of the liberties of England, and an enemy to the same.

Rushworth, I, 670

28. A proclamation for suppressing of false rumours touching parliaments, 27 March 1629

Whereas, notwithstanding our late Declaration for satisfying of the minds and affections of our loving subjects, some ill-disposed persons do spread false and pernicious rumours abroad, as if the scandalous and seditious proposition in the House of Commons, made by an outlawed man, desperate in mind and fortune, which was tumultuously taken up by some few, after that by our royal authority we had commanded their adjournment, had been the vote of the whole House, whereas the contrary was the truth. For it was then descried by the wisest and best affected, and is since disavowed upon examination by such as were suspected to have consented thereunto, and affirmed as well by them as others who served in the House that day to be a thing of most wicked and dangerous consequence to the good estate of this kingdom, which appeareth to be so by those impressions which this false rumour hath made in men's minds, whereby out of causeless fears the trade of the kingdom is disturbed, and merchants discouraged to continue in their wonted traffic.

We have thought it expedient, not only to manifest the truth hereof, but to make known our royal pleasure, that those who raise or nourish such false reports shall be severely punished, and such as cheerfully go on with their trade have all good encouragement, not purposing to overcharge our subjects by any new burdens, but to satisfy ourselves with those duties that were received by the King our father, of blessed memory, which we neither can nor will dispense withal, but shall esteem them unworthy of our protection who shall deny the same, we intending to employ it for defence for our kingdom, dominion of our seas, and safeguard of our merchants, especially by such shipping as are now making ready, and such further preparation for aid of our friends and allies as need shall require.

And whereas, for several ill ends, the calling again of a parliament is divulged; howsoever we have shown by our frequent meeting with our people our love to the use of parliaments, yet the late abuse having for the present driven us unwillingly out of that course, we shall account it presumption for any to prescribe any time unto us for parliaments, the calling, continuing and dissolving of which is always in our own power; and we shall be more inclinable to meet in parliament again when our people shall see more clearly into our intentions and actions, when such as have bred this interruption shall have received their condign punishment, and those who are misled by them and by such ill reports as are raised upon this occasion shall come to a better understanding of us and themselves. *Foedera*, XIX, 62–3

III. EPILOGUE: THE 1630's

Impositions continued to be levied in the 1630's, and monopolies were extended again, the pretence of new inventions taking many of them out of the scope of the Act of 1624. Indeed, after the collapse of the merchants' revolt in 1631 the government became more and more closely identified with the trading and manufacturing classes in the exploitation of the favourable situation created by the war in Europe, which was hampering the trade of Holland, France and Spain. Peace was made with France in 1629 and Spain in 1630, and the old 'war party' of the 'twenties, led by Wentworth, accepted the fact that more was to be gained by economic infiltration. Even in the later 'thirties, when his political position began to collapse, Charles retained his standing with the City of London, and had he been able to persue any economic policy consistently, and restrain the religious extravagances of Archbishop Laud, he might have carried England over into the parliament-less condition of so many continental countries.[1]

Meanwhile the exploitation of the parliamentary classes, the landowners, continued. Elizabeth in 1599 had appointed a Commission to compound with tenants of the Crown whose titles to their land were defective or non-existent; this Commission was renewed in 1603, and again in 1605, 1606, 1608, 1609, 1611 and 1613.[2] A new Commission was issued in 1618, but by 1621 the opposition was too strong to be ignored. In 1606 the Commons had called the Secretary to the Commission, William Tipper, to the bar; in 1621 he and his son Robert were again sharply criticised, and it seemed for a time that they might go the way of Mitchell and Mompesson.[3] Coke brought in a bill 'for the general quiet of the subjects against all pretences of concealment', but it was not passed until 1624.[4] Even then this statute only protected those who could prove continuous possession for the past sixty years, and in December 1628 Charles appointed yet another Commission for Defective Titles, to compound with those outside the terms of the act, as well as those occupying reclaimed land, those who had encroached on the royal forests, and those who had enclosed wastes and common land contrary to the stream of statutes and proclamations forbidding it. The secretary was Robert Tipper.[5] In 1630 the Commission for Defective Titles was reissued, and the king's subjects were chided for being so slow to take advantage of his grace; but another commission had to be appointed in 1635.[6] Meanwhile, encroachment on the Forest, which had proceeded with little let or hindrance for over two hundred years, was specifically dealt with by special commissions of Justice in Eyre, beginning in 1634.[7] Again, this was no new problem, and as early as 1604 the Commons had passed a bill to protect the holders of

[1] The general argument is put by Kearney, *Eleven Years' Tyranny*. See also Ashton, *Money Market*, p. xv; Dietz, *Public Finance*, ch. XI; R. W. K. Hinton, 'The Decline of Parliamentary Government under Elizabeth and the Early Stuarts', *Cambridge Historical Journal*, XIII (1957), 116.

[2] *Commons Debates 1621*, VII, 350–5.

[3] *Diary of Robert Bowyer*, pp. 106–7, 132–4, 147–8; *Commons Debates 1621*, II, 149, 272, V, 264.

[4] 21 Jac. I, c. 2. See *ibid*. IV, 180. Charles I remarked in 1635 that his father 'gave way' to this act (*Foedera*, XIX, 671).

[5] 'A proclamation declaring his majesty's royal grace and pleasure to confirm to his subjects their defective titles, estates and possessions, as well by colour of former grants, as without any grants from the Crown, by his commission granted to that purpose' (6 December 1628, *Foedera*, XIX, 4–6).

[6] *Ibid*. pp. 167–8, 670–81.

[7] George Hammersley, 'The Revival of the Forest Laws under Charles I', *History*, XLV (1960), 85–102.

assart lands, taken from the Forest under the authority of royal grants which were often somewhat nebulous.[1] Now such landowners, even potentates like the second earl of Salisbury, Sir Christopher Hatton and the earl of Warwick, had to compound for their offences. An even more irritating way of mulcting the landowner was the revival of the dormant obligation on all those holding land worth £40 a year or more to assume the honour of knighthood at the king's coronation, or as soon thereafter as possible. In January 1630 a commission was appointed to compound with offenders, and the court of exchequer upheld the king's right, which had been exercised under the Tudors. Between 1630 and 1635 the government secured £165,000 from this source.[2]

Ship-money had something in common with these devices, but it differed in kind as well as extent. The right of the king to demand ships from the maritime towns and counties for the defence of the realm and the suppression of piracy was undoubted; it had been exercised as recently as 1627, and in 1634 the situation in the Channel, traversed by the contending warships of Spain and France, in the North Sea, where the Dutch and the English were competing fiercely for fish, and on the western coasts, troubled increasingly by marauding barbary corsairs, justified Charles I's request for a further contribution.[3] The following year, however, writs were sent to the inland counties, too, demanding money in lieu of ships, and the landed classes were obliged to subsidise the merchants, who ought to profit directly from the protection of a new English fleet, and support the king's foreign policy, which involved an unpopular *detente* with Spain. Moreover, ship-money was in effect the new land-tax the Commons had jibbed at in 1610. The lump sum initially decided upon was divided by the Privy Council amongst the various counties, according to their estimated population and wealth. The Council also fixed the amount for towns, and the remainder was divided by the sheriff amongst the hundreds and then amongst the parishes, where the basis of the assessment was houses and land.[4] In 1636 John Hampden and Lord Saye and Sele refused to pay, and the government made Hampden's a test case. It came on in 1637, and in 1638 a majority of the judges gave the verdict to the king.[5]

Just how opposed to ship-money the gentry were, and how far they were alarmed by the verdict in *Rex v. Hampden*, we do not know. Certainly in its early years it was paid willingly or collected stringently—one or the other—

[1] *House of Lords Manuscripts*, XI, no. 3281. Cf. The Form of Apology and Satisfaction, 1604 (*TCD*, p. 227).

[2] Gardiner, *History of England*, VII, 167; Dietz, *English Public Finance*, pp. 262–3.

[3] A specimen writ is printed in *GCD*, p. 105.

[4] M. D. Gordon, 'The Collection of Ship Money in the Reign of Charles I', *Transactions of the Royal Historical Society*, 3rd series, IV (1910), 141–62.

[5] No. **34**, p. 109 below. Ship-money is discussed more fully in ch. 3.

for from 1634 through 1637 the yield of the tax was never less than 90% of the estimate, and often more; a remarkable record for any seventeenth-century tax. In 1638 only £69,750 was demanded and more than one third was unpaid, and in 1639 £214,000 was demanded and only £43,417 paid.[1] But in these latter years Charles's whole position was collapsing anyway, and the refusal of the gentry to pay probably reflected opposition to his Scots policy rather than opposition to ship-money; certainly Hampden's legal battle from 1636 to 1638 did not have an immediate effect on the yield of the tax. The truth probably is that in the 1630's the need for a stronger English fleet was obvious, and to oppose it was unpatriotic. Not until it became clear that the ship-money fleet was to be used in support of Spain, in support of the Catholic side in the Thirty Years War, did opposition harden. It was probably the raising of the siege of Dunkirk in 1635 by Admiral Pennington that nerved Hampden to make his refusal, and the inaction of the fleet from 1635 to 1639, while Spanish and Dutch warships trespassed with impunity on English territorial waters, contributed to the myth of a pro-Catholic plot. As so often in this period, disputes which on the surface concerned law and the subject's rights really revolved around foreign policy and the great international struggle between Protestantism and the Counter-Reformation.[2]

[1] Gordon, *op. cit.* p. 143.
[2] Charles I's foreign policy has received little attention in recent years, except from C. V. Wedgwood in 'The Causes of the English Civil War, a New Analysis', *History Today*, v (1955), 670–7.

CHAPTER 3

THE JUDICIARY

I. THE ASCENDANCY OF COKE

In the early seventeenth century the judges of the courts of Common Law, King's Bench, Common Pleas and Exchequer were the king's judges, appointed by him and dismissable at will. Whether their patents read *quamdiu se bene gesserint* or *durante bene placito*—a distinction to which much importance was later attached—was largely immaterial. The holder of the former patent could sue out a writ of *scire facias* demanding that the king show cause, but it took a bold man to do this, and only one man in this period is known to have exercised the right, Chief Baron Walter in 1629.[1] In general the position of the judges was not strong. Weakened by the corruption and intimidation of the fifteenth century, the courts did not recover until the closing years of the sixteenth. The jury system, now commonly regarded as the singular glory of the Common Law, was then one of its most serious weaknesses. Before 1563 witnesses could not be subpœnaed by the central courts except through the lord chancellor, and even when this was rectified it was extremely difficult to break jurors of the habit of regarding themselves as witnesses to fact, and even interested parties.

A solution was found in the suppression of the jury as far as possible in civil cases; in criminal cases there evolved a breed of forthright and authoritative judges who could cow most juries. (This breed found its highest, or lowest, expression in Scroggs and Jeffreys.) As a last resort a delinquent or obstinate jury, and the sheriff that empanelled it, could be severely punished, and this was one of the principal concerns of Star Chamber.

Indeed, the uncertainties of the jury system, the frailty of judges in weighing the crimes of great men, and their reluctance to extend the criminal law, particularly in the field of conspiracy and constructive treason, caused Tudor governments to use Star Chamber increasingly. On the other hand, the horrid complexities of the land law, with its attendant expense, and the endless delays that could be imposed by obstructive defendants and malicious plaintiffs, induced many private litigants to seek a short cut through Chancery.[2] Chancery was subject to delays enough, but under lord chancellors of the quality of Ellesmere (1603–17) and Bacon (1617–21) it attracted an in-

[1] The king denied him the writ and suspended him until his death. Gardiner, *History of England*, VII, 112–13; Aylmer, *King's Servants*, pp. 111–13.
[2] For the state of the land law at this time, see for instance A. W. B. Simpson, *An Introduction to the History of the Land Law* (1961).

90

creasing amount of business. So, too, did the High Commission Court under Bancroft.[1]

Finally, the attitude of James I to the Common Law was ambiguous. His Scots upbringing had naturally given him a liking for the Roman or Civil Law, practised now only in the church courts and the court of Admiralty. He was prepared to tolerate Common Law as the Law of State, but in his early years he was given a bad jolt when the judges declined to authorise his assumption of the title King of Britain.[2] He showed an increasing tendency to favour the prerogative courts, and particularly High Commission.

In this emergency the leadership of the common lawyers (barristers as well as judges) was undertaken by Sir Edward Coke, one of the foremost jurists of his generation and a noted supporter of the Crown, with a temper and a character that intimidated most of his contemporaries—'We shall never see his like again', wrote his harassed widow, 'praises be to God!'[3] Solicitor general in 1592, Speaker of the Commons in 1593, and attorney general in 1594, he was appointed Chief Justice of Common Pleas in 1606.

Even before he joined the bench the judges had begun to retaliate against the encroachments of High Commission, the Court of Requests, the Council of the North and the Council of the Marches and Wales by the increasing use of writs of prohibition, which halted cases in other courts and removed them to Westminster Hall. With his arrival, armed with immense legal learning, overweening self-assurance and a combative temper, the tempo of the conflict quickened. Archbishop Bancroft's spirited defence of High Commission provoked a long series of acrimonious exchanges and pacifying conferences presided over by the king, who showed remarkable tolerance and common sense under the most intense provocation, and at no time tried to force the Common Law judges.[4] Eventually even his patience was exhausted and in March 1610 he told Parliament that he had proclaimed a truce; at the same time he also gave his unvarnished opinion of the Common Law and its practitioners.[5] But two years later Coke was still issuing prohibitions against the Council of the North, referring with contempt to its 'English bills' (29 c).

Coke was nothing if not a professional. He took his stand on the antiquity

---

[1] See pp. 176–9 below.

[2] D. H. Willson, 'King James I and Anglo-Scottish Unity', in *Conflict in Stuart England*, ed. W. A. Aiken and B. D. Henning (1960), pp. 43–55.

[3] S. E. Thorne, *Sir Edward Coke, 1552–1952* (Selden Society, 1952), p. 4.

[4] See pp. 177–8 below. The most famous encounter between Coke and James I was in February 1609, when Coke told him that High Commission was a foreign jurisdiction, 'after which his Majesty fell into that high indignation as the like was never known in him, looking and speaking with bended fist, etc., which the Lord Coke perceiving fell flat on all fours'. It is a good story but it is not confirmed by the testimony of those present. See R. G. Usher, 'James I and Sir Edward Coke', *EHR*, xviii (1903), 664.

[5] 21 March 1610, *Works*, pp. 532–5.

and authority of the law, and it is a mistake to regard him as an ally of the parliamentary opposition before 1621. The insistence of the judges in 1605 that only Parliament could arbitrate between them and the High Commission delighted Gardiner, who remarked: 'It is this appeal to Parliament which raises the dispute from a mere quarrel about jurisdiction to the dignity of a constitutional event.'[1] But they were not 'appealing to Parliament', they were merely remarking, quite casually, that the body that framed new statutes was the ultimate authority in Common Law.[2] Certainly there was no trace of an alliance between the judges and the parliamentary opposition, though one sometimes stimulated the other, and part at least of their motive stemmed from the fact that the greater part of their income was from fees. James was not being entirely unfair when he spoke of 'every court striving to bring in most moulture to their own mill'.[3]

Coke's greatest service to the Common Law was the publicity he secured for it, a publicity which was heightened by James I's incorrigible loquaciousness and his essential fairmindedness. He stiffened his colleagues, and he encouraged in every way he knew that almost superstitious reverence for the Common Law which was prevalent in the 1620's. He drove this lesson home by his personal intervention in the parliaments of the 1620's and by his published *Institutes* and *Reports*. When he was appointed Chief Justice of King's Bench in 1613, and removed from the main arena of contestation, his influence continued notwithstanding.

In his contest with rival courts, which threatened their professional dignity and their personal income, his colleagues were willing enough to follow his lead; but when he launched himself into a personal battle with King James they naturally fell back. In 1615, in Peacham's Case, he insisted in the face of established custom and precedent that the king had no right to consult the judges individually before they tried a case.[4] The letters of his great enemy, Bacon (whom he had defeated for the attorney-generalship in 1594 and for the hand of Lady Frances Hatton in 1598), suggest his growing awkwardness and cantankerousness, which erupted again the following year, when he declined to postpone the hearing of a case involving commendams—the Crown's right to collate a bishop to an additional benefice—until the king had taken further advice.[5] He was at once suspended for rank disobedience and shortly afterwards dismissed.

The dismissal of an obstructive chief justice who had flouted the king's commands did not surprise or particularly displease contemporaries; it is

---

[1] *History of England*, II, 36.
[2] The vexed question as to whether Coke did or did not support judicial review is not relevant here, but Dr R. W. K. Hinton makes some interesting points in 'The Decline of Parliamentary Government under Elizabeth I and the Early Stuarts', *Cambridge Historical Journal*, XIII (1957), 127–30.
[3] *Works*, pp. 532–5.   [4] *TCD*, pp. 188–92.   [5] *Ibid*. pp. 192–8.

posterity that has magnified the incident into an event of great constitutional significance. Coke was appointed to the Privy Council in 1617 and for four years pursued a career at court, using all the flattery and unction at his command to secure the alliance of the favourite, Buckingham, against Francis Bacon. But the disastrous marriage between his only daughter and Buckingham's mentally defective brother soured him, and in the parliament of 1621 his conduct led to his dismissal from the Council and the final end of his official career.

In 1621 he was at once faced with the problem of bringing to justice those who had misused the king's patents of monopoly. It would be unwise to leave them to the Common Law; on the other hand, the House of Commons' right to sit as a court of first instance had never been established. Sir Francis Mitchell was brought before the House in February and dispatched to the Tower, but although high words flew about on the back benches Coke and other lawyers were firm in their insistence that they could only imprison him for the duration of the session, and then only on the forced plea that his conduct was a breach of privilege; they could not even examine him on oath. The Lords, however, had such powers. On petition from the Commons they could impose an oath on witnesses, try the evidence with the help of the judges (who sat in the Upper House as assistants), and award punishment.[1] These powers had last been used to try Lord Stanley in 1459, but they had never been denied, and Coke was able to convince both Houses that they could and should adopt this method (30). The Lords, restless and dissatisfied with the Marquess of Buckingham, could be trusted to give a true verdict, and Mitchell and Sir Giles Mompesson were soon disposed of by this process, and the king was forced to associate himself with this campaign against corruption in high places, even when it reached out to one of his most valued servants, Francis Bacon.[2]

The word 'impeachment' was not formally used in 1621, nor the formula of arraignment usual in later times: 'We, in the name of the House of Commons and all the Commons of England, impeach N. of....' Nor were the Commons invited to present their case personally, as in 1626, 1628 or 1641. The procedure was comparatively informal. The Commons Committee on Grievances held a conference with a Lords Committee, to whom they made a brief statement, then handed over their evidence and lists of witnesses in writing. In the three cases before them in 1621 a formal trial was scarcely necessary, since one defendant fled the country, another (Bacon) made a full confession, and the guilt of the other was obvious. Moreover, the process was seen merely as a practical means of dealing with an immediate problem which none of the normal courts of law could solve. It is significant that

---

[1] See Frances Helen Relf's introduction to *Notes of Debates in the House of Lords*.
[2] *TCD*, pp. 324 ff.

whereas the Lords gave judgement on Mompesson in the name of 'The Lords Spiritual and Temporal of this High Court of Parliament', and against Bacon as 'this High Court', they sentenced Lionel Cranfield in 1624 in the name of 'this High Court of Parliament', a phrase which may have been intended to associate the Commons with the verdict.[1] On this last occasion, too, Coke made a long speech to the Lords in which he asserted that the Commons, as the representative element in the constitution, could act as 'inquisitor general' of the commonwealth (31).

This was partly due to the fact that Cranfield pleaded not guilty, and had to have a six-day trial in which the prosecution was led by the attorney-general.[2] But in other respects it was a borderline case. Cranfield had been guilty of corruption, like his predecessors in 1621, but the real motive of the attack was to remove a minister in whom the king still had confidence but who was distrusted by the Commons as well as by the Duke of Buckingham.[3] James realised that Parliament was now asserting a right to influence his choice of ministers, and he warned Charles and Buckingham of the danger in establishing this kind of precedent.

This danger came on perhaps earlier than James himself had feared. The impeachment of Buckingham in 1626[4] was the first attempt to remove a minister whom the king was determined to retain. It was only a qualified success. Buckingham remained, but Charles was forced to dissolve Parliament without obtaining the money necessary to carry out Buckingham's policies. The impeachment of Strafford in 1641 also broke down, and had to be supplemented by a bill of attainder. Buckingham was simply accused of misusing the king's favour to enrich himself and of failing in his duties as Lord High Admiral, but Strafford's accusers went so far as to assert that a man could commit high treason while obeying the king's orders; the first attempt to divide the person of the king from his office. They also attempted to prove that a cumulative series of actions, none of them treasonable, could constitute treason when taken together.[5]

However, even before Strafford's case impeachment was being obviously misused, against small men guilty of small crimes. The use of impeachment against divines, from Manwaring in 1628 to Sacheverell in 1710, was taking a sledgehammer to crack a nut. In the crisis of 1641–2 so many men were impeached—the ship-money judges, the bench of bishops, the Five Members, the peers who joined the king at York—and so few were brought to trial, that the whole process fell into disrepute.

[1] *ST*, ii, 1132, 1250; *LJ*, iii, 106.
[2] He sat as an assistant in the Lords; it is reasonably certain that he was not regarded as leading for the Crown on this occasion.
[3] R. H. Tawney, *Business and Politics under James I* (Cambridge, 1958), pp. 251 ff.
[4] The articles of impeachment are printed in *GCD*, pp. 3 ff.
[5] No. **55 b**, p. 207 below.

29. Prohibitions

(a) Pierrepoint's Case. Hil. 6 Jacobi [1609], Common Pleas

Pierrepoint procured one to convey the daughter of a gentleman and to marry her to a ploughman in the night, and procured a priest to marry them, and was there present. For which matter he was excommunicate[d] by the Ordinary of the Diocese, and after absolution he was for the same committed to prison by the High Commissioners. It was holden by the court that matters concerning tithes, marriage or testaments are not examinable before them; yet because that he had suffered imprisonment for such things, and that neither the statute of 23 Hen. VIII nor the canon doth extend to the High Commissioners, it was resolved that if upon submission to the Commissioners they would not set him at liberty, then this court would do it.

Godbolt, p. 158

(b) Candict and Plomer's Case. Pasch. 8 Jacobi [1610], Common Pleas

The parishioners had used time out of memory of man to choose the parish clerk of the church of St Augustine in Canterbury, and the old clerk being dead they chose a new clerk and the parson by force of a new canon[1] chose another man for the clerk. Upon which the clerk chosen by the parishioners was sued in the Spiritual Court, and he had a prohibition; and afterwards he was sued again in the Spiritual Court, for setting of the bread upon the Communion Table, and for singing in another tune than the parishioners and the other clerk[2] did, and was deprived by sentence there.

Haughton, Serjeant, moved for a prohibition, and said that although the last suit in the Spiritual Court was not directly for the using of the office of clerk, yet by the matters contained in the libel it is drawn in question whether he were lawful clerk or not, and therefore prayed a prohibition.

Coke. You shall have a prohibition, for the canon is against the Common Law, for particular customs are part of the Common Law; and said, that the Canon Law would not endure gun-shot. And he said that by the suit in the Spiritual Court they would examine whether he were a lawful clerk or not, for if he be a lawful clerk, then he hath good authority to set the bread upon the Communion Table.

[1] By canon XCI of 1604 (Cardwell, *Synodalia*, I, 298), the parson was to appoint the clerk.
[2] One of the clerk's duties, of course, was to set the key and lead the singing.

95

Haughton. But what shall we do, for we are deprived by sentence given there?

Coke. There is no question but that the prohibition lieth, notwithstanding the sentence there, and for the deprivation it is merely void. For the clerkship is a lay office, and may be executed by a layman, and therefore the Ordinary hath no power to deprive him....And I wish that an Information be drawn against them for holding plea of a thing which is a mere lay thing....

Warmersley, Justice. The office is lay, and the deprivation by the Ordinary is void; for he cannot deprive him because he hath nothing to do in the election.

And a prohibition was granted.

At another day the case was moved again, and the court was of the same opinion, that the clerk could not be deprived because the clerkship was a lay office....But *Coke* said, the same day in another case which was moved in court, and gave it for a rule, that after sentence given in the spiritual court he would not grant a prohibition if there were not matter apparent within the proceedings. For I will not allow [he said] that the party shall, to have a prohibition, show anything not grounded on the sentence, because he hath admitted of the jurisdiction; and there is no reason for him to try if the spiritual court will help him, and afterwards at the Common Law to sue forth a prohibition. All which was agreed by the whole court.[1]   *Ibid.* pp. 163–4

(c) *The Archbishop of York and Sedgwick's Case.* Trin. 10 Jacobi [1612]

The Archbishop of York and Doctor Ingram brought and exhibited a bill in the Exchequer at York upon an obligation of seven hundred pounds, and declared in their bill [it was] in the nature of an action for debt brought at the Common Law. Which matter being showed unto the Court of Common Pleas by Sedgwick, the defendant there, a prohibition was awarded to the archbishop and to the said court at York.

And *Coke,* Chief Justice, gave the reasons wherefore the court granted the prohibition. He said: (1) because the matter was merely determinable at the Common Law, and therefore ought to be proceeded in according to the course of the Common Law. (2) Although the

---

[1] The inconsistency is only apparent. Coke was not prepared to challenge the verdict of an ecclesiastical court on the petition of the loser unless it could be shown that that court had never possessed jurisdiction.

King had granted to the Lord President and the Council of York to hold pleas of all personal actions, yet (he said) they cannot alter the form of the proceedings. For as 6 Hen. VII, c. 5 is, the King by his grant cannot make that inquirable in a Leet which was not inquirable there by the law, nor a Leet to be of other nature than it was at the Common Law. And in 11 Hen. IV it is holden that the Pope nor any other person can change the Common Law, without a Parliament. And Coke vouched a record in 8 Hen. IV, that the King granted to both the universities that they should hold pleas of all causes arising within the universities according to the course of the Civil Law; and all the judges of England were then of opinion that the grant was not good, because the King could not by his grant alter the law of the land. With which case agrees 37 Hen. VI, 26, 2 Ed. IV, 16 and 7 Hen. VII. But at this day, by a special Act of Parliament, made 13 Eliz., not printed, the universities have now power to proceed and judge according to the Civil Law. (3) He said that the oath of judges is, viz. 'You shall do and procure the profit of the King and his Crown, in all things wherein you may reasonably effect and do the same'. And he said that upon every judgement upon debt of forty pounds the King was to have ten shillings paid to the Hanaper, and if the debt were more, then more. But he said by this manner of proceeding by English Bill[1] the King should lose his fine. (4) He said that it was against the statute of Magna Carta, viz., *Nec super eum ibimus, nec super eum mittemus, nisi per legale judicium parium suorum, vel per legem terrae*. And the law of the land is, that matters of fact shall be tried by verdict of twelve men; but by their proceedings by English Bill, the party should be examined upon his oath, and it is a rule in law that *nemo tenetur seipsum prodere*. And also he said, that upon their judgement there no writ of error lieth, so as the subject should by such means be deprived of his birth-right. (5) It was said by all the justices, with which the justices of the King's Bench did agree, that such proceedings were illegal, and the Lord Chancellor of England would have cast such a bill out of the Court of Chancery. And they advised the Court of York so to do, and a Prohibition was awarded accordingly.

Ibid. pp. 201–2

---

[1] The writ or indictment in the Common Law courts was in Latin.

30. The revival of impeachment: Sir Giles Mompesson

[Commons, 28 February 1621: in a committee appointed to examine precedents.]

Sir Edward Coke. The court of Parliament a Court of Counsel and a Court of Pleas. When the Houses were divided the indivisible things remained with the Lords; pleas continued in the upper House long after the statute. Complaints and examinations of grievances have been ancient in the House of Commons, the matter of fact tried there; they have often resorted to the Lords for judicature. The proceedings have been with some variety. In some cases the House of Commons made plaintiffs and delinquents to answer there, sometimes the Steward of the House made a complaint and the Commons were made a party, and sometimes the Commons would have the cognizance alone. Never any that was found guilty hath been able to bear out the storm of the Commons forces. *Commons Debates 1621,* IV, 115–16

[Later, in the House.]

Sir Edward Coke made report from the committee for the search of precedents, that the searchers have discharged their duties. I thank God for three unities of this Parliament: 1, betwixt our sovereign and us; 2, betwixt the Lords and us; 3, betwixt ourselves. This is as weighty a cause as any in my time, because it concerns not us only but the Lords also. Therefore we are resolved according to former precedents to address ourselves to the Lords, for so it was in Henry the Sixth's time, in whose reign we have two precedents: 2 Hen. 6 [Sir John Mortimer], and the 31 Hen. 6 [Thomas Thorpe].

So it was agreed to go to the Lords, and that the committee examine all his offences. *Ibid.* II, 148–9

[3 March.] A message from the lower House, delivered by Sir Edward Coke, with divers knights, citizens and burgesses:

That the House of Commons had entered into a due consideration of divers heavy grievances, and about that matter they desired a conference with their Lordships....

Answer was returned by the same messengers that the Lords are willing and do yield to such conference as is desired; the number to be the whole house.... [33]

[12 March.] The Lord Chancellor, removing from his place to his seat as a peer, reported what passed at the conference of both houses on Saturday last [10 March], the inducement of which conference was to clear the King's honour touching grants to Sir Giles Mompesson, and the passages procuring the same. The effect of which conference was, ...that the authority granted by the King was much abused in the execution thereof, to the intolerable grievance of the subject, and much imposture was used in the trade. [42]

[22 March.] The Lord Chief Justice related the message delivered yesterday from the lower House by Sir Robert Phelips and others.... They acknowledged the good correspondence between both the Houses, especially in the examination of the grievances complained of, and presented to the Lords, with humble thanks for the supply the Lords added to their labours in giving the oath unto the examinants, which they cannot do. [61]

[26 March. King's Speech.]...I am ashamed (these things proving so, as they are generally reported to be) that it was not my good fortune to be the only author of the reformation and punishment of them by some ordinary course of justice. Nevertheless, since these things are now discovered by Parliament, which before I knew not of, nor could so well be discovered otherwise, in regard of that representative body of the kingdom which comes from all parts of the country, I will be never a wit the slower to do my part for the execution....

I intend not to derogate or infringe any of the liberties or privileges of this House, but rather to fortify and strengthen them, for never any king hath done so much for the nobility of England as I have done, and will ever be ready to do. And whatsoever I shall now say and deliver unto you as my thought, yet, when I have said what I think, I will afterwards freely leave the judgement wholly to your House. I know ye will do nothing but what the like hath been done before, and I pray you be not jealous that I will abridge you in anything that hath been used, for whatsoever the precedents in times of good government can warrant I will allow. For I acknowledge this to be the Supreme Court of Justice, wherein I am ever present by representation, and in this ye may be better satisfied by my own presence, coming divers times amongst you; neither can I give you any greater assurance or better pledge of this my purpose, than that I have done you the honour to set my only son amongst you, and hope that ye with him shall have the means to make this the happiest parliament that ever was in England.... [69]

[26 March, afternoon.] Message sent to the lower House..., that if the Commons, with their Speaker, will according to the ancient custom of Parliament come to demand of the Lords that judgement be given against Sir Giles Mompesson for the heinous offences by him committed, they shall be heard....

The knights, citizens and burgesses of the House of Commons, accompanied with their Speaker, came to the Bar, where the Speaker repeated the message which the Lords had sent unto them, and said:

The Commons, by me their Speaker, demand judgement to be given against Sir Giles Mompesson, according as the heinousness of his offence doth require.

The Lord Chief Justice, being in place of the Lord Chancellor,[1] answered:

Mr Speaker, the Lords Spiritual and Temporal have taken knowledge of the great pains the Commons have taken to inform their Lordships of many complaints brought unto them against Sir Giles Mompesson and others, whereof their Lordships received divers instructions from them, and thereupon, proceeding by examinations of divers witnesses upon oath, they find Sir Giles Mompesson, and divers others, guilty of many heinous crimes, against the King's Majesty and against the Commonwealth....

And so his Lordship pronounced the judgement of the Lords against Sir Giles Mompesson.... [72]   *LJ*, III, 33–72

31. The impeachment of Cranfield, 1624

[15 April.] Message from the House of Commons, by Lord Cavendish and others: That whereas they have received divers and sundry complaints against a member of this House, which are of a high and grievous nature, they desire a conference, thereby to impart the same unto their Lordships. The time and place, and number of committees, they humbly leave unto their Lordships.

Answered: The Lords will be ready to give them meeting and conference, with a committee of their whole house, about this business, this afternoon at three, in the Hall at Whitehall. [306]

[16 April.] The Lord Keeper reported on the conference yesterday at Whitehall between the two Houses in this manner, *videlicet*: At this conference *Sir Edward Coke* (on the behalf of the Commons) showed that the knights, citizens and burgesses assembled in Parliament are

---

[1] Bacon had been accused of corruption the previous week, and had retired to his bed.

always elected; the knights by the counties, the citizens by the cities, and the burgesses by the boroughs of the kingdom. That your Highness and my Lords do enjoy your places by blood and descent; some of your Lordships by creation, and the Lords Ecclesiastical by succession; but the members of the House of Commons by free election. They appear for multitudes, and bind multitudes, and therefore they have no proxies. They are the representative body of the realm, for all the people are present in Parliament by person representative; and therefore, by the wisdom of the State, and by parliament orders, the Commons are appointed the Inquisitors-General of the grievances of the kingdom, and that for three causes:

1. Because they have best notice from all parts thereof.

2. They are most sensible it is not your Lordships, but the weakest Commons, that go to the wall.

3. As in a natural body, not the disease but the neglect of cure killeth, *non morbus sed morbi neglecta curatio interfecit*; so the long delay of cure of grievances *corpus politicum interfecit*; and this would happen if they were not found out by the Commons.

In their inquisition they found (what they scarce ever did before in this kind) many great, exorbitant and heinous offences against a member of this House, the Lord Treasurer; and they found him guilty after a strange manner, for in all the House no man said 'no' but [it was] concluded against him *nemine dissentiente*.

That the House appointed him (Sir Edward Coke) to present these enormities unto your Lordships, much against his mind; others were far more sufficient, as well in regard of his great years, as of other accidents. Yet, he said, he would do it truly, plainly and shortly.

There were two great offences in general, which they had distributed into two parts, one of them which should be represented by him, and the other by his colleague.

That which he should represent was to consist of two charges: (1) Gross and sordid bribery. (2) For procuring good orders of the Court of Wards to be altered—for it was done by his principal procurement—to the deceit of the King, oppression of the subject, [and] enriching of his own servants.

He would begin with presenting unto your Lordships the bribery....
[307]

*   *   *   *   *   *

[5 May. King's Speech to the Lords.]

...It is my judgement, next under God, which you are to exercise at this time; and therefore, as a judge instructs the jury before the prisoner departs from the bar, so it becomes me to tell you how to carry yourselves in this great business. And the cause hereof is this, because I am bound in conscience to be careful of your carriage herein, for if your judgement should fall contrary to my approbation I protest to God it would be a great misery to me, and a greater grief unto your hearts. Before the last parliament I never saw any precedents of this nature. In the last, against another great officer of mine, there needed no admonition, because ye had *reum confitentem*. In this the party stands upon his justification, and therefore you have more need to take heed and examine it well. There is no doubt at all of your doing justice,...you are the most honourable jury of England; nor do I intend further to instruct you than to open your eyes (many eyes see more than one)....

Now I shall recommend unto you some generals, not for his respect or particular but mine own, my son's, and posterity's; and your own (my Lords), whose part, God knows when, it may fall unto. Let no man's particular ends bring forth a precedent that may be prejudicial to you all, and your heirs after you. Precedents there were none, of many years, before this and the last sessions. The informers are the lower House, and the upper House are the judges. If the accusations come in by the parties wronged, then you have a fair entrance for justice; if by men that search and hunt after other men's lives and actions, beware of it; it is dangerous, it may be your own case another time.... [343-4]

[7 May.] The Lord Keeper signified to the Lords that his Majesty said, he did not deliver this speech out of any suspicion of their Lordships, but only in discharge of his own duty and conscience. Which the House ordered to be entered. [344]

[On 13 May Cranfield was found guilty, and sentenced to be dismissed all his offices, barred from court and parliament, fined £50,000 and imprisoned during the king's pleasure. James at once cancelled the fine and the imprisonment.]   *LJ*, III, 306-83

II. THE REACTION AGAINST COKE

The climax of Sir Edward Coke's career was reached in the Petition of Right, which was in many ways the embodiment of his concept of the law and the functions of the judiciary. In his years on the bench he had always held that judges were not bound entirely by case law or precedent, that it was possible for a new case to raise a new principle (a more daring idea than it seems), and that in some cases the judges must fall back on the law of reason, or the fundamental unwritten law of England. He also held that in some respects the king was below the law, and that judges must not hesitate to find against him if their precedents, or the fundamental law, demanded it.

But in this Coke was running clean counter to the traditional view of the judicial function, which was summed up by his successor, Lord Chief Justice Hobart, in the ironically titled *Sir Edward Coke's Case* in 1623 (**32**). He held that in cases of doubt the verdict must always be for the king in the king's courts, and this was rigidly adhered to by King's Bench in 1627, when five gentlemen imprisoned by Charles for refusing a forced loan sued out a writ of *habeas corpus*.[1] The judges were given every opportunity to discuss whether the king could levy forced loans or imprison men without cause shown, or whether by Magna Carta the subject had a general right to 'due process of law', but they studiously ignored them. There is something pathetic in Lord Chief Justice Hyde's remark, 'The precedents are all against you, every one of them, and what shall guide our judgements, since there is nothing alleged in this case but precedents?' (**33**).

Coke's answer was the Petition of Right, the first attempt to commit to the statute book what were regarded as certain fundamental rights, which would bind the judges henceforward. But he was wasting his time. They only heard Charles I's appeal for their support when he prorogued Parliament in June 1628: 'My Lords the judges,...to you only, under me, belongs the interpretation of laws.'[2] In the months and years that followed they showed again and again that they were not prepared to abandon the professional mystique of case law, crabbed but certain, for the misty profundities and vague generalisations of the fundamental law, on the lips of every amateur. Nor were they prepared to abandon their traditional role as servants of the Crown, comfortable and honourable men, for the hazardous demagogic role of arbiters between Crown and Parliament. In 1628 the Court of Exchequer decided that the king had the right to distrain the goods of merchants who refused to pay tunnage and poundage, and it supported him steadily through 1629 and 1630 in his attempt to break the merchants' resistance, accepting his argument that tunnage and poundage was not covered by the Petition of Right. King's Bench also upheld the imprisonment of Sir John Eliot and other Members of Parliament, rejecting the plea that it was not only against parliamentary privilege but against the Petition of Right.[3]

Judges who felt a disposition to stray were perhaps deterred by the suspension of the Chief Baron of the Exchequer in 1629, and the dismissal of Sir

---

[1] See p. 59 above.   [2] *PH*, II, 434 (26 June 1628).
[3] See p. 51 above.

Robert Heath, Chief Justice of Common Pleas, in 1634.[1] But this does not explain the defection of the younger generation of lawyers who had supported Coke in the parliaments of the 1620's. Edward Lyttelton accepted the Recordership of London in 1631 and the solicitor-generalship in 1634; he argued against Hampden in 1637, of course, and was made Lord Keeper in 1641. William Noy and Dudley Digges had an even more distinguished record of opposition to Charles I; but Noy was appointed attorney-general in 1634, and was surely marked out for further promotion when he died in 1637, while Digges ended up on the High Commission. John Selden was another opposition lawyer turned courtier.

It was not just that these men did not expect another parliament to sit in the near future; they were disillusioned, too, by the manifest failure of the Petition of Right, and the obstructive conduct of the Opposition in 1629. Charles took steps to seize Coke's papers on his death in 1634,[2] but his posthumous influence on the professional lawyers of this generation was slight. In the same year the king consulted the judges before he issued the first writs of ship-money (this was when he dismissed Heath), and again in 1635 before he extended the writs to the inland counties. In February 1637, when Hampden and Saye and Sele showed a disposition to contest the issue he again consulted the judges, and *Rex versus Hampden* was finally heard in November 1637 before all the judges of the three benches, sitting in Exchequer Chamber. Hampden's counsel agreed with the judges that the king could call upon his subjects for aid, in the form of ships, arms, men or money, in an emergency, but they denied that an emergency existed in the years 1634–6, and they insisted that there had been time to call Parliament into consultation. The answer was that the king was sole judge of an emergency, and if he must call parliament on every such occasion this must lead, sooner or later, to disaster (34). In many ways the judges were much less sweeping in their judgement than they had been in Bate's Case; they stuck close to the issue in hand—whether the king, in a war emergency, could demand aid from his subjects—and Mr Justice Berkeley's careful proviso that their judgement did not confer on the Crown any general right of arbitrary taxation was not contradicted by any of his colleagues. Moreover, five out of twelve judges had the courage to find for Hampden, two of them on technical grounds.[3] Unfortunately, Sir John Finch, Chief Justice of King's Bench, caused grave offence by reflecting on the conduct of parliaments in general and the last parliament in particular, in which he had been Speaker.

---

[1] Gardiner, *History of England*, VII, 112–13, 361. There is no direct evidence that Heath was dismissed for his refusal to countenance ship-money.

[2] It should be said that this was part of a general movement; Charles also wanted to secure the papers of Lord Conway, an eminently loyal servant of the Crown (*CSPD 1629–31*, p. xxvi).

[3] The legal issues are thoroughly discussed by D. L. Keir, 'The Case of Ship Money', *Law Quarterly Review*, LII (1936), 546. For the political and financial background, see p. 88 above.

More generally, Clarendon pointed out that, whereas in 1627 the judges had resolutely declined to consider any issues or factors outside the narrow limits of case law or precedent, ten years later they had no hesitation in discussing the state of Europe or the war in the Narrow Seas, and allowing such considerations to influence their decision. Clarendon was sharply critical of this (35), but in some ways the judges were only following Coke's advice, and it was ironical that it should have been used against the subject's property rights.

The case of ship-money finally wrecked the reputation of the judges, and brought on their impeachment in the summer of 1641. But the law had suffered too. In the 1620's the law and lawyers had been regarded with superstitious reverence, as priests who could exorcise the devils that possessed the king and commonwealth; through the law and the judges the ancient constitution would find its true balance again. The failure of the Petition of Right, and the policy of the judges in the 'thirties, were a complete disillusionment, and the Long Parliament accordingly turned to remedial legislation which would leave the bench no freedom of action at all. Lawyers like Coke, Lyttelton, Digges, Noy, Hakewill and Whitelocke had played a decisive part in opposition from 1604 to 1629; they played no such part after 1640.

The disillusionment of the upper classes with the Common Law left it unprotected against the criticisms of the lower classes, which were directed at its slowness, its incomprehensibility, its defectiveness and its expense. In the 1640's men came forward, for the first time for a century, to demand the codification of the law, the abandonment of law French and a revision of the judicial system; they even demanded the exclusion of lawyers from parliament. Throughout the Interregnum this demand for reform was insistent, and not easily countered.

32. 'Sir Edward Coke's case' (Pasch: 21 Jacobi [1623] in the Court of Wards)

[The Crown was attempting to recover debts to Queen Elizabeth incurred by Sir Christopher Hatton as Remembrancer and Collector of the First Fruits and Tenths. The issue was complicated by the fact that Hatton had made a deed settling his lands on his son and his son's heirs in tail, with a power of revocation in his own lifetime. Sir Edward Coke represented the interests of his wife Frances, Hatton's daughter. The Court of Wards was assisted by Ley, Chief Justice of King's Bench, Hobart, Chief Justice of Common Pleas, Tanfield, Chief Baron of Exchequer, and Dodderidge, Justice of King's Bench.]

Hobart, Lord Chief Justice of the Common Pleas, argued to the same purpose.... He said in this case it was not material whether the Inquisition find the Deed to be with power of revocation, for he said that the land is extended, and that the extent remains good until it be avoided;[1] and he said that a revocable conveyance is sufficient to bind the parties themselves, but not to bind the King, but that the lands are liable into whose hands soever they come. When a man is said to forfeit his body, it is not to be intended his life, but the freedom of his body; imprisonment. At the Common Law a common person could neither take the body nor the lands in execution, but yet at the Common Law a *capias* lay upon a force,[2] although it did not lie in case of debt, agreement, etc. The King is *parens legum*, because the laws flowed from him; he is *maritus legum*, for the Law is as it were under *covert baron*;[3] he is *tutor legum*, for he is to direct the laws, and they desire aid of him. And he said that all the land of the King's debtor are liable to his debt. The word (*debitor*) is *nomen equivocum*, and he is a debtor who is any way chargeable for debt, damages, duty, rent behind, etc. The Law amplifies everything which is for the King's benefit, or made for the King. If the King releaseth all his debts, he releaseth only debts by recognisance, judgement, obligation, specialty,[4] or contract. Every thing for the benefit of the King shall be taken largely, as every thing against the King shall be taken strictly; and the reason why they shall be taken for his benefit is because the King cannot so nearly look to his particular, because he is intended to consider *ardua regni pro bono publico*. The Prerogative Laws are not the Exchequer Law, but is the Law of the Realm for the King, as the Common Law is the Law of the Realm for the subject. The King's Bench is a Court for the Pleas of the Crown; the Common Pleas is for Pleas betwixt subject and subject; and the Exchequer is the proper court for the King's revenues. Godbolt, p. 295

33. The Five Knights' case, King's Bench, 15–28 November 1627

[Letter from the Council to the Warden of the Fleet, on a writ of *habeas corpus* from King's Bench.]

Whereas Sir Walter Earl, Knight, was heretofore committed to your custody, these are to will and require you still to detain him, letting you

---

[1] The writ of extent was the peculiar means open to the Crown to sue for debt; it differed from the remedies available to the subject in that the debtor's lands, goods and person could all be seized at the same time.

[2] A writ of *capias* required the sheriff to seize the person of the defendant, and could be used in cases of forcible entry or disseisin.

[3] A *covert baron* was a married woman. Hobart meant that the law stood in relation to the king as a wife to her husband.　　　　[4] A contract under seal.

know that both his first commitment and this direction for the continuance of him in prison were and are by his Majesty's special commandment.

From Whitehall, 7 November 1627.

To the Guardian of the Fleet or his deputy. *ST, III, 12*

[Sergeant Bramston, 22 November 1627.]

If this return shall be good, then his imprisonment shall not continue on for a time, but for ever; and the subjects of this kingdom may be restrained of their liberties perpetually, and by law there can be no remedy for the subject: and therefore this return cannot stand with the laws of the realm or that of Magna Carta, nor with the statute of 28 Edw. 3, c. 3; for if a man be not bailable upon this return, they cannot have the benefit of these two laws, which are the inheritance of the subject.... We are not to reflect upon the present time and government, where justice and mercy floweth, but we are to look what may betide us in the time to come, hereafter. *Ibid. III, 6–8*

[John Selden, 22 November.]

...Now, my Lord, I will speak a word or two to the matter of the return; and that is touching the imprisonment *per speciale mandatum domini regis*, by the Lords of the Council, without any cause expressed....

The statute of Magna Carta, cap. 29, that statute [which] if it were fully executed as it ought to be, every man would enjoy his liberty better than he doth...out of the very body of this Act of Parliament, besides the explanation of other statutes, it appears, *nullus liber homo capiatur vel imprisonetur nisi per legem terrae*. My Lords, I know these words, *legem terrae*, do leave the question where it was, if the interpretation of the statute were not. But I think, under your Lordships' favour, there it must be intended, by 'due course of law', to be either by presentment or by indictment.

My Lords, if the meaning of these words *per legem terrae* were but, as we use to say, 'according to the law', which leaves the matter very uncertain; and [if] *per speciale mandatum, &c.* be within the meaning of these words 'according to law', then this Act had done nothing.

Ibid. III, 16–18

[Heath, Attorney-General, 26 November.]

And now, my Lord, we are where we were, to find out the true meaning of Magna Carta, for there is the foundation of our case; all this that hath been said concerneth other things, and is nothing to the thing in question. There is not a word either of the commitment of the King, or commandment of the Council, in all the statutes and records ...[and] they on the other side cannot cite one book, statute or other thing to prove that they that have been committed *per speciale mandatum* are bailable....

My Lords, there be *arcana Dei, et arcana imperii*....There shall be as much prejudice come to the kingdom, if God direct not the heart of the King, which is in the hand of God, as the rivers of waters; I say there may as much hazard come to the commonwealth in many other things with which the King is trusted, as in this particular there can accrue to the subject....It may be divers men do suffer wrongfully in prison, but therefore shall all prisoners be delivered? That were a great mischief. No doubt but the King's power is absolutely over his coins; if then he shall command his coin shall be turned to brass or leather...can your Lordship hinder it, as being an inconvenience?...The King may pardon all traitors and felons; and if he should do it, may not the subjects say, If the King do this, the bad will overcome the good? But shall any say, The King cannot do this? No, we may only say, he will not do this.

Ibid. III, 35–50

[Lord Chief Justice Hyde, 28 November.]

...I am sure you expect justice from hence, and God forbid we should sit here but to do justice to all men according to our best skill and knowledge, for it is our oaths and duties so to do, and I am sure there is nothing else expected of us. We are sworn to maintain all prerogatives of the King, that is one branch of our oath; and we are likewise sworn to administer justice equally to all people.

...That which is now to be judged by us is this: whether one that is committed by the King's authority, and no cause declared of his commitment, according as here it is upon this return, whether we ought to deliver him by bail, or to remand him back again? Wherein you must know this, which your counsel will tell you, we can take notice only of this return; and when the case appears to come to us no otherwise than by the return we are not bound to examine the truth of the return, but the sufficiency of it, for there is a great difference between the sufficiency and the truth.

We cannot judge upon rumours nor reports, but upon that which is before us on record, and therefore the return is examinable by us, whether it be sufficient or not....

The cause of the detention is sufficiently answered,...and therefore we resolve that the form of this return is good. The next thing is the main point in law, whether the substance or matter of the return be good or no, wherein the substance is this, he [the warder] doth certify that they are detained in prison by the special command of the King; and whether this be good in law or no, that is the question....

[He then examined in detail all the cases and statutes cited by counsel, and dismissed them.]

...Then the precedents are all against you, every one of them, and what shall guide our judgements, since there is nothing alleged in this case but precedents? [We find] that if no cause of the commitment be expressed it is to be presumed to be for matters of state, which we cannot take notice of. You see we find none, no not one, that hath been delivered by bail in the like cases, but by the hand of the King or his direction....

[He then examined in detail a number of cases in favour of the crown, ending with a declaration by the judges in 1592, with which the attorney-general had made great play.]

...You see what hath been the practice in all the Kings' times heretofore, and your own records, and this resolution of the judges teacheth us; and what can we do but walk in the steps of our forefathers? If in justice we ought to deliver you, we would do it. But upon these grounds, and these records, and the precedents and resolutions, we cannot deliver you, but you must be remanded....   *Ibid.* III, 51–9

34. Rex *v*. Hampden, 1637–8 (ship-money)
[Oliver St John, November 1637.]

My Lords,...it must needs be granted that in this business of defence the *suprema potestas* is inherent in his Majesty, as part of his crown and kingly dignity.

So that as the care and provision of the law of England extends in the first place to foreign defence, and secondly lays the burden upon all, and for ought I have to say against it, it maketh the quantity of each man's estate the rule whereby this burden is to be equally apportioned upon each person; so likewise hath it in the third place made his Majesty the sole judge of dangers from foreigners, and when and how the same are to be prevented, and to come nearer, hath given him power by writ under the Great Seal of England, to command the inhabitants of each county to provide shipping for the defence of the kingdom, and may by law compel the doing thereof.

So that, my Lords, as I still conceive [it] the question will not be *de persona*, in whom the *suprema potestas* of giving the authorities or powers to the sheriff, which are mentioned in this writ, doth lie, for that is in the King; but the question is only *de modo*, by what medium or method this supreme power, which is in his Majesty, doth infuse and let out itself into this particular....

His Majesty is the fountain of justice; and though all justice which is done within the realm flows from this fountain, yet it must run in certain and known channels: an assize in the King's Bench, or an appeal of death in the Common Pleas, are *coram non judice*, though the writ be his Majesty's command; and so of the several jurisdictions of each Court....If the process be legal, and in a right court, yet I conceive that his Majesty alone, without assistance of the judges of the court, cannot give judgement. I know that King John, H.3 and other Kings have sat on the King's Bench, and in the Exchequer; but for ought appears they were assisted by their judges....

And as without the assistance of his judges, who are his settled counsel at law, his Majesty applies not the law and justice in many cases unto his subjects; so likewise in other cases neither is this sufficient to do it without the assistance of his great Council in Parliament. If an erroneous judgement was given before the Statute of 27 Eliz. in the King's Bench, the King could not relieve his grieved subjects any way but by Writ of Error in Parliament; neither can he out of Parliament alter the old laws, nor make new, or make any naturalisations or legitimations, nor do some other things; and yet is the Parliament his Majesty's court too, as well as other his Courts of Justice. It is his Majesty that gives life and being to that, for he only summons, continues and dissolves it, and by he his *le volt* enlivens all the actions of it; and after the dissolution of it, by supporting his Courts of Justice, he keeps them still alive, by putting them in execution. And although in the Writ of Waste, and some other writs, it is called *commune concilium regni*, in respect that the whole kingdom is representatively there, and secondly, that the whole kingdom have access thither in all things that concern them, other courts affording relief but in special causes, and thirdly, in respect that the whole kingdom is interested in, and receive benefit by the laws and things there passed; yet it is *concilium regni* no otherwise than the Common Law is *lex terrae*.... [484-6]

My Lords, the Parliament, as it is best qualified and fitted to make this supply for some of each rank, and that through all the parts of the kingdom being there met, his Majesty having declared the danger, they best knowing the estates of all men within the realm, are fittest, by comparing the danger and men's estates together, to proportion the aid accordingly.

And secondly, as they are fittest for the preservation of that fundamental propriety which the subject hath in his lands and goods, because each subject's vote is included in whatever is there done.... [505]

My Lords, it appears not by anything in the writ, that any war at all was proclaimed against any state, or that if any his Majesty's subjects had taken away the goods of any prince's subjects in Christendom, but that the party might have recovered them before your Lordships in any his Majesty's Courts; so that the case in the first place is, whether in times of peace his Majesty may, without consent in Parliament, alter the property of the subject's goods for the defence of the realm.

Secondly, the time that will serve the turn for the bringing in of supplies and means of the defence, appears to your Lordships judicially by the writ, that is seven months within four days, for the writ went out 4 August, and commands the ship to be at Portsmouth, the place of rendezvous, the first of March following; and thereby it appears that the necessity in respect of the time was not such, but that a parliamentary consent might in that time have been endeavoured for the effecting of the supply.... [526-7]   Rushworth, II, 484-527

The Judgement, 1638

[Sir Robert Berkeley, 10 February 1638.]

...I hope that none doth imagine that it either is, or can be drawn by consequence, to be any part of the question in this case, whether the King may at all times and upon all occasions impose charges upon his subjects in general, without common consent in Parliament. If that were made the question, it is questionless that he may not. The people of the kingdom are subjects, not slaves, freemen, not villeins to be taxed *de alto et basso*.

Though the King of England hath a monarchical power, and hath *jura summae majestatis*, and hath an absolute trust settled in his crown and person for government of his subjects, yet his government is to be *secundum leges regni*....By those laws the subjects are not tenants at the King's will, of what they have....They have in their goods a propriety, a peculiar interest, a *meum et tuum*. They have a birthright in the laws of the kingdom. No new laws can be put upon them, none of their laws can be altered or abrogated, without common consent in Parliament.... [1090]

[He then examined the precedents for ship-money, and dismissed the idea that it was an aid or subsidy. He pointed out that ships, not money, were to be provided, and in theory they remained the property of the contributors. He admitted that the kingdom was not on the very verge of war, but he argued that there was sufficient danger on the high seas to warrant the king's action (1090–96).]

Now, whether to set the commonwealth free and in safety from this peril of ruin and destruction the King may not of his own royal authority, and without common assent in Parliament, impose a charge upon his subjects in general to provide such shipping as is necessary in his royal judgement, to join with his Majesty's own ships to attend them for such time as his Majesty in his royal wisdom shall think fit, and also to enjoin them to be themselves at the expenses...? [That is the question.]

I would be loth to irritate any differing from me with provoking or odious terms, but I cannot more fully express myself (and so I desire it may be taken as an expression, and not as a comparison) than in saying, that it is a dangerous tenet, a kind of judaizing opinion, to hold that the weal public must be exposed to peril of utter ruin and subversion, rather than such a charge as this, which may secure the commonwealth, may be imposed by the King upon the subject, without common consent in Parliament. So that the security of the commonwealth, for the very subsistence of it, must stay and expect until a Parliament provide for it, in which interim of time it is possible, nay, apparently probable, yea, in a manner to be presumed, that all may be, yea, will be brought to a final period of destruction and desolation....

I now come to my second general head, wherein I proposed to consider of the fundamental policy and maxims and rules of law for the government of this realm, and of the reasons of law pertinent to our case, which are very many. I will briefly and severally point at those which make impression on me.

1. It is plain that as originally, even before the Romans' time, the

frame of this kingdom was a monarchical state, so for divers hundreds of years past, upon the Romans' desertion of it, and after the heptarchy ended, it was, and continued and still continueth monarchical. And our gracious sovereign is a monarch, and the rights of free monarchy appertain unto him....

2. Where Mr Holborne[1] supposed a fundamental policy in the creation of the frame of this kingdom, that in case the monarch of England should be inclined to exact from his subjects at his pleasure he should be restrained, for that he could have nothing from them, but upon a common consent of Parliament, he is utterly mistaken herein. I agree the Parliament to be a most and supreme court, where the King and peers, as judges, are in person, and the whole body of the commons representatively. There peers and Commons may, in a fitting way, *parler leur ment*, and shew the estate of every part of the kingdom; and amongst other things, make known their grievances (if there be any) to their sovereign, and humbly petition him for redress.

But the former fancied policy I utterly deny. The law knows no such king-yoking policy. The law is of itself an old and trusty servant of the King's; it is his instrument or means which he useth to govern his people by. I never read nor heard that *lex* was *rex*; but it is common and most true that *rex* is *lex*, for he is *lex loquens*, a living, a speaking, an acting law....

There are two maxims of the law of England, which plainly disprove Mr Holborne's supposed policy. The first is, 'that the King is a person trusted with the state of the commonwealth'. The second of these maxims is, 'that the King cannot do wrong'. Upon these two maxims the *jura summae majestatis* are grounded, with which none but the King himself (not his high court of Parliament without leave) hath to meddle, as, namely, war and peace, value of coin, Parliament at pleasure, power to dispense with penal laws, and divers others; amongst which I range these also, of regal power to command provision (in case of necessity) of means from the subjects, to be adjoined to the King's own means for the defence of the commonwealth, for the preservation of the *salus reipublicae*. Otherwise I do not understand how the King's Majesty may be said to have the majestical right and power of a free monarch.

It is agreed that the King is by his regal office bound to defend his people...against all disturbers of the general peace amongst them, most chiefly in my judgement against dangerous foreigners....

---

[1] One of Hampden's counsel.

3. Though I have gone already very high, I shall go yet to a higher contemplation of the fundamental policy of our laws, which is this: that the King of mere right ought to have, and the people of mere duty are bound to yield unto the King, supply for the defence of the kingdom. And when the Parliament itself doth grant supply in that case it is not merely a benevolence of the people, but therein they do an act of justice and duty to the King.... [1097–9]

4. I confess that by the fundamental law of England the Parliament is *commune concilium regis et regni*, that it is the greatest, the most honourable and supreme court in the kingdom, that no man ought to think any dishonourable thing of it. Yet give me leave to say that it is but a *concilium*, to say so is no dishonour to it; the King may call it, prorogue it, dissolve it, at his pleasure, and whatsoever the King doth therein is always to be taken for just and necessary. We must consider that it is a great body, [and] moves slowly; sudden despatches cannot be expected in it. Besides, though the Parliament cannot err, parliament men may *de facto*. Every particular member of the House hath his free voice; some of them may chance to make scruples where there is no cause; it is possible some of them may have sinister ends. These things breed delays, so they may disturbances; I would to God the late woeful experience of this kingdom had not verified these speculations.... [1101]

ST, III, 1090–1101

[Sir John Finch, Lord Chief Justice of Common Pleas.]

...A parliament is an honourable court, and I confess it is an excellent means of charging the subject, and defending the kingdom, but yet it is not the only means. An honour the last Parliament was pleased to bestow on me, which never any shall with more respect remember than myself, when they were pleased to choose me for their Speaker. And as my brother Hutton said, I conceive it a fit way to charge the subject, and I wish that some, for their private humour, had not sowed the tares of discontent in that field of the commonwealth, then might we have expected and found good fruit. But now the best way to redeem this lost privilege (for which we may give those thanks only) is to give all opportune appearance of obedience and dutifulness to his Majesty's command. The two houses of Parliament without the King cannot make a law, nor without his royal assent declare it; he is not bound to call it but when he pleaseth, nor to continue it but at his pleasure. Certainly there was a King before a Parliament, for how else could there be an assembly of King, Lords and Commons? And then what sovereignty was there in the kingdom but this? His power then was limited by the positive law; then it cannot be denied but originally the King had the sovereignty of the whole kingdom both by sea and land, who hath a power of charging the whole kingdom.

The law that hath given that power hath given means to the King by this authority to put it in execution. It is a very true rule, the law commands nothing to be done, but it permits the ways and means how it may be done, else the law should be imperfect, lame and unjust. Therefore the law that hath given the interest and sovereignty of defending and governing the kingdom to the King doth also give the King power to charge his subjects for the necessary defence and good thereof. And as the King is bound to defend, so the subjects are bound to obey, and to come out of their own country, if occasion be, and to provide horse and arms in foreign war.... Then if sea and land be but one entire kingdom, and the King lord of both, the subject is bound as well to the defence of the sea as of the land, and then all are bound to provide ships, men, ammunition, victuals and necessaries for that defence.... But here the maritime towns shall not help the inland, nor the inland the maritime, but each of them bear their own charge.... [1226–7]

* * * * * *

...There hath been, and may be, as great danger when the enemy is not discerned as when in arms and on the land. In the time of war when the course of law is stopped, when judges have no power or place, when the courts of justice can send out no process, in this case the King may charge his subjects, you grant. Mark what you grant: when there is such a confusion as no law, then the King may do it.... Expectancy of danger, I hold, is sufficient ground for the King to charge his subjects, for if we stay till the danger comes it will be then too late, it may be. And his averment of the danger is not traversable, it must be binding when he perceives and says there is a danger; as in 1588, the enemy had been upon us, if it had not been foreseen and provided for before it came.

But I will not determine the danger now. Do not we see our potent neighbours, and our great enemies heretofore, were they not prepared for war; and was there not another navy floated upon the sea? and was not the dominion of the sea threatened to be taken away? As long as this danger remains I shall bless God for such a King as will provide for the defence of the kingdom timely, and rejoice to see such a navy as other nations must veil to; and we are not in case of safety without it, and should lose our glory besides.... [1234]

Acts of Parliament may take away flowers and ornaments of the crown, but not the crown itself; they cannot bar a succession, nor can they be attainted by them, and acts that bar them of possession are void. No Act of Parliament can bar a King of his regality, as that no lands should hold of him; or bar him of the allegiance of his subjects; or the relative on his part, as trust and power to defend his people. Therefore Acts of Parliament to take away his royal power in the defence of his kingdom are void....They are void Acts of Parliament to bind the King not to command the subjects' persons and goods, and I say their money too, for no Acts of Parliament make any difference.... [1235]

Ibid. 1226-35

35. Clarendon on ship-money

And here the damage and mischief cannot be expressed, that the Crown and State sustained by the deserved reproach and infamy that attended the judges, by being made use of in this and like acts of power; there being no possibility to preserve the dignity, reverence and estimation of the laws themselves but by the integrity and innocency of the judges. And no question, as the exorbitancy of the House of Commons this Parliament[1] hath proceeded principally from their contempt of the laws, and that contempt from the scandal of that judgement, so the concurrence of the House of Peers in that fury can be imputed to no one thing more than to the irreverence and scorn the judges were justly in; who had been always before looked upon there as the oracles of the law, and the best guides and directors of their opinions and actions: and they now thought themselves excused for swerving from the rules and customs of their predecessors (who in altering and making of laws, in judging of things and persons, had always observed the advice and judgement of those sages) in not asking questions of those whom they knew nobody would believe; and thinking it a just reproach upon them (who out of their gentilesses had submitted the difficulties and mysteries of the law to be measured by the standard of general reason and explained by the wisdom of state), to see those men make use of the licence they had taught, and determine that to be law which they thought

---

[1] The Long Parliament.

reasonable or found to be convenient. If these men had preserved the simplicity of their ancestors in severely and strictly defending the laws, other men had observed the modesty of theirs in humbly and dutifully obeying them.

Clarendon, History, bk I, § 151

III. STAR CHAMBER

The history, function and procedure of the Court of Star Chamber under the Tudors have now been definitively established, and under the Stuarts there were no new developments.[1] Ostensibly its main purpose remained to punish breaches of the king's peace by riot, assault or intimidation, and in 1633 it could still be called upon to suppress local opposition to schemes of reclamation and resettlement, in this case Vermuyden's draining of the Fens (36a). It also remained the principal court for cases of fraud, forgery or perjury, which were inadequately covered by the courts of Common Law. Some of its most spectacular cases were originated by the government, but the great majority of plaintiffs before it were private individuals already engaged in parallel litigation in Chancery or Common Pleas, who sought to strengthen their plea or simply embarrass their opponents by accusing them —often on the flimsiest evidence—of riot, defamation, conspiracy or assault; charges which 'the Tudor–Stuart monarchy's almost compulsive preoccupation with good order' would not allow it to ignore.[2] By the end of Elizabeth's reign the court had become so popular that when Egerton was appointed Lord Keeper, in 1596, he had to issue a series of orders clarifying and expediting its procedure, but even then the pressure of litigation was so great that in the reign of Charles I it was in danger of suffocation, and in 1632 its doors were closed to common informers under penal statutes, whose suits, initiated merely to substantiate their accusations, rarely proceeded to judgement.[3]

It is clear that right up to 1640 the court retained its popularity with litigants, nor did it arouse the jealousy of the Common Law courts. The three chief justices normally sat on it, and its president was the Lord Keeper, who under Charles I was usually a common lawyer, too. This was natural enough, since it was merely administering the Common Law by means of a different procedure, which admitted written depositions as evidence and permitted the cross-examination of the accused under oath. It was well understood that its functions and personnel were not limited by the statute of 1487,[4]

---

[1] Elton's account, though brief (*Tudor Constitution*, pp. 158–61), supersedes all others, and is a good guide to the bibliography of the subject. For the court under the Stuarts, see H. E. I. Phillips, 'The Last Years of the Court of Star Chamber, 1630–1641', *Transactions of the Royal Historical Society*, 4th ser., XXI (1938), 103, and Thomas G. Barnes, 'Due Process and Slow Process in the late Tudor early Stuart Star Chamber', *American Journal of Legal History*, VI (1962), 221, 315.

[2] Barnes, *op. cit.* p. 226.   [3] Barnes, *op. cit.* pp. 331–3.   [4] Elton, *loc. cit.*

which so confused the nineteenth century, and it had the unqualified endorsement of the great Coke himself.[1] As Professor Barnes insists:

> Star Chamber was latterly and throughout the period under discussion [1558–1640] a court of law, fixed solidly in the firmament of English judicature, administering the historically founded yet changing Common Law by a procedure different from that of Common Law though acceptable to the common lawyers and sanctioned by the judges of the Common Law courts.[2]

With this in mind, it is difficult to explain its precipitate abolition in the summer of 1641. Of course, on this occasion the Long Parliament acted with more emotion than logic,[3] but it showed no such reckless animus against the Court of Requests or the Court of Wards, which were most unpopular with the lawyers and the landowners respectively; in fact, both of them survived into the Civil War.

The explanation may lie in the severe corporal punishments meted out by the court in the 1630's, and its use in the same period to support a controversial religious and economic policy. In the absence of a prison system all seventeenth-century courts had to impose fines, corporal punishment or public penance; this was especially so of Star Chamber, which could not inflict the death penalty. But in an age when the Poor Law prescribed that women who would not work should be whipped 'till their backs be bloody', the ear-cropping ordered by Star Chamber was not out of line, and in fact, out of 236 known sentences of the Court between 1630 and 1641 only 19 included corporal punishment, and of these only 9 or 10 aroused any great public interest.[4] But William Prynne's second trial in 1637, with Bastwick and Burton, and the trial of that arch-publicist John Lilburne, caught the attention of the public, no doubt in part because they were campaigning against the unpopular bishops.[5] Another factor which roused public opinion was the fact that most of the men who were sentenced to gross physical mutilation were gentlemen, who were rarely sentenced to the pillory or the branding iron by the ordinary courts. Most remarkable in this respect was the case of Sir Thomas Wiseman, who was convicted in 1638 of slandering Lord Keeper Finch and the court of Star Chamber itself. He was fined £10,000, with £7,000 damages; he was degraded from the order of knighthood and his patent of baronetcy was cancelled; his ears were cut off, he was placed in the pillory, and he was ordered to be imprisoned during

---

[1] See the extract from his *Institutes*, printed Elton, *op. cit.* pp. 165–7.
[2] Barnes, *op. cit.* p. 224.
[3] Phillips outlines the circumstances, *op. cit.* pp. 103–6.
[4] *Ibid.* p. 118. Cf. Thomas G. Barnes, 'Star Chamber Mythology', *American Journal of Legal History*, v (1961), 1.
[5] Phillips, *op. cit.* p. 124; Haller, *Rise of Puritanism*, p. 280.

the king's pleasure.[1] Wiseman brought his case before Parliament in 1641, as did Prynne and the others, and this must have influenced its deliberations.

The court was also besmirched by its association in the public mind with the Laudian hierarchy. One of its main uses was to strengthen and sustain other courts, and the ecclesiastical courts were particularly weak in this era. So we find Lady Grenville in 1632 using her husband's casual and almost irrelevant slander on the earl of Suffolk to enforce her demands for alimony, he having ignored the sentence of the church courts (36 b). This was straightforward enough; it was a different matter when a minister, having found the High Commission insufficient, prosecuted his parishioners for riot because they refused to take the sacrament kneeling (36 c), or when a clergyman was arraigned for 'irreligious and profane speeches to the disgrace of the State and his Majesty's government'.[2] When another clergyman prosecuted a pedlar for accusing him of adultery with his wife the Lord Keeper protested that the case belonged to the ecclesiastical courts, but he did not press the point.[3] Such cases emphasised the presence of bishops on the board. Laud sat regularly, as bishop of London and archbishop, and so did Richard Neile, bishop of Winchester and later archbishop of York. Juxon of London also sat occasionally after his appointment to the Treasury in 1635. It was noticed that these bishops always pressed for the heaviest and cruellest punishment, whether their order was involved or not. The presence of bishops was not an innovation, of course, but it had been easier to ignore it in previous generations when bishops were not committed to a controversial theory of Church and State.

However, the most important single cause of Star Chamber's unpopularity was the role it was called upon to play in the 1630's in the enforcement of the king's fiscal and social policies. In the absence of parliaments the government also had to make increasing use of proclamations, and the enforcement of proclamations had always been a function peculiar to Star Chamber. Between 1631 and 1641 the attorney-general brought 175 actions in Star Chamber, most of them on the simplified procedure of ore tenus[4]—in itself something of an abuse. Of these 175 about 40 were brought to a conclusion, and the great majority of these were concerned with breaches of proclamations; proclamations against enclosures, against unlawful residence in London,[5] against builders of tenements in the suburbs, fraudulent manufacturers, exporters of prohibited commodities and victuallers who sold meat in

---

[1] *CSPD*, 1637–8, p. 491. This case is rather obscure; the savagery of the sentence may have reflected the sensitivity of the judges to accusations of corruption after Bacon's fall.

[2] Gardiner, *Cases in Star Chamber*, p. 89.   [3] *Ibid.* pp. 70–1.

[4] When the accused stood mute, which was held to imply a confession; or when he confessed of his own accord, of course. See Phillips, *op. cit.* pp. 113–14.

[5] By the terms of the proclamation of 20 June 1632 (no. **143**, p. 502 below).

Lent.[1] Other prosecutions involving questions of public policy were those of sheriffs who failed to collect ship-money, hoarders of corn, and those who infringed patents of monopoly. So intense was this activity that Professor Barnes concludes: 'In the 1630's Star Chamber became...a tribunal for the trial of cases of public import, involving profit for and the safety of the State.'[2] Or, as Pym said in 1640: 'The Star Chamber now is become a court of revenue; it was not used that *meum et tuum* should be disputed there.'[3] Its comparative success in enforcing a centralised economic policy ensured its unpopularity with the landed classes, who always hankered after decentralisation even at the cost of efficient government.

36. Cases before the Star Chamber

(a) *Attorney-general versus Charles Moody, Richard Strode and others.*
    Michaelmas Term 1633

Present: Lord Keeper
Lord Privy Seal
Earl of Arundel
Earl of Bridgewater
Lord Wentworth
Lord Falkland

Bishop of London
Bishop of Winchester
Sir Thomas Jermyn
Sir John Coke
Sir Thomas Richardson, CJ
Sir Robert Heath, CJ.

The bill set forth that his Majesty, being seized of divers lands and waste grounds called the Fens, in the counties of Lincoln and Nottingham, etc., these lands were surrounded with water and barren, his Majesty by advice of his Council took order with Sir Cornelius Vermuyden for the draining of the Fens if it might be, and articles of agreement were made between his Majesty and the said Sir Cornelius Vermuyden, and authority given by virtue of the King's letters patent under the Great Seal of England for the doing thereof, and a special provision that those that had any title of common should repair to the commissioners appointed for that purpose by commission, and upon their showing their title or interest they should have full recompense. The King's letters were sent to warn them to come to the Commission and demand their recompense 23 February, 3 *Caroli* [1628]. They were all agreed the commoners should have one part of [blank]. The King

[1] Barnes, 'Due Process and Slow Process in the late Tudor early Stuart Star Chamber', *American Journal of Legal History*, VI (1962), 336. Cf. Phillips, *op. cit.* p. 116, where he puts the number of cases arising directly from proclamations as seventeen (out of approximately forty settled).   [2] Barnes, *loc. cit.*
[3] 17 April 1640, no. **53**, p. 202 below.

provided workmen, the work was brought to good forwardness, and divers ditches and banks made, and Sir Cornelius Vermuyden was at great charge thereabouts.

That the defendants, with others, came together in companies to throw down and demolish what was done, although divers proclamations were made, and no right they could pretend, and 4 *Caroli* they made their assemblies by hundreds and five hundreds, they demolish[ed] the work, they beat the workmen, and burne[d] the spades, shovels, wheelbarrows, planks, set up a pair of gallows for to terrify the workmen, threw some of them into the water and held them under a while. They had a signal to assemble themselves by sometimes a bell, sometimes by a horn, they threatened to kill the workmen if they came thither to work again. That they had fourteen several times in riotous and rebellious manner assembled themselves and done these riots, etc., to the slander of his Majesty's government, to the hindrance of the works, and to the damage of Sir Cornelius Vermuyden £5,000, and that some of them put those that served the King's process out of this court upon them into the stocks. [59–60]

*   *   *   *   *   *

It was unanimously declared by the whole court that his Majesty proceeded herein legally and rightfully for the benefit of his crown and people, for the draining of these Fens; and many of the defendants were found guilty of the several riots charged in the bill; viz., Toxie, James Moody, Henry Scott, and Hezekias Browne, who were fined £1,000 apiece. The widow Smith, who married the minister after the riots,[1] £500, and the several women who were proved to be at the said riots, 500 marks apiece, and they were adjudged to pay for damages unto Sir Cornelius Vermuyden, the relator, £2,000.

After this sentence Mr Attorney moved the court to take it into their consideration, whether it were not fit to fine the adjoining towns where these riots and rebellious assemblies were made; he showed that here were fourteen several riots, wherein the poorer sorts of people were set on work, but the rich, they escape, and these were committed three years ago, and never any are brought to be presented or indicted at any assizes or sessions. He taketh it that by the law these towns ought to be fined. [The Statute of] Westm[inster] 2, ch. 4, [said] that the towns

---

[1] 'Katherine Smith had since married with a minister, a grave divine, who was not called to answer...' [p. 64].

adjoining shall be distrained in such a case, etc., which was but a declaration of the Common Law. My Lord Keeper directed that the precedents should be considered, and if it agreed therewith they should be fined, but [it was] objected that these towns and villages were not called here to answer. Mr Attorney answered that upon a *rescusse* returned into a court of record if it appeared to be done the village or town where it was done is amerced, though not called, etc. Whereupon my Lord Keeper said it was a good motion and was not fit to die; yet nothing more was done for this time. Gardiner, *Cases in Star Chamber*, pp. 59–60, 64–5

(b) Theophilus, Earl of Suffolk, versus Sir Richard Grenville, Bt.

3 February 1632

The earl of Suffolk complained by his bill of Sir Richard Grenville, but [?that] whereas he had been a means to procure his lady, in a just cause, alimony against the said Sir Richard till the cause were heard in the ecclesiastical court, and the said earl of Suffolk sent a messenger with the order to give Sir Richard notice to pay the said alimony. Whereupon the said Sir Richard broke out in words before the said messenger, and the Lady Grenville, and others, saying: The earl of Suffolk is a base lord and hath dealt basely with me; and sent a message to him with these reproachful words: Tell him he is a base lord and hath used me basely, and he shall know as much, etc.

The defendant pleaded not guilty, and endeavoured to excuse himself for not defending himself in examining his witnesses to the contrary, and upon the reputation of the witnesses.

This cause came to be heard and sentenced this day.

My Lord Richardson showed that the earl of Suffolk was a noble lord, and a man of great office and trust, and honourable in his birth and actions, and not base. These words were very foul and dishonourable, it is a tainting of all honour. The old law was to cut off the tongues of such men; all honour is founded in the King. This is against the statutes of Westminster 2, ch. 34, and 12 Rich. II, c. 30, and [the] Book of Assizes. [A] Lord Chief Baron brought his writ against a lady that called him traitor, and his declaration was that it was *in despite le Roy*.

The bishop of Winchester said that Sir Richard Grenville had touched the highest blood in the kingdom, that his actions are according to his degree and parentage, and related what he heard the Lord Treasurer Burleigh say long ago, upon the coming forth of Dollmann's book, that he would boldly justify the House of Suffolk from the earls of Norfolk to be descended of Edward IV. The offices of my Lord Suffolk were great, Captain of the Pensioners and Lord Warden of the Cinque Ports. Sir Richard Grenville is a soldier, and a colonel, a man of good deserts otherwise.

But the tongue should not be the soldier's weapon, said the *bishop of London*.

So by the vote of the court Sir Richard Grenville was fined £4,000 to the King, and adjudged to pay £4,000 damages to the said earl of Suffolk, and to be imprisoned during the King's pleasure.

Ibid. pp. 108–10

(c) Allen versus Jemmat and others[1]

A motion was made by one Allen, a minister of Sudbury in Suffolk, that whereas he had put in a bill in this court against one Samuel Jemmat, clerk, and others for divers riots and misdemeanours committ[ed] by the defendants in the church, of which they endeavoured to dispossess the pl[ain]tiff because he would not suffer them to receive the sacrament sitting, and for refusing to kneel at the sacrament, and for throwing the holy sacrament most contemptuously and irreligiously under their feet. The pl[ain]tiff desired, being admitted to prosecute this cause *in forma pauperis*, that in regard he is poor and hath but £11 a year, that the suit might be undertaken to be presented by the King's attorney.

The bishop of London commended this cause to the court as concerning the ecclesiastical jurisdiction as much as any ever did.[2]

Mr Prynne for the defend[an]ts showed that this was complained of in the High Commission court, and there dismissed, and that for the same things that are here charged; that Mr Jemmat was lawfully presented, etc., and that therefore the court would dismiss the cause or dispauper the pl[ain]t[iff] for that by his confession he hath £11 *per annum*.

The bishop of Winchester showed the court that the archb[isho]p of York brought this into the High Commission court, that upon the defend[an]ts' submissions and promises of amendment and quietness they were there dismissed; but that since they were more refractory, etc.

My Lord Keeper pronounced this order, that the plaintiff should continue *pauper*, and to be considered if it can be proved by certificate that

---

[1] This case is undated, but it was heard before 1 February 1633, when Prynne was imprisoned.
[2] Clearly by 'ecclesiastical jurisdiction' Laud meant the dignity and authority of the priesthood rather than the jurisdiction of ecclesiastical courts.

any of these things being so foul as they seem to be by the charge of the bill; his Lordship thought it a fit thing for Mr Attorney to take care of and to present it.

Mr Prynne desired my Lord Keeper to give him leave to open the truth of the cause to his Lordship shortly. He showed that Allen, being a vicar in Sudbury and beneficed and unqualified, accepted of another living, and his lordship for that cause did grant the first living to another, one Samuel Jemmat; that he was admitted and inducted at five of the clock in the morning, when nobody was there in the church, and this he chargeth as a riot; and that in the afternoon of the same day there was a burial to be solemnised, and there coming the said Jemmat and thirty persons more to bury the dead corpse, when he had locked up the doors, this was the second riot. And for the other things charged, they were exhibited by articles into the High Commission court and there dismissed.

The bishop of London reproved Mr Prynne for saying that the articles in the Commission court were at the suit of the party; he averred that to his knowledge they were at the preferring of the late [arch]bishop of York. So the order aforesaid stood. *Ibid.* pp. 72–3

CHAPTER 4

THE ESTABLISHED CHURCH

I. THE JACOBEAN CHURCH

Any study of the early seventeenth-century Church must be principally devoted to its critics and opponents. The standard interpretation of Puritanism portrays it as a movement steadily developing and growing, posing an increasing challenge to successive kings and archbishops until it overwhelmed all kings and all archbishops in the 'Puritan Revolution'. In fact, this runs clean counter to any number of obvious and well-known facts. In Elizabeth's reign many Puritans, inside and outside parliament, demanded that the Book of Common Prayer be rewritten from end to end and that the institution of episcopacy be abolished or drastically modified—changes that implied nothing less than the complete refoundation of the Church. It is important to realise that this challenge was not renewed under James I, nor was it renewed in the reign of his son with the same unanimity and zeal as it had been, for instance, in the parliament of 1572–81. Many laymen had been induced to support Puritanism in the 1570's on the plea that only radical ecclesiastical reform could strengthen the Church against the dangers of the Counter-Reformation; this argument lost its force with the execution of Mary Stuart and the failure of the Armada, and the emergence of Brownism or separatism in the 1590's provoked a strong reaction against the reformers, a reaction encouraged and reinforced by Archbishop Whitgift. Parliament had abandoned its support for the Puritan cause, in so far as it implied fundamental church reform, and its more aggressive leaders amongst the clergy had died off, fled abroad, or been silenced by High Commission.

So, by 1603 Puritanism no longer implied a desire to overthrow the establishment, but a feeling on the part of a minority of the clergy,[1] and perhaps a larger proportion of the middle-class laity, that the time had come for the relaxation of the iron discipline established by Whitgift at a time of crisis. It was safe now to make slight alterations in the Prayer Book, for instance, and to reopen the question of the wearing of the surplice, that potent piece of linen. Perhaps the most serious issue was 'subscription'. The

[1] Usher, *Reconstruction*, I, 249–51, calculates that the number of Puritan ministers in 1603 was 281, and no contemporary estimate exceeds 300. (The total number of clergymen was about 6,000.) The number of Puritan laymen is almost impossible to assess, but Usher (*ibid.* I, 269) suggests that only 2% of the population were Puritan, as against 5% Catholic and 18% committed supporters of the Establishment, the rest being indifferent.

Subscription Act of 1571[1] required every clergyman to 'declare his assent and subscribe to all the Articles of Religion which only concern the confession of a true Christian faith and the Doctrine of the Sacraments'. This appeared to exclude those of the Thirty-Nine Articles which concerned the government of the Church and its doctrine on vexed questions like predestination, and this was the view taken by the Convocation of 1575; but from 1583 Whitgift had demanded subscription to all the articles, with the result that many scrupulous clergymen had been ejected or silenced.[2] This particularly vexed the laity, who pointed out that the enforcement of conformity had done nothing to raise the standards of preaching, rather the opposite. They pressed for the licensing of the 'silenced brethren', the removal of the 'dumb dogs', and the energetic provision of 'a godly, learned and sober ministry'. Finally, both clergy and laity were concerned at the increasing activity of the High Commission, and its free use of the oath *ex officio mero*, which infringed the basic Common Law principle that no man could be made to bear witness against himself.[3]

The first shot was fired by a group of clergymen who presented James with a moderate and undogmatic series of proposals, the Millenary Petition, on his way south in 1603 (37). James readily agreed to their suggestion that he summon a conference of both sides, which sat at Hampton Court 14–16 January 1604.[4] The king was not uncritical of the bishops, and during the conference he echoed the general concern at the low standard of the English parish clergy and the abuse of pluralism and non-residence; and though he refused to contemplate any change in the centralised and hierarchical government of the Church he was prepared to amend anything that could be proved dissonant with scripture or with the practice of the primitive Church. Finally, he agreed to certain changes in the Prayer Book, particularly the rubrics, a reform of the procedure in the lesser ecclesiastical courts, and measures to improve the income from tithes, and so make many incumbencies attractive to a better type of clergyman.

The conference ended amicably, but no compromise had been reached on such vital questions as subscription, and since the Convocation which assembled with Parliament at once began drafting a new series of canons for the government and discipline of the Church, the Opposition in the Commons felt obliged to espouse the cause of reform. In May they drew up a list of articles to be discussed at a conference with the Lords which were sub-

---

[1] 13 Eliz., c. 12, an Act to reform certain disorders touching ministers of the Church, printed *PCD*, pp. 64–5.

[2] Cardwell, *Synodalia*, I, 58–62 nn.; Makower, *Constitutional History*, p. 171 n. But see Sir John Neale, 'Parliament and the Articles of Religion, 1571', *EHR*, LXVII (1952), 510.

[3] See § III, p. 176 below.

[4] The account which follows is based on Mark H. Curtis, 'The Hampton Court Conference and its Aftermath', *History*, XLVI (1961), 1.

stantially a repetition of the Millenary Petition,[1] and when the Lords proved uncooperative they began translating this programme into bills, though most of them arrived in the upper House so late in the session that they could be safely ignored.[2] These bills,[3] for providing 'a learned and godly ministry', for preventing plurality of benefices, for removing 'scandalous and unworthy ministers', and for preventing clergymen being appointed magistrates, sum up the seventeenth-century layman's view of the clergy, that they should be poor, pure, learned and unworldly.

James was furious at this encroachment on his right to legislate for the Church with the assistance of Convocation, and he gave the Opposition a tongue-lashing when he prorogued parliament in July 1604.[4] Gone was the former spirit of accommodation. On 16 July he issued a proclamation which gave clergymen until 30 November to conform or suffer the consequences (38), and in September he licensed the Canons drawn up by Convocation, which were an unqualified endorsement of orthodoxy. In particular, canon xxxv demanded that candidates for holy orders 'willingly and *ex animo* subscribe' to three articles similar to those drawn up by Whitgift in 1583, asserting that the Prayer Book contained 'nothing contrary to the word of God', and that all the Thirty-Nine Articles were 'agreeable to the word of God' (39).[5]

This drive for conformity produced an unprecedented reaction amongst the gentry, and petitions on behalf of the threatened ministers were addressed to the king by the leading men in several counties.[6] James was furious, and three of the men who signed the Northamptonshire petition were cross-examined by the council and banished for a time to the country.[7] But the king's anger was never long lasting. At Hampton Court he had commanded the bishops to treat the Puritans gently,[8] an instruction repeated in the proclamation of 16 July and apparently obeyed by Richard Bancroft, who succeeded Whitgift at Canterbury in October.[9] For the rest of this parliament the Commons were anxious and agitated by the sufferings of the 'silenced ministers', though contemporaries only put their number at 300, and modern research has wittled this down to 150, of which only 80 or 90

[1] Printed TCD, pp. 69–70.

[2] Usher, *Reconstruction*, I, 345 ff.

[3] They are, in the order cited, nos. 3278, 3279, 3287(a) and 3285 in *House of Lords Manuscripts*, XI. Other bills would have prohibited the residence of married men in universities and cathedral precincts, restricted the lease of episcopal lands, and made new provisions to prevent simony (*ibid.* nos. 3283, 3284, 3288).

[4] No. **12**, p. 39 above.

[5] Cf. Elton, *Tudor Constitution*, pp. 444–5.

[6] *HMC*, Salisbury, XVII, 7–8, 34–5, 56–7; Babbage, *Puritanism and Richard Bancroft*, pp. 125ff.

[7] He regarded this petition as treasonable (see Gardiner, *History*, I, 198–9, and p. 446 below), but it is difficult to see why. The original is P.R.O., S.P. 14/12, 69.

[8] Mark H. Curtis, *op. cit.* p. 9.

[9] *TCD*, pp. 73–7; *HMC*, Salisbury, XVII, 34–5, 46–7, 58–9, 133.

were deprived of their benefices.[1] Either figure is very low, and, fractious and irresponsible as the House of Commons often was, it is difficult to believe that it would have concerned itself so actively with the fate of less than 1% of the clergy. (However, it must be admitted that it was always anxious to restrict the numbers—surely never very large—of clergymen who habitually frequented ale-houses and brothels.) However this may be, in 1606 the Commons passed a bill 'to enable suspended and deprived ministers to sue and prosecute their appeals',[2] and in 1607 another to modify or explain the Subscription Act of 1571. It failed in the Lords, of course, but another was passed in 1610,[3] and in the Petition on Religion submitted to James in July of that year (40) the Commons repeated with emphasis this and other points already made in previous sessions.

The bishops were equally concerned with the state of the clergy, and the canons of 1604 laid down high minimum qualifications for candidates for holy orders and tried to restrict pluralism. But the Commons would never admit that Convocation had independent legislative powers, and one of their first acts in the session of 1606 was to bring in a bill 'for the more sure establishing and assurance of true religion', which 'required that no alteration should be of any substantial point of religion but by parliament with the advice and consent of the clergy in Convocation'.[4] They then proceeded to bring in their own measures 'for the providing of a learned and godly ministry' and 'against scandalous and unworthy ministers', very similar to those of the previous session, and subject to the same fate in the Lords.[5]

Throughout this period the Commons ignored the fact that the remedy for the ills of the Church lay to a great extent with their own class.[6] Out of a total of 9,244 livings 3,849 were in the hands of lay patrons, who collected the tithes and usually only passed a proportion of this income on to the incumbent; and even where there was no lay patron, and the incumbent received the full tithe, the levy had usually been fixed in the Middle Ages, when it was designed to support an unmarried, unlettered *curé*, and had never been adjusted to the rise in prices since. Any attempt to increase the rate was sure to meet with opposition from the local landlords. The main cause of pluralism and non-residence was that many, if not most, livings simply could not support an educated, married man; yet the Commons

---

[1] R. G. Usher, 'The deprivation of Puritan Ministers', *EHR*, XXIV (1909), 232; *idem, Reconstruction*, bk II, ch. vii; Babbage, *op. cit.* ch. vi. Babbage points out that many who did not conform were not punished.

[2] *House of Lords Manuscripts*, XI, 3295.

[3] *Ibid.* 3307, 3316.

[4] Some anti-clericals even objected to this last phrase, but Sir Edwin Sandys told them 'that the papists would say, not without show, that we professed only a statute religion' (Bowyer, *Diary*, p. 52 (24 February)).

[5] *House of Lords Manuscripts*, XI, 3293, 3287 (b).

[6] The condition of the clergy is thoroughly discussed by Usher, *Reconstruction*, I, 205–43.

persistently rejected any proposals, either from the king or the Lords, to remedy the situation.[1]

However, none of James's subsequent parliaments, after 1610, was so bold or pertinacious in its opposition to the establishment. The problem of the silenced ministers probably receded as their numbers diminished; we simply do not know. Not even the most inexact or suspect statistics are available. But it is clear that by 1620 the problem was not to find preaching ministers but to restrain them from preaching too much. George Abbott, who succeeded Bancroft at Canterbury in 1611, was a much less rigid prelate; but like Bancroft he was determined to curb pluralism, force incumbents to preach or hire a curate who would, and establish a university degree as an essential qualification for the priesthood. In response to this demand the universities were expanding and new colleges were being founded, often specifically dedicated to the production of a better clergy.[2] The result was that in the 1620's and 1630's there was an obvious surplus of preachers, many of them with no cure of souls, either because of their disinclination to conform or lack of suitable benefices for them.[3]

The problem posed by this intelligentsia of 'lecturers' outside the disciplinary structure of the Church had been recognised as early as 1604,[4] but the control of men who did not present themselves for collation to a benefice was difficult, and accordingly in 1605 James ordered the three articles of Canon XXXVI to be imposed on all graduands of the universities, though Cambridge did not comply until 1613.[5] But with the outbreak of the German War in 1618 the increasing vigour of extreme Protestant sermons, directed against the archbishop of Canturbury as well as the bishop of Rome, could not be ignored, and in August 1622 the king issued his Directions to Preachers (41). These not only ordered bishops to exercise greater care in the licensing of lecturers—'a new body, severed from the ancient clergy'—but also sharply restricted the topics on which the ancient clergy themselves could preach, be they never so eminent. The printed word was covered by a proclamation of September 1623, reviving the Star Chamber decree of 1586 against unlicensed printing,[6] though a year later a further proclamation admitted that the number of 'seditious, puritanical books and pamphlets, scandalous to our person and state' had if anything increased, and declared

---

[1] *Ibid.* pp. 352–3. Cf. Hill, *Economic Problems of the Church, passim.*

[2] Mark H. Curtis, *Oxford and Cambridge in Transition.*

[3] Mark H. Curtis, *op. cit.*, and 'The Alienated Intellectuals of Early Stuart England', *Past and Present*, no. 23 (1962), 25.

[4] See, for instance, canons L and LVI (39).

[5] Even then, they were only required of doctors and bachelors of divinity; James had to intervene again, in 1616, before they were extended to all graduands. See C. H. Cooper, *Annals of Cambridge*, 5 vols (London, 1842–1908), III, 59–60, and J. B. Mullinger, *The University of Cambridge, 1535–1625* (London, 1884), pp. 456–8.

[6] Printed *TCD*, pp. 143–5.

that henceforth no works on religion or church government were to be published without the imprimatur of an archbishop, the bishop of London, or one of the vice-chancellors of the universities.[1]

Much of this new agitation was provoked by the situation abroad; in this sense English Puritanism and the Counter Reformation were still closely linked. The death of Philip II in 1598 had relaxed the tension between Catholic and Protestant Europe; so had the promulgation of the Edict of Nantes in the same year. The peace between England and Spain in 1604 and the truce between Spain and the Dutch in 1609 confirmed a pattern which was only slightly disturbed by isolated acts of regression like the Gunpowder Plot or the assassination of Henry IV. Thus the outbreak of war in Germany in 1618, leading rapidly to the annexation of the Palatinate and the renewal of the Hispano-Dutch war, were an even greater shock to public opinion, coming as they did out of a clear sky. There was widespread sympathy for the Elector Palatine and his Electress, James's popular daughter Elizabeth, and the parliament of 1621 was electric with the realisation that once more the very survival of Protestantism was in the balance. As Sir John Perrott said:

> Salvation is the centre of religion, God's service the circumference, piety and godliness the direct lines, superstition and heresy the oblique lines and angles. Religion is shaken everywhere; if it decrease not fearfully at home, 'tis near to withering and ruin abroad.[2]

In similar circumstances under Elizabeth the gentry had accepted the argument that the Church could only be strengthened by radical reform of liturgy and government, and the disasters of European Protestantism in the 1620's produced much the same effect.

At first this was not obvious, except in the mounting frenzy of the pulpit and the unlicensed press.[3] The parliament of 1621, except in its closing weeks, was more interested in suppressing papists at home than combating them in Europe, and the parliament of 1624 was unnaturally docile, its anger appeased by the breaking off of the Spanish marriage negotiations. But there were significant straws in the wind. One was the decision of a group of wealthy laymen, the 'lay feoffees', to buy up impropriations as they came on the market and use the income to the full to support worthy incumbents or pay the stipends of lecturers. The number of purchases made is perhaps not impressive, but it was a new method by which the laity could by-pass the hierarchy and influence, or even secure control of, the ministry.[4] Another

---

[1] *Foedera*, XVII, 616–17 (15 August 1624).   [2] *Commons Debates 1621*, V, 200 (4 June).

[3] The Rev. Thomas Scott's *Vox Populi* (1620) is an outstanding example of the kind of propaganda which preceded the assembly of parliament. Cf. Louis B. Wright, 'Propaganda against James I's Appeasement of Spain', *Huntington Library Quarterly*, VI (1942–3).

[4] E. W. Kirby, 'The Lay Feoffees', *Journal of Modern History*, XIV (1942), 1; Isabel M. Calder, *The Activities of the Puritan Faction of the Church of England, 1625–33* (London, 1957); Hill, *Economic Problems*, ch. xi.

straw in the wind was the increasing concern of Parliament with Lord's Day observance.[1] This was only one aspect of the middle classes' concern for the morals of the poor; for instance, James's first parliament passed no less than four statutes for repressing drunkenness, regulating alehouses, and restraining 'inordinate haunting and tippling in inns, alehouses and other victualling houses'.[2] But attempts to make the Sabbath holy were less successful, though they were always at the head of the Commons' agenda; in 1606 a bill for this purpose was sent up to the Lords as early as 17 February, and in 1614 a similar bill was read on the first day of the session.[3] Both were abortive, of course, and the situation was decisively changed by the king's intervention in May 1618. Returning from a visit to Scotland, he issued his Declaration of Sports, in which he blamed the increase of papists in Lancashire on the justices' over-precise enforcement of Lord's Day observance.[4] He therefore ordered that once they had attended Divine Service 'our good people be not disturbed, letted or discouraged from any lawful recreation, such as dancing, either men or women, archery for men, leaping, vaulting or any other such harmless recreation, nor from having May games, Whitsun ales and morris dances, and the setting up of maypoles and other sports therewith used', although he forbade 'bear and bull baitings, interludes and, at all times in the meaner sort of people by law prohibited, bowling'.[5] The order that this should be read out in churches caused many clergymen great heart-searching, though some eased their conscience by taking it to apply only to Lancashire, while others were consoled by the fact that they did not have to signify their agreement with it.[6]

The parliament of 1621 lost no time in debating a bill 'for punishing of abuses on the Sabbath day', and they incontinently expelled an over-clever young lawyer from Lincoln's Inn who pointed out that the Sabbath was Saturday, and that King David had danced before the Ark of the Lord.[7] But James forbade them to legislate against any recreations allowed by the Declaration of Sports, which left them small scope, and they heeded his recommendation that they turn to more important matters. The parliament of 1624 produced an act 'for repressing of drunkenness', and another 'to prevent and reform profane swearing and cursing',[8] but James vetoed a bill to punish abuses committed on the Lord's day, and in Charles I's first parliament they had to content themselves with an act reinforcing the Declaration of Sports,[9] though their abortive bill of 1606 had also prohibited 'morris

[1] Hill, *Society and Puritanism*, ch. 5.
[2] 1 Jac. I, c. 9; 4 Jac. I, cc. 4–5; 7 Jac. I, c. 10.
[3] *House of Lords Manuscripts*, XI, 3291; *Commons Debates 1621*, VII, 634.
[4] James Tait, 'The Declaration of Sports for Lancashire', EHR, XXXII (1917), 561.
[5] TCD, pp. 54–6. [6] Fuller, *Church History*, III, 303–6.
[7] *Commons Debates 1621*, II, 82, IV, 52–3. [8] 21 Jac. I, cc. 7, 20.
[9] 1 Car. I, c. 1.

dances, hunting, coursing, hawking, church ales, dancing, rush-bearing, may games, whitsun ales, outhurlings, inhurlings and wakes'.[1] This act was renewed in 1628 until the end of the first session of the next parliament; that is, May 1640.

37. The Millenary Petition, 1603

The humble petition of the ministers of the Church of England, desiring reformation of certain ceremonies and abuses of the Church

To the most Christian and excellent prince, our gracious and dread sovereign, James, by the grace of God, [&c.], We, the ministers of the Church of England that desire reformation, wish a long, prosperous and happy reign over us in this life, and in the next everlasting salvation.

Most gracious and dread sovereign, seeing it hath pleased the Divine Majesty, to the great comfort of all good Christians, to advance your Highness according to your just title, to the peaceable government of this Church and Commonwealth of England; we the ministers of the gospel in this land, neither as factious men affecting a popular parity in the Church, nor as schismatics aiming at the dissolution of the state ecclesiastical; but as the faithful servants of Christ, and loyal subjects to your Majesty, desiring and longing for the redress of divers abuses of the Church, could do no less, in our obedience to God, service to your Majesty, love to his Church, than acquaint your princely Majesty with our particular griefs. For, as your princely pen writeth: 'The king, as a good physician, must first know what peccant humours his patient naturally is most subject unto, before he can begin his cure.' And, although divers of us that sue for reformation have formerly, in respect of the times, subscribed to the [Prayer] Book, some upon protestation, some upon exposition given them, some with condition[s], rather than the Church should have been deprived of their labour and ministry; yet now we, to the number of more than a thousand, of your Majesty's subjects and ministers, all groaning as under a common burden of human rites and ceremonies, do with one joint consent, humble ourselves at your Majesty's feet to be eased and relieved in this behalf. Our humble suit, then, unto your Majesty is, that [of] these offences following, some may be removed, some amended, some qualified:

I. *In the church-service.* That the cross in baptism, interrogatories ministered to infants, confirmation, as superfluous, may be taken away:

[1] *HMC*, 3rd report, p. 28b; *House of Lords Manuscripts*, XI, 3291.

baptism not to be ministered by women, and so explained: the cap and surplice not urged: that examination may go before the communion: that it be ministered with a sermon; that divers terms of *priests* and *absolution*, and some others used, with the ring in marriage, and other such like in the Book, may be corrected: the longsomeness of service abridged: church-songs and music moderated to better edification: that the Lord's day be not profaned, the rest upon holy-days not so strictly urged: that there may be a uniformity of doctrine prescribed: no popish opinion to be any more taught or defended: no ministers charged to teach their people to bow at the name of Jesus: that the canonical scripture only be read in the church.

II. *Concerning church ministers.* That none hereafter be admitted into the ministry but able and sufficient men; and those to preach diligently, and especially upon the Lord's day: that such as be already entered, and cannot preach, may either be removed, and some charitable course taken with them for their relief; or else be forced, according to the value of their livings, to maintain preachers: that non-residency be not permitted: that King Edward's statute for the lawfulness of ministers' marriage be revived: that ministers be not urged to subscribe but according to the law to the Articles of Religion, and the King's Supremacy only.

III. *For church-livings and maintenance.* That bishops leave their commendams; some holding prebends, some parsonages, some vicarages with their bishoprics: that double-beneficed men be not suffered to hold some two, some three, benefices with cure, and some two, three, or four dignities besides: that impropriations annexed to bishoprics and colleges be demised only to the preachers-incumbents, for the old rent: that the impropriations of laymen's fees may be charged with a sixth or seventh part of the worth, to the maintenance of the preaching minister.

IV. *For church-discipline.* That the discipline and excommunication may be administered according to Christ's own institution; or, at the least, that enormities may be redressed: as, namely, that excommunication come not forth under the name of lay persons, chancellors, officials, &c.: that men be not excommunicated for trifles, and twelve-penny matters: that none be excommunicated without consent of his pastor: that the officers be not suffered to extort unreasonable fees: that none having jurisdiction, or registers' places, put out the same to farm: that diverse popish canons (as for restraint of marriage at certain times) be reversed: that the longsomeness of suits in ecclesiastical courts, which hang sometimes two, three, four, five, six, or seven years, may be restrained: that the oath *ex officio*, whereby men are forced to accuse themselves, be more sparingly used: that licences for marriage, without banns asked, be more cautiously granted.

These, with such other abuses yet remaining, and practised in the Church of England, we are able to show not to be agreeable to the scriptures, if it shall please your Highness farther to hear us, or more at large by writing to be informed, or by conference among the learned to be resolved. And yet we doubt not but that, without any farther process, your Majesty, of whose Christian judgement we have received so good a taste already, is able of yourself to judge the equity of this cause. God, we trust, hath appointed your Highness our physician to heal these diseases. And we say with Mordecai to Esther, 'Who knoweth, whether you are come to the kingdom for such a time?' Thus your Majesty shall do that which, we are persuaded, shall be acceptable to God; honourable to your Majesty in all succeeding ages; profitable to his Church, which shall be thereby increased; comfortable to your ministers, who shall be no more suspended, silenced, disgraced, imprisoned, for men's traditions; and prejudicial to none, but to those that seek their own quiet, credit and profit in the world. Thus, with all dutiful submission, referring ourselves to your Majesty's pleasure for your gracious answer, as God shall direct you; we most humbly recommend your Highness to the Divine Majesty; whom we beseech for Christ's sake to dispose your royal heart to do herein what shall be to his glory, the good of his Church, and your endless comfort.

Your Majesty's most humble subjects, the ministers of the gospel, that desire not a disorderly innovation, but a due and godly reformation.

Fuller, *Church History*, III, 215–17

38. A proclamation enjoining conformity to the form of the service of God established, 16 July 1604

The care which we have had, and pains which we have taken, to settle the affairs of this Church of England in a uniformity, as well of doctrine as of government, both of them agreeable to the Word of God, the doctrine of the primitive Church, and the laws heretofore established for these matters in this realm, may sufficiently appear by our former actions. For no sooner did the infection of the plague, reigning immediately after our entry into this kingdom, give us leave to have any assembly, but we held at our honour of Hampton Court for that purpose a conference between some principal bishops and deans of this Church and such other learned men as understood or favoured the opinions of those that seek alteration, before ourself and our Council.

Of which conference the issue was, that no well-grounded matter appeared to us or our said Council why the state of the Church here by law established should in any material point be altered. Nor did those that before had seemed to affect such alteration, when they heard the contrary arguments, greatly insist upon it, but seemed to be satisfied themselves, and to undertake within reasonable time to satisfy all others that were misled with opinion that there was any just cause of alteration. Whereupon we published by our proclamation[1] what had been the issue of that conference, hoping that when the same should be made known, all reasonable men would have rested satisfied with that which had been done, and not have moved further trouble or speech of matters whereof so solemn and advised determination had been made.

Notwithstanding, at the late assembly of our Parliament there wanted not many that renewed with no little earnestness the questions before determined, and many more as well, about the Book of Common Prayer, as other matters of church government, and importuned us for our assent to many alterations therein; but...the end of all their motions and overtures falling out to be none other in substance than was before at the conference at Hampton Court, that is, that no apparent or grounded reason was shown why either the Book of Common Prayer or the church discipline here by law established should be changed, which were unreasonable considering that particular and personal abuses are remediable otherwise than by making general alterations, we have thought good once again to give notice thereof to all our subjects by public declaration, who we doubt not but will receive great satisfaction when they shall understand that after so much impugning there appeareth no cause why the form of the Service of God wherein they have been nourished so many years should be changed; and consequently to admonish them all in general to conform themselves thereunto, without listening to the troublesome spirits of some persons who never receive contentment, either in civil or ecclesiastical matters, but in their own fantasies, especially of certain ministers who, under pretended zeal of reformation, are the chief authors of divisions

[1] Of 5 March 1604, *Foedera*, XVI, 574–6.

and sects among our people. Of many of which we hope that now, when they shall see that such things as they have proposed for alteration prove upon trial so weakly grounded as [to] deserve not admittance, they will out of their own judgment conform themselves to better advice, and not omit the principal and substantial parts of their duties for shadows and semblances of zeal, but rather bend their strength with our intent to join in one end, that is, the establishing of the Gospel and recovering of our people seduced out of the hands of the common adversaries of our religion, which shall never be well performed but by a uniformity of our endeavours therein.

But if our hope herein fail us, we must advertise them that our duty towards God requireth at our hands that what intractable men do not perform upon admonition they must be compelled unto by authority, whereof the supreme power resting in our hands by God's ordinance we are bound to use the same in nothing more than in preservation of the Church's tranquillity, which by God's grace we are fully purposed to do. And yet by advice of our Council, and opinion of the bishops, although our former proclamations, both before the conference and since, ought to be a sufficient warning and admonition to all men who are within the danger of them, we have thought good to give time to all ministers disobedient to the orders of the Church and to ecclesiastical authority here by law established, and who for such disobedience, either in the days of the Queen our sister of famous memory deceased or since our reign, have incurred any censures of the Church or penalties of laws, until the last of November now next ensuing to bethink themselves of the course they will hold therein.

In which mean time both they may resolve either to conform themselves to the Church of England and obey the same, or else to dispose of themselves and their families some other ways as to them shall seem meet, and the bishops and others whom it concerneth provide meet persons to be substitutes in the place of those who shall wilfully abandon their charges upon so slight causes, assuring them that after that day we shall not fail to do that which princely providence requireth at our hands, that is, to put in execution all ways and means that may take from among our people all grounds and occasions of sects, divisions and unquietness; whereof, as we wish there may never be occasion given us to make proof, but that this our admonition may have equal force in all men's hearts to work a universal conformity, so we do require all archbishops, bishops and other ecclesiastical persons to do their utmost endeavours, by conferences, arguments, persuasions, and by all other ways of love and gentleness, to reclaim all that be in the ministry to the obedience of our church laws, for which purpose only we have enlarged the time formerly prefixed for their remove or reformation, to the end that if it be possible that uniformity which we desire may be wrought by clemency and by weight of reason, and not by rigour of law. And the like advertisement do we give to all civil magistrates, gentlemen, and others of understanding, as well abroad in the counties as in cities and towns, requiring them also not in any sort to support, favour or countenance any such factious ministers in their obstinacy, of whose endeavours we doubt not but so good success may follow, as this our admonition, with their endeavours, may prevent the use of any other means to retain our people in their due obedience to us, and in unity of mind to the service of Almighty God.

Cardwell, *Documentary Annals*, II, 80–84

39. The canons of 1604

OF THE CHURCH OF ENGLAND

*   *   *   *   *   *

IV. *Impugners of the public worship of God established in the Church of England censured*

Whosoever shall hereafter affirm, That the form of God's worship in the Church of England established by law and contained in the Book of Common Prayer...is a corrupt, superstitious or unlawful worship of God, or containeth anything in it that is repugnant to the Scriptures, let him be excommunicated *ipso facto*, and not restored but only by the archbishop, and after his repentance and public revocation of those his wicked errors.

*   *   *   *   *   *

V. *Impugners of the Articles of Religion established in the Church of England censured*

Whosoever shall hereafter affirm, That any of the nine and thirty Articles agreed upon by the archbishops and bishops of both provinces and the whole clergy in the Convocation holden at London in the year of our Lord God 1562, for avoiding diversities of opinions and for the establishing of consent touching true religion, are in any part superstitious or erroneous, or such as he may not with a good conscience subscribe unto; let him be excommunicated...[etc.]

VI. *Impugners of the rites and ceremonies established in the Church of England censured*

Whosoever shall hereafter affirm, That the rites and ceremonies of the Church of England by law established are wicked, anti-christian, or superstitious, or such as, being commanded by lawful authority, men who are zealously and godly affected may not with any good conscience approve them, use them, or, as occasion requireth, subscribe unto them; let him be excommunicated...[etc.]

VII. *Impugners of the government of the Church of England by archbishops, bishops, &c., censured*

Whosoever shall hereafter affirm, That the government of the Church of England under his Majesty by archbishops, bishops, deans, archdeacons and the rest that bear office in the same, is anti-Christian or repugnant to the Word of God; let him be excommunicated...[etc.]

* * * * * *

X. *Maintainers of schismatics in the Church of England censured*

Whosoever shall hereafter affirm, That such ministers as refuse to subscribe to the form and manner of God's worship in the Church of England prescribed in the Communion Book, and their adherents, may truly take unto them the name of another Church not established by law, and dare presume to publish it, That this pretended Church hath of long time groaned under the burden of certain grievances imposed upon it, and upon the members thereof before mentioned, by the Church of England, and the orders and constitution therein by law established; let them be excommunicated...[etc.]

* * * * * *

MINISTERS, THEIR ORDINATION, FUNCTION AND CHARGE

* * * * * *

XXXIV. *The quality of such as are to be made ministers*

No bishop shall henceforth admit any person into sacred orders, which is not of his own diocese, except he be either of one of the universities of this realm, or except he shall bring letters dimissory (so termed) from the bishop of whose diocese he is; and desiring to be a deacon is three and twenty years old, and to be a priest four and twenty years complete; and hath taken some degree of school in either of the said universities; or at the least, except he be able to yield an account of his faith in Latin, according to the Articles. . .[of 1562], and to confirm the same by sufficient testimonies out of the Holy Scriptures, and except moreover he shall then exhibit letters testimonial of his good life and conversation, under the seal of some college in Cambridge or Oxford, where before he remained, or of three or four grave ministers, together with the subscription and testimony of other credible persons who have known his life and behaviour by the space of three years next before.

* * * * * *

XXXVI. *Subscription required of such as are to be made Ministers*

No person shall hereafter be received into the ministry, nor either by institution or collation admitted to any ecclesiastical living, nor suffered to preach, catechize, or to be a lecturer or reader of divinity in either university, or in any cathedral or collegiate church, city or market-town, parish church, chapel or in any other place within this realm, except he be licensed either by the archbishop, or by the bishop of the diocese where he is to be placed, under the hands and seals, or by one of the two universities under their seal likewise; and except he shall first subscribe to these three articles following, in such manner and sort as we have here appointed.

(I) That the King's Majesty, under God, is the only supreme governor of this realm, and of all other his Highness's dominions and countries, as well in all spiritual or ecclesiastical things or causes as temporal; and that no foreign prince, person, prelate, state or potentate hath, or ought to have, any jurisdiction, power, superiority, pre-eminence or authority, ecclesiastical or spiritual, within his Majesty's said realms, dominions and countries.

(II) That the Book of Common Prayer, and of ordering of bishops, priests and deacons, containeth in it nothing contrary to the Word of God, and that it may lawfully so be used; and that he himself will use the form in the said Book prescribed in public prayer and administration of the sacraments, and none other.

(III) That he alloweth the Book of Articles of Religion agreed upon by the archbishops and bishops of both provinces, and the whole clergy, in the Convocation holden at London in the year of our Lord God

1562; and that he acknowledgeth all and every the articles therein contained, being in number nine and thirty, besides the ratification, to be agreeable to the Word of God.

To these three articles whosoever will subscribe, he shall, for the avoiding of all ambiguities, subscribe in this order and form of words, setting down both his Christian and surname, viz.:

'I, N.N., do willingly and *ex animo* subscribe to these three articles above mentioned, and to all things that are contained in them.'

And if any bishop shall ordain, admit or license any as is aforesaid, except he first have subscribed in manner and form as here we have appointed, he shall be suspended from giving of orders and licenses to preach for the space of twelve months. But if either of the universities shall offend therein, we leave them to the danger of the law, and his Majesty's censure.

* * * * * *

XLI. *Licences for plurality of benefices limited, and residence enjoined*

No licence or dispensation for the keeping of more benefices with cure than one shall be granted to any but such only as shall be thought very well worthy for his learning, and very well able and sufficient to discharge his duty; that is, who shall have taken the degree of Master of Arts at the least in one of the universities of this realm, and be a public and sufficient preacher licensed. Provided always that he be by a good and sufficient caution bound to make his personal residence in each of his said benefices for some reasonable time in every year, and that the said benefices be not more than thirty miles distant asunder; and lastly, that he have under him in the benefice where he doth not reside a preacher lawfully allowed, that is able sufficiently to teach and instruct the people.

* * * * * *

XLV. *Beneficed preachers, being resident upon their livings, to preach every Sunday*

Every beneficed man allowed to be a preacher, and residing on his benefice, having no lawful impediment, shall in his own cure, or in some other church or chapel where he may conveniently, near adjoining (where no preacher is), preach one sermon every Sunday of the year wherein he shall soberly and sincerely divide the word of truth, to the glory of God and to the best edification of the people.

XLVI. *Beneficed men, not preachers, to procure monthly sermons*

Every beneficed man, not allowed to be a preacher, shall procure sermons to be preached in his cure once in every month at the least, by preachers lawfully licensed, if his living in the judgement of the ordinary will be able to bear it. And upon every Sunday, when there shall not be a sermon preached in his cure, he or his curate shall read some one of the homilies prescribed or to be prescribed by authority, to the intents aforesaid.

* * * * * *

L. *Strangers not admitted to preach without showing their licence*

Neither the minister, churchwardens, nor any other officers of the Church shall suffer any man to preach within their churches or chapels but such as by showing their licence to preach shall appear unto them to be sufficiently authorised thereunto, as is aforesaid.

* * * * * *

LVI. *Preachers and lecturers to read Divine Service and administer the Sacraments twice a year at the least*

Every minister being possessed of a benefice that hath cure and charge of souls, although he chiefly attend to preaching, and hath a curate under him to execute the other duties which are to be performed for him in the church, and likewise every other stipendiary preacher that readeth any lecture, or catechiseth, or preacheth in any church or chapel, shall twice at the least every year read himself the Divine Service upon two several Sundays publicly, and at the usual times, both in the forenoon and afternoon, in the church which he so possesseth, or where he readeth, catechiseth, or preacheth, as is aforesaid; and shall likewise as often in every year administer the sacraments of baptism (if there be any to be baptized), and of the Lord's Supper, in such manner and form, and with the observation of all such rites and ceremonies, as are prescribed by the Book of Common Prayer in that behalf; which if he do not accordingly perform, then shall he that is possessed of a benefice (as before) be suspended; and he that is but a reader, preacher, or catechiser, be removed from his place by the bishop of the diocese, until he or they shall submit themselves to perform all the said duties in such manner and sort as before is prescribed.

* * * * * *

LVIII. *Ministers reading Divine Service and administering the Sacraments to wear surplices, and graduates therewithal hoods*

Every Minister saying the public prayers, or ministering the Sacraments, or other rites of the Church, shall wear a decent and comely surplice with sleeves, to be provided at the charge of the parish. And if any question arise touching the matter, decency, or comeliness thereof, the same shall be decided by the discretion of the ordinary. Furthermore, such ministers as are graduates shall wear upon their surplices at such times, such hoods as by the orders of the universities are agreeable to their degrees, which no minister shall wear (being no graduate) under pain of suspension....

*   *   *   *   *   *

THINGS APPERTAINING TO CHURCHES

*   *   *   *   *   *

LXXXII. *A decent communion table in every church*

Whereas we have no doubt but that in all churches within the realm of England convenient and decent tables are provided and placed for the celebration of the Holy Communion, we appoint that the same tables shall from time to time be kept and repaired in sufficient and seemly manner, and covered in time of Divine Service with a carpet of silk or other decent stuff thought meet by the ordinary of the place, if any question be made of it, and with a fair linen cloth at the time of the ministration, as becometh that table, and so stand, saving when the said Holy Communion is to be administered, at which time the same shall be placed in so good sort within the church or chancel as thereby the minister may be more conveniently heard of the communicants in his prayer and ministration, and the communicants also more conveniently and in more number may communicate with the said minister.... Cardwell, *Synodalia*, I, 248-93

40. Commons' petition on religion, July 1610

Most Gracious and Dread Sovereign,

Since it hath pleased Almighty God of his unspeakable goodness and mercy towards us to call your Majesty to the government of this kingdom, and hath crowned you with supreme power, as well in the Church as in the Commonwealth, for the advancement of his glory and the general benefit of all the subjects of this land, we do in all humility present at the feet of your excellent Majesty ourselves and our desires, full of confidence in the assurances of your religious mind and princely disposition that you will be graciously pleased to give life and effect to these our petitions, greatly tending (as undoubtedly we conceive) to the Glory of God, the good of his Church, and safety of your most royal person, wherein we acknowledge our greatest happiness to consist.

I. Whereas good and provident laws have been made for the maintenance of God's true religion, and safety of your Majesty's royal person, issue and estate, against Jesuits, seminary priests and Popish recusants; and although your Majesty by your godly, learned and judicious writings have declared your Christian and princely zeal in the defence of the religion established, and have very lately (to the comfort of your best affected subjects) published to both Houses of Parliament your princely will and pleasure that recusants should not be concealed, but detected and convicted; yet for that the laws are not executed against the priests, who are the corrupters of the people in religion and loyalty, and many recusants have already compounded, and (as it is to be feared) more and more (except your Majesty in your great wisdom prevent the same) will compound with those that beg their penalties, which maketh the laws altogether fruitless, or of little or none effect, and the offenders to become bold, obdurate and unconformable.[1]

Your Majesty therefore would be pleased, at the humble suit of your Commons in this present Parliament assembled, in the causes so highly concerning the Glory of God, the preservation of true religion, of your Majesty and State, to suffer your Highness's natural clemency to retire itself, and give place to justice, and to lay your royal command upon all your ministers of justice, both ecclesiastical and civil, to see the laws made against Jesuits, seminary priests and recusants (of what kind and sort soever) to be duly and exactly executed without dread or delay; and that your Majesty would be pleased likewise to take into your own hands the penalties due for recusancy, and that the same be not converted to the private gain of some, to your infinite loss, the emboldening of the Papists, and decay of true religion.

II. Whereas also divers painful and learned pastors, that have long travailed in the work of the ministry with good fruit and blessing of their labours, who were ever ready to perform the legal subscription

---

[1] Petyt has *uncomfortable*.

appointed by the statute of the 13th of Elizabeth, which only concerneth the confession of the true Christian Faith, and doctrine of the Sacraments; yet for not conforming in points of ceremonies, and refusing the subscription directed by the late Canons, have been removed from their ecclesiastical livings, being their freehold, and debarred from all means of maintenance, to the great grief of sundry your Majesty's well-affected subjects, seeing the whole people that want instruction are by this means punished, and through ignorance lie open to the seducements of Popish and ill-affected persons.

We therefore most humbly beseech your Majesty would be graciously pleased that such deprived and silenced Ministers may, by licence or permission of the Reverend Fathers, in their several dioceses, instruct and preach unto the people, in such parishes and places where they may be employed, so as they apply themselves in their Ministry to wholesome doctrine and exhortation, and live quietly and peaceably in their callings, and shall not by writing or preaching impugn things established by public authority.

III. Whereas likewise through plurality of benefices, and toleration of non-residency in many who possess not the meanest of livings with cure of souls, the people in divers places want instruction, and are ignorant and easy to be seduced, whereby the adversaries of our religion gain great advantage; and although the pluralities and non-residents do frame excuse of the smallness[1] of some livings, and pretend the maintenance of learning, yet we find by experience that they, coupling many of the greatest livings, do leave the least helpless, and the best as ill served and supplied with preachers as the meanest. And where[as] pluralists, heaping up many livings into one hand, do by that means keep divers learned men from maintenance, to the discouragement of students and the hindrance of learning, and the non-residents (forsaking or absenting themselves from their pastoral charges) do leave the people as a prey to the Popish seducers; it might therefore please your most excellent Majesty, for remedy of those evils in the Church, to provide that dispensations for plurality of benefices with cure of souls may be prohibited, and that the toleration of non-residency may be restrained. So shall all true religion be better upheld, and the people more instructed in divine and civil duties.

* * * * * *

Petyt, *Jus Parliamentarium*, pp. 318–21

[1] Petyt has *smallest*.

41. Directions to Preachers, 1622

[The king to the archbishop of Canterbury, 4 August 1622.]

Most Reverend Father in God, right trusty and entirely beloved counsellor, we greet you well.

Forasmuch as the abuses and extravagances of preachers in the pulpit have been in all times suppressed in this realm by some act of council or state with the advice and resolution of grave and learned prelates,... and whereas at this present divers young students, by reading of late writers and ungrounded divines, do broach many times unprofitable, unsound, seditious and dangerous doctrines, to the scandal of the Church and disquiet of the State and present government, we upon humble representation unto us of these inconveniences by yourself and sundry other grave and learned prelates of this Church, as also of our princely care and zeal for the extirpation of schism and dissension growing from these seeds, and for the settling of a religious and peaceable government both in Church and Commonwealth, do by these our special letters straitly charge and command you to use all possible care and diligence that these limitations and cautions herewith sent unto you concerning preachers be duly and strictly from henceforth put in practice and observed by the several bishops within your jurisdiction. And to this end our pleasure is, that you send them forthwith copies of these directions, to be speedily sent and communicated unto every parson, vicar, curate, lecturer and minister, in every cathedral or parish church within their several dioceses; and that you do earnestly require them to employ their utmost endeavours in the performance of this so important a business, letting them know that we have a special eye unto their proceedings and expect a strict account thereof, both from you and every of them. And these our letters shall be your sufficient warrant and discharge in that behalf.

[Directions enclosed.]

I. That no preacher under the degree and calling of a bishop or dean of a cathedral or collegiate church (and they upon the King's days and set festivals) do take occasion, by the expounding of any text of scripture whatsoever, to fall into any set discourse or common place [sc. theme], otherwise than by opening the coherence and division of the text, which shall not be comprehended and warranted, in essence, substance, effect or natural inference, within some one of the Articles of Religion. . . ., or in some of the homilies set forth by authority of the Church of England not only for a help for the non-preaching but withal for a pattern and boundary (as it were) for the preaching ministers. . . .

II. That no parson, vicar, curate or lecturer shall preach any sermon or collation hereafter upon Sundays and holy days in the afternoon in any cathedral or parish church throughout the kingdom but upon some part of the Catechism or some text taken out of the Creed, Ten Commandments, or the Lord's Prayer (funeral sermons only excepted). . . .

III. That no preacher of what title soever under the degree of bishop, or dean at the least, do from henceforth presume to preach in any popular auditory the deep points of predestination, election, reprobation, or of the universality, efficacy, resistibility or irrestibility, of God's grace; but leave those themes rather to be handled by the learned men, and that moderately and modestly by way of use and application rather than by way of positive doctrines, being fitter for the schools and universities than for simple auditories.

IV. That no preacher, of what title or denomination soever, from henceforth shall presume in any auditory within this kingdom, to declare, limit, or bound out, by way of positive doctrine, in any lecture or sermon the power, prerogative, and jurisdiction, authority, or duty of sovereign princes, or otherwise meddle with these matters of State and the differences betwixt princes and the people. . . .

V. That no preacher, of what title or denomination soever, shall presume causelessly (and without invitation from the text) to fall into bitter invectives and indecent railing speeches against the persons of either Papists or Puritans, but modestly and gravely (when they are occasioned thereunto by the text of Scripture), free both the doctrine and discipline of the Church of England from the aspersions of either adversary, especially where the auditory is suspected to be tainted with the one or the other infection.

VI. Lastly, that the archbishops and bishops of the kingdom (whom his Majesty hath good cause to blame for their former remissness) be more wary and choice in licensing of preachers, . . . and that all the lecturers throughout the kingdom of England (a new body severed from the ancient clergy, as being neither parsons, vicars, nor curates) be licensed henceforward in the Court of Faculties only by recommendation of the party from the bishop of the diocese under his hand and seal, with a *fiat* from the lord archbishop of Canterbury, and a confirmation under the Great Seal of England. . . . Cardwell, *Documentary Annals*, II, 198–203

II. THE LAUDIAN REVOLUTION

Charles I was well equipped to handle the difficult ecclesiastical conditions of the 1620's; a sincere Protestant and an upright young man, he and his chief henchman Buckingham had many contacts with the reformist wing of the clergy.[1] But his chief reliance was on the controversial young bishop of St David's, William Laud. Laud believed that the *ecclesia anglicana* was the only true survivor of the primitive church of the Apostles and the Fathers, preserved by its isolation from the manifold corruptions of the medieval papacy. The emphasis he placed on the sacraments, and thereby on the liturgy, and his willingness to accept the re-introduction of ceremonies and ceremonial equipment which many regarded as popish, were controversial from the beginning; and his insistence that episcopacy was of divine right, of the *esse*, not the *bene esse* of the Church drove a serious doctrinal or theological wedge between Anglican and Puritan (47).[2]

The advent of Laud and Charles I therefore killed the vague assumption, encouraged by Elizabeth and not vigorously discouraged by James I,[3] that the episcopal establishment, abolished in all the other reformed churches, would soon wither away in England, too. The new king was soon committed to a policy which envisaged the glorification and enhancement of episcopal authority, and Laud's emphasis on the uniqueness and worthiness of English Church was a nationalist counterblast to the Puritans, who had always stressed England's mission as the chosen race, the leader of European Protestantism: in place of the Elect Nation Laud offered the Elect Church.[4] Attempts to smear him as an Arminian, a believer in free will as against predestination, were not notably successful. His own theological views are obscure, but it was possible to combine strictly orthodox Calvinism with a belief in episcopacy by divine right;[5] 'Arminian' in this context is little more than a term of abuse, and religious thought in the seventeenth century was much less precise than is often supposed.[6] Laud put his opponents on the defensive, and on the defensive they remained until 1640. Even then, though he and his suffragans had virtually no supporters in the Long Parliament his Church had many, and it was his Church that survived. The failure of

---

[1] James F. Maclear, 'Puritan Relations with Buckingham', *Huntington Library Quarterly*, XXI (1957–8), 111.

[2] New, *Anglican and Puritan*, pp. 55 ff.

[3] James insisted on the maintenance of bishops as a prop to the political order, but he was an orthodox Calvinist, and his episcopal appointments were slovenly and ill considered. See H. R. Trevor Roper, *Historical Essays* (London, 1957), pp. 130 ff.

[4] W. Haller, *Foxe's Book of Martyrs and the Elect Nation* (London, 1963).

[5] As did Joseph Hall. See Charles H. George, 'A Social Interpretation of English Puritanism', *Journal of Modern History*, XXV (1953), 327.

[6] There is still room for disagreement as to whether Puritan and Anglican theology differed at all. See George, *Protestant Mind*, and New, *Anglican and Puritan*.

Puritanism in the 1640's and 1650's was not entirely due to its internal disagreements and inconsistencies; men were always conscious of the fact that there was an acceptable alternative. The verdict of 1661 was in favour of that alternative.

Laud's influence was not fully exerted until his appointment to the see of London in 1628, but as early as June 1625 he preached a sermon before Parliament exalting the kingly power (42a). At the opening of the next parliament, in February 1626, he preached another sermon, in which he exalted episcopal authority under the king and made an assertion that was to run like a refrain through his later speeches and writings, that his opponents meditated a revolution in the State as well as the Church (42b).

This was particularly provocative in that both parliaments were concerned in the case of Richard Montague, a clergyman who not only rejected the doctrine of predestination and sanctioned auricular confession in certain cases, but had the temerity to assert that there were several points on which Catholics and Protestants were in agreement, and that the bishop of Rome did not always err. In 1625 he dedicated his latest work, *Appello Caesarem*, to the king, but Parliament fell on him in a fury. Laud intervened on his behalf, and the dispute was continued in 1626. When his second parliament rose Charles issued a proclamation 'for the establishing of the peace and quiet of the Church of England' which betrayed a certain irritation with both sides (43). This was exacerbated by the controversy over Manwaring's notorious sermons,[1] especially when the Commons, not content with impeaching Manwaring and forcing him to retract, sent up a remonstrance on 11 June 1628 in which they complained of the growth of Arminianism and innovations in religion, accusing Laud by name. 'It being now generally held the way to preferment and promotion in the Church', they said, 'many scholars do bend the course of their studies to maintain those errors.'[2]

There is really no reason to doubt Charles's sincerity when he declared in 1626 that he desired no innovations in religion, and it is clear that these theological disputations bored him. Questions were coming to the surface which had never troubled the waters of his father's reign (now amazingly calm in retrospect), and he was determined that they should be pushed under again. Soon after the prorogation of parliament he suppressed Manwaring's sermons, and in November 1628, 'with the advice of so many of our bishops as might conveniently be called together', he republished the Thirty-Nine Articles and asserted that any differences as to their interpretation must be settled by the clergy in Convocation.[3] Like most of his other public utterances on religion, this declaration was profoundly Erastian in tone, and the manner in which he referred to 'those curious points', or 'these both curious and unhappy differences', indicates a certain lack of interest in theology. Finally,

---

[1] No. **5**, p. 14 above.   [2] Rushworth, I, 633.   [3] *GCD*, p. 75.

in January 1629 he made what he regarded as a final gesture of conciliation. Having appointed Montague bishop of Chichester, he ordered *Appello Caesarem* to be suppressed, as being 'the first cause of those disputes and differences which have sithence much troubled the quiet of the Church', 'hoping thereby that men will no more trouble themselves with these unnecessary questions'. But he ended with a characteristic threat:

> But if we shall be deceived in this our expectation, and that by reading, preaching and making books either pro or contra concerning these differences men begin anew to dispute, we shall take such order with them and those books, that they shall wish they had never thought upon these needless controversies.[1]

But these pronouncements were pointless when it was obvious that Laud and his disciples enjoyed a monopoly of Church patronage. Men, not measures, were the real danger, and the House of Commons was alarmed and incensed at the great reshuffle of bishops that took place during the recess in the second half of 1628. Laud was already established at Bath and Wells, Richard Neile at Winchester, Joseph Hall at Exeter and John Buckeridge at Ely. Now Laud moved to London, Samuel Harsnet to the archbishopric of York, John Howson to Durham, Richard Corbet to Oxford, Richard Montague to Chichester—a particularly controversial appointment—and Francis White to Norwich. Only Lincoln, Salisbury and Worcester were unaffected by these changes; and the incumbents of Lincoln and Salisbury, John Williams and John Davenant respectively, were two of Laud's greatest crosses. But apart from them, and apart from George Abbott, who lived on at Canterbury until 1633, all the English sees were now occupied by Laudians or neutrals, and the wealthy and influential southern sees by his closest lieutenants.

The Commons were alive to the significance of these changes, and in January 1629 they initiated an investigation of the state of the Church in which Neile and Montague came in for particularly violent criticism. The resolutions on religion prepared by a subcommittee on 24 February asserted that the Thirty-Nine Articles had been modified by the Lambeth Articles of 1595, the Articles of the Irish Church in 1615 (which were markedly anti-Arminian in tone), and by the resolutions of the Synod of Doort in 1619 (44). This was the most extreme pronouncement on religion made by the Commons during this period.

During the eleven years that followed without a parliament, Laud could carry on his policy with very little resistance. Even in 1628 Lord Keeper Coventry had told the bishops that 'his Majesty took special notice not only of the increase of priests and papists but of the infinite swarms of sectaries'.[2]

---

[1] *Foedera*, XIX, 26 (17 January 1629).
[2] 'A Charge to the Judges of Assize' [13 February 1628], ed. Thomas G. Barnes, *Huntington Library Quarterly*, XXIV (1960–1), 255.

And indeed there was a serious problem of discipline; Laud was not merely intent on eliminating his critics. The emphasis in Calvinist theology on the personal confrontation of the individual with God, coupled with the remorseless criticism of the discipline and government of the national Church carried on by some of its members, had tended as early as 1590 to encourage separatism or congregationalism among the lower classes. If all men were equal in God's eyes, and if the mediation of the priest was unnecessary to salvation, what need was there of a church? Brownism had been virtually stamped out by Whitgift, but the sects were forming again, and Laud had more than one brush with them on the High Commission.[1] Moreover, the easy episcopal discipline of the past decade had allowed the survival of too many clergymen whose eccentricity bordered on lunacy, and whose sermons were one continuous libel. When he succeeded Abbott at Canterbury in 1633, one of Laud's first acts was to secure new Instructions from the king which placed further restrictions on lecturers without cure of souls and ordered the bishops of his province to look into the kind of sermons preached by their lower clergy (45). The bishops' reports were subsumed in an annual report from Laud to the king, who took a keen personal interest (46).

The most controversial, though not the most important part of Laud's work was his emphasis on the liturgical and sacramental functions of the church service, which frequently involved the moving of the communion table. The siting of this table had never been precisely fixed since the Reformation. The compromise favoured by the Elizabethan bishops was that the table should ordinarily stand in the nave, east and west, whence it was to be carried up to the chancel and placed north and south for the celebration of communion. It seems that most churches soon abandoned this tiresome procedure, and the table settled down in the nave or the chancel. Once in the chancel it was placed permanently against the east wall, covered with a cloth or a carpet, and in many churches replaced by a stone altar. Laud never committed himself to the view that this siting of the table, or altar, implied a Real Presence at the Communion, but rasher souls like Richard Montague did. There is no doubt where Laud's sympathies lay, but in 1637, when he defended his policy at length before Star Chamber, he maintained that this was 'a thing indifferent',[2] and he was able to cite in support a decision of John Davenant, bishop of Salisbury, scarcely one of his firmest supporters.[3] His views on the altar were finally summed up in canon VII of 1640. (48).

The aspect of this controversy which most alarmed Laud was lay interference, by churchwardens or vestries, with arrangements made by a priest. This still held when he himself did not approve of these arrangements; thus he insisted on the punishment of the Recorder of Salisbury for smashing a stained-glass window which represented the first person of the Trinity as

---

[1] No. 52, p 185 below. [2] *Works*, VI, 59. [3] *Ibid.* VI, 61.

THE LAUDIAN REVOLUTION

'an old gaffer in red and blue', though he subsequently ordered the cathedral authorities not to replace it. It is not surprising that he lost no time in forcing the disbandment of the lay feoffees, who offered a machinery by which laymen might eventually take over the Church entirely, and the King's Instructions of 1633 even forbade gentlemen to keep domestic chaplains (45). In 1632 Richardson, Chief Justice of Common Pleas, supported the local justices of peace in their efforts to suppress the Somerset Wakes, and his order to this effect was read in churches. For this assumption of episcopal, or even regal authority he was savagely criticised by Laud at the council table, and suspended from the western circuit.[1] The following year Charles reissued his father's Declaration of Sports, which roused a far greater furore than it had in 1618.[2]

On the other hand, this rule did not apply in reverse; the clergy were perfectly at liberty to assume the functions of the laity. Bishop Juxon succeeded the earl of Portland as lord treasurer in 1635, while Laud was always one of the king's chief advisers, in secular policy as well as ecclesiastical.

This exaggeration of clerical authority made Laud bitterly unpopular, in an age when the nobility and gentry were particularly sensitive to any slight on their honour,[3] and when so many bishops were of mean parentage.[4] But it was Laud's blind insistence on uniformity that finally brought him down. The Irish Church was forced to adopt the Thirty-Nine Articles in 1634, and in 1637 he turned to Scotland. The Scottish revolt against the new bishops and the new Prayer Book led directly to the collapse of Charles I's regime.

But he was defiant to the last. The Convocation of Canterbury which assembled with the Short Parliament in 1640 took the unprecedented step of remaining in session after the dissolution. It voted the king taxes, which Parliament had refused, and it passed a series of canons which included an elaborate defence of the Laudian standpoint on 'innovations', and a number of 'explanations' of the Divine Right of Kings and the unlawfulness of resistance to constituted authority, which every clergyman was to read out to his congregation four times a year (48). But the most controversial was canon VI, which imposed on all clergymen the notorious 'etcetera' oath, which bound them not to consent to the alteration of 'the government of this Church by archbishops, bishops, deans and archdeacons, etc.'. It was primarily directed at lurking Romanists, and indeed, it soon revealed Goodman, bishop of

[1] Thomas G. Barnes, 'County Politics and a Puritan cause célèbre: Somerset Church Ales, 1633', Transactions Royal Historical Society, 5th ser., IX (1959), 103.
[2] Printed GCD, p. 99. It was usually known as the 'Book of Sports'.
[3] Stone, Crisis of the Aristocracy, ch. III.
[4] Of the thirty-four clergymen promoted to sees between 1625 and 1641, only one had any connection with the nobility or gentry (and this was Williams of Lincoln, said to be 'of an ancient Welsh family'). Harsnet, archbishop of York, was a baker's son, and Corbet of Oxford a gardener's son. The rest were of yeoman or merchant stock, or the sons of clergymen; Laud's father was a clothier.

Gloucester, as a secret convert; but this did nothing to reconcile Laud's enemies, particularly in the Long Parliament. On 11 December 1640 a petition signed by 15,000 Londoners was presented to the House of Commons calling for the extirpation of episcopacy 'root and branch' (48). On the 15th the Commons declared that the late canons were binding on neither clergy nor laity, and next day they voted them illegal, since Convocation had no power to legislate without consent of Parliament.[1] On the 18th Laud was impeached of high treason and taken into custody. The authoritarian rule he had established over the Church now proved its greatest weakness, for with his disappearance into the Tower the machinery of episcopal discipline at once collapsed.

42. William Laud: two sermons

(a) On the opening of Parliament, 19 June 1625

Psalms 75. 2, 3. When I shall receive the congregation I will judge uprightly.[2] The earth and all the inhabitants thereof are dissolved; I bear up the pillars of it.

*　*　*　*　*　*

...'I will judge according unto right' is not only the King's engagement, between God and the people, but it is the engagement of every judge, magistrate and officer between God, the King and the State. The King's power, that's from God: the judges' and the subordinate magistrates' power, that's from the King. Both are for the good of the people....

All judges and courts of justice, even this great congregation, this great council now ready to sit, receive influence and power from the King, and are dispensers of his justice as well as their own, both in the laws they make and in the laws they execute, in the causes which they hear and in the sentences which they give; the King God's High Steward, and they stewards under him....For inferior governors of all sorts the King is the sun. He draws up some vapours, some support some supply from us, 'tis true. He must do so. For if the sun draws up no vapours it can pour down no rain, and the earth may be too hard, as well as too soft and too melting. Now this rain which descends, and is first caused by the sun, is prepared in the clouds before it falleth on the earth. And all great men that are raised higher than the rest,

---

[1] CJ, II, 51, 52.
[2] Or, as Laud would have it, 'according to right'. He seems to have been using his own translation of the Vulgate.

especially judges and magistrates of all sorts, they are the clouds. They receive the more immediate influence from the King, and if they be God's clouds, and retain what he gave them, they drop fatness upon the people, but if they be clouds without water they transmit no influence; if they be light clouds in the wind, then no certain influence; if they be clouds driven...by a whirlwind, then it is passionate and violent influence. And the clouds I hope are not, I am sure should not be, thus between the King and his people....

*   *   *   *   *   *

Sermons, pp. 112–13

(b) On the opening of Parliament, 6 February 1626

Psalms 122. 3–5: Jerusalem is builded as a city that is united in itself. For thither the tribes go up, even the tribes of the Lord, to the testimony of Israel, to give thanks unto the name of the Lord. For there are the seats of judgement; even the thrones of the House of David.

*   *   *   *   *   *

I know there are some that think the Church is not yet far enough beside the cushion, that their seats are too easy yet, and too high too. A parity they would have, no bishop, no governor, but a parochial consistory, and that should be lay enough too. Well, first, this parity was never left to the Church by Christ; he left Apostles, and Disciples under them. It was never in use with the Church since Christ; no church ever, anywhere (till this last age) without a bishop. If it were in use it might perhaps govern some petty city, but make it common once, and it can never keep unity in the Church of Christ. And for their seats being too high, God knows they are brought low, even to contempt. They were high in Jerusalem. For all divines agree that this in prime reference is spoken of ecclesiastical censures, and seats. And the word is thrones, no less. So in the original, so the Septuagint, and so many of the later divines, forgetting their own invention of the presbytery.

And one thing more I'll be bold to speak, out of a like duty to the Church of England and the House of David. They, whoever they be, that would overthrow *sedes ecclesia*, the seats of ecclesiastical government, will not spare (if ever they get power) to have a pluck at the Throne of David. And there is not a man that is for parity, all fellows

153

in the Church, but he is not for monarchy in the State. And certainly either he is but half-headed to his own principles, or he can be but half-hearted to the House of David....

Ibid. pp. 91–3

43. A proclamation for the establishing of the peace and quiet of the Church of England, 16 June 1626

The King's most excellent Majesty, in his most religious care and princely consideration of the peace of this Church and commonwealth of England and other his dominions, whereof God in his goodness hath, under his son Christ Jesus, made him his Supreme Governor, observing that in all ages great disturbances both in Church and State have ensued out of small beginnings when the seeds of contention were not timely prevented, and finding that of late some questions and opinions seem to have been broached or raised in matters of doctrine and the tenets of our religion, which at first only being meant against the Papists, but afterwards by the sharp and indiscreet handling and maintaining some of either parts have given much offence to the sober and well-grounded readers and hearers of these late written books on both sides, which [it] may justly be feared will raise some hopes in the professed enemies of our religion, the Romish Catholics, that by degrees the professors of our religion may be drawn first to schism and after to plain Popery.

His Majesty therefore, in the integrity of his own heart and singular providence of the peaceable government of that people which God hath committed to his charge, hath thought fit, by the advice of his reverend bishops, to declare and publish not only to his own people but also to the whole world his utter dislike to all those who, to show the subtlety of their wit, or to please their own humours, or vent their own passions, do or shall adventure to stir or move any new opinions not only contrary [to] but differing from the sound and orthodoxal grounds of the true religion sincerely professed and happily established in the Church of England; and also to declare his full and constant resolution that neither in matter of doctrine or discipline of the Church, nor in the government of the State, he will admit of the least innovation, but by God's assistance will so guide the sceptre of these his kingdoms and dominions, by the Divine Providence put into his hand, as shall be for the comfort and assurance of his sober, religious and well-affected subjects, and for the repressing and severe punishing of the insolencies of such as out of any sinister respects or disaffection to his person and government shall dare either in Church or State to disturb or disquiet the peace thereof.

And therefore his most excellent Majesty doth hereby admonish, and also straightly charge and command all his subjects of this realm and of his realm of Ireland, of whatsoever degree, quality or condition they be of, especially those who are churchmen, and by their profession and places ought to be lights and guides to others, that from henceforth they carry themselves so wisely, warily and conscionably that neither by writing, preaching, printing, conferences or otherwise they raise any doubts, or publish or maintain any new inventions or opinions concerning religion than such as [are] clearly grounded and warranted by the doctrine and discipline of the Church of England heretofore published and happily established by authority. And if any person of what degree soever shall at any time hereafter adventure to break this rule of sobriety and due obedience to his Majesty and his laws, and to this religious duty to the Church of God, his Majesty doth hereby straitly charge and command all his reverend archbishops and bishops, in their several dioceses, speedily to reclaim and repress all such spirits as shall in the least degree attempt to violate this bond of peace.

And his Majesty doth also charge and command all his councillors of estate, judges, justices and ministers of justice whatsoever, that they in their several places take especial care to observe and execute his Majesty's pious and royal pleasure herein expressed.

And lastly, his Majesty doth hereby give assurance to all to whom it may concern, that such as shall take the boldness wilfully to neglect this his Majesty's gracious admonition, and for the satisfying of their unquiet and restless spirits, and to express their rash and undutiful insolencies, shall wilfully break that circle of order, which without apparent danger to Church and State may not be broken, that his Majesty shall and will proceed against all such offenders and wilfull contemners of his gracious and religious government with that severity as upon due consideration had of the quality of their offences and contempts they shall deserve, that so by the exemplary punishment of some few, who by lenity and mercy cannot be won, all others may be warned to take heed how they fall into the just indignation of their Sovereign, and that all his Majesty's good and loving subjects who are studious of the peace and prosperity of this Church and commonwealth may bless God for his Majesty's pious, religious, wise, just and gracious government.

Foedera, xviii, 719–20

44. Heads of articles to be insisted on, and agreed upon, at a sub-committee for religion (House of Commons, 24 February 1629)

I. That we call to mind, how that, in the last session of this Parliament, we presented to his Majesty a humble declaration of the great danger threatened to this Church and State, by divers courses and practices tending to the change and innovation of religion.[1]

II. That what we then feared, we do now sensibly feel; and therefore have just cause to renew our former complaints herein.

III. That yet, nevertheless, we do with all thankfulness acknowledge the great blessing we have received from Almighty God, in setting a king over us, of whose constancy in the profession and practice of the true religion here established, we rest full assured; as likewise of his most pious zeal and careful endeavour for the maintenance and propagation thereof; being so far from having the least doubt of his Majesty's remissness therein that we, next under God, ascribe unto his own princely wisdom and goodness, that our holy religion hath yet any countenance at all amongst us.

IV. And for that the pious intention and endeavours, even of the best and wisest princes, are often frustrated through the unfaithfulness and carelessness of their ministers; and that we find a great unhappiness to have befallen his Majesty this way; we think that, being now assembled in Parliament to advise of the weighty and important affairs concerning Church and State, we cannot do a work more acceptable than, in the first place, according to the dignity of the matter, and necessity of the present occasions, faithfully and freely to make known, what we conceive may conduce to the preservation of God's religion, in great peril now to be lost; and, therewithal, the safety and tranquillity of his Majesty and his kingdoms now threatened with certain dangers. For the clearer proceedings therein, we shall declare: (1) What those dangers and inconveniencies are. (2) Whence they arise. (3) In some sort, how they may be redressed.

The dangers may appear partly from the consideration of the state of religion abroad; and partly from the condition thereof within his Majesty's own dominions, and especially within this kingdom of England.

From abroad we make these observations: (1) By the mighty and prevalent party, by which true religion is actually opposed, and the

---

[1] The Remonstrance of 11 June 1628; Rushworth, I, 631.

contrary maintained. (2) Their combined counsels, forces, attempts, and practices, together with a most diligent pursuit of their designs, aiming at the subversion of all the Protestant Churches in Christendom. (3) The weak resistance that is made against them. (4) Their victorious and successful enterprises, whereby the Churches of Germany, France, and other places, are in a great part already ruined, and the rest in the most weak and miserable condition.

*　　*　　*　　*　　*　　*

Here in England we observe an extraordinary growth of Popery, insomuch that in some counties, where in Queen Elizabeth's time there were few or none known recusants, now there are above 2,000, and all the rest generally apt to revolt. A bold and open allowance of their religion, by frequent and public resort to mass, in multitudes, without control, and that even to the Queen's Court, to the great scandal of his Majesty's government. Their extraordinary insolence; for instance, the late erecting of a College of Jesuits in Clerkenwell, and the strange proceedings thereupon used in favour of them. The subtle and pernicious spreading of the Arminian faction; whereby they have kindled such a fire of division in the very bowels of the State, as if not speedily extinguished, it is of itself sufficient to ruin our religion; by dividing us from the Reformed Churches abroad, and separating amongst ourselves at home, by casting doubts upon the religion professed and established, which, if faulty or questionable in three or four articles, will be rendered suspicious to unstable minds in all the rest, and incline them to Popery, to which those tenets, in their own nature, do prepare the way: so that if our religion be suppressed and destroyed abroad, disturbed in Scotland, lost in Ireland, undermined and almost outdared in England, it is manifest that our danger is very great and imminent.

*　　*　　*　　*　　*　　*

The points wherein the Arminians differ from us and other the Reformed Churches, in the sense of the Articles confirmed in Parliament, 13 Eliz., may be known and proved in these controverted points, viz.: (1) By the Common Prayer, established by Parliament. (2) By the book of Homilies, confirmed by the Articles of Religion. (3) By the Catechism concerning the points printed in the Bible, and read in churches, and divers other impressions published by authority. (4) Bishop Jewel's works, commanded to be kept in all churches, that every parish may have one of them. (5) The public determination of divinity professors, published by authority. (6) The public determination of divines in both the universities. (7) The Resolution of the archbishop of Canterbury and other reverend bishops and divines assembled at Lambeth, for this very purpose, to declare their opinions concerning those points, anno 1595, unto which the archbishop of York and all his province did likewise agree. (8) The Articles of Ireland, though framed by the Convocation there, yet allowed by the clergy and State here. (9) The suffrage of the British divines, sent by King James to the Synod of Dort. (10) The uniform consent of our writers published by authority. (11) The censures, recantations, punishments, and submissions made, enjoined and inflicted upon those that taught contrary thereunto, as Barrow and Barrett in Cambridge, and Bridges in Oxford.

The remedy of which abuses we conceive may be these:

1. Due execution of laws against Papists.

2. Exemplary punishments to be inflicted upon teachers, publishers, and maintainers of Popish opinions, and practising of superstitious ceremonies, and some stricter laws in that case to be provided.

3. The orthodox doctrine of our Church, in these now controverted points by the Arminian sect, may be established and freely taught, according as it hath been hitherto generally received, without any alteration or innovation; and severe punishment, by the same laws, to be provided against such as shall, either by word or writing, publish anything contrary thereunto.

* * * * * *

5. That such as have been authors, or abettors, of those Popish and Arminian innovations in doctrine, may be condignly punished.

* * * * * *

7. That his Majesty would be graciously pleased to confer bishoprics, and other ecclesiastical preferments, with the advice of his Privy Council, upon learned, pious and orthodox men.

8. That bishops and clergymen being well chosen, may reside upon their charge, and with diligence and fidelity perform their several duties, and that accordingly they may be countenanced and preferred.

9. That some course may in this parliament be considered of, for providing competent means to maintain a godly, able minister in every parish church of this kingdom.

10. That his Majesty would be graciously pleased to make a special choice of such persons, for the execution of his ecclesiastical commissions, as are approved for integrity of life and soundness of doctrine.

PH, II, 483–7

45. The instructions of 1633

Instructions for the most Reverend Father in God our right trusty and right entirely beloved counsellor William lord archbishop of Canterbury, concerning certain orders to be observed and put in execution by the several bishops of his province, Anno Dom. 1633

I. That the Lords the Bishops respectively be commanded to their several sees, there to keep residence, excepting those which are in necessary attendance at our court.

* * * * * *

III. That they give charge in their triennial Visitations, and at other convenient times, both by themselves and the archdeacons, that our declaration for settling all questions in difference[1] be strictly observed by all parties.

IV. That there be a special care taken by them all, that their ordinations be solemn, and not of unworthy persons.

V. That they likewise take great care concerning the lecturers within their several dioceses, for whom we give them special directions following.

(1) That in all parishes the afternoon sermons be turned into catechising by questions and answers, where and whence ever there is not some great cause apparent to break this ancient and profitable order.

(2) That every bishop take care in his diocese that all the lecturers do read Divine Service according to the liturgy printed by authority, in their surplices and hoods, before the lecture.

(3) That where a lecture is set up in a market town it may be read by a company of grave and orthodox divines near adjoining and of the same diocese, and that they ever preach in such seemly habits as belong to their degrees, and not in cloaks.

(4) That if a corporation maintains a single lecturer he be not suffered to preach till he professes his willingness to take upon him a

---

[1] In 1628; see p. 148 above.

living with cure of souls within that corporation, and that he do actually take such benefice or cure so soon as it shall be fairly procured for him.

* * * * * *

VII. That the bishops suffer none under noblemen or men qualified by law, to keep any private chaplain in his house.

* * * * * *

XIV. Lastly, we command every bishop respectively to give his account in writing to his Metropolitan of all these our instructions, or as many of them as may concern him, at or before the tenth day of December yearly, and likewise that you out of them make a brief of your whole province, and present it to us yearly by the second day of January following, that so we may see how the Church is governed and our commands obeyed. And hereof in any wise fail you not.

Foedera, XIX, 470–2

46. My Lord of Canterbury's return to his Majesty's instructions, for the year 1636

May it please your sacred Majesty,

According to your royal commands expressed in your late instructions for the good of the Church, I do here most humbly present my yearly account for my diocese and province of Canterbury for this last year, ending at Christmas 1636.

And first for my own diocese.

I have every year acquainted your Majesty, and so must do now, that there are still about Ashford and Edgerton divers Brownists and other Separatists; but they are so very mean and poor people that we know not what to do with them. They are said to be the disciples of one Turner and Fenner, who were long since apprehended and imprisoned by order of your Majesty's High Commission Court; but how this part came to be so infected with such a humour of Separation I know not, unless it were by too much connivance at their first beginning, neither do I see any remedy like to be, unless some of their chief seducers be driven to abjure the kingdom, which must be done by the Judges at the Common Law, but it is not in our power. [*Inform me of the particulars and I shall command the judges to make them abjure.*][1] . . .

[1] Marginal comment by the king.

There have been heretofore many in Canterbury that were not conformable to church discipline, and would not kneel at the Communion, but they are all now very conformable, as I hear expressly by my officers, and that there is no falling away of any to recusancy....

In the diocese of *London* I find that my lord the bishop there (now by your Majesty's grace and favour Lord High Treasurer of England) hath very carefully observed those instructions which belong to his own person, and for the diocese his lordship informs me of three great misdemeanours: the one committed by Dr Cornelius Burgess, who in a Latin sermon before the clergy of London uttered divers insolent passages against the bishops and government of the Church, and refused to give his lordship a copy of the sermon, so there was a necessity of calling him into the High Commission Court, which is done.

The second misdemeanour is of one Mr Wharton, a minister in Essex, who in a sermon at Chelmsford uttered many unfit and some scurrilous things, but for this he hath been convented, and received a canonical admonition, and upon his sorrow and submission any further censure is forborne.

The third misdemeanour which my Lord complains of is the late spreading and dispersing of some factious and malicious pamphlets against the bishops and government of the Church of England, and my lord further certifies that he hath reasonable ground to persuade him that those libellous pamphlets have been contrived, or abetted and dispersed, by some of the clergy of his diocese; and therefore desires me to use the authority of the High Commission for the discovery of this notorious practice, to prevent the mischiefs that will otherwise ensue upon the government of the Church. This, God willing, I shall see performed; but if the High Commission shall not have power enough, because one of these libels contains seditious matter in it, and that which is very little short of treason (if any thing at all), then I humbly beg leave to add this to my Lord Treasurer's motion, and humbly to desire, that your Majesty will call it into a higher court, if you find cause, since I see no likelihood but that these troubles in the Church, if they be permitted, will break out into some sedition in the Commonwealth....
[*What the High Commission cannot do in this I shall supply as I shall find cause, in a more powerful way.*][1]

*   *   *   *   *   *

[1] Marginal comment by the king.

[*Norwich.*] His Lordship found a general defect in catechising quite through the diocese, but hath settled it. And in Norwich, where there are thirty four churches, there was no sermon in the morning on Sundays save only in four, but all put off till the afternoon, and so no catechising; but now he hath ordered that there shall be a sermon every morning and catechising in the afternoon in every church.

For lectures, they abound in Suffolk, and many set up by private gentlemen, even without so much as the knowledge of the Ordinary, and without any due observation to the Canons of the discipline of the Church. Divers of these his Lordship hath carefully regulated according to order, especially at St Edmundsbury [Bury St Edmunds], and with their very good content, and suspended no Lecturer of whom he might obtain conformity.... At Yarmouth, where there was great division heretofore for many years, their lecturer being censured in the High Commission about two years since went into New England, since which time there hath been no lecture, and very much peace in the town, and all ecclesiastical orders well observed. [*Let him go, we are well rid of him.*][1] But in Norwich one Mr Bridge, rather than he would conform, hath left his lecture and is gone into Holland, the lecturers in the Country generally observing no Church Orders at all; and yet the Bishop hath carried it with that temper, and upon their promise and his hope of conformity, that he hath inhibited but three in Norfolk and as many in Suffolk, of which one is no graduate and hath been a common stage-player.

His Lordship humbly craves direction what he shall do with such scholars (some in Holy Orders and some not) as knights and private gentlemen keep in their houses, under pretence to teach their children, as also with some divines that are beneficed in towns, or near, but live in gentlemen's houses. For my part, I think it very fit the beneficed men were presently commanded to reside upon their cures, and for the rest, your Majesty's Instructions allow none to keep chaplains but such as are qualified by law; all which notwithstanding, I most humbly submit (as the Bishop does) to your Majesty's judgement. [*I approve your judgement in this. I only add that care must be taken that even those qualified by law keep none but conformable men.*][1] ...

Worcester. My lord the bishop of this see certifies that your Majesty's instructions are carefully observed, and that there are only two lectures in the city of Worcester, but very conformable, and that they shall no

---

[1] Marginal comment by the king.

longer continue than they are so, and that one of them preaches on Sundays in the afternoons after catechising and service in the parish churches, and ending before evening prayers in the Cathedral....

* * * * * *

[*St Davids.*] Baronet Ridd is in this diocese, the son of a late bishop there, who is a sober gentleman. He hath built him a chapel, and desires the bishop to consecrate it, but his lordship finding one of your Majesty's Instructions to be, that none shall keep a chaplain in his house but such as are qualified by law, which he conceives a baronet is not, hath hitherto forborne to consecrate this chapel, as being to be of small use without a chaplain, and humbly craves direction herein, what he shall do.

I humbly propose to your Majesty, whether, considering the charge this gentleman hath been at, and the ill ways which many of them there have to church, it may not be fit to consecrate this chapel, and then that he may have a licence to use the minister of the parish, or any other lawfully in orders; always provided that he use this chapel but at times of some necessity, and not making himself and his family strangers to the Mother Church, and that there be a clause expressed in the licence for recalling thereof, upon any abuse there committed, and that this licence be taken, either from the bishop under his seal, or from the archbishop of the province. [*Since he hath been at the charge and hath so good testimony, let him have his desire, with those restrictions mentioned.*][1]

* * * * * *

St Asaph. In the diocese of St Asaph there is no complaint but the usual, that there is great resort of recusants to Holy Well, and that this summer the Lady Falkland and her company came as pilgrims thither, who were the more observed because they travelled on foot, and dissembled neither their quality nor their errand; and this boldness of theirs is of very bad construction among your Majesty's people. My humble suit to your Majesty is, that whereas I complained of this in open council in your Majesty's presence you would now be graciously pleased that the order then resolved on for her confinement may be put in execution. [*It is done.*][1]

Bangor. For Bangor, I find that the catechising was quite out of use in those remote parts (the more the pity), but the bishop is now in hope

---

[1] Marginal comment by the king.

to do much good, and seeth some reformation in that particular already. And I would say for this and the other dioceses in Wales, that much more good might be done there in a Church way if they were not over-borne by the Court of the Marches there. And this present year in this diocese of Bangor my Commissioner for my Metropolitical Visitation there complains unto me that the power which belongs to my place hath been in them very much wronged and impeached by that court, and I do most humbly beseech your Majesty in your own good time to give this my cause a hearing, if it take not a fair end without trouble. [*I doubt not but by the Grace of God to agree these differences, by hearing of them.*][1]

Rochester. For Rochester (God comfort him) the bishop is very ill of a palsy, and that I fear hath made him forget his account. Neither hath the bishop of Gloucester sent me any, but why I know not; and for Bristol the see is void.

*   *   *   *   *   *

And so I most humbly submit this my yearly account of my province of Canterbury to your Majesty's princely wisdom.

Whitehall

21 February 1637.

Foedera, xx, 109–113

47. Archbishop Laud's Apologia: delivered in Star Chamber, 14 June 1637, at the condemnation of Bastwick, Burton and Prynne

...'Tis unworthy in itself, and preposterous in demeanour, for a man to be ashamed for doing good because other men glory in speaking ill. And I can say it clearly and truly, as in the presence of God, I have done nothing as a prelate, to the uttermost of what I am conscious, but with a single heart, and with a sincere intention for the good government and honour of the Church, and the maintenance of the orthodox truth and religion of Christ, professed, established and maintained in this Church of England.

For my care of this Church, the reducing of it into order, the up-holding of the external worship of God in it, and the settling of it to the rules of its first reformation, are the causes (and the sole causes, whatever are pretended) of all this malicious storm, which hath lowered

---

[1] Marginal comment by the king.

so black upon me and some of my brethren. And in the meantime, they, which are the only or the chief innovators of the Christian world, having nothing to say, accuse us of innovation; they themselves and their complices in the meantime being the greatest innovators that the Christian world hath almost ever known. I deny not but others have spread more dangerous errors in the Church of Christ; but no men, in any age of it, have been more guilty of innovation than they, while [they] themselves cry out against it. *Quis tulerit Gracchos?*

And I said well, *Quis tulerit Gracchos?* For 'tis most apparent to any man that will not wink, that the intention of these men and their abettors was and is to raise a sedition, being as great incendiaries in the State (where they get power) as they have ever been in the Church.…

Our main crime is (would they all speak out, as some of them do) that we are bishops; were we not so, some of us might be as passable as other men. And a great trouble 'tis to them that we maintain that our calling of bishops is *jure divino*, by divine right: of this I have said enough, and in this place, in Leighton's case,[1] nor will I repeat [it]. Only this I will say, and abide by it, that the calling of bishops is *jure divino*, by divine right, though not all adjuncts to their calling. And this I say in as direct opposition to the Church of Rome, as to the Puritan humour. And I say further, that from the Apostles' times, in all ages, in all places, the Church of Christ was governed by bishops, and lay elders never heard of till Calvin's newfangled device at Geneva.

Now this is made by these men as if it were *contra regem*, against the King, in right or in power. But that's a mere ignorant shift, for our being bishops *jure divino*, by divine right, takes nothing from the King's right or power over us. For though our office be from God and Christ immediately, yet we may not exercise that power, either of order or jurisdiction, but as God hath appointed us, that is, not in his Majesty's or any Christian king's kingdoms, but by and under the power of the King given us so to do. And were this a good argument against us, as bishops, it must needs be good against priests and ministers too, for themselves grant that their calling is *jure divino*, by divine right; and yet I hope they will not say that to be priests and ministers is against the King, or any his royal prerogatives.

Next, suppose our calling as bishops could not be made good *jure divino*, by divine right, yet *jure ecclesiastico*, by ecclesiastical right, it cannot be denied. And here in England the bishops are confirmed, both

---

[1] The trial of Dr Alexander Leighton, 4 June 1630.

in their power and means, by Act of Parliament. So that here we stand in as good case as the present laws of the realm can make us. And so we must stand till the laws shall be repealed by the same power that made them.

...No man can libel against our calling (as these men do), be it in pulpit, print or otherwise, but he libels against the King and the State, by whose laws we are established. Therefore all these libels, so far forth as they are against our calling, are against the King and the Law, and can have no other purpose than to stir up sedition among the people....

Works, VI, 42–6

48. The canons of 1640

Constitutions and canons ecclesiastical, treated upon by the . . . convocations . . . of Canterbury and York, . . . and now published for the due observation of them by his Majesty's authority under the great seal of England [16 June 1640]

Charles, by the Grace of God king of England, Scotland, France and Ireland, Defender of the Faith, etc., to all to whom these presents shall come, greeting.... Forasmuch as we are given to understand that many of our subjects, being misled against the rites and ceremonies now used in the Church of England, have lately taken offence at the same, upon an unjust supposal that they are not only contrary to our laws but also introductive unto Popish superstitions; whereas it well appeareth unto us...that the authors and fomenters of these jealousies, though they colour the same with a pretence of zeal, and would seem to strike only at some supposed iniquity in the said ceremonies, yet, as we have cause to fear, aim at our own royal person, and would fain have our good subjects imagine that we ourselves are perverted, and do worship God in a superstitious way, and that we intend to bring in some alteration of the religion here established. Now, how far we are from that, and how utterly we detest every thought thereof, we have by many public declarations and otherwise upon sundry occasions given such assurance to the world, as that from thence we also assure ourself, that no man of wisdom and discretion could ever be so beguiled as to give any serious entertainment to such brainsick jealousies; and for the weaker sort, who are prone to be misled by crafty seducers, we rest no less confident that even of them as many as are of loyal, or indeed but of charitable, hearts, will from henceforth utterly banish all such causeless fears and surmises, upon these our sacred professions so often made by us, a Christian Defender of the Faith, their King and Sovereign. ...

We therefore, out of our princely inclination to uniformity and peace, in matters especially that concern the holy worship of God,...and..., having fully advised herein with our metropolitan, and with the commissioners authorised under our Great Seal for causes ecclesiastical, have thought good to give them free leave to treat in Convocation, and agree upon certain other canons necessary for the advancement of God's glory, the edifying of his Holy Church, and the due reverence of his blessed Mysteries and Sacraments; that, as we have ever been and by God's assistance (by whom alone we reign) shall ever so continue, careful and ready to cut off superstition with one hand, so we may no less expel irreverence and profaneness with the other....

* * * * * *

I. *Concerning the regal power*

Whereas sundry laws, ordinances and constitutions have been formerly made for the acknowledgement and profession of the most lawful and independent authority of our dread sovereign lord the King's most excellent Majesty, over the State ecclesiastical and civil,...for the fuller and clear instruction and information of all Christian people within this realm in their duties in this particular we do further ordain and decree that every parson, vicar, curate or preacher upon some one Sunday in every quarter of the year, at morning prayer, shall, in the place where he serves, treatably and audibly read these explanations of the regal power here inserted:

The most high and sacred Order of Kings is of Divine Right, being the ordinance of God himself, founded in the prime laws of nature, and clearly established by express texts both of the Old and New Testaments. A supreme power is given to this most excellent Order by God himself in the Scriptures, which is, that kings should rule and command in their several dominions all persons of what rank or estate soever, whether ecclesiastical or civil, and that they should restrain and punish with the temporal sword all stubborn and wicked doers.

The care of God's Church is so committed to kings in the Scripture that they are commended when the Church keeps the right way, and taxed when it runs amiss, and therefore her government belongs in chief unto kings; for otherwise one man would be commended for another's care, and taxed but for another's negligence, which is not God's way.

The power to call and dissolve Councils, both national and provincial, is the true right of all Christian kings within their own realms and territories; and when in the first times of Christ's Church prelates used this power, it was therefore only because in those days they had no Christian kings; and it was then so only used as in times of persecution, that is, with supposition (in case it were required) of submitting their very lives unto the very laws and commands even of those pagan princes that they might not so much as seem to disturb their civil government, which Christ came to confirm, but by no means to undermine.

For any person or persons to set up, maintain or avow in any their said realms or territories respectively, under any pretence whatsoever, any independent coactive power, either papal or popular (whether directly or indirectly), is to undermine their great royal office, and cunningly to overthrow that most sacred ordinance which God himself hath established, and so is treasonable against God as well as against the King.

For subjects to bear arms against their kings, offensive or defensive, upon any pretence whatsoever, is at least to resist the powers which are ordained of God; and though they do not invade but only resist, St Paul tells them plainly they shall receive to themselves damnation.

And although tribute, and custom, and aid, and subsidy, and all manner of necessary support and supply be respectively due to kings from their subjects by the Law of God, Nature and Nations, for the public defence, care and protection of them; yet nevertheless subjects have not only possession of but a true and just right, title, and property to and in all their goods and estates, and ought to have. And these two are so far from crossing one another that they mutually go together for the honourable and comfortable support of both. For as it is the duty of the subjects to supply their king so it is part of the kingly office to support his subjects in the property and freedom of their estates....

*   *   *   *   *   *

[Canons II, III, IV and V were, respectively, 'For the better keeping of the day of his Majesty's most happy Inauguration', 'For the suppressing of the growth of Popery', 'Against Socinianism' and 'Against Sectaries'.]

VI. An oath enjoined for the preventing of all innovations in doctrine and government

This present synod (being desirous to declare their sincerity and constancy in the profession of the doctrine and discipline already established in the Church of England, and to secure all men against any suspicion of revolt to Popery, or any other superstition) decrees, that all archbishops and bishops, and all other priests and deacons, in places exempt or not exempt, shall before the second day of November next ensuing take this oath following, against all innovation of doctrine or discipline, and this oath shall be tendered [to] them and every of them, and all others named after in this canon, by the bishop in person, or his chancellor, or some grave divines named and appointed by the bishop under the seal; and the said oath shall be taken in the presence of a public notary, who is hereby required to make an act of it, leaving the universities to the provision which follows.

The oath is:

I, A.B., do swear that I do approve the doctrine and discipline, or government established in the Church of England, as containing all things necessary to salvation, and that I will not endeavour by myself or any other, directly or indirectly, to bring in any Popish doctrine, contrary to that which is so established; nor will I ever give my consent to alter the government of this Church by archbishops, bishops, deans and archdeacons, etc.,[1] as it stands now established, and as by right it ought to stand, nor yet ever subject it to the usurpations and superstitions of the See of Rome. And all these things I do plainly and sincerely acknowledge and swear, according to the plain and common sense and understanding of the same words, without any equivocation, or mental evasion, or secret reservation whatsoever. And this I do heartily, willingly and truly, upon the faith of a Christian. So help me God in Jesus Christ.

*   *   *   *   *   *

We likewise constitute and ordain that all masters of arts (the sons of noblemen only excepted), all bachelors and doctors in divinity, law or physic, all that are licensed to practise physic, all registrars, actuaries and proctors, all schoolmasters, all such as being natives or naturalised

---

[1] This is what made it notorious as the 'Etcetera Oath'.

do come to be incorporated into the universities here, having taken a degree in any foreign university, shall be bound to take the said oath. And we command all governors of colleges and halls in either of the universities that they administer the said oath to all persons resident in their several houses that have taken the degrees before-mentioned in this canon within six months after the publication hereof.

And we likewise constitute, that all bishops shall be bound to give the said oath unto all those to whom they give Holy Orders at the time of their ordination, or to whomsoever they give collation, institution, or licence to preach or serve any cure.

VII. A declaration concerning some rites and ceremonies

Because it is generally to be wished that unity of faith were accompanied with uniformity of practice in the outward worship and service of God, chiefly for the avoiding of groundless suspicions of those who are weak, and the malicious aspersions of the professed enemies of our religion; the one fearing the innovations, the other flattering themselves with the vain hope of our backslidings unto their Popish superstition, by reason of the situation of the Communion Table, and the approaches thereunto, the synod declareth as followeth:

That the standing of the Communion Table sideway[s] under the east window of every chancel or chapel is in its own nature indifferent, neither commanded nor condemned by the word of God, either expressly or by immediate deduction, and therefore that no religion is to be placed therein, or scruple to be made thereon. And albeit at the time of reforming this Church from that gross superstition of Popery it was carefully provided that all means should be used to root out of the minds of the people both the inclination thereunto and memory thereof, especially of the idolatry committed in the Mass, for which cause all Popish altars were demolished; yet notwithstanding it was then ordered by the Injunctions and Advertisements of Queen Elizabeth of blessed memory,[1] that the Holy Tables should stand in the place where the altars stood, and accordingly have been continued in the royal chapels of three famous and pious princes, and in most cathedral and some parochial churches, which doth sufficiently acquit the manner of placing the said tables from any illegality, or just suspicion of Popish

[1] It was convenient to invoke Elizabeth's name, but in fact she had refused to license these Injunctions and Advertisements, which had been issued on the sole authority of the archbishops.

superstition or innovation. And therefore we judge it fit and convenient that all churches and chapels do conform themselves in this particular to the example of the cathedral or mother-churches, saving always the general liberty left to the bishop by law, during the time of administration of the Holy Communion. And we declare that this situation of the Holy Table doth not imply that it is or ought to be esteemed a true and proper altar, whereon Christ is again really sacrificed, but it is and may be called an altar by us in that sense in which the Primitive Church called it an altar, and in no other.

And because experience hath shewed us how irreverent the behaviour of many people is in many places, some leaning, others casting their hats, and some sitting upon, some standing [on], and others sitting under the Communion Table in time of Divine Service, for the avoiding of these and the like abuses it is thought meet and convenient by this present synod that the said Communion Tables in all chancels or chapels be decently severed with rails, to preserve them from such or worse profanations....

*   *   *   *   *   *

Cartwright, *Synodalia*, I, 380–92, 402–6

49. The Root and Branch Petition, 11 December 1640

To the Right Honourable the Commons House of Parliament.

The humble petition of many of his Majesty's subjects in and about the City of London, and several counties of the kingdom, showeth,

That whereas the government of archbishops and lord bishops, deans and archdeacons, etc., with their courts and ministrations in them, have proved prejudicial and very dangerous both to the Church and Commonwealth, they themselves having formerly held, that they have their jurisdiction or authority of human authority, till of these later times, being further pressed about the unlawfulness, that they have claimed their calling immediately from the Lord Jesus Christ, which is against the Laws of this kingdom, and derogatory to his Majesty and his state royal. And whereas the said government is found by woeful experience to be a main cause and occasion of many foul evils, pressures and grievances of a very high nature unto his Majesty's subjects in their own consciences, liberties and estates, as in a schedule of particulars hereunto annexed may in part appear.

We therefore most humbly pray and beseech this honourable assembly, the premisses considered, that the said government, with all its dependencies, roots and branches, may be abolished, and all laws in their behalf made void, and the government according to God's Word may be rightly placed amongst us. And we your humble suppliants, as in duty we are bound, will daily pray for his Majesty's long and happy reign over us, and for the prosperous success of this high and honourable Court of Parliament.

A particular of the manifold evils, pressures and grievances caused, practised and occasioned by the prelates and their dependants

1. The subjecting and enthralling all ministers under them and their authority, and so by degrees exempting them from the temporal power; whence follows:

2. The faint-heartedness of ministers to preach the Truth of God, lest they should displease the prelates; as namely, the doctrine of Pre-destination, of Free-Grace, of Perseverance, of Original Sin remaining after baptism, of the Sabbath, the doctrine against Universal Grace, Election for Faith foreseen, Free Will, against Anti-Christ, Non-Residents, human Inventions in God's Worship; all which are generally withheld from the people's knowledge, because not relishing to the bishops.

3. The encouragement of ministers to despise the temporal magistracy, the nobles and gentry of the land, to abuse the subjects and live contentiously with their neighbours, knowing that they, being the bishops' creatures, shall be supported.

4. The restraint of many godly and able men from the ministry, and thrusting out of many congregations their faithful, diligent and powerful ministers, who lived peaceably with them, and did them good, only because they cannot in conscience submit to and maintain the bishops' needless devices; nay, sometimes for no other cause but for their zeal in preaching or great auditories.

*　　*　　*　　*　　*　　*

6. The great increase of idle, lewd and dissolute, ignorant and erroneous men in the ministry, which swarm like the locusts of Egypt over the whole kingdom, and will they but wear a canonical cap, a surplice, a hood, bow at the name of Jesus, and be zealous of superstitious ceremonies, they may live as they list, confront whom they please, preach

and vent what errors they will, and neglect preaching at their pleasures without control.

* * * * * *

9. The hindering of godly books to be printed, the blotting out or perverting those which they suffer, all or most of that which strikes either at Popery or Arminianism, the adding of what or where pleaseth them, and the restraint of reprinting books formerly licensed, without relicensing.

* * * * * *

11. The growth of Popery and increase of Papists, priests and Jesuits in sundry places, but especially about London since the Reformation; the frequent venting of crucifixes and Popish pictures both engraved and printed, and the placing of such in Bibles.

* * * * * *

13. Moreover, the offices and jurisdictions of archbishops, lord-bishops, deans, archdeacons, being the same way of Church government which is in the Romish Church, and which was in England in the time of Popery, little change thereof being made (except only the head from whence it was derived), the same arguments supporting the Pope which do uphold the prelates, and overthrowing the prelates which do pull down the Pope; and other Reformed Churches having, upon their rejection of the Pope, cast the prelates out also, as members of the Beast; hence it is that the prelates here in England, by themselves or their disciples, plead and maintain that the Pope is not Anti-Christ, and that the Church of Rome is a true Church, hath not erred in fundamental points, and that salvation is attainable in that religion, and therefore have restrained to pray for the conversion of our Sovereign Lady the Queen. Hence also hath come:

14. The great conformity and likeness both continued and increased of our Church to the Church of Rome, in vestures, postures, ceremonies and administrations, namely as bishops' rotchets and the lawn-sleeves, the four-cornered cap, the cope and surplice, the tippet, the hood and the canonical coat, the pulpits clothed, especially now of late, with the Jesuits' badge upon them every way.

15. The standing up at *Gloria Patri*, and at the reading of the Gospel, praying towards the east, bowing at the name of Jesus, the bowing to the altar towards the east, cross in baptism, the kneeling at the Communion.

16. The turning of the Communion Table altar-wise, setting images, crucifixes and conceits over them, and tapers and books upon them, and bowing or adoring to, or before them,...which is a plain device to usher in the Mass.

* * * * * *

19. The multitude of canons formerly made, wherein among other things excommunication, *ipso facto*, is denounced for speaking of a word against the devices above said, or subscription thereunto, though no law enjoined a restraint from the ministry without subscription, and appeal is denied to any that should refuse subscription or unlawful conformity, though he be never so much wronged by the inferior judges. Also the canons made in the late sacred synod, as they call it, wherein are many strange and dangerous devices to undermine the Gospel, and the subjects' liberties, to propagate Popery, to spoil God's People, ensnare ministers and other students, and so to draw all into an absolute subjection and thraldom to them and their government, spoiling both the King and the Parliament of their power.

20. The countenancing plurality of benefices, prohibiting of marriages without their licence, at certain times almost half the year, and licensing of marriages without banns asking.

21. Profanation of the Lord's Day, pleading for it, and enjoining ministers to read a declaration set forth (as 'tis thought) by their procurement for tolerating of sports upon that day, suspending and depriving many godly ministers for not reading the same, only out of conscience, because it was against the Law of God so to do, and no law of the land to enjoin it.

* * * * * *

25. ...The pride and ambition of the prelates being boundless, unwilling to be subject either to man or laws, they claim their office and jurisdiction to be *jure divino*, exercise ecclesiastical authority in their own names and rights, and under their own seals, and take upon them temporal dignities, places and offices in the Commonwealth, that they may sway both Swords.

26. Whence follows the taking commissions in their own courts and consistories, and where else they sit, in matters determinable of right at Common Law, the putting of ministers upon parishes without the patron's and people's consent.

* * * * * *

28. The exercising of the oath *ex officio*, and other proceedings by way of Inquisition, reaching even to men's thoughts, the apprehending and detaining of men by pursuivants, the frequent suspending and depriving of ministers, fining and imprisoning of all sorts of people, breaking up of men's houses and studies,... and the doing of many other outrages, to the utter infringing of the laws of the realm and the subjects' liberties, and ruining of them and their families; and of later time the judges of the land are so awed with the power and greatness of the prelates, and other ways promoted, that neither prohibition, *habeas corpus*, nor any other lawful remedy can be had, or take place, for the distressed subjects in most cases; only Papists, Jesuits, priests and such others as propagate Popery or Arminianism, are countenanced, spared, and have much liberty; and from hence followed amongst others these dangerous consequences:

First, The general hope and expectation of the Romish party, that their superstitious religion will ere long be fully planted in this kingdom again, and so they are encouraged to persist therein, and to practice the same openly in divers places, to the high dishonour of God, and contrary to the laws of the realm.

2. The discouragement and destruction of all good subjects, of whom are multitudes, both clothiers, merchants and others, who being deprived of their ministers and overburdened with these pressures have departed the kingdom, to Holland and other parts, and have drawn with them a great manufacture of cloth, and trading, out of the land into other places where they reside, whereby wool, the great staple of the kingdom, is become of small value, and vends not, trading is decayed, many poor people want work, seamen lose employment and the whole land is much impoverished, to the great dishonour of this kingdom, and blemishment to the government thereof.

3. The present wars and commotions happened between his Majesty and his subjects of Scotland, wherein his Majesty and all his kingdoms are endangered, and suffer greatly, and are like to become a prey to the common enemy, in case the wars go on, which we exceedingly fear will not only go on, but also increase, to an utter ruin of all, unless the prelates with their dependencies be removed out of England, and also they and their practises, who, as we under your Honours' favours do verily believe and conceive, have occasioned the quarrel.

All which we humbly refer to the consideration of this Honourable Assembly, desiring the Lord of Heaven to direct you in the right way to redress all these evils.

Rushworth, v, 93–6

III. HIGH COMMISSION[1]

In the first ten years of James I's reign the High Commission met the most serious attack of its career to date. The evolution of an *ad hoc* commission for the enforcement of clerical discipline into a regular court, not only the highest court of first instance in the Church but also a court of appeal, had not gone unchallenged. But in Caudry's case, in 1592, the Common Law judges had ruled that it was a valid court.[2] However, the renewed attempt to impose conformity on the clergy after 1604 brought a reaction, and Puritan ministers and patrons of livings appealed increasingly to the Court of Common Pleas to transfer cases to its own list, or even re-try cases in which the Commission had given its verdict. Whether the judges were activated by religious prejudice or not, they were now much more willing to issue writs of prohibition, ordering a case before them to determine whether it appertained to the lay or the clerical jurisdiction, and their final verdict was rarely in favour of the commissioners. The king was unwilling to force the judges, who had proved quite amenable when it was a question of enforcing the canons of 1604,[3] and it is probable that many of his advisers, like Elizabeth's advisers, were resentful of the bishops and suspicious of the High Commission. Certainly its enemies found plenty to criticise in the letters patent under which it operated, which were so loosely phrased as to give it jurisdiction over almost any crime and the right to award any punishment short of death.[4] It seemed evident that its scope should be limited to the offences enumerated in section VIII of the Act of Supremacy,[5] and to the punishments awarded by the other ecclesiastical courts (that is, excommunication, deprivation and penance). These objections were not yet precisely formulated, but the attitude of the judges so alarmed Bancroft that in 1605 he drew up twenty-five leading questions on the relations of the lay and clerical jurisdiction, which he asked the king to submit to the judges.[6] The judges replied at length to the *Articuli Cleri*, rebutting with vigour the charge that prohibitions could not be issued against the spiritual courts, that they were obliged under oath to defend the royal supremacy, and that their use of prohibitions was undermining the authority of the Crown. The only result seems to have been a hardening in the attitude of the Common Law judges, who had now been forced to define their position.

---

[1] Usher's *Rise and Fall of High Commission* is still the only complete study, but see Babbage, *Puritanism and Richard Bancroft*, ch. 9, and, for its work under Elizabeth, Elton, *Tudor Constitution* pp. 217 ff.

[2] Elton, *op. cit.* pp. 226–7.

[3] Babbage, *op. cit.* pp. 120–3.

[4] The commission of 1559 is printed by Elton, *op. cit.* pp. 221–5, and those of 1562, 1572, 1576 and 1601, in *PCD*, pp. 232–41.

[5] Elton, *op. cit.* p. 365.

[6] See *TCD*, pp. 177 ff.

The following year the House of Commons took up the attack, emboldened, no doubt, by this obvious division between the king's ecclesiastical and judicial officers. Its criticism was particularly directed at the *ex officio* oath, which obliged the accused to answer questions of which he had no prior warning. The oath itself was used by Star Chamber without provoking any significant opposition; the difference was that in Star Chamber a man usually had a copy of the indictment, or a precise knowledge of the crimes with which he was charged, and he was not usually cross-examined on his beliefs, religious or political. In view of this agitation, during the summer recess in 1606 the Privy Council asked the Chief Justices of King's Bench and Common Pleas in what circumstances such an oath could legally be tendered. Coke and Popham replied that the accused must be provided with a list of the heads under which he was to be examined, and that even then no layman could be cross-examined on matters of theology and personal belief.[1] It was probably something more than a coincidence that in December of that year the Commons passed a bill to make the *ex officio* oath illegal; and in June 1607 the advocate Nicholas Fuller introduced another bill to restrict High Commission to the powers granted it under the Act of Supremacy.[2] Fuller had already criticised the Commission in public in Westminster Hall, and as soon as Parliament rose he was imprisoned for contempt. King's Bench responded to his appeal for a writ of prohibition, but the Commission avoided a head-on conflict by altering the charge from contempt to schism.[3] All the same, the judges gave their opinion that the interpretation of the Act of Supremacy, and therefore the Commission's powers, lay with them.[4] Coke then went on to argue, by a strained interpretation of the statute, that the Commission had power only over 'enormous' crimes, the importance of this being that it removed from its orbit such questions as tithe and alimony.

At Bancroft's suggestion the king now intervened, on the grounds that since he was supreme judge under God he could arbitrate between rival jurisdictions (50). Coke rejected this claim, and in the next two years Common Pleas issued writs of prohibition with such frequency and lack of scruple as to threaten the very existence of the High Commission.[5] The

---

[1] *Coke's Reports*, pt XII, 26 (vi, 227–8). Usher (*op. cit.* p. 169) questions the authenticity of this report, but it is accepted by Mary H. Maguire, 'The Attack of the Common Lawyers on the Oath *ex officio*', pp. 221–2. After all, Coke was only recommending the adoption of standard Star Chamber procedure, and the *ex officio* oath had always been the weakest point in the High Commission's defence. It had been sharply criticised by Burleigh (Tanner, *Tudor Constitutional Documents*, pp. 373 ff.), and it is not unreasonable to suppose that his son Salisbury, and others on James's Council, shared his dislike.

[2] Bowyer, *Diary*, pp. 344–9 (23 June 1607); *House of Lords Manuscripts*, XI, 3305.

[3] Maguire, *op. cit.* pp. 224 ff.

[4] *Coke's Reports*, pt XII, 41–5 (vi, 250–4); Usher, *Reconstruction*, bk 3, ch. v.

[5] And the Council of the North and the Council of the Marches and Wales. But since Bancroft was the most influential spokesman with the king he usually took these other courts under his protection.

judges, referring again to the Act of Supremacy, denied the right of the Commission to imprison, and they rejected the canons of 1604 in so far as they conflicted with Common Law or statute.[1] A number of conferences between the king, the judges and Council brought no solution, and early in 1610 James imposed a truce.[2] This was largely ineffective, and did not bind the House of Commons, which produced another bill to abolish the *ex officio* oath in 1610,[3] and sharply criticised its use in their Petition on Religion.[4] Moreover, there was now considerable doubt as to whether the Commission could imprison, and this was a crucial point, for if the accused refused to take the oath he could only be imprisoned for contumacy, and until he submitted the process came to a standstill.

Finally the government gave way, and the new Letters Patent issued in 1611 (51) exactly defined the crimes on which the Commission should adjudicate and gave it power to imprison and use the *ex officio* oath. Coke at first refused to sit, but the other judges complied, and the death of Bancroft in 1611, followed by Coke's dismissal in 1616, seems to have taken much of the bitterness out of the controversy. But the objections of the judges had been answered only by a manifest illegality; there was no doubt that the Crown could appoint commissions for ecclesiastical causes, but there was considerable legitimate doubt as to whether it could create a court of law by letters patent, which is in effect what it did in 1611.[5] When its time came in 1641 it had no legal case whatsoever.

By 1641 the High Commission was thoroughly unpopular, but the general impression, then and later, that it was a key weapon in Laud's offensive against the Puritans, is incorrect. It proceeded against non-conforming clergymen, and against sectaries (who were as odious to middle-class Puritans as anybody), but this did not comprise a large proportion of its business, nor was it the most notable. The most notorious cases in Laud's drive for conformity—the prosecution of Leighton, Prynne, Bastwick, the lay feoffees, and so on—were heard in Star Chamber. Between 1611 and 1640 80% of the cases before the commission were brought by private litigants, many of whom were seeking to remove drunken, immoral or eccentric clergymen, and of the remaining 20% only a quarter were initiated by the commissioners.[6] Some of these were of a trifling nature, too; when Laud was bishop of London he haled an unfortunate peasant before the High Commission for pissing in St Paul's.[7] However, it should be noticed that by the 1630's a

---

[1] No. 29b, p. 95 above.
[2] Usher, *Reconstruction*, bk 3, ch. x.
[3] *House of Lords Manuscripts*, XI, 3315.
[4] No. 40, p. 142 above.
[5] Usher, *High Commission*, pp. 254–5.
[6] See Usher, *High Commission*, ch. XII, and particularly the table on p. 279. The minute book of the Commission for February 1634 through February 1636 is P.R.O., S.P. 9/261; summarised in *CSPD*.
[7] Gardiner, *Cases in Star Chamber*, pp. 380, 298. See also the case of the men arraigned for christening a cat, *ibid.* p. 275.

high proportion of its business could loosely be described as 'matrimonial'. The trial of matrimonial offences and the imposition of alimony was the business of the church courts, but with the feeble means of coercion at their command they had usually failed to enforce their judgements, especially amongst the upper classes. In 1613, to ease the strain on the Privy Council, which was besieged by injured husbands and starving wives, the High Commission was called in. With the power to fine and imprison it reduced many delinquent spouses to order, and the successful prosecution of Sir Giles Allington for incest and Viscountess Purbeck for adultery showed that wealthy and well-born offenders no longer enjoyed the right to order their private lives as they wished, irrespective of the laws of God and the Church.[1] To some this must have been a profound shock.

But the opposition to the High Commission was just part of the general opposition to divines exercising jurisdiction at all. So general was the belief that the bishops had no power to hold courts in their own name that in 1637 Laud asked Charles to consult the judges and publish their reply, which was, of course, favourable.[2] But a much greater menace was the persistent refusal of many offenders, like the Newington sectaries (52), to take the oath *ex officio* at all. They purged their contempt in prison, of course, but in the meanwhile the commission was unable to proceed. Finally in 1638 Charles published an extraordinary letter to the commissioners, authorising them 'of our own mere motion and knowledge, and by our supreme power ecclesiastical' to proceed against those who refused to take the oath as though they had confessed to the crimes of which they stood accused—the procedure *ore tenus*.[3]

The judges clearly never authorised this patent illegality. In a decade when the judges were regarded as mere tools of despotism, and the influence of the hierarchy is supposed to have been all-pervading and omnipotent, the successors of Coke continued his policy of obstruction as best they could, in the inferior church courts. In 1640 the Dean of Arches, Sir John Lambe, complained bitterly to Laud that the Common Law courts were encroaching on his jurisdiction as unscrupulously as ever:

> They will adjudge incest to be lawful matrimony, as that I may marry my wife's sister, which they will take upon themselves not to be in the Levitical law forbidden....The statute saith that nothing shall be held heresy unless [it is] against the express Scripture or the first four General Councils, [and they claim] they are judges and interpreters of statutes, and so must judge what is against the Word of God and the four first Councils.[4]

[1] Gardiner, *History of England*, vii, 251, viii, 145. For the Commission of 1613, see *PCD* pp. 431–2.　　[2] *Foedera*, xx, 168–9 (18 August 1637).　　[3] *Ibid.* pp. 190–1 (4 February 1638).
[4] *CSPD 1640–1641*, p. 348. Cf. *ibid. 1639–1640*, pp. 350–51.

The truth is, seventeenth-century Englishmen were reluctant to admit that priests were capable of interpreting any law, even the Law of God, and the High Commission perished in 1641 in a wave of hostility against all ecclesiastical jurisdiction.[1]

50. Prohibitions del Roy, Michaelmas 5 Jac. I. [1607]

Note, upon Sunday the 10th of November in this same term the King, upon complaint made to him by Bancroft, archbishop of Canterbury, concerning prohibitions, the King was informed that when the question was made of what matters the ecclesiastical judges have cognisance, either upon the exposition of the statute concerning tithes, or any other thing ecclesiastical, or upon the statute 1 Eliz. concerning the High Commission, or in any other case in which there is not express authority in law, the King himself may decide it in his royal person, and that the judges are but the delegates of the King, and that the King may take what causes he shall please to determine from the determination of the judges, and may determine them himself. And the archbishop said that this was clear in divinity, that such authority belongs to the King by the word of God in the Scripture.

To which it was answered by me, in the presence and with the clear consent of all the judges of England and barons of the exchequer, that the King in his own person cannot adjudge any case, either criminal (as treason, felony, &c.) or betwixt party and party, concerning his inheritance, chattels or goods, &c., but this ought to be determined and adjudged in some court of justice according to the law and custom of England. And always judgements are given, *ideo consideratum est per curiam*, so that the court gives the judgement; and the King hath his court, viz., in the Upper House of Parliament, in which he with his Lords is the supreme judge over all other judges; for if error be in the Common Pleas, that may be reversed in the King's Bench; and if the Court of King's Bench err, that may be reversed in the Upper House of Parliament, by the King with the assent of the Lords spiritual and temporal, without the Commons, and in this respect the King is called the Chief Justice. . . . And it appears in our books that the King may sit

---

[1] We have dealt with the High Commission for the province of Canterbury, but the Crown could and did establish others. Thus there was a High Commission at York, whose extensive records have never been fully investigated, and another at Durham. See R. A. Marchant, *The Puritans and the Church Courts in the diocese of York, 1560–1642* (1960), and *The Acts of the High Commission Court for the Diocese of Durham*, ed. W. H. D. Longstaffe (Surtees Society, 1858).

in the Star Chamber, but this was to consult with the justices upon certain questions proposed to them, and not *in judicio*; so in the King's Bench he may sit, but the court gives the judgement, and it is commonly said in our books that the King is always present in court in the judgement of law, and upon this he cannot be nonsuit[ed]; but the judgements are always given *per curiam* and the judges are sworn to execute justice according to law and the custom of England....And the judges informed the King that no king after the Conquest assumed to himself to give any judgement in any cause whatsoever which concerned the administration of justice within this realm, but these were solely determined in the courts of justice..., and it was greatly marvelled that the archbishop durst inform the King that such absolute power and authority, as is aforesaid, belonged to the King by the word of God....

Then the King said, that he thought the law was founded upon reason, and that he and others had reason, as well as the judges. To which it was answered by me, that true it was that God had endowed his Majesty with excellent science and great endowments of nature, but his Majesty was not learned in the laws of his realm of England, and causes which concern the life, or inheritance, or goods, or fortunes of his subjects are not to be decided by natural reason but by the artificial reason and judgement of law, which law is an act which requires long study and experience before that a man can attain to the cognisance of it, and that the law was the golden mete-wand and measure to try the causes of the subjects, and which protected his Majesty in safety and peace. With which the King was greatly offended, and said, that then he should be under the law, which [it] was treason to affirm, as he said. To which I said, that Bracton saith, *quod rex non debet esse sub homine, sed sub Deo et lege.*

Coke, Reports, VI, 280–2 (pt XII, 63–5)

51. The High Commission, 29 August 1611

James, by the Grace of God...[etc.], to the most reverend father our right and trusty and right well-beloved councillor, George, lord archbishop of Canterbury,...[and 89 others], greeting.

[1.] Whereas at the parliament holden at Westminster in the first year of the reign of our dear sister Elizabeth late Queen of England one Act was made amongst others entitled, An Act restoring to the Crown the ancient jurisdiction over the state ecclesiastical...,[1] by the express

---

[1] Act of Supremacy, 1559; Elton, *Tudor Constitution*, pp. 363–7.

words of which said Act, authorising our said dear sister, her heirs and successors, to grant such commissions when and as often and for such and so long time as should be thought meet and convenient, it appeareth that the said parliament purposed plainly...that such commissions... might be accommodated to the accidents and varieties of times and occasions; we have now thought good, for divers weighty causes, and out of our princely care and desire to ease and content our loving subjects as far as may stand with good government and justice, by the advice of our Privy Council to grant forth our commissions in manner and form following.

[2.] Know ye therefore that we for sundry good, weighty, and necessary causes and considerations us thereunto especially moving, of our own mere motion and certain knowledge, by force and virtue of our supreme authority and prerogative royal and of the said Act, do by these our letters patent under our Great Seal of England give and grant full, free and lawful power and authority unto you the said...[commissioners]...to inquire as well by examination of witnesses or presentments as also by examination of the parties accused themselves upon their oath...of all and singular apostacies, heresies, great errors in matters of faith and religion, schisms, unlawful conventicles tending to schisms against the religion or government of the Church now established, and also of all other persons which have or shall refuse to have their children baptised, or which have or shall administer or procure or willingly suffer the sacrament of baptism to be administered by any Jesuit, seminary or other popish priest, or which have or shall celebrate the mass or procure the same to be celebrated, or willingly hear or be present at the same, and of their said offences, and also of all blasphemous and impious acts and speeches, scandalous books, libels and writings against the doctrine of religion, the Book of Common Prayer, or ecclesiastical state or government now established in the Church of England, or against any archbishop or bishop touching any offence or crime of ecclesiastical cognisance, profanation of the sacraments of baptism and the Lord's Supper and of all other things and places consecrated or dedicated to divine service, wilful and unlawful digging up of buried bodies in any church or chapel or churchyard, violent and wilful disturbances and interruptions of divine service or sermons in any church, chapel or public preaching place, violent and wilful laying of hands upon the person of any archbishop or bishop, simonies, incests, infamous and notorious adulteries, and also of all corruptions, contempts and abuses in any ecclesiastical judges, officers or their deputies or clerks or other ministers whatsoever belonging to any ecclesiastical courts or attending or...employed in or by the same, committed...within these our realms....

* * * * * *

[4.] And also we...give...authority unto you...[etc.] to search for, apprehend and imprison...all and singular Jesuits, seminaries and other Popish priests, obstinate and dangerous Popish recusants suspected of practice against the state, and sectaries, and likewise all and every such person which shall send or convey, or cause to be sent or conveyed, any children of their own or of any others or any persons whatsoever into the parts beyond the seas, to be there kept, taught or brought up in the Romish religion, either in any school or seminary or in any other place whatsoever, and also all such as shall send and convey...any money or other things towards the relief or maintenance of any such child or children, or of the said seminaries or schools themselves, or any persons living or abiding in the same, and to proceed against and punish them in manner and form hereafter following, or otherwise to deliver them over to our temporal courts, judges and justices as their several cases shall require.

[5.] And also we...do give...authority unto you...to inquire and search for...all heretical, schismatical and seditious books, libels and writings, and all makers, devisers, printers and wilful dispersers of any such...books...[etc.], and their procurers, counsellors and abettors, and the same books...[etc.] and the printing presses themselves likewise to seize, and also to take, apprehend and imprison...the offenders in that behalf.

[6.] And we do further give...authority unto you...to send your letters missive to or for any person which shall be charged, accused or upon notorious fame suspected to have offended in any of the premises, thereby willing, requiring and commanding them to appear before you ...at a day and place certain to answer thereunto; and where you... shall find it necessary in any of the cases aforesaid only we give you... authority, by our messengers or pursuivants or by attachment to be directed to the sheriff to whom the execution in that behalf shall appertain, to cause such person so charged...to be arrested...and kept in safe custody till he shall be brought before you....

* * * * * *

[10.] And we do also give full power and authority unto you...to call before you...all and every offender and offenders in any of the premisses and also all such as shall be charged, accused or upon notorious fame suspected to have offended in any of the premisses and every of them, to examine [them] upon their corporal oaths touching every or any of the premisses which you shall object against them, in case it do first appear that the parties unto which the said oath shall be so ministered are thereof detected either by examination of witnesses or by presentments or by public or notorious fame or by information of the Ordinary where the offence was committed. And if any person or persons shall refuse to take the said oath in the cases aforesaid or having taken the oath shall refuse to answer upon their oath directly and fully unto the articles and matters objected against them..., then it shall and will be lawful to and for you...to apprehend...such persons...and to commit them to prison, there to remain...until they have taken the said oath and made full and direct answer respectively unto the said articles....

* * * * * *

[13.] And if you...shall find by confession of the party or other sufficient proof any person to have offended in the premisses,...or refusing to obey or perform your orders, decrees and commandments in anything touching the premisses, that then you...shall have full power and authority...to punish the same person so offending by censures ecclesiastical or by reasonable fine or imprisonment according to the quality and quantity of their offence, or by all or any the said means according to your discretions.

* * * * * *

[24.] Provided always...that no sentence definitive of any cause or matter determinable by virtue of this commission shall hereafter be given without the personal presence, hearing and full assent of five or more of you, whereof...[the archbishop of Canterbury, the Lord Chancellor, Lord Treasurer, Lord Privy Seal, the bishops of London, Winchester, Exeter, Lichfield, Chichester, Rochester or Gloucester, and five other named persons] to be one, anything before in these presents contained to the contrary in anywise notwithstanding.

* * * * * *

[26.] And our will and pleasure is, and we do hereby signify and declare unto you our said commissioners and to all other our loving subjects, that it shall be lawful for any persons that shall hereafter be sentenced by you by virtue of this our commission which shall find themselves grieved by reason of any such sentence, to become suitors unto us by way of supplication as of our grace to have a commission of review to be granted by us for the re-examination of their cause.

* * * * * *

P.R.O. Patent Roll, 9 Jac. I.

52. The Newington Sectaries: High Commission, 14 June 1632

Rawlins, Harvy, Arthur Goslin, Howland, Robert Bye, John Smith and others were taken at a conventicle in a wood near Newington, in Surrey, upon the Sabbath day last, and being now brought to the court they were required to take their oaths to answer the articles put in against them. Two of them answer[ed] they will not swear at this time, and as they were going out Harvy put on his hat, which was presently taken off and he was complained on, and being called back to answer it, he said he was shifting away, and put on his hat. Another saith that a lawful magistrate had examined them already, and therefore he will not swear to be here examined.

[*The bishop of*] *London* [Laud]: 'Your examinations taken before Sir [blank] he sent to me; there is nothing in it but that you met together to confer upon the word of God as far as you understand the same, and to pray, which you might answer here. But you tell this court that it is not a lawful power and authority, and of the same mind are those that were taken at Blackfriars, for they petitioned the King to be tried by his judges, by his lords, declining the ecclesiastical jurisdiction. This they tendered the last Sunday. This your obstinacy will cause you to be proceeded against at the Common Law, and be made [to] abjure the kingdom, and if you return, be hanged.'

[*The*] *King's Advocate* speaketh to another of them: 'You are required to take your oath to answer the articles put in against you.'

Prisoner: 'I cannot swear, because I know them not in certainty....'

Andrew Sherle will not lay his hand upon the book.

Robert Bye coming into the court, the *bishop of London* spoke kindly to him, saying: 'Come, thou lookest like a good fellow, that will take thy oath.' *Bye*: 'I am Christ's freeman; I owe obedience to God and the King, and those that are lawfully sent by him, but to no others.' At which there being some laughter, he said: 'I am indeed in good earnest, I dare not take this oath. An oath is for the ending of a controversy, but this is made to be but the beginning of the controversy.'

[*The*] *archbishop of Canterbury*: 'You do show yourselves the most ungrateful to God and to his Majesty the King and to us the fathers of the Church. If you have any knowledge of God, it hath come through and by us, or some of our predecessors. We have taken care, under God, to give milk to the babes and younglings and strong meat for the men of understanding; you have the word of God to feed you, the Sacraments to strengthen you, and we support you by prayer. For all this what despite do you return us? You call us abominable men, to be hated of all, that we carry the mark of the Beast, that we are his members. We do bear this patiently, not because we have no law to right us, but because of your obstinacy. But for your dishonouring of God and disobeying the King, it is not to be endured. When you have reading, preaching, singing, teaching, you are your own ministers; the blind lead the blind. Whereas his Majesty is God's vice-regent in the Church, the Church is nothing with you, and his ministers not to be regarded, and you run into woods as if you lived in persecution. Such a one you make the King, to whom we are so much bound for his great care for the truth to be preserved among us; and you would have men believe he is a tyrant—this besides your wickedness, unthankfulness and ungraciousness towards us, the fathers of the Church. Therefore let these men be put two and two in several prisons.'

Gardiner, Cases in Star Chamber, pp. 308–10

BOOK II

THE ERA OF EXPERIMENT
1640–1660

Men go away, but constitutions never fall.

GEORGE DOWNING

CHAPTER 5

THE BREAKDOWN, 1640–1642

Unable to suppress the Scots revolt, Charles I summoned a parliament for 13 April 1640. The initiative in the Commons fell to John Pym, who was well prepared.[1] On 17 April he delivered a long speech in which he took up the petitions from each county laid on the table of the House, and transformed these complaints of local grievances into a national indictment of the king's advisers (53). Some Members demanded the impeachment of ministers, but Pym was not ready for that; first it was necessary to repair the dreadful damage done by Eliot in 1629, particularly to the relations between the two Houses, and he ended by calling upon the Commons to consult with the Lords on how best their grievances could be remedied. Strafford and the king made a direct appeal to the Lords at the same time, asking them to put supply before the satisfaction of grievances, reversing the traditional order. The Commons then launched a bitter attack on the military charges levied on many counties to defray the expenses of the army, and on the news that they were preparing a petition asking the king to seek terms with the Scots, Strafford advised an immediate dissolution, on 5 May.

Charles's persistence with the Scottish war that summer, Strafford's negotiations with Spain, the implied threat that the Commons leaders might be arraigned as traitors for conspiring with the Scots; all this changed Pym's attitude. Moreover, when Charles summoned another parliament for 3 November his position was even weaker than in April; his campaign had failed, at York he had been met by the active resistance of the nobility, and the Treaty of Ripon now obliged him to pay the Scots £25,000 a month pending a full settlement of their claims. On the other hand, he had numerous opportunities of making mischief. The English army remained, and there was every prospect of help from abroad; from Spain, from the queen's French relatives, or from Holland. Negotiations were soon opened with the Stadtholder Frederick Henry which eventually led to the betrothal of his eldest son, William, to Charles's elder daughter, Mary, on 10 February.

The king's attitude provoked the leaders of the Opposition to raise their demands, and by the time the Long Parliament met they had clearly decided to remove the king's ministers, beginning with Strafford, and change his

---

[1] On the dissolution Pym's house was searched, and he 'had a trunkful of papers, written books and journals of Parliament taken from him, there being some arguments of the ecclesiastical jurisdiction of bishops, how far their power extends, and some other things of the proceedings in Parliament' (CSPD, 1640, p. 153).

methods of rule as well as his policy. The convention that the king could do no wrong encouraged the belief in a Catholic plot engineered by his advisers, and this rapidly became a test of Opposition orthodoxy and, indirectly, a programme of action. The majority of the Commons were still concerned with the settlement of their own grievances,[1] but their leaders now had more ambitious plans—to make Parliament a permanent part of the constitution with a voice in the appointment of the king's servants. In this respect a comparison between the speech Pym delivered on 17 April 1640 and his speech of 7 November (54) is instructive.

In November grievances, which had been the body of his previous speech, were simply swept aside; there was no time to draft statutes now, when the safety of the nation hung in the balance; simple resolutions would suffice. The core of his speech was an examination of the great Catholic conspiracy to alter religion and government, in which the king's chief ministers and the Anglican hierarchy were implicated, and which had already gone so far that swift action was necessary to frustrate it. This thesis was elaborated in the Grand Remonstrance, a year later (64), but it was not developed. In April Laud's ecclesiastical policy had been an attempt to reintroduce 'those superstitious and infirm ceremonies which accompanied the most decrepit age of Popery'; something mistaken, wrongheaded, even mischievous, but without an ulterior motive. But by November it was clear to Pym that the hierarchy were working for reunion with Rome, as part of a plan for the subversion of the State as well as the Church. Therefore he now moved for 'a settled committee to find out the danger the king and kingdom is in'.

A Committee on the State of the Kingdom was appointed on 10 November, and the next day Pym impeached the earl of Strafford of high treason. From then until the following spring Strafford and his accusers were locked in a struggle which was vital to both; for if the Commons could not destroy one of the most unpopular men in England they could destroy no one, and if Strafford went free he would be a focus for royalist reaction and perhaps even the establishment of non-parliamentary government. Pym himself opened the preliminary charges against the earl, on 25 November, and argued that an attempt to sow discord between king and people was treason. His speech was reminiscent of many of Strafford's own ideas (55a). In January the Articles of Impeachment propounded another novel idea, of cumulative treason; the commission of a series of acts, none of them in themselves treasonable, but amounting to treason in the whole (55b). In a brilliant and moving speech before the Lords in April Strafford rebutted these ideas (55c), and he was answered by Pym in a speech equally brilliant and much

---

[1] The best account of Members' feelings is in the introduction to Mary F. Keeler, *The Long Parliament*.

more intellectual, in which he once again summed up his views on the seventeenth-century constitution (55 d). The tragedy is that the ideas of these two great men were almost identical. After this it is an anti-climax to record that Strafford was finally disposed of in May 1641 by act of attainder.

So there were always two processes at work in the Long Parliament during this first session: the punishment of the guilty men, principally Strafford, and the passing of reform statutes. During the first few months, the first task was easily the most demanding, as appears from the number of Commons committees engaged in it (56)—as Notestein remarks: 'The work of first importance was to be the attack on particular men; other select committees were to be retained only if they aided in that work.'[1] Ecclesiastical questions were swept aside for the time being, not entirely by accident, and though several committees were set to work drafting reform statutes Pym was unwilling to give them priority until Strafford had been destroyed. Meanwhile he played upon the public's fears by means familiar enough to Edward Hyde, later earl of Clarendon, but then one of Pym's lieutenants (57), and in the queen's relations with officers of the English army, the king's negotiations with Holland, his persistent refusal to disband the Irish army, and the continued clemency shown to Catholic priests, he had plenty of ammunition. On May 3 the Commons issued a protestation of support for the Protestant religion which was at once distributed in the provinces for signature; it was intended to rally popular support behind them and stampede the House of Lords (60).

Stripped of his few feeble advisers, the king was adrift; he refused to come to terms with the Opposition leaders (though he did appoint Oliver St John solicitor-general), and he declined to come forward as the leader of the moderates against the radical leadership of Pym and Hampden (58). On 15 January 1641 he announced that henceforth judges would hold office during good behaviour, not during pleasure, but five days later his hand was forced when the first reform statute, the bill for triennial parliaments, was sent up to the Lords. On 25 January, in a speech to both Houses, he agreed to cancel all innovations in Church and State, reform the courts of law, and strip the bishops of their temporal authority outside Parliament; but he warned them that he would never consent to the exclusion of the bishops from the House of Lords, nor would he consent to the Triennial Bill, which he characterised as a direct encroachment on his prerogative.[2] However, the Triennial Bill, which would oblige him to meet parliament every three years for a session of fifty days (59), passed the Lords, and such was the public agitation in the City and at Westminster that on 16 February he gave way. Naturally, this convinced the Opposition leaders that however inflexible Charles might appear he could be induced to agree to anything under pressure. When the

---

[1] *D'Ewes Journal*, ed. Notestein, p. 243, n. 5.   [2] No. 8, p. 19 above.

impeachment of Strafford broke down they rushed through a bill of attainder, and to prevent a snap dissolution they brought forward a revolutionary bill prohibiting the adjournment, prorogation or dissolution of the present parliament without its own consent.[1] Charles gave his assent to both on 10 May.

With Strafford dead and the king firmly tied to Parliament, the Opposition had secured the conditions necessary for the nation's safety and their own survival. The great Popish Plot had been scotched for the time being, and parliament could turn to reform and redress of grievances. In June, July and August 1641 a whole series of statutes was passed to this end. The Tunnage and Poundage Act gave Charles the ancient customs, plus all the impositions which were being levied when parliament met, but for two months only; it was subsequently renewed at two-monthly intervals up to July 1642.[2] The Court of Star Chamber was abolished on a number of flimsy and unhistorical excuses (61), and with it went the Council of the Marches and Wales and the Council of the North, another statute disposed of the Court of High Commission (62). Finally, the levy of ship-money was declared illegal,[3] the limits of the royal forest were defined once and for all,[4] and the exaction of fines in distraint of knighthood was prohibited.[5] The Court of Requests, moribund for some years, was pardonably overlooked, and so was the Court of Wards, more surprisingly. A bill to abolish another old grievance, purveyance, was in progress at the end of the session, but it was abandoned in the subsequent crisis; all that survived was an act to restrict the activities of the Clerk of the Market.[6] Wardship was abolished by an ordinance in 1646, confirmed by Cromwell ten years later and by the Cavalier Parliament in 1661.[7] These reform statutes were never repealed; in fact, they were the basis of the Restoration Settlement. In a sense, from August 1641 until May 1660 the constitution just marked time.

The events of May 1641 left each side deeply mistrustful of the other. The Triennial Act was not a crucial measure; it did not come into operation until the next parliament, and the machinery for enforcing it would almost certainly have broken down in practice. But the act which prevented the king from dissolving, proroguing or even adjourning the present parliament was a direct invasion of the prerogative which alarmed him as much as it angered him. The belief to which he had given expression as early as 1629— that the Commons would not be content with rectifying what they termed

[1] GCD, p. 158.
[2] 17 Car. I, c. 8, printed GCD, p. 159.
[3] 17 Car. I, c. 14, ibid. p. 189.
[4] 17 Car. I, c. 16, ibid. p. 192.
[5] 17 Car. I, c. 20, ibid. p. 196.
[6] 17 Car. I, c. 19. Purveyance was suspended by order of Parliament in December 1642 and abolished by ordinance in 1657; G. E. Aylmer, 'The Last Years of Purveyance, 1610-60', Economic History Review, x (1957), 84, 90. See p. 361 below.
[7] Firth and Rait, I, 833, II, 1043; 12 Car. II, c. 4. See Bell, Court of Wards, pp. 158 ff.

the abuses of executive power, but would seize that power for themselves; that their aim was 'to erect a universal, over-swaying power to themselves, which belongs only to us, and not to them',[1]—was now confirmed. The death of Strafford, echoing the assassination of Buckingham, merely added emotional overtones to this belief.

On the other side, the Opposition had by now swallowed their own propaganda; they believed that there was indeed a Catholic plot, and the Protestation of 3 May seemed to assume the imminence of civil war (60). Two days later Pym's revelation of the First Army Plot accelerated the passage of Strafford's attainder and the bill to prevent a dissolution; but any good Charles might have done by consenting to both these measures he threw away at once by announcing his imminent departure for Edinburgh. In his public speeches since the crisis began he had been sensible enough to admit the need for reform, but it was not clear who was to implement a reform policy. Clandestine negotiations for the admission of Pym and Hampden to the Privy Council, with offices of responsibility, had already broken down. As Clarendon points out, Charles would not accept such men into his service unless they demonstrated their change of heart in Parliament, but this they could not do without jeopardising their standing in the Commons; yet it was their standing in the Commons that brought them to the king's attention (58). Charles's reluctance to come to terms with the Opposition leaders betrayed the fact that he regarded the present situation as transitory. His only motive in going to Edinburgh could be to seek the aid of the Scots nobility against the Covenanters and their English allies in the Long Parliament.

Consequently, the Opposition came to the conclusion that the reform statutes they had pushed through would eventually be set aside unless they could ensure the appointment of ministers and advisers who would be prepared to abide by them. This issue had only been raised once before, in 1626, and then in a negative way; the Commons had demanded the exclusion from the king's counsels of one man, and even then they had proceeded against him by impeachment. On 24 June 1641 Pym took a long step forward when he submitted to the Lords Ten Propositions governing the king's conduct; of which number three requested the king to commit 'his own business, and the affairs of the kingdom, to such councillors and officers as the Parliament may have cause to confide in', adding that if this were refused they would 'reduce this petition to names of particulars'.[2] Control of the executive had not even been on the Opposition's programme in November 1640; henceforward it was the only serious point at issue between them and the king.

[1] The King's Declaration showing the causes of the late Dissolution, 10 March 1629, GCD, p. 95.   [2] GCD, p. 163.

Charles's ill-judged attempt in Edinburgh to arrest the earl of Argyle and the duke of Hamilton was fresh grist to Pym's mill, and when Parliament reassembled on 20 October after a six-week recess he was able to call up the London trained-bands to guard the precincts of Westminster, a measure which in itself heightened the atmosphere of crisis and revolution. In this atmosphere the arrival of the news of the Irish Rebellion on 1 November confirmed the whole idea of a great Catholic conspiracy, and put Charles's persistent refusal to disband the Irish army in a most sinister light. Worse, it raised in a particularly acute form the question of Charles's suitability to wield executive power. Another large army must now be raised; the king would be its commander-in-chief, and even if he did not lead it in person he and he alone could appoint its generals and commission its officers. In view of the question-mark that hung over Charles's policy for the past two years, if not the past ten, this was unthinkable. Therefore on 5 November Pym proposed an Additional Instruction to the joint parliamentary committee in attendance upon the king at Edinburgh, that they were to inform the king that unless he changed his policy and his advisers Parliament must decline to assist him in the reconquest of Ireland. The House would not stomach this, but—rather surprisingly—on 8 November it accepted a new draft embodying a much more revolutionary proposition, that if Charles did not comply with their request they would take their own measures to suppress the rebellion (63).

From this moment Parliament was on the slope leading down into civil war, but the king was still without a party. Charles's one hope was the religious question, which had seriously divided the Commons in February and March, and had divided Lords from Commons in August and September.[1] Therefore at the end of October he announced: 'I am constant for the doctrine and discipline of the Church of England as it was established by Queen Elizabeth and my father, and resolved (by the Grace of God) to live and die in the maintenance of it.'[2] The answer of the Opposition was to bring on at last the Grand Remonstrance on the state of the kingdom which had been in preparation since the previous November (64). In it was now incorporated the demand that the king should only employ ministers approved by Parliament, and that they should be removed at the request of Parliament without formal evidence against them (§§ 197–8), and its sponsors tried to smother the Church question by asking that it be referred to a synod of divines drawn not only from England but from the other Protestant communities of Europe (§ 185). It led to one of the longest and fiercest debates in this Parliament, and it finally passed, on 22 November, by a mere eleven votes.

[1] See pp. 251–3 below.
[2] *Memoirs Illustrative of the Life and Writings of John Evelyn*, ed. W. Bray, 2nd ed. (London, 1819), II, app., p. 37. The remark was in a marginal note on a letter of Edward Nicholas's dated 12 October, and received back on the 23rd.

Three days later Charles at last returned to London and came to terms with the 'constitutional royalists' headed by Edward Hyde. On his arrival he repeated to the aldermen of London his pledge to the Established Church, and on 10 December he issued a proclamation ordering that religious services be carried on according to law. His answer to the Grand Remonstrance, on 23 December, also made the preservation of the Church his main concern.[1] Meanwhile the increasingly violent rioting of the London unemployed round the palaces of Whitehall and Westminster convinced Charles that the Commons intended to force his hand as they had in May, by an oblique threat to the queen. Also the Common Council elections in December showed that he was losing control of the City government.[2] On their side the Opposition leaders were alarmed by the gathering in London of large numbers of gentlemen volunteers and soldiers of fortune, ostensibly for service in Ireland or in the Portuguese war of independence. With some reason they feared a military *coup d'état,* and Charles's attempt on 23 December to replace the governor of the Tower by one of his own creatures roused such fierce resistance that he had to give way. On 28 December Lord Digby took the alternative, constitutionalist line by proposing to the Lords that in view of the ferocious rioting around Westminster their deliberations were not free and they should adjourn to a place of safety. Unfortunately, these same riots caused most of the bishops to stay away, and the motion was lost by four votes. When the bishops returned the following day, asserted that they had been kept away by deliberate intimidation, and tried to have the vote set aside, a majority of the Lords suddenly lost all patience with these unpopular and troublesome ecclesiastics. They sent the bishops' petition down to the Commons, who gratefully impeached the lot, and the Lords at once sequestered them.

This sudden *volte face* on the part of the Lords, and the serious reduction of his majority there, panicked the king. On 3 January 1642, the lord keeper was instructed to impeach Lord Kimbolton and five members of the Commons—Pym, Hampden, William Strode, Denzil Holles and Sir Arthur Haslerigg—on the grounds that they had 'endeavoured to subvert the fundamental laws and government of the kingdom'; almost exactly the same charge as had been levelled against the bishops a few days before (65). Next day, 4 January, the king appeared at Westminster with a posse of his gentlemen volunteers, armed, and burst into the House of Commons to arrest the five Members. Forewarned, they had already fled down the river to the City. This gross violation of parliamentary privilege, which could be represented as an attempt to overawe Parliament by force of arms, lost Charles London, as well as doing his reputation permanent harm. Such was

[1] GCD, p. 233.
[2] V. Pearl, *London and the Outbreak of the Puritan Revolution* (1961), pp. 132 ff.

the attitude of the Lords, the Commons, the Inns of Court, even the city government, that he left with the queen on 10 January.

During the succeeding nine months the struggle was focused on the control of the forces which both sides wanted to raise for the relief of Ireland. Other questions which hitherto had seemed incapable of solution were simply pushed aside; the bill to exclude the bishops from the House of Lords, for instance, which had been a bone of contention between the two Houses for nearly a year, passed the Lords on 5 February, and the king gave his assent a week later.[1] Meanwhile on 31 January the Commons drew up a Militia Bill giving Parliament the power to name the lord-lieutenant in each county. Though they refused to pass the bill, the Lords associated themselves with the demand, and on 12 February a list of suitable lord-lieutenants was drawn up for submission to the king.

But Charles, understandably enough, declined point-blank to give up control of the armed forces, and in March, having put his wife on a ship for the Continent, where she was to seek what aid she could, he withdrew to York, where he hoped for a better reception than in the south, and whence he hoped to seize the important arsenal of Hull, still stocked with the arms gathered for the campaigns of 1639 and 1640. But on 5 March the two Houses finally passed the Militia Ordinance,[2] put Hull in charge of Sir John Hotham, and on 29 March reinforced the garrison. When Charles presented himself before the town on 23 April—too late, as always—he was denied admission until Hotham had consulted his masters at Westminster. Charles now began assembling volunteers in a much more purposeful way than hitherto and opened a veritable propaganda war with the Long Parliament; for the next three months messages and replies, declarations and answers flew to and fro between London and York. On 20 May the two Houses resolved 'that it appears that the king, seduced by wicked counsel, intends to make war against the Parliament', and on the 26th they drew up a Remonstrance on Hull which remained to many the most decisive and acceptable statement of their case (66). On 1 June they published the Nineteen Propositions (67), which they could never have expected the king to accept; but he still had no sizeable party, and these were to be the terms of a dictated peace. He was to accept the Militia Ordinance, consent to the reformation of the Church by synod, place the education and marriage of his children in Parliament's hands and surrender his rights of appointment in every sphere of government, even his right to issue patents of nobility. Meanwhile on 27 May Charles had published a proclamation forbidding his subjects to obey the Militia Ordinance,[3] and in their reply, on 6 June, Parliament finally enunciated the doctrine that was to see them through the first civil war—that the person of the king was distinguishable from his office, and the functions of his office could be

---

[1] See p. 254 below.   [2] Printed *GCD*, pp. 245–7.   [3] *Ibid.* pp. 248–9.

exercised by Parliament 'after a more eminent and obligatory manner than it can be by personal act or resolution of his own' (68).

In his answer to the Nineteen Propositions, on 18 June, Charles's advisers produced a most remarkable document, upon which they never succeeded in improving.[1] They argued that England's was a mixed constitution, of monarchy, aristocracy and democracy, and that no one of those elements could be too closely restricted without damaging the whole structure. They reaffirmed the king's acceptance of the Triennial Act, and the act preventing the dissolution of this parliament, but they insisted that if Parliament secured the right of appointing ministers this would be an unwarranted encroachment of the legislature on the executive and could only lead to anarchy and disorder. (Indeed, they foretold the general course of events for the next ten years with remarkable accuracy.)

On any academic judgement, there can be no doubt that the king had won this constitutional and legal debate. Parliament, stripped of more and more of its members, was soon driven to policies quite as arbitrary as any of Charles's, even to levying forced loans by distraint, despite the Petition of Right. It made its position no better by declining to assert its own sovereignty and hiding under the king's skirts. But this dialectical victory was not so easily translated into military terms. Reverence for the kingly office was universal, but so was distrust of the kingly person (which was why Parliament tried so hard to separate the two), and when Charles raised his standard at Nottingham on 22 August the response was lukewarm. It needed Parliament to provide him with a nucleus of supporters, which they did with incomparable clumsiness on 6 September, when they declared that the charges and expense of the war must be borne by those persons who had been, or were to be, voted delinquents by both Houses—a declaration which was a suspended sentence on any man of property who did not at once join them (69).

53. Pym's speech on grievances, 17 April 1640[2]

He that takes away weights from the motions doth as good service as he that adds wings unto them. These weights are old grievances. He therefore will do a good work for the King who, to expedite his designs, will set good rules and patterns for effecting thereof.

When God made the world he did it by a pattern which [he] himself had conceived, and Moses did according to the pattern he saw on the Mount. I shall therefore offer you a model of the grievances which

---

[1] No. 9, p. 21 above.

[2] This speech survives in a number of versions, of which one (Rushworth, v, 21–4; PH, II, 640–3) is dated 7 November 1640. The elaborate 'literary' version published in 1642 (Somers Tracts, IV, 391–404) is similarly misdated.

afflict the Commonwealth, and which have disabled us to administer any supply until they be redressed, and which still disable us; which grievances may be reduced to three heads.

The first are those grievances which during these eleven years' interval of parliaments are against the liberties and privileges of Parliament.

The second are innovations in matters of religion.

The third, grievances against the propriety of our goods.

Which grievances I will first propound, and secondly show that the permission of them is as prejudicial to his Majesty as to the Commonwealth; and thirdly, I will show in what way they may be remedied.

In all these I shall take care to maintain the great prerogative of the King, which is, that the King can do no wrong.

And first, I will begin with the grievances against the privileges and liberties of Parliament. We all know that the intellectual part, which ought to govern the rest, ought to be kept from distemper, for it is that which purgeth us from all errors, and prevents other mischiefs for time to come. If the understanding part be hurt the mind cannot perform her function. A Parliament is that to the Commonwealth which the soul is to the body, which is only able to apprehend and understand the symptoms of all such diseases which threaten the body politic. It behoves us therefore to keep the faculty of that soul from distempers. I shall briefly therefore give you a view of such occurrences as have altered the happy and healthful constitution of it; and in the first place I must remember the breaches of our liberties and privileges of Parliament, which are:

First, in that the Speaker the last Parliament (the last day of it), being commanded to put the question, the House was commanded they should not speak. These are conceived to be the grounds of whatsoever befell those gentlemen which so lately suffered. 'Tis true, the House was commanded to adjourn presently, yet whilst the House sat God forbid we should be barred from offering the last sighs and groans to his Majesty.

Secondly, in that the Parliament was then dissolved, before our grievances had redress, or before we could make our wills known, which is the privilege of dying men; and to be heard before [being condemned] is not denied to private persons.

Thirdly, that the judges presume to question the proceedings of the House. It is against nature and order that inferior courts should undertake to regulate superior. The Court of Parliament is a court of the highest jurisdiction, and cannot be censured by any other law or sentence but by its own.

Fourthly, the several imprisonments of divers gentlemen, for speaking freely in Parliament.

Fifthly, that inferior courts should be informed to punish acts done in this court, whereby divers members of the House were so kept in prison till they had put in security for their good behaviour; and some of them died in prison, others not released until writs came for this parliament.

Lastly (which I conceive to be the greatest), that the Parliament was punished without being suffered to make its own defence. I call the dissolution of the Parliament a punishment, and justly; the breaking of the Parliament is death to a good subject.

But it is to be observed that in this and the other grievances, though the King be no party (for his Highness's prerogative is to do no wrong) yet most of these distempers of state arise and do invade the subjects by means of misinforming him; as the celestial bodies of themselves send forth nothing but wholesomeness to man, but by the ill distemper in inferior bodies much hurt ariseth from them.

The next sort of grievances I deliver are those that concern matters of religion. Wherein I will first observe the great encouragement which is given to them of the Popish religion by a universal suspension of all laws that are against them, and some of them admitted into public places of trust and power. I desire not to have any new laws made against them (God be thanked, we have enough), nor a strict execution of the old ones, but only so far forth as tends to the safety of his Majesty, and such a practice of them that the religion that can brook no co-rival may not be the destruction of ours by being too concurrent with it. There is an intention of a Nuncio from the Pope, who is to be here to give secret intelligence to Rome how we incline here, and what will be thought fit to win us thither.

I observe as a great grievance, there are divers innovations in religion amongst ourselves, to make us more capable of a translation, to which purpose Popish books have been published in print, and disputations of Popish points are and have been used in the universities and elsewhere with privilege, and preached in the pulpit, and maintained for sound doctrine, whereby Popish tenets are maintained. The introducing of Popish ceremonies, as altars, bowing towards the east, pictures, crosses, crucifixes and the like, which of themselves considered, are so many dry bones, but being put together make the man. We are not now contented with the old ceremonies, I mean such as the constitution of the reformed religion hath continued unto us, but we must introduce again many of those superstitious and infirm ceremonies which accompanied the most decrepit age of Popery—bowing to the altar, and the like.

I shall observe the daily discouraging of all godly men who truly profess the Protestant religion, as though men could be too religious. Some things are urged by ecclesiastical men without any ground by any canon or article established, and without any command from the King, either under his Great Seal or by proclamation. The Parliament ever since Queen Elizabeth's time desired the bishops to deal moderately, but how they have answered those desires we all know, and these good men for the most part feel. I may not forget that many of the ministers are deprived for refusing to read the Book for Sports and Recreation upon the Sabbath, which was a device of their own heads, which book I may affirm hath many things faulty in it.

Then the encroaching upon the King's authority by ecclesiastical courts, as namely the High Commission, which takes upon it to fine and imprison men, enforcing them to take the oath *ex officio*, with many of the like usurpations, which are punishments belonging only to temporal jurisdiction, and it hath been resolved in the time of King James that the statute of 1 Eliz., c. 1 gives them no such power; moreover, the power which they claim they derive not from the King, nor from any law or statute, but they will immediately have it from heaven *jure divino*. Divers particular ordinaries, chancellors and archdeacons take upon them to make and ordain constitutions within their particular limits. All these things are true to the knowledge of most that hear me.

I now come to the general head of grievances, which is the grievances belonging to our goods, and are in civil matters. The heads thereof are too many.

[1.] The taking of tunnage and poundage, and divers other impositions, without any grant or law for to do so, is a great grievance. There are divers ancient customs due to the King, but they are certain what they are and are due by prescription. These customs being too narrow for his service, and the affections of the people growing stronger and stronger to their prince, tunnage and poundage were granted for years to the King, and afterwards by this House granted for lives, but never were taken by the King's own act without a Parliament, for doing which there is no precedent, unless a year or two in the latter end of Queen Elizabeth.

[2.] In the next place of these grievances I rank knighthood, the original whereof was, that persons fit for chivalry might be improved. But this after was stretched for another end, for money, and extended not only to terre tenants [sc. freeholders] but to lessees and merchants, who were first to appear, and then to plead for themselves, at the Council board, but were delayed from day to day, to their great charge and inconvenience, and notwithstanding the just defence they have made for themselves there have been infinite distresses laid upon them until the fines were paid, which were imposed not by courts but by commissioners assigned for that purpose, and this being a continuing offence they are by the same rule as liable now to fines as ever.

[3.] Monopolies, and inundations of them, whereby a burden is laid not only upon foreign but upon native commodities, as soap, salt, drink, etc., the particulars whereof are fit for the Committee of Grievances.

[4.] Fourthly, ship-money, and although there be a judgement for it, yet I dare be bold to say it's against all former precedents and laws, and not one judgement that ever maintained it. This is a grievance that all are grieved at, having no limits either for time or proportion; if therefore any shall endeavour to defend this he must know that both his reputation and conscience lie at stake in the defence.

[5.] The enlarging the bounds of the Forest. Though our ancestors were heretofore questioned for the same thing, yet upon the satisfaction of all the objections that were or could be made they then saved themselves. Yet now the same things are turned upon us.

[6.] The sale of public nuisances, for so they are pretended to be. Many great nuisances have been complained of, but when there hath been money given, and compositions made, then they are no more nuisances, as buildings and depopulations.

[7.] Military charges and impositions upon counties, by letters only from the council table, whereby soldiers' conduct money and coats are to be provided at the county's charge, and horses also provided without ground or law, many things in this kind being done by deputy-lieutenants of their own accord.

[8.] Extrajudicial judgements and impositions of the judges without any cause before them, whereby they have anticipated the judgement which is legal and public and circumvented one of the parties of just remedies, in that no writ of error lies, but only upon the judicial proceedings.

The next sort of grievances is that the great courts do countenance the oppressions, as I may instance in the Court of Star Chamber advancing and countenancing of monopolies, which should be instead of this great council of the kingdom; and the Star Chamber now is become a court of revenue, informations there being put in against sheriffs for not making returns of money upon the writs of ship-money. It was not used that *meum et tuum* should be disputed there.

The Privy Councillors should be Lights of the Realm. Sure in them is the greatest trust, and they by Magna Carta are to do justice (as was urged by one in this House the last Parliament), but now if these councillors should so far descend below themselves as to countenance, nay, to plot projects and monopolies, what shall we think of this? Surely it is much beneath their dignity. This is a great grievance, but I must go higher.

I know the King hath a transcendent power in many cases, whereby by proclamation he may prevent and guard against sudden accidents, but that this power should be applied to countenance monopolies (the projectors being not content with their private grants without a proclamation) is without precedent. But yet I must go higher than this; it hath been in the pulpit applied and also published in books and disputations, asserting a power unlimited in the King, that he may do what he pleaseth. This grievance was complained of in the last parliament, in the case of Dr Manwaring, who for maintaining that opinion in a sermon, that a subject had no propriety in his goods, but that all was at the King's pleasure, made his submission upon his knees in this place, and then was brought so low that I thought he would not have leaped so soon into a bishopric.[1]

I have by this time wearied you as well as myself, but I am come to the last grievance, which is the fountain of all these, and that is the intermissions of Parliaments, whereas by two statutes not repealed or expired, a Parliament ought to be once in a year.

These grievances are as prejudicial to his Majesty as to the Commonwealth. The breach of Parliaments is much prejudicial, for by this means the great union and love which should be kept and communicated betwixt the King and his subjects is interrupted. They cannot make known their petitions, nor the King his wants, to have supplies. Where the intercourse of the spirits betwixt the head and the members is

---

[1] Manwaring was now bishop of St Davids. For an extract from his famous sermon, and Pym's speech on his impeachment in 1628, see Nos. 6, 7, pp. 14–18 above.

hindered the body prospers not. If Parliaments had been more frequent the King had had more supplies.

By our grievance in religion the King's party abroad is much weakened, and that great part of this aids [sc. allies] abroad do forsake us is for that they think we are forsaking our religion.

Many of the King's subjects, for that they cannot be quiet in things indifferent, and know not where they shall have an end of them, have departed this land with their goods, estates and posterities.

The preferment of men ill-deserving, and neglecting others of great integrity and merit, hath much weakened and discouraged us. There are but a few now that apply themselves either to do well or to deserve well, finding flattery and compliance to be the easier way to attain their ends and expectations.

The not observing of laws, but countenancing of monopolies and such like, breeds jealousies in the minds of many, and may prepare a way for distempers, though (thanks be to God) as yet there have been none; our religion hath preserved us. But if anything but well should happen one summer's distempers would breed great change, and more than all unlawful courses would recompense. We know how unfortunate Henry III and other princes have been, by the occasion of such breaking of their laws. I pray God that we never see such times....

I come now to the last thing, the remedy of these grievances.

First, I advise to present them to the House of Peers, that they may join with us to go to the King, and pray that these grievances being clear in fact may be voted. If anything in the vote be stuck upon, that it may be debated and drawn according to the course of the House, into a remonstrance, with a humble petition of both Houses for redress. I hope the wisdom of this House will prepare such a remedy as will make the King a great king, and the people happy.   Rushworth, IV, 1131–6

54. Pym's speech, 7 November 1640[1]

Mr Pym moved for a reformation, etc., finding out authors and punishment of them. [The] actual declaration of offences needs no statutes, and that is a step to reformation.[2]

---

[1] This is the fullest version available. I have omitted the more obscure passages, and supplemented others by quotations, usually in the footnotes, from the brief version published in *Speeches and Passages* the following year (pp. 458–60), which I have also compared with the MS. in P.R.O., S.P. 16/472, 81–2.

[2] 'The distempers of this kingdom are well known, they need no repetition, for though we have good laws yet they want their execution; if they are executed it is in a wrong sense.'

[There is] a design to alter the kingdom both in religion and government. This is the highest of treason, this blows up by piecemeal, and almost goeth through [to] their ends. This concerns the King as well as we, and that I say with reverence and care of his Majesty.

So there are many heads of grievances.[1]

1. The Papists' party alter religion, and this by setting differences between the King and his subjects; and tenets of Papists undermine our religion.

2. The corrupt part of our clergy[2] that make things for their own ends and with a union between us and Rome.

3. Agents for Spain and other kingdoms by pensions to alter religion and government.[3]

4. Those that [are] for their own preferments and further all bad things are worse than Papists; those [who] are willing to run with Popery.[4] Steps of these things that have proceeded in motion, first softly, now by strides, which are near their end if they be not prevented. [These] designs [are] carried upon four feet.

The first foot is [religion].

1. Ecclesiastical courts.

2. Discountenancing of forward men in our religion.

3. Countenancing their own party, or else no promotion.

4. By negotiating agents from hence to Rome and from Rome to this place to extirpate our religion, [of which] proof will appear.

5. Frequent preaching for monarchy, Doctor Beale[5] and others.

The second foot: policy for [the] State and Courts of Justice.

1. The Council endeavouring to make [a] difference between King and people by taxes against laws and wrong ways....

2. By keeping the King in constant necessity, [that he may seek their counsels for relief; to this purpose to keep the parliaments in distaste,][6] that he might be for them. Still, [there is] no imputation to be laid

---

[1] This hackneyed reference to grievances may have been inserted by d'Ewes or his informant. Pym had already swept the usual grievances aside, and in the printed version he firmly couples the Papists with the design to alter the government: 'There is a design to alter law and religion. That party that affects this are papists, who are obliged by a maxim in their doctrine, that they are not only to maintain their religion, but also extirpate others.'

[2] 'Our hierarchy, which cannot amount to the height they aim at without a breach of our law.'

[3] 'There they intend chiefly the Spanish white gold, works which are of most effect.'

[4] The printed version refers directly to Charles's ministers: 'Favourites, such as for promotion prize not conscience; and such are our judges spiritual and temporal, such are also our councillors of state.'

[5] Dr William Beale of Paulersbury, Northants.   [6] From *Speeches and Passages*.

upon the King for any irregular actions, but upon them that he entrusted.

3. Arbitrary proceedings of courts of justice; law and precedent were nothing, expunging of matters, all defence of the subject taken away for the dissolution of the kingdom.

4. To make a difference between England and Scotland, [that when we had well wearied ourselves against one another we might be both brought to what scorn they pleased].[1] A sermon [was] preached in the North before the King [that] to make an agreement between Popery and our religion the partition wall must be pulled down, which was the Puritans. The Scots have been [made] the first authors of all.

5. By misguiding the King's approbation. [Ingratiating of Papists and saying they are the best subjects, to bring the King in love with them].[2]

The third foot: discontent and breach of Parliaments.

1. He would not mention the breach of old privileges, but late instances in new, as Mr Crewe's case.[3] The Clerk is not bound to deliver any petitions, nor so any member. If no safety here, then nowhere.

2. Great slanders in the declaration[4] for which he desired reparation. The King took it upon credit of others, he never saw it.

[3.] By moulding the Irish government into an illegal course, with intent to do [the same] here, [and] so we [ought] to have an interest with them; we are all the same subjects and no new thing.

The fourth foot: military steps.

1. Putting Papists or suspected persons into command of armies.

2. Power to Papists to muster by commission.[5]

3. To bring soldiers from beyond sea, and endeavours have been and haply are, but that means are wanted to do it. No account of Spaniards coming here.[6] Great jealousies.

4. The Irish army to bring us to a better order; we are not fully conquered....

He moved that there might be a settled committee to find out the danger the King and kingdom is in.   D'Ewes Journal, ed. Notestein, pp. 7–11

[1] From Speeches and Passages.
[2] This sentence has been transferred from the next paragraph, on Parliament.
[3] See no. 19, p. 53 above.
[4] Giving the king's reasons for dissolving Parliament, May 1640, PH, II, 572–9.
[5] 'To whom their armour is delivered contrary to the statute.'
[6] An obscure reference to Strafford's negotiations with the Spanish government, or to the arrival of a Spanish fleet in English territorial waters in the autumn of 1639.

55. Strafford's impeachment, 1640–41

(a) *John Pym's speech to the preliminary charges, 25 November 1640*

These articles have expressed the character of a great and dangerous treason, such a one as is advanced to the highest degree of malice and mischief. It is enlarged beyond the limits of any description or definition, it is so heinous in itself as that it is capable of no aggravation; a treason against God, betraying his truth and worship; against the King, obscuring the glory and weakening the foundations of his throne; against the Commonwealth, by destroying the principles of safety and prosperity. Other treasons are against the rule of the law: this is against the being of the law. It is the law that unites the King and his people, and the author of this treason hath endeavoured to dissolve that union, even to break the mutual, irreversible, indissoluble band [?bond] of protection and allegiance whereby they are, and I hope ever will be, bound together.

If this treason had taken effect our souls had been enthralled to the spiritual tyranny of Satan, our consciences to the ecclesiastical tyranny of the Pope, our lives, our persons and estates, to the civil tyranny of an arbitrary, unlimited, confused government.

Treason in the least degree is an odious and horrid crime. [But] other treasons are particular: if a fort be betrayed, or an army, or any other treasonable fact committed, the kingdom may outlive any of these. This treason would have dissolved the frame and being of the Commonwealth; it is a universal, a Catholic treason; the venom and malignity of all other treasons are abstracted, digested, sublimated into this.

The law of this kingdom makes the King to be the fountain of justice, of peace, of protection; therefore we say, the King's courts, the King's judges, the King's laws; the royal power and majesty shines upon us in every public blessing and benefit we enjoy. But the author of this treason would make him the fountain of injustice, of confusion, of public misery and calamity.... There cannot be a greater lesion or diminution of majesty, than to bereave a king of the glory of his goodness. It is a goodness, my lords, that can produce not only to his people, but likewise to himself honour and happiness. There are principalities, thrones and dominions amongst the devils, greatness enough; but being incapable of goodness they are made incapable both of honour and happiness.

The laws of this kingdom have invested the royal crown with power sufficient for the manifestation of his goodness and of his greatness; if more be required it is like to have no other effects but poverty, weakness and misery, whereof of late we have had very woeful experience. It is far from the Commons to desire any abridgement of those great prerogatives which belong to the King; they know that their own liberty and peace are preserved and secured by his prerogative....A king and his people make one body: the inferior parts confer nourishment and strength, the superior, sense and motion. If there be an interruption of this necessary intercourse of blood and spirits, the whole body must needs be subject to decay and distemper. Therefore obstructions are first to be removed before restoratives can be applied. This, my lords, is the end of this accusation, whereby the Commons seek to remove this person, whom they conceive to have been a great cause of the obstructions between his Majesty and his people; for the effecting whereof they have commanded me to desire your lordships that your proceedings against him may be put into as speedy a way of despatch as the courses of Parliament will allow.... *Somers Tracts*, IV, 216–17

(*b*) *Articles of impeachment against Strafford, 28 January 1641*

[The first article accused him of exercising an arbitrary and tyrannical government in the north parts, as Lord President of the Council there.]

II

That shortly after the obtaining of the said Commission...[as Lord President], to wit, the last day of August then next following [1633], he the said earl (to bring his Majesty's liege people into a dislike of his Majesty and of his government, and to terrify the justices of the peace from executing of the laws)...did publicly at the assizes held for the county of York, in the city of York,...declare and publish before the people there attending for the administration of justice according to law, and in the presence of the justices sitting, that some of the justices were all for law, and nothing would please them but law, but they should find that the King's little finger should be heavier than the loins of the law.

III

That the realm of Ireland having been time out of mind annexed to the imperial crown of this his Majesty's realm of England, and governed by the same laws, the said earl being Lord Deputy of that realm, to bring his Majesty's liege subjects of that kingdom likewise into dislike of his Majesty's government, and intending the subversion of the fundamental laws and settled government of that realm, and the destruction of his Majesty's liege people there, did upon the 30th day of September, in the ninth year of his Majesty's reign [1633], in the city of Dublin..., in a public speech before divers of the nobility and gentry of that kingdom, and before the mayor, aldermen and recorder, and many citizens, of Dublin, and other his Majesty's liege people, declare and publish that Ireland was a conquered nation, and that the King might do with them what he pleased; and speaking of the charters of former kings of England made to that city he further then said, that their charters were nothing worth, and did bind the King no further than he pleased.

*   *   *   *   *   *

[Articles IV–XIX dealt in detail with Strafford's rule in Ireland.]

XX

That the said earl hath in the 15th and 16th years of his Majesty's reign 1639–40, and divers years past, laboured and endeavoured to breed in his Majesty an ill opinion of his subjects, namely, of those of the Scotch nation, and divers and sundry times, and especially since the pacification made by his Majesty with his said subjects [in 1639]...he the said earl did labour and endeavour to persuade, incite and provoke his Majesty to an offensive war against his said subjects of the Scottish nation, and the said earl by his counsels, actions and endeavours hath been and is a principal and chief incendiary of the war and discord between his Majesty and his subjects of England, and the said subjects of Scotland, and hath declared and advised his Majesty that the demands made by the Scots in their Parliament were a sufficient cause of war against them.

The said earl having formerly expressed the height and rancour of his mind towards his Majesty's subjects of the Scottish nation, viz., the tenth day of October...[1639] he said that the nation of the Scots were rebels and traitors, and he being then about to come to England, he then further said that if it pleased his Master...to send him back again he would root out of the said kingdom...[of Ireland] the Scottish nation both root and branch....

XXI

That the said earl of Strafford, shortly after his speeches mentioned in the last precedent article..., came into this realm of England, and was made lord-lieutenant of Ireland, and continued his government of that kingdom by a deputy. At his arrival here, finding that his Majesty with much wisdom and goodness had composed the Troubles in the North, and had a pacification with his subjects of Scotland, he laboured by all means to procure his Majesty to break that pacification, incensing his Majesty against his subjects of that kingdom and the proceeding[s] of the Parliament there.

And having incited his Majesty to an offensive war against his subjects of Scotland by sea and land, and by pretext thereof to raise forces for the maintenance of that war, he counselled his Majesty to call a Parliament in England. Yet the said earl intended that if the said proceedings of that Parliament should not be such as would stand with the said earl of Strafford's mischievous designs he would then procure his Majesty to break the same, and by ways of force and power to raise monies upon the subjects of this kingdom. And for the encouragement of his Majesty to hearken to his advice he did before his Majesty and his Privy Council...make a large declaration, that he would serve his Majesty in any other way, in case the Parliament should not supply him.

* * * * * *

[Article XXII dealt with Strafford's visit to Ireland, March 1640.]

XXIII

That upon the thirteenth day of April last the Parliament of England met, and the Commons House...did accordingly to the trust reposed in them enter into debate and consideration of the great grievances of this kingdom, both in respect of religion and the public liberty of the kingdom; and his Majesty's referring chiefly to the said earl of Strafford and the archbishop of Canterbury the ordering and disposing of all matters concerning the Parliament, he the said earl of Strafford, with the assistance of the said archbishop, did procure his Majesty by sundry speeches and messages to urge the said Commons House to enter into some resolution for his Majesty's supply...before any course taken for the relief of the great and pressing grievances wherewith this kingdom was then afflicted...and while the said Commons then assembled (with expression of great affection to his Majesty and his service) were in debate and consideration of some supply, before any resolution by them made, he the said earl of Strafford, with the help and assistance of the said archbishop, did procure his Majesty to dissolve the said Parliament upon the fifth day of May last; and upon the same day...did treacherously, falsely and maliciously endeavour to incense his Majesty against his loving and faithful subjects who had been Members of the said House of Commons, by telling his Majesty they had denied to supply him. And afterwards upon the same day he did traitorously and wickedly counsel and advise his Majesty to this effect; viz., that having tried the affections of his people, he was loosed and absolved from all rules of government, and that he was to do everything that power would admit, and that his Majesty had tried all ways, and was refused, and should be acquitted towards God and Man, and that he had an army in Ireland...which he might employ to reduce this kingdom.[1]

* * * * * *

XXV

...And a great loan of a hundred thousand pounds was demanded of the City of London, and the lord mayor, and sheriffs and aldermen of the said city were often sent for by his advice to the Council table to give an account of their proceedings in raising of ship-money, and furthering of that loan...[and] he the said earl of Strafford did use these and the like speeches, viz., that they deserved to be put to fine and ransom, and that no good would be done with them till an example were made of them, and that they were laid by the heels, and some of the aldermen hanged up.

* * * * * *

[Articles XXVI–XXVIII dealt in detail with Strafford's activities in the remaining months of 1640.]

All and every which words, counsels and actions of the said earl of Strafford were spoken, given and done by...[him] traitorously, and contrary to his allegiance to our sovereign lord the King, and with an intention and endeavour to alienate and withdraw the hearts and affections of the King's liege people of all his realms from his Majesty, and

[1] See no. 136, p. 481 below.

to set division between them, and to ruin and destroy his Majesty, and [his] Majesty's said kingdoms, for which they do further impeach him the said Thomas, earl of Strafford, of high treason against our sovereign lord the King, his Crown and Dignity.... Rushworth, II, 61–75

(c) *Strafford's last speech in his defence, 13 April 1641*[1]

...My lords, I have all along my charge watched to see that poisoned arrow of treason that some would have to be feathered in my breast, and that deadly cup of wine that hath so intoxicated some petty mis-alleged errors as to put them in the elevation of high treason; but in truth it hath not been my quickness to discern any such monster yet within my breast, though perhaps now by a sinister imputation sticking to my clothes. They tell me of a twofold treason, one against the statute, another by the Common Law; this direct, that constructive; this individual, that accumulative; this in itself, that by way of construction. ...To make up this constructive treason, or treason by accumulation, many articles are brought against me, as if in a heap of felonies or mis-demeanours—for in their own conceit they reach no higher—some prolific seed apt to produce what is treasonable could lurk.

Here I am charged to have designed the overthrow both of religion and the State. The first seemeth to me to have been used rather for making me odious than guilty, for there is not the least probation alleged concerning my confederacy with the Popish faction, nor could there be any indeed. Never a servant in authority beneath the King my master who was more hated and maligned, and am still, by these men than myself, and that for a strict and impartial execution of the laws against them. Hence your Lordships may observe that the greater number of the witnesses used against me either from Ireland or York-shire are men of that religion; and for my own resolution I thank God I am ready every minute of the day to seal my disaffection to the Church of Rome with my dearest blood....

As to my designs about the State, I dare plead as much innocency here as in the matter of my religion. I have ever admired the wisdom of our ancestors, who have so fixed the pillars of this monarchy that each of them keeps due measure and proportion with [the] other, and have so handsomely tied up the nerves and sinews of the State that the

[1] From a MS. in the Public Record Office drawn up by or for Sir Edward Nicholas. Rush-worth (II, 633–60) prints another version of the speech with very different wording but much the same sense.

straining of one may bring damage and sorrow to the whole economy. The prerogative of the Crown and the propriety of the subject have such mutual relations that this took protection from that, that foundation and nourishment from this; and as on the lute, if anything be too high or too low wound up you have lost the harmony, so here the excess of a prerogative is oppression, of a pretended liberty in the subject disorder and anarchy. The prerogative must be used, as God doth his omnipotency, at extraordinary occasions; the laws...must have place at all other times, and yet there must be a prerogative if there must be extraordinary occasions. The propriety of the subject is ever to be maintained if it go in equal pace with this; they are fellows and companions that have been and ever must be inseparable in a well-governed kingdom; and no way so fitting, so natural to nourish and intertex both as the frequent use of parliaments. By this a commerce and acquaintance is kept between the King and the subject; this thought hath gone along with me these fourteen years of my public employments, and shall, God willing, to my grave. God, his Majesty and my own conscience, yea, all who have been accessory to my most inward thoughts and opinions, can bear me witness I ever did inculcate this: the happiness of a kingdom consists in [the] just poise of the King's prerogative and the subject's liberty, and that things should never be well till these went hand in hand together. I thank God for it, by my master's favour and the prudence of my ancestors I have an estate which so interests me in the Commonwealth that I have no great mind to be a slave, but a subject. Nor could I wish the cards to be shuffled over again upon hope to fall on a better set; neither did I ever keep such base mercenary thoughts as to become a pander to the tyranny, the ambition of the greatest man living. No, I have and shall ever aim at a fair but a bounded liberty, remembering always that I am a freeman, but a subject; that I have a right, but under a monarch. But it hath been my misfortune now under my grey hairs to be charged with the mistakes of the times, which are now so high bent that all appears to them to be in the extremes for monarchy which is not for themselves....

My lords, you see what may be alleged for this constructive, rather this destructive treason. For my part, I have not the judgement to conceive that such a treason is either agreeable to the fundamental grounds of reason or law. Not of reason, for how can that be treason in the whole which is not in any of the parts? Or how can that make a thing treasonable which in itself is nothing so? Nor of law, since neither statute, Common Law nor practice hath from the beginning of this government ever mentioned such a thing. And where, I pray you, my lords, hath this fire without the least token of smoke lain his so many hundreds of years, and now breaks forth in a violent flame to destroy me and my posterity from the earth? My lords, do we not live by laws, and must we be punishable by them ere they be made? Far better it were to live by no law at all, but be governed by those characters of discretion and virtue stamped in us, than to put this necessity of divination upon a man and to argue him of the breach of a law ere it be a law at all.... My lords, if this crime which they call arbitrary treason had been marked by any discernment of the law, the ignorance of the same should not excuse me; but if it be no law at all, how can it in rigour, in strictness itself, condemn me?

Beware you do not awake these sleeping lions by the raking up of some neglected, some moth-eaten records—they may sometime tear you and your posterity in pieces. It was your ancestors' care to chain them up within the barrier of a statute; be not you ambitious to be more skilful, more curious than your fathers were in the art of killing. ...I leave it to your lordships' consideration to foresee what may be the issue of so dangerous, so recent precedencies. These gentlemen tell me they speak in defence of the commonweal against my arbitrary laws; give me leave to say that I speak in defence of the commonweal against their arbitrary treason. For if this latitude be admitted, what prejudice shall follow to the King, to the country, if you and your posterity be disabled by the same from the great affairs of the kingdom? ...Let me be a Pharos to keep you from shipwreck, and do not put such rocks in your own way, which no prudence nor circumspection can eschew or satisfy but by utter ruin. And whether judgement in my case—I wish it were not the case of you all—be it life or death, it shall be righteous in mine eyes, and received with a *te deum laudamus*. Now, *in te Domine confido, ne confundar in eternum*.

CSPD, 1640–41, pp. 540–5

(d) John Pym's reply

...We have passed through our evidence, and the result of all this is, that the earl of Strafford hath endeavoured by his words, actions and counsels to subvert the fundamental law of England and Ireland, and to introduce an arbitrary and tyrannical government. This is the envenomed arrow for which he inquired, in the beginning of this replication this day, which hath infected all his blood; this is that intoxicating cup (to use his own metaphor) which hath tainted his judgement and poisoned his heart; from hence was infused that specifical difference, which turned his speeches, his actions, his counsels into treason—not cumulative, as he expressed it, as if many misdemeanours could make one treason; but formally and essentially. It is the end that doth inform actions, and doth specificate the nature of them, making not only criminal but even indifferent words and actions to be treason, being done and spoken with a treasonable intention.

That which is given to me in charge, is to show the quality of the offence, how heinous it is in the nature, how mischievous in the effect of it, which will best appear if it be examined by that law to which he himself appealed, that universal, that supreme law, *salus populi*. This is the element of all laws, out of which they are derived, the end of all laws, to which they are designed, and in which they are perfected. How far it stands in opposition to this law I shall endeavour to show in some considerations which I shall present to your lordships, all arising out of the evidence which hath been opened.

The first is this, it is an offence comprehending all other offences; here you will find several treasons, murders, rapines, oppressions, perjuries. The earth has a seminary virtue, whereby it doth produce all herbs and plants, and other vegetables. There is in this crime a seminary of all evils hurtful to a State; and if you consider the reasons of it it must needs be so. The law is that which put as difference between good and evil, between just and unjust; if you take away the law all things will fall into a confusion, every man will become a law to himself, which in the depraved condition of human nature must needs produce many grave enormities. Lust will become a law, and envy will become a law, covetousness and ambition will become laws; and what dictates, what decisions such laws will produce may easily be discerned in the late government of Ireland. The law hath a power to prevent, to restrain, to repair evils; without this all kinds of mischief and distempers will break in upon a State.

It is the law that doth entitle a king to the allegiance and service of his people; it entitles the people to the protection and justice of the King.... The law is the boundary, the measure between the King's prerogative and the people's liberty. Whilst these move in their own orbs they are a support and a security to one another; the prerogative a cover and defence to the liberty of the people, and the people by their liberty are entitled to be a foundation to the prerogative; but if these bounds be so removed that they enter into contestation and conflict one of these mischiefs must ensue: if the prerogative of the King over-whelm the liberty of the people it will be turned into tyranny; if liberty undermine the prerogative, it will grow into anarchy....

The second consideration is this: this arbitrary power is dangerous to the King's person, and dangerous to his crown; it is apt to cherish ambition, usurpation and oppression in great men, and to beget sedi-tion and discontent in the people, and both these have been, and in reason must ever be, causes of great trouble and alteration to princes and states. If the histories of those eastern countries be perused, where princes order their affairs according to the mischievous principles of the earl of Strafford, loose and absolved from all rules of government, they will be found to be frequent in combustions, full of massacres and of the tragical ends of princes. If any man shall look into our own stories, in the times when the laws were most neglected, he shall find them full of commotions, of civil distempers, whereby the kings that then reigned were always kept in want and distress, the people con-sumed with civil wars; and by such wicked counsels as these some of our princes have been brought to such miserable ends as no honest heart can remember without horror, and earnest prayer that it may never be so again.

The third consideration is this: the subversion of the laws. And this arbitrary power, as it is dangerous to the King's person, and to his crown, so is it in other respects very prejudicial to his Majesty in his honour, profit and greatness. And yet these are the gildings and paint-ings that are put upon such counsels: 'These are for your honour, for your service'—whereas in truth they are contrary to both. But if I shall take off this varnish I hope they shall then appear in their own native deformity....

It cannot be for the honour of the King that his sacred authority should be used in the practice of injustice and oppression, that his name should be applied to patronise such horrid crimes as have been repre-sented in evidence against the earl of Strafford. And yet how frequently how presumptuously, his commands, his letters, have been vouched throughout the course of this defence? Your lordships have heard, when the judges do justice, it is the King's justice, and this is for his honour, because he is the fountain of justice; but when they do in-justice the offence is their own. But those officers and ministers of the

King who are most officious in the exercise of this arbitrary power, they do it commonly for their advantages, and when they are questioned for it, then they fly to the King's interest, to his direction. And truly, my lords, this is a very unequal distribution for the King, that the dishonour of evil courses should be cast upon him, and they to have the advantage....

Rushworth, II, 661–3

56. Select committees of the Long Parliament (Journal of Sir Thomas Peyton, 12 January 1641)

Sir John Hotham reported from the committee appointed to consider what committees were fit to stand and what to be suspended, that the more general should only subsist for the present, which were these:

1. That of My Lord Canterbury.
2. That of My Lord Strafford.
3. That of Mr Secretary Windebank and the recusants.[1]
4. That for my Lord Keeper, the judges, and ship-money.
5. That of the bishop of Bath and Wells [William Piers].
6. That of the bishop of Ely [Matthew Wren].
7. That for elections and other privileges of the House.
8. That for the breach of privileges of former Parliaments.
9. That concerning the Star Chamber and Proclamation Law, and the High Commission, and undue proceedings at the Council Table.
10. That of the twenty-four persons to draw a Remonstrance of all the present evils and grievances of the kingdom, to present to the King.[2]
11. That for the frequent holding of parliaments.
12. That for the northern parts.
13. That for my Lord Marshal's Court.[3]
14. That for the rigorous levying of ship-money.
15. That for the abuses of lord-lieutenants and deputy-lieutenants, and for drawing a bill for restraining their power.
16. That for salt, soap and leather.

---

[1] Windebank had issued orders to justices to relax the execution of the recusancy laws.

[2] The Committee on the State of the Kingdom, which eventually produced the Grand Remonstrance.

[3] The Earl Marshal's Court, which had roused a disproportionate amount of hostility.

These only are thought fit to be in being, and the five Grand Committees:

1. That of religion.
2. That of trade.
3. That of grievances.
4. That of Irish affairs.
5. That of courts of justice.   *D'Ewes Journal*, ed. Notestein, p. 242, n. 4

57. Opposition tactics, 1641

[It was] always their custom, when they found the heat and distemper of the House (which they endeavoured to keep up by the sharp mention and remembrance of former grievances and pressures) in any degree allayed by some gracious act or gracious profession of the King, to warm and inflame them again with a discovery, or promise of a discovery, of some notable plot and conspiracy against themselves, to dissolve the Parliament by the Papists, or some other way, in which they would be sure that somewhat always should reflect upon the Court. Thus they were sometimes informing of great multitudes of Papists gathering together in Lancashire; then of secret meetings in caves and under ground in Surrey; letters from beyond sea of great provisions of arms making there for the Catholics of England, and the like; which upon examination always vanished, but for the time (and they were always applied in useful articles of time) served to transport common minds with fears and apprehensions, and so induced them to comply in sense with those who were like soonest to find remedies for those diseases which none but themselves could discover. And in this progress there sometimes happened strange accidents for the confirmation of their credit.   Clarendon, *Rebellion*, III, 179

58. The king's tactics, 1641

The King besides had at that time a greater disadvantage (besides the concurrence of ill and extraordinary accidents) than himself or any of his progenitors had ever had before, having no servant of the House of Commons of interest, ability and reputation, and of faithfulness and affection to his service....So that...they who out of the most abstracted sense of loyalty to the King and duty to their country severed from any relations to the King, or hopes from the court, preserved their own innocence, and endeavoured to uphold the good old frame of government, received neither countenance [n]or conduct from those who were naturally to have taken care of that province. And sure the raging and fanatic distempers of the House of Commons (to which all other distempers are to be imputed) must most properly be attributed to the want of good ministers of the Crown in that assembly, who, being unawed by any guilt of their own, could have watched other men's, and informed, encouraged and governed those who stood well inclined to the public peace.

To which purpose, if that stratagem (though none of the best) of winning men by places had been practised as soon as the resolution was taken at York to call a Parliament (in which it was apparent dangerous attempts would be made, and that the Court could not be able to resist those attempts), and if Mr Pym, Mr Hampden and Mr Holles had then been preferred with Mr St John, before they were desperately embarked in their desperate designs, and had innocence enough about them to trust the King and be trusted by him, having yet contracted no personal animosities against him, it is very possible that they might either have been made instruments to have done good service, or at least been restrained from endeavouring to subvert the royal building, for supporting whereof they were placed as principal pillars.

But the rule the King gave himself (very reasonable at another time), that they should first do service and compass this or that thing for him before they should receive favour, was then very unseasonable, since, besides that they could not in truth do him that service without the qualification, it could not be expected they would desert that side by the power of which they were sure to make themselves considerable without an unquestionable mark of interest in the other, by which they were to keep up their power and reputation. And so, whilst the King expected they should manifest their inclinations to his service by their temper and moderation in those proceedings that most offended him, and they endeavoured by doing all the hurt they could to make evident the power they had to do him good, he grew so far disobliged and provoked that he could not in honour gratify them, and they so obnoxious and guilty that they could not think themselves secure in his favour; and thence, according to the policy and method of injustice, combined to oppress that power they had injured, and to raise a security for themselves by disenabling the King to question their transgressions.

Ibid. IV, 75–7

59. The Triennial Act, 1641

16 Car. I, c. 1: *An Act for the preventing of inconveniences happening by the long intermission of parliaments*

Whereas by the laws and statutes of this realm the parliament ought to be held at least once every year for the redress of grievances, but the appointment of the time and place for the holding thereof has always belonged, as it ought, to his Majesty and his royal progenitors; and whereas it is by experience found that the not holding of parliaments accordingly hath produced sundry and great mischiefs and inconveniences to the King's Majesty, Church and Commonwealth, for the prevention of the like mischiefs and inconveniences in time to come:

II. Be it enacted...that in case there be not a parliament summoned by writ under the Great Seal of England and assembled and held before the tenth day of September which shall be in the third year next after the last day of the last meeting and sitting in this present parliament,... and so from time to time and in all times hereafter if there shall not be a parliament assembled and held...[as aforesaid], then...the parliament shall assemble and be held in the usual place at Westminster in such manner and by such means only as is hereafter in this present Act declared and enacted and not otherwise, on the second Monday which shall be in the month of November then next ensuing.

And in case this present parliament now assembled and held, and any other parliament which shall at any time hereafter be assembled and held,...shall be prorogued or adjourned or continued by prorogation or adjournment until the tenth day of September which shall be in the third year next after the last day of the last meeting and sitting in parliament,...that then in every such case every such parliament... shall from the said tenth day of September be thenceforth clearly and absolutely dissolved. And the lord chancellor of England, the lord keeper of the Great Seal of England, and every commissioner and commissioners for the keeping of the Great Seal of England for the time being shall within six days after the said tenth day of September ...in due form of law and without any further warrant or direction from his Majesty, his heirs or successors, seal, issue forth and send abroad several and respective writs to the several and respective peers of this realm, commanding every such peer that he personally be at the parliament to be held at Westminster on the second Monday which shall be in November next following the said tenth day of September, ...and shall also seal, issue forth and send abroad several and respective writs to the several and respective sheriffs of the several and respective counties, cities and boroughs of England and Wales...for the electing of the knights, citizens, barons and burgesses of and for the said counties ...[etc.] in the accustomed form, to sit and serve in parliament to be held at Westminster on the second Sunday...in November....Which said peers after the said writs received, and which said knights, citizens, barons and burgesses chosen by virtue of the said writs shall then and there appear and serve in Parliament accordingly. And the said lord chancellor...[etc.] shall respectively take a solemn oath upon the Holy Evangelist for the due issuing of writs according to the tenor of this act, ...which oath is forthwith to be taken by the present lord keeper. ...And if the said lord chancellor...[etc.] shall fail or forbear so to issue out the said writs..., then he or they respectively shall beside the incurring of the grievous sin of perjury be disabled and become by virtue of this Act incapable *ipso facto* to bear his and their said offices respectively, and be further liable to such punishments as shall be inflicted on him or them by the next or any ensuing parliament.

And in case the said lord chancellor, lord keeper, commissioner or commissioners aforesaid shall not issue forth the said writs as aforesaid, or in case that the parliament do not assemble and be held at the time and place before appointed, then the parliament shall assemble and be held in the usual place at Westminster in such manner and by such means only as is hereafter in this present Act declared and enacted and not otherwise, on the third Monday which shall be in the month of January then next ensuing. And the peers of this realm shall by virtue of this Act be enabled and are enjoined to meet in the Old Palace of Westminster in the usual place there on the third Monday in the said month of November, and they or any twelve or more of them then and there assembled shall, on or before the last Monday of November next following the tenth day of September aforesaid, by virtue of this Act without other warrant issue out writs in the usual form in the name of the King's Majesty, his heirs or successors, attested under the hands and seals of twelve or more of the said peers, to the several and respective sheriffs...for the electing of the knights, citizens, barons and burgesses...to be and appear at the parliament...on the third Monday in January....And it is enacted that the said writs so issued shall be of the same force and power to all intents and purposes as the writs or summons to parliament under the Great Seal of England have ever been....

[III. If the peers fail to act, and no parliament assembles by 23 January, then a parliament must be elected in the following manner, to assemble on the second Tuesday in March, when the peers must also assemble as if summoned by writ.]

IV. And for the better assembling of the knights, citizens, barons and burgesses to the said parliament as aforesaid, it is further enacted that the several and respective sheriffs of their several and respective counties, cities and boroughs of England and Wales, and the chancellor, masters and scholars of both and every of the universities, and the mayor and bailiffs of the borough of Berwick upon Tweed, shall at the several courts and places to be held and appointed for their respective counties, universities, cities and boroughs next after the said three and twentieth day of January cause such knight and knights, citizen and citizens, burgess and burgesses of their said counties, universities, cities and boroughs respectively, to be chosen by such persons and in such manner as if several and respective writs of summons to parliament under the Great Seal of England had issued and been awarded. And in case any of the several sheriffs, or the chancellor, masters and scholars of either of the universities, or the mayor and bailiffs of Berwick respectively do not before ten of the clock in the forenoon of the same day wherein the several and respective courts and places shall be held or appointed for their several and respective counties, universities, cities and boroughs, begin and proceed on according to the meaning of this law in causing elections to be made...as aforesaid, then the freeholders of each county, and the masters and scholars of every of the universities, and the citizens and others having voices in such election respectively in each university, city and borough, that shall be assembled at the said courts or places...shall forthwith without further warrant or direction proceed to the election of such knight or knights, citizen or citizens, burgess or burgesses aforesaid in such manner as is usual in case of writs of summons issued and awarded.

VI. And it is further enacted that no parliament henceforth to be assembled shall be dissolved or prorogued within fifty days at the least after the time appointed for the meeting thereof, unless it be by assent of his Majesty, his heirs or successors, and of both Houses of Parliament assembled. And that neither the House of Peers nor the House of

Commons shall be adjourned within fifty days at least after the meeting thereof unless it be by the free consent of every the said houses respectively.

*   *   *   *   *   *

XI. And it is lastly provided and enacted that his Majesty's royal assent to this bill shall not thereby determine this present session of parliament, and that all statutes and acts of Parliament which are to have continuance unto the end of this present session shall be of full force after his Majesty's assent until this present session be fully ended and determined. And if this present session shall determine by dissolution of this present parliament then all the acts and statutes aforesaid shall be continued until the end of the first session of the next parliament.

SR, v, 54–7

60. Protestation of the House of Commons, 3 May 1641

We the knights, citizens and burgesses of the Commons House in Parliament, finding to the grief of our hearts that the designs of the priests and Jesuits, and other adherents to the see of Rome, have of late been more boldly and frequently put in practice than formerly, to the undermining and danger of the ruin of the true Reformed Religion in his Majesty's dominions established, and finding also that there hath been, and having cause to suspect there still are, even during the sitting in Parliament, endeavours to subvert the fundamental laws of England and Ireland, and to introduce the exercise of an arbitrary and tyrannical government by most pernicious and wicked counsels, practices, plots and conspiracies; and that the long intermission and unhappier breach of parliaments hath occasioned many illegal taxations, whereby the subjects have been prosecuted and grieved; and that divers innovations and superstitions have been brought into the Church, multitudes driven out of his Majesty's dominions, jealousies raised and fomented between the King and people, a Popish army levied in Ireland, and two armies brought into the bowels of this kingdom, to the hazard of his Majesty's royal person, the consumption of the revenue of the Crown and the treasure of this realm; and lastly, finding the great causes of jealousy, [that] endeavours have been, and are used, to bring the English army into [a] misunderstanding of this Parliament, thereby to incline that army by force to bring to pass those wicked counsels, have therefore thought good to join ourselves in a declaration of our united affections and resolutions; and to make this ensuing Protestation:

I, A. B., do, in the presence of God, promise, vow and protest to maintain and defend, as far as lawfully I may, with my life, power and estate, the true reformed religion, expressed in the doctrine of the Church of England,[1] against all Popery and Popish innovation within this realm, contrary to the said doctrine, and according to the duty of my allegiance to his Majesty's royal person, honour and estate; as also the power and privilege of Parliament, the lawful rights and liberties of the subjects, and every person that shall make this Protestation in whatsoever he shall do, in the lawful pursuance of the same: And to my power, as far as lawfully I may, I will oppose, and, by all good ways and means, endeavour to bring to condign punishment all such as shall by force, practice, counsels, plots, conspiracies or otherwise do anything to the contrary in this Protestation contained:

And further, I shall in all just and honourable ways endeavour to preserve the union and peace betwixt the three kingdoms of England, Scotland and Ireland, and neither for hope, fear, nor other respect, shall relinquish this promise, vow and protestation.

CJ, II, 132

61. 16 Car. I, c. 10: An Act for the regulating the Privy Council and for taking away the court commonly called the Star Chamber

…Whereas by the statute made in the third year of King Henry the Seventh[2] power is given to the Chancellor, the Lord Treasurer of England for the time being, and the Keeper of the King's Privy Seal, or two of them, calling unto them a bishop and a temporal lord of the King's most honourable council and the two chief justices of the King's Bench and Common Pleas for the time being or other two justices in their absence, to proceed as is in that Act expressed for the punishment of some particular offences therein mentioned,…but the said judges have not kept themselves to the points limited by the said statute, but have undertaken to punish where no law doth warrant, and to make decrees for things, having no such authority, and to inflict heavier punishments than by any law is warranted: And forasmuch as all matters examinable or determinable before the said judges or in the court commonly called the Star Chamber may have their proper

---

[1] A week later the House issued an explanation of this passage, see no. 70, p. 258 below.
[2] 3 Hen. VII, c. 1, printed Elton, *Tudor Constitution*, p. 163.

remedy and redress, and their due punishment and correction, by the Common Law of the Land and in the ordinary course of justice elsewhere; and forasmuch as the reasons and motives inducing the erection and continuance of the court do now cease, and the proceedings, censure and decrees of that court have by experience been found to be an intolerable burden to the subjects, and the means to introduce an arbitrary power and government; and forasmuch as the Council Table hath of late times assumed unto itself a power to intermeddle in civil causes and matters only of private interest between party and party, and have adventured to determine of the estates and liberties of the subject, contrary to the law of the land and the rights and privileges of the subject, by which great and manifold mischiefs and inconveniences have arisen and happened, and much more uncertainty by means of such proceedings hath been conceived concerning men's rights and estates.

For settling whereof and preventing the like in time to come, be it ordained and enacted by the authority of this present Parliament that the said court commonly called the Star Chamber, and all jurisdiction, power and authority belonging unto or exercised in the same court or by any the judges, officers or ministers thereof be from the first day of August in the year of our Lord God 1641 clearly and absolutely dissolved, taken away and determined....

II. And be it likewise enacted that the like jurisdiction now used and exercised in the court before the President and Council in the Marches of Wales, and also before the President and Council established in the Northern Parts, and also in the court commonly called the Court of the Duchy of Lancaster held before the chancellor and council of the court, and also in the Court of Exchequer of the County Palatine of Chester held before the chamberlain and council of that court, the like jurisdiction being exercised there, shall from the same first day of August 1641 be also repealed and absolutely revoked and made void, any law, prescription, custom or usage, or the said statute made in the third year of King Henry the Seventh,...or any Act or Acts of Parliament heretofore had or made to the contrary thereof in any wise notwithstanding, and that from henceforth no court, council or place of judicature shall be erected, constituted or appointed within this realm of England or dominion of Wales which shall have use or exercise the same or the like jurisdiction as is or hath been used, practised or exercised in the said Court of Star Chamber.

III. Be it likewise declared and enacted by authority of this present parliament, that neither his Majesty nor his Privy Council have or ought to have any jurisdiction, power or authority by English bill, petition, articles, libel or any other arbitrary way whatsoever to examine or draw into question, determine or dispose of the lands, tenements, hereditaments, goods or chattels of any the subjects of this kingdom, but that the same ought to be tried and determined in the ordinary courts of justice and by the ordinary course of the law.

* * * * * *

62. 16 Car. I, c. 11: An Act for repeal of a branch of a statute primo Elizabeth concerning commissioners for causes ecclesiastical

[The preamble rehearses § VIII of the Act of Supremacy of 1559;[1] then proceeds:]

...And whereas by colour of some words in the foresaid branch of the said Act whereby commissioners are authorised to execute their commission according to the tenor and effect of the King's Letters Patent..., the said commissioners have to the great and insufferable wrong and oppression of the King's subjects used to fine and imprison them, and exercise another authority not belonging to [the] ecclesiastical jurisdiction restored by that Act, and divers other great mischiefs and inconveniences have also ensued to the King's subjects by occasion of the said branch and commissions issued thereupon, and the executions thereof; Therefore, for the repressing and preventing of the foresaid abuses, mischiefs and inconveniences in time to come, be it enacted by the King's most excellent Majesty and the Lords and Commons in this present Parliament assembled and by the authority of the same, that the foresaid branch, clause, article or sentence contained in the said Act, and every word, matter and thing contained in that branch, clause, article or sentence, shall from henceforth be repealed, annulled, revoked, annihilated and utterly made void for ever, any thing in the said Act to the contrary in any wise notwithstanding.

II. And be it also enacted by the authority aforesaid that no archbishop, bishop or vicar-general, nor any ordinary whatsoever, nor any other spiritual or ecclesiastical judge, officer, or minister of justice, nor any other person or persons whatsoever exercising spiritual or ecclesi-

[1] See Elton, *Tudor Constitution*, pp. 365–6.

astical power, authority or jurisdiction by any grant, licence or commission of the King's Majesty, his heirs or successors, or by any power or authority derived from the King, his heirs or successors, or otherwise, shall from and after the first day of August which shall be in the year of our Lord God 1641 award, impose or inflict any pain, penalty, fine, amercement, imprisonment or other corporal punishment upon any of the King's subjects for any contempt, misdemeanour, crime, offence, matter or thing whatsoever belonging to spiritual or ecclesiastical cognisance or jurisdiction, or shall *ex officio* or at the instance or promotion of any other person whatsoever urge, enforce, tender, give or minister unto any churchwarden, sideman or other person whatsoever any corporal oath whereby he or she shall or may be charged or obliged to make any presentment of any crime or offence or to confess or to accuse him or herself of any crime, offence, delinquency or misdemeanour, or any neglect, matter or thing whereby or by reason whereof he or she shall or may be liable or exposed to any censure, pain, penalty or punishment whatsoever....

*   *   *   *   *   *

IV. And be it further enacted that from and after the said first day of August no new court shall be erected, ordained or appointed within this realm of England or dominion of Wales which shall or may have the like power, jurisdiction or authority as the said High Commission court now hath or pretendeth to have, but that all and every such letters patent, commissions and grants made or to be made by his Majesty, his heirs or successors, and all powers and authorities granted or pretended or mentioned to be granted thereby and all acts, sentences and decrees to be made by virtue or colour thereof shall be utterly void and of none effect. *SR*, v, 112–13

63. The Additional Instruction, 5–8 November 1641

[5 November. Taking into consideration the Irish Rebellion, the House of Commons issued five 'instructions' to the Committee of both Houses in Edinburgh.]

The Instructions being agreed on...Mr Pym stood up and moved that no man should be more ready and forward to engage his estate, person, life and all than himself for the suppression of this rebellion in Ireland or for the performance of any other service for his Majesty's honour and safety, but he feared that as long as he gave ear to those evil counsellors about him all that we did would prove in vain, and therefore desired that we might add some declaration in the end of these instructions that howsoever we had engaged ourselves for the assistance of Ireland, yet unless the King would remove his evil counsellors and take such counsellors as might be approved by Parliament we should account ourselves absolved from this engagement.

Divers would have had it speedily assented unto, but Mr Hyde stood up and first opposed it, and said amongst other things that by such an addition we should as it were prevail the King.

Mr Waller spake also against it, and said that as the Earl of Strafford had advised the King that because we did not relieve him he was absolved from all rules of government, so by this addition on the contrary we should pretend that if the King did not remove his ill counsellors we were absolved from our duties in assisting him in the recovery of Ireland.

Mr Pym stood up and interrupted him, and spake to the Orders of the House,[1] and said that if his motion he had made were of the same nature with the earl of Strafford's then he deserved the like punishment, and therefore he craved the justice of the House either to censure him, or to cause the gentleman who had last spoken to make him reparation.

Divers called on Mr Waller to explain himself, which he not doing fully, he was commanded after some debate to withdraw, and went accordingly into the committee chamber...but after a little debate [he] was called down out of the committee chamber and publicly asked the pardon of the House and of Mr Pym.

[Next day, Saturday, this sixth article caused further debate, and over Sunday Pym decided to amend it.]

[8 November.] Mr Pym brought in the Instructions to be sent into Scotland to our Committee there, of which we had agreed the first five articles on Saturday last, and had long debated the sixth article..., but now Mr Pym had left out that last condition and had added this new one, viz., that if his Majesty should not be graciously pleased to grant it, though we would continue in that obedience and loyalty to him which was due by the laws of God and this kingdom, yet we should

---

[1] That is, on a point of order.

take such a course for the securing of Ireland as might likewise secure ourselves.[1]

Divers spoke to this, and most against the sixth article, and some for it..., till at last it came to a question; and though the ayes were apparently more than the noes, yet neither side yielding...[a vote was taken]. The ayes were 151 and the noes were 110, and so it was ordered that the said sixth article should be sent into Scotland as part of our instructions to our Committee there. (I was a no, conceiving this article to be of very dangerous consequence.)

D'Ewes Journal, ed. Coates, pp. 94–105

64. The Grand Remonstrance, 1641

The Petition of the House of Commons which accompanied the Remonstrance of the state of the kingdom, when it was presented to His Majesty at Hampton Court, 1 December 1641

Most Gracious Sovereign,

Your Majesty's most humble and faithful subjects the Commons in this present parliament assembled do with much thankfulness and joy acknowledge the great mercy and favour of God, in giving your Majesty a safe and peaceable return out of Scotland into your kingdom of England, where the pressing dangers and distempers of the State have caused us with much earnestness to desire the comfort of your gracious presence, and likewise the unity and justice of your royal authority, to give more life and power to the dutiful and loyal counsels and endeavours of your Parliament for the prevention of that eminent ruin and destruction wherein your kingdoms of England and Scotland are threatened. The duty which we owe to your Majesty and our country cannot but make us very sensible and apprehensive that the multiplicity, sharpness and malignity of those evils under which we have now many years suffered are fomented and cherished by a corrupt and ill-affected party, who amongst other their mischievous devices for the alteration of religion and government have sought by many false scandals and imputations, cunningly insinuated and dispersed

---

[1] The Instructions read: 'And, if herein his Majesty shall not vouchsafe to condescend to our humble supplication,...we shall be forced, in discharge of the trust which we owe to the State, and to those whom we represent, to resolve upon some such way of defending Ireland from the rebels as may concur to the securing of ourselves from such mischievous counsels and designs as have lately been and are still in practice and agitation against us, as we have just cause to believe; and to commend those aids and contributions which this great necessity shall require to the custody and disposing of such persons of honour and fidelity as we have cause to confide in' (*LJ*, IV, 431).

amongst the people, to blemish and disgrace our proceedings in this parliament, and to get themselves a party and faction amongst your subjects for the better strengthening themselves in their wicked courses, and hindering those provisions and remedies which might, by the wisdom of your Majesty and counsel of your Parliament, be opposed against them.

For preventing whereof, and the better information of your Majesty, your Peers and all other your loyal subjects, we have been necessitated to make a Declaration of the State of the Kingdom, both before and since the assembly of this parliament unto this time, which we do humbly present to your Majesty, without the least intention to lay any blemish upon your royal person, but only to represent how your royal authority and trust have been abused, to the great prejudice and danger of your Majesty, and of all your good subjects.

And because we have reason to believe that those malignant parties whose proceedings evidently appear to be mainly for the advantage and increase of Popery, is [sic] composed, set up and acted by the subtle practice of the Jesuits and other engineers and factors for Rome, and to the great danger of this kingdom and most grievous affliction of your loyal subjects have so far prevailed as to corrupt divers of your bishops and others in prime places of the Church, and also to bring divers of those instruments to be of your Privy Council, and other employments of trust and nearness about your Majesty, the prince, and the rest of the royal children.

And by this means have had such an operation in your counsel and the most important affairs and proceedings of your government, that a most dangerous division and chargeable preparation for war betwixt your kingdoms of England and Scotland, the increase of jealousies betwixt your Majesty and your most obedient subjects, the violent distraction and interruption of this parliament, the insurrection of the Papists in your kingdom of Ireland, and bloody massacre of your people, have been not only endeavoured and attempted but in a great measure compassed and effected.

For preventing the final accomplishment whereof, your poor subjects are enforced to engage their persons and estates to the maintaining of a very expensive and dangerous war, notwithstanding they have already since the beginning of this parliament undergone the charge of 150,000 pounds sterling, or thereabouts, for the necessary support and supply of your Majesty in these present and perilous designs. And because all our most faithful endeavours and engagements will be ineffectual for the peace, safety and preservation of your Majesty and your people if some present, real and effectual course be not taken for suppressing this wicked and malignant party, we your most humble and obedient subjects do with all faithfulness and humility beseech your Majesty:

1. That you will be graciously pleased to concur with the humble desires of your people in a parliamentary way, for the preserving the peace and safety of the kingdom from the malicious designs of the Popish party:

For depriving the bishops of their votes in Parliament, and abridging their immoderate power usurped over the clergy, and other your good subjects, which they have perniciously abused to the hazard of religion and great prejudice and oppression to the laws of the kingdom and just liberty of your people;

For the taking away such oppressions in religion, church government and discipline as have been brought in and fomented by them;

For uniting all such your loyal subjects together as join in the same fundamental truths against the Papists, by removing some oppressive and unnecessary ceremonies by which divers weak consciences have been scrupled, and seem to be divided from the rest, and for the due execution of those good laws which have been made for securing the liberty of your subjects.

2. That your Majesty will likewise be pleased to remove from your council all such as persist to favour and promote any of those pressures and corruptions wherewith your people have been grieved, and that for the future your Majesty will vouchsafe to employ such persons in your great and public affairs, and to take such to be near you in places of trust, as your Parliament may have cause to confide in; [and] that in your princely goodness to your people you will reject and refuse all mediation and solicitation to the contrary, how powerful and near soever....

Which humble desires of ours being graciously fulfilled by your Majesty, we will, by the blessings and favour of God, most cheerfully undergo the hazard and expenses of this war, and apply ourselves to such other courses and counsels as may support your real estate with honour and plenty at home, with power and reputation abroad, and by our loyal affections, obedience and service, lay a sure and lasting foundation of the greatness and prosperity of your Majesty, and your royal posterity in future times.

The Grand Remonstrance

The Commons in this Parliament assembled, having with much earnestness and faithfulness of affection and zeal to the public good of this kingdom and his Majesty's honour and service, for the space of twelve months wrestled with great dangers and fears, the pressing miseries and calamities, the various distempers and disorders which had not only assaulted but even overwhelmed and extinguished the liberty, peace and prosperity of this kingdom, the comfort and hopes of all his Majesty's good subjects, and exceedingly weakened and undermined the foundation and strength of his own royal throne, do yet find an abounding malignity and opposition in those parties and factions who have been the cause of those evils, and do still labour to cast aspersions upon that which hath been done, and to raise many difficulties for the hindrance of that which remains yet undone, and to foment jealousies between the King and Parliament, that so they may deprive him and his people of the fruit of his own gracious intentions, and their humble desires of procuring the public peace, safety and happiness of this realm.

For the preventing of those miserable effects which such malicious endeavours may produce, we have thought good to declare the root and growth of these mischievous designs; the maturity and ripeness to which they have attained before the beginning of the parliament; the effectual means which have been used for the extirpation of those dangerous evils, and the progress which hath therein been made by his Majesty's goodness and the wisdom of the parliament; the ways of obstruction and opposition by which that programme hath been interrupted; the courses to be taken for the removing those obstacles, and for the accomplishing of our most dutiful and faithful intentions and endeavours of restoring and establishing the ancient honour, greatness and security of this Crown and nation.

The root of all this mischief we find to be a malignant and pernicious design of subverting the fundamental laws and principles of government, upon which the religion and justice of this kingdom are firmly established. The actors and promoters thereof have been:

1. The Jesuited Papists, who hate the laws, as the obstacles of that change and subversion of religion which they so much long for.
2. The bishops, and the corrupt part of the clergy, who cherish

formality and superstition as the natural effects and more probable supports of their own ecclesiastical tyranny and usurpation.

3. Such councillors and courtiers as for private ends have engaged themselves to further the interests of some foreign princes or states to the prejudice of his Majesty and the State at home.[1]

The common principles by which they moulded and governed all their particular counsels and actions were these:

First, to maintain continual differences and discontents between the King and the people, upon questions of prerogative and liberty, that so they might have the advantage of siding with him, and under the notions of men addicted to his service gain to themselves and their parties the places of greatest trust and power in the kingdom.

A second, to suppress the purity and power of religion, and such persons as were best affected to it, as being contrary to their own ends, and the greatest impediment to that change which they thought to introduce.

A third, to conjoin those parties of the kingdom which were most propitious to their own ends, and to divide those who were most opposite, which consisted in many particular observations: to cherish the Arminian part in those points wherein they agree with the Papists; to multiply and enlarge the difference between the common Protestants and those whom they call Puritans; to introduce and countenance such opinions and ceremonies as are fittest for accommodation with Popery; to increase and maintain ignorance, looseness and profaneness in the people; that of those three parties, Papist, Arminians and Libertines, they might compose a body fit to act such counsels and resolutions as were most conducible to their own ends.

A fourth, to disaffect the King to parliaments by slander and false imputations, and by putting him upon other ways of supply, which in show and appearance were fuller of advantage than the ordinary course of subsidies, though in truth they brought more loss than gain both to the King and people, and have caused the great distractions under which we both suffer.

* * * * * *

[§§ 1–87 of the Remonstrance recount in detail the machinations of the Popish faction from the accession of Charles I, reaching a climax in the promulgation of the canons of 1640.]

[1] Cf. the similar phraseology used by Pym on 7 November 1640, no. 54, p. 204 above.

88. The Popish party enjoyed such exemptions from penal laws as amounted to a toleration, besides many other encouragements and court favours.

89. They had a Secretary of State, Sir Francis Windebank, a powerful agent for speeding all their desires.

90. A Pope's nuncio residing here, to act and govern them according to such influences as he received from Rome, and to intercede for them with the most powerful concurrence of the foreign princes of that religion.

91. By his authority the Papists of all sorts, nobility, gentry and clergy, were convocated after the manner of a Parliament.

92. New jurisdictions were erected of Romish archbishops, taxes levied, another State, moulded within this State, independent in government, contrary in interest and affection, secretly corrupting the ignorant or negligent professors of our religion, and closely uniting and combining themselves against such as were found in this posture, waiting for an opportunity by force to destroy those whom they could not hope to seduce.

93. For the effecting whereof they were strengthened with arms and munitions, encouraged by superstitious prayers, enjoined by the nuncio to be weekly made for the prosperity of some great design.

94. And such power had they at court that secretly a commission was issued out, or intended to be issued to some great men of that profession for the levying of soldiers, and to command and employ them according to private instructions, which we doubt were framed for the advantage of those who were the contrivers of them.

* * * * * *

[§§ 95–104 deal briefly with the campaign of 1640, leading up to the summons of the Long Parliament.]

105. At our first meeting all oppositions seemed to vanish; the mischiefs were so evident which those evil counsellors produced that no man durst stand up to defend them; yet the work itself afforded difficulty enough.

106. The multiplied evils and corruptions of fifteen years, strengthened by custom and authority, and the concurrent interest of many powerful delinquents, were now to be brought to judgement and reformation. . . .

107. The difficulties seemed to be insuperable, which by the Divine Providence we have overcome, the contrarieties incompatible, which yet in a great measure we have reconciled.

* * * * * *

[§§ 111–36 are a summary of the activities and achievements of this parliament during its first session, particularly its legislative record.]

137. Many excellent laws and provisions are in preparation for removing the inordinate power, vexation and usurpation of bishops, for reforming the pride and idleness of many of the clergy, for easing the people of unnecessary ceremonies in religion, for censuring and removing unworthy and improfitable ministers, and for maintaining godly and diligent preachers through the kingdom.

138. Other things of main importance for the good of this kingdom are in proposition, though little could hitherto be done in regard of the many other more pressing businesses, which yet before the end of this session we hope may receive some progress and perfection.

139. The establishing and ordering the King's revenue, that so the abuse of officers and superfluity of expenses may be cut off, and the necessary disbursements for his Majesty's honour, the defence and government of the kingdom, may be more certainly provided for.

140. The regulating of courts of justice, and abridging both the delays and charges of law suits.

141. The settling of some good courses for preventing the exportation of gold and silver, and the inequality of exchanges between us and other nations, for the advancing of native commodities, increase of our manufactures, and well balancing of trade, whereby the stock of the kingdom may be increased, or at least kept from impairing, as through neglect hereof it hath done for many years last past.

142. Improving the herring fishing upon our coasts, which will be of mighty use in the employment of the poor, and a plentiful nursery of mariners for enabling the kingdom in any great action.

143. The oppositions, obstructions and the difficulties wherewith we have been encountered, and which still lie in our way with some strength and much obstinacy, are these; the malignant party, whom we have formerly described to be the actors and promoters of all our misery, they have taken heart again.

144. They have been able to prefer some of their own factors and agents to degrees of honour, to places of trust and employment, even during the parliament.

145. They have endeavoured to work in his Majesty ill impressions and opinions of our proceedings, as if we had altogether done our own work, and not his; and had obtained from him many things very prejudicial to the Crown, both in respect of prerogative and profit....

* * * * * *

154. As to the second branch of this slander, we acknowledge with much thankfulness that his Majesty hath passed more good bills to the advantage of the subjects that have been in many ages....

* * * * * *

156. And for both Houses of Parliament we may with truth and modesty say thus much: that we have ever been careful not to desire anything that should weaken the Crown either in just profit or useful power.

157. The triennial parliament [Act], for the matter of it, doth not extend to so much as by law we ought to have required (there being two statutes still in force for a parliament to be once a year); and for the manner of it, it is in the King's power that it shall never take effect, if he by a timely summons shall prevent any other way of assembling.

158. In the bill for continuance of this present parliament there seems to be some restraint of the royal power in dissolving of parliaments, not to take it out of the Crown, but to suspend the execution of it for this time and occasion only, which was so necessary for the King's own security and the public peace, that without it we could not have undertaken any of these great charges, but must have left both the armies to disorder and confusion, and the whole kingdom to blood and rapine.

* * * * * *

161. In the rest there will not be found so much as a shadow of prejudice to the Crown.

162. [Yet] they [the 'malignant party'] have sought to diminish our reputation with the people, and to bring them out of love with parliaments.

163. The aspersions which they have attempted this way have been such as these:

164. That we have spent much time and done little, especially in those grievances which concern religion.

* * * * * *

166. To which there is a ready answer: if the time spent in this parliament be considered in relation backward to the long growth and deep root of those grievances which we have removed, to the powerful supports of those delinquents which we have pursued, to the great necessities and other charges of the Commonwealth for which we have provided; [167] or if it be considered in relation forward to many advantages, which not only the present but future ages are like to reap by the good laws and other proceedings in this Parliament, we doubt not but it will be thought by all indifferent judgements that our time hath been much better employed than in a far greater proportion of time in many former parliaments put together....

* * * * * *

170. [Moreover], they have had such a party of bishops and Popish lords in the House of Peers as hath caused much opposition and delay in the prosecution of delinquents, [and] hindered the proceedings on divers good bills passed in the Commons' House concerning the reformation of sundry great abuses and corruptions both in Church and State.

171. They have laboured to seduce and corrupt some of the Commons' House to draw them into conspiracies and combinations against the liberty of the Parliament, [172] and by their instruments and agents they have attempted to disaffect and discontent his Majesty's army, and to engage it for the maintenance of their wicked and traitorous designs: the keeping up of bishops in votes and functions, and by force to compel the parliament to order, limit and dispose their proceedings in such manner as might best concur with the intentions of this dangerous and potent faction.

* * * * * *

[§§ 173-4 are concerned with the First and Second Army Plots.]

175. Thus they have been continually practising to disturb the peace, and plotting the destruction even of all the King's dominions; and have employed their emissaries and agents in them all for the pro-

moting their devilish designs, which the vigilancy of those who were well affected hath still discovered and defeated before they were ripe for execution in England and Scotland.

176. Only in Ireland, which was farther off, they have had time and opportunity to mould and prepare their work, and had brought it to that perfection that they had possessed themselves of that whole kingdom, totally subverted the government of it, rooted out religion, and destroyed all the Protestants whom the conscience of their duty to God, their King and country, would not have permitted to join with them, if by God's wonderful providence their main enterprise, upon the city and castle of Dublin, had not been detected and prevented upon the very eve before it should have been executed.

177. Notwithstanding, they have in other parts of that kingdom broken out into open rebellion, surprising towns and castles, committed murders, rapes and other villainies, and shaken off all bonds of obedience to his Majesty and the laws of this realm; [178] and in general have kindled such a fire as nothing but God's infinite blessing upon the wisdom and endeavours of this State will be able to quench it.

179. And certainly had not God in his great mercy unto this land discovered and confounded their former designs we had been the prologue to this tragedy in Ireland, and had by this been made the lamentable spectacle of misery and confusion.

180. And now what hope have we but in God, when as the only means of our subsistence and power of reformation is under him in the Parliament?

181. But what can we the Commons [do] without the conjunction of the House of Lords, and what conjunction can we expect there, when the bishops and recusant lords are so numerous and prevalent that they are able to cross and interrupt our best endeavours for reformation, and by that means give advantage to this malignant party to traduce our proceedings?

182. They infuse into the people that we mean to abolish all church government, and leave every man to his own fancy for the sacrifice and worship of God, absolving him of that obedience which he owes under God unto his Majesty, whom we know to be entrusted with the ecclesiastical law as well as with the temporal, to regulate all the members of the Church of England by such rules or order and discipline as are established by Parliament, which is his great council, in all affairs both in Church and State.

183. We confess our intention is, and our endeavours have been, to reduce within bounds that exorbitant power which the prelates have assumed unto themselves, so contrary to the Word of God and to the laws of the land, to which end we passed the bill for the removing them from their temporal power and employments, that so the better they might with meekness apply themselves to the discharge of their functions, which bill themselves opposed, and were the principal instruments of crossing it.

184. And we do here declare that it is far from our purpose or desire to let loose the golden reins of discipline and government in the Church, to leave private persons or particular congregations to take up what form of Divine Service they please, for we hold it requisite that there should be throughout the whole realm a conformity to that order which the laws enjoin according to the Word of God. And we desire to unburden the consciences of men of needless and superstitious ceremonies, suppress innovations, and take away the monuments of idolatry.

185. And the better to effect the intended reformation, we desire there may be a general synod of the most grave, pious, learned and judicious divines of this island, assisted with some from foreign parts professing the same religion with us, who may consider of all things necessary for the peace and good government of the Church, and represent the results of their consultations unto the Parliament, to be there allowed of and confirmed, and receive the stamp of authority, thereby to find passage and obedience throughout the kingdom.

186. They have maliciously charged us that we intend to destroy and discourage learning, whereas it is our chiefest care and desire to advance it, and to provide a competent maintenance for conscionable and preaching ministers throughout the kingdom, which will be a great encouragement to scholars, and a certain means whereby the want, meanness and ignorance to which a great part of the clergy is now subject will be prevented.

187. And we intend likewise to reform and purge the fountains of learning, the two universities, that the streams flowing from thence may be clear and pure, and an honour and comfort to the whole land.

* * * * * *

191. For the perfecting of the work begun, and removing all future impediments, we conceive these courses will be very effectual, seeing

the religion of the Papists hath such principles as do certainly tend to the destruction and extirpation of all Protestants whom they shall have opportunity to effect it.

192. It is necessary in the first place to keep them in such condition as that they may not be able to do us any hurt, and for avoiding of such connivance and favour as hath heretofore been shown unto them.

193. That his Majesty be pleased to grant a standing commission to some choice men named in Parliament, who may take notice of their increase, their counsels and proceedings, and use all due means by execution of the laws to prevent all mischievous designs against the peace and safety of this kingdom.

194. That some good course be taken to discover the counterfeit and false conformity of Papists to the Church, by colour whereof persons very much disaffected to the true religion have been admitted into places of greatest authority and trust in the kingdom.

195. For the better preservation of the laws and liberties of the kingdom, that all illegal grievances and exactions be presented and punished at the sessions and assizes.

196. And that judges and justices be very careful to give this in charge to the grand jury, and both the sheriff and justices to be sworn to the due execution of the Petition of Right and other laws.

197. That his Majesty be humbly petitioned by both Houses to employ such councillors, ambassadors and other ministers, in managing his business at home and abroad, as the parliament may have cause to confide in, without which we cannot give his Majesty such supplies for support of his own estate, not such assistance to the Protestant party beyond the sea, as is desired.

198. It may often fall out that the Commons may have just cause to take exception at some men for being councillors, and yet not charge those men with crimes, for there be grounds of difference which lie not in proof, [and, 199,] there are others which, though they may be proved, yet are not legally criminal.

200. To be a known favourer of Papists, or to have been very forward in defending or countenancing some great offenders questioned in Parliament; or to speak contemptuously of either House of Parliament, or parliamentary privilege; [201,] or such as are factors or agents for any foreign prince of another religion; such [as] are justly suspected to get councillors' places, or any other of trust concerning public

employment, for money: for all these and divers others we may have great reason to be earnest with his Majesty not to put his great affairs into such hands, though we may be unwilling to proceed against them in any legal ways of charge or impeachment.

202. That all Councillors of State may be sworn to observe those laws which concern the subject in his liberty, that they may likewise take an oath not to receive or give reward or pension from any foreign prince, but such as they shall within some reasonable time discover to the lords of his Majesty's Council.

203. And although they should wickedly forswear themselves, yet it may herein do good to make them known to be false and perjured to those who employ them, and thereby bring them into as little credit with them as with us.

204. That his Majesty may have cause to be in love with good counsel and good men, by showing him in a humble and dutiful manner how full of advantage it would be to himself to see his own estate settled in a plentiful condition to support his honour; to see his people united in ways of duty to him, and endeavours of the public good; to see happiness, wealth, peace and safety derived to his own kingdom, and procured to his allies by the influence of his own power and government.

Rushworth, IV, 437–51

65. The impeachment of the Five Members, 3 January 1642

The lord keeper signified to the House [of Lords], that he was commanded by the King, to let their lordships know, that his Majesty hath given Mr Attorney-General command to acquaint their lordships with some particulars from him. Hereupon Mr Attorney, standing at the Clerk's table, said that the King had commanded him to tell their lordships, that divers great and treasonable designs and practices against him and the State have come to his Majesty's knowledge, for which the King hath given him command, in his name, to accuse, and did accuse, six persons of high treason, and other high misdemeanours, by delivery of the Articles in writing which he had in his hand, which he received from his Majesty, and was commanded to desire your lordships to have it read, in which Articles the persons' names, and the heads of the treason, were contained. Which Articles were commanded to be read, *in haec verba*.

Articles of high treason and other high misdemeanours against the

Lord Kimbolton, Mr Denzil Holles, Sir Arthur Haslerigg, Mr John Pym, Mr John Hampden and Mr William Strode.

1. That they have traitorously endeavoured to subvert the fundamental laws and government of the kingdom of England, to deprive the King of his regal power, and to place in subjects an arbitrary and tyrannical power over the lives, liberties and estates of his Majesty's liege people.

2. That they have traitorously endeavoured, by many foul aspersions upon his Majesty and his government, to alienate the affections of his people, and to make his Majesty odious unto them.

3. That they have endeavoured to draw his Majesty's late army to disobedience to His Majesty's commands, and to side with them in their traitorous designs.

4. That they have traitorously invited and encouraged a foreign power to invade his Majesty's kingdom of England.

5. That they have traitorously endeavoured to subvert the rights and the very being of parliaments.

6. That for the completing of their traitorous designs they have endeavoured (as far as in them lay) by force and terror to compel the parliament to join with them in their traitorous designs, and to that end have actually raised and countenanced tumults against the King and Parliament.

7. And that they have traitorously conspired to levy, and actually have levied, war against the King.

* * * * * *

Ordered, That this business shall be taken into consideration by a committee of the whole House, and to consider whether this accusation of Mr Attorney-General, of the Lord Kimbolton and others, of high treason, be a regular proceeding, according to law,...and whether an accusation of treason may be brought into this House by the King's attorney against a Peer in Parliament and whether any person ought to be committed to custody upon a general accusation from the King or the House of Commons, before it be reduced into particulars.

LJ, IV, 500–501

66. Remonstrance of both Houses, in answer to the King's declaration concerning Hull, 26 May 1642

* * * * * *

And as for 'the duty and modesty of former times', from which we are said to have varied, and to want the warrant of any precedents therein, but what ourselves have made; if we have made any precedents in this parliament, wc have made them for posterity, upon the same or better grounds of reason and law than those were upon which our predecessors first made any for us. And as some precedents ought not to be rules for us to follow, so none can be limits to bound our proceedings, which may and must vary according to the different condition of times....If we have done more than ever our ancestors have done we have suffered more than they have ever suffered, and yet, in point of modesty and duty, we shall not yield to the best of former times, and we shall put this in issue: Whether the highest and most unwarrantable proceedings of any of his Majesty's predecessors do not fall short of, and much below, what hath been done to us this parliament; and on the other side, whether, if we should make the highest precedents of other parliaments our pattern, there would be cause to complain of 'want of modesty and duty' in us, when we have not so much as suffered such things to enter our thoughts which all the world knows they have put in action?

Another charge which is laid very high upon us (and which were indeed a very great crime if we were found guilty thereof), is, that by avowing this act of Sir J. Hotham[1] we do in consequence confound and destroy the title and interest of all his Majesty's good subjects to their lands and goods, and that upon this ground, 'that his Majesty hath the same title to his own town of Hull which any of his subjects hath to their houses or lands....'

Here that is laid down for a principle which would indeed pull up the very foundation of the liberty, property and interest of every subject in particular, and of all the subjects in general, if we should admit it for a truth that his Majesty hath the same right and title to his towns and magazines (bought with the public monies, as we conceive that at Hull to have been) that every particular man hath to his house, lands and goods, for his Majesty's towns are no more his own than his king-

[1] In refusing the king entrance to Hull.

dom is his own, and his kingdom is no more his own that his people are his own.... This erroneous maxim, being infused into princes, that their kingdoms are their own, and that they may do with them what they will (as if their kingdoms were for them, and not they for their kingdoms) is the root of all the subjects' misery, and of all the invading of their just rights and liberties. Whereas, indeed, they are only entrusted with their kingdoms, and with their towns, and with their people, and with the public treasure of the commonwealth and whatsoever is bought therewith. By the known law of this kingdom the very jewels of the crown are not the king's proper goods, but are only entrusted to him for the use and ornament thereof, as the towns, forts, treasure, magazine, offices and people of the kingdom, and the whole kingdom itself, are entrusted unto him for the good and safety and best advantage thereof; and as this trust is for the use of the kingdom, so ought it to be managed by the advice of the Houses of Parliament, whom the kingdom hath trusted for that purpose....

But, admitting his Majesty had indeed a property in the town and magazine of Hull, who doubts but that a parliament may dispose of any thing wherein his Majesty or any subject hath a right, in such a way as that the kingdom may not be exposed to hazard or danger thereby? Which is our case in the disposing of the town and magazine of Hull. And whereas his Majesty doth allow this, and a greater, power to a parliament, but in that sense only as he himself is a part thereof, we appeal to every man's conscience that hath observed our proceedings, whether we disjoined his Majesty from his parliament, who have in all humble ways sought his concurrence with us,...or whether these evil counsellors about him have not separated him from his parliament, not only in distance of place, but also in the discharge of this joint trust with them for the peace and safety of the kingdom....

* * * * * *

We are so far from believing 'that his Majesty is the only person against whom treason cannot be committed' that, in some sense, we acknowledge he is the only person against whom it can be committed, that is, as he is king; and that treason which is against the kingdom is more against the King than that which is against his person because he is King; for that very treason is not treason as it is against him as a man, but as a man that is a king, and as he hath relation to the kingdom, and stands as a person entrusted with the kingdom, and discharging that trust....

[As] for the Order of assistance to the committees of both Houses; as they have no directions or instructions but what have the law for their limits and the safety of the land for their ends, so we doubt not but all persons mentioned in that Order, and all his Majesty's good subjects, will yield obedience to his Majesty's authority signified therein by both Houses of Parliament. . . .

* * * * * *

PH, II, 1298–1314

67. The Nineteen Propositions, 1 June 1642

Your Majesty's most humble and faithful subjects, the Lords and Commons in Parliament. . .do in all humility and sincerity present to your Majesty their most dutiful petition and advice, that, out of your princely wisdom, for the establishing of your own honour and safety, and gracious tenderness of the welfare and security of your subjects and dominions, you will be pleased to grant and accept these our humble desires and propositions, as the most necessary effectual means, through God's blessing, of removing those jealousies and differences, which have unhappily fallen betwixt you and your people, and procuring both your Majesty and them a constant course of honour, peace and happiness.

1. That the Lords and others of your Majesty's Privy Council and such great officers and ministers of state, either at home or beyond the seas, may be put from your Privy Council, and from those offices and employments, excepting such as shall be approved of by both Houses of Parliament; and that the persons put into the places and employments of those that are removed, may be approved of by both Houses of Parliament; and that all Privy Councillors shall take an oath for the due execution of their places, in such form as shall be agreed upon by both Houses of Parliament.

2. That the great affairs of the kingdom may not be concluded or transacted by the advice of private men, or by any unknown or un-sworn councillors, but that such matters as concern the public, and are proper for the High Court of Parliament, which is your Majesty's great and supreme council, may be debated, resolved and transacted only in Parliament, and not elsewhere: and such as shall presume to do any thing to the contrary shall be reserved to the censure and judgement of Parliament: and such other matters of state as are proper for your Majesty's Privy Council shall be debated and concluded by such of the

nobility and others as shall, from time to time, be chosen for that place, by approbation of both Houses of Parliament: and that no public act concerning the affairs of the kingdom, which are proper for your Privy Council, may be esteemed of any validity, as proceeding from the royal authority, unless it be done by the advice and consent of the major part of your council, attested under their hands: and that your council may be limited to a certain number, not exceeding twenty-five, nor under fifteen: and if any councillor's place happen to be void in the intervals of Parliament, it shall not be supplied without the assent of the major part of the council, which choice shall be confirmed at the next sitting of Parliament, or else be void.

3. That the Lord High Steward of England, Lord High Constable, Lord Chancellor, or Lord Keeper of the Great Seal, Lord Treasurer, Lord Privy Seal, Earl Marshall, Lord Admiral, Warden of the Cinque Ports, Chief Governor of Ireland, Chancellor of the Exchequer, Master of the Wards, Secretaries of State, two Chief Justices, and Chief Baron, may always be chosen with the approbation of both Houses of Parliament; and in the intervals of Parliament, by assent of the major part of the council, in such manner as is before expressed in the choice of councillors.

4. That he or they, unto whom the government and education of the King's children shall be committed, shall be approved of by both Houses of Parliament; and in the intervals of Parliament, by the assent of the major part of the Council, in such manner as is before expressed in the choice of councillors; and that all such servants as are now about them, against whom both Houses shall have any just exception, shall be removed.

5. That no marriage shall be concluded or treated, for any of the King's children, with any foreign prince, or other person whatsoever, abroad or at home, without the consent of Parliament, under the penalty of a Praemunire, unto such as shall conclude or treat any marriage as aforesaid; and that the said penalty shall not be pardoned, or dispensed with but by the consent of both Houses of Parliament.

6. That the laws in force against Jesuits, priests, and Popish recusants, be strictly put in execution, without any toleration or dispensation to the contrary; and that some more effectual course may be enacted, by authority of Parliament, to disable them from making any disturbance in the State, or eluding the law, by trusts, or otherwise.

7. That the votes of the Popish Lords in the House of Peers may be

taken away, so long as they continue Papists; and that His Majesty would consent to such a bill as shall be drawn for the education of the children of Papists by Protestants, in the Protestant religion.

8. That your Majesty would be pleased to consent, that such a reformation be made of the Church government and liturgy, as both Houses of Parliament shall advise; wherein they intend to have consultations with divines, as is expressed in their declaration to that purpose; and that your Majesty will contribute your best assistance to them, for the raising of a sufficient maintenance for preaching ministers throughout the kingdom; and that your Majesty will be pleased to give your consent to laws for the taking away of innovations and superstitions, and of pluralities, and against scandalous ministers.

9. That your Majesty will be pleased to rest satisfied with that course that the Lords and Commons have appointed, for ordering the militia, until the same shall be further settled by a bill; and that your Majesty will recall your declarations and proclamations against the ordinance made by the Lords and Commons concerning it.

10. That such Members of either House of Parliament as have, during this present parliament, been put out of any place and office, may either be restored to that place or office, or otherwise have satisfaction for the same, upon the petition of that House whereof he or they are Members.

11. That all privy councillors and judges may take an oath, the form whereof to be agreed on and settled by Act of Parliament, for the maintaining of the Petition of Right and of certain statutes made by Parliament, which shall be mentioned by both Houses of Parliament: and that an inquiry of all the breaches and violations of those laws may be given in charge by the justices of the King's Bench, every term, and by the judges of assize in their circuits, and justices of the peace at the sessions, to be presented and punished according to law.

12. That all the judges, and all officers placed by approbation of both Houses of Parliament, may hold their places *quam diu bene se gesserint.*

13. That the justice of Parliament may pass upon all delinquents, whether they be within the kingdom or fled out of it; and that all persons cited by either House of Parliament may appear and abide the censure of Parliament.

14. That the general pardon offered by your Majesty may be granted with such exceptions as shall be advised by both Houses of Parliament.

15. That the forts and castles of this kingdom may be put under the command and custody of such persons as your Majesty shall appoint

with the approbation of your Parliament: and in the intervals of Parliament, with approbation of the major part of the Council, in such manner as is before expressed in the choice of councillors.

16. That the extraordinary guards and military forces now attending your Majesty may be removed, and discharged; and that, for the future, you will raise no such guards or extraordinary forces, but according to the law, in case of actual rebellion or invasion.

17. That your Majesty will be pleased to enter into a more strict alliance with the States of the United Provinces, and other neighbouring princes and states of the Protestant religion, for the defence and maintenance thereof, against all designs and attempts of the Pope and his adherents to subvert and suppress it; whereby your Majesty will obtain a great access of strength and reputation, and your subjects be much encouraged and enabled, in a parliamentary way, for your aid and assistance, in restoring your royal sister and [her] princely issue to those dignities and dominions which belong unto them, and relieving the other Protestant princes who have suffered in the same cause.

18. That your Majesty will be pleased, by Act of Parliament, to clear the Lord Kimbolton, and the Five Members of the House of Commons, in such manner that future parliaments may be secured from the consequence of that evil precedent.

19. That your Majesty will be graciously pleased to pass a bill for restraining Peers made hereafter from sitting or voting in Parliament, unless they be admitted thereunto with the consent of both Houses of Parliament.

And these our humble desires being granted by your Majesty, we shall forthwith apply ourselves to regulate your present revenue in such sort as may be for your best advantage; and likewise to settle such an ordinary and constant increase of it, as shall be sufficient to support your royal dignity in honour and plenty, beyond the proportion of any former grants of the subjects of this kingdom to your Majesty's royal predecessors. We shall likewise put the town of Hull into such hands as your Majesty shall appoint, with the consent and approbation of Parliament, and deliver up a just account of all the magazine, and cheerfully employ to the uttermost our power and endeavours, in the real expression and performance of our most dutiful and loyal affections, to the preserving and maintaining the royal honour, greatness and safety of your Majesty and your posterity. *LJ,* v, 97–9

68. A Declaration of the Lords and Commons in Parliament concerning His Majesty's Proclamation of the 27th May 1642, 6 June 1642

The Lords and Commons, having perused his Majesty's proclamation forbidding all his Majesty's subjects belonging to the Trained Bands or Militia of this kingdom to rise, march, muster or exercise by virtue of any order or ordinance of one or both Houses of Parliament, without consent or warrant from his Majesty, upon pain of punishment according to the laws:

Do thereupon declare, that neither the statute of the seventh of Edward the First, therein vouched, nor any other law of this kingdom, doth restrain or make void the ordinance agreed upon by both Houses of Parliament, for the ordering and disposing the Militia of the kingdom in this time of extreme and imminent danger, nor expose his Majesty's subjects to any punishment for obeying the same, notwithstanding that his Majesty hath refused to give his consent to that ordinance, but [it] ought to be obeyed by the fundamental laws of this kingdom....

The question is not, whether it belong to the King or no, to restrain such force, but, if the King shall refuse to discharge that duty and trust, whether there is not a power in the two Houses to provide for the safety of the Parliament and peace of the kingdom, which is the end for which the ordinance concerning the Militia was made, and, being agreeable to the scope and purpose of the law, cannot in reason be adjudged to be contrary to it....

It is acknowledged that the King is the fountain of justice and protection, but the acts of justice and protection are not exercised in his own person, nor depend upon his pleasure, but by his courts, and by his ministers, who must do their duty therein, though the King in his own person should forbid them; and therefore if judgements should be given by them against the King's will and personal command, yet are they the King's judgements.

The High Court of Parliament is not only a court of judicature, enabled by the laws to adjudge and determine the rights and liberties of the kingdom, against such patents and grants of his Majesty as are prejudicial thereunto, although strengthened both by his personal command and by his proclamation under the Great Seal; but it is likewise a council, to provide for the necessities, prevent the imminent dangers, and preserve the public peace and safety of the kingdom, and to declare the King's pleasure in those things as are requisite thereunto; and what they do herein hath the stamp of royal authority, although his Majesty, seduced by evil counsel, do in his own person oppose or interrupt the same; for the King's supreme and royal pleasure is exercised and declared in this high court of law and counsel, after a more eminent and obligatory manner than it can be by personal act or resolution of his own.

Seeing therefore, the Lords and Commons, which are his Majesty's great and high Council, have ordained that, for the present and necessary defence of the realm, the trained bands and militia of this kingdom should be ordered according to that ordinance,....all his Majesty's loving subjects, as well by that law as by other laws, are bound to be obedient thereunto; and what they do therein is (according to that law) to be interpreted to be done in aid of the King, in discharge of that trust which he is tied to perform; and it is so far from being liable to punishment, that, if they should refuse to do it, or be persuaded by any commission or command of his Majesty to do the contrary, they might justly be punished for the same, according to the laws and usages of the realm; for the King, by his sovereignty, is not enabled to destroy his people, but to protect and defend them; and the High Court of Parliament, and all other his Majesty's officers and ministers, ought to be subservient to that power and authority which the law hath placed in His Majesty to that purpose, though he himself in his own person should neglect the same.

Wheretofore the Lords and Commons do declare the said proclamation to be void in law, and of none effect; for that, by the constitution and policy of this kingdom, the King by his proclamation cannot declare the law contrary to the judgement and resolution of any of the inferior courts of justice, much less against the High Court of Parliament....

* * * * * *

LJ, v, 112–13

69. Answer to the King, from both Houses of Parliament, 6 September 1642

Whereas his Majesty, in a message received the 5th of September, requires that the parliament would revoke their declaration against such persons as have assisted his Majesty in this unnatural war against his kingdom: It is this day ordered and declared by the Lords and Commons that the arms which they have been forced to take up, and shall be forced to take up, for the preservation of the Parliament, religion, the laws and liberties of the kingdom, shall not be laid down, until his Majesty shall withdraw his protection from such persons as have been voted by both Houses to be delinquents, or that shall by both Houses be voted to be delinquents, and shall leave them to the justice of Parliament, to be proceeded with according to their demerits; to the end that both this and succeeding generations may take warning with what danger they incur the like heinous crimes and also to the end that those great charges and damages wherewith all the Commonwealth hath been burdened in the premises since his Majesty's departure from the Parliament may be borne by the delinquents and other malignant and disaffected persons; and that all his Majesty's good and well-affected subjects who, by loans or monies, or otherwise at their charge, have assisted the Commonwealth, or shall in like manner hereafter assist the Commonwealth in time of extreme danger, may be repaid all sums of money by them lent for these purposes, and be satisfied their charges so sustained, out of the estates of the said delinquents and of the malignant and disaffected party in this kingdom. *LJ*, v, 341

CHAPTER 6

THE PURITAN FAILURE, 1641-1648

The Root and Branch Petition[1] submitted to Parliament in December 1640 voiced a detestation of the bishops which was general amongst all classes, and was one of the principal reasons for the government's weakness in this crisis. However, it soon became evident that much of this hostility was directed not against the institution of episcopacy but against its present representatives. In December 1640 the Commons had no hesitation in declaring the canons made in convocation that summer illegal, nor in impeaching Laud, but when they debated the Root and Branch Petition in February 1641 it was soon apparent that the firm majority which was behind all secular reforms was going to break up on the Church question. The elder Vane remarked soothingly that, 'We all tended to one end, that was reformation, only we differed in the way', a remark which summed up the failure of the Puritans to profit from the opportunity for which they had waited so long.[2]

One influential group, led by Falkland, Hyde and Culpeper, was willing to reduce the bishops' coercive powers and punish individuals for specific crimes, but was not even willing to exclude them from the Lords. Others regarded their exclusion from the Lords as an absolute minimum; others toyed with the concept of a 'primitive reformed episcopacy'; others envisaged them as chairmen of diocesan synods; but only a small minority of 'Root and Branchers', or Independents, wanted them removed altogether. Pym and his henchmen were alarmed, though not surprised, by the emergence of differences which might easily break the unity of Parliament and set House against House, as well as Member against Member, particularly since the Root-and-Branchers included some of their staunchest supporters in the struggle to bring down Strafford. On 30 March a bill to remove the bishops from the House of Lords and the Council was given its first reading, and on 1 May it was sent up to the Lords. On the 24th the Lords informed the Commons that they could not agree to remove members of their own House by statute, and on the 27th, as a result, the Root-and-Branchers introduced a bill to abolish episcopacy altogether. However, it made little progress before the end of the session, and it was not revived. Nothing is more impressive in this Parliament than the leaders' skill in suppressing contentious legislation.

[1] No. 49, p. 171 above.
[2] D'Ewes Journal, ed. Notestein, p. 337. Cromwell was still saying the same thing in 1647: 'I cannot see but that we all speak to the same end, and the mistakes are only in the way' (Woodhouse, Puritanism and Liberty, p. 104).

251

However, with the removal of Laud episcopal discipline had virtually collapsed, and it was essential that another form of church government be substituted; for on one thing only the great majority of the parliamentary gentry agreed with Laud—the necessity for suppressing 'the cankers of public liberty' in religion.[1] Already in London and other towns the removal of episcopal supervision had revealed the existence of large numbers of congregations which denied the necessity or the spiritual efficacy of any superior ecclesiastical power. These separatists, sectarians or congregationalists had their supporters in the Commons, and they were regarded with some complacency by the parliamentary leaders because they were an important element of support in the City. Many more Members of Parliament were under pressure from ministers whom they respected who were anxious for the reform of the liturgy and doctrine of the Church, as well as the suppression of Laudian innovations. These were matters, unfortunately, on which there were almost as many opinions as votes in the House, and though the Commons swore in the Protestation of 3 May 1641[2] to defend 'the true reformed Protestant religion expressed in the doctrine of the Church of England', they found themselves obliged to issue a public explanation of these terms a week later (70).

Few of the Commons leaders had any programme of Church reform. When Hyde asked the influential Nathaniel Fiennes what he would put in place of the bishops if they were abolished he replied 'that there would be time enough to think of that'.[3] Cromwell returned a similar answer to the same question—'I can tell you, sir, what I would not have, though I cannot, what I would.'[4] In secular matters this negative attitude was reasonable; there it was considered necessary to remove certain illegal accretions on the body of the constitution, which after this operation would function perfectly; only in the case of the Church was there an apparent need in the spring of 1641 for constructive statesmanship, and that was because the Church had never been settled to any man's satisfaction since the Reformation. The obvious alternative to episcopacy was Presbyterianism, the solution naturally pressed with vigour by the influential Scots Committee in London; but the truth was, Presbyterianism was very little understood even by influential English divines, for the union of the Crowns had done little to close the gulf between England and Scotland.[5] But the more they saw of Presbyterianism, the less the parliamentarians liked it, and the more they laboured to keep it out of sight. With some success, for as late as 20 November one Member remarked that neither Presbyterianism nor Independency had yet been discussed in the House.[6]

[1] CSPD, 1640–41, p. 307.
[2] No. 60, p. 222 above.
[3] Clarendon, Life (1759), I, 80–1.
[4] Qu. Miller, Orthodoxy in Massachuset s, p. 73.
[5] Shaw, I, 6; Miller, op. cit. p. 74.
[6] Shaw, I, 101.

The attitude of the Lords was even more nebulous. The Root and Branch bill was talked out in the Commons at the end of July, but Church ceremonial was soon to prove as explosive a topic as Church government. Early in 1641 many ministers, churchwardens or parishioners began removing altars and altar rails and breaking down statues recently installed in their churches, while many clergymen abandoned in whole or in part the form of divine service in the Book of Common Prayer, despite an Order of the House of Lords on 16 January that services should be conducted according to the laws of the land. This Order could be directed against either Laudians or Puritans, and another Order of the Lords on 1 March, that the communion table 'should stand in the ancient place where it ought to do by the law, and as it hath done for the great part of these three score years last past',[1] was even more two-faced, for the whole altarian controversy hinged on conflicting interpretations of canon LXXXII of 1604. The Commons were equally cautious. They introduced a bill 'for abolishing superstition and idolatry, and for the better advancing of the the true worship and service of God' on 5 February; it was read a second time and committed on 13 February, but the committee was not called upon for its report until 8 August, six months later.[2] The bill then expired, but not before the Commons had decided that it must take notice of the spontaneous wave of iconoclasm that was still proceeding. Meanwhile the king had left London, and on 14 August he entered Edinburgh, having passed through the English and Scots armies without the expected incident; there was an immediate relaxation of tension, and it seemed safe to let the ghost of ecclesiastical reform walk again. So, on 1 September the Commons passed a series of resolutions on ecclesiastical innovations which ordered the removal of altars, altar rails and statues, forbade bowing at the name of Jesus, and enjoined the proper observance of the Lord's Day (71). The Lords agreed to the destruction of altars, but without discussing the other resolutions they provocatively reissued their Order of 16 January, and had it printed (72). The session ended on 10 September with the Houses deadlocked. The only achievement of this great reforming Parliament in the ecclesiastical sphere was the abolition of High Commission.

The atmosphere when Parliament reassembled on 20 October was not conducive to reform of any kind, and though the next day a bill was introduced and speedily passed the Commons to prohibit any of the clergy from exercising any temporal jurisdiction whatsoever (commonly described as 'The Bishops' Exclusion Bill') it was still lingering in the House of Lords at the end of the year. However, the king's announcement in November that he would be steadfast in the defence of the Anglican Church established by law[3] rallied its supporters, as was evident in the preliminary debates on the Grand Remonstrance. Indeed, the authors of the Remonstrance were very

---

[1] *Ibid.* I, 105.   [2] *Ibid.* I, 104.   [3] See p. 194 above.

much on the defensive; they denied any intention 'to let loose the golden reins of discipline and government in the Church', and set forth as their aim 'a conformity to that order which the laws enjoin, according to the Word of God'.[1] The bishops could not have asked for more. Even then, on 15 November strong exception was taken to a clause referring to the 'errors and superstitions' of the Book of Common Prayer, and the following day it was moved, 'that the clause that has been now read concerning the liturgy shall be recommended to the same committee, that a clause may be brought in that may not cast any aspersions or scandal upon the Book of Common Prayer established by law'. And it was finally decided, 'that the clause or anything therein contained that concerns the Common Prayer Book shall be totally left out of this declaration'.[2]

Under a lesser man than Pym this might have produced a violent reaction, but he was determined that religious questions should not again threaten the unity of the Commons, as they had in September; he was content to water down this aspect of the Remonstrance, and take refuge in the idea that the reform of Church government should be left to a synod, whose assembly could be indefinitely postponed.[3] Even the king's departure from London, and the drift into civil war, scarcely affected the Church question. In January 1642 the Lords passed the Bishop's Exclusion Bill, and the king gave his assent, after some hesitation, the following month (73)—an indication that the struggle now impending had long since ceased to involve the reform of the Church. Nevertheless, the difficulty of reaching agreement with the Lords, and the attempt to secure the king's assent, delayed until August the passing of an Ordinance to demolish all 'monuments of superstition and idolatry' which embodied the Commons' Resolutions of the previous September.[4]

However, the secession of the royalist Members in 1642 doomed the bishops at last, and so did the intervention of the Scots. When Parliament tentatively approached the Edinburgh government in September 1642 to see what aid it would lend, the Scots inquired what measures they intended to take for the reform of the Church. Both Houses at once docilely agreed that bishops, deans and chapters were 'a great impediment to the perfect reformation and growth of religion, and very prejudicial to the State and government of this kingdom',[5] but although the military disasters of 1643 made Scots aid more and more desirable, there was an increasing disposition on the part of Parliament to evade the establishment of Presbyterian Church government, which the Scots would almost certainly demand as the first condition of an alliance. One delaying tactic was to appoint at last the synod of divines

[1] § 184, p. 238 above.
[2] CJ, II, 598.
[3] See § 185 of the Remonstrance, p. 238 above.
[4] Firth and Rait, I, 265–6.
[5] CJ, II, 747.

called for by the Grand Remonstrance, and an Ordinance of 12 June 1643 (74) set up an Assembly of 121 ministers, all selected by Members of Parliament, and stiffened by the addition of ten Lords and twenty Members of the Commons, all men of influence and power. It could only discuss questions put before it by Parliament and make recommendations in return; it had no legislative power of its own, and it was even forbidden to publish its recommendations. The preamble to this Ordinance pledged Parliament once more to the abolition of episcopacy, but in the Solemn League and Covenant (75) their delegates insisted on the insertion of the words 'according to the Word of God', which meant that they were obliged to accept Presbyterian Church government only in so far as it was demonstrably sanctioned by Scripture.

So, progress towards Presbyterianism was always slow and halting, and became more so in 1645, when the military importance of the Scots sharply declined. The majority of the Westminster divines, in fact, were in favour of Presbytery, but an able and voluble minority were not, and they had the support of a majority of the lay members, who in turn were supported by an influential group of Independents in the Commons. The Independents believed in the viability of each separate congregation, though they were not necessarily in favour of complete sectarianism (for even Independent congregations could be 'federated' in a national Church), and they were supported by other Members of Parliament who feared that the establishment of Presbyterianism would only erect a clerical despotism akin to Archbishop Laud's, and insisted that the lay central government must retain an overriding control.

Thus the Westminster Assembly met on 1 July 1643, but it was not until 5 February following that it embarked on a discussion of the theoretical basis of Presbyterianism, and its justification by scripture. After more than five weeks this had to be laid aside while Parliament and the Assembly dealt with the urgent questions or ordination and public worship. A scheme for the ordination of new ministers had been delayed in the hope that it could be handed over to the presbyteries, as in Scotland; but since the presbyteries were no nearer, Parliament would only appoint a committee of London ministers to examine the qualifications of ordinands for the time being. Significantly, it declined to impose any doctrinal test, or commit itself to a statement that ministers were ordained of God.[1]

This done, in October 1644 the Assembly was asked to frame a new Directory of Worship, to replace the Prayer Book, which could be put to the king in the negotiations now pending at Uxbridge. It was hurried through with remarkable speed and very little debate, and published as a schedule to an ordinance of 4 January 1645. But the ordinance provided no machinery

[1] 'An ordinance...for the ordination of ministers *pro tempore*', Firth and Rait, I, 521–6. Cf. Shaw, I, 318 ff.

for distributing the new Directory, let alone enforcing it, nor did it impose penalties for the use of the Book of Common Prayer, though it repealed all the Tudor legislation enforcing its use.[1] The failure of the Uxbridge negotiations left the country with two prayer books, neither of them prescribed by law, and no Church government; and the only question on which the Assembly and Parliament seemed able to agree was the imposition of that personal austerity commonly associated with the word 'Puritan'. As far back as September 1642 Parliament had forbidden the performance of stage plays, and in April 1644 a new ordinance 'for the better observation of the Lord's Day' even forbade travel on a Sunday.[2] In December 1644 it surpassed itself by abolishing Christmas (76). Regular public fasts were preceded by orgies of self-examination and self-accusation.[3]

Meanwhile, under pressure from the Scots the Assembly resumed its discussion of Presbyterianism, this time in a more practical spirit, and Parliament took its recommendations into consideration in January 1645, spurred on by a petition from the Presbyterian ministers of London—a formidable pressure group—calling their attention to the spread of sectarianism and the need for strong Church government. On 27 January the Commons agreed with the Assembly's recommendations that each congregation should be governed by lay elders, that congregations should be grouped in presbyteries, and that presbyteries should be grouped in provincial assemblies. But it had taken two-and-a-half years to reach this basic position, and there was no likelihood of very rapid progress now that the Presbyterian generals had been removed and the Independent Members were firmly allied with Oliver Cromwell, a passionate advocate of religious toleration. Nevertheless, the spread of sectarianism in London and in the army was causing grave concern, and led many who were at best lukewarm towards Presbyterianism to support it as the only means of restoring order. These contrary influences produced deadlock. On 26 April 1645 Parliament dealt a blow at the sects by forbidding preaching except by ordained ministers but it was not until 19 August that it issued an ordinance 'regulating the election of Elders' (77). Even then, this was precisely what it said: it described the form which Presbyterian Church government was to take in England—with careful provision for a majority of laymen at every stage of the governing pyramid, with Parliament firmly in control of the National Assembly—but it did nothing to put it into effect. However, as if in compensation, a week later it issued an ordinance to enforce the use of the Directory of Worship and penalise the use of the Prayer Book;[4] but this only made the situation more anomalous still.

[1] Firth and Rait, I, 582 ff.   [2] Ibid. I, 20, 420.
[3] Typical was the ordinance of 15 February 1643, exhorting the nation 'to the duty of repentance, as the only remedy for their present calamities, with an earnest confession and deep humiliation for all particular and national sins' (ibid. I, 80).
[4] Ibid. I, 755 (26 August 1645).

As if all this were not enough, Parliament and the Assembly of Divines then broke out into open quarrelling over the powers that were to be given to Ruling Elders, especially the power to reserve the sacrament. Parliament was anxious that ministers should not have this power; but to grant it outright to any group of laymen seemed worse still. So it was not until 14 March 1646 that Parliament took another step forward. Then it ordered the formation of the Church government described the previous August to be undertaken, but it set up a body of parliamentary commissioners in each Province to hear appeals against decisions of the congregational elders.[1] In face of the almost unanimous opposition of the Presbyterian ministers this had to be withdrawn, and another ordinance of 5 June merely set up a central committee of appeal nominated by Parliament.[2] But even then little attempt was made to set up the Presbyterian system outside London.

Meanwhile, the disorderly legislative procedure of this parliament had left the bishops unscathed in law, though it was generally assumed that they had in fact been abolished, and Laud had been attainted and executed in 1645.[3] It was not until October 1646 that the offices of archbishop and bishop were finally abolished by ordinance, thus implementing the programme laid down in September 1642, and even then the first sentence of the ordinance, 'for the abolishing of archbishops and bishops, and providing for the payment of the just and necessary debts of the kingdom', betray the fact that the financial embarrassments of the government rather than a desire for Church reform lay behind this move.[4]

The negotiations with Charles I in 1646 and 1647 further hindered the introduction of Presbyterianism, and it was not until 29 January 1648, on the eve of the second Civil War, that Parliament finally committed itself by passing an ordinance implementing the legislation of 1645.[5] But it was far too late. Hatred of the Scots, and with them their religion, had reached new heights, and a violent hostility to all priests, Catholic, Anglican or Presbyterian was noticeable in all classes, and particularly in the New Model Army.[6] The religious settlement was now at the mercy of the opponents of organised religion, and the attempt to preserve the Church of England in a Puritan form had been a miserable failure.

[1] *Ibid.* I, 833. Like the ordinance of 26 August, it also excluded the private chapels of the nobility from the presbyterian system altogether.

[2] *Ibid.* I, 852–5.

[3] Parliament always acted as though it had in fact abolished episcopacy, and in the ordinance of 14 March 1646 congratulated itself on having done so, but see Shaw, I, 119 ff.

[4] *Ibid.* I, 879–83 (9 October 1646). Deans and chapters were not abolished until 1649 (*ibid.* II, 81).

[5] *Ibid.* I, 1062–3. See Shaw, II, 19 ff.

[6] James F. Maclear, 'Popular Anti-Clericalism in the Puritan Revolution', *Journal of the History of Ideas*, XVII (1956), 443.

70. An Explanation of the Protestation, 12 May 1641

An Explanation, brought from the Committee for the Bill for the Protestation, was this day reported; and upon the Question, ordered, *in haec verba*:

Resolved, upon the Question, That whereas some doubts have been raised by several persons, out of this House, concerning the meaning of these words contained in the Protestation lately made by the Members of this House, viz. 'the true reformed Protestant religion, expressed in the doctrine of the Church of England, against all Popery and Popish innovations within this realm, contrary to the same doctrine'. This House doth declare, that by these words was and is meant only, the public doctrine professed in the said Church, so far as it is opposite to Popery, and Popish innovations; and that the said words are not to be extended to the maintaining of any form of worship, discipline, or government; nor of any rites or ceremonies of the said Church of England.

CJ, II, 144–5

71. Resolutions of the Commons on ecclesiastical innovations, 1 September 1641

Whereas divers innovations in or about the worship of God have been lately practised in this kingdom, by enjoining some things and prohibiting others, without warrant of law, to the great grievance and discontent of his Majesty's subjects; for the suppression of such innovations, and for preservation of the public peace, it is this day ordered by the Commons in Parliament assembled:

That the churchwardens of every parish church and chapel respectively do forthwith remove the communion table from the east end of the church, chapel or chancel into some other convenient place, and that they take away the rails, and level the chancels as heretofore they were before the late innovations.

That all crucifixes, scandalous pictures of any one of more persons of the Trinity, and all images of the Virgin Mary, shall be taken away and abolished, and that all tapers, candlesticks and basins be removed from the communion table.

That all corporal bowing at the name Jesus, or towards the east end of the church, chapel or chancel, or towards the communion table, be henceforth forborne.

*　*　*　*　*　*

That the Lord's Day shall be duly observed and sanctified; all dancing, or other sports, either before or after divine service, be forborne and restrained, and that the preaching of God's word be permitted in the afternoon in the several churches and chapels of this kingdom, and that ministers and preachers be encouraged thereunto.

* * * * * *

CJ, II, 279

72. The Lords on ecclesiastical innovations

[16 January 1641]

[The king brought to the notice of the House that the previous Sunday the constables and churchwardens of St Saviour's, Southwark, had surprised a large number of sectarians worshipping in a private house.]

1. They [the ringleaders] being brought before Sir John Lenthall [J.P.], he demanded why they would not go and resort to their parish church, according to the Law of 35 Eliz. They answered that the Law of 35 Eliz. was not a true law, but that it was made by the bishops, and they would not obey it.

2. That they would not go to their parish churches, that those churches were not true churches, and that there was no true church but where the faithful met.

3. That the King could not make a perfect law, for that he was not a perfect man.

4. That they ought not to obey him but in civil things....

[Having dealt with the offenders,] upon this occasion the House thought fit, and ordered: That this order following shall be read publicly in all the parish churches of London and Westminster, the borough of Southwark, and all the liberties and suburbs of them;

That the Divine Service be performed as it is appointed by the Acts of Parliament of this realm; and that all such as shall disturb that wholesome order shall be severely punished according to law; and that the parsons, vicars and curates in [the] several parishes shall forbear to introduce any rites or ceremonies that may give offence, otherwise than those which are established by the laws of the land.

[9 September 1641]

It being in debate concerning the printing and publishing of an order touching Divine Service; it was resolved upon the question, by the major part, that this House will vote the printing and publishing of the order made the 16th of January 1640[-41] concerning Divine Service, before this House desires a conference with the House of Commons concerning that particular....[1] Resolved upon the question, by the major part, that the order made the 16th of January 1640[-41]...shall be printed and published.

Hereupon it is ordered, to have a conference with the House of Commons, to desire them to join herein with this House.

LJ, IV, 133–4, 395

73. The Bishops' Exclusion Act

17 Car. I, c. 27: *An Act for disenabling all persons in Holy Orders to exercise any temporal jurisdiction or authority*

Whereas bishops and other persons in holy orders ought not to be entangled with secular jurisdiction, the office of the ministry being of such great importance that it will take up the whole man, and for that it is found by long experience that their intermeddling with secular jurisdictions hath occasioned great mischiefs and scandal both to Church and State, his Majesty, out of his religious care of the Church, and [the] souls of his people, is graciously pleased that it be enacted, and by authority of this present parliament be it enacted, that no archbishop or bishop or other person that now is or hereafter shall be in holy orders shall at any time after the 15th day of February in the year of Our Lord one thousand six hundred [and] forty-one [1642] have any seat or place, suffrage or voice, or use or execute any power or authority in the parliaments of this realm, nor shall be of the Privy Council of his Majesty, his heirs or successors, or justice of the peace of *oyer and terminer* or gaol delivery, or execute any temporal authority by virtue of any commission, but shall be wholly disabled and be incapable to have, receive, use or execute any of the said offices, places, powers, authorities and things aforesaid.

*   *   *   *   *   *

SR, V, 138

[1] Six peers—Warwick, Newport, Clare, Bedford, Kimbolton and Wharton—entered a protest; not against the order, but against reissuing it without consulting the Commons.

74. The Westminster Assembly, 1 July 1643

An ordinance for the calling of an assembly of learned and Godly divines, to be consulted with by the Parliament, for the settling of the government of the Church [12 June 1643]

Whereas amongst the infinite blessings of Almighty God upon this nation none is or can be more dear unto us than the purity of our religion; and for that as yet many things remain in the liturgy, discipline and government of the Church which do necessarily require a further and more perfect reformation than as yet hath been attained; and whereas it hath been declared and resolved by the Lords and Commons assembled in Parliament that the present Church government by archbishops, bishops, their chancellors, commissaries, deans, deans and chapters, archdeacons, and other ecclesiastical officers depending upon the hierarchy is evil, and justly offensive and burdensome to the kingdom, a great impediment to reformation and growth of religion, and very prejudicial to the State and government of this kingdom, and that therefore they are resolved that the same shall be taken away, and that such a government shall be settled in the Church as may be most agreeable to God's Holy Word, and most apt to procure and preserve the peace of the Church at home, and nearer agreement with the Church of Scotland, and other reformed churches abroad; and for the better effecting hereof, and for the vindicating and clearing of the doctrine of the Church of England from all false calumnies and aspersions, it is thought fit and necessary to call an assembly of learned, godly and judicious divines, to consult and advise of such matters and things, touching the premises, as shall be proposed unto them by both or either of the Houses of Parliament, and to give their advice and counsel therein to both or either of the said Houses when and as often as they shall be thereunto required.

Be it therefore ordained by the Lords and Commons in this present parliament assembled, that all and every the persons hereafter in this present ordinance named, that is to say: Algernon, earl of Northumberland, William, earl of Bedford, Philip, earl of Pembroke and Montgomery, William, earl of Salisbury, Henry, earl of Holland, Edward, earl of Manchester, William, Lord Viscount Saye and Sele, Edward, Lord Viscount Conway, Philip, Lord Wharton, Edward, Lord Howard of Escrick; John Seldon, esquire, Francis Rouse, esquire, Edmund Prideaux, esquire, Sir Henry Vane, knight, senior, John Glyn, esquire, recorder of London, John White, esquire, Bulstrode Whitelocke, esquire, Humphrey Salloway, esquire, Mr Serjeant Wilde, Oliver St John, esquire, his Majesty's solicitor, Sir Benjamin Rudyard, knight, John Pym, esquire, Sir John Clotworthy, knight, John Maynard, esquire, Sir Henry Vane, knight, junior, William Pierrepoint, esquire, William Wheller, esquire, Sir Thomas Barrington, knight, Mr Young, esquire, Sir John Evelyn, knight...[and 121 named clergymen] and such other person and persons as shall be nominated and appointed by both Houses of Parliament, or so many of them as shall not be letted by sickness or other necessary impediment shall meet and assemble, and are hereby required and enjoined upon summons signed by the Clerks of both Houses of Parliament, left at their several respective dwellings, to meet and assemble themselves at Westminster, in the chapel called King Henry the Seventh's Chapel, on the first day of July in the year of Our Lord one thousand six hundred and forty three. And after the first meeting, being at least of the number of forty, shall from time to time sit, and be removed from place to place, and also that the said assembly shall be dissolved in such manner as by both Houses of Parliament shall be directed.

And the said persons, or so many of them as shall be so assembled or sit, shall have power and authority, and are hereby likewise enjoined from time to time during this present parliament, or until further order be taken by both the said Houses, to confer and treat amongst themselves of such matters and things touching and concerning the liturgy, discipline and government of the Church of England, or the vindicating and clearing of the doctrine of the same from all false aspersions and misconstructions as shall be proposed unto them by both or either of the said Houses of Parliament, and no other, and to deliver their opinions and advices of or touching the matters aforesaid, as shall be most agreeable to the Word of God, to both or either of the said Houses from time to time, in such manner and sort as by both or either of the said Houses of Parliament shall be required; and the same not to divulge by printing, writing or otherwise without the consent of both or either House of Parliament.

And be it further ordained by the authority aforesaid, that William Twist, Doctor in Divinity, shall sit in the Chair as prolocutor of the said assembly; and if he happen to die, or be letted by sickness or other necessary impediment, then such other person to be appointed in his place as shall be agreed on by both the said Houses of Parliament. And in case any difference of opinion shall happen amongst the said persons so assembled, touching any of the matters that shall be proposed to them as aforesaid, that then they shall represent the same, together with the reasons thereof, to both or either the said Houses respectively, to the end such further direction may be given as shall be requisite in that behalf.

* * * * * *

Provided always, that this ordinance, or anything therein contained, shall not give unto the persons aforesaid, or any of them, nor shall they in this assembly assume to exercise, any jurisdiction, power or authority ecclesiastical whatsoever, or any other power than is herein particularly expressed.

Firth and Rait, I, 180–4

75. 'A solemn league and covenant for reformation and defence of religion, the honour and happiness of the King, and the peace and safety of the three kingdoms of England, Scotland and Ireland'[1]

We noblemen, barons, knights, gentlemen, citizens, burgesses, ministers of the Gospel, and commons of all sorts in the kingdoms of England, Scotland and Ireland, by the providence of God living under one king, and being of one reformed religion; having before our eyes the glory of God and the advancement of the kingdom of Our Lord and Saviour Jesus Christ, the honour and happiness of the King's Majesty and his posterity, and the true public liberty, safety and peace of the kingdom, wherein everyone's private condition is included; and calling to mind the treacherous and bloody plots, conspiracies, attempts and practices of the enemies of God against the true religion and professors thereof in all places, especially in these three kingdoms, ever since the reformation of religion; and how much their rage, power and presumption are of late at this time increased and exercised, whereof the deplorable estate of the Church and kingdom of Ireland, the distressed estate of the Church and kingdom of England, and the dangerous estate of the Church and kingdom of Scotland, are present and public testimonies: we have now at last, after other means of supplication, remonstrance, protestation and sufferings, for the preservation of ourselves and our religion from utter ruin and destruction, according to the commendable

---

[1] Taken by the Convention of Estates, 17 August 1643, and by the Westminster Assembly and the House of Commons, 25 September.

practice of these kingdoms in former times, and the example of God's people in other nations, after a mature deliberation, resolved and determined to enter into a mutual and solemn league and covenant, wherein we all subscribe, and each one of us for himself, with our hands lifted up to the most high God, do swear:

I. That we shall sincerely, really and constantly, through the grace of God, endeavour in our several places and callings, the preservation of the reformed religion in the Church of Scotland, in doctrine, worship, discipline and government, against our common enemies; the reformation of religion in the kingdoms of England and Ireland in doctrine, worship, discipline and government, according to the Word of God and the example of the best reformed churches; and we shall endeavour to bring the churches of God in the three kingdoms to the nearest conjunction and uniformity in religion, confessing of faith, form of church government, directory for worship, and catechising, that we and our posterity after us may, as brethren, live in faith and love, and the Lord may delight to dwell in the midst of us.

II. That we shall in like manner, without respect of persons, endeavour the extirpation of Popery, prelacy (that is, Church government by archbishops, bishops, their chancellors and commissaries, deans, deans and chapters, archdeacons, and all other ecclesiastical officers depending on that hierarchy), superstition, heresy, schism, profaneness, and whatsoever shall be found to be contrary to sound doctrine and the power of godliness, lest we partake in other men's sins, and thereby be in danger to receive of their plagues; and that the Lord may be one and his name one in the three kingdoms.

III. We shall with the same sincerity, reality and constancy in our several vocations endeavour with our estates and lives mutually to preserve the rights and privileges of the parliaments, and the liberties of the kingdoms, and to preserve and defend the King's Majesty's person and authority, in the preservation and defence of the true religion and liberties of the kingdoms, that the world may bear witness with our consciences of our loyalty, and that we have no thoughts or intentions to diminish his Majesty's just power and greatness.

IV. We shall also with all faithfulness endeavour the discovery of all such as have been or shall be incendiaries, malignants, or evil instruments, by hindering the reformation of religion, dividing the King from his people, or one of the kingdoms from another, or making any faction or parties amongst the people, contrary to the league and covenant, that they may be brought to public trial and receive condign punishment, as the degree of their offences shall require or deserve, or the supreme judicatories of both kingdoms respectively, or others having power from them for that effect, shall judge convenient.

V. And whereas the happiness of a blessed peace between these kingdoms, denied in former times to our progenitors, is by the good providence of God granted to us, and hath been lately concluded and settled by both parliaments; we shall each one of us, according to our places and interest, endeavour that they may remain conjoined in a firm peace and union to all posterity, and that justice may be done upon the wilful opposers thereof, in manner expressed in the precedent articles.

VI. We shall also, according to our places and callings, in this common cause of religion, liberty and peace of the kingdoms, assist and defend all those that enter into this league and covenant in the maintaining and pursuing thereof, and shall not suffer ourselves, directly or indirectly, by whatsoever combination, persuasion or terror, to be divided and withdrawn from this blessed union and conjunction, whether to make defection to the contrary part, or give ourselves to a detestable indifferency or neutrality in this cause, which so much concerneth the glory of God, the good of the kingdoms and the honour of the King; but shall all the days of our lives zealously and constantly continue therein, against all opposition, and promote the same according to our power, against all lets and impediments whatsoever; and what we are not able ourselves to suppress or overcome we shall reveal and make known, that it may be timely prevented or removed; all which we shall do as in the sight of God.

And because these kingdoms are guilty of many sins and provocations against God and his son Jesus Christ, as is too manifest by our present distress and dangers, the fruits thereof, we profess and declare before God and the world our unfeigned desire to be humbled for our own sins and for the sins of these kingdoms, especially that we have not as we ought valued the inestimable benefit of the Gospel, that we have not laboured for the purity and power thereof, and that we have not endeavoured to receive Christ in our hearts, nor to walk worthy of Him in our lives, which are the causes of other sins and transgressions so much abounding amongst us; and our true and unfeigned purpose, desire and endeavour, for ourselves and all others under our power and charge, both in public and in private, in all duties we owe to God and man, to amend our lives, and each one to go before another in the example of a real reformation, that the Lord may turn away his wrath and heavy indignation, and establish these Churches and kingdoms in truth and peace. And this covenant we make in the presence of Almighty God, the searcher of all hearts, with a true intention to perform the same, as we shall answer at that great day when the secrets of all hearts shall be disclosed, most humbly beseeching the Lord to strengthen us by his Holy Spirit for this end, and to bless our desires and proceedings with such success as may be a deliverance and safety to his people, and encouragement to the Christian Churches groaning under or in danger of the yoke of anti-Christian tyranny, to join in the same or like association and covenant, to the glory of God, the enlargement of the kingdom of Jesus Christ, and the peace and tranquillity of Christian kingdoms and commonwealths.   Rushworth, VI, 478-9

76. **An ordinance for the better observation of the monthly fast; and more especially the next Wednesday, commonly called the Feast of the Nativity of Christ, throughout the kingdom of England and dominion of Wales, 19 December 1644**

Whereas some doubts have been raised whether the next fast shall be celebrated, because it falleth on the day which heretofore was usually called the Feast of the Nativity of Our Saviour, the Lords and Commons in Parliament assembled do order and ordain that public notice be given that the fast appointed to be kept on the last Wednesday in every month ought to be observed until it be otherwise ordered by both Houses of Parliament; and that this day in particular is to be kept with the more solemn humiliation, because it may call to remembrance our sins, and the sins of our forefathers, who have turned this feast, pretending the memory of Christ, into an extreme forgetfulness of him, by giving liberty to carnal and sensual delights, being contrary to the life which Christ himself led here upon earth, and to the spiritual life of Christ in our souls, for the sanctifying and saving whereof Christ was pleased both to take a human life, and to lay it down again.

Firth and Rait, I, 580

77. An Ordinance regulating the election of Elders, 19 August 1645

1. That the Ruling Elders of a parochial and congregational Eldership shall be chosen by the several ministers and members of their congregation respectively, being of such as have taken the National Covenant, and are not persons under age, nor servants that have no families.

2. That notice of such election, and of the day when, shall be given by the minister in the public assembly the next Lord's Day but one before; and on the said Lord's Day a sermon be preached preparatory to that weighty business.

3. That no man be chosen for a Ruling Elder, but only for one congregation; and that in the place where his most settled dwelling and employment doth lie.

4. That it shall be lawful for the congregations respectively, or any other person, to exhibit exceptions against any person elected as aforesaid, touching the right of his election, or touching matter of ignorance or scandal hereafter mentioned, within fourteen days next after the said election, to such persons, ministers and others, as shall be appointed by authority of Parliament to receive the said exceptions; which said persons shall have power to receive, hear and determine all complaints against any Elder...and shall have power to approve the person so elected in case no just exception as aforesaid shall be proved against him; but if he shall upon just proof be found ignorant or scandalous as aforesaid, then to remove him; and if any of the said Elders shall be adjudged to be removed as aforesaid, then another shall be chosen in his place as aforesaid.

5. That such shall be chosen for Ruling Elders as are men of good understanding in matters of religion, sound in faith, prudent, discreet, grave and of unblameable conversation, and willing to undergo the said office.

6. That all parishes and places whatsoever (as well privileged places and exempt jurisdictions as others) be brought under the government of Congregational, Classical, Provincial and National Assemblies; provided that the chapels or places in the houses of the peers of this realm shall continue free for the exercise of divine duties, to be performed according to the Directory.

[Clauses 7–9 make detailed provision for the division of the Province of London into *classes*.]

Concerning the members of the Classical and Congregational Assemblies in the several counties

That in the several counties certain persons, ministers and others, shall be appointed by authority of Parliament, who shall consider how their several counties respectively may be most conveniently divided into distinct Classical Presbyteries, and what ministers and others are fit to be of each Classis; and they shall accordingly make such division and nomination of persons for each Classical Presbytery, which divisions, and persons so named for every division, shall be certified up to the Parliament.

That the chancellors, vice-chancellors and heads of the universities shall consider how the colleges may be most conveniently put into Classical Presbyteries, and do certify the same up unto the Parliament.

And the said several Classes respectively, being approved by Parliament within their several precincts, shall have power to constitute Congregational Elderships, where a competent number of persons so qualified for Elders as aforesaid, shall be found; and where no persons shall be found fit to be Elders as aforesaid, then that congregation shall be immediately under the Classical Presbytery until that congregation shall be enabled with members fit to be Elders as aforesaid.

The Congregational Assembly shall meet once every week, and oftener if occasions shall serve.

The Classical Assembly shall meet once every month.

Concerning members of the Provincial Assembly

The Provincial Assembly shall be constituted of members sent from every Classis within the Province. The number of the members sent from each classis shall be so proportioned as that the Provincial Assembly may be more in number than any Classical Presbytery within that Province, and to that end there shall be at least two ministers and four Ruling Elders out of every Classis; and that, where there shall be need the number may be increased, as to the persons appointed for the bounding of the Provincial Assembly shall seem meet; provided that the number do not exceed nine of each, ministers and ruling members, from any one Classis, and that there be always two Ruling Elders to one minister.

That the Provincial Assembly, being constituted, shall meet twice every year; the first meeting shall be determined by the persons appointed for the bounding of the Provincial and Classical Assemblies.

Concerning the National Assembly

That the National Assembly shall be constituted of members sent from the several Provinces aforesaid. The number of the members from each Province to the National Assembly shall be two ministers and four Ruling Elders.

The National Assembly is to meet when they shall be summoned by Parliament, and to sit and continue as the Parliament shall order, and not otherwise.

Firth and Rait, I, 749–54

CHAPTER 7

THE GOVERNMENT OF THE LONG PARLIAMENT, 1642–1648

During the first Civil War no theoretical advance was made on the messages and declarations exchanged in the summer of 1642. Charles continued to insist, of course, that the Long Parliament was in revolt, but he dare not take the obvious step of dissolving it by proclamation, because that would infringe the Act of May 1641 and thereby jeopardise the whole programme of reform legislation upon which his moderate support depended. Parliament, on the other hand, insisted that it was exercising the office of the king because the person of its holder had been led astray by evil counsel, and in 1643 it imposed a new oath to this effect (**82**). It was hampered by the king's possession of the Great Seal, and it is significant that it dare not introduce another until the end of 1643;[1] but the courts of law, despite the king's attempts at interference, continued to function at Westminster, and assizes were held in those areas not immediately affected by the war. The Solemn League and Covenant between the English and the Scots in 1643[2] had as one of its principal aims an accommodation with the king, and it was not until June 1644 that the royalist Members who had deserted were expelled from the Commons and by-elections ordered.[3]

The principal innovations were in the field of administration and taxation. In March 1642 an Act was passed to raise £4,000,000, half by June, the other half by December, to pay the troops now being raised.[4] Somewhat ironically it was modelled on ship-money, in that a lump sum was first named, then apportioned amongst the counties, leaving each to levy the tax as best it could. For this purpose a committee of twelve or fifteen gentry was appointed in each county. Subsequent ordinances for the assessment and the sequestration of royalist estates named other committees, with roughly the same personnel, and these county committees in the areas under the control of Parliament soon came to administer every aspect of local government: the levy of troops (and sometimes, as in Staffordshire, their deployment), the collection of taxes, and the implementation of the various ordinances on

---

[1] Firth and Rait, I, 340 (10 November 1643).   [2] No. **75**, p. 264 above.

[3] Ordinance of 29 June 1644 (Firth and Rait, I, 458). See R. N. Kershaw, 'The Recruiting of the Long Parliament, 1645–47', *History*, VIII (1924), 169, and Godfrey Davies and E. L. Klotz, 'List of Members Expelled from the Long Parliament', *Huntington Library Quarterly*, II (1939), 479.

[4] 16 Car. I, c. 32, *SR*, V, 145; one of the last bills to which the king gave his assent.

religion—and this in addition to the normal duties which many committee members performed as justices of the peace (81).[1]

However, Parliament's decision to group several of the counties well-affected to their cause in Associations, with their combined forces under one general, did something to ease the strain. On 15 December 1642 the counties of Derby, Nottingham, Leicester, Northampton, Rutland, Huntingdon, Bedford and Buckingham were formed into the Midlands Association; the more famous Eastern Association, of Norfolk, Suffolk, Essex, Cambridge and Hertford, followed five days later; and on 31 December Stafford and Warwick were united under the command of Lord Brooke, Shropshire being added the following April.[2]

Meanwhile Parliament decided in June 1642 to raise a special force of 10,000 men in the London area, and soon found itself short of money. In November it passed an ordinance to raise money, plate, horse, horsemen and arms by voluntary contributions,[3] but such old-fashioned remedies were no longer sufficient, and an ordinance of 24 February 1643 (78) established the weekly Assessment, which persisted with little change right up to the Restoration.[4] Like the Act of March 1642, the new ordinance was silent on the question of how the money was to be raised; each county was merely ordered to pay a weekly sum, and the county committee then appointed assessors who determined at what rate the local landowners must be taxed. Attempts were made to include personal property and the income from fees and offices, but like all seventeenth-century direct taxes the assessment soon became in effect a land-tax. From 1649 to 1653 an attempt was made to levy a pound rate on every £20 personalty, but it broke down.[5]

The idea of a land-tax was so abhorrent to the landed gentry that it threw some of them into hysteria. Sir William Strickland said in the Parliament of 1656–7: 'I am sorry to hear any land-tax mentioned here. The people would never have chosen us if they had thought we would ever have moved that. Nothing is so like to blast your settlement as a land-tax. Pardon me if I speak confusedly; any man will justify my distraction in this.'[6] Only the pressing needs of war could justify so sinister an innovation.

[1] Some research has been done on these committees in recent years. See Pennington and Roots, *The Committee at Stafford*; Everitt, *The County Committee of Kent*, and *Suffolk in the Great Rebellion*; and D. H. Pennington, 'The Accounts of the Kingdom, 1642–1649', in Fisher, *Tawney Essays*, p. 182. Extracts from the minutes of the York Committee are printed in *Yorks Archaeological Society, Record Series*, cxviii (1953).

[2] Firth and Rait, I, 49, 51, 53, 124. There were many minor alterations, of course; Shropshire from February to April 1643 was grouped with Gloucester, Worcester, Wiltshire and Somerset under Sir William Waller, and Huntingdon was soon transferred to the Eastern Association.

[3] Firth and Rait, I, 38 (26 November 1642).

[4] It became a monthly assessment in 1645; *ibid.* I, 630 (21 February).

[5] Kennedy, *English Taxation*, pp. 38 ff.; Ashley, *Financial and Commercial Policy*, ch. viii.

[6] Burton, *Parliamentary Diary*, II, 24 (24 April 1657). For the expression of similar views in 1670, see Grey, *Debates*, I, 314 ff.

The novelty of the Assessment was its efficiency and the devolution of greater responsibility on the local authorities, who soon found themselves saddled with even more onerous duties by the Sequestration Ordinance of 27 March 1643 (**79**), which ordered the estates of all those who had contributed money to the king or appeared in arms against Parliament to be confiscated and placed in the charge of committees, who managed them and remitted the profits to the parliamentary treasurers at the Guildhall.

But all this was not enough to meet the rising expense of war, and in March 1643 Pym proposed an excise on alcoholic beverages manufactured in England. A similar proposal had been discussed in 1628, and the principle of the excise was familiar enough; but the more familiar the notion became the less it was liked, and it was already firmly linked in the popular mind with arbitrary government, and the surrender of the liberties of the subject.[1] But Parliament accepted it in 1643 for the same reason as their successors reluctantly continued it in 1660; because the only alternative was a further direct tax on property. The ordinance of 22 July 1643 (**80**) established a 'New Impost' (the word 'excise' being carefully avoided in the title) on tobacco, wine, cider and beer, on imported silks, furs, hats, leather, lace and linen, and on imported 'grocery'—raisins, figs, currants, pepper and sugar. To supervise the collection of the tax eight commissioners were established in London, with subordinate officers in the provinces, who were immediately given those broad powers of entry to premises and the authority to examine suspects under oath which were always to be the main grievances against the excise service. On 8 September the ordinance was re-enacted,[2] with the addition of soap, paper, cloth and imported glassware to the schedule of dutiable goods, and from then on new commodities were added almost every year: in January 1644, meat and salt;[3] in July 1644, 'industrial chemicals' like alum, copperas, hops and saffron, as well as hats and English made silks;[4] in November 1645, lead, gold and silver thread, fish and vegetable oils and imported woollen cloth;[5] and so on. The new tax, and the men who levied it, were always ferociously unpopular, and especially after the end of the first Civil War. By February 1647 riots against the excise were so frequent and so menacing that Parliament issued a declaratory ordinance justifying its imposition, promising to abandon it as soon as the army was demobilised, and in the meanwhile establishing special machinery for the speedier investigation of complaints against excise officers (**83**). Even then, in June 1647 it had to cancel the two most unpopular duties, on meat and salt. But the duty on salt was reinstated in 1649, and in March 1654 Cromwell extended the excise to virtually all saleable commodities. Its unpopularity never waned, but it

---

[1] Hughes, *Studies in Administration and Finance*, pp. 116–17.   [2] Firth and Rait, I, 274.
[3] *Ibid.* I, 364. The title of this ordinance incorporated the word 'excise' for the first time.
[4] *Ibid.* I, 466.   [5] *Ibid.* I, 806.

continued to be the financial mainstay of the interregnum governments, and after 1650 its collection was largely farmed out to private individuals, with some increase in efficiency.[1]

Meanwhile, the principle of sequestration was pressed to its logical conclusion. Prisoners of war were soon given the opportunity to 'compound' for their delinquency by paying a fine proportionate to their participation in the war. In September 1644 the Committee at Goldsmith's Hall (it appears to have had no formal name) was authorised by Parliament to negotiate with those who had been declared delinquents by proclamation but now wished to withdraw from the war.[2] The following March the committee suggested to Parliament that it go outside those limits, by summoning men before it and entertaining voluntary applications from those who had not been officially proclaimed delinquent. In August the minimum composition was fixed at two years' rent, and the proportion could be as much as two-thirds the estimated value of an estate.[3] After the Civil Wars the estates of those who had gone abroad or refused to compound were confiscated outright, and most of them were eventually sold on the open market, with the lands of the Crown and the Church.[4]

Parliament's administration was efficient enough, by the standards of the time, but its patent lack of war aims and its failure to settle the Church were the disillusionment of many of its supporters. The death of Pym, Hampden and Brooke, all in 1643, removed the ablest and most respected of the parliamentary leaders, and they were never replaced. At Westminster Sir Henry Vane the Younger was perhaps the most able manager and speaker left, but his views were so extreme that he could never command a regular majority; it was only natural that he and the other Independents should look for support outside Parliament, and especially to Oliver Cromwell, who was emerging as the best general on either side. The alliance with the Scots was never popular, and the first great parliamentary victory, at Marston Moor in 1644, was not followed up. The incompetence and indecision of the 'Presbyterian' generals, Essex, Manchester and Waller, was now exposed, and the following winter Parliament decided to hand over the conduct of the war to those who were prepared to prosecute it to the bitter end without regard to the ultimate effects. On 17 February 1645 an ordinance was passed creating a new army of mercenaries, 6,600 horse, 14,400 foot and 1000 dragoons, to replace the 'volunteer' armies of the County Associations. Raised 'for the

---

[1] Kennedy, *English Taxation*, pp. 52–5; Ashley, *Financial and Commercial Policy*, pp. 62–71; Hughes, *op. cit.* pp. 120 ff. Parliament also continued to collect tunnage and poundage; see the ordinances of 1 August 1642 and 20 February 1645 (Firth and Rait, I, 16, 627).

[2] *Calendar of the Committee for Compounding*, I, 10.

[3] *Ibid.* I, 17, 24. Cf. p. vii.

[4] Hardacre, *The Royalists during the Puritan Revolution*, chs. II and V, has a good summary of this legislation, and an up-to-date bibliography of the whole question.

defence of the king and Parliament, the true Protestant religion, and the laws and liberties of the kingdom', it was placed under the command of Sir Thomas Fairfax, with Oliver Cromwell Lieutenant-General of Horse.[1] Finally, on 3 April 1645 the Self-Denying Ordinance obliged Members of both Houses to resign all their offices, military and civil.[2] Henceforward, though Parliament continued to govern, the ascendancy of the army in politics was assured.

78. **An ordinance for the speedy raising and levying of money for the maintenance of the army raised by the Parliament, and other great affairs of the Commonwealth, by a weekly assessment upon the cities of London and Westminster, and every county and city of the kingdom of England, and dominion of Wales, 24 February 1643**

The Lords and Commons now assembled in Parliament, being fully satisfied and resolved in their consciences that they have lawfully taken up arms, and may and ought to continue the same for the necessary defence of themselves and the Parliament from violence and destruction, and of this kingdom from foreign invasion, and for the bringing of notorious offenders to condign punishment, which are the only causes for which they have raised and do continue an army and forces which cannot possibly be maintained, nor the kingdom subsist, without the speedy raising of large and considerable sums of money proportionable to the great expenses which now this kingdom is at for the supporting of the said army, and for the saving of the whole kingdom, our religion, laws and liberties from utter ruin and destruction; which, that it may be done with as much ease and indifferency to the good subject as the exigency of the time will permit, the said Lords and Commons do ordain, and be it ordained by the said Lords and Commons in the present Parliament assembled, that for the intents and purposes aforesaid the several and weekly sums of money hereafter in this ordinance mentioned shall be charged, rated, taxed and levied upon all and every the several counties, cities, towns, liberties, places and persons hereafter mentioned, according to the proportions, rates and distributions in this present ordinance expressed, the same to be paid in weekly to the several collectors appointed by this ordinance for the receiving hereof; that is to say, upon the city of London the weekly sum of ten thousand pounds....

[1] Firth and Rait, I, 614.   [2] GCD, pp. 287–8.

[Westminster, £1,250; Anglesey, £25; Bedford, £250; Berkshire, £550; Brecon, £50; Bristol, £55. 15s.; Buckingham, £420; Caernarvon, £35; Cambridge, £375; Carmarthen, £50; Cardigan, £62. 10s.; Cheshire, £175; Chester, £62; Cornwall, £625; Coventry, £37. 10s.; Cumberland, £37. 10s.; Denbigh, £25; Derby, £175; Devon, £1,800; Dorset, £437. 10s.; Durham, £62. 10s.; Essex, £1,125; Exeter, £50. 10s.; Flint, £16. 10s.; Glamorgan, £67. 10s.; Gloucestershire, £750; Gloucester, £62. 10s.; Hampshire, £750; Haverfordwest, £5; Hereford, £437. 10s.; Hertford, £450; Hull, £25; Huntingdon, £220; Isle of Ely, £147. 10s.; Kent, £1,250; Lancashire, £500; Leicester, £187. 10s.; Lichfield, £5; Lincoln, £812. 10s.; Merioneth, £12. 10s.; Middlesex, £750; Monmouth, £62. 10s.; Montgomery, £62. 10s.; Newcastle, £25; Norfolk, £1,250; North-ampton, £425; Northumberland, £50; Nottingham, £187. 10s.; Oxford, £650; Poole, £5; Radnor, £37. 10s.; Rutland, £62. 10s.; Shropshire, £375; Somerset, £1,050; Southwark, £300; Stafford, £212. 10s.; Suffolk, £1,250; Surrey, £400; Sussex, £625; Warwick, £562. 10s.; Westmorland, £27. 5s.; Wiltshire, £725; Worcester (city), £16. 13s.; Worcester, £550; York, £62. 10s.; Yorkshire, £1,062. 10s.]

And be it further ordained, that as well every person of the estate of baron or baroness, and every estate above, and all and every other person and persons born within this realm of England, Wales or other the King's dominions, as well ecclesiastical as temporal, and every fraternity, guild, corporation, mystery, brotherhood and commonalty corporate or not corporate, as well ecclesiastical as temporal, within the realm of England, Wales or other the King's dominions, for the value of every pound which every such person, fraternity, guild...[etc.] hath of his or their own, or that any other hath to his or their use or uses, as well in coin, in plate, stock of merchandise, any manner of corn or grain, household stuff, and of all other goods, moveables, as well within this realm as without, and of all such sum and sums of money as to him or them is, are or shall be owing, whereof he or they trust in his or their conscience to be paid,...shall pay towards the said weekly sum and sums of money so assessed as aforesaid. And every alien and stranger born out of the King's obedience, as well denizens as others, inhabiting within the realm, and also every Popish recusant convict or not convict, shall pay towards the sums aforesaid a proportion double to those of the like estates being no aliens or recusants.

And that every person born within the King's obedience, as well ecclesiastical as temporal, and every corporation, fraternity...[etc.], for every estate that every such person or persons, and every corporation, fraternity...[etc.] or any other to his or their use in trust or otherwise, hath in fee-simple, fee-tail, for term of life, term of years, by execution, wardship, or by copy of court-roll, of and in any honours, castles, manors, lands, tenements, rents, services, tithes, oblations, obventions, annuities, offices of profit, fees, corrodies, or other yearly profits or hereditaments, as well within ancient demesne and other places privileged as elsewhere, shall pay to and towards the said weekly sums his and their proportionable part and proportion of such sum or sums of money as are imposed, charged and set upon each several county, according as the same shall be divided, distributed, taxed or set upon each several town, hamlet, parish or place where such person or persons is or shall be chargeable by this ordinance....

And the said several sums so charged, set upon the said several counties, cities, towns, liberties, places and persons aforesaid, shall by authority of this ordinance be taxed, cessed and rated according to this ordinance, in every shire, riding, lathe, wapentake, rape, city, borough, town, and every other place within this realm of England and dominion of Wales, before the twenty-sixth day of February in the year of Our Lord 1642[-3]. And the first payment of the said weekly sums so assessed by this ordinance shall be made at or before the first day of March 1642[-3], and the said weekly payments to continue weekly for three months next ensuing from the said first day of March, unless the King's army shall be disbanded in the meantime. And for the better expediting of the said service, be it further ordained by the said Lords and Commons, that the persons hereafter named shall be committees for the several and respective counties and places hereafter mentioned: That is to say... [The names of the members of the committee in each county and county borough follow.]

Which said several committees[1] of the said several and respective counties and places, or the greatest part of them, shall with all convenient speed after notice of this ordinance given to them, or any two of them, meet together within the several counties and places respectively, where they are committees, in some convenient place within the same counties or places, and may there agree to sever and divide themselves for the execution of the said service, unto such hundreds, places and divisions within their respective counties and places as to them shall seem meet and expedient; and afterwards the said committees, or any two of them, respectively, shall direct their warrants to

---

[1] That is, 'committee men'.

such number of persons as they shall think fit within their several and respective divisions, to appear before them, or any two of them, and upon their appearance the said respective committees, or any two of them, shall nominate and appoint such persons as they shall think fit within their respective divisions; which said persons so nominated, or any two of them, shall have power to assess all and every person or persons, fraternity, guild... [etc.] chargeable by this ordinance, according to the weekly rates and proportions in this ordinance mentioned.

* * * * * *

Firth and Rait, 1, 85–100

79. An ordinance for sequestring notorious delinquents' estates, 27 March 1643

The Lords and Commons assembled in Parliament, taking into their serious consideration the heavy pressures and calamities which now lie upon this kingdom by this unnatural war raised against the Parliament; and that notwithstanding all their faithful and incessant endeavours for the preserving of his Majesty and the whole kingdom from the mischievous and restless designs of Papists and ill affected persons whose aim is the extirpation of our religion, laws and liberties, yet their counsels and practices are still so prevalent with his Majesty, and the hearts of many people so misled and beguiled by their false pretences and insinuations, that nothing can be expected but ruin and desolation unless God in mercy prevent it, and incline his Majesty's heart to the faithful advice of his great council of Parliament, which hath ever been and is under God the chief support of his royal dignity and the security of all that we have or can enjoy. And for that it is most agreeable to common justice that the estates of such notorious delinquents as have been the causers or instruments of the public calamities, which have been hitherto employed to the fomenting and nourishing of these miserable distractions, should be converted and applied towards the support of the great charges of the Commonwealth, and for the easing of the good subjects therein, who have hitherto borne the greatest share in these burdens.

Be it therefore ordained by the said Lords and Commons, that the estates as well real as personal of the several bishops hereafter mentioned, that is to say, of William, archbishop of Canterbury, John, archbishop of York,... and of all such bishops, deans, deans and chapters, prebends, archdeacons, and of all other person and persons, ecclesiastical or temporal, as have raised or shall raise arms against the Parliament, or have been, are or shall be in actual war against the same, or have voluntarily contributed, or shall voluntarily contribute (not being under the power of any part of the King's army at the time of such contributing) any money, horse, plate, arms, munition or other aid or assistance, for or towards the maintenance of any forces raised against the Parliament, or for the opposing of any force or power raised by authority of both Houses of Parliament, and of all such as have joined or shall join in any oath, or act of association against the Parliament, or have imposed, or shall impose any tax or assessment upon his Majesty's subjects for or towards the maintenance of any forces against the Parliament, or have, or shall use any force or power to levy the same, shall be forthwith seized and sequestered into the hands of the sequestrators and committees hereafter in this ordinance named, and of such other persons as shall at any other time hereafter be appointed and nominated by both Houses of Parliament, for any county, city or place within the realm of England or dominion of Wales. Which said sequestrators and committees, or any two or more of them, in each several county, city or place respectively are hereby authorised and required by themselves, their agents and deputies, to take and seize into their hands and custodies as well all the money, goods, chattels, debts and personal estate, as also all and every the manors, lands, tenements and hereditaments, rents, arrearages of rents, revenues and profits of all and every the said delinquents, or persons before specified...; and also two parts of all the money, goods, chattels, debts, and personal estate, and two parts of all and every the manors, lands, tenements and hereditaments, rents, arrearages of rents, revenues and profits of all and every Papist, or which any other person hath in trust for any Papists, or to the use or uses of any Papists, and to let, set and demise the same, or any part thereof, as the respective landlord or owner thereof may or might have done from year to year; and shall have power to call before them, or any two of them, all stewards, bailiffs, rent gatherers, auditors or other officers or servants, as well of the said archbishops, bishops, deans, deans and chapters, prebends, archdeacons, as of all and every other of the said delinquents or persons before specified, and to send for or take any books of accounts, rentals, copies of court rolls, or other evidences, writings, or memorials touching the premises or any of them, and thereby, and by all other ways and means which to the said sequestrators, or any two or more of them, shall seem meet and necessary to inform themselves, as well of the said several delinquents and every of them as of their several estates and possessions, rents, arrearages of rents, revenues and profits, goods and chattels, estates real and personal, and the true value thereof, and of all things concerning the same or any part thereof, and to appoint any officer or officers, or other person or persons under them, for the better expediting of this service....

* * * * * *

And the said sequestrators...shall be accountable from time to time for the same, and for all such other things as shall be had or taken by them, their agents or deputies; and for all their receipts and payments and other acts, for or in respect of the premises, to both Houses of Parliament, or to such as they shall appoint; and shall pay in all such sums of money as they or any of them shall receive out of the said estates unto the treasurers at Guildhall, London, and shall keep books of accounts, and shall be from time to time subject to the further orders and directions of both Houses of Parliament,...as cause shall require....

* * * * * *

Firth and Rait, 1, 106–10

80. An ordinance for the speedy raising and levying of monies, set by way of charge or new impost,...as well for...the maintenance of the forces raised for the defence of the King and Parliament, both by sea and land, as for and towards the payment of the debts of the Commonwealth, 22 July 1643

...Forasmuch as many great levies have been already made for the purpose first above mentioned, which the well-affected party to the Protestant religion have hitherto willingly paid, to their great charge, and the malignants of this kingdom have hitherto practised by all cunning ways and means how to evade and elude the payment of any part thereof, by reason whereof the Lords and Commons do hold it fit that some constant and equal way for the levying of monies for the future maintenance of the Parliament forces, and other great affairs of the Commonwealth, may be had and established, whereby the said malignants and neutrals may be brought to and compelled to pay their proportionable parts of the aforesaid charge, and that the levies hereafter to be made for the purposes aforesaid may be borne with as much indifferency to the subject in general as may be.

279

I. Be it therefore ordered, ordained and declared by the said Lords and Commons, that the several rates and charges in a schedule hereunto annexed and contained, shall be set and laid, and are hereby set and laid, charged and imposed upon all and every the commodities in the said schedule particularly expressed, as the same are particularly therein taxed and rated, as well upon those that are already brought into this realm, or the dominion of Wales, and town of Berwick, and every of them, and are remaining in the hands of any merchant, buyer or seller, or other owner thereof respectively, as upon any of the commodities in the schedule mentioned which hereafter shall be imported into this kingdom of England, dominion of Wales, and town of Berwick, or any of them.

II. And be it further ordained by the said Lords and Commons, that for the better levying of the monies hereby to be raised, that an office from henceforth by force and virtue of these presents shall be and is hereby erected, made and appointed in the city of London, called or known by the name of the Office of Excise or New Impost, whereof there shall be eight commissioners to govern the same, and one of them to be treasurer, with several registers, collectors, clerks and other subordinate officers, as the eight commissioners (or the major part of them) for the time being shall with the approbation of the Committee of Lords and Commons appointed for the Advance of Money, and making of other provisions for the army (sitting at Haberdashers' Hall, London) nominate and appoint....

*   *   *   *   *   *

IV. And it is further ordered and ordained that the said commissioners and treasurer shall be from time to time nominated by both Houses of Parliament.... And all parts of the cities of London and Westminster, with their several suburbs, and all other places within seven miles of either of the said cities and suburbs, shall be subject to the rule and government of the said Office.

V. That the like Office, and so many of such Officers, shall be and is hereby erected, and appointed in all and every the counties of the realm of England, dominion of Wales and town of Berwick, and in all other the cities and such other places thereof as the said eight Commissioners, or the major part of them, shall for the time being think fit....

*   *   *   *   *   *

X. That all and every the merchants and importers of any of the several foreign commodities in the schedule mentioned, and all ale and common beer brewers shall weekly cause to be entered into the said office a true and perfect list or account, as well of all and every the said commodities by them respectively and weekly sold, as of the names of the buyers thereof, and of those to whose use the same is bought, and that they shall not deliver any of the said commodities unto any of the buyers thereof, or other person or persons, until the same shall be so entered, and that the buyer hath procured a ticket under the hand of the treasurer for the time being signifying that he hath paid tho rates set upon the said commodities, or given security for the same.

XI. That if any of the sellers of the said commodities shall refuse or neglect to make a true entry of the said commodities, according to the next precedent article, or do anything contrary to the said article, that then he or they so refusing, neglecting or doing contrary to the said article, shall forfeit to the use of the Commonwealth four times the true value or worth of the goods and commodities so by him or them neglected to be entered or delivered contrary to the said article, for which he shall be distrained.... And if it shall happen that no distress can be conveniently taken of the goods of the party so offending, that then it may and shall be lawful to and for the said commissioners, or the major part of them, their deputy or deputies, by some one or more of their officers, to arrest the party so offending, and commit him to some common prison next adjoining to his place of dwelling or abode, there to remain without bail or mainprize until he pay the penalties by him forfeited as aforesaid....

XII. That if any common brewer, alehouse keeper, cider or perry maker, in the country or in any city, town or place therein, which doth brew ale or beer, or make cider and perry, in their houses or elsewhere, do not make a true entry in manner aforesaid,...then they shall incur the like penalty as aforesaid....

XIII. That all and every person and persons whatsoever that keep or shall keep private houses and families,...which brew, or shall cause to be brewed their own ale and beer for the sustenance of their families, ...shall monthly cause the like entries to be made...or the like penalties to be levied on the offenders herein....

* * * * * *

XX. That the said commissioners...shall have power and authority to call before them any person or persons whom they shall think fit, to inform or testify touching the premises, and to examine them upon oath for the better discovery of any fraud or guile in the not entering, or not payment, of the rates of excise or new impost herein mentioned, and that the testimony of two credible witnesses shall be sufficient, and that the said commissioners...shall have full power by virtue of this ordinance to administer an oath to any person or persons for the purposes aforesaid.

XXI. That the said commissioners...shall from time to time appoint any officer or officers belonging to the said office to enter into cellars, shops, warehouses, store-houses, or other places of every person or persons that selleth, buyeth or spendeth any of the said commodities, to search and see what quantities of any of the said commodities every such hath on his hands, or any other person or persons to his use.

*   *   *   *   *   *

XXIV. That the said commissioners and other officers, and every of them appointed by this ordinance, shall have power to call the trained bands, volunteers or other forces of any county, city or place respectively to be aiding and assisting to them, to compel obedience in this ordinance, where any resistance shall be made, which said trained bands, volunteers and other forces, and their several commanders, and other officers, are hereby required and enjoined to give their aid and assistance accordingly, as need shall require.

XXV. And be it further ordained that as well all and every the said commissioners, deputies, treasurer, registers, receivers or other officers whatsoever belonging to the said several offices, as all and every other person and persons which shall do anything in execution or performance of this present ordinance, shall be therein from time to time protected and saved harmless by the power and authority of both Houses of Parliament.

*   *   *   *   *   *

Firth and Rait, I, 202–9

81. Minutes of the Committee for Staffordshire

[18 March 1643]

The fornicator gunner

Ordered that the gunner which did commit fornication shall be set upon the great gun with a mark upon his back through the garrison and then disgracefully expulsed....

Brett

Whereas Alexander Brett of Pencle holds a farm there of Mr Ralph Keeling of Newcastle and is behind of his rent, as the said Mr Keeling informs, the sum of £18, for which he took a distress of his cattle, which he afterwards by the help of the enemy then in those parts rescued and took again: It is therefore now ordered that the said Mr Keeling shall have liberty to distrain for the said arrears, and to take to his assistance so many of Captain Stone's soldiers as shall be thought necessary, giving them satisfaction for their pains therein... [75].

[24 April]

1. That Mr Ferne of Crackmarsh be committed to the marshal to bide in prison until he pay the sum of one hundred pounds demanded of him upon the proposition according to the ordinance of Parliament.

2. That Jo. Hichecok [*sic*] be desired to fetch the cistern of lead, three long ladders, and a pair of gates from the Grange and bring them to Stafford.

3. That Mrs Eliz. Hamersley quietly enjoy those lands formerly by deed made over to her by her husband for the maintenance of her and children, she paying all levies assessed upon those lands by the committee of Parliament. And that the remainder of Mr Hamersley's estate only be sequestered....

Beer at 1d. the quart

Forasmuch as there hath been of late much drunkenness in the soldiers, which hath been occasioned by the excessive strong beer brewed contrary to the rate ordained by the statute. It is therefore ordered that no inn or alehouse keepers shall brew any ale or beer other than what they will sell for a penny a quart *intus et foras* [*sc.* on or off the premises]. And if they shall demand more, for every such offence that shall pay 10s., to be levied on their goods, and not suffered to brew any more... [103].

[7 May 1645]

Tovey

Ordered that Capt. Tovey (in respect his troop is wholly squandered and lost, and that there is not horse in the county to recruit nor need of more officers, the contribution of the county not being able to bear those we have already) be dismissed his attendance here for command, and if he stay to have no more allowance from the committee.

M. Snowe

Ordered that Major Snowe's Company march to the leaguer at Chester, and that Major Snowe himself march with them and command all the Staffordshire Foot in the absence of Colonel Bowyer, and when Col. Bowyer comes he to stay with those companies until he be dismissed by Sir Will. Brereton.

Winkle and Lees

Whereas it is informed that there are two orchards, the one of Mrs Winkles and the other of Mrs Dorothy Lees, which have been converted to the State's use ever since the taking of this garrison by the Parliament's forces, which orchards were formerly valued at 40s. per annum as is informed. It is ordered that the solicitors for sequestration shall pay yearly to the said Mrs Winkle and Mrs Lees the sum of £1. 13s. 4d. out of delinquents' rents to be equally divided betwixt them. And likewise shall pay the arrears for the time past, and the £1. 13s. 4d. so long as the state holdeth them.

[8 May]

Davenport

Ordered that Mr Bargh shall let widow Davenport have a cow's grass rent free, for the maintaining of two poor orphans whose father was killed in service.

Blakemore

Ordered that Mr Blakemore look to the buildings, grass and corn which belong to the parsonage of Swynerton and preserve them for the next incumbent [303–4].

Pennington and Roots, *The Committee at Stafford*, pp. 75, 103, 303–4

82. Declaration to be tendered to officers and members of the Committee and those rated to lend to Parliament

April 27th...1643

I do acknowledge that the Parliament orders and ordinances, as they issue forth now, are as fully to be yielded obedience unto as the orders and ordinances of former parliaments, and this I testify with my heart, and that because the king's authority and power is there, though his person be not.

Witness my hand.

Everitt, *Suffolk and the Great Rebellion*, p 58

83. An ordinance concerning the excise, with additional instructions for the better regulating the same, 22 February 1647

The Lords and Commons assembled in Parliament, taking notice of the many tumults and great riots which have of late happened and been privily fomented in several parts of the kingdom against the receipts and collections of the excise, by the secret and subtle designs and practices of malignants, and such who by their false and feigned pretences do endeavour to breed misunderstanding and impatience in the people, have for the better manifesting of the justice of their proceeding, and reality of their intentions, thought fit to make this declaration to the whole kingdom:

That as nothing did or could have drawn them to resolve upon this imposition but the preservation of this kingdom, the religion, laws and liberties from utter ruin and destruction, all which at that time was threatened by the restless and cruel designs, practices and treacheries of Papists and malignant persons, so they could then find no other means, after the well-affected had so willingly born so many great levies, which the malignants had endeavoured by all cunning ways to evade, as any longer to maintain the Parliament forces, and other great affairs of the Commonwealth, and to draw in the malignants and neutrals to bear their proportional parts of the charge, than by some such constant and indifferent way. And what great difficulties, expenses and charges the said Lords and Commons have by the receipt and credit of the excise, with some other helps as occasion did require, been enabled ever since, through God's blessing, to overcome and maintain, by continually keeping on foot so many several armies, as they were by the King's party in arms against the Parliament enforced to raise in divers parts of the kingdom; by maintaining so many garrisons; by relieving of Ireland from time to time, when other supplies could not be timely raised; by satisfying our brethren of Scotland, is by this time so evident to the whole kingdom that they hope no well-affected person can or will look back upon what he hath contributed in this way for his part with any regret or repining, as if the same had or can be fruitless to him or his posterity.

And [as] for the present continuance of this levy; when it shall be considered for what great sums, and to how many well-affected persons they have already engaged the excise for monies borrowed and justly due unto them; what expenses they must yet be at before they can settle this kingdom; what charges are requisite to reduce the kingdom of Ireland; and what great engagements do otherwise lie upon the Parliament for many supplies and services, for satisfying whereof the public faith and honour of the Parliament and kingdom is engaged; they are confident that no well-affected or understanding person can or will desire or expect that this levy, which they still find the most equal and indifferent course to go through so many great affairs, should cease while the Parliament is thus deeply engaged and have [sic] so many pressing occasions for monies for the necessary support and preservation of the kingdom.

And therefore the said Lords and Commons assembled in Parliament do hereby declare to the whole kingdom that they shall and do expect that all persons whatsoever shall duly pay all sums of money imposed by any ordinance of Parliament by way of excise upon all and every the commodities, merchandises and things therein mentioned and comprised; and that the same ordinances shall be duly observed according to the rules therein prescribed until further order of both Houses of Parliament. Whereunto the said Lords and Commons do hereby require all persons to yield all ready obedience, conformity and assistance accordingly, as they tender the honour of the Parliament, the welfare of the kingdom, and as they would approve themselves well-affected to both.

And we the said Lords and Commons assembled in Parliament, to manifest our constant and sincere intentions in the continuance of this receipt of the excise, do hereby declare, that as hitherto the revenue thereof hath been wholly employed for the public uses and occasions of the kingdom, and diverted to no private use whatsoever so they are still resolved to dispose thereof in the same public and necessary service of the Commonwealth only; and shall no longer continue this charge upon the subject than they shall find the public affairs wherewith they are entrusted necessarily to require the same. And when it shall please God by the continuance of his mercy to enable them to settle the peace of the kingdom, and to overcome the engagements thereof in some good measure, they shall then make it appear to the whole world how much more ready they are to ease the people of this charge then they were willing at first to impose the same.

*　　*　　*　　*　　*　　*

Firth and Rait, I, 916–20

CHAPTER 8

THE ARMY AND REFORM
1647–1649

The 'classical' Independents who had so successfully sabotaged the programme of the Westminster Assembly have been described as 'decentralised Calvinists'.[1] They asserted the right of each congregation to discipline itself, and they rejected the overriding authority of either presbytery or bishop, yet they accepted the existence of a national Church and the need for the secular magistrate to suppress the grosser forms of blasphemy and heresy. Moreover, they held to the belief that each 'gathered' congregation must include both the elect and the reprobate.

However, the relaxation of ecclesiastical discipline and the profound, though temporary, social disturbances caused by the first Civil War brought to the surface a lower-class Independency[2] which had much more in common with sixteenth-century Brownism. The distinguishing mark of these sects was that they consisted only of the elect; they also rejected any association, however tenuous, with the Church, and they permitted, even encouraged, lay preaching. The members of many sects soon became convinced that not only were they of the elect but they *were* the elect—they, and nobody else; therefore cooperation with any other sect was undesirable and even impossible. Finally, the teaching of most of these sects was strongly chiliastic, though few of them defined their theories with such accuracy as the Fifth Monarchists, who prophesied the Second Coming in 1656. This encouraged a sublime indifference to political forms which, together with the mutual intolerance of the sects, undermined many of the reforms attempted by their leaders. Even Cromwell believed that the most perfect constitution was 'dross and dung in comparison of Christ'.

The Independents, therefore, sought religious toleration as a defence against Presbyterianism; the Sectaries demanded it as a natural right, an essential part of their Christian belief. But until the king was dead these two groups were forced into alliance by the fear that he and the Long Parliament would join to impose a Presbyterian Church on the nation and persecute all independent congregations or sects out of existence.

The popular view that the New Model Army was the peculiar breeding-ground of left-wing democracy and religious radicalism has been criticised

---

[1] See Yule, *The Independents*, ch. I; Miller, *Orthodoxy in Massachusetts*, ch. IV.
[2] Henceforward described as 'sectarianism' for the sake of clarity.

on the ground that much of the preaching to which it was exposed was conservative and even authoritarian in nature.[1] But the myth that the Army was an army of saints, in which each individual soldier had enlisted to fight for England's freedom and her people's natural rights, and to carry out God's Intention for His Nation, was a contemporary creation, the work of the junior officers and N.C.O.s who supported the programme of the London Levellers. It was asserted with great confidence by the Levellers at Putney in 1647, and was restated in a particular pure form by the junior officers of Cromwell's army in 1650 (91). But it was simply not true. Many of the soldiers of the New Model were pressed men, many more had simply enlisted for pay; they would follow their officers wherever they led, provided they could satisfy their demands for back-pay and good terms of future service.[2] Thus in the crises of 1647 and 1649 the army commanders faced a revolt on the part of a few officers and N.C.O.s, not a general mutiny, and this is why the Levellers could never force the Council of the Army to accept more of their programme than suited them. Nevertheless, the Army was a privileged enclave in that it enjoyed complete freedom of preaching and theological speculation, free from interference by magistrates, county committees or Presbyterian clerics; and the continuance of this de facto toleration was always high on its list of priorities, for officers as well as men.

But in the conditions of 1647 and 1648 the Army's claim to represent the nation was plausible enough. Immediately the war ended Parliament's lack of war aims, formerly an embarrassment, became a grievance. By assessment and excise, not to mention sequestration and confiscation, it had imposed on the nation taxation of an unprecedented intensity and efficiency; it had killed thousands of men; it had ridden roughshod over legal and constitutional forms—but why it had done all this it had never clearly explained, and the Levellers were not the only ones who were disillusioned with rulers whose sole aim seemed to be the perpetuation of their own authority. Intellectual republicans like John Milton shared this disillusion.[3] The Long Parliament had long ago exceeded the mandate given it in October 1640 (and half the men elected then had fallen by the way), and it would be difficult to find any element in the nation, apart perhaps from the Presbyterian clergy, that supported it out of conviction. The Propositions for a settlement which it presented to the king at Newcastle in July 1646[4] were conceived in a narrow

[1] Leo F. Solt, Saints in Arms; also 'Puritanism and Democracy in the New Model Army', Archiv für Reformationsgeschichte, L (1959), 234.

[2] It is worth noting that even S. R. Gardiner did not regard this as an army of fanatics or reformers; he remarks that arrears and indemnity 'were all that the greater number of the soldiers really cared for', and that 'the religious enthusiasts' were in a minority (Civil War, III, 228).

[3] See Milton's remarkable 'Character of the Long Parliament', too long for inclusion here (Works, X, 318), and his poem 'On the New Forcers of Conscience' (ibid. I, 71). The most cogent Leveller attack was by William Walwyn in The Bloody Project, August 1648, printed by Haller and Davies, Leveller Tracts, pp. 135–40.   [4] GCD, p. 290.

spirit of revenge and repression, padded out with so many exceptions that they would have removed from public life any and every person who had ever opposed it or even disagreed with it.

Yet it was essential that they reach agreement with the king. Any permanent government without him was unthinkable, and in any case the paradox of war had left the vanquished more popular than the victor. Charles's public reception on his return from Newcastle confirmed that his position was potentially very strong, theirs weak. They must insist on Presbyterianism, but both sides knew that this had virtually no popular support and would attract the particular disfavour of the Army. The Army was also personally hostile to Charles I, as the author of the war, and the publication of his correspondence, captured at Naseby, had confirmed his duplicity in their eyes. Even so, all might have been well had Parliament been able to pay the soldiers' arrears of wages—eighteen weeks for the infantry and forty-three for the cavalry—and had it been willing to pass an ordinance indemnifying them for crimes committed during the war. But it hesitated to pass an Act of Oblivion, which might lead to a demand from the king for the inclusion of his own supporters, and it simply dare not increase taxation in time of peace to pay off the Army. Its clumsy attempts to demobilise most of the Army without arrears of pay and ship the rest to Ireland infuriated the troops, and only Cromwell and Fairfax kept them from open mutiny. All this played into Charles's hands, and his third answer to the Propositions of Newcastle, in May 1647,[1] was studiously moderate. To Parliament's demand that he surrender control of the militia for twenty years he offered ten; he proposed that the Church should be reformed and settled by the Westminster Assembly, with twenty divines of his own choosing added; and he declined to permit the punishment of his supporters and friends.

At this stage it became clear that Parliament was so weak that the king would in time secure his own terms; in any case both sides were agreed on the need for an authoritarian Church. The Army now intervened on the plea that it was more representative of the nation than the present parliamentary junto. Thus began its attempt to represent itself as an Army with a mission, even a mandate. On 4 June Charles was seized at Holdenby and brought to headquarters, and the next day officers and men subscribed to a Solemn Engagement not to disband until their immediate claims had been met and the constitution in Church and State had been settled along lines acceptable to them. A Council of the Army was formed, representing officers and men, and some regiments were moved up on London. On 14 June, at St Albans, the Council issued the *Declaration of the Army* (84), demanding that Parliament expel those Members hostile to the army, appoint a date for its own dissolution, and make provision for the regular assembly of subsequent parliaments.

[1] *GCD*, p. 311.

'We are not a mere mercenary army', they wrote, 'hired to serve any arbitrary power of a state, but called forth and conjured by the several Declarations of Parliament to the defence of our own and the people's just rights and liberties.' They therefore demanded that the Long Parliament, before it dispersed, should reduce the power of the county committees, publish its accounts and pass an Act of Oblivion for both sides in the late war. All subsequent declarations and petitions of the Army, right down to 1652, were just elaborations on this basic text.

Under continued pressure from the Army eleven of the Commons leaders did withdraw on 26 June, but Parliament made no further attempt to comply with the *Declaration*, and in July the Council of the Army, guided by John Lambert and Henry Ireton, Cromwell's son-in-law, drafted a more detailed exposition of its views: a draft constitution together with further proposals for reform. These *Heads of the Proposals* were informally handed to the king on 23 July, and published on 1 August (85). Meanwhile the Commons' former leaders, strongly supported in the City, had resumed their seats amidst wild rioting, and on 30 July the Speaker with the greater part of the Independent Members fled to the army camp. On 6 August the Army took London, suppressed the mobs, and brought Parliament to heel.

The only difficulty now was, how to persuade the king to accept the *Heads of the Proposals*. These differed most noticeably from Parliament's proposals in their leniency to the royalists and their demand for religious toleration. Only a handful of major delinquents were to be subject to the full rigour of the law, as a public example; the rest were to compound on easy terms and were only to be excluded from public office for five years. No provision was made for church government, but all legislation compelling attendance at church was to be repealed, and other means found to suppress the Papists and 'Prelatists'. For the rest, the Army Council put its faith in biennial parliaments, with the king in the hands of a Council of State; for ten years control of the militia and of appointments to the great offices of state were to be in the hands of Parliament, and after that under its close supervision. Perhaps the most interesting proposals, indicative of the influence of the lesser gentry in the Army, were those calling for reform of the electoral system (I, 5) and for the election of sheriffs and justices of the peace indirectly by the county freeholders (I, 11). Finally, like the *Declaration*, the *Proposals* had to take notice of popular grievances voiced by the Levellers in London and in the Army: the reform of the law, the replacement of excise and tithe, the abolition of monopolies, and so on.

The Levellers were unique in that they were the only 'party' thrown up during these troubles that did not also constitute a religious sect or have a religious programme. The basis of their power was the London mob, swelled by unemployment in years of slump, and this was reflected in their

291

programme of social reform; the abolition of restraints on trade, the implementation of the poor laws, the reduction of indirect taxation, and so on. But the Leveller leaders had moved beyond this. John Lilburne in particular, profiting by his study of Sir Edward Coke's works, had evolved a theory of natural right which asserted that every free man in England, irrespective of wealth or property, had the right to vote, and that this right had been suppressed at the Conquest, which had ushered in a period of foreign tyranny which still continued.[1] He and his followers therefore demanded a large extension of the franchise and the abolition of the monarchy and the House of Lords. Their influence in the Army steadily increased during the course of 1647, and men infected by their doctrines were naturally alarmed and incensed at the sight of their own leaders, Fairfax, Cromwell and Ireton, negotiating a future constitution with Charles Stuart, that man of 'bloody and tyrannical spirit'. If anything they were even more appalled when Cromwell resumed his negotiations with the Presbyterian leaders in the Commons in October. Each regiment had already elected agents or agitators (the two words were synonymous) to represent them in the pay negotiations, and on 18 October five of these agents, led by the Leveller John Wildman, issued *The Case of the Army Truly Stated*,[2] in which they called upon the senior officers to implement the *Declaration* of 14 June at once. Fairfax being ill, Cromwell had to summon a full meeting of the Army Council, with additional Leveller representatives, to Putney on 28 October. As a basis for discussion the Levellers at once tabled the *Agreement of the People*, which called for a unicameral legislature, elected on a broad franchise, which was to be omnipotent except in certain reserved matters, such as religion and conscription (86).

It is not clear that at this stage the Levellers wanted to abolish the kingship. The king is nowhere mentioned, but the *Agreement* was specifically a proposal for dealing with Parliament; in the debate at Putney the powers of the king were discussed at length, and not all the Levellers questioned the necessity for his existence. Similarly, it has now been shown that their demand for universal manhood suffrage did not extend to wage-earners.[3] In some respects, then, the *Agreement* was not as radical as is sometimes supposed, but it was too radical for Henry Ireton, the officers' chief spokesman, who showed himself steadfastly resolved to limit the administration of government and the exercise of direct political power to the landed gentry (87). After a lengthy debate extending over several days the whole matter was

[1] See Hill, *Puritanism and Revolution*, pp. 50 ff., and, more generally, J. Frank, *The Levellers* (Harvard, 1955), and H. N. Brailsford, *The Levellers and the English Revolution* (London, 1961).
[2] Printed by Haller and Davies, *Leveller Tracts*, pp. 65 ff.; excerpts in Woodhouse, *Puritanism and Liberty*, pp. 429 ff.
[3] C. B. Macpherson, *The Political Theory of Possessive Individualism*, ch. III. However, see Peter Laslett's criticisms, in *Historical Journal*, VII (1964), 151–2.

referred to a committee, which eventually produced what is sometimes known as the *Second Agreement of the People*,[1] incorporating the kingship, and the Council of State outlined in the *Heads of the Proposals*. This was not a popular move, but Fairfax issued a lengthy statement justifying the senior officers' stand,[2] and at a rendezvous of the more disaffected regiments called for 15 November any signs of mutiny were crushed. Meanwhile on 11 November the king had escaped to the Isle of Wight, and on 26 December he signed a secret *Engagement* with representatives of the Scots nobility, in which he bound himself, in return for the establishment of the constitution as in 1642, to introduce Presbyterianism for a trial period of three years and suppress all sectarian deviations.[3]

The situation was now as confused as it possibly could be. The *Engagement*, of course, was still secret, but on 28 December the king had rejected Parliament's latest proposals, and on 17 January 1648 Parliament replied with the *Vote of No Addresses*, breaking off all negotiations.[4] Yet Parliament, including the Independent Members, still believed, most of them, in government by king, Lords and Commons; and so did the senior officers of the Army, despite the attitude of so many of their juniors. But with the realisation that the king had fomented another civil war the feeling in the Army overwhelmed its leaders. At the end of April a great prayer meeting was held at Windsor before the Army dispersed to the war, and there it was finally agreed that Charles Stuart, 'that man of blood', must be brought to trial (88). This was entirely unofficial, but it was all the programme the Army now had.

The utter defeat of the Scots at Preston in August 1648 and the speedy elimination of the Welsh and English royalists gave the Army another mandate, but it had to seek inspiration again from the Levellers, and its renewed attempts to found a new constitution were steadily undermined by Parliament, which reopened negotiations with the king at Newport in September —bringing forth a trenchant restatement of Leveller principles from Lilburne, the *Humble Petition* (89). The Leveller leaders now demanded that the Army Council appeal beyond Parliament to the people, but the insistence of Fairfax (Cromwell was in Scotland) on preserving constitutional forms to the end frustrated them, and brought chaos. On 20 November the council presented yet another *Remonstrance of the Army* to Parliament.[5] In its assertion of the ultimate sovereignty of the people and its demand for the king's removal, this document shows the extent to which Ireton had moved over to the Leveller position. But, Parliament remaining obdurate, he could only secure

---

[1] Printed Woodhouse, *op. cit.* pp. 356 ff. For a bibliographical analysis and some description of the various documents bearing this title, see J. W. Gough, 'The Agreements of the People, 1647–1649', *History*, xv (1931), 334–41.

[2] Abbott, I, 557–60.

[3] *GCD*, pp. 347–52.

[4] *Ibid.* pp. 353–6.

[5] Printed Woodhouse, *op. cit.* pp. 456–65.

his aims by force. Finding that Parliament was still negotiating with the king, he ordered Charles to be arrested and on 2 December reoccupied London. He then pleaded with the Council of Officers that Parliament be dispersed by force if it refused to dissolve itself, but he was overruled, and on 6 December Colonel Pride was merely ordered to exclude the Presbyterian members. Pride's Purge appears a dreadful blow to the independence of Parliament, but the opposite was the case; by proceeding to these lengths the Army betrayed its absolute need of the sanction of the House of Commons, *some* House of Commons, any House of Commons. When the Lords refused to follow them any longer, on 4 January 1649, the Rump, as it was now called, passed three resolutions; that ultimate power resided in the people, that the people had delegated this power to their chosen representatives, and that legislation by the Commons alone, without king or Lords, was of perfect legal validity (90). Two days later it passed an Act[1] setting up a High Court of Justice to try the king.[2]

Ironically enough, Parliament had now accepted the Levellers' main tenet —that all power was derived from the people—but because of the maladroitness and misplaced constitutionalism of the Council of Officers it was now being used to prop up a mere oligarchy, a handful of discredited men who dare not face the electors. It had been their main aim to force a dissolution of the Long Parliament, but they had made the elementary error of seeking from it first the authority to try the king. Once it had authorised the trial of the Lord's Anointed it was itself unassailably the chief legal authority in the land. Yet the High Court of Justice was a farce; so the officers did not even have the satisfaction of giving Charles a dignified public trial.[3] They would have done much better to have tried him by court-martial and shot him.

Attempts to regain lost ground were hopeless. In December Lilburne had produced an amended and expanded version of the *Agreement of the People*, which now offered a complete working constitution, without king or Lords. It was further amended by the Council of Officers and presented by them to the Commons on 20 January 1649.[4] This new Agreement was of use to the men who drew up the *Instrument of Government* four years later, but for the time being it was a dead letter. The Rump was not obliged to accept it, and had no intention of setting a term to its own power now the Army had exhausted its means of coercion; and if it needed an excuse for delay it could always plead the necessity of dealing with the king first.

Charles was in a handsome position legally, too, though it was obvious that he had only a week or two to live. He had pursued a perfectly consistent

---

[1] Henceforward the term 'ordinance' was abandoned.
[2] *GCD*, pp. 357–8.   [3] See C. V. Wedgwood, *Trial of Charles I.*
[4] *GCD*, pp. 359–71. Cf. Gough, *op. cit.* pp. 338–40.

policy ever since 1642, rejecting or ignoring all proposals which limited his command of the army or his choice of ministers. The only treaty he had signed, the *Engagement* with the Scots, was the only one which did not impose such restrictions. (It does not appear that the position of episcopacy was so vital to him as it was to many of his apologists, who were anxious to associate the martyred king with the restored Church. It may be significant that on the scaffold Juxon had to remind him to say something on this score.) Moreover, he could assert with truth that the Army's every action since June 1647 had been illegal and unconstitutional, and therefore its proposals for constitutional reform had no validity at all. This attitude he maintained by refusing to plead before the High Court, and he argued that if the Army could treat him like this—the king, the fountain of law and justice—then no lesser man was safe. His argument that kingship was the sole guarantee of social order was a commonplace, and echoed Strafford's arguments in 1628 and 1641; his insistence that for the mass of the people liberty consisted in having government, not in governing, was an echo of Ireton at Putney. In Westminster Hall and on the scaffold he appealed with unconscious skill to the conservative parliamentary gentry who had rebelled in 1642 and had now been suppressed by the Army. His words established a programme on which his son was to be restored in 1660.[1]

84. A declaration, or representation from His Excellency Sir Thomas Fairfax, and of the army under his command, Humbly tendered to the Parliament, St Albans, 14 June 1647

That we may no longer be the dissatisfaction of our friends, the subject of our enemies' malice (to work jealousies and misrepresentations) and the suspicions (if not the astonishment) of many in the kingdom, in our late or present transactions and conduct of business, we shall in all faithfulness and clearness profess and declare unto you those things which have of late protracted and hindered our disbanding, the present grievances which possess our army and are yet unremedied, with our desires as to the complete settlement of the liberties and peace of the kingdom, which is that blessing of God than which (of all worldly things) nothing is more dear unto us, or more precious in our thoughts, we having hitherto thought all our present enjoyments, whether of life, or livelihood, or nearest relation, a price but sufficient to the purchase of so rich a blessing, that we and all the free-born people of this nation may sit down in quiet under our vines, under the glorious

[1] The King's indictment, the sentence of the court and the death warrant are printed in *GCD* pp. 371–4, 377–80.

administration of justice and righteousness, and in the full possession of those fundamental rights and liberties without which we can have little hopes (as to human considerations) to enjoy either any comforts of life or so much as life itself, but at the pleasures of some men ruling merely according to will and power.

It cannot be unknown what hath passed betwixt the Parliament and the army as to the service of Ireland. By all which, together with the late proceedings against the army in relation to their petition and grievances, all men may judge what hath hindered the army from a ready engagement in that service; and without further account or apology as to that particular, than what passages and proceedings themselves already made public do afford, we do appeal to yourselves whether those courses to which the Parliament hath (by the designs and practices of some) been drawn, have rationally tended to induce a cheerful and unanimous undertaking of the army to that service, or rather to break or pull the army in pieces with discontent and dishonour, and to put such disobligations and provocations upon it as might drive it into distemper, and indeed discourage both this army and other soldiers from any further engagement in the Parliament's service....

* * * * * *

Nor will it now, we hope, seem strange or unseasonable to rational and honest men, who consider the consequence of our present case to their own and the kingdom's (as well as our) future concernment in point of right, freedom, peace and safety, if from a deep sense of the high consequence of our present case, both to ourselves in [the] future and all other people, we shall before disbanding proceed in our own and the kingdom's behalf to propound and plead for some provision for our and the kingdom's satisfaction and future security in relation to those things, especially considering that we were not a mere mercenary army, hired to serve any arbitrary power of a state, but called forth and conjured by the several Declarations of Parliament to the defence of our own and the people's just rights and liberties. And so we took up arms in judgement and conscience to those ends, and have so continued them, and are resolved, according to your first just desires in your Declarations, and such principles as we have received from your frequent informations, and our own common sense concerning those our fundamental rights and liberties, to assert and vindicate the just power and rights of this kingdom in Parliament, for those common ends premised against all arbitrary power, violence and oppression, and against all particular parties or interest whatsoever. The said Declarations still directing us to the equitable sense of all laws and constitutions, as dispensing with the very letter of the same, and being supreme to it when the safety and preservation of all is concerned, and assuring us that all authority is fundamentally seated in the office, and but ministerially in the person; neither do or will these our proceedings (as we are fully and in conscience persuaded) amount to any thing not warrantable before God and Men, being thus far much short of the common proceedings in other nations to things of a higher nature than we have yet appeared to. And we cannot but be sensible of the great complaints that have been made generally to us of the kingdom, from the people where we march, of arbitrariness and injustice to their great and insupportable oppressions.

And truly such kingdoms as have, according both to the Law of Nature and Nations, appeared to the vindication and defence of their just rights and liberties, have proceeded much higher; as our brethren of Scotland, who in the first beginning of these late differences associated in Covenant from the very same grounds and principles, having no visible form either of parliament or king to countenance them; and as they were therein justified and protected by their own and this kingdom also, so we justly shall expect to be.

We need not mention the state of the Netherlands, the Portugals, and others, all proceeding from the same principles of right and freedom; and accordingly the Parliament hath declared it no resistance of magistracy to side with the just principles and the Law of Nature and Nations, being that law upon which we have assisted you, and that the soldiery may lawfully hold the hands of the general who will turn his cannon against his army on purpose to destroy them, the seamen the hands of the pilot who wilfully runs the ship upon a rock (as our brethren of Scotland argued). And such were the proceedings of our ancestors of famous memory, to the purchasing of such rights and liberties as they have enjoyed through the price of their blood, and we (both by that and the later blood of our dear friends and fellow soldiers, with the hazard of our own) do now lay claim to.

Nor is that supreme end (the glory of God) wanting in these cases, to set a price upon all such proceedings of righteousness and justice, it being one witness of God in the world to carry on a testimony against the injustice and unrighteousness of men, and against the miscarriages of governments, when corrupted or declining from their primitive or original glory.

These things we mention but to compare proceedings, and to show that we are so much the more justifiable and warranted in what we do by how much we come short of that height and measure of proceedings which the people in free kingdoms and nations have formerly practised.

Now, having thus far cleared our way in this business, we shall proceed to propound such things as we do humbly desire for the settling and securing of our own and the kingdom's common right, freedom, peace and safety, as followeth.

First, That the Houses may be speedily purged of such members as for their delinquency, or for corruptions, or abuse to the State, or undue exactions, ought not to sit there; whereof the late elections in Cornwall, Wales and other parts of the kingdom afford too many examples to the great prejudice of the people's freedoms in the said elections.

Secondly, That those persons who have in the unjust and high proceedings against the army appeared to have the will and confidence, credit and power to abuse the Parliament and the army, to endanger the kingdom, in carrying on such things against us (while an army), may be some way speedily disabled from doing the like or worse to us when disbanded and dispersed....

But because neither the granting of this alone would be sufficient to secure our own and the kingdom's rights, liberties and safety, either for the present age or posterity, nor would our proposing of this singly be free from the scandal and appearance of faction and design, only to weaken one party (under the notion of unjust or oppressive) that we may advance another (which may be imagined more our own), we therefore declare:

That indeed we cannot but wish that such men and such only might be preferred to the great power and trust of the Commonwealth as are approved at least for moral righteousness; and of such we cannot but in our wishes prefer those that appear acted [*sc.* activated] thereunto by a principle of conscience and religion in them. And accordingly we do and ever shall bless God for those many such worthies who through his providence have been chosen into this Parliament.... But yet we are so far from designing or complying to have an absolute or arbitrary power settled, for continuance, in any persons whatsoever, as that (if we might be sure to obtain it) we cannot wish to have it so in the persons of any whom we could most confide in, or who should appear most of our own opinions or principles, or whom we might have most personal assurance of, or interest in. But we do and shall much rather wish that the authority of this kingdom, in Parliaments rightly constituted—that is, freely, equally and successively chosen, according to its original intention—may ever stand and have its course; and therefore we shall apply our desires chiefly to such things as, by having Parliaments settled in such a right constitution, may give most hopes of justice and righteousness to flow down equally to all in that its ancient channel, without any overtures tending either to overthrow that foundation of order and government in this kingdom, or to engross that power for perpetuity into the hands of any particular persons or party whatsoever....

We therefore humbly conceive that...the main thing to be intended in this case...seems to be this, viz., to provide that however unjust or corrupt the persons of parliament men in present or future may prove, or whatever ill they may do to particular parties (or to the whole in particular things) during their respective terms or period, yet they shall not have the temptation or advantage of an unlimited power fixed in them during their own pleasure, whereby to perpetuate injustice or oppression upon any, without end or remedy, or to advance or uphold any one particular party, faction or interest whatsoever, to the oppression or prejudice of the community and the enslaving of the kingdom to all posterity.... Yet in this we would not be misunderstood in the least, to blame those worthies of both Houses whose zeal to vindicate the liberties of this nation did procure that Act for the continuance of this Parliament, whereby it was secured from being dissolved at the king's pleasure, as former Parliaments had been, and reduced to such a certainty as might enable them the better to assert and vindicate the liberties of this nation, immediately before so highly invaded, and then also so much endangered. And this we take to be the principal ends and grounds for which in that exigency of time and affairs it was procured, and to which we acknowledge it hath happily been made use of; but we cannot think it was by those worthies intended or ought to be made use of to the perpetuating of that supreme trust and power in the persons of any during their own pleasures, or to the debarring of the people from their right of elections totally now, when these dangers or exigencies were past, and the affairs and safety of the Commonwealth would admit of such a change.

Having thus cleared our grounds and intentions, as we hope, from all scruples and misunderstandings,...we further humbly desire as followeth:

Thirdly, That some determinate period of time may be set for the continuance of this and future parliaments, beyond which none shall continue, and upon which new writs may of course issue out, and new elections successively take place, according to the intent of the bill for triennial parliaments.

And herein we would not be misunderstood to desire a present or sudden dissolution of this parliament, but only, as is expressed before, that some certain period may be set for the determining of it, so as it may not remain, as now, continuable for ever, or during the pleasure of the present Members.... And for further securing the rights and liberties, and settling the peace of the kingdom...we further humbly offer:

Fourthly, That secure provision may be made for the continuance of future parliaments so that they may not be adjournable or dissolvable at the King's pleasure, or any other ways than by their own consent during their respective periods, but at those periods each parliament to determine of course as before. This we desire may be now provided for, if it may be, so as to put it out of dispute for [the] future, though we think of right it ought not to have been otherwise before....

These things we desire may be provided for by bill or ordinance of Parliament, to which the royal assent may be desired; and when his Majesty in these things, and what else shall be proposed by the parliament necessary for securing the rights and liberties of the people, and for settling the militia, and peace of the kingdom, shall have given his concurrence to put them past dispute, we shall then desire that the rights of his Majesty and his posterity may be considered of and settled in all things so far as may consist with the right and freedom of the subject, and with the security of the same for the future.

Fifthly, We desire that the right and freedom of the people to represent to the Parliament, by way of humble petition, their grievances, in such things as cannot otherwise be remedied than by Parliament, may be cleared and vindicated. That all such grievances of the people may be freely received and admitted into consideration, and put into an equitable and speedy way to be heard, examined and redressed, if they appear real; and that in such things for which men have remedy by law, they may be freely left to the benefit of the law, and the regulated course of justice, without interruption or check from the Parliament....

Sixthly, That the large powers given to the committees, or deputy-lieutenants, during the late time of war and distraction may be speedily taken into consideration; that such of those powers as appear not necessary to be continued may be taken away, and such of them as are necessary may be put into a regulated way, and left to as little arbitrariness as the nature and necessity of the things wherein they are conversant will bear.

Seventhly, We could wish that the kingdom might both be righted and publicly satisfied in point of accounts for the vast sums that have been levied and payed; as also in divers other things wherein the Commonwealth may be conceived to have been wronged and abused....

Eighthly, That public justice being first satisfied by some few examples to posterity, out of the worst of excepted persons, and other delinquents having passed their composition, some course may be taken by a general Act of Oblivion, or otherwise, whereby the seeds of future war or fears, either to the present age or posterity, may the better be taken away, by easing that sense of present and satisfying those fears of future ruin or undoing to persons or families which may drive men into any desperate ways for self-preservation or remedy; and by taking away the private remembrances and distinctions of parties, as far as may stand with safety to the rights and liberties we have hitherto fought for.

...These proposals aforegoing being the principal things we bottom and insist upon, we shall, as we have said before, for our parts acquiesce for other particulars in the wisdom and justice of Parliament. And whereas it has been suggested or suspected, that in our late or present proceedings our design is to overthrow Presbytery or hinder the settlement thereof, and to have the Independent Government set up, we do clearly disclaim and disavow any such design. We only desire that, according to the declarations promising a provision of tender consciences there may be some effectual course taken according to the intent thereof, and that such who upon conscientious grounds may differ from the established forms may not for that be debarred from the common rights, liberties or benefits belonging equally to all, as men and members to the Commonwealth, while they live soberly and inoffensively towards others, and peaceably and faithfully towards the State.

* * * * * *

Rushworth, VII, 564–70

301

85. The Heads of the Proposals, 1 August 1647

The Heads of the Proposals agreed upon by his Excellency Sir Thomas Fairfax and the Council of the Army, to be tendered to the Commissioners of Parliament residing with the army, and with them to be treated on by the Commissioners of the Army: containing the particulars of their desires in pursuance of their former declarations and papers, in order to the clearing and securing of the rights and liberties of the kingdom; and the settling a just and lasting peace....

I. That (things hereafter proposed being provided for by this Parliament) a certain period may by Act of Parliament be set for the ending of this Parliament (such period to be put within a year at most), and in the same Act provision to be made for the succession and constitution of Parliaments in future, as followeth:

1. That parliaments may biennially be called and meet at a certain day, with such provision for the certainty thereof as in the late Act was made for triennial parliaments; and what further or other provision shall be found needful by the Parliament to reduce it to more certainty; and upon the passing of this, the said Act for triennial parliaments to be repealed.

2. Each biennial parliament to sit 120 days, unless adjourned or dissolved sooner by their own consent; afterwards to be adjournable or dissolvable by the King; and no parliament to sit past 240 days from their first meeting, or some other limited number of days now to be agreed on; upon the expiration whereof each parliament to dissolve of course, if not otherwise dissolved sooner.

3. The King, upon the advice of the Council of State, in the intervals betwixt biennial parliaments, to call a Parliament extraordinary, provided it meet above 70 days before the next biennial day, and be dissolved at least 60 days before the same, so as the course of biennial elections may never be interrupted.

4. That this parliament and each succeeding biennial parliament, at or before adjournment or dissolution thereof, may appoint committees to continue during the interval for such purposes as are in any of these proposals referred to such committees.

5. That the elections of the Commons for succeeding parliaments may be distributed to all counties, or other parts or divisions of the kingdom, according to some rule of equality or proportion, so as all

counties may have a number of Parliament members allowed to their choice proportionable to the respective rates they bear in the common charges and burdens of the kingdom, according to some other rule of equality or proportion, to render the House of Commons as near as may be an equal representative of the whole; and in order thereunto, that a present consideration be had to take off the elections of burgesses for poor, decayed or inconsiderable towns, and to give some present addition to the number of Parliament members for great counties that have now less than their due proportion, to bring all at present, as near as may be, to such a rule of proportion as aforesaid.

6. That effectual provision be made for future freedom of elections, and certainty of due returns.

7. That the House of Commons alone have the power from time to time to set down further orders and rules for the ends expressed in the two last preceding articles, so as to reduce the elections of members for that House to more and more perfection of equality in the distribution, freedom in the election, order in the proceeding thereto, and certainty in the returns, with orders and rules in that case to be in laws.

8. That there be a liberty for entering dissents in the House of Commons, with provision that no member be censurable for ought said or voted in the House further than to exclusion from that trust; and that only by the judgement of the House itself.

9. That the judicial power, or power of final judgement, in the Lords and Commons (and their power of exposition and application of law, without further appeal) may be cleared; and that no officer of justice, minister of state or other person adjudged by them, may be capable of protection or pardon from the King without their advice or consent.

10. That the right and liberty of the commons of England may be cleared and vindicated as to a due exemption from any judgement, trial or other proceedings against them by the House of Peers, without the concurring judgement of the House of Commons; as also from any other judgement, sentence or proceeding against them, other than by their equals, or according to the law of the land.

11. The same Act to provide that grand jurymen may be chosen by and for [the] several parts or divisions of each county respectively in some equal way, and not to remain as now, at the discretion of an under-sheriff to be put on or off, and that such grand jurymen for their respective counties may at each assize present the names of persons to be made justices of the peace from time to time, as the county hath need

for any to be added to the commission, and at the summer assize to present the names of three persons, out of whom the King may prick one to be sheriff for the next year.

II. For the future security of Parliament and the militia in general, in order thereunto, that it be provided by Act of Parliament:

1. That the power of the militia by sea and land during the space of ten years next ensuing shall be ordered and disposed by the Lords and Commons assembled, and to be assembled, in the parliament or parliaments of England, by such persons as they shall nominate and appoint for that purpose from time to time during the said space.

2. That the said power shall not be ordered, disposed or exercised by the King's Majesty that now is, or by any person or persons by any authority derived from him, during the said spare, or at any time hereafter by his said Majesty, without the advice and consent of the said Lords and Commons, or of such committees or council in the intervals of Parliament as they shall appoint.

3. That during the same space of ten years the said Lords and Commons may by bill or ordinance raise and dispose of what moneys and for what forces they shall from time to time find necessary; as also for payment of the public debts and damages, and for all other the public uses of the kingdom.

4. And to the end the temporary security intended by the three particulars last precedent may be the better assured, it may therefore be provided, that no subjects that have been in hostility against the Parliament in the late war shall be capable of bearing any office of power or public trust in the Commonwealth during the space of five years without the consent of Parliament or of the Council of State; or to sit as members or assistants of either House of Parliament until the second biennial parliament be passed.

III. For the present form of disposing the militia in order to the peace and safety of this kingdom and the service of Ireland:

[The navy was to be put under commissioners, the army under a general, the militia under county commissioners. A Council of State, for seven years in the first instance, was to control the militia and conduct foreign policy, subject to Parliament's ultimate control over war and peace.]

IV. That an Act be passed for disposing the great offices for ten years by the Lords and Commons in Parliament; or by such committees as they shall appoint for that purpose in the intervals (with submission to the approbation of the next parliament), and after ten years they to nominate three, and the King out of that number to appoint one for the succession upon any vacancy.

* * * * * *

XI. An Act to be passed to take away all coercive power, authority and jurisdiction of bishops and all other ecclesiastical officers whatsoever, extending to any civil penalties upon any; and to repeal all laws whereby the civil magistracy hath been, or is bound upon any ecclesiastical censure to proceed *ex officio* unto any civil penalties against any persons so censured.

XII. That there be a repeal of all Acts or clauses in any Act enjoining the use of the Book of Common Prayer, and imposing any penalties for neglect thereof; as also of all Acts or clauses of any Act imposing any penalty for not coming to church, or for meetings elsewhere for prayer or other religious duties, exercises or ordinances; and some other provision to be made for discovering of Papists and Popish recusants, and for disabling of them, and of all Jesuits or priests, from disturbing the State.

XIII. That the taking of the Covenant be not enforced upon any, nor any penalties imposed on the refusers, whereby men might be restrained to take it against their judgements or consciences, but all orders and ordinances tending to that purpose to be repealed.

XIV. That (the things herebefore proposed being provided, for settling and securing the rights, liberties, peace and safety of the kingdom) his Majesty's person, his Queen and royal issue, may be restored to a condition of safety, honour and freedom in this nation, without diminution to their personal rights, or further limitation to the exercise of the regal power than according to the particular foregoing.

XV. For the matter of composition.

[The proposals here were complicated, but much more merciful than those put forward by Parliament in 1646. Apart from the Irish rebels—whom everyone regarded as lepers—only five persons were to be totally excepted from pardon, as against thirty-eight named by Parliament. The rates at which other royalists could compound were slashed, and those having less than £200 in land or goods were to be discharged without further penalty.

Lastly, this section ended with a proposal to which the army officers attached the highest importance:]

6. That the faith of the army, or other forces of the Parliament, given in articles upon surrenders to any of the King's party, may be fully made good; and where any breach thereof shall appear to have been made, full reparation and satisfaction may be given to the parties injured, and the persons offending, being found out, may be compelled thereto.

XVI. That there may be a general Act of Oblivion to extend unto all (except the persons to be continued in exception as before), to absolve from all trespasses, misdemeanours &c., done in prosecution of the war; and from all trouble or prejudice for or concerning the same (after their compositions passed), and to restore them to all privileges, &c., belonging to other subjects, provided as in the fourth particular under the second general head aforegoing concerning security.

And whereas there have been of late strong endeavours and practices of a factious and desperate party to embroil this kingdom in a new war, and for that purpose to induce the King, the Queen and the Prince to declare for the said party, and also to excite and stir up all those of the King's late party to appear and engage for the same, which attempts and designs many of the King's party, out of their desires to avoid further misery to the kingdom, have contributed their endeavours to prevent (as for divers of them we have had particular assurance): we do therefore desire that such of the King's party who shall appear to have expressed, and shall hereafter express, that way their good affections to the peace and welfare of the kingdom, and to hinder the embroiling of the same in a new war, may be freed and exempted from compositions, or to pay but one year's revenue, or a twentieth part.

Next to the proposals aforesaid for the present settling of a peace, we shall desire that no time may be lost by the Parliament for despatch of other things tending to the welfare, ease and just satisfaction of the kingdom, and in special manner:

I. That the just and necessary liberty of the people to represent their grievances and desires by way of petition may be cleared and vindicated, according to the fifth head in the late Representation or Declaration of the Army sent from St Albans.[1]

[1] Printed above, no. 84.

II. That in pursuance of the same head in the said Declaration the common grievances of this people may be speedily considered of, and effectually redressed, and in particular:

1. That the excise may be taken off from such commodities whereon the poor people of the land do ordinarily live, and a certain time to be limited for taking off the whole.

2. That the oppressions and encroachments of forest laws may be prevented for the future.

3. All monopolies (old or new) and restraints on the freedom of trade be taken off.

4. That a course may be taken and commissioners appointed to remedy and rectify the inequality of rates lying upon several counties, and several parts of each county in respect of others, and to settle the proportion of land rates to more equality throughout the kingdom; in order to which we shall offer some further particulars, which we hope may be useful.

5. The present unequal, troublesome and contentious way of ministers' maintenance by tithes to be considered of, and some remedy applied.

6. That the rules and course of law, and the officers of it, may be so reduced and reformed as that all suits and questions of right may be more clear and certain in the issues, and not so tedious nor chargeable in the proceedings as now; in order to which we shall offer some further particulars hereafter.

7. That prisoners for debt or other creditors, who have estates to discharge them, may not by embracing imprisonment, or any other ways, have advantage to defraud their creditors, but that the estates of all men may be some way made liable to their debts (as well as tradesmen are by commissions of bankrupt), whether they be imprisoned for it or not; and that such prisoners for debt who have not wherewith to pay, or at least do yield up what they have to their creditors, may be freed from imprisonment or some way provided for, so as neither they nor their families may perish by their imprisonment.

8. Some provision to be made that none may be compelled by penalty or otherwise to answer unto questions tending to the accusing of themselves or their nearest relations in criminal causes; and no man's life to be taken away [by] under two witnesses.

9. That consideration may be had of all statutes, and the laws and customs of corporations, imposing any oaths; either to repeal or else

to qualify and provide against the same, so far as they may extend or be construed to the molestation or ensnaring of religious and peaceable people merely for nonconformity in religion.

[§§ III and IV repeated, respectively, sections six and seven of the Declaration of 15 June (p. 301 above).]

* * * * * *

V. That provision may be made for payment of arrears to the army, and the rest of the soldiers of the kingdom who have concurred with the army in the late desires and proceedings thereof; and in the next place for payment of the public debts and damages of the kingdom; and that to be performed first to such persons whose debt or damages upon the public account are great, and their estates small, so as they are thereby reduced to a difficulty of subsistence: in order to all which, and to the fourth particular last preceding, we shall speedily offer some further particulars (in the nature of rules) which we hope will be of good use towards public satisfaction.

August 1, 1647   Signed by the appointment of his Excellency
                  Sir Thomas Fairfax and the Council of War

Rushworth, VII, 731-6

86. The First Agreement of the People, 28 October 1647

An Agreement of the People for a firm and present peace upon grounds of common right

Having by our late labours and hazards made it appear to the world at how high a rate we value our just freedom, and God having so far owned our case as to deliver the enemies thereof into our hands, we do now hold ourselves bound in mutual duty to each other to take the best care we can for the future to avoid both the danger of returning into a slavish condition and the chargeable remedy of another war; for, as it cannot be imagined that so many of our countrymen would have opposed us in this quarrel if they had understood their own good, so may we safely promise to ourselves that, when our common rights and liberties shall be cleared, their endeavours will be disappointed that seek to make themselves our masters. Since therefore our former oppressions and scarce-yet-ended troubles have been occasioned either by want of frequent national meetings in council, or by rendering those

308

meetings ineffectual, we are fully agreed and resolved to provide that hereafter our representatives be neither left to an uncertainty for the time nor made useless to the ends for which they are intended. In order whereunto we declare:

That the people of England, being at this day very unequally distributed by counties, cities and boroughs for the election of their deputies in Parliament, ought to be more indifferently proportioned according to the number of the inhabitants; the circumstances whereof for number, place and manner are to be set down before the end of this present parliament.

II. That, to prevent the many inconveniences apparently arising from the long continuance of the same persons in authority, this present parliament be dissolved upon the last day of September which shall be in the year of Our Lord 1648.

III. That the people do of course choose themselves a Parliament once in two years, viz., upon the first Thursday in every second March, after the manner as shall be prescribed before the end of this parliament, to begin to sit upon the first Thursday in April following at Westminster, or such other place as shall be appointed from time to time by the preceding representatives, and to continue till the last day of September then next ensuing, and no longer.

IV. That the power of this and all future representatives of this nation is inferior only to theirs who choose them, and doth extend, without the consent or concurrence of any other person or persons, to the enacting, altering and repealing of laws, to the erecting and abolishing of offices and courts, to the appointing, removing and calling to account magistrates and officers of all degrees, to the making war and peace, to the treating with foreign states, and generally to whatsoever is not expressly or implicitly reserved by the represented to themselves.

Which are as followeth:

1. That matters of religion and the ways of God's worship are not at all entrusted by us to any human power, because therein we cannot remit or exceed a tittle of what our consciences dictate to be the mind of God without wilful sin. Nevertheless, the public way of instructing the nation (so it be not compulsive) is referred to their discretion.

2. That the matter of impressing and constraining any of us to serve in the wars is against our freedom; and therefore we do not allow it in

our representatives; the rather because money (the sinews of war) being always at their disposal, they can never want numbers of men apt enough to engage in any just cause.

3. That after the dissolution of the present parliament no person be at any time questioned for anything said or done in reference to the late public differences, otherwise than in execution of the judgements of the present representatives, or House of Commons.

4. That in laws made or to be made every person may be bound alike, and that no tenure, estate, charter, degree, birth or place do confer any exemption from the ordinary course of legal proceedings whereunto others are subjected.

5. That as the laws ought to be equal, so they must be good, and not evidently destructive to the safety and well-being of the people.

These things we declare to be our native rights, and therefore are agreed and resolved to maintain them with our utmost possibilities against all opposition whatsoever; being compelled thereunto not only by the examples of our ancestors, whose blood was often spent in vain for the recovery of their freedoms, suffering themselves through fraudulent accommodations to be still deluded of the fruit of their victories, but also by our own woeful experience, who, having long expected and dearly earned the establishment of these certain rules of government, are yet made to depend for the settlement of our peace and freedom upon him that intended our bondage and brought a cruel war upon us.   Gardiner, *Civil War*, III, 392–4

87. The Putney Debates, 28–29 October 1647

[28 October. The proceedings opened with a reading of *The Agreement of the People*, which clearly took the officers by surprise. Cromwell's reply, on the spur of the moment, betrays his innate conservatism, and its style—hesitant, repetitive, and full of qualifications—was typical of his subsequent contributions, which did little to clarify the debate.]

Cromwell.... Truly this paper does contain in it very great alterations of the very government of the kingdom, alterations from that government that it hath been under, I believe I may almost say, since it was a nation—I say, I think I may almost say so.... Therefore, although the pretensions in it, and the expressions in it, are very plausible, and if we could leap out of one condition into another that had so specious things in it as this hath, I suppose there would not be much dispute—

though perhaps some of these things may be very well disputed. How do we know if, whilst we are disputing these things, another company of men shall [not] gather together, and put out a paper as plausible perhaps as this?...And not only another, and another, but many of this kind? And if so, what do you think the consequence of that would be? Would it not be confusion? Would it not be utter confusion?... Give me leave to say this. There will be very great mountains in the way of this...and therefore we ought to consider the consequences, and God hath given us our reason that we may do this. It is not enough to propose things that are good in the end, but suppose this model were an excellent model, and fit for England and the kingdom to receive, it is our duty as Christians and men to consider consequences, and consider the way [7–8].

[There followed an argument between Cromwell and Ireton on the one hand and Rainborough and Wildman on the other, as to how far the Army was bound by the previous documents published in its name, such as the *Declaration of 15 June*, or the *Heads of the Proposals*. Colonel Gough (19–20) suggested a prayer-meeting the following day to seek enlightenment, and this was eagerly taken up by Cromwell. It was decided to hold prayers the following morning, and another business meeting in the afternoon. But the discussion continued for a while, and Ireton issued a passionate rebuttal of Gough's assertion that they could freely break engagements which they now saw to be unjust.]

Ireton....I am far from holding that if a man have engaged himself to a thing that is not just—to a thing that is evil, that is sin if he do it— that that man is still bound to perform what he hath promised; I am far from apprehending that. But when we talk of 'just', it is not so much of what is sinful before God (which depends upon many circumstances of indignation to that man, and the like), but it intends of that which is just according to the foundations of justice between man and man. And for my part, I account that the great foundation of justice [is] that we should keep covenant one with another, without which I know nothing of justice between man and man....There is no other foundation of right I know, of right to any one thing from another man, no foundation of that justice or that righteousness, but this general justice, and this general ground of righteousness, that we should keep covenant one with another....Take away that, I do not know what ground there is of anything you can call any man's right. I would very fain know what you gentlemen, or any other, do account the right you have to anything in England—anything of estate, land or goods that you have, what right you have to it. What right hath any man to any thing if you lay not down that principle, that we are to keep covenant? If you will resort only to the law of nature you have no more right to this land, or anything else, than I have. I have as much right to take hold of anything that is for my sustenance, take hold of anything that I have a desire to for my satisfaction, as you. But here comes the foundation of all right that I understand to be betwixt men, as to the enjoying of one thing or not enjoying of it; we are under a contract, we are under an agreement, and that agreement is, what a man has for matter of land that he hath received by a traduction from his ancestors, which according to the law does fall upon him to be his right; that he shall enjoy, he shall have the property of, the use of, the disposing of, with submission to that general authority which is agreed upon amongst us for the preserving of peace, and for the supporting of this law.... This is the foundation of all the right any man has to anything but his own person. This the general thing: that we must keep covenant one with another when we have contracted one with another.... And therefore when I hear men speak of laying aside all engagements to [take up] that wild or vast notion of what in every man's conception is just or unjust, I am afraid, and I do tremble at the boundless and endless consequences of it...[26–7].

[29 October. This gave warning of what Ireton's attitude was to be throughout, and as soon as the discussion was resumed the following day he returned to the attack. He admitted that engagements entered into by individuals like himself could not stand against the general feeling of the meeting, but he went on to speak of the Will of God in terms that made it clear that he regarded Him as a defender of the existing social order.]

Ireton....Neither do I care for the engagements of the army so much for the engagements' sake, but I look upon this army as having carried with it hitherto the name of God, and having carried with it hitherto the interest of the people of God, and the interest which is God's interest, the honour of his name, the good and freedom and safety and happiness of his people. And for my part I think that it is that that is the only thing for which God hath appeared with us, and led us, and gone before us, and honoured us....We have professed to endeavour to follow the counsels of God, and to have him president in our councils, and I hope it hath been so in our hearts....We have been carried on with a confidence in him; we have made him our trust, and we have held forth his name, and we have owned his hand towards us....And therefore by this means, and by that appearance of God amongst us, the name and honour of God, the name and reputation of the people of God, and of that Gospel that they profess, is deeply and dearly and nearly concerned in the good or ill management of this army, in their good or ill carriage; and therefore, for my part I profess it, that's the only thing to me. [It is] not to me so much as the vainest or lightest thing you can imagine, whether there be a king in England or no, whether there be lords in England or no. For whatever I find the work of God tending to, I should desire quietly to submit to. If God saw it good to destroy not only king and lords but all distinctions of degrees —nay, if it go further, to destroy all property, [so] that there's no such thing left, that there be nothing at all of civil constitution left in the kingdom—if I see the hand of God in it I hope I shall with quietness acquiesce, and submit to it, and not resist it. But still I think that God certainly will so lead those that are his, and I hope too he will so lead this army, that they may not incur sin, or bring scandal upon the name of God, and the name of the people of God, that are both so nearly concerned in what this army does...I would have us consider of this; that our ways and workings and actings, and the actings of the army, so far as the counsels of those prevail in it who have everything of the spirit of Jesus Christ, may appear suitable to that spirit...[49–50].

[They then fell to discussing the extent of the franchise, and whether it was to extend to the whole male population, apart from wage-earners.]

Rainborough. I desired that those that had engaged in it [might vote]. For I really think that the poorest he that is in England hath a life to live, as the greatest he; and therefore truly, sir, I think it's clear that every man that is to live under a government ought first by his own counsel to put himself under that government; and I do think that the poorest man in England is not at all bound in a strict sense to that government that he hath not had a voice to put himself under...[53].

Ireton.....Give me leave to tell you, that if you make this the rule I think you must fly for refuge to an absolute natural right, and you must deny all civil right....For my part, I think it is no right at all. I think that no person hath a right to an interest or share in the disposing of the affairs of the kingdom, and in determining or choosing those that shall determine what laws we shall be ruled by here—no person hath a right to this, that hath not a permanent fixed interest in this kingdom, and those persons together are properly the represented of this kingdom, and consequently are to make up the representers of this kingdom, who taken together to comprehend whatsoever is of real or permanent interest in the kingdom.... We talk of birthright. Truly [by] birthright there is thus much claim. Men may justly have by birthright, by their very being born in England, that we should not refuse to give them air and place and ground, and the freedom of the highway, and other things, to live amongst us.... That I think is due to a man by birth. But that by a man's being born here he shall have a share in that power that shall dispose of lands here, and of all things here, I do not think it a sufficient ground... [53-4].

   Rainborough.... I do hear nothing at all that can convince me, why any man that is born in England ought not to have his voice in election of burgesses. It is said that if a man have not a permanent interest he can have no claim, and we must be no freer than the laws will let us be, and that there is no chronicle will let us be freer than that we enjoy. Something was said to this yesterday. I do think that the main cause why Almighty God gave men reason, it was that they should make use of that reason, and that they should improve it for that end and purpose that God gave it them.... I do not find anything in the Law of God, that a lord shall choose twenty burgesses, and a gentleman but two, or a poor man shall choose none; I find no such thing in the law of nature, nor in the law of nations. But I do find that all Englishmen must be subject to English laws, and I do verily believe that there is no man but will say that the foundation of all law lies in the people... [55-6].

   Ireton.... All the main thing that I speak for, is because I would have an eye to property. I hope we do not come to contend for victory, but let every man consider with himself that he do not go that way to take away all property. For here is the case of the most fundamental part of the constitution of the kingdom, which if you take away, you take away all by that. Here men of this and this quality are determined to be the electors of men to the Parliament, and they are all those who have any permanent interest in the kingdom, and who, taken together, do comprehend the whole interest of the kingdom.... Now I wish we may all consider of what right you will challenge that all the people should have right to elections. Is it by the right of nature? If you will hold forth that as your ground, then I think you must deny all property too, and this is my reason... [57-8].

Rainborough.....As for estates and those kind of things, and other things that belong to men, it will be granted that they are property; but I deny that that [i.e., the right to vote] is a property, to a lord, to a gentleman, to any man more than another in the kingdom of England. If it be a property, it is a property by a law—neither do I think that there is very little property in this thing by the law of the land, because I think that the law of the land in that thing is the most tyrannical law under heaven. And I would fain know what we have fought for...[61].

Petty.....'Tis true, that somewhat may be derived in the paper against the King, the power of the King, and somewhat against the power of the Lords; and the truth is, when I shall see God going about to throw down King and Lords and property, then I shall be contented. But I hope that they may live to see the power of the King and the Lords thrown down, that yet may live to see property preserved. And for this of changing the representative of the nation, of changing those that choose the representative, making of them more full, taking more into the number than formerly, I had verily thought we had all agreed in it that more should have chosen, all that had desired a more equal representation than we now have. For now those only choose who have forty shillings freehold. A man may have a lease for one hundred pounds a year, a man may have a lease for three lives, [but has not the vote].....But I judge every man is naturally free; and I judge the reason why men [chose representatives] when they were in so great numbers that every man could not give his voice [directly] was that they who were chosen might preserve property; and therefore men agreed to come into some form of government that they might preserve property, and I would fain know, if we were to begin a government [would you say], 'You have not forty shillings a year, therefore you shall not have a voice'?...[61–2].

Rich.....Some men [have] ten, some twenty servants, some more, some less. If the master and servant shall be equal electors, then clearly those that have no interest in the kingdom will make it their interest to choose those that have no interest. It may happen that the majority may by law, not in a confusion, destroy property; there may be a law enacted, that there shall be an equality of goods and estate. I think that either of the extremes may be urged to inconveniency...[63].

Wildman.....Our case is to be considered thus, that we have been under slavery. That's acknowledged by all. Our very laws were made by our conquerors; and whereas it's spoken much of chronicles, I conceive there is no credit to be given to any of them; and the reason is because those that were our lords, and made us their vassals, would suffer nothing else to be chronicled. We are now engaged for our freedom. That's the end of parliaments: not to constitute what is already, [but to rule] according to the just rules of government. Every person in England hath as clear a right to elect his representative as the greatest person in England. I conceive that's the undeniable maxim of government: that all government is in the free consent of the people. If [so], then upon that account there is no person that is under a just government, or hath justly his own, unless he by his own free consent be put under that government. This he cannot be unless he be consenting to it, and therefore, according to this maxim, there is never a person in England [but should have the vote]...[65–6].

Ireton....If a foreigner come within this kingdom...it is a piece of hospitality, of humanity, to receive that man amongst us; I think that man may very well be content to submit himself to the law of the land, that is, the law that is made by those people that have a property, a fixed property, in the land. I think, if any man will receive protection from this people, though [neither] he nor his ancestors, nor any betwixt his and Adam, did ever give concurrence to this constitution, I think this man ought to be subject to those laws, and to be bound by those laws, so long as he continues amongst them. That is my opinion. A man ought to be subject to a law, that did not give his consent, but with this reservation, that if this man do think himself unsatisfied to be subject to this law he may go into another kingdom. If he hath money, his money is as good in another place as here; he hath nothing that doth locally fix him to this kingdom...[66–7].

Sexby....I see that though liberty were our end, there is a degeneration from it. We have engaged in this kingdom and ventured our lives, and it was all for this: to recover our birthrights and privileges as Englishmen; and by the arguments urged there is none. There are many thousands of us soldiers that have ventured our lives; we have had little propriety in the kingdom as to our estates, yet we have had a birthright. But it seems now, except a man hath a fixed estate in this kingdom he hath no right in this kingdom. I wonder we were so much deceived. If we had not a right to the kingdom, we were mere mercenary soldiers...[69].

Rainborough....Sir, I see that it is impossible to have liberty but all property must be taken away. If it be laid down for a rule, and if you will say it, it must be so. But I would fain know what the soldier hath fought for all this while? He hath fought to enslave himself, to give power to men of riches, men of estates, to make him a perpetual slave... [71].

Ireton....I [will] tell you what the soldier of the kingdom hath fought for. First, the danger that we stood in was that one man's will must be a law. The people of the kingdom must have this right at least, that they should not be concluded [but] by the representative of those that had the interest of the kingdom. Some men fought in this [war] because they were immediately concerned and engaged in it. Other men who had no interest in the kingdom but this, that they should have the benefit of those laws made by the representative, yet [fought] that they should have the benefit of this representative. They thought it was better to be concluded by the common consent of those that were fixed men, and settled men, that had the interest of this kingdom—'And from that way' [they said], 'I shall know a law and have a certainty.'....Here was a right that induced men to fight, and those men that had this interest, though this be not the utmost interest that other men have, yet they had some interest. Now [tell me] why we should go to plead whatsoever we can challenge by the right of nature against whatsoever any man can challenge by [the] constitution. I do not see where that man will stop, as to point of property, that he shall not use that right he hath by the law of nature against that constitution... [72].

[Cromwell then intervened, and threatened to withdraw.]

Audley....I see you have a long dispute [and] that you do intend to dispute here till the tenth of March. You have brought us into a fair pass, and the kingdom into a fair pass, for if your reasons are not satisfied, and we do not fetch all our waters from your wells, you threaten to withdraw yourselves. I could wish, according to our several protestations, we might sit down quietly, and there throw down ourselves where we see reason... [75].

[The discussion continued a while longer without achieving much, since Ireton's views were not to be reconciled with the Levellers'. On 1 November they discussed the veto powers of king and Lords, but from then on the discussion apparently turned in favour of the Levellers. Finally, on 8 November, the Agitators were ordered to their regiments in preparation for a general rendezvous of the Army summoned for the 15th, while a committee was appointed to eliminate from the *Agreement* those points inconsistent with the Army's previous engagements.]   Woodhouse, *Puritanism and Liberty*, pp. 7–75

88. The Windsor prayer-meeting, 1 May 1648

William Allen: *A faithful memorial of that remarkable meeting of many officers of the army in England, at Windsor Castle, in the year 1648.*[1] 1659.

[Allen describes the 'divisions, confusions, tumults and every evil work' that came upon the Army as a result of their negotiations with Charles I. They accordingly spent 29 April 1648 in prayer at Windsor, 'inquiring into the causes of that sad dispensation'. Next day they undertook an examination of their own conduct from the foundation of the New Model Army in 1645. On the third day, 1 May, they came to the conclusion that they had sinned in holding 'those cursed carnal conferences' with the king.]

... And in this path the Lord led us not only to see our sin, but also our duty; and this so unanimously sat with weight upon each heart that none was able hardly to speak a word to each other for bitter weeping, partly in the sense and shame of our iniquities of unbelief, base fear of men, and carnal consultations (as the fruit thereof), with our own wisdoms, and not with the Word of the Lord, which only is a way of wisdom, strength and safety, and all besides it ways of snares; and yet we were also helped with fear and trembling to rejoice in the Lord, whose faithfulness and loving-kindness we were made to see, yet failed us not; but remembered us still, even in our low estate, because his mercy endures for ever. Who no sooner brought us to his feet, acknowledging him in that way of his, viz., searching for, being ashamed of and willing to turn from our iniquities, but he did direct our steps, and presently we were led and helped to a clear agreement amongst ourselves, not any dissenting, that it was the duty of our day, with the forces we had, to go out and fight against those potent enemies which that year in all places appeared against us, with a humble confidence in the name of the Lord only, that we should destroy them; also enabling us then, after serious seeking his face, to come to a very clear and joint resolution, on many grounds at large then debated amongst us, that it was our duty, if ever the Lord brought us back again in peace, to call

[1] *As also a discovery of the great goodness of God, in his gracious meeting of them, hearing and answering their suit or supplications, while they were yet speaking to him. All which is humbly presented as a precious pattern and precedent unto the officers and soldiers of the said army (or elsewhere) who are, or shall be, found in the like path of following the Lord in this evil day, searching and trying their ways, in order to a thorough return and reformation.* Dedicated by Allen, a former adjutant-general, to Fleetwood, the commander of the army in 1659.

Charles Stuart, that man of blood, to an account for that blood he had shed, and mischief he had done to his utmost against the Lord's cause and people in these poor nations. *Somers Tracts, VI, 501*

89. The Leveller programme: the Humble Petition

To the Right Honourable the Commons of England in Parliament assembled, the humble petition of divers well-affected persons inhabiting the City of London, Westminster, the Borough of Southwark, hamlets and places adjacent. [Presented 11 September 1648.]

Showeth,

That although we are as earnestly desirous of a safe and well-grounded peace, and that a final end were put to all the troubles and miseries of the Commonwealth, as any sort of men whatsoever, yet considering upon what grounds we engaged on your part in the late and present wars, and how far (by our so doing) we apprehend ourselves concerned, give us leave (before you conclude us by the treaty in hand)[1] to acquaint you first with the ground and reason which induced us to aid you against the King and his adherents; secondly, what our apprehensions are of this treaty; thirdly, what we expected from you, and do still most earnestly desire.

Be pleased therefore to understand that we had not engaged on your part, but that we judged this honourable House to be the supreme authority of England, as chosen by and representing the people, and entrusted with absolute power for redress of grievances and provision for safety; and that the King was but at most the chief public officer of this kingdom, and accountable to this House (the representative of the people, from whom all just authority is or ought to be derived) for discharge of his office. And if we had not been confident hereof we had been desperately mad to have taken up arms or to have been aiding and assisting in maintaining a war against him, the laws of the land making it expressly a crime no less than treason for any to raise war against the King.

But when we considered the manifold oppressions brought upon the nation by the King, his lords and bishops, and that this honourable House declared their deep sense thereof; and that (for continuance of that power which had so oppressed us) it was evident the King intended

[1] The negotiations between Parliament and the king which opened at Newport, I.O.W., on 18 September (Gardiner, *Civil War*, IV, 214).

to raise forces and to make war, and that if he did set up his standard it tended to the dissolution of the government—upon this, knowing the safety of the people to be above law, and that to judge thereof appertained to the Supreme Authority, and not to the Supreme Magistrate, and being satisfied in our consciences that the public safety and freedom was in imminent danger, we concluded we had not only a just cause to maintain but the Supreme Authority of the nation to justify, defend and indemnify us in time to come, in what we should perform by direction thereof, though against the known law of the land or any inferior authority, though the highest.

And as this our understanding was begotten in us by principles of right reason, so were we confirmed therein by your own proceedings: as by your condemning those judges who in the case of ship-money had declared the King to be judge of safety; and by your denying him to have a negative voice in the making of laws, where you wholly exclude the King from having any share in the Supreme Authority; and by your declaring to the Lords that if they would not join with you in settling the militia (which they long refused) you would settle it without them,[1] which you could not justly have done had they had any share in the Supreme Authority.

* * * * * *

But to our exceeding grief we have observed that no sooner God vouchsafeth you victory, and blesseth you with success, and thereby enableth you to put us and the whole nation into an absolute condition of freedom and safety, but, according as you have been accustomed, passing by the ruin of a nation, and all the blood that hath been spilled by the King and his party, you betake yourselves to a treaty with him, thereby putting him, that is but one single person, and a public officer of the Commonwealth, in competition with the whole body of the people, whom you represent, not considering that it is impossible for you to erect any authority equal to yourselves; and declared to all the world that you will not alter the ancient government from that of King, Lords and Commons, not once mentioning (in case of difference) which of them is supreme, but leaving that point (which was the chiefest

---

[1] The farthest the Commons went in this direction was on 1 February 1642, when they sent an oral message to the Lords asking them to join in a petition to the King requesting him to put the militia into the hands of men acceptable to Parliament. The messenger was instructed to say that, 'if they will not join with this House now that things are brought to the last gasp...they must not expect this House to come to them again in this business' (*CJ*, II, 408). The Lords complied.

cause of all our public differences, disturbances, wars and miseries) as uncertain as ever.

* * * * * *

And whereas a personal treaty, or any treaty with the King, hath been long time held forth as the only means of a safe and well-grounded peace, it is well known to have been cried up principally by such as have been disaffected unto you, and though you have contradicted it yet it is believed that you much fear the issue; as you have cause sufficient, except you see greater alteration in the King and his party than is generally observed, there having never yet been any treaty with him but was accompanied with some underhand dealing; and whilst the present force upon him (though seeming liberty) will in time to come be certainly pleaded against all that shall or can be agreed upon. Nay, what can you confide in if you consider how he hath been provoked, and what former Kings upon less provocations have done, after oaths, laws, charters, bonds, excommunications and all ties of reconciliations, to the destruction of all those that had provoked and opposed them; yea, when yourselves so soon as he had signed those bills in the beginning of this parliament saw cause to tell him that even about the time of passing those bills some design or other was on foot, which if it had taken effect would not only have rendered those bills fruitless but have reduced you [to] a worse condition of confusion than that wherein the Parliament found you.

* * * * * *

The truth is (and we see we must either now speak it [or] for ever be silent), we have long expected things of another nature from you, and such as we are confident would have given satisfaction to all serious people of all parties:

1. That you would have made good the Supreme [Authority] of the people in this honourable House from all pretence of negative voices, either in King or Lords.

2. That you would have made laws for election of representatives yearly and of course, without writ or summons.

3. That you would have set express times for their meeting, continuance and dissolution, [so] as not to exceed 40 or 50 days at the most, and to have fixed an expressed time for the ending of this present parliament.

4. That you would have exempted matters of religion and gospel from the compulsive or restrictive power of any authority upon earth, and reserved to the Supreme Authority an uncompulsive power only of appointing a way for the public [worship], whereby abundance of misery, persecution and heart-burning would for ever be avoided.

5. That you would have disclaimed in yourselves and all future representatives a power of pressing and forcing any sort of men to serve in wars. . . .

6. That you would have made both kings, queens, princes, dukes, earls, lords and all persons alike liable to every law of the land, made or to be made. . . .

7. That you would have freed all commoners from the jurisdiction of the Lords in all cases, and to have taken care that all trials should be only of twelve sworn men, and no conviction but upon two or more sufficient known witnesses.

8. That you would have freed all men from being examined against themselves, and from being questioned or punished for doing of that against which no law hath been provided.

9. That you would have abbreviated the proceedings in law, mitigated and made certain the charge thereof in all particulars.

10. That you would have freed all trade and merchandising from all monopolising and engrossing, by companies or otherwise.

11. That you would have abolished excise, and all kinds of taxes except subsidies, the old and only just way of England.

12. That you would have laid open all late enclosures of fens and other commons, or have enclosed them only or chiefly to the benefit of the poor.

13. That you would have considered the many thousands that are ruined by perpetual imprisonment for debt, and provided to their enlargement.

14. That you would have ordered some effectual course to keep people from begging and beggary in so fruitful a nation as through God's blessing this is.

15. That you would have proportioned punishments more equal[ly] to offences, that so men's lives and estates might not be forfeited upon trivial and slight occasions.

16. That you would have removed the tedious burden of tithes, satisfying all impropriators and providing a more equal way of maintenance for the public ministers.

17. That you would have raised a stock of money out of those many confiscated estates you have had, for payment of those who contributed voluntarily above their abilities, before you had provided for those that disbursed out of their superfluities.

18. That you would have bound yourselves and all future parliaments from abolishing propriety, levelling men's estates, or making all things common.

19. That you would have declared what the duty or business of the kingly office is, and what not, and ascertained the revenue, past increase or diminution, that so there might never be more quarrels about the same.

20. That you would have rectified the election of public officers for the City of London, [and] of every particular company therein, restoring the commonalty thereof to their just rights, most unjustly withheld from them, to the producing and maintaining of corrupt interest opposite to common freedom, and exceedingly prejudicial to the trade and manufactures of this nation.

21. That you would have made full and ample reparations to all persons that had been oppressed by sentences in High Commission, Star Chamber and Council Board, or by any kind of monopolisers or projectors, and that out of the estates of those that were authors, actors or promoters of so intolerable mischiefs, and that without much attendance.

22. That you would have abolished all Committees, and have conveyed all businesses into the true method of the usual trials of the Commonwealth.

23. That you would not have followed the example of former tyrannous and superstitious parliaments, in making orders, ordinances or laws, or in appointing punishments concerning opinions or things supernatural, styling some blasphemies, others heresies,[1] when as you know yourselves easily mistaken, and that divine truths need no human helps to support them, such proceedings having been generally invented to divide the people amongst themselves and to affright men from that liberty of discourse by which corruption and tyranny would be soon discovered.

24. That you would have declared what the business of the Lords is, and ascertained their condition, not derogating from the liberties of other men, that so there might be an end of striving about the same.

[1] The reference is to an Ordinance of 2 May 1648, Firth and Rait, I, 1133–6.

25. That you would have done justice upon the capital authors and promoters of the former or late wars, many of them being under your power, considering that mercy to the wicked is cruelty to the innocent, and that all your lenity doth but make them the more insolent and presumptuous.

26. That you would have provided constant pay for the army, now under the command of the Lord General Fairfax, and given rules to all judges, and all other public officers throughout the land, for their indemnity, and for the saving harmless all that have any ways assisted you, or that have said or done anything against the King....

27. That you would have laid to heart all the abundance of innocent blood that hath been spilled, and the infinite spoil and havoc that hath been made of peaceable, harmless people by express commissions from the King, and seriously to have considered whether the justice of God be likely to be satisfied, or his yet continuing wrath appeased, by an Act of Oblivion.

These and the like we have long time hoped you would have minded, and have made such an establishment for the general peace and contentful satisfaction of all sorts of people, as should have been to the happiness of all future generations, and which we most earnestly desire you would set yourselves speedily to effect, whereby the almost dying honour of this most honourable House would be again revived, and the hearts of your petitioners and all other well affected people be afresh renewed unto you....

Haller and Davies, *Leveller Tracts*, pp. 148–55

90. Commons' Resolutions, 4 January 1649

Resolved, &c. That the Commons of England, in Parliament assembled, do declare, That the people are, under God, the original of all just power:

And do also declare, That the Commons of England, in Parliament assembled, being chosen by, and representing the people, have the supreme power in this nation:

And do also declare, That whatever is enacted, or declared for law, by the Commons, in Parliament assembled, hath the force of law; and all the people of this nation are concluded thereby, although the consent and concurrence of King, or House of Peers, be not had thereunto.

CJ, VI, 111

91. A retrospect: the Army of the Lord of Hosts

A declaration of the English army now in Scotland, 1 August 1650.[1]

At the beginning of the great and wonderful workings of God in these two nations of England and Scotland, we, the under-officers and soldiers of the English army now in Scotland, were most of us—if not all—men of private callings, and not at all interested in matters of public and state affairs. But yet very many of us, in whom the Lord had begun to reveal himself in the face of Jesus Christ, were sensible of the Antichristian tyranny that was exercised by the late King and his prelates over the consciences, bodies and estates of the true spiritual Church of Jesus Christ.... Under these sad sufferings of the People of God our souls mourned, and understanding by the manifold gracious promises in the Word of God that a time of deliverance was to be expected to the Church of Christ, and destruction and ruin to Babylon, our hearts, together with all the truly godly in England, were exceedingly stirred up to pray to the Lord, even day and night, that he would arise to destroy Antichrist, and to save his people.

*   *   *   *   *   *

Let us remember how the Lord was pleased graciously to answer the prayers of his people at that time, in their deliverance from the army raised by the late King and his prelates for the destruction of all the people of God in England and Scotland; insomuch that soon after Scotland sits in peace, enjoying their former liberties without being imposed upon by the Antichristian prelacy in England. And England obtains a Parliament to whom they have opportunity to complain of their grievances, and through the great goodness of God so constituted those grievances are heard, and overtures made to the late King for their redress. Which was so irksome to his oppressing, tyrannical and bloody spirit that he again betook himself to overthrow the Parliament by force, and to that end entertains the officers of the army that had gone forth against our brethren of Scotland; and [he] withdrawing himself from his Parliament, an appearance of a civil war begins. Which being made known to us, the inferior officers and soldiers of this army (then in our private callings), we found our hearts extraordinarily stirred up by the Lord to assist the Parliament against the King, being abundantly satisfied in our judgements and consciences that we were called forth by

[1] In answer to a paper addressed by the Scots 'to the under-officers and soldiers of the English army'.

the Lord to be instrumental to bring about that which was our continual prayer to God, viz., the destruction of Antichrist and the deliverance of his Church and people. And upon this simple account we engaged, not knowing the deep policies of worldly statesmen, and have ever since hazarded our lives in the high places of the field (where we have seen the wonders of the Lord) against all the opposers of this work of Jesus Christ, whom we have all along seen going with us, and making our way plain before us.

* * * * * *

But when we saw that under pretence of the Covenant a corrupt party in Parliament by their worldly policy, after the war was ended in England, and the late King's party subdued, with the loss of thousands of the lives of the saints (whose death is precious in the sight of the Lord), did endeavour to set up the King upon his own terms, and with him to establish a national church-government, not in all things agreeable to the Word of God, but [such as] is destructive to the just liberties of the true spiritual Church of Christ, which he hath by his own most precious blood purchased for them, and is now come forth to bestow upon them. Which did sufficiently demonstrate itself by the dealings of the then master-builders with the churches of Jesus Christ in and about London, that were then threatened to be dissolved, and laws made to prevent the communion of saints with one another, except only in that one public form then about to be established, to the astonishment of many of us that had lifted up our hands to God and sworn to endeavour a reformation according to the Word of God. And therefore after much waiting upon God in prayer, and examining our own hearts about the ends and sincerity thereof, we were abundantly satisfied that it was not only lawful but our duty to keep our arms in our hands till the ends beforementioned should be accomplished. And to that end the army whereof we are a part did refuse to disband, did march up to London to propose to the Parliament a way of establishment that might be more for the carrying on the ends of religion and liberty, [and] though therein we were not at that time successful, yet [we were] most wonderfully and graciously preserved by the Lord, and extraordinarily convinced, after much seeking the face of God, that our failing was in endeavouring to set up the King upon any terms, he being a man of so much blood that the Lord would have no peace with him, nor any that should go about to establish him. Whereupon— after his own hard heart had hindered him from yielding to any overtures that were made to him by the Parliament (through whom all the army's proposals were to be tendered), and a second war, more dangerous than the former, contrived by him and his son (now with you), together with those in Scotland that hated us of the army of England under the name of Sectaries, being by the unspeakable goodness and mighty power of God waded through, and a second testimony given from heaven to justify the proceedings of his poor servants against that bloody Antichristian brood, though with the loss of many precious saints—we were then powerfully convinced that the Lord's purpose was to deal with the late King as a man of blood. And being persuaded in our consciences that he and his monarchy was one of the ten horns of the Beast (spoken of, Rev. xvii. 12–15), and being witnesses to so much of the innocent blood of the saints that he had shed in supporting the Beast, and considering the loud cries of the souls of the saints under the altar, we were extraordinarily carried forth to desire justice upon the King, that man of blood, and to that purpose petitioned our superior officers and Parliament to bring him to justice. Which accordingly by a high hand of providence was brought to pass, which act we are confident the Lord will own in preserving the Commonwealth of England against all kingdoms and nations that shall adventure to meddle with them upon that account. When God executes his justice upon malefactors, let none go about to resist.

*   *   *   *   *   *

And here give us leave (not in a boasting spirit, but in meekness and fear) to tell you that we are persuaded we are poor unworthy instruments in God's hand, to break his enemies and preserve his people.... We value the churches of Jesus Christ, who are the lot of God's inheritance, ten thousand times above our own lives; yea, we do bless the Lord we are not only a rod of iron to dash the common enemies in pieces, but also a hedge (though very unworthy) about Christ's vineyard.... We are not soldiers of fortune, we are not merely the servants of men; we have not only proclaimed Jesus Christ, the King of Saints, to be our King by profession, but desire to submit to him upon his own terms, and to admit him to the exercise of his royal authority in our hearts, and to follow him whithersoever he goeth, he having of his own good will entered into a Covenant of Grace with his poor saints.

*   *   *   *   *   *

Woodhouse, Puritanism and Liberty, pp. 474–8

CHAPTER 9

THE INTERREGNUM, 1649–1660

On 1 February 1649, two days after Charles I's execution, the House of Commons appointed a committee to review the list of Members and suspend all those who had voted for further negotiations with the king on 5 December last.[1] Pride's Purge was therefore confirmed by the House itself. On 6 February it resolved to abolish the House of Lords, and next day the monarchy, though the necessary statutes were not passed until the middle of March (92).[2] Meanwhile as early as 11 February an Act was passed changing the name of King's Bench to 'Upper Bench', and on the 17th another Act removed the word 'king' from all legal documents and substituted the grandiose phrase 'Keepers of the Liberties of England'; even the King's Highway was renamed 'The Common Highway'.[3] On 13 February the executive functions of monarchy were vested for a year in a Council of State with forty members, thirty-one of them Members of Parliament,[4] and on 10 March the council elected its first president. However, the process of constitutional revision was ragged and haphazard, and it was not until 19 May that an Act was passed declaring England to be 'a Commonwealth or Free-State'.[5]

The institution of this narrow, oligarchic government brought a howl of protest from the Levellers, and on 26 February Lilburne laid before Parliament a petition with the self-explanatory title of *England's New Chains Discovered*.[6] But in the two months that followed, Leveller influence in the Army was ruthlessly and permanently destroyed, and on 30 July Cromwell sailed for Dublin. During the next two years he and his generals carried the arms of the republic to success after success. Irish resistance was smashed by Cromwell in 1649 and 1650, and mopped up by Ireton in 1651. The Scots were defeated at Dunbar in 1650 and again at Worcester a year later, when they were led by Charles II in person. Both countries were put under military rule and in 1654 Scotland was united with England, in ironic fulfilment of the dreams of James I. Meanwhile the outlying islands—Jersey, Scilly, Man—were cleared, and the Caribbean plantations and the colonies of the American South came to heel after Worcester, that 'crowning mercy'.

[1] *CSPD, 1649–50*, p. 1; *CJ*, VI, 93. These Members were expelled on 9 June.
[2] The Act abolishing the House of Lords is printed in *GCD*, p. 387.
[3] Firth and Rait, II, 6–9; *CJ*, VI, 138.
[4] *GCD*, pp. 381–3.
[5] *Ibid.* p. 388.
[6] Haller and Davies, *Leveller Tracts*, pp. 156 ff.

But the regicides found it more difficult to establish their authority in England itself. Six High Court judges refused to accept the new patents offered them, and not until June 1649 could their places be filled. Even greater difficulty was experienced in finding a city government that would support the new order.[1] In October Lilburne was brought to trial before a special judicial commission on a charge of high treason, only to be acquitted; at the other extreme it was well known that Fairfax had not approved Charles's execution and was reluctant to give his unqualified support to the republic. In these circumstances the government decided (with no great reluctance) that it could not fulfil the pledge it had made in the Act abolishing the monarchy (92), to dissolve Parliament in the near future and hold new elections. Moreover, the maintenance of large forces by land and sea, and in Ireland and Scotland as well as England, forced them to continue the bitterly unpopular taxation of the war years, and in this way the officers and civilians at Westminster became even more dependent one upon the other; and though Parliament had to make a few concessions here and there, the steady pressure of the Council of Officers for the implementation of the programme of social and legal reform they had first put forward in 1647 had little effect.

In September 1649 Parliament passed an Act to relieve those imprisoned for debt,[2] but it was not until November 1650 that the courts were ordered to abandon the use of Law French.[3] On the key question of religion the Rump was particularly dilatory, and in June 1649 it passed an Act for the maintenance of preaching ministers which made express provision for the payment of tithe, though ever since 1647 the Army had been on record as demanding its abolition.[4] In August Parliament grudgingly resolved that in the future government of the Church (not yet decided) tithes would not be compulsory, but until then they were, and it ignored a petition from the Council of Officers on 16 August requesting the repeal of the statutes enforcing attendance at church, and the suppression of drunkenness, swearing, and 'uncleanness' in general. On the contrary, it issued a public declaration on 28 September that it would never allow 'a universal toleration'.[5]

Meanwhile the unpopularity of the government, and the threat from Scotland, had the paradoxical effect of setting the Rump more firmly in the saddle. On 11 October 1649, ostensibly in an attempt to frustrate a hostile electorate, it decreed that all its Members, present and future, must take the Engagement to the Commonwealth without king or House of Lords. The following day this obligation was extended to all office-holders, state pensioners, local government officials, officers of the armed forces, judges,

---

[1] Gardiner, *Commonwealth and Protectorate*, I, 42–3, 65.
[2] An Act for discharging poor prisoners unable to satisfy their creditors (Firth and Rait, II, 240–1). Re-enacted in an expanded form on 21 December (*ibid.* 321–4).
[3] *Ibid.* II, 455–6 (22 November 1650).   [4] *Ibid.* II, 142–8.
[5] Gardiner, *Commonwealth and Protectorate*, I, 192–3.

barristers, clergy, schoolmasters, and fellows of the universities.[1] On 2 January 1650 an Act was passed confirming this, and imposing the obligation on the whole of the male population over the age of eighteen (93). How far this was enforced it is difficult to say; partly as a result of Fairfax's uncooperative attitude an Act had to be rushed through postponing the deadline for a month;[2] but evidently Parliament wanted to divide the whole nation into the sheep and the goats as the Act of Classes had divided Scotland. A further step in this plan was the report of the standing committee on elections in February, adopted by the House, which recommended that sitting Members should retain their seats even at a general election.[3]

This bill went no further for the time being, but the Rump's intentions were now clear, and the Army was not pacified by an Act for the better observation of the Lord's Day, in April 1650,[4] followed the next month by a remarkable statute which made incest and adultery punishable by death and fornication by three months' imprisonment,[5] and in June by an Act laying down fines, graduated according to rank and social station, for 'profane swearing and cursing'.[6] It was not until the autumn, with Charles II at Edinburgh and an invasion imminent, that Parliament turned to the more serious part of the Army's religious programme. The Blasphemy Act of 9 August, by outlawing only those who asserted that they or their leader was the reincarnation of Christ and those who taught that any sin was permitted to the Elect, legalised by implication any religious deviation less outrageous than these.[7] Moreover, on 27 September, in the wake of the great victory at Dunbar, Parliament at last acceded to the Army's demand for the repeal of all standing legislation enforcing weekly attendance at church.[8] It even revitalised its standing committee on the reform of the Common Law, again under pressure from the Army.[9]

But it took another twelve months, and the victory of Worcester, to produce another reluctant jerk forward. In November 1651 a rough bargain was struck. The army establishment was to be reduced, and in return the Rump abandoned the plan to give its Members seats in perpetuity; but even then it postponed its dissolution until 3 November 1654. The Army's demand that Parliament account in detail for all the taxes collected in its name since 1642 then forced further concessions, such as the passage of the long-delayed Act of Oblivion in February 1652.[10] Once again law reform was taken up, despite the steady opposition of the legal profession.

[1] CJ, VI, 306–7.
[2] Firth and Rait, II, 348 (23 February).
[3] CJ, VI, 345.
[4] Firth and Rait II, 383–7 (19 April).
[5] Ibid. 387–9 (10 May).
[6] Ibid. 393–6 (28 June).
[7] Ibid. 409–12.
[8] GCD, pp. 391–4.
[9] G. B. Nourse, 'Law Reform under the Commonwealth', Law Quarterly Review, LXXV (1959), 512.
[10] Firth and Rait, II, 565. Even this did not satisfy one of the officers' main grievances, the setting aside of Articles of Surrender concluded with royalist commanders. (See no. 85, p. 306 above.)

Religion, however, remained the most controversial subject, and one which divided the Council of Officers as well as Parliament. Cromwell supported the dean of Christ Church, John Owen, who favoured a state church accompanied by a wide degree of toleration. He strongly influenced the Committee for the Propagation of the Gospel appointed by Parliament in February 1652, which made its report a year later. The committee recommended no doctrinal test, but it added socinianism (or unitarianism) to be the heresies already proscribed by the Blasphemy Act. It recommended that two committees, of laymen and clergy, examine candidates for the ministry and recommend the removal of unsuitable pastors—the 'Triers' and the 'Ejectors', as they were later called. Most controversial of all, the committee assumed the continuance of tithes and private patronage.[1] The Rump began to debate these proposals, but it was interrupted in April 1653, and the scheme had to be taken up later by Cromwell.[2]

The outbreak of war with Holland in June 1652 might have been expected to damp down the controversy between the Army and Parliament, but in fact the nature of the war left the land forces as idle as ever, and a prey to all manner of frustrations and discontents. On 13 August the Council of Officers could no longer restrain themselves, and they presented another strongly worded petition to the Rump calling once more for the implementation of the programme of 1647: that Parliament be dissolved, handing over to its successor the task of reforming the common law, reducing the excise, publishing its accounts, settling the army's arrears of pay, abolishing tithes, suppressing vagabondage, and so on.[3] It is an astonishing demonstration of the Army's impotence, at a time when it was supposed to be in a position to dictate its own terms, that it had been pushing this programme for five years now without result.

Cromwell persuaded the Council of Officers to drop their peremptory demand for an immediate dissolution, but the petition did produce action in this direction. The postponement of the dissolution until 3 November 1654 was tacitly abandoned, and on 14 September a new Committee on Elections was appointed. Much now depended on Cromwell. His prestige, already high in 1649, had been rising steadily ever since, and the retirement of Fairfax in 1650 had left him without a rival. But he was uneasily aware that what little constitutional or legal authority survived in the England of 1652 was still vested in the Rump, that tiny fragment of a freely elected Parliament. He did not move, and he restrained his supporters from moving, until his hand was forced. In April 1653 the leaders of the Rump produced another bill to make the tenure of sitting Members perpetual. Cromwell's counterproposal, that in the present emergency, and in view of the hostility of a

[1] CJ, VII, 258–9.   [2] Ibid. 262, 264, 269, 274. See p. 335 below.
[3] Summarised by Gardiner, Commonwealth and Protectorate, II, 167–8.

large part of the electorate, the parliamentary constitution be suspended and a nominated assembly summoned, only caused the Rump to hasten its plans, not unnaturally. Once the bill on elections was passed, it proposed to dismiss Cromwell from the post of commander-in-chief and adjourn until the autumn. On 20 April therefore Cromwell brought troops down to Westminster and dispersed Parliament, but there is no reason to doubt the truth of his remark: 'I have sought the Lord night and day, that he would rather slay me than put me upon the doing of this work.'[1]

The Council of Officers at once issued a declaration justifying their action,[2] but in fact the forcible dissolution of the Long Parliament produced remarkably little public reaction. Even the judges soothed their consciences by pretending that Parliament was only temporarily interrupted. The events of 1659 were to show that there was still a strong republican sentiment amongst the junior officers of the army, but they had no means of expressing themselves in 1653. But Cromwell knew well enough the implications of what he had done. When the Council of Officers on 11 March had called for just this course of action he and Desborough had asked them, 'if they destroyed that Parliament what they should call themselves, a State they could not be. They answered that they would call a new Parliament. Then, says the general, the Parliament is not the supreme power, but that is the supreme power that calls it'.[3]

Cromwell was right. All the constitutional experiments that followed were initiated by him and his officers, and the supreme authority they assumed was always resisted by elected parliaments which had a much better claim to represent the nation. The removal in 1654 of religious visionaries like Thomas Harrison and dedicated republicans like Edmund Ludlow exposed the remainder of the army high command as ruthless politiques, without principles or convictions, determined to secure by any means that offered the continuation of their own authority—every bit as bad, in fact, as the Rump. Cromwell could have retired into private life, as Fairfax had done, but this would have been to abandon the nation to probable chaos and the possible return of the Stuarts; moreover, he was inspired by the sincere belief that he had been singled out by God for a purpose, and that this selection had been confirmed by the great victories of '50 and '51. The solution found by eighteenth-century revolutionaries, of summoning a constituent convention which would frame a constitution and subsequently take no part in its operation, was apparently never considered.

Indeed, from April to July 1653 England was simply ruled by Cromwell by virtue of his post as commander-in-chief, and nothing else. But he was

---

[1] Abbott, *Cromwell's Writings*, II, 640–5. See also C. H. Firth, 'Cromwell and the Expulsion of the Long Parliament', *EHR*, VIII (1893), 526.
[2] *GCD*, pp. 400–4. [3] Firth, *op. cit.* 528.

anxious to lay down this authority, and he was still committed to the idea of a nominated assembly, suggested to him by Thomas Harrison. In May the separated congregations of England and Wales were asked to submit to the Council of Officers lists of men 'fearing God and of approved fidelity and honesty'; from them the council chose 129[1] for England and Wales, adding five for Scotland and six for Ireland. Cromwell then issued a personal summons to these 140 men, requesting them to assemble in the Council Chamber at Whitehall on 4 July and assume responsibility for the government of the three nations. The use of the name 'parliament' was sedulously avoided, but the new assembly at once assumed the title and removed itself to the Parliament House at Westminster.

The experiment was a dismal failure. The Nominated Parliament[2] was swayed by a minority of fanatics, which at once began to put into operation the radical reforms demanded by many of the sects. They alienated the lawyers by abolishing the Court of Chancery outright and bringing forward proposals to codify the Common Law. They offended the Army by suggesting that in order to reduce taxation officers should serve for a year without pay, and early in December they rejected the report of the Committee for the Propagation of the Gospel and brought in a bill to abolish all ecclesiastical patronage. This was enough for the moderates. It is rather astonishing that despite the eccentric method of selection used this Parliament still contained a majority of 'normal' parliamentary gentry, of the kind which had been elected for generations before and would be elected for generations after. These men went down to the House early on 12 December and voted to surrender their authority to the Lord General, whence it came.

Cromwell was grievously disappointed, but not surprised, and he was ready with the Instrument of Government (94), which had been prepared by John Lambert and the Council of Officers. On 16 December Cromwell took the oath as Lord Protector and the Instrument was published. It was a sensible, workmanlike document which tried to translate into action, under very different circumstances, the Heads of the Proposals of 1647. The executive was vested in a Protector, advised and assisted by triennial parliaments, which must each sit for at least five months. Parliament—consisting only of the lower House, of course—was to be elected from constituencies redistributed and reformed along lines laid down by Ireton and the Levellers. Some 'decayed' boroughs were suppressed, many more were reduced to one member each, and some of the surplus seats thus created were distributed amongst the counties (§ x), where the franchise was now confined to those having £200 in real or personal property (§ xviii). Yet the overall number

[1] One seat was kept in vain for Fairfax (Gardiner, *Commonwealth and Protectorate*, II, 231–2).
[2] The nickname 'Barebones Parliament' came later. For a stimulating analysis of this and Cromwell's other parliaments, see H. R. Trevor-Roper. 'Oliver Cromwell and his Parliaments'.

of Members was reduced to 400 from England and Wales, plus 30 each from Scotland and Ireland (§ IX). Those elected must be 'of known integrity', etc. (§ XVII), but otherwise there were few restrictions on candidates, except that delinquents could not elect or be elected to the first four parliaments.[1]

The resultant changes in the composition of the House were more startling than might appear at first glance. The number of borough members was reduced from 419 to 136, while county members now took 264 out of 400 seats, as against 90 out of 509 in the Long Parliament. The percentage of borough members dropped from 83 to 34, while the percentage of county members rose from 17 to 66.[2] The result was a parliament of more than ordinarily independent country gentry. The officers had dreamed of an independent parliament, but it had not occurred to them, apparently, that it would be independent of government, too. A machinery devised by Ireton to guard the liberties of the people from Charles I was too readily taken over into a new era.

To Parliament, when it was elected, the most offensive aspect of the Instrument was the exaltation of the Protector's authority. He had no veto on legislation, unless such legislation infringed the Instrument itself, but he could issue ordinances which had the force of law until or unless they were rejected by the next parliament, which was not due to sit until September 1654 (§ XXX). Moreover, the Instrument granted Cromwell £200,000 a year for the costs of the civil administration, and maintenance for an army of 10,000 horse and 20,000 foot, which financial settlement was not subject to parliamentary interference (§ XXVII); he was also granted the remainder of the Crown lands and other perquisites of royalty (§ XXXI). The Council of State was designed to act as a brake on the Protector, but fifteen of its members were named in the Instrument, and subsequent vacancies were to be filled by a cumbersome method obviously subject to manipulation by the executive (§ XXV). The chief officers of state were to be chosen by 'the approbation of parliament', a sufficiently vague term (§ XXXIV), and in the absence of any statement to the contrary it must be assumed that all other appointments were in the hands of the Protector. Finally, though this was a constitution drafted by men having no relevant authority, there was no machinery for revision or amendment; indeed, the Protector had a veto over legislation to that end (§ XXIV). Difficulties were foreseen, and though the Council of Officers did not make the mistake of trying to impose a prospective oath on new Members they obliged the returning officer, on the electors' behalf, to certify 'that the person elected shall not have power to alter the government as it is hereby settled in one single person and parliament'

---

[1] Gardiner offers two different interpretations of the relevant section (XIV), in *Commonwealth and Protectorate*, II, 286, and *GCD*, p. liv, and indeed everything hinges on the placing of a comma.

[2] Trevor-Roper, *op. cit.* p. 28; Vernon F. Snow, 'Parliamentary Reapportionment Proposals in the Puritan Revolution', *EHR*, LXXIV (1959), 420 ff.

(§ xII).[1] The great questions which had provoked the civil wars, and were summed up in the Militia Ordinance of 1642, the control of the Army and the negative voice, were not settled in a way satisfactory to any sincere patriot who had fought in those wars.

This was not all. In the first half of 1654 Cromwell proceeded to use the powers granted him by the Instrument to promulgate a whole series of controversial ordinances. For many of them there was a good case; it was clearly essential that the customs and excise and the monthly assessment should continue to be collected,[2] and it was only logical, as well as sensible, to repeal the Act imposing the Engagement.[3] But by redefining treason so as to include the public assertion 'that the Lord Protector and the people in Parliament assembled are not the supreme authority of this Commonwealth', the Treason Ordinance of 19 January 1654[4] begged a most important question; and the decision to settle religion by ordinance was more controversial still. Ignoring the decisions of the Nominated Parliament, the Instrument (§ xxxv) declared that tithes should be paid until some alternative could be found, and called for the regulation of the public ministry. In March 1654 Cromwell began to carry into effect the proposals of the Committee for the Propagation of the Gospel, though they had been rejected by the Nominated Parliament, and set up by ordinance a central committee of 'Triers' to investigate the background and qualifications of candidates for collation to benefices or appointment to lectureships. In August a further ordinance appointed commissioners in each county to eject 'scandalous, ignorant and insufficient ministers and schoolmasters',[5] though it attempted no definition of ignorance or insufficiency. The government remained silent on the vexed question of tithes, but it could take advantage of the fact that public opinion was deeply divided on this question, and that the only alternative—voluntary contributions—was felt by many to give the congregation too tight a grip on their minister. In fact, tithes continued to be collected.[6]

The fact that the first parliament of the Protectorate, to the horror of the righteous, was ordered to assemble on the Lord's Day, just because it was the anniversary of Dunbar and Worcester (3 September 1654), indicated the personal nature of the new regime. The foundation of its authority was demonstrated by the extraordinary precautions taken when the Protector ventured down to Westminster to address them. The Members were locked out of their own House, which was guarded by troops, and soldiers also

---

[1] This was not, however, mentioned in the writs for the first parliament (Abbott, *Cromwell's Writings*, III, 307–8).

[2] Ordinances to this end were published on 24 December 1653, 17 February and 20 March 1654 respectively; Firth and Rait, II, 823, 842–4, 854.

[3] *Ibid.* 830–1 (19 January 1654).　　　　　　　　　　[4] *Ibid.* 831–5.

[5] *Ibid.* 855–8, 968–90 (20 March, 28 August).

[6] Margaret James, 'The Tithes Controversy in the English Revolution', *History*, XXVI (1942), 1.

patrolled all the corridors; Cromwell arrived at the Painted Chamber flanked by senior officers and surrounded by life-guards and halberdiers.[1] But military force could not overawe the Members, who at once set out to amend the Instrument, and would submit to no curb or check. Only a week later, on 12 September, Cromwell had to harangue them again, and bind them by an oath of recognition.[2] But it was no use; they insisted on tampering with his control of the Army, his veto on legislation, and his income,[3] and he dissolved them at the earliest opportunity, on 22 January 1655, with 'turbid oratory, protestations of his own virtue and their waywardness, romantic reminiscences, proprietory appeals to the Lord, and great broken gobbets from the Pentateuch and the Psalms'.[4]

Two months later the first considerable royalist plot of the Interregnum, though it fizzled out in a pathetic rural uprising in Wiltshire, called attention to the government's pressing security problems. Nevertheless, Cromwell was determined to reduce the numbers of the Army, which was not only a serious drain on the national finances but the principal cause of the government's unpopularity, and on 31 July 1655 he cut down the army establishment, reduced its pay, and promulgated measures designed to strengthen the local militia. But at the same time he allowed the Council of Officers to perpetrate their most unpopular move. In August they divided England and Wales into ten districts or groups of counties and placed each under a senior army officer, whose duty it was to reinvigorate the militia and coordinate and stimulate the work of the officers of the peace in suppressing royalism (95). The surrender to naked military rule was bad enough, but the Major-Generals were made even more unpopular because the expenses of their regime were defrayed by a tax of 10% on the estates of royalists, who were thus punished twice for the same crime. Moreover, one of their twenty-one tabulated instructions from the council saddled them with execution of the intemperate anti-vice laws of the Commonwealth, and this, together with the decision to forbid race meetings and close brothels, as being habitual haunts of royalists, set the seal on their unpopularity.

Cromwell survived this; he even survived a serious outbreak of mutiny in the legal profession. Nothing is more remarkable than the way in which the administration of justice had proceeded under the old forms, or something very close to them, through every military and constitutional upheaval. Individual judges might object and lay down their commissions, but suitable replacements were always available: the terms were kept, the High Court sat in Westminster Hall, the assize judges rode their circuits, the Commissioners

---

[1] Burton, I, p. xxxiii (Guibon Goddard's account).
[2] Abbott, *Cromwell's Writings*, III, 451 ff.
[3] Their amendments were collected into a Constitutional Bill, which is printed by *GCD*, pp. 427–47 (see also pp. lviii–lix).
[4] Trevor-Roper, *op. cit.* p. 2; Abbott, *Cromwell's Writings*, III, 579–93.

of the Great Seal continued to appoint justices of the peace, who themselves maintained the fabric of the legal system in the provinces. At the same time the profession resisted the demand voiced by the Levellers in 1647, and taken up with increasing persistence by the army, for the reform of legal procedure and the reduction of costs.[1] The Nominated Parliament had been the most serious threat to their position, but Cromwell had apparently rejected that line of policy; his ordinance reforming the Court of Chancery[2] was therefore all the greater shock. In 1655 an increasing number of judges served notice, in effect, that although for the sake of good government they had accepted an illegal constitution they would not allow the executive to infringe that constitution.[3] Cromwell had scrupulously refrained from issuing further ordinances, but dispute now arose as to whether his earlier ordinances, never confirmed by Parliament, were valid—particularly the taxation ordinances. It was also becoming increasingly difficult to find judges and juries who would convict royalist conspirators unless the government's case was absolutely watertight. The only solution was another parliament, which could confirm the Instrument or extend it, and one was summoned for 17 September 1656.

At first Cromwell was unusually cunning. The major-generals were encouraged to influence borough elections as much as they could, and the Council of Officers were induced to remove about 100 of the more obstreperous Members;[4] then Cromwell disowned them both, and viewed with complacency the storm of complaint against them. He did not foresee a monarchist reaction, but it was inevitable, especially now that the republicans had been excluded. Cromwell had now so far dissociated himself from his officers that he could be regarded as a spokesman of opposition to them. As early as 28 October a back-bencher proposed to make the Protectorship hereditary, and on 19 January 1657 James Ashe moved that Cromwell 'take upon him the government according to the ancient constitution'. The discovery of a Leveller plot to assassinate Cromwell caused a stampede; on 29 January Parliament snubbed the major-generals by throwing out the bill for a decimation tax, and on 23 February it took into consideration a remonstrance, later entitled the Humble Petition and Advice, which called upon Cromwell to assume the crown and revised the Instrument in such a way as to give him every inducement to do so.

The events of the next two or three months are still the subject of con-

[1] G. B. Nourse, 'Law Reform under the Commonwealth', Law Quarterly Review, LXXV (1959), 512.

[2] 21 August 1654, Firth and Rait, II, 949–67. See Stuart E. Prall, 'Chancery Reform and the Puritan Revolution', American Journal of Legal History, VI (1962), 28. R. Robinson's 'Anticipations under the Commonwealth of Changes in the Law', in Select Essays in Anglo-American Legal History, ed. E. Freund et al. (Boston 1907), I, 467, is also still useful.

[3] Gardiner, Commonwealth and Protectorate, III, 149 ff.

[4] About 100 were excluded, and 50 or 60 then voluntarily absented themselves in protest; exact figures cannot be established. See Firth, Last Years, I, 12–16.

troversy.[1] It is still in doubt whether Cromwell declined the crown because of the pressure of the Council of Officers, and, if he did, whether he was justified in acceding to this pressure. However this may be, the compromise eventually agreed upon included the worst of both worlds. Cromwell rejected the Humble Petition on 3 April; after prolonged negotiations he rejected it a second time on 8 May. Parliament then agreed to delete the clause asking him to take the kingship and settle for a semi-hereditary protectorate, and the amended petition was submitted on 25 May and accepted.

The Humble Petition and Advice, clarified by an Additional and Explanatory Petition on 26 June (96), gave Cromwell the right to nominate his successor and an 'Other House' of forty, which would henceforth fill gaps in its ranks by co-option. The Protector was granted £1,300,000 a year, of which £1,000,000 was allocated to the armed forces, though some of the value of this was removed by the stipulation that it should not be raised by a land-tax. Finally, disdaining the evasions of the Instrument, the Petition tried to lay down the framework of a national Independent Church.

But the constitution as amended by the Petition had a short life. Parliament adjourned on 26 June, and in the next six months the members of the Other House were chosen, removing from the Commons some of the ablest supporters of the regime. When the Commons met again on 20 January 1658 the excluded Members were admitted on swearing a simple oath of loyalty to the Protector. But the republicans did not consider that this bound them to support the other House, and their criticisms of this institution so angered Cromwell that he dissolved them on 4 February.

Cromwell's death on 3 September, and the accession of his son, Richard, only exacerbated the problem. The Instrument of Government had never been approved by Parliament, and the Humble Petition had not been passed in a full Parliament, and so little confidence did the Council of State feel in either document that they abandoned the system of representation laid down in 1654 and summoned a parliament in January 1659 on the old franchise, with the Other House.[2] From the beginning its debates were disordered by the republicans, who declined to admit that Richard Cromwell had succeeded his father by law, and refused to recognise the Other House. In April the Council of Officers forced the Protector to dissolve Parliament on the grounds that it was invincibly hostile to the Army, but their plan to use Richard as a mask for their own authority was wrecked by their own junior

---

[1] The most recent statement is by Trevor-Roper, 'Oliver Cromwell and His Parliaments', pp. 40–41. See also Firth, *Last Years*, I, chs. v–vi; *idem*, 'Cromwell and the Crown', *EHR*, XVII (1902), 429, XVIII (1903), 52; R. C. H. Catterall, 'The Failure of the Humble Petition and Advice', *American Historical Review*, IX (1903), 36, and Paul, *The Lord Protector*, pp. 366 ff.

[2] The reasons for this are, in fact, unknown. See G. Davies, 'The Elections to Richard Cromwell's Parliament', *EHR*, LXIII (1948), 488–9.

officers, who, with the rank and file behind them, demanded and secured the return of the Rump. The Rump, like the Bourbons, learnt nothing and forgot nothing, and in October the army generals dispersed it once more. By this time, however, the irresponsibility of the republicans, the sheer incompetence of the army high command, and the threat of a recession in trade had strained the patience of the public beyond endurance. George Monk, commander-in-chief of the army of Scotland, now came forward as the spokesman of those who demanded a return to constitutional parliamentary government, and in the New Year he marched his hand-picked, carefully purged force south on London. Under this threat the Rump was hastily recalled.

Monk reached London in February 1660, and rapidly and efficiently dispersed the English army to far-distant garrisons. But he soon realised, if he did not know already, that the Rump had nothing to offer, and on 21 February he readmitted the Members excluded by Colonel Pride in 1648. He thus enabled the Long Parliament to dissolve itself at last, and order a general election. On 4 April Charles II, acting on suggestions secretly made by Monk himself, issued a pacific declaration from Breda; subject to the approval of a freely elected Parliament, he offered a free pardon to all, full payment of arrears to the Army, the confirmation of land sales made since 1642, and the possibility of general toleration (97). On these terms the new Parliament, or Convention, which assembled on 25 April, voted for the king's restoration, and on 27 May he landed at Dover.

92. An Act for the abolishing the kingly office in England and Ireland, and the dominions thereunto belonging, 17 March 1649

Whereas Charles Stuart, late King of England...[etc.], hath by authority derived from Parliament been, and is hereby declared to be justly condemned, adjudged to die, and put to death, for many treasons, murders and other heinous offences committed by him, by which judgement he stood, and is hereby declared to, be attainted of high treason, whereby his issue and posterity, and all other pretending title under him, are become incapable of the said crowns, or of being king or queen of the said kingdom or dominions, or either or any of them; be it therefore enacted and ordained...by this present parliament and by the authority thereof, that all the people of England and Ireland..., of what degree or condition soever, are discharged of all fealty, homage and allegiance which is or shall be pretended to be due unto any of the issue and posterity of the said late King, or any claiming under him;

and that Charles Stuart, eldest son, and James called Duke of York, second son, and all other the issue and posterity of him the said late King, and all and every person and persons pretending title from, by or under him, are and be disabled to hold or enjoy the said Crown of England and Ireland. . . .

And whereas it is and hath been found by experience that the office of a king in this nation and Ireland, and to have the power thereof in any single person, is unnecessary, burdensome and dangerous to the liberty, safety and public interest of the people, and that for the most part use hath been made of the regal power and prerogative to oppress and impoverish and enslave the subject, and that usually and naturally any one person in such power makes it his interest to encroach upon the just freedom and liberty of the people, and to promote the setting up of their own will and power above the laws, that so they might enslave these kingdoms to their own lust, be it therefore enacted and ordained by this present Parliament. . . that the office of a king in this nation shall not henceforth reside in or be exercised by any one single person, and that no one person whatsoever shall or may have or hold the office, style, dignity, power or authority of king of the said kingdoms and dominions, or any of them, or of the Prince of Wales, any law. . . notwithstanding.

And whereas by the abolition of the kingly office provided for in this Act a most happy way is made for this nation (if God see it good) to return to its just and ancient right of being governed by its own Representatives[1] or National Meetings in Council, from time to time chosen and entrusted for that purpose by the people; it is therefore resolved and declared by the Commons assembled in Parliament, that they will put a period to the sitting of this present Parliament, and dissolve the same, so soon as may possibly stand with the safety of the people that hath betrusted them, and with what is absolutely necessary for the preserving and upholding the government now settled in the way of a Commonwealth, and that they will carefully provide for the certain choosing, meeting and sitting of the next and future Representatives with such other circumstances of freedom in choice and equality in distribution of Members to be elected thereunto as shall most conduce to the lasting freedom and good of this Commonwealth.

And it is hereby further enacted and declared, notwithstanding anything contained in this Act, [that] no person or persons of what condi-

---

[1] That is, 'representative assemblies'.

tion and quality soever, within the Commonwealth of England and Ireland, Dominion of Wales, the Islands of Guernsey and Jersey, and [the] town of Berwick upon Tweed, shall be discharged from the obedience and subjection which he and they owe to the government of this nation, as it is now declared, but all and every of them shall in all things render and perform the same, as of right is due unto the Supreme Authority hereby declared to reside in this and the successive Representatives of the people of this nation, and in them only.

Firth and Rait, II, 18-20

93. An Act for subscribing the Engagement, 2 January 1650

Whereas divers disaffected persons do by sundry ways and means oppose and endeavour to undermine this present government, so that unless special care be taken a new war is likely to break forth, for the preventing whereof, and also for the better uniting of this nation, as well against all invasions from abroad as the common enemy at home, and to the end that those which receive benefit and protection from this present government may give assurance of their living quietly and peaceably under the same, and that they will neither directly or indirectly contrive or practice anything to the disturbance thereof, the Parliament now assembled do enact and ordain,... that all men whatsoever within the Commonwealth of England, of the age of eighteen years and upwards, shall as is hereafter in this present Act directed take and subscribe this Engagement following, viz., *I do declare and promise, that I will be true and faithful to the Commonwealth of England as it is now established, without a king or House of Lords.*

And for the due taking and subscribing thereof, be it further enacted..., that all and every person and persons that now hath, or hereafter shall have, hold or enjoy any place or office of trust or profit, or any place or employment of public trust whatsoever within the said Commonwealth,... that hath not formerly taken the said Engagement, by virtue of any order or direction of Parliament, shall take and subscribe the said Engagement at or before the twentieth day of February, 1650....

*   *   *   *   *   *

And it is further enacted and declared, that all and every person or persons that expects benefit from the courts of justice of this Commonwealth, and that either now are or hereafter shall be plaintiff or plaintiffs, demandant or demandants, in any suit, plaint, bill, action, information, writ, demand, execution, or any other process whatsoever, in any of the courts...[of justice] within the Commonwealth of England... shall take and subscribe, and are hereby required to take and subscribe the aforesaid Engagement....And that it shall be lawful for all and every person or persons that are or shall be defendant or defendants, or that are or shall be sued, impleaded, attached, arrested, molested or complained against in any such courts...from and after the twentieth of April, 1650, to plead, aver, or to move in arrest of judgement... that the plaintiff or plaintiffs...have not taken and subscribed the said Engagement....

* * * * * *

Firth and Rait, II, 325–8

94. The Instrument of Government, 1653

The government of the Commonwealth of England, Scotland and Ireland, and the dominions thereunto belonging [16 December 1653]

I. That the supreme legislative authority of the Commonwealth of England...[etc.] shall be and reside in one person, and the people assembled in Parliament; the style of which person shall be, 'The Lord Protector of the Commonwealth of England, Scotland and Ireland'.

II. That the exercise of the chief magistracy, and the administration of the government over the said countries and dominions, and the people thereof, shall be in the Lord Protector, assisted with a Council, the number whereof shall not exceed twenty-one nor be less than thirteen.

III. That all writs, process[es], commissions, patents, grants and other things, which now run in the name and style of the Keepers of the Liberties of England by Authority of Parliament, shall run in the name and style of the Lord Protector, from whom for the future shall be derived all magistracy and honours in these three nations; and [he] shall have the power of pardons (except in case of murders and treason) and benefit of all forfeitures for the public use; and shall govern the said countries and dominions in all things by the advice of the Council, and according to these presents, and the laws.

IV. That the Lord Protector, the Parliament sitting, shall dispose and order the militia and forces, both by sea and land, for the peace and good of the three nations, by consent of Parliament; and that the Lord Protector, with the advice and consent of the major part of the Council, shall dispose and order the militia for the ends aforesaid in the intervals of Parliament.

v. That the Lord Protector, by the advice aforesaid, shall direct in all things concerning the keeping and holding of a good correspondency with foreign kings, princes and states; and also, with the consent of the major part of the Council, have the power of war and peace.

vi. That the laws shall not be altered, suspended, abrogated, or repealed, nor any new law made, nor any tax, charge or imposition laid upon the people, but by common consent in Parliament (save only as is expressed in the 30th article).

vii. That there shall be a parliament summoned to meet at Westminster upon the third day of September, 1654, and that successively a parliament shall be summoned once in every third year, to be accounted from the dissolution of the present parliament.[1]

viii. That neither the parliament to be next summoned, nor any successive parliaments, shall during the time of five months, to be accounted from the day of their first meeting, be adjourned, prorogued or dissolved, without their own consent.

ix. That as well the next as all other successive parliaments shall be summoned and elected in manner hereafter expressed. That is to say, the persons to be chosen within England, Wales, the isles of Jersey, Guernsey and the town of Berwick upon Tweed...shall be and not exceed the number of four hundred. The persons to be chosen within Scotland...shall be and not exceed...thirty; and...for Ireland... thirty.

x. That the persons to be elected to sit in Parliament from time to time for the several counties of England [and] Wales...and all places within the same respectively, shall be according to the proportions and numbers hereafter expressed....[2]

[xi. If the Protector fails to issue the writs, they are to be issued by the Commissioners of the Great Seal.]

xii. That at the day and place of elections the sheriff of each county, and...mayors...[etc.] within their cities...[etc.] shall take view of the said elections, and shall make return into the Chancery within

---

[1] That is, the parliament to assemble in 1654.

[2] This redistribution is discussed in detail by Vernon F. Snow, 'Parliamentary Re-apportionment Proposals in the Puritan Revolution', *EHR*, lxxiv (1959), 409.

twenty days after the said elections of the persons elected,...wherein shall be contained [an acknowledgement] that the persons elected shall not have power to alter the government as it is hereby settled in one single person and a Parliament.

[XIII. Sheriffs neglecting their duty to be punished.]

XIV. That all and every person and persons who have aided, advised, assisted or abetted in any war against the Parliament since the first day of January 1641 [1642] (unless they have been since in the service of the Parliament, and given signal testimony of their good affection thereunto) shall be disabled and incapable to be elected, or to give any vote in the election of any Members to serve in the next parliament, or in the three succeeding triennial parliaments.

XV. That all such who have advised, assisted or abetted the Rebellion of Ireland shall be disabled and incapable for ever to be elected or to give any vote in the election of any Member to serve in Parliament; as also all such who do or shall profess the Roman Catholic religion.

[XVI. Heavy penalties to be imposed on disqualified men who vote.]

XVII. That the persons who shall be elected to serve in Parliament shall be such (and no other than such) as are persons of known integrity, fearing God, and of good conversation, and being of the age of twenty-one years.

XVIII. That all and every person and persons seized or possessed to his own use of any estate, real or personal, to the value of £200, and not within the aforesaid exceptions, shall be capable to elect Members to serve in Parliament for counties.

[XIX. For failing to do their duty under § XI above, the Commissioners of the Great Seal shall be liable to the penalties of high treason.

XX. If no writs are issued, elections are to be held by the returning officers notwithstanding.]

XXI. That the clerk called the Clerk of the Commonwealth in Chancery for the time being, and all others who shall afterwards execute that office, to whom the returns shall be made, shall for the next parliament, and the two succeeding triennial parliaments, the next day after such return, certify the names of the several persons so returned...unto the Council, who shall peruse the said returns, and examine whether the persons so elected and returned be such as is agreeable to the qualifications, and not disabled to be elected; and that every person and persons being so duly elected, and being approved of by the major part of the Council to be persons not disabled, but qualified as aforesaid, shall be esteemed a Member of Parliament and be admitted to sit in Parliament, and not otherwise.

XXII. That the persons so chosen and assembled in manner aforesaid, or any sixty of them, shall be and be deemed the Parliament of England, Scotland and Ireland; and the supreme legislative power to be and reside in the Lord Protector and such Parliament, in manner herein expressed.

XXIII. That the Lord Protector, with the advice of the major part of the Council, shall at any other time than is before expressed, when the necessities of the State shall require it, summon parliaments in manner before expressed, which shall not be adjourned, prorogued, or dissolved without their own consent during the first three months of their sitting; and in case of future war with any foreign state a parliament shall be forthwith summoned for their advice concerning the same.

XXIV. That all bills agreed unto by the Parliament shall be presented to the Lord Protector for his consent, and in case he shall not give his consent thereto within twenty days after they shall be presented to him, or give satisfaction to the Parliament within the time limited, that then upon declaration of the Parliament that the Lord Protector hath not consented nor given satisfaction, such bills shall pass into and become law, although he shall not give his consent thereunto; provided such bills contain nothing in them contrary to the matters contained in these presents.

XXV. That Henry Lawrence, Esq., [John Lambert, Charles Fleetwood, Philip Skippon, John Desborough, Edward Montague, William Sydenham,[1] Philip Sydney (Viscount Lisle), Sir Anthony Ashley Cooper, Sir Charles Wolseley, Sir Gilbert Pickering, Francis Rous, Richard Major and Walter Strickland], or any seven of them, shall be a Council for the purposes expressed in this writing and upon the death or other removal of any of them the Parliament shall nominate six persons of ability, integrity, and fearing God, for every one that is dead or removed; out of which the major part of the Council shall elect two and present them to the Lord Protector, of which he shall elect one. And in case the Parliament shall not nominate within twenty days after notice given unto them thereof, the major part of the Council shall

[1] The first seven were army officers.

345

nominate three as aforesaid to the Lord Protector, who out of them shall supply the vacancy....

XXVI. That the Lord Protector and the major part of the Council aforesaid may, at any time before the meeting of the next parliament, add to the Council such persons as they shall think fit, provided the number of the Council be not made thereby to exceed twenty-one; and the quorum to be proportioned accordingly by the Lord Protector and the major part of the Council.

XXVII. That a constant yearly revenue shall be raised, settled and established for maintaining of 10,000 horse and dragoons and 20,000 foot, in England, Scotland and Ireland, for the defence and security thereof, and also for a convenient number of ships for guarding of the seas; besides £200,000 per ann. for defraying the other necessary charges of administration of justice, and other expenses of the government; which revenue shall be raised by the customs, and such other ways and means as shall be agreed upon by the Lord Protector and the Council, and shall not be taken away or diminished, nor the way agreed upon for raising the same altered, but by the consent of the Lord Protector and the Parliament.

XXVIII. That the said yearly revenue shall be paid into the public treasury, and shall be issued out for the uses aforesaid.

XXIX. That in case there shall not be cause hereafter to keep up so great a defence both at land or sea, but that there be an abatement made thereof, the money which will be saved thereby shall remain in bank for the public service, and not be employed to any other use but by consent of Parliament; or, in the intervals of Parliament, by the Lord Protector and major part of the Council.

XXX. That the raising of money for defraying the charge of the present extraordinary forces, both at sea and land, in respect of the present wars, shall be by consent of Parliament and not otherwise; save only that the Lord Protector, with the consent of the major part of the Council, for preventing the disorders and dangers which might otherwise fall out both by sea and land, shall have power, until the meeting of the first parliament, to raise money for the purposes aforesaid; and also to make laws and ordinances for the peace and welfare of these nations, where it shall be necessary, which shall be binding and in force until order shall be taken in Parliament concerning the same.

XXXI. That the lands, tenements, rents, royalties, jurisdictions and hereditaments which remain yet unsold or undisposed of by Act or

Ordinance of Parliament, belonging to the Commonwealth...shall be vested in the Lord Protector to hold, to him and his successors Lords Protectors of these nations, and shall not be alienated but by consent in Parliament....

[XXXII. On the Protector's death his successor shall be elected by the Council, with a quorum of thirteen.]

XXXIII. That Oliver Cromwell, Captain General,...shall be, and is hereby declared to be, Lord Protector....

XXXIV. That the chancellor, keeper or commissioners of the Great Seal, the treasurer, admiral, chief governors of Ireland and Scotland, and the chief justices of both the Benches, shall be chosen by the approbation of Parliament, and in the intervals of Parliament by the approbation of the major part of the Council, to be afterwards approved by the Parliament.

XXXV. That the Christian religion, as contained in the Scriptures, be held forth and recommended as the public profession of these nations; and that as soon as may be a provision, less subject to scruple and contention, and more certain than the present, be made for the encouragement and maintenance of able and painful teachers, for instructing the people, and for discovery and confutation of error, heresy and whatever is contrary to sound doctrine. And that until such provision be made the present maintenance shall not be taken away nor impeached.

XXXVI. That to the Public Profession held forth none shall be compelled by penalties or otherwise; but that endeavours be used to win them by sound doctrine and the example of a good conversation.

XXXVII. That such as profess faith in God by Jesus Christ (though differing in judgement from the doctrine, worship or discipline publicly held forth) shall not be restrained from, but shall be protected in, the profession of the Faith, and exercise of their religion; so as they abuse not this liberty to the civil injury of others, and to the actual disturbance of the public peace on their parts. Provided this liberty be not extended to Popery nor Prelacy, nor to such as, under the profession of Christ, hold forth and practice licentiousness.

XXXVIII. That all laws, statutes and ordinances, and clauses in any law, statute or ordinance to the contrary of the aforesaid liberty, shall be esteemed as null and void.

[XXXIX. Confirmed financial engagements entered into by the Long Parliament.

XL. Confirmed treaties and agreements undertaken by the Long Parliament.]

* * * * * *

Firth and Rait, II, 813–22

95. Instructions to the major-generals, October 1655

1. They are to endeavour the suppressing all tumults, insurrections, rebellions or other unlawful assemblies which shall be within the said counties respectively, as also all invasions from abroad, and to that purpose shall have power to draw together the said forces or troops, and march in such places as they shall judge convenient in England and Wales.

2. They are to take care and give order, that all Papists and others who have been in arms against the Parliament, or assisted the late King or his son in the late wars, as also all others who are dangerous to the peace of the nation, be disarmed, and their arms secured in some adjacent garrisons, or otherwise disposed of, as may be for the public service.

3. And to the end that all the highways and roads may be more safe for travellers, and the many robberies and burglaries daily committed may be prevented, they with the said captains and officers shall use their best endeavours to find out all such thieves, robbers, highwaymen and other dangerous persons as lurk and lie hid in any place within the several counties, and the houses and places which they frequent and usually lodge in, and take such course for the apprehending of them, and also for the prosecuting them and their receivers, as is agreeable to law. And they have hereby power to appoint such reward, not exceeding ten pounds, to such person or persons as shall discover and apprehend any such thief, highwayman or robber, to be paid into them after the conviction of the party so discovered and apprehended, which the sheriff for the time being shall pay....

4. They are to have a strict eye upon the conversation and carriage of all disaffected persons within the several counties; and they shall give the like direction to all the said captains and officers at their meetings, to be watchful and diligent in the same kind. As also that no horse-races, cock-fighting, bear-baitings, stage plays, or any unlawful assemblies be suffered or permitted within their counties, forasmuch as treason and rebellion is usually hatched and contrived against the State upon such occasions, and much evil and wickedness committed.

5. They and the aforesaid officers shall labour to inform themselves of all such idle and loose people that are within their counties who have no visible way of livelihood, nor calling or employment, and shall consider by what means they may be compelled to work, or be sent out of the Commonwealth; as also how the poor and impotent of those counties may be employed and better provided for than now they are, and certify the same to us and the Council, for our further direction thereupon; and in the meantime shall endeavour as far as in them lies that the laws in such cases made and provided be put in effectual execution.

6. They shall in their constant carriage and conversation encourage and promote godliness and virtue, and discourage and discountenance all profaneness and ungodliness; and shall endeavour with the other justices of the peace, and other ministers and officers who are entrusted with the care of those things, that the laws against drunkenness, blaspheming and taking of the name of God in vain, by swearing and cursing, plays and interludes, and profaning the Lord's Day, and such-like wickedness and abominations, be put in more effectual execution than they have been hitherto.

7. They shall take an exact account of what proceedings have been put upon the ordinance for ejecting of ignorant, insufficient and scandalous ministers and schoolmasters, and take care that the same be effectually put in execution for the time to come....

[8. The servants of delinquents or suspect persons, as defined in § 2, to be bound over.

9–15. A central registry is to be set up for recording the existence and the movements of all Papists, delinquents, and suspect persons.]

16. That a more than ordinary regard be had to the securing of the roads, chiefly about London.

17. That no house standing alone and out of a town be permitted to sell ale, beer or wine, or to give entertainment, but that such licenses be called in and suppressed.

[18. Riding post is to be restricted and closely regulated.]

19. And for the effecting more particularly a reformation in the city of London and Westminster, that all gaming houses and houses of evil fame be industriously sought out and suppressed within the cities of London and Westminster and all the liberties thereof.

20. That all house keepers within the same who have no trade or calling, or do not labour in such trade or calling, or have no other visible estate, but are observed generally to lodge and harbour loose and dissolute persons, be bound to their good behaviour and compelled to work, and for want of security be sent to Bridewell.

21. That all alehouses, taverns and victualling houses towards the outskirts of the said cities, or either of them, be suppressed, except such as are necessary and convenient to travellers; and that the number of alehouses in all other parts of the town be abated, and none continued but such as can lodge strangers and are of good repute.

Abbott, Cromwell's Writings, III, 844–8

96. The Humble Petition and Advice, 25 May 1657

To his Highness the Lord Protector of the Commonwealth of England, Scotland and Ireland, and the dominions thereto belonging, The Humble Petition and Advice of the knights, citizens and burgesses now assembled in the Parliament of this Commonwealth

We, the knights, citizens and burgesses in this present parliament assembled, taking into our most serious consideration the present state of the three nations joined and united under your Highness's protection, cannot but in the first place with all thankfulness acknowledge the wonderful mercy of Almighty God in delivering us from that tyranny and bondage, both in our spiritual and civil concernments, which the late King and his party designed to bring us under, and pursued the effecting thereof by a long and bloody war; and also that it hath pleased the same gracious God to preserve your person in many battles, to make you an instrument for preserving our peace, though environed with enemies abroad and filled with turbulent, restless and unquiet spirits in our own bowels, that as in the treading down the common enemy and restoring us to peace and tranquillity the Lord hath used you so eminently, and the worthy officers and soldiers of the army (whose faithfulness to the common cause we and all good men shall ever acknowledge, and put a just value upon); so also that he will use you and them in the settling and securing our liberties as we are men and Christians to us and our posterity after us, which are those great and glorious ends which the good people of these nations have so freely, with the hazard of their lives and estates, so long and earnestly contended for. We consider likewise the continual danger which your life is in from the bloody practices both of the malignant and discontented party (one whereof through the goodness of God you have been lately delivered from), it being a received principle amongst them that, no order being settled in your lifetime for the succession in the government, nothing is wanting to bring us into blood and confusion, and them to their desired ends, but the destruction of your person. And in case things should thus remain at your death we are not able to express what calamities would in all human probability ensue thereupon, which we trust your Highness (as well as we) do hold yourself obliged to provide against, and not to leave a people, whose common peace and interest you are entrusted with, in such a condition as may hazard both, especially in this conjecture, when there seems to be an opportunity of coming to a settlement upon just and legal foundations. Upon these considerations we have judged it a duty incumbent upon us to present and declare these our most just and necessary desires to your Highness.

1. That your Highness will be pleased, by and under the name and style of Lord Protector of the Commonwealth of England, Scotland and Ireland, and the dominions and territories thereunto belonging, to hold and exercise the office of chief magistrate of these nations, and to govern according to this Petition and Advice in all things therein contained, and in all other things according to the laws of these nations, and not otherwise. That your Highness will be pleased during your lifetime to appoint and declare the person who shall immediately after your death succeed you in the government of these nations.

2. That your Highness will for the future be pleased to call parliaments consisting of two Houses (in such manner as shall be more particularly afterwards agreed and declared in this Petition and Advice) once in three years at furthest, or oftener, as the affairs of the nations shall require....

3. That...those persons who are legally chosen by a free election of the people to serve in Parliament may not be excluded from sitting in Parliament to do their duties, but by judgement and consent of that House whereof they are members.

4. That those who have advised, assisted or abetted the Rebellion of Ireland, and those who do or shall profess the Popish religion, be disabled and made incapable for ever to be elected or to give any vote in the election of any Member to sit and serve in Parliament;...[also] all and every person and persons who have aided, abetted, advised or assisted in any war against the Parliament since the first day of January

1641[–2] (unless he or they have since borne arms for the Parliament or your Highness, or otherwise given signal testimony of his or their good affection to the Commonwealth, and continued faithful to the same), and all such as have been actually engaged in any plot, conspiracy or design against the person of your Highness, or in any insurrection or rebellion in England or Wales since the 16th day of December 1653....

* * * * * *

And that the persons who shall be elected to serve in Parliament be such, and no other than such as are persons of known integrity, fearing God, and of good conversation, and being of the age of twenty-one years, and not such as are...in Holy Orders,... ministers, or public preachers of the Gospel. Nor such as are guilty of any of the offences mentioned in an Act of Parliament bearing date the 9th of August 1650 entitled, an Act against several atheistical, blasphemous and execrable opinions derogatory to the honour of God and destructive to human society, no common scoffer nor reviler or religion, or of any person or persons for possessing thereof, no person that hath married or shall marry a wife of the Popish religion, or hath trained or shall train up his child or children, or any other child or children under his tuition or government, in the Popish religion, or that shall permit or suffer such child or children to be trained up in the said religion, or that hath given or shall give his consent that his son or daughter shall marry any of that religion, no person that shall deny the Scriptures to be the Word of God, or the Sacraments, prayer, magistracy and ministry to be of the Ordinances of God, no common profaner of the Lord's Day, no profane swearer or cursers, no drunkard or common haunter of taverns or alehouses.

[Commissioners were instituted to scrutinise returns and inform Parliament if men so disqualified were elected. Elaborate precautions were taken to control these commissioners, but in the *Additional Petition and Advice*[1] the whole clause was repealed and a fine of £1,000 was merely imposed on offenders.]

* * * * * *

5. That your Highness will consent that none be called to sit and vote in the Other House but such as are not disabled...in the former article, being such as shall be nominated by your Highness and approved

[1] Firth and Rait, II, 1183–4.

by this House,[1] and that they exceed not seventy in number, nor be under the number of forty (whereof the quorum to be one and twenty) who shall not give any vote by proxies; and that as any of them do die, or be legally removed, no new ones be admitted to sit and vote in their rooms but by consent of the House itself.[2]

That the Other House do not proceed in any civil causes, except in writs of error, in cases adjourned from inferior courts into the Parliament for difficulty, in cases of petition against proceedings in courts of equity, and in cases of the privileges of their own House. That they do not proceed in any criminal causes whatsoever, against any person criminally, but upon an impeachment of the Commons assembled in Parliament, and by their consent. That they do not proceed in any cause, either civil or criminal, but according to the known laws of the land, and the due course and custom of Parliament. That no final determinations or judgements be by any Members of that House, in any cause there depending either civil, criminal or mixed, as commissioners or delegates, to be nominated by that House; but all such final determinations and judgements to be by the House itself, any law or usage to the contrary notwithstanding.

6. That in all other particulars which concern the calling and holding of parliaments, your Highness will be pleased that the laws and statutes of the land be observed and kept, and that no laws be altered, suspended, abrogated or repealed, or new law made, but by Act of Parliament.

7. And to the end that there may be a constant revenue for support of the government, and for the safety and defence of these nations by sea and land, we declare our willingness to settle forthwith a yearly revenue of £1,300,000, whereof £1,000,000 for the navy and army, and £300,000 for the support of the government, and no part thereof to be raised by a land-tax, and this not be altered without the consent of the three estates in Parliament;[3] and to grant such other temporary

---

[1] However, the *Additional Petition and Advice* authorised Cromwell to summon the members of the Other House during the next recess, and declared that at the beginning of the next session 'the persons so summoned and assembled together shall be, and are hereby declared to be the Other House of Parliament, and shall and may without further approbation of this House... proceed to do and perform all such matters and things as the other House of Parliament ought to do and perform...by the aforesaid Humble Petition and Advice...' (Firth and Rait, II, 1186).

[2] The *Additional Petition and Advice* added: 'That the nomination of the persons to supply the place of such Members of the House as shall die or be removed shall be by your Highness and your successors' (*ibid.* 1184).

[3] 'That the monies directed to be for the supply of the sea and land forces be issued by advice of the Council, and that the treasurer, or commissioners of the treasury, shall give an account of all the said money to every parliament' (*ibid.* 1184).

supplies according to the Commons assembled in Parliament shall from time to time adjudge the necessities of these nations to require; and do pray your Highness that it be enacted and declared that no charge be laid, nor person be compelled to contribute to any gift, loan, benevolence, tax, tallage, aid or any other like charge, without common consent by Act of Parliament, which is a freedom the people of these nations ought by the laws to inherit.

8. That none may be admitted to the Privy Council of your Highness or successors, but such as are of known piety and undoubted affection to the rights of these nations, and a just Christian liberty in matters of religion, nor without consent of the Council to be afterwards approved by both Houses of Parliament, and shall not afterwards be removed but by consent of Parliament, but may in the intervals of Parliament be suspended from the exercise of his place by your Highness, by your successors and the Council, for just cause; and that the number of the Council shall not be above twenty-one, whereof the quorum be seven, and not under; as also that after your Highness's death [the appointment of] the commander-in-chief under your successors of such army or armies as shall be necessary to be kept in England, Scotland or Ireland, as also all such field-officers at land, or generals at sea, which after that time shall be newly made and constituted by your successors be by consent of the Council and not otherwise. And that the standing forces of this Commonwealth shall be disposed of by the chief magistrate by the consent of both Houses of Parliament, the Parliament sitting, and in the intervals of Parliament by the chief magistrate by the advice of the Council; and also that your Highness and successors will be pleased to exercise your government over these nations by the advice of your Council.

9. And that the chancellor, keeper or commissioners of the Great Seal of England, the treasurer, or commissioners of the treasury, the admiral, the chief governor of Ireland, the chancellor, keeper or commissioners of the Great Seal of Ireland, the chief justices of both the Benches, and the chief baron in England and Ireland, the commander-in-chief of the forces in Scotland, and such officers of state there as by Act of Parliament in Scotland are to be approved by Parliament, and the judges in Scotland hereafter to be made, shall be approved by both Houses of Parliament.[1]

---

[1] The *Additional Petition and Advice* provided that in the intervals of Parliament these officers should be chosen 'by the consent of the Council, to be afterwards approved by Parliament' (*ibid.* 1184).

10. And whereas your Highness, out of your zeal to the glory of God and the propagation of the Gospel of the Lord Jesus Christ, hath been pleased to encourage a godly ministry in these nations, we earnestly desire that such as do openly revile them or their assemblies, or disturb them in the worship and service of God, to the dishonour of God, scandal of good men, or breach of the peace, may be punished according to law, and where the laws are defective, that your Highness will give consent to such laws as shall be made in that behalf.

11. That the true Protestant Christian religion, as it is contained in the Holy Scriptures of the Old and New Testament, and no other, be held forth and asserted for the public profession of these nations; and that a Confession of Faith, to be agreed by your Highness and the Parliament, according to the rule and warrant of the Scriptures, be asserted, held forth and recommended to the people of these nations, that none may be suffered or permitted by opprobrious words or writing maliciously or contemptuously to revile or reproach the Confession of Faith to be agreed upon as aforesaid. And such who profess faith in God the Father, and in Jesus Christ his eternal Son, the true God, and in the Holy Spirit, God co-equal with the Father and the Son, One God blessed for ever, and do acknowledge the Holy Scriptures of the Old and New Testament to be revealed Will and Word of God, and shall in other things differ in doctrine, worship or discipline from the public profession held forth, endeavours shall be used to convince them by sound doctrine and the example of a good conversation, but they may not be compelled thereto by penalties, nor restrained from their profession, but protected from all injury and molestation in the profession of the faith, and exercise of their religion, whilst they abuse not this liberty to the civil injury of others or the disturbance of the public peace; so that this liberty be not extended to Popery or Prelacy, or to the countenancing such who publish horrid blasphemies, or practice to hold forth licentiousness or profaneness under the profession of Christ.

And that those ministers or public preachers who shall agree with the public profession aforesaid in matters of faith, although in their judgement and practice they differ in matters of worship and discipline, shall not only have protection in the way of their churches and worship respectively, but be esteemed fit and capable, notwithstanding such difference (being otherwise duly qualified and duly approved) of any trust, promotion or employment whatsoever in these nations that any ministers who agree in doctrine, worship and discipline with the public profession aforesaid are capable of. And all others who agree with the public profession in matters of faith, although they differ in matters of worship and discipline as aforesaid, shall not only have protection as aforesaid, but be esteemed fit and capable (notwithstanding such difference, being otherwise duly qualified) of any civil trust, employment or promotion in these nations. But for such persons who agree not in matters of faith with the public profession aforesaid, they shall not be capable of receiving the public maintenance appointed for the ministry.

Provided, that this clause shall not be construed to extend to such ministers or public preachers, or pastors of congregations; but that they be disenabled to hold any civil employment which those in holy orders were or are disenabled to hold by an Act entitled, an Act for disenabling all persons in holy orders to exercise any temporal jurisdiction or authority.

And that your Highness will give your consent that all laws, statutes, ordinances, and clauses in any law, statute and ordinance, so far as they are contrary to the aforesaid liberty, be repealed.

[12. Reconfirmed the financial obligations of the Long Parliament, the sale of lands and the abolition of episcopacy, etc.

13. Those excluded from Parliament by § 4 above are also excluded from public service.]

14. And that your Highness will be pleased to consent that nothing in this Petition and Advice contained, nor your Highness's assent thereto, shall be construed to extend to the dissolving of this present Parliament....

15.[1] And that nothing contained in this Petition and Advice, nor your Highness's consent thereunto, shall be construed to extend to the repealing or making void of any Act or Ordinance which is not contrary hereunto, or to the matters herein contained....

[16. Confirmed the validity of all existing writs, indictments, etc., and the efficacy of the actions started by them.]

17. And that your Highness and your successors will be pleased to take an oath in such a form as shall be agreed upon by your Highness and this present Parliament.[2]

---

[1] This and the following clauses are misnumbered in the original, 16, 17, etc.
[2] This was set out in the *Additional Petition and Advice* (Firth and Rait, II, 1185).

And in case your Highness shall not be satisfied to give your consent to all the matters and things in this Humble Petition and Advice, that then nothing in the same be deemed of force to oblige the people of these nations in any particulars therein contained.

*   *   *   *   *   *

Firth and Rait, II, 1048–56

97. The Declaration of Breda, 1660

Charles, by the Grace of God, King of England, Scotland, France and Ireland, Defender of the Faith, &c., to all our loving subjects, of what degree or quality soever, greeting. If the general distraction and confusion which is spread over the whole kingdom doth not awaken all men to a desire and longing that those wounds which have so many years together been kept bleeding may be bound up, all we can say will be to no purpose. However, after this long silence we have thought it our duty to declare how much we desire to contribute thereunto, and that, as we can never give over the hope in good time to obtain the possession of that right which God and Nature hath made our due, so we do make it our daily suit to the Divine Providence that he will, in compassion to us and our subjects, after so long misery and sufferings, remit and put us into a quiet and peaceable possession of that our right, with as little blood and damage to our people as is possible. Nor do we desire more to enjoy what is ours, than that all our subjects may enjoy what by law is theirs, by a full and entire administration of justice throughout the land, and by extending our mercy where it is wanted and deserved.

And to the end that the fear of punishment may not engage any, conscious to themselves of what is passed, to a perseverance in guilt for the future, by opposing the quiet and happiness of their country in the restoration both of king, peers and people to their just, ancient and fundamental rights, we do by these presents declare, that we do grant a free and general pardon, which we are ready upon demand to pass under our Great Seal of England, to all our subjects, of what degree or quality soever, who within forty days after the publishing hereof shall lay hold upon this our grace and favour, and shall by any public act declare their doing so, and that they return to the loyalty and obedience of good subjects (excepting only such persons as shall hereafter be excepted by Parliament). Those only excepted, let all our loving subjects, how faulty soever, rely upon the word of a king, solemnly given by this present Declaration, that no crime whatsoever committed against us or our royal father before the publication of this shall ever rise in judgement or be brought in question against any of them, to the least endamagement of them either in their lives, liberties or estates, or (as far forth as lies in our power) so much as to the prejudice of their reputations by any reproach or term of distinction from the rest of our best subjects, we desiring and ordaining that henceforward all notes of discord, separation and difference of parties be utterly abolished among all our subjects, whom we invite and conjure to a perfect union among themselves, under our protection, for the resettlement of our just rights and theirs in a free Parliament, by which, upon the word of a king, we will be advised.

And because the passion and uncharitableness of the times have produced several opinions in religion, by which men are engaged in parties and animosities against each other, which, when they shall hereafter unite in a freedom of conversation, will be composed and better understood, we do declare a liberty to tender consciences, and that no man shall be disquieted or called in question for differences of opinion in matter of religion which do not disturb the peace of the kingdom; and that we shall be ready to consent to such an act of parliament as, upon mature deliberation, shall be offered to us, for the full granting that indulgence.

And because, in the continued distractions of so many years and so many and great revolutions, many grants and purchases of estates have been made, to and by many officers, soldiers and others, who are now possessed of the same, and who may be liable to actions at law upon several titles, we are likewise willing that all such differences, and all things relating to such grants, sales and purchases, shall be determined in Parliament, which can best provide for the just satisfaction of all men who are concerned.

And we do further declare, that we will be ready to consent to any Act or Acts of parliament to the purposes aforesaid, and for the full satisfaction of all arrears due to the officers and soldiers of the army under the command of General Monck, and that they shall be received into our service upon as good pay and conditions as they now enjoy.

Given under our Sign Manual and Privy Signet, at our Court at Breda, this 4/14 day of April, 1660, in the twelfth year of our reign.

LJ, XI, 7–8

BOOK III

THE RESTORED CONSTITUTION

A constitution cannot make itself; somebody made it, not at once but at several times. It is alterable, and by that draweth nearer perfection; and without suiting itself to differing times and circumstances, it could not live.

HALIFAX

CHAPTER 10

THE RESTORATION SETTLEMENT

The Restoration Settlement was based on the undertakings given in the Declaration of Breda, and on the legislation of 1641 and 1642 to which Charles I had given his assent. Only two of these statutes were repealed: the Act of 1642 excluding bishops from the House of Lords,[1] and the Triennial Act, which was hastily repealed in 1664 on the mistaken ground that it might oblige Charles to dissolve his present parliament.[2] It was replaced by a simple declaratory Act, which obliged the king to meet parliament every three years, but provided no machinery of compulsion (**104**). It is worth noting that Charles II did not infringe this Act until March 1684, James II not until November 1688.

Very little of the legislation of 1660-2 was designed to strengthen or protect the executive. The Act for the Preservation of the King's Person and Government[3] confirmed the existing law of treason and imposed penalties on those who declared the king to be a Papist, or who upheld the jurisdiction and authority of the Long Parliament. Another Act of 1661, forbidding the submission of petitions to the king or to Parliament by more than ten persons, was obviously framed with the events of 1641 in mind.[4] Also, the dispute which had led to the outbreak of civil war was finally settled by the Militia Act of 1661 (**100**), which unequivocally vested the command of the armed forces in the king. On the other hand, the Convention Parliament of 1660 completed the work of reform which the Long Parliament had abandoned in the autumn of 1641 by abolishing purveyance and feudal tenures in return for a grant in perpetuity of a portion of the excise.[5]

Meanwhile the implementation of the Declaration of Breda did not prove easy. By a prodigious burst of taxation in 1660 and 1661 the greater part of the army and navy was demobilised with full arrears of pay, and a serious and successful effort was made to absorb the veterans into civilian society.[6]

---

[1] By 13 Car. II, c. 12 (*SR*, v, 306).

[2] Caroline Robbins, 'The Repeal of the Triennial Act in 1664', *Huntington Library Quarterly*, xII (1948), 121. It should be noted that the Acts of 1641 and 1664, unlike the Act of 1695, did not lay down any maximum period for a Parliament, so long as the king met it at least once in three years.   [3] 13 Car. II, st. 1, c. 1, printed Browning, *Documents*, p. 63.

[4] *Ibid.* p. 66. The preamble to the Act reversing Strafford's attainder (*SR*, v, 424) makes the same point.

[5] 12 Car. II, c. 24. The important sections are printed by Costin and Watson, I, 2–5. See p. 192 above.

[6] For instance, Parliament at last passed an Act for which the army had agitated since 1647, obliging corporations to waive or modify apprenticeship rules for veterans (12 Car. II, c. 16; *SR*, v, 237).

Charles also fulfilled in a handsome manner his promise of a full indemnity and oblivion. The Act of Indemnity and Oblivion is a remarkable document (98); with the exception of those who had signed Charles I's death warrant or officiated at his execution, plus a few particularly obnoxious individuals, like Vane, Lambert and Haslerigg, everyone received a full pardon, and all process of revenge or retribution was halted. More remarkable still, for three years penalties were imposed for reflecting, by speech or writing, on any man's conduct during the past twenty years.

But the government's approach to the land question was tentative and hesitant, as well it might be. The wholesale confiscation and sale of lands during the Interregnum had created a tangled situation, and at Breda Charles had promised to recognise existing titles to lands, however they had been acquired. He and his lord chancellor, Edward Hyde, earl of Clarendon, finally decided that they must distinguish between those whose land had been forcibly confiscated and sold, and those who had sold it voluntarily, even to pay delinquency fines. The latter must suffer, because any other course would impugn the validity of legal proceedings during the Interregnum, with chaotic results. But the government was not anxious to publicise its decision. By reversing all treasons and attainders since 1642, and proceedings on them, the Act of Oblivion, § II (98) freed the estates of royalists proscribed by the Long Parliament, but those seeking further enlightenment had to read through to § XLVIII, which declared that those who had purchased estates not formerly belonging to the Crown or the Church and not sold by order of one of the Interregnum governments, had a sound title. Similarly, § X of the Act confirming Judicial Proceedings (99) again safeguarded the lands of Crown and Church, but § VI specifically excluded all other land sales from its scope. This left the legal position so uncertain that many prominent royalists, particularly those who had fled abroad during the Interregnum, secured private Acts of parliament for the recovery of their estates. Though there was some grumbling, of course, it never came to a head, or looked like doing so, and modern research has tended to invalidate the former assumption that large amounts of land changed hands permanently during the Interregnum and that this caused a serious displacement in the land-owning classes. Very few new landed families appeared in the reign of Charles II whose rise can be attributed to the purchase of delinquents' lands, and very few disappeared because they had had to dispose of their estates.[1]

Charles II's final undertaking in the Declaration of Breda, that he would

---

[1] The old view is trenchantly put by H. E. Chesney, 'The Transference of Land in England, 1640–60', *Transactions Royal Historical Society*, 4th ser., xv (1933), 181; but see Joan Thirsk, 'The Sale of Royalist Land during the Interregnum', *Economic History Review*, 2nd ser., v (1952), 188, and 'The Restoration Land Settlement', *Journal of Modern History*, xxv (1945), 315; also Brunton and Pennington, *Members of the Long Parliament*, pp. 183–4, and Hardacre, *The Royalists during the Puritan Revolution*, ch. VIII.

give his assent to any legislation that offered a measure of religious toleration, was never implemented, because no such legislation was ever presented. The position of the Puritans, apparently so strong even in 1660, rapidly crumbled. The great mass of sectarians or congregationalists were members of the lower classes, divided amongst themselves and regarded with aversion by both sides. The upper-class Presbyterian ministers were deluded by hopes of comprehension—bishoprics were offered to the more prominent among them, and Stephen Reynolds accepted—and betrayed by prominent laymen like Monk and Montague, on whom they relied. The Convention Parliament, which contained a powerful 'Presbyterian' element in Lords and Commons, and was without the bishops,[1] was skilfully prevented from legislating on religious matters by the promise of a national synod to decide the future of the Church. The Fifth Monarchy uprising in London in January 1661 compromised all Dissent, however respectable and law-abiding, and the elections in March and April 1661 returned a Parliament opposed to any compromise. One of their first Acts sent the bishops back to the House of Lords, and they then busied themselves with a stringent Uniformity bill. They were restrained from further action during their first session, however, by the need to await the close of the Savoy Conference between the bishops and the leading Dissenting ministers.[2] The failure of this conference gave the persecutors their head, and in November 1661 they produced the Corporation Act, which excluded from the government or management of borough corporations those who would not take the Anglican sacrament and the oaths of allegiance and supremacy, and make two solemn declarations, one abjuring or rejecting the Solemn League and Covenant, the other declaring that it was in no circumstances lawful to take up arms against the king—the famous 'Non-Resistance Oath' (102). For three years the Act was to be administered by Crown commissioners, who had the power to remove officials from corporations without even tendering the oaths to them. Secondly, in May 1662 a new Uniformity Act (103) laid it down that all those in holy orders, with or without cure of souls, must take all the oaths and declarations imposed on members of corporations, and a declaration of their 'unfeigned acceptance' of the Book of Common Prayer. Those who failed to comply by the Feast of St Bartholomew (24 August 1662) were removed, and patrons could present to their livings as if they were legally dead. Finally, an Act of 1663 compelled vestrymen to take the non-resistance oath and an oath 'to conform to the liturgy of the Church of England as it is now by law established'.[3]

[1] L. F. Brown, 'Religious Factors in the Convention Parliament', *EHR*, XXII (1907), 51, and G. F. Trevallyn Jones, 'The Composition and Leadership of the Presbyterian Party in the Convention', *ibid.* LXXIX (1964), 307.

[2] E. C. Ratliff, 'The Savoy Conference and the Revision of the Book of Common Prayer', in Nuttall and Chadwick, pp. 89 ff.

[3] 15 Car. II, c. 5, 'An Act for Regulating Select Vestries', *SR*, v, 446-7.

There is still room for argument between those who believe that this reactionary Church settlement was planned with Machiavellian cunning from the beginning and those who hold that Charles's government merely drifted with the tide. Others are convinced that Clarendon, in particular, had to accept a less tolerant solution than he had originally contemplated.[1] What is certain is that the Church as re-established would have pleased John Pym more than William Laud. This was evident in the first session of 1661, when the House of Commons firmly resisted an attempt on the part of the bishops to revive the High Commission. Moreover, though it agreed to repeal those parts of the Act of 1641 that might be said to impugn the bishops' powers to hold their ordinary ecclesiastical courts, Parliament expressly stated that the clause of the Act of Supremacy which was held to authorise the High Commission was still repealed, and it again forbade, rather neurotically, the administration of the *ex officio* oath. Finally, in the same statute it settled an old quarrel by declining to authorise the canons of 1640, or any other canons promulgated without its approval (**101**).

It was thus decided that Parliament would exercise a censorship on the discipline of the Church, and the Uniformity Act at the same time confirmed its right, established a century earlier, to lay down forms of public worship and impose qualifications on clergymen. In 1664 a private agreement between Clarendon and Archbishop Sheldon ended the clergy's right to tax themselves separately in Convocation; as a result Convocation did not meet again until 1689. Clarendon's attempt to use the Corporation Act as a means to increase the power of the government over parliamentary corporations in the name of religious orthodoxy was handsomely defeated,[2] and so, too, was the king's attempt to secure a measure of toleration for Catholics and Dissenters.[3]

The Restoration Settlement could not help but damage the Church. For the first time it was admitted that she did not command a monopoly of all Protestant believers in England, and whereas Laud had always endeavoured to coerce the Puritans into conformity and obedience, Sheldon simply rejected them. The Uniformity Act of 1662 was far from producing uniformity, and the Conventicle Act of 1664, which forbade meetings held 'under colour or pretence of any exercise of religion' of five or more persons not members of the same household, accepted the existence of a separate Protestant community. This Act expired in 1668, and though it was re-enacted in 1670 in an amended form (**105**) the effect of the two-year intermission was disastrous; so, too, was the shorter intermission imposed by the

---

[1] The chief exponent of the 'planned *coup*' theory is Bosher, *The Making of the Restoration Settlement*. His views have been criticised by George R. Abernethy, 'Clarendon and the Declaration of Indulgence', *Journal of Ecclesiastical History*, XI (1960), 55. The best survey of the whole question is by Anne Whiteman in Nuttall and Chadwick, pp. 19 ff.

[2] J. H. Sacret, 'The Restoration Government and the Municipal Corporations', *EHR*, XLV (1933), 232.

[3] See p. 401 below.

Declaration of Indulgence in 1672. The Elizabethan Acts enforcing attendance at church services, directed against Papists, were inadequate, and it proved particularly difficult to deal with ministers ejected by the Uniformity Act. By the Five Mile Act of 1665[1] such ministers, and other unlicensed preachers, were forbidden to come within five miles of the parish where they had been incumbent or of any city or town.

However, as fear of Rome mounted again in the late 'sixties and early 'seventies, so did the desire for the reunion of the Protestant community. § x of the Conventicles Act of 1670 (105) is a public admission of what was generally known, that many constables and even some magistrates were making little effort to enforce the Clarendon Code.[2] During the Exclusion Crisis the Opposition called for the repeal of this legislation, with the result that in the subsequent reaction beginning in 1681, a serious attempt was made to enforce it, perhaps for the first time, and especially against the Quakers, whose refusal to take an oath was regarded as deeply subversive. This left it open for James II, with what sincerity it is impossible to say, to appeal for the support of the Dissenters in his Declaration of Indulgence in 1687.[3] The apparent ability of a Catholic king to split the Protestant nation confirmed the worst fears of those Anglicans who had been arguing ever since 1662 for comprehension and even toleration.[4] The result was the comprehension proposals of 1689 and the Toleration Act, which were foreshadowed even in the Petition of the Seven Bishops in June 1688.[5]

98. 12 Car. II, c. 11: An Act of free and general pardon, indemnity and oblivion (1660)

The King's most excellent Majesty, taking into his gracious and serious consideration the long and great troubles, discords and wars that have for many years past been in this kingdom, and that divers of his subjects are by occasion thereof and otherwise fallen into and be obnoxious to great pains and penalties, out of a hearty and pious desire to put an end to all suits and controversies that by occasion of the late distractions have arisen and may arise between all his subjects, and to the intent that no crime whatsoever committed against his Majesty or his Royal Father shall hereafter rise in judgement or be brought in question against any of them to the least endamagement of them either in their lives, liber-

---

[1] Browning, *English Historical Documents*, p. 382.
[2] See also the remarks of Sir Peter Leicester, no. **131**, p. 464 below.
[3] No. **115**, p. 410 below. The latest discussion of James's motives is by Maurice Ashley, in *Historical Essays, 1600–1750*, ed. H. E. Bell and R. L. Ollard (1963), pp. 185 ff.
[4] Sykes, *From Sheldon to Secker*; Roger Thomas, 'Comprehension and Indulgence', in Nuttall and Chadwick.
[5] Thomas, *loc. cit.*; Every, *High Church Party*, pp. 22–3, 41–2.

ties, estates or to the prejudice of their reputations by any reproach or term of distinction, and to bury all seeds of future discords and remembrance of the former, as well in his own breast as in the breasts of his subjects one towards another, and his performance of his royal and gracious word signified by his letters to the several Houses of Parliament now assembled, and his declarations in that behalf published, is pleased that it may be enacted, and be it enacted by the King's most excellent Majesty with the advice and consent of the Lords and Commons in this present parliament assembled, first that all and all manner of treasons, misprisions of treason, murders, felonies, offences, crimes, contempts and misdemeanours counselled, commanded, acted or done since the first day of January in the year of Our Lord 1637[-8] by any person or persons before the twenty-fourth day of June in the year of Our Lord 1660 (other than the persons hereafter by name excepted, in such manner as they are hereafter excepted) by virtue or colour of any command, power, authority, commission, warrant or instructions from his late Majesty King Charles or his Majesty that now is, or from any other person or persons deriving or pretending to derive authority mediately or immediately from both or either of their Majesties, or by virtue or colour of any authority derived mediately or immediately of or from both Houses or either House of Parliament, or of or from any convention or assembly called or reputed or taking on them the name of a Parliament, or by, from or under any authority styled or known by the name of The Keepers of the Liberty of England by Authority of Parliament, or by virtue or colour of any writ, commission, letters patents, instruction or instructions of or from any person or persons titled, reputed or taken to be Lord Protector of the Commonwealth of England, Scotland and Ireland..., or assuming the authority or reputed to be Chief Magistrate of the Commonwealth, or Commander in Chief of the Forces or Armies of this nation by sea or land, or by any pretended warrant or command whatsoever from them or any of them, or their or either of their respective councils or council, or any members of such council or councils, or from any person or persons whatsoever deriving or pretending to derive authority from them or any of them, be pardoned, released, indemnified, discharged and put in utter oblivion.

II. And that all and every the person and persons acting, advising, assisting, abetting and counselling the same, they, their heirs, executors and administrators (except as before is excepted) be and are hereby

366

pardoned, released, acquitted, indemnified and discharged from the same, and of and from all pains of death and other pains, judgements, indictments, convictions, attainders, outlawries, penalties, escheats and forfeitures therefore had or given, or that might accrue for the same, and that all such judgements...[etc.], and all grants thereupon made, and all estates derived under the same, be...from henceforth null and void, and that all mesne profits not yet received by such grantees shall be and are here hereby discharged; and that all and every person and persons, bodies politic and corporate, their and every of their heirs, executors, administrators and successors shall be and are hereby restored to all and every their lands, tenements and hereditaments, goods, chattels and other things forfeited, which to his Majesty do or shall appertain by reason of any offence herein before mentioned, and not hereafter in this present Act excepted and foreprised.

*   *   *   *   *   *

v. And it is further by the authority aforesaid enacted in the second place that all and every the subject of these his Majesty's realms of England and Ireland, the dominion of Wales, the Isles of Jersey and Guernsey and the town of Berwick upon Tweed, and other his Majesty's dominions, the heirs, executors and administrators of them and every of them, and all and singular bodies in any manner or wise corporated, cities, boroughs, shires, ridings, hundreds, lathes, rapes, wapentakes, towns, villages, hamlets and tithings and every of them, and the successors and successor of every of them, shall be and are by the authority of this present Parliament acquitted, pardoned, released, indemnified and discharged against the King's Majesty, his heirs and successors and every of them, of and from all manner of treasons, misprisions of treason, felonies, offences, contempts, trespasses, entries, wrongs, deceits, misdemeanours, forfeitures, penalties and sums of money, intrusions, mesne profits, wardships, marriages, reliefs, liveries, ouster le maines, mesne rates, respites of homage, fines and seizures for alienation without licence, arrearages of rents (other than the arrearages of rents due from the late farmers or pretended farmers of the excise or customs...), and of and from all arrearages of tenths and first-fruits, fines, post-fines, issues and amercements, and all recognisances, bonds or other securities given for payment of them or any of them, concealments of customs and excise, arrearages of purveyance and of compositions for the same, and of and from all pains of death, pains corporal and pecuniary, and generally of and from all other things, causes, quarrels, suits, judgements and executions in this present Act hereafter not excepted nor foreprised which may be or can be by his Majesty in any wise or by any means pardoned before and unto...24 June 1660, to every or any of his said subjects, bodies corporate, cities, boroughs, shires, ridings,...[etc.].

*   *   *   *   *   *

XXIII. And be it further enacted by the authority aforesaid that all acts of hostility and injuries, whether between the late King and the Lords and Commons then in Parliament assembled, or between any of the people of this nation, which did arise upon any action, attempt, assistance, counsel or advice having relation unto or falling out by reason of the late troubles or in the late wars and public differences between the late King and Parliament or between his now Majesty or any of his subjects, and which are not in this Act excepted, that the same and whatsoever hath ensued thereupon, whether trenching upon the laws and liberties of this nation or upon the honour of his Majesty, or upon the honour or authority of the Parliament, or to the prejudice of any particular or private person, shall in no time from and after... 24 June 1660 be called in question, whatsoever be the quality of the person, or of whatsoever kind or degree, civil or criminal, the injury is supposed to be, and that no mention be made thereof in time to come in judgement or judicial proceedings.

XXIV. And to the intent and purpose that all names and terms of distinction may likewise be put into utter oblivion, be it further enacted by the authority aforesaid that if any person or persons within the space of three years next ensuing shall presume maliciously to call or allege of, or object against any other person or persons, any name or names, or other word of reproach anyway tending to revive the memory of the late differences or the occasions thereof, that then every such person so as aforesaid offending shall forfeit and pay unto the party grieved, in case such party offending shall be of the degree of gentleman or above, ten pounds, and if under that degree, forty shillings, to be recovered by the party grieved by action of debt to be therefore brought in any of his Majesty's Courts of Record....

X.[1] Except and always foreprised out of this free and general pardon ...[murder or piracy unconnected with the late wars, buggery, rape,

---

[1] The order of the clauses has been rearranged in the interests of clarity.

forced marriage, bigamy, and witchcraft]; and also excepted all and singular the accounts of all and every person and persons appointed by any of the authorities or pretended authorities aforesaid to be treasurer, receiver, farmer or collector (other than the subcollectors of the several parishes, towns and hamlets... [before 24 June 1659]) who have received or collected any subsidy, custom, subsidy of tunnage and poundage, prize-goods, assessment, sequestration, new impost or excise, or any of the rents and revenues of any land or hereditaments of or belonging to the late King, Queen or Prince or King that now is, or belonging to the late archbishoprics, bishoprics, deans or deans and chapters, canons, prebends and other officers belonging to any cathedral or collegiate church, or Popish recusants convict, or of persons sequestered for their recusancy, or other sequestered estates received or collected by or paid unto them since... 30 January 1643, and of all monies and other duties grown due or contracted upon the sale or disposition of them or any of them.[1]

*   *   *   *   *   *

xxix. And be it further enacted by the authority aforesaid that no person or persons who by virtue of any order or warrant mediately or immediately derived from his late Majesty or his Majesty that now is, or by virtue of any act, ordinance or order of any or both Houses of Parliament, or any of the authorities aforesaid, or any committee or committees acting under them or any of them, have seized, sequestered, levied, advanced or paid to any public use or into any public treasury within this kingdom any goods, chattels, debts, rents, sum or sums of money belonging to any person or persons whatsoever shall hereafter be sued, molested or drawn into question for the same, but that they and every of them shall be discharged against all persons for so much and no more of the said goods, chattels, debts, rents, sum or sums of money as their several and respective orders of discharge or acquittances extend unto.

*   *   *   *   *   *

xlviii. Provided always... that no conveyance, assurance, grant, bargain, sale, charge, lease, assignment of lease, grants and surrenders by copy of court roll, estate, interest, trust or limitation of any use or

---

[1] But no proceedings could be taken under this clause after 24 June 1662 (§ xiv), and military and naval officers could not be called to account for the pay or allowances or subsistence of their men (§ xiii).

uses of any manors, lands, tenements or hereditaments, not being the land nor hereditaments of the late King, Queen, Prince or of any archbishops, bishops, deans, deans and chapters, nor being land or hereditaments sold or given or appointed to be sold or given for the delinquency or pretended delinquency of any person or persons whatsoever by virtue or pretext of any Act, Order or Ordinance, or reputed Act, Order or Ordinance, since...1 January 1642, nor any statute, judgement, or recognisance had, made, acknowledged or suffered to any person or persons, bodies politic or corporate before...29 September 1659 by any of the persons before in this Act by name excepted or their heirs..., nor any conveyance, assurance, grant or estate made before 25 April 1660 by any person or persons to any such person or persons excepted by name as aforesaid, in trust and for the benefit of any other person or persons, bodies politic or corporate not excepted by name as aforesaid, shall be impeached, defeated, made void, or frustrated hereby, or by the attainder or conviction of any such excepted person or persons, but that the same shall be held and enjoyed by the purchasers, grantees, lessees, assignees, *cestuy que use*, *cestuy que trust*, and every of them their heirs, executors, administrators and assigns respectively, as if this Act had not been made, and as if the said person or persons had not been excepted, attainted or convicted, any law, statute, usage or custom to the contrary thereof in any wise notwithstanding.

* * * * * *

[The statute was full of exceptions, though in total the number of men involved was few and their importance slight.

It was natural that those guilty of bribery, forgery, perjury and subornation of witnesses should be excepted (§ xv), and Roman Catholic priests and Jesuits (xviii), and those committing thefts and felonies since 4 March 1660 (xxvii). Charles also took care to make his own servants responsible for money collected on his behalf since his accession in 1649 (xxx) and for traitorous correspondence with foreign powers over the same period (xxxii).

The general moratorium on debts and receipts also had many exceptions. The proceeds of the Decimation Tax of 1655–6 could be recovered (xxxi), and so could the ancient rents collected by sheriffs (xvii), and tithes (xliv). The proceeds of the excise since 1658, and debts against the excise since 1657, were accountable for (xxxiii, xlvi), as were sums owed by the army for billeting since 2 July 1659 (xlvii). Charles also gave himself the power to proceed against those who had stolen or confiscated the goods and chattels of the Royal Family, except munitions and stores, at any time since 1642 (xvi).

But the most important exceptions were penal. The only general category of men excepted were those responsible for the Irish Rebellion of 1641, which still generated more heat than any other single incident in the past twenty years (xxv), and even those responsible for trying, sentencing or executing Charles I were listed by name in so far as they were known (xxxiv). Cromwell, Ireton and John Bradshaw were excepted entirely out of the Act (xxxvi), as were the other regicides who had died (xxxvii), and John Lambert and Sir Henry Vane (xli). Six men whose conduct in January 1649 was doubtful (xxxviii) and Sir Arthur Haslerigg (xxxxi) were excepted, but with the proviso that they should not be subject to the death penalty. In addition a number of men who were not regicides but who were regarded as particularly dangerous, such as Lenthall, Speaker of the Long Parliament, Oliver St John, Henry Ireton's brother John, Fleetwood, Desborough, Cobbet and several other army officers, were forbidden to take office under the government or any public employment under pain of exclusion from the benefits of the Act (xlii).] SR, v, 226–34

99. 12 Car. II, c. 12: An Act for confirmation of judicial proceedings (1660)

Be it enacted and it is enacted by his Majesty and the Lords and Commons in Parliament assembled and by the authority of the same, that no fines, nor final concords, chirographs nor proclamations of fines, nor any recoveries, verdicts, judgements, statutes, recognisances nor enrolments of any deed or wills or of any such fines, proclamations, recoveries, verdicts, judgements, statutes, or recognisances, nor any exemplifications of them nor any of them, nor any inquisitions, indictments, presentments, informations, decrees, sentences, probates of will, nor letters of administration, nor any writs nor actings on, nor returns of writs, orders or other proceedings in law and equity, had, made, given, taken or done or depending in the Courts of Chancery, King's Bench, Upper Bench, Common Pleas and Court of Exchequer and Courts of Exchequer Chamber or any of them, sitting at Westminster or in the Courts of the Great Sessions in Wales, the Courts of any Counties Palatine or Duchy of Lancaster or town of Berwick-upon-Tweed, or in any other inferior courts of law or equity, or by any the judges, clerks, officers, sheriffs, coroners or ministers or others acting in obedience to them or any of them, or by any the Courts of Admiralty, Delegates, Justices of Assize, Nisi Prius, Oyer and Terminer, Gaol Delivery, Justices of the Peace, Commissioners of Sewers, Bankrupts or Charitable Uses, nor any actings, process, proceedings, nor executions thereupon had, made, given, done or suffered in the kingdom of England since the first of May 1642 shall be avoided for any want or defect of any legal power in the said courts, judges, commissioners, justices or any of them, or for or by reason that the premisses or any of them were commenced, prosecuted, had, made, held or used in the name, style or title of the late King, or in the name, style, title or test of *custodes libertatis angliae authoritate parliamenti*, or...of the Keepers of the Liberties of England, or...of Oliver, Lord Protector..., or...of Richard, Lord Protector..., or for or by reason of any alteration of the said names, styles or titles, or for that the said fines, recoveries, process, pleadings, proceedings and other things before mentioned, or the entry and enrolment of them or any of them were in the Latin or English tongue; but that all and every such fines, recoveries and other things above mentioned, and the actings, doings and proceedings thereupon, shall be of such and of no other force, effect and virtue than as of such courts, judges...[etc.] had acted by virtue of a true, just and legal authority, and as if the same and the entry and enrolment thereof were in Latin, and as if the several Acts and Ordinances or pretended Acts or Ordinances made by both or either Houses of Parliament, or any Convention assembled under the name of a Parliament, or by Oliver Cromwell...and his Council warranting or directing such proceedings had been good, true and effectual Acts of Parliament.

* * * * * *

v. And whereas since the first day of May 1641, and before the five and twentieth day of April 1660, there were divers persons that adhered to both Houses of Parliament who for or in respect of such their adherence were indicted, charged or impeached of treason; and whereas ...[during the same period] divers persons who adhered to his Majesty or to the late King were for such their allegiance charged, impeached or indicted of high treason, be it further provided and enacted that the said charges, impeachments, indictments, and all exigents, outlawries, convictions and attainders thereupon, and all letters patents and grants thereupon made of any manors, lands, tenements or hereditaments escheated or forfeited by reason of such attainder, and all title to any mesne profits by reason of such conviction, outlawry, attainder or grant be from henceforth repealed and discharged, and that all escheats, forfeitures and confiscations by reason of such outlawries, conviction or attainder be and are hereby restored unto such persons so outlawed, convicted or attainted, their heirs, executors and administrators respectively, as if no such attainder had been.

VI. Provided nevertheless...that this Act or anything herein contained shall not extend to avoid or confirm any sales of estates made by virtue of any Act, Order or Ordinance, or reputed Act, Order or Ordinance of Parliament since the first day of May 1642, nor any confirmation thereof made, or to be made thereof in this present parliament, but that such sales stand and be in the same plight and condition as they should or might have done if this Act had not been made.

*　*　*　*　*　*

X. Provided always...that no non-claim upon or after any fine or fines hereby made good or confirmed shall extend or be construed to bar or prejudice any person or persons, their heirs or successors, or their feoffees or trustees...as concerning such right, claim and interest as they had in or to any land, tenements or other hereditaments which by colour of any Act, Order or Ordinance of both or either Houses of Parliament or any Convention sitting at Westminster under the name or style or assuming the name or style of a parliament since...1 May 1642 and before...25 April 1660, were sold, conveyed or disposed [of, such] as then or late the land, tenements and hereditaments of the King, Queen or Prince, or of archbishops, bishops, deans, deans and chapters, or other ecclesiastical persons, or [such] as the lands, tenements and hereditaments of any other persons for their adherency to the late King or his Majesty that now is, or for any their actings relating to or in respect of the late Troubles, so always that the said person or persons aforesaid, their heirs or successors, pursue their title, claim or interest by way of action of lawful entry within five years next after...29 May 1660.

XI. And although in this confirmation of Judicial Proceedings it was necessary to mention divers pretended Acts and Ordinances by the names and styles which those persons then usurped...took upon them to pass the same,...yet this present Parliament doth declare, and it is enacted by authority of the same, that the names and styles aforesaid and every of them are most rebellious, wicked, traitorous and abominable usurpations, detested by this present Parliament as opposite in the highest degree to his sacred Majesty's most just and undoubted right, to whom and to his heirs and lawful successors the imperial crowns of the realms of England, Scotland and Ireland, with their and every of their dominions and territories, do of right appertain, and as violating and infringing the just rights and privileges of Parliament and of both Houses thereof now assembled, or that hereafter shall be called and assembled.

SR, v, 234-6

100. 13 Car. II, c. 6: An Act declaring the sole right of the militia to be in the King (1661)

Forasmuch as within all his Majesty's realms and dominions the sole supreme government, command and disposition of the militia and of all forces by sea and land and of all forts and places of strength is and by the laws of England ever was the undoubted right of his Majesty and his royal predecessors, Kings and Queens of England, and that both or either of the Houses of Parliament cannot nor ought to pretend to the same, nor can nor lawfully may raise or levy any war, offensive or defensive, against his Majesty, his heirs or lawful successors, and yet the contrary thereof hath of late years been practised, almost to the ruin and destruction of this kingdom, and during the late usurped governments many evil and rebellious principles have been distilled into the minds of the people of this kingdom, which unless prevented may break forth, to the disturbance of the peace and quiet thereof; and whereas an Act is under consideration for exercising the militia with most safety and ease to the King and his people,[1] which Act cannot as yet be perfected, be it therefore enacted by the King's most excellent Majesty, by and with the advice and consent of the Lords and Commons assembled in Parliament, that the militia and land forces of this kingdom, and of the dominion of Wales and town of Berwick-upon-Tweed, now under the power of Lieutenants or their Deputies, shall be exercised, ordered and managed until the 25th day of March next ensuing in such manner as the same now is actually exercised, ordered and managed, according to such commissions and instructions as they formerly have or from time to time shall receive from his Majesty.[2]

*   *   *   *   *   *

SR, v, 308

[1] This emerged as the Militia Act of 1662 (SR, v, 358).

[2] The Act was occasioned not so much by the king's desire to settle a question which had brought about civil war in 1642—though that was undoubtedly a part of it—but by Venner's rising in London in January 1661, and the need to indemnify the trained bands which had helped suppress it.

101. 13 Car. II, c. 12: An Act for explanation of a clause contained in an Act of Parliament made in the seventeenth year of the late King Charles...concerning commissioners for causes ecclesiastical (1661)

Whereas in an Act of Parliament made in the seventeenth year of the late King Charles entitled 'An Act for repeal of a branch of a statute primo Elizabethae concerning commissioners for causes ecclesiastical'[1] it is amongst other things enacted that no...person or persons whatsoever exercising spiritual or ecclesiastical power, authority or jurisdiction by any grant, licence or commission of the King's Majesty, his heirs or successors or otherwise shall, from and after...[1 August 1641] award, impose or inflict any pain, penalty, fine, amercement, imprisonment or other corporal punishment upon any of the King's subjects for any contempt, misdemeanour, crime, offence, matter or thing whatsoever belonging to spiritual or ecclesiastical cognisance or jurisdiction; whereupon some doubt hath been made that all ordinary power of coercion and proceedings in causes ecclesiastical were taken away, whereby the ordinary course of justice in causes ecclesiastical hath been obstructed; be it therefore enacted...that neither the said Act nor anything therein contained doth or shall take away any ordinary power or authority from any of the said archbishops, bishops or any other person or persons named as aforesaid, but that they and every of them exercising ecclesiastical jurisdiction may proceed, determine, sentence, execute and exercise all manner of ecclesiastical jurisdiction...in as ample manner and form as they did and might lawfully have done before the making of the said Act.

II. And be it further enacted...that the afore-recited Act of decimo septimo Caroli and all the matters and clauses therein contained) excepting what concerns the High Commission Court, or the erecting of some such like court by commission) shall be and is hereby repealed....

III. Provided always, and it is hereby enacted, that neither this Act nor anything herein contained shall extend or be construed to revive or give force to the said branch of the said statute made in the first year of the reign of the said late Queen Elizabeth mentioned in the said Act of Parliament [above]..., but that the said branch of the said statute made ...shall stand and be repealed in such sort as if this [present] Act had never been made.

[1] 13 Car. I, c. 11, no. 62, p. 225 above.

IV. Provided also, and it is hereby further enacted, that it shall not be lawful for any archbishop, bishop, vicar-general, chancellor, commissary or other spiritual or ecclesiastical judge, officer, or minister, or any other person having or exercising spiritual or ecclesiastical jurisdiction to tender or administer unto any person whatsoever the oath usually called the oath *ex officio*....

V. Provided always that this Act or anything therein contained shall not extend or be construed to extend...to confirm the canons made in the year 1640 nor any of them, nor any other ecclesiastical laws or canons not formerly confirmed, allowed or enacted by Parliament or by the established laws of the land as they stood in the year...1639.

SR, v, 315–16

102. 13 Car. II, st. 2, c. 1: An Act for the well governing and regulating of corporations (The Corporation Act, 1661)

Whereas questions are likely to arise concerning the validity of elections of magistrates and other officers and members in corporations, as well in respect of removing some as placing others during the late Troubles, contrary to the true intent and meaning of their charters and liberties, and to the end that the succession in such corporations may be most probably perpetuated in the hands of persons well affected to his Majesty and the established government, it being too well known that notwithstanding all his Majesty's endeavours and unparalleled indulgence in pardoning all that is past nevertheless many evil spirits are still working, wherefore for prevention of the like mischief for the time to come and for preservation of the public peace both in Church and State, be it enacted...that commissions shall before 24 February next be issued forth under the Great Seal of England unto such persons as his Majesty shall appoint for the executing of the powers and authorities hereinafter expressed....

II. And be it enacted...that no charter of any corporation...shall at any time hereafter be avoided for or by reason of any act or thing done or omitted to be done before the first day of this present parliament.

III. And be it further enacted...that all persons who upon 24 December, 1661, shall be mayors, aldermen, recorders, bailiffs, town clerks, common councilmen and other persons then bearing any office or offices of magistracy, or places or trusts or other employment relating to or concerning the government of the said respective cities, corporations and boroughs and cinque ports and their members, and other port towns, shall at any time before 25 March 1663, when they shall be thereunto required by the said respective commissioners or any three of them, take the Oaths of Allegiance and Supremacy and this oath following:

> I, A.B., do declare and believe that it is not lawful upon any pretence whatsoever to take arms against the King, and that I do abhor the traitorous position of taking arms by his authority against his person or against those that are commissioned by him. So help me God.

And also at the same time shall publicly subscribe before the said commissioners or any three of them the following declaration:

> I, A.B., do declare that I hold that there lies no obligation upon me or any other person from the oath commonly called the Solemn League and Covenant, and that the same was in itself an unlawful oath and imposed upon the subjects of this realm against the known laws and liberties of the kingdom.

IV. And that all such of the said mayors and other the persons aforesaid...who shall refuse to take and subscribe the same within the time and in manner aforesaid shall from and immediately after such refusal be by authority of this Act (*ipso facto*) removed and displaced of and from the said offices and places respectively; and the said offices and places from and immediately after such refusal shall...be void to all intents and purposes as if the said respective persons so refusing were naturally dead.

V. And nevertheless be it enacted...that the said commissioners or any five or more of them shall have full power by virtue of this Act by order and warrant under their hands and seals to displace or remove any of the persons aforesaid from the said respective offices...if the said commissioners or the major part of them then present shall deem it expedient for the public safety, although such persons shall have taken and subscribed or be willing to take and subscribe the said oaths and declaration.

VI. And be it also enacted that the said respective commissioners or any five or more of them as aforesaid shall have power to restore such person or persons as have been illegally or unduly removed into the places out of which he or they were removed, and also to put and place into the offices and places which by any of the ways aforesaid shall be void respectively some other person or persons then being or which have been members or inhabitants of the said respective cities...[etc.], and that the said persons, from and after the taking of the said oaths and subscribing the said declaration shall hold and enjoy and be vested in the said offices and places as if they had been duly elected and chosen according to the charters and former usages of the said respective cities...[etc.]

VII. And be it further enacted...that...from and after the expiration of the said respective commissions the said three oaths and declaration shall be from time to time administered...by such person or persons respectively who by the charters or usages of the said respective cities...[etc.] ought to administer the oath for due executing the said places or offices respectively, and in default of such by two justices of the peace of the said cities...[etc.] if any such there be, or otherwise by two justices of the peace for the time being of the respective counties where the said cities...[etc.] are.

* * * * * *

IX. Provided also...that from and after the expiration of the said commissions no person or persons shall for ever hereafter be placed, elected or chosen in or to any the offices or places aforesaid that shall not have within one year next before such election or choice taken the Sacrament of the Lord's Supper according to the rites of the Church of England,...and in default hereof every such placing, election and choice is hereby enacted and declared to be void.

* * * * * *

XI. Provided also...that the powers granted to the commissioners by virtue of this Act shall continue and be in force until 25 March 1663 and no longer.

SR, v, 321-3

103. 14 Car. II, c. 4: An Act for the uniformity of public prayers and administration of sacraments and other rites and ceremonies (The Uniformity Act, 1662)

Whereas in the first year of the late Queen Elizabeth there was one uniform Order of Common Service and Prayer and of the administration of Sacraments, Rites and Ceremonies in the Church of England (agreeable to the Word of God and usage of the Primitive Church) compiled by the reverend bishops and clergy, set forth in one book, entitled 'The Book of Common Prayer and Administration of Sacraments and other Rites and Ceremonies in the Church of England', and enjoined to be used by Act of Parliament holden in the said first year of the said late Queen entitled 'An Act for the Uniformity of Common Prayer and Service in the Church, and Administration of the Sacraments',[1] very comfortable to all good people desirous to live in Christian conversation and most profitable to the estate of this realm, …and yet, this notwithstanding, a great number of people in divers parts of this realm, following their own sensuality and living without knowledge and due fear of God, do wilfully and schismatically abstain and refuse to come to their parish churches…, and whereas by the great and scandalous neglect of ministers in using the said order or liturgy so set forth and enjoined as aforesaid great mischiefs and inconveniences during the times of the late unhappy troubles have arisen and grown, and many people have been led into factions and schisms, to the great decay and scandal of the reformed religion of the Church of England, and to the hazard of many souls; for prevention whereof in time to come, for settling the peace of the Church, and for allaying the present distempers which the indisposition of the time hath contracted, the King's Majesty, according to his Declaration of 25 October, 1660, granted his commission under the Great Seal of England to several bishops and other divines to review the Book of Common Prayer and…make such additions and alterations…as to them should seem meet and convenient, and should exhibit and present the same to his Majesty in writing for his further allowance or confirmation. Since when time, upon full and mature deliberation, they…have accordingly reviewed the said books, and have made some alterations…and have exhibited and presented the same unto his Majesty in writing in one book, entitled 'The Book of Common Prayer and Administration of the Sacraments and other Rites and Ceremonies of the Church according to the use of the Church of England, together with the Psalter or Psalms of David appointed as they are to be sung or said in churches, and the form and manner of making, ordaining and consecrating of Bishops, Priests and Deacons'. All which his Majesty having duly considered, hath fully approved and allowed the same, and recommended to this present Parliament. …

Now in regard that nothing conduceth more to the settling of the peace of this nation (which is desired by all good men) nor to the honour of our religion and the propagation thereof than a universal

[1] 1 Eliz., c. 2, printed Elton, *Tudor Constitution*, pp. 401 ff.

agreement in the public worship of Almighty God, and to the intent that every person within this realm may certainly know the rule to which he is to conform in public worship..., be it enacted...that all and singular ministers in any cathedral, collegiate or parish church or chapel or other place of public worship within this realm...shall be bound to say and use the Morning Prayer, Evening Prayer, celebration and administration of both the Sacraments, and all other the public and common prayer in such order and form as is mentioned in the said Book annexed and joined to this present Act and entitled...[as above]. And that the Morning and Evening Prayers therein contained shall upon every Lord's day and upon all other days and occasions and at the times therein appointed be openly and solemnly read by all and every minister or curate in every church, chapel or other place of public worship...aforesaid.

II. And to the end that uniformity in the public worship of God (which is so much desired) may be speedily effected, be it further enacted...that every parson, vicar or other minister whatsoever who now hath and enjoyeth any ecclesiastical benefice or promotion within this realm of England or places aforesaid shall in the church, chapel or place of public worship belonging to his said benefice or promotion upon some Lord's day before the Feast of St Bartholomew [24 August], 1662, openly, publicly and solemnly read the Morning and Evening Prayer appointed to be read by and according to the said Book of Common Prayer at the times thereby appointed, and after such reading thereof shall openly and publicly before the congregation there assembled declare his unfeigned assent and consent to the use of all things in the said Book contained and prescribed, in these words and no other:

> I, A.B., do declare my unfeigned assent and consent to all and every thing contained and prescribed in and by the book entitled the Book of Common Prayer and...[etc., as above].

III. And that all and every such person who shall...neglect or refuse to do the same within the time aforesaid...shall *ipso facto* be deprived of all his spiritual promotions, and that from henceforth it shall be lawful to and for all patrons and donors of all and singular the said spiritual promotions or any of them according to their respective rights and titles to present or collate to the same as though the person or persons so offending or neglecting were dead.

[IV. Henceforward any new incumbent was obliged to make this declaration within two months of entering upon his benefice, under pain of deprivation as above.]

* * * * * *

VI. And be it further enacted...that every dean, canon and prebendary of every cathedral or collegiate church, and all masters and other heads, fellows, chaplains and tutors of or in any college, hall, house of learning or hospital, and every public professor and reader in either of the universities and in every college elsewhere, and every parson, vicar, curate, lecturer and every other person in holy orders, and every schoolmaster keeping any public or private schools, and every person instructing or teaching any youth in any house or private family as a tutor or schoolmaster, who upon the first day of May, 1662, or at any time thereafter shall be incumbent or have possession of any deanery, canonry, prebend, mastership, headship, fellowship, professor's place or reader's place, parsonage, vicarage, or any other ecclesiastical dignity or promotion, or of any curate's place, lecture or school, or shall instruct or teach any youth as tutor or schoolmaster, shall before the Feast Day of St Bartholomew [24 August], 1662, or at or before his or their respective admission to be incumbent or have possession aforesaid subscribe the Declaration or Acknowledgement following:

> I, A.B., do declare that it is not lawful upon any pretence whatsoever to take arms against the King, and that I do abhor that traitorous position of taking arms by his authority against his person or against those that are commissioned by him, and that I will conform to the liturgy of the Church of England as it is now by law established. *And I do declare that I do hold there lies no obligation upon me or on any other person from the oath commonly called the Solemn League and Covenant to endeavour any change or alteration of government either in Church or State. And that the same was in itself an unlawful oath and imposed upon the subjects of this realm against the known laws and liberties of this kingdom.*[1]

[To be subscribed before the vice-chancellor, the archbishop, bishop or other ordinary as appropriate under pain of deprivation as above.]

[1] § VIII of the Act decreed that the sentences in italics should be dropped after 25 March 1682.

VII.... And after such subscription made every such parson, vicar, curate and lecturer shall procure a certificate under the hand and seal of the respective...ordinary..., and shall publicly and openly read the same, together with the Declaration and Acknowledgement aforesaid upon some Lord's day within three months then next following in his parish church where he is to officiate in the presence of the congregation there assembled in the time of Divine Service...[under pain of deprivation as above].

* * * * * *

SR, v, 364–8

104. 16 Car. II, c. 1: An Act for the assembling and holding of parliaments once in three years at the least (The Triennial Act, 1664)

Whereas the Act made in the parliament begun at Westminster the third day of November in the sixteenth year of the reign of our late Sovereign Lord King Charles of blessed memory entitled *An Act for the preventing of inconveniences happening by the long intermission of Parliaments*[1] is in derogation of his Majesty's just rights and prerogative inherent to the Imperial Crown of this realm for the calling and assembling of parliaments, and may be an occasion of manifold mischiefs and inconveniences, and much endanger the peace and safety of his Majesty and all his liege people of this realm, be it therefore enacted by the King's most excellent Majesty by and with the advice and consent of the Lords spiritual and temporal and the Commons in this present parliament assembled and by the authority of the same, that the said Act...and all and every the articles, clauses and things therein contained, is, shall be and are hereby wholly annulled and utterly made void, and are hereby declared to be null and void to all intents and purposes whatsoever as if the said Act had never been had or made, anything in the said Act contained to the contrary notwithstanding.

II. And because by the ancient laws and statutes of this realm made in the reign of King Edward the Third parliaments are to be held very often, your Majesty's humble and loyal subjects the Lords spiritual and temporal and the Commons in this present parliament assembled most humbly do beseech your most excellent Majesty that it may be declared and enacted, and be it declared and enacted by the authority aforesaid,

---

[1] No. 59, p. 219 above.

that hereafter the sitting and holding of parliaments shall not be intermitted or discontinued above three years at the most, but that within three years from and after the determination of this present parliament, and so from time to time within three years after the determination of any other parliament or parliaments, or if there be occasion, more often, your Majesty, your heirs and successors do issue out your writs for calling, assembling and holding of another parliament, to the end that there may be a frequent calling, assembling and holding of parliaments once in three years at the least.

SR, v, 513

105. 22 Car. II, c. 1: An Act to prevent and suppress seditious conventicles[1] (The Conventicles Act, 1670)

For providing further and more speedy remedies against the growing and dangerous practices of seditious sectaries and other disloyal persons, who under pretence of tender consciences have or may at their meetings contrive insurrections (as late experience hath shown), be it enacted... that if any person of the age of sixteen years or upwards, being a subject of this realm, at any time after May 10th next shall be present at any assembly, conventicle or meeting under colour or pretence of any exercise of religion in other manner than according to the liturgy and practice of the Church of England..., at which conventicle...there shall be five persons or more assembled together over and besides those of the same household if it be in a house where there is a family inhabiting—or if it be in a house, field or place where there is no family inhabiting, then where any five persons or more are so assembled as aforesaid—it shall and may be lawful for any one or more justices of the peace of the county, limit, division, corporation or liberty wherein the offence aforesaid shall be committed,...and he and they are hereby required and enjoined, upon proof to him or them respectively made of such offence, either by confession of the party, or oath of two witnesses,...or by notorious evidence and circumstance of the fact, to make a record of every such offence under his or their hands and seals respectively, which...shall to all intents and purposes be in law taken and adjudged to be a full and perfect conviction....And thereupon the said justice...shall impose on every such offender so convicted as aforesaid a fine of five shillings for such first offence,[2] which record and

---

[1] The marked differences between this and the Act of 1664 for the same purpose (16 Car. II, c. 4, SR v, 516–20), which had expired in 1668, are outlined in the footnotes.

[2] In 1664 a maximum of three months' imprisonment or a £5 fine.

conviction shall be certified by the said justice...at the next Quarter Sessions of the Peace....

II. And be it further enacted...that if such offender so convicted as aforesaid shall at any time again commit the like offence or offences... and be thereof in manner aforesaid convicted, then such offender... shall for every such offence incur the penalty of ten shillings,[1] which fine and fines for the first and every other offence shall be levied by distress and sale of the offender's goods and chattels; or in case of the poverty of such offender upon the goods and chattels of any other person or persons who shall be then convicted in manner aforesaid of the like offence at the same conventicle at the discretion of the said justice..., so as the sum to be levied on any one person in case of the poverty of other offenders amount not in the whole to above the sum of ten pounds upon occasion of any one meeting....[2]

III. And be it further enacted by the authority aforesaid that every person who shall take upon him to preach or teach in any such meeting, assembly or conventicle and shall thereof be convicted as aforesaid shall forfeit for every such first offence the sum of twenty pounds....[3] And if the said preacher or teacher so convicted be a stranger, and his name and habitation not known, or his fled and cannot be found, or in the judgement of the justice...shall be thought unable to pay the same, the said justice, justices or chief magistrate respectively are hereby empowered and required to levy the same by warrant as aforesaid upon the goods and chattels of any such persons who shall be present at the same conventicle, anything in this or any other Act, law or statute to the contrary notwithstanding....[4] And if such offender so convicted as aforesaid shall at any time again commit the like offence...and be thereof convicted...then [he]...shall for every such offence incur the penalty of forty pounds....

IV. And be it further enacted...that every person who shall wittingly and willingly suffer any such conventicle, meeting or unlawful assembly aforesaid to be held in his or her house, outhouse, barn, yard or backside, and be convicted thereof in manner

---

[1] In 1664 a maximum of six months' imprisonment or a £10 fine; and for the third offence he was sent to the assizes, and if convicted, sentenced to seven years' transportation or £100 fine. (It is probable that this last proviso was dropped partly because of the difficulty of persuading the colonies to accept such convicts; as it was, Virginia and New England were excluded from the Act.)

[2] Despite the much higher fines imposed, the Act of 1664 did not offer this device.

[3] The Act of 1664 did not proceed against preachers.

[4] However, § v of this Act again restricts the liability of any one person to £10.

aforesaid, shall forfeit the sum of twenty pounds, to be levied in manner aforesaid....

* * * * * *

VI. Provided also, and be it further enacted, that in all cases of this Act where the penalty or sum charged upon any offender exceeds the sum of ten shillings, and such offender shall find himself aggrieved, it shall and may be lawful for him within one week after...to appeal in writing...to the judgement of the justices of the peace in their next Quarter Sessions,...whereupon such offender may plead and make [his] defence and have his trial by a jury...[which shall be final].

* * * * * *

VIII. And be it further enacted...that the justice, justices of the peace and chief magistrates respectively, or the respective constables, headboroughs and tithingmen by warrant from the said justice, justices or chief magistrate respectively, shall and may, with what aid, force and assistance they shall think fit for the better execution of this Act after refusal or denial to enter, break open and enter into any house or other place where they shall be informed any such conventicle as aforesaid is or shall be held, as well within liberties as without, and take into their custody the persons there unlawfully assembled, to the intent that they may be proceeded against according to this Act. And that the lieutenants or deputy-lieutenants or any commissioned officer of the militia or other of his Majesty's forces, with such troops or companies of horse and foot, and also the sheriffs and other magistrates and ministers of justice, or any of them, jointly or severally, within any the counties or places within this kingdom..., with such other assistance as they shall think meet or can get in readiness with the soonest, on certificate made to them respectively under the hand and seal of any one justice of the peace or chief magistrate, of his particular information or knowledge, of such unlawful meeting or conventicle held or to be held in their respective counties or places, and that he with such assistance as he can get together is not able to suppress and dissolve the same, shall and may and are hereby required and enjoined to repair unto the place where they are so held or to be held, and by the best means they can to dissolve, dissipate or prevent all such unlawful meetings, and take into their custody such and so many of the said persons so unlawfully assembled as they shall think fit....

IX. Provided always that no dwelling house of any peer of this realm where he or his wife shall be then resident shall be searched by virtue of this Act but by immediate warrant from his Majesty...or in the presence of the lieutenant or one deputy-lieutenant or two justices of the peace, whereof one to be of the quorum of the same county or riding.

X. And be it further enacted...that if any constable, headborough, tithingman, churchwarden or overseer of the poor who shall know or be credibly informed of any such meetings or conventicles held within his precincts, parish or limits, and shall not give information thereof to some justice of the peace...and endeavour the conviction of the parties according to his duty,...he shall forfeit for every such offence the sum of five pounds....And that if any justice of the peace or chief magistrate shall wilfully and wittingly omit the performance of his duty in the execution of this Act he shall forfeit the sum of £100....[1]

* * * * * *

XVII. Provided also that neither this Act nor anything therein contained shall extend to invalidate or avoid his Majesty's supremacy in ecclesiastical affairs, but that his Majesty and his heirs and successors may from time to time and at all times hereafter exercise and enjoy all powers and authorities in ecclesiastical affairs as fully and as amply as himself or any of his predecessors have or might have done the same, anything in this Act notwithstanding.[2]   *SR*, v, 648–51

[1] This clause had no counterpart in the Act of 1664, and obviously reflects the sympathy of many magistrates and constables for the Dissenters.
[2] Not found in the Act of 1664.

CHAPTER II

PARLIAMENT, 1660–1688

There is nothing after 1660 to match the monographs that have appeared on the individual parliaments of James I and Charles I, not to mention the very full accounts of debates, published or unpublished, for the session of 1610, the parliaments of 1621, 1625 and 1628–9, and the Long Parliament.[1] In part this reflects a shortage of material; the only debates that have been published are Anchitel Grey's collection, from 1667 onwards, John Milward's brief diary for 1666–8, and a few printed speeches delivered during the Exclusion Crisis; nor does it seem that much remains unpublished, apart from such indirect sources as the Muddiman newsletters at Longleat.

So, there are many problems with regard to Charles II's parliaments, and particularly the Long Parliament of 1661–79, that are still insoluble, or whose solution is a matter of guesswork. Why did this parliament turn so decisively against Charles II, and was it inevitable that it should? Were the old Cavaliers an important element, and was there any change in the wealth or social status of Members after 1660, a decline that some historians have discerned in the calibre of local justices at this time? How far did 'the old parliamentary gang' survive the constant changes of personnel at bye-elections? In 1661, 103 voted against burning the Solemn League and Covenant, a dead document if ever there was one, and the Corporation Act only passed by 185 votes to 136:[2] does the presence of this 'Presbyterian' element explain the increasing disposition to tolerate Protestant Dissenters which is one of the most surprising developments of the late 'sixties and early 'seventies? More important, what apart from religion motivated the 'country' opposition in the 'seventies, later to swell into the Exclusion Movement?[3] There has been some suggestion that the gentry were now economically a declining class, increasingly preoccupied by local government, and regarding central government as a necessary but burdensome evil; in this case the Exclusion Movement may well have been in large part a class protest against the growing power of the nobility, a view which finds some support in the bad relations between Commons and Lords throughout this reign. But this is a theory expounded many years ago,[4] and it has not been consolidated and fully proved by detailed research.

---

[1] Research into Charles's parliaments begins and virtually ends with Wilbur C. Abbott's 'Long Parliament of Charles II', *EHR*, xxi (1906), 21, 254 (2 pts), though some work has been done on electioneering during the Exclusion Crisis, and rather less on the House of Lords.

[2] Abbot, *op. cit.* pp. 28, 29.   [3] See J. R. Jones, *The First Whigs.*

[4] H. J. Habbakuk, 'English Landownership, 1680–1740', *Economic History Review*, 1st ser., x (1940), 2.

A work of this kind cannot pretend to answer such questions, but they should be posed at this stage. What follows is merely a review of the more important constitutional questions which divided Parliament and the Crown, or the two Houses of Parliament, in this reign.

I. FINANCE

The financial provisions of the Restoration Settlement are well enough known. The Commons in 1661 granted the king tunnage and poundage for life, tacitly abandoning an old quarrel, but rather than perpetuate the monthly assessments of the Interregnum it continued the excise. This was divided into two halves: the Hereditary Excise[1] was granted to Charles and his successors in perpetuity, in respect of his surrender of feudal tenures and purveyance, while the other half, the Additional Excise, was granted him for life.

Parliament estimated that this, plus his normal income, would amount to £1,200,000, which would pay the expenses of the court and the government, as well as a modest peace-time naval and military establishment. In fact, it was not sufficient, and in any case the anticipated yield was not obtained until the 1670's; and chronic shortage of money caused the usual bitterness between king and Parliament, who were now obliged to work together much more regularly and frequently than before.

The Commons made one or two hit-and-miss attempts at a working agreement. On the king's side there was a vacuum. Charles, a much over-rated monarch, could not be bothered, and the earl of Southampton, lord treasurer from 1661 to 1667, was too old and inexperienced. The Second Dutch War (1665–7) showed up all the deficiencies of the administration, and the king's quarrelling ministers, Ashley, Arlington, Clifford, Buckingham and Clarendon, did nothing to restore the government's public image. There was an explanation for England's poor showing at sea, and the money voted for the war could have been accounted for, most of it, but the government was too divided within itself to present its case fairly and straightforwardly to Parliament or the public. Incompetence was therefore denounced as treachery, and extravagance as corruption. As early as 1665 the Commons were deeply suspicious, and in their Supply Act of that year (**106**) they ordered a register to be kept in the Exchequer of the receipts from the taxes voted and the nature of the disbursements. They also usurped the functions of the chancellor and the auditor of the Exchequer by insisting that repayment of loans to the government be made in strict chronological rotation—'in course'. The fact that this was proposed by Sir George Downing, one of the tellers of the Exchequer, made it no more palatable to the government. The Supply Act of 1666 went a step further by directing that

[1] On beer, cider, mead, crude spirits, coffee, chocolate, sherbert and tea.

£380,000 of the money voted be applied to the payment of seamen's wages (**107**). By 1678 this practice of 'appropriation' had become customary, and when Parliament was induced to vote money for the disbandment of the army the king had raised for the Flanders campaign the most stringent precautions were taken to ensure that it was used for that purpose and no other, and the Commons even wrote into the Act the date of demobilisation —a clear infringement of the king's prerogative of peace and war (**109**).[1]

The parliament of 1685, subservient in most things, abandoned these precautions, and granted James II extra impositions on tobacco, sugar, wines and vinegar for eight years without appropriation. The preambles to the supply bills stated that the money was to be used for the navy and the ordnance, but there was no effort to supervise its expenditure.[2] Since James II used a great deal of this money to build up a standing army, after the Revolution strict appropriation became the general rule.

Meanwhile in 1667, despairing of obtaining comprehensible accounts of receipt and expenditure from the Treasury, and strongly suspecting large-scale fraud, particularly in seamen's pay, the Commons brought in a bill to appoint a commission for taking the public accounts. This was blocked by the Lords, and the king prepared to appoint his own carefully chosen commission, but all hopes of compromise were swept away by the Medway disaster in the early summer. Charles was forced to dismiss Clarendon and give his assent to a statutory commission with power to subpœna any royal servant and cross-examine him under oath, and access to all records (**108**). The commission was only appointed for three years, and its report to Parliament was confused and inconclusive, but it was an invaluable precedent which was taken up after the Revolution.

106. Payment in Course, 1665

17 Car. II, c. 1: *An Act for granting the sum of twelve hundred and fifty thousand pounds to the King's Majesty for his present further Supply*

*   *   *   *   *   *

v. And that to the intent that all monies to be lent to your Majesty and monies that shall be due upon such contracts for wares and goods which shall be delivered for this service may be well and sufficiently

---

[1] W. A. Shaw's introductions to the *Calendars of Treasury Books* are still the best authority on the public finance of Charles II's reign, though they must be used with caution. Stephen Baxter has dealt thoroughly and conclusively with the Treasury as a department of state.

[2] 1 Jac. II, cc. 3–4 (*SR*, VI, 2–7). Another Act of the same session, granting the Crown further impositions, on imported silks, linens and brandies, for five years to pay for the suppression of Monmouth's Rebellion, did have a clause (§ 10) requiring debts to be repaid 'in course', but that was all (1 Jac. II, c. 5; *ibid.* 7–9).

secured out of the monies arising and payable by this Act, be it further enacted...that there be provided and kept in his Majesty's Exchequer, to wit, in the office of the auditor of the Receipt, one book or register, in which...all monies that shall be paid into the Exchequer by this Act shall be entered and registered, apart and distinct from... all other monies or branches of your Majesty's revenue whatsoever; and that also there be one other book or register provided or kept in the said office, of all Orders or Warrants to be made by the Lord Treasurer and Under Treasurer or by the Commissioners of the Treasury for the time being for payment of all and every sum and sums of money to all persons for monies lent, wares or goods bought, or other payments directed by his Majesty relating to the service of this war; and that no monies levyable by this Act be issued out of the Exchequer during this war but by such order or warrant mentioning that the monies payable by such order or warrant are for the service of your Majesty in the said war respectively.

*   *   *   *   *   *

VII. That it shall be lawful for any person or persons willing to lend any money or to furnish any wares, victuals, necessities or goods on the credit of this Act at the usual times when the Exchequer is open to have access unto and view and peruse all or any of the said books for their information of the state of those monies and all engagements upon them, for their better encouragement to lend any monies or furnish any goods or wares as aforesaid. And...that all and every person and persons who shall lend any monies to your Majesty and pay the same into the Receipt of the Exchequer shall immediately have a tally of loan struck for the same, and an order for his repayment bearing the same date with his tally, in which order shall be also a warrant contained for payment of interest for forbearance after the rate of 6 % per annum for his consideration, to be paid every six months until the repayment of his principal; and that all person and persons who shall furnish your Majesty, your Officers[1] of the Navy or Ordnance with any wares, good, victuals or other necessaries for the service aforesaid shall upon certificate of the Commissioners and Officers of the Navy, or of the Masters or Commissioners and Officers of the Ordnance, or some of them, without delay forthwith have made out to them warrants or orders for the payment of the monies due or payable unto them....

---

[1] That is, the principal administrative officers who comprised the Navy Board.

And that all orders for the repayment of money lent shall be registered in course according to the date of the tallies respectively. And that all orders signed by the Lord Treasurer and Under Treasurer for payment of money for goods, wares, victuals and other necessaries furnished to his majesty...shall be registered in course according to the time of bringing to the office of the Auditor of Receipt the certificates above mentioned, and that all orders so signed for payments directed by his Majesty shall be entered in course according to their respective dates, and none of the sorts of orders above mentioned...shall have preference one before another, but shall all be entered in their course according to the dates of the tallies, the times of bringing the certificates, and the dates of the orders for payments directed by his Majesty, as they are in point of time respectively before each other. And that all and every person and persons shall be paid in course according as their orders shall stand entered in the said register book....

*   *   *   *   *   *

SR, v, 573–4.

107. Appropriation, 1666

18 & 19 Car. II, c. 13: *An Act for granting the sum of twelve hundred, fifty six thousand three hundred forty seven pounds thirteen shillings to the King's Majesty towards the maintenance of the present war*

*   *   *   *   *   *

x. Provided always and be it enacted by the authority aforesaid, that the sum of £380,000 shall be charged and registered in the Book of Register appointed by this Act to be kept in the office of the Auditor of the Receipt of the Exchequer, to be paid to the Treasurer of the Navy for the time being out of the money payable for the last ten months of the eleven months' assessment granted by this Act, for the salaries and wages of such officers, seamen, mariners and soldiers as are or shall be employed aboard your Majesty's Navy for this present winter, beginning at 1 January 1667 and aboard your Majesty's Navy for the summer in the year 1667....

xi. And it is hereby further enacted that if the Treasurer of the Navy do divert or employ the said £380,000 or any part thereof to any use or service whatsoever other than for the payment of the salaries and wages of such officers, seamen, mariners and soldiers...as aforesaid until the said wages and salaries shall be fully and entirely paid and discharged, that then and in such case he shall forfeit treble the value of the money diverted or employed contrary to the intent and meaning hereof, to be recovered in any of his Majesty's courts at Westminster..., one moiety whereof to be to such person as shall sue for the same and the other moiety to your Majesty, your heirs and successors.

* * * * * *

SR, v, 621

108. The Commission for Public Accounts, 1667

19 & 20 Car. II, c. 1: *An Act for taking the accounts of the several sums of money therein mentioned*

Whereas many and great aids and provisions have been given, raised and assigned for the necessary defence of your Majesty and your kingdoms in the late great and important wars, to the end that both your Majesty and this whole kingdom may be satisfied and truly informed whether all the same monies and provisions have been faithfully issued out and expended in and about the preparing and setting forth of your Royal Navy, and other the management and carrying on the said war, and with such care, fidelity and good husbandry as the nature of such services would admit of, according to your Majesty's own gracious and princely desires and the earnest expectations of your most loyal subjects, than which nothing can encourage them more cheerfully to undergo the like burdens in time to come for the necessary defence of your Majesty and your realms, may it therefore please your Majesty that it be enacted...that William, Lord Brereton, baron of Laughtyn in the kingdom of Ireland, William Pierrepoint, esquire, Sir George Savile, baronet, Giles Dunster, esquire, Sir James Langham, knight, Henry Osborne, esquire, Sir William Turner, alderman of the city of London, George Thompson, esquire, and John Gregory, esquire, or any five or more of them shall be Commissioners for the taking of the accounts of...[the direct taxation voted since 1664, in total £5,183,847], and of all such monies as have arisen by the Customs granted to his Majesty by an Act of the present Parliament and have been applied to the service of the war, and such prizes as have been taken during the said late war for his Majesty's use, and of all other monies, provisions and things whatsoever which have been raised or assigned for or towards the fitting, furnishing or setting out to sea any of the navies or ships employed in the said late war, or for or touching the management or maintenance thereof.

And to that end the said Commissioners or any five or more of them are hereby authorised and required to call before them all treasurers, receivers, paymasters, principal officers and commissioners of the navy and ordnance respectively, victuallers, pursers, mustermasters and clerks of the cheque, accountants and all officers and keepers of his Majesty's stores and provisions for war, as well for land as sea, and all other persons whatsoever employed in the management of the said war, or requisite for the discovery of any frauds relating thereunto, to make true and perfect accounts of all such of the monies as have come to any of their hands respectively and to bring in and deliver the same to the said Commissioners...without delay, and also to bring in their several books of accounts, vouchers and acquittances, contracts, muster rolls, cheque rolls, cheque books, and all other books and writings whatsoever touching or concerning the premises, to be perused, tried and examined by the said Commissioners:

Whereby it may appear what monies they have received and how the same have been disbursed, and what ammunition, provisions and stores of any kind which were in his Majesty's storehouses or yards or elsewhere have been employed in the said war after 1 September, 1664, and what ships or other vessels his Majesty then had for the service of the war, together with their several equipages and furniture, and what monies or other provisions or materials have been paid or delivered to the hands of the said treasurers, receivers, paymasters, victuallers, pursers or other accountants, or any of the said officers or keepers of his Majesty's stores, and when the same was so paid and delivered, and how and at what time or times the same have been disposed of and to whom and for what use or uses, and to examine the rates and prices set upon any provisions, wares, or materials bought or provided for the service of the said war, and what the same were then truly worth, and what was really paid for the same, and by whom and to whom, and when the same was so bought or paid for, and how the same provisions, wares and materials have been employed and disposed of and by what warrant.

And [they are] to examine all such merchants and tradesmen, and their books, receipts and acquittances, and all such seamen and others as shall be thought fit to be heard touching any frauds, oppressions or exactions practised or used by any person or persons entrusted or employed in or about the payment or receipt of any of the said monies or the buying or providing of any of the said provisions, wares or materials, or the custody, ordering or disposing of the same and to what value, and what gain or advantage was made thereby and by whom, and where and about what time the same was so done.

And [they are] to inquire and find out whether any and which of the seamen and others have been defrauded of any of their premiums or rewards, victuals, clothes, pillage or other allowances or benefits assigned, promised or appointed to any of them for or in respect of their service in the said war, and by whom and to what value. And [they are] to inquire and find out what monies have been or ought to have been set apart for the Chest[1] from 24 June 1660, and how the same have been paid or disposed of, and whether any part thereof hath been defalked or detained from the persons to whom it was due and payable, and how much, when and by whom and by what pretence the same was done.

And [they are to inquire] whether any sums of money and how much arising by the customs and subsidy of tunnage and poundage ever since 1 September, 1664, hath been issued and allowed for and towards the maintenance of the said war, and also to inquire and find out the numbers and values of all the prize ships and goods which hath been taken for his Majesty's use during the said war, and their several bills of lading, and how the same ships and goods or any of them have been apprised, valued, sold, embezzled or otherwise disposed of, and how the price and monies thereof arising have been accounted for to his Majesty, and what frauds or abuses have been committed therein and by whom and for what value. And [they are] to inquire whether any and how much of the said monies given for the maintenance of the said war by Act of Parliament as aforesaid hath been bestowed or disposed of to or for any other use or purpose, and to what other uses or persons the same are or any part thereof was so bestowed and disposed.

And [they are] also to inquire by whose means, counsel or procurement it came to pass that the ships, seamen, mariners and others were generally discharged by tickets and not paid with money, by the cheque roll of the respective ships or vessels wherein they served as formerly, and how any of the land forces came to be so paid, and what loss or disadvantage his Majesty or any of the seamen or land soldiers have sustained thereby, and what advantage or benefit hath been made

---

[1] The Chatham Chest: chiefly for the payment of disablement grants and pensions to seamen.

by any person or persons by means of such payment or by buying, selling or assigning of any such tickets, and by whom particularly and to what value; and how much of the wages due to any of the said seamen or land soldiers is yet remaining unpaid and to whom particularly the same is due or payable.[1]

And further [they are] to search into, examine and find out all other frauds, exactions, negligences and defaults and abuses which have been practised or committed by any person or persons whatsoever touching the premisses, and when and by whom the same were so practised and committed, and what damage hath been sustained thereby, and to what value. And for that end and purpose [they are] also to inspect and examine all such former accounts as they shall think necessary, and to send for seamen and cause to appear before...[them] all or any of the said accountants and other officers and keepers of stores, and all such merchants, tradesmen, seamen, soldiers and other persons as they shall think meet, and to examine them severally upon their corporal oaths (which the said Commissioners or any five or more of them shall and may administer by virtue of this Act), and also to send for and peruse all such records, books, vouchers, acquittances and other writings as they shall think fit to be produced for the better discovery of any the said frauds, exactions, negligences and defaults or abuses, and to do, execute and perform all such other act and acts as they...in their judgement shall find requisite whereby all such person and persons as shall appear guilty...may be brought to condign punishment in Parliament or otherwise....[And any official refusing to answer under oath, or refusing to produce his books, could be committed to prison by the Commissioners indefinitely.]

[II. The Commissioners can call upon sheriffs to summon Grand Juries in the provinces, to examine witnesses under oath, and report.]

III. ...And the said Commissioners are hereby required from time to time as they shall see cause, and at the determination of their examinations and proceedings by virtue of this Act, to give an account thereof in writing...to the King's Majesty and to both Houses of Parliament if then sitting....

* * * * * *

SR, v, 624–7

[1] The greatest single scandal of a scandalous war. Paid off at the ports by tickets redeemable only in London, many seamen had sold them at an outrageous discount to waiting profiteers.

109. Appropriation, 1678

30 Car. II, c. 1: *An Act for granting a Supply to his Majesty...for disbanding the army and other uses therein mentioned*

We your Majesty's most loyal and obedient subjects the Commons now in Parliament assembled, perceiving that there is no further occasion for the Forces raised since 29 September last, and being sensible that the continuance of them must be a great burden and unnecessary charge to your Majesty, to the intent therefore that the said charge may not continue, and to enable your Majesty completely to pay and to disband all the said Forces as hereafter is mentioned and expressed, we ...have given and granted...for the aims and purposes aforesaid... the sum of £206,462. 17s. 3d.....

*   *   *   *   *   *

XIII. And be it further enacted that all the respective Forces, regiments, troops and companies, officers and soldiers, whether in garrison or out of garrison within this kingdom of England and dominion of Wales and the town of Berwick-upon-Tweed and the islands of Guernsey and Jersey, raised at any time since the said 29 September 1677, be paid, disbanded and discharged at or before 30 July 1678 in such manner and by such orders and directions as his Majesty shall appoint, and by such other rules and directions as are herein limited and appointed.

XIV. And be it further enacted that all other regiments, troops and companies, officers and soldiers, being his Majesty's subjects,...in any part of the Spanish Netherlands raised at any time since the said 29 September 1677 be paid, disbanded and discharged on or before 26 August 1678....

XV. And be it further enacted...that all monies hereinbefore named and mentioned, collected, levied and paid by virtue of this Act, except the allowances therein made to the respective collectors, clerks and receivers general, and the usual fees of the officers of the Exchequer, and what shall be issued thence for the repayment of loans made in pursuance of this Act upon the credit of the said £206,462. 17s. 3d. into the Exchequer and interest for the same, shall be applied and appropriated, and are hereby appropriated to and for the speedy and complete paying and disbanding the forces, officers and soldiers raised since 29 September 1677, and to no other intent, use or purpose whatsoever.

*   *   *   *   *   *

SR, v, 867, 871

II. FOREIGN POLICY

The Commons' control of finance inevitably strengthened their influence on foreign policy. At the Restoration the king's right to control foreign policy had been tacitly confirmed, but ever since 1603, and before, Parliament had been demanding that this control be exercised in full view of the public. James I's surrender on this point in 1624 had been decisive, and in 1625 Buckingham had expounded his master's foreign policy at length to both Houses.[1] However, Charles I returned to secret, or confidential, diplomacy after Buckingham's death, and his son naturally adopted the same tactic. Foreign policy and war were not only one of the few remaining prerogatives left to the Crown, they were also one of the most important, a seventeenth century king was at his most magnificent, and his most effective, in the preparation for or the prosecution of war.

In the 1660's there was no serious disagreement on foreign policy, though Arlington and Clarendon were criticised for allowing the French to ally with the Dutch in 1662; but after 1670 the problem became acute. By the Treaty of Dover in 1670 Charles agreed to join France in the forcible partition of the United Netherlands. The fact that he had also undertaken to declare himself a Roman Catholic was a profound secret, but it was widely suspected that the treaty contained more than had ever been made public, especially since the heir-presumptive, James, Duke of York, had been converted to Rome and the declaration of war in 1672 was immediately preceded by the Declaration of Indulgence, which favoured Roman Catholics as much as Protestant Dissenters.[2] Early in 1674 Charles solemnly denied to Parliament that there were any secret clauses in the Treaty of Dover, but the Commons insisted on cross-examining the second duke of Buckingham on the circumstances that led up to the war (110).

Buckingham and Arlington, the secretary of state chiefly responsible for foreign policy, resigned, and Charles was obliged to make peace with the Dutch. The Commons had won, and for the next four years the king's foreign policy see-sawed to and fro; Charles tempted Parliament with the project of a war against France, but the Commons were reluctant to provide him with an army, and he was quite content not to be forced. In May 1677 the Commons tried to break the deadlock by presenting a memorial threatening to withhold supply unless the king made an alliance with Holland against France (111a). The secretaries of state, Coventry and Williamson, protested that this was an invasion of one of the most cherished prerogatives of the Crown, and Charles rejected the memorial, on the grounds that while they could advise him in general terms they could not force him to make specific

---

[1] See E. R. Turner, 'Parliament and Foreign Affairs, 1603–1760', *EHR*, xxxiv (1919), 172 ff.
[2] See p. 402 below.

alliances (**111b, c**). The following year the whole incident was repeated almost exactly.[1] Charles was on the point of rejoining the European war at last when it was terminated by the Peace of Nimwegen, and his attempt to form a European coalition against France in 1679 and 1680 was viewed with cynicism by the Exclusion Parliaments.[2] The secret alliance with France in March 1681 is sometimes represented as a victory for the king. In fact it was merely a negative measure, which emphasised that Charles could not pursue a positive foreign policy without the approval and assistance of Parliament.

110. Buckingham's examination: second day: 14 January 1674

...Intimation being given to the House, that the duke now had recollected himself, and could give the House information of some matters relating to public affairs; and thereupon several questions being agreed to by the House to be proposed to his lordship, which are as followeth, viz.,

1. Whether any persons have at any time declared to him any of their advices, or evil purposes, against the liberty of this House, or propounded any ways to him for altering our government; and if they did, what was that advice, and by whom?

2. What was meant by this expression yesterday, that he had gotten nothing, and that others had gotten, three, four and five hundred thousand pounds; who they were that had gotten it, and by what means?

3. By whose advice the army was raised, and Papists set to officer them, and M. Schomberg to be their general?

4. Whether he knows that any have advised to make use of the army to awe the debates and resolutions of this House?

5. By whose counsel and ministry the Triple League was made?

6. And the first treaty with France, whereby it was broken, and the articles thereof?

7. And the Orders of Assignment and Credit of the Exchequer broken and destroyed?

8. And the Declaration about matters of religion made?

9. And the Smyrna Fleet fallen upon before war was declared?

10. And the second treaty with the French king, at Utrecht, and the articles thereof?

11. And by whose counsels the war was made without advice of Parliament, thereupon prorogued?   *CJ*, IX, 293

[1] Commons Address, 31 January 1678, King's Answer, 4 February (*CJ*, IX, 430, 431).
[2] Kenyon, *Sunderland*, pp. 40 ff.

III. Commons Address, 25 May 1677

(a) *Commons Address*

May it please your most excellent Majesty,

Your Majesty's most loyal and dutiful subjects, the Commons in Parliament assembled, having taken into their serious consideration your Majesty's gracious speech, do beseech your Majesty to believe, it is a great affliction to them to find themselves obliged at present to decline the granting your Majesty the supply your Majesty is pleased to demand, conceiving it is not agreeable to the usage of Parliament to grant supplies for maintenance of wars and alliances before they are signified in Parliament—which the two wars against the States of the United Provinces since your Majesty's happy Restoration, and the League made with them in January 1667[-8] for preservation of the Spanish Netherlands, sufficiently prove, without troubling your Majesty with instances of greater antiquity. From which usage if we should depart, the precedent might be of dangerous consequence in future times, though your Majesty's goodness gives us great security during your Majesty's reign, which we beesech God long to continue.

This consideration prompted us, in our last Address to your Majesty before our late recess, humbly to mention to your Majesty our hopes that before our meeting again your Majesty's alliances might be so fixed as that your Majesty might be graciously pleased to impart them to us in Parliament, that so our earnest desires of supplying your Majesty for prosecuting those great ends we had humbly laid before your Majesty might meet with no impediment or obstruction, being highly sensible of the necessity of supporting as well as making the alliances humbly desired in our former Addresses; and which we still conceive so important to the safety of your Majesty and your kingdom that we cannot, without unfaithfulness to your Majesty and those we represent, omit upon all occasions humbly to beseech your Majesty, as we now do, to enter into a league, offensive and defensive, with the States General of the United Provinces against the growth and power of the French king and for the preservation of the Spanish Netherlands, and to make such other alliances with such other of the Confederates as your Majesty shall think fit and useful to that end.... *CJ*, ix, 425

(b) *Commons debate on the Address, 25 May*

Sir Joseph Williamson [secretary of state]. He agrees as far in the end of the Address as any gentleman does, but he fears that the success will show, that this way will not do it. He cannot but think this is a new thing, and that it will be far from acknowledging the King's condescension, and that we encroach upon his prerogative.... Why must alliances, offensive and defensive, be the matter of the Address? The people cannot consider it; that is proper only for the royal breast. Defensive consideration is more proper for the people; he never knew an *offensive* league declared here before. You are told that the Parliament advised the Palatinate War. There is nothing too great for this House, but he never knew anything done of this nature, but the House was first called up to it. They were called to consult of the Palatinate War, and of the late Dutch War. If there be no precedent of it, and if but one, he begs of gentlemen to consider what reception this Address will have, though from the best and kindest of princes from such a House of Commons. You desire freedom of speech and privilege of Parliament. The King has but few prerogatives, as coining money, and making peace and war, and they are as landmarks, and are known; they are but few, and a curse is upon him that removes them. You are told of the alliances that saved Holland, &c. He will not compare those with the fears upon you at present, but in Queen Elizabeth's time, before she could be brought to a league offensive and defensive with them, we had two cautionary towns, and a fort, put into our hands. You by this hasty Address are cut off from all hopes of any such caution from them. He has acquitted himself as his allegiance and duty to this House obliges him, and he knows not what to advise you. But would have reasons as strong in the thing as may be, before you go to the King with this Address.... Grey, *Debates*, IV, 379

(c) *The King's Reply, 28 May*

Gentlemen,

Could I have been silent, I would rather have chosen to be so than to call to mind things so unfit for you to meddle with as are contained in some part of your Address, wherein you have entrenched upon so undoubted a right of the Crown that I am confident it will appear in no age (when the sword was not drawn) that the prerogative of making peace and war hath been so dangerously invaded. You do not content yourselves with desiring me to enter into such leagues as may be for the safety of the kingdom, but you tell me what sort of leagues they must be, and with whom. And, as your Address is worded, it is more liable to be understood to be by your leave than your request that I should make such other alliances as I please with other of the Confederates. Should I suffer this fundamental power of making peace and war to be so far invaded (though but once) as to have the manner and circumstances of leagues prescribed to me by Parliament, it is plain that no prince or State would any longer believe that the sovereignty of England rests in the Crown; nor could I think myself to signify any more to foreign princes than the empty sound of a king. Wherefore you may rest assured, that no condition shall make me depart from, or lessen, so essential a part of the monarchy. And I am willing to believe so well of this House of Commons, that I am confident these ill consequences are not intended by you. ...

CJ, IX, 426

III. THE SUSPENDING AND DISPENSING POWER

One of the gravest causes of dispute between king and Parliament arose from the religious settlement of 1661-2. Charles II was always sympathetic towards Roman Catholicism, and he had good reason to feel gratitude to many individual Catholics. Moreover, whatever his feelings about the Church settlement as a whole, he was anxious that the conditional promise of a 'liberty for tender consciences' he had made at Breda should not be absolutely rejected. On 17 March 1662 he sent down to the Lords two provisos to be added to the Uniformity Bill then under debate. One confirmed his 'supreme power and authority in ecclesiastical affairs', which gave him the right to dispense from the provisions of the Act all those who were not ministers of the Church, and was so clearly in favour of the Catholics that the Lords rejected it two days later.[1] The second proviso merely gave him power to dispense ministers of whose loyalty he was assured from the necessity of wearing the surplice or using the sign of the cross in baptism. This passed the Lords, but it was thrown out by the Commons on 22 April.[2]

As a result Charles seriously considered suspending the Act of Uniformity altogether, and on 10 June the Privy Council consulted the judges and the bishops.[3] But the judges questioned the legality of the suspending power, and

---

[1] LJ, XI, 411; House of Lords Manuscripts, XI, no. 3699.
[2] CJ, VIII, 414; HMC, 7th Report, pp. 162-3.
[3] George R. Abernethy, 'Clarendon and the Declaration of Indulgence', Journal of Ecclesiastical History, XI (1960), 62.

the proposal was dropped. On 26 December Charles made one final effort. He issued a long declaration defending himself against charges of ill faith, undue tolerance of Catholics, and an ambition to set up military government; at the end he suggested that Parliament in its next session pass an Act 'as may enable us to exercise with a more universal satisfaction that power of dispensing which we conceive to be inherent in us' (112).[1] It was an ill-judged and incautiously drafted pronouncement, and the tone of approval with which he referred to his Catholic subjects was long remembered against him. In his speech at the opening of the next session, 18 February 1663, he again defended himself against charges of partiality to the Catholics and explained that he had no desire to admit them to office under the Crown. In their reply, on 27 February, the Commons accepted these assurances with gratitude but politely dismissed the proposed 'Dispensation Act', which they said, 'will establish schism by a law'.[2] After a long delay Charles returned an evasive reply which left the question hanging.

However, the king's right to dispense occasional individuals from compliance with certain statutes was not seriously questioned, even in 1689, and throughout his reign the Catholics who had assisted Charles in his escape after the battle of Worcester enjoyed the benefit of such dispensations. On the other hand, Parliament was not prepared to allow the application of this principle to large numbers, or whole categories, of men, and in any case dispensations from the Uniformity Act were ineffective, since they could not reinstate a minister in his living. In March 1672, therefore, Charles tried to solve the problem by suspending the penal legislation altogether by his Declaration of Indulgence; the only restriction on religious freedom was that Protestant ministers must be licensed and Catholics were not allowed to worship in public (113). But the judges were hostile, as in 1662, and when Parliament met again, in February 1673, the Commons asserted that statutes could be suspended only by subsequent statutes, not by royal edict, and Charles was forced to cancel the Declaration (114). Parliament then passed the Test Act,[3] which, though it was directed at Catholics, was also an effective bar to most Protestant Dissenters.

The accession of a Catholic monarch in 1685 exacerbated the whole problem, and James II's dispensations to Roman Catholic army officers, relieving them of compliance with the Test Act, roused a storm in the House of Lords in November 1685.[4] There was a growing feeling that though the king did possess a power of dispensation it should not be applied to statutes

---

[1] This is sometimes called the 'First Declaration of Indulgence'; there is no objection to this, provided the edict of 1672 is not described as the 'Second Declaration of Indulgence'. The first was a request to Parliament to pass a bill; the second was a suspension by proclamation of existing legislation.

[2] *PH*, IV, 262. [3] No. **130**, p. 461 below.

[4] Browning, *English Historical Documents*, pp. 81 ff.

which imposed a religious test or qualification. In *Godden v. Hales* the judges decided that no such distinction existed.[1] But they continued to regard the suspending power with suspicion, and this may have influenced the drafting of James's Declaration of Indulgence issued in April 1687 (**115**), which was far less sweeping than his brother's. It suspended the penal laws outright, but with regard to the Test Act of 1673 it merely ordered that the oaths and declaration therein required of all office holders should not be tendered; the offer of individual dispensations as well implied that there was a need to be doubly sure. Many Protestant office-holders, like Godolphin and Herbert, rather provocatively continued to comply with the first Test Act, appearing in Chancery and King's Bench to take the oaths of supremacy and allegiance and tender certificates to prove they had taken the Anglican sacrament.

James himself dragged the whole question out into the open when he reissued the Declaration in April 1688 and ordered the Anglican clergy to read it from their pulpits. The archbishop of Canterbury and six of his bishops petitioned against this order, on the grounds that the suspending power had been declared illegal by Parliament, and were indicted for seditious libel.[2] Their acquittal underlined the doubts of the judges, and the Bill of Rights in 1689 abolished the suspending power outright, though it only condemned the dispensing power 'as it hath been assumed and exercised of late'.[3]

112. His Majesty's declaration to all his loving subjects, 26 December 1662

...Our principal aim [in this declaration] is to apply proper antidotes to all those venomous insinuations by which (as we are certainly informed) some of our subjects of inveterate and unalterable ill principles do daily endeavour to poison the affections of our good people by misleading their understandings, and that principally by four sorts of most false and malicious scandals....

The first, by suggesting unto them, that having attained our ends in re-establishing our regal authority, and gaining the power into our own hands by a specious condescension to a general Act of Indemnity, we intend nothing less than the observation of it; but on the contrary by degrees to subject the persons and estates of all such who stand in need of that law to future revenge, and to give them up to the spoil of those who had lost their fortunes in our service.

[1] No. **124**, p. 438 below.
[2] Nos. **126-7**, pp. 441-2 below.
[3] Williams, *Eighteenth-century Constitution*, p. 28.

Secondly, that upon pretence of plots and practices against us, we intend to introduce a military way of government in this kingdom.

Thirdly, that having made use of such solemn promises from Breda, and in several declarations since, of ease and liberty to tender consciences, instead of performing any part of them, we have added straiter fetters than ever, and new rocks of scandal to the scrupulous, by the Act of Uniformity.

Fourthly and lastly,...that at the same time [as] we deny a fitting liberty to those other sects of our subjects, whose consciences will not allow them to conform to the religion established by law, we are highly indulgent to Papists, not only exempting them from the penalties of the law, but even to such a degree of countenance and encouragement as may even endanger the Protestant Religion.

* * * * * *

As for the third, concerning the non-performance of our promises, we remember well the very words of those from Breda, viz:

> *We do declare a liberty to tender consciences, and that no man shall be disquieted or called in question for differences of opinion in matters of religion which do not disturb the peace of the kingdom; and that we shall be ready to consent to such an Act of Parliament as upon mature deliberation shall be offered to us for the full granting that indulgence.*

We remember well the confirmations we have made of them since upon several occasions in Parliament, and as all these things are still fresh in our memory, so are we still firm in the resolution of performing them to the full. But it must not be wondered at, since that Parliament to which those promises were made in relation to an Act never thought fit to offer us any to that purpose, and being so zealous as we are (and by the Grace of God shall ever be) for the maintenance of the true Protestant religion, finding it so shaken (not to say overthrown) as we did, we should give its establishment the precedency before matters of indulgence to dissenters from it. But that once done (as we hope it is sufficiently by the Bill of Uniformity), we are glad to lay hold on this occasion to renew unto all our subjects concerned in those promises of indulgence by a true tenderness of conscience this assurance:

That as in the first place we have been zealous to settle the uniformity of the Church of England, in discipline, ceremony and government, and shall ever constantly maintain it; so as for what concerns the penalties upon those who (living peaceable) do not conform thereunto through scruple and tenderness of misguided conscience, but modestly and without scandal perform their devotions in their own way, we shall make it our special care so far forth as in us lies, without invading the freedom of Parliament, to incline their wisdom at this next approaching sessions to concur with us in the making some such Act for that purpose as may enable us to exercise with a more universal satisfaction that power of dispensing which we conceive to be inherent in us. Nor can we doubt of their cheerful co-operating with us in a thing wherein we do conceive ourselves so far engaged, both in honour and in what we owe to the peace of our dominions, which we profess we can never think secure whilst there shall be a colour left to the malicious and disaffected to inflame the minds of so many multitudes upon the score of conscience, with despair of ever obtaining any effect of our promise for their case.

In the last place, as to that most pernicious and injurious scandal, so artificially spread and fomented, of our favour to Papists; as it is but a repetition of the same detestable arts by which all the late calamities have been brought upon this kingdom in the time of our royal father of blessed memory (who, though the most pious and zealous Protestant that ever reigned in this nation, could never wash off the stains cast upon him by that malice, but by his martyrdom), we conceive all our subjects should be sufficiently prepared against that poison by memory of those disasters, especially since nothing is more evident than that the wicked authors of this scandal are such as seek to involve all good Protestants under the odious name of Papists, or Popishly affected. Yet we cannot but say upon this occasion that our education and course of life in the true Protestant religion has been such, and our constancy in the profession of it so eminent in our most desperate condition abroad among Roman Catholic princes, when the appearance of receding from it had been the likeliest way in all human forecast to have procured us the most powerful assistances of our re-establishment, that should any of our subjects give but the least admission of that scandal unto their beliefs we should look upon it as the most unpardonable offence that they can be guilty of towards us.

'Tis true, that as we shall always according to justice retain, so we think it may become us to avow to the world a due sense we have of the greatest part of our Roman Catholic subjects of this kingdom having deserved well from our royal father of blessed memory, and from us, and even from the Protestant religion itself, in adhering to us with their lives and fortunes for the maintenance of our Crown in the religion established against those who under the name of zealous Protestants employed both fire and sword to overthrow them both. We shall with as much freedom profess unto the world, that it is not our intention to exclude our Roman Catholic subjects, who have so demeaned themselves, from all share in the benefit of such an act as in pursuance of our promises the wisdom of our Parliament shall think fit to offer unto us for the ease of tender consciences. It might appear no less than injustice, that those who deserved well and continued to do so should be denied some part of that mercy which we have obliged ourselves to afford to ten times the number of such who have not done so. Besides, such are the capital laws in force against them, although[1] justified in their rigour by the times wherein they were made, we profess it would be grievous unto us to consent to the execution of them, by putting any of our subjects to death for their opinions in matter of religion only. But at the same time that we declare our little liking of those sanguinary ones, and our gracious intentions already expressed to such of our Roman Catholic subjects as shall live peaceably, modestly and without scandal, we would have them all know, that if for doing what their duties and loyalties obliged them to, or from our acknowledgement of their well-deserving, they shall have the presumption to hope for a toleration of their profession, or a taking away either those marks of distinction, or of our displeasure, which in a well-governed kingdom ought always to be set upon dissenters from the religion of the State, or to obtain the least remission in the strictness of those laws which either are or shall be made to hinder the spreading of their doctrine, to the prejudice of the true Protestant religion; or that upon our expressing (according to Christian charity) our dislike for bloodshed for religion only, priests shall take the boldness to appear and avow themselves, to the offence and scandal of good Protestants, and of the laws in force against them, they shall quickly find we know as well to be severe, when wisdom requires, as indulgent when charity and sense of merit challenge it from us.... Cardwell, *Annals*, II, 312-13, 316-19

[1] Original reads *as though.*

113. Declaration of Indulgence, 1672

His Majesty's Declaration to all his loving subjects (15 March 1672)

Our care and endeavours for the preservation of the rights and interests of the Church have been sufficiently manifested to the world by the whole course of our government since our happy restoration, and by the many and frequent ways of coercion that we have used for reducing all erring or dissenting persons, and for composing the unhappy differences in matters of religion which we found among our subjects upon our return. But it being evident by the sad experience of twelve years that there is very little fruit of all those forcible courses, we think ourself obliged to make use of that supreme power in ecclesiastical matters which is not only inherent in us but hath been declared and recognised to be so by several statutes and acts of Parliament; and therefore we do now accordingly issue this our Declaration, as well for the quieting the minds of our good subjects in these points, for inviting strangers in this conjuncture to come and live under us, and for the better encouragement of all to a cheerful following of their trade and callings, from whence we hope by the blessing of God to have many good and happy advantages to our government; as also for preventing for the future the danger that might otherwise arise from private meetings and seditious conventicles.

And in the first place we declare our express resolution, meaning and intention to be, that the Church of England be preserved and remain entire in its doctrine, discipline and government, as now it stands established by law; and that this be taken to be, as it is, the basis, rule and standard of the general and public worship of God, and that the orthodox, conformable clergy do receive and enjoy the revenues belonging thereunto; and that no person, though of a different opinion and persuasion, shall be exempt from paying his tithes or other dues whatsoever. And further, we declare that no person shall be capable of holding any benefice or preferment of any kind in this our kingdom of England who is not exactly conformable.

We do in the next place declare our will and pleasure to be, that the execution of all and all manner of penal laws in matters ecclesiastical, against whatsoever sort of nonconformists or recusants, be immediately suspended; and all judges, judges of assize and gaol-delivery, sheriffs, justices of the peace, mayors, bailiffs and other officers whatsoever, whether ecclesiastical or civil, are to take notice of it, and pay due obedience thereunto.

And that there may be no pretence for any of our subjects to continue their illegal meetings and conventicles, we do declare that we shall from time to time allow a sufficient number of places, as they shall be desired, in all parts of this our kingdom, for the use of such as do not conform to the Church of England, to meet and assemble in in order to their public worship and devotion, which places shall be open and free to all persons.

But to prevent such disorders and inconveniences as may happen by this our indulgence, if not duly regulated, and that they may be the better protected by the civil magistrate, our express will and pleasure is that none of our subjects do presume to meet in any place until such place be allowed, and the teacher of that congregation be approved by us.

And lest any should apprehend that this restriction should make our said allowance and approbation difficult to be obtained, we do further declare that this our indulgence, as to the allowance of the public places of worship and approbation of the teachers, shall extend to all sorts of nonconformists and recusants, except the recusants of the Roman Catholic religion, to whom we shall in no way allow public places of worship, but only indulge them their share in the common exemption from the execution of the penal laws, and the exercise of their worship in their private houses only.

And if after this our clemency and indulgence any of our subjects shall presume to abuse this liberty and shall preach seditiously, or to the derogation of the doctrine, discipline or government of the Established Church, or shall meet in places not allowed by us, we do hereby give them warning, and declare, that we will proceed against them with all imaginable severity; and we will let them see we can be as severe to punish such offenders, when so justly provoked, as we are indulgent to truly tender consciences. Cardwell, *Annals*, II, 333–7

114. The King's Surrender, 1673

(a) The King's Reply,[1] 24 February 1673

His Majesty hath received an Address from you, and he hath seriously considered of it, and returneth you this answer.

[1] To the Commons' Address of the 14th requesting him to withdraw the Declaration of Indulgence.

That he is very much troubled that that Declaration, which he put out for ends so necessary to the quiet of his kingdom, and especially in that conjuncture, should have proved the cause of disquiet in his House of Commons, and give occasion to the questioning of his power in ecclesiastics, which he finds not done in the reigns of any of his ancestors. He is sure he never had thoughts of using it otherwise than as it hath been entrusted in him, to the peace and establishment of the Church of England, and the ease of all his subjects in general; neither did he pretend to the right of suspending any laws wherein the properties, rights or liberties of any of his subjects are concerned; nor to alter anything in the established doctrine or discipline of the Church of England; but his only design in this was, to take off the penalties the statutes inflict upon Dissenters, and which he believes, when well considered of, you yourselves would not wish executed according to the rigour and letter of the law. Neither hath he done this with any thought of avoiding or precluding the advice of his Parliament, and if any bill shall be offered him, which shall appear more proper to attain the aforesaid ends, and secure the peace of the Church and Kingdom, when tendered in due manner to him, he will show how readily he will concur in all ways that shall appear good for the kingdom.

CJ, IX, 256

(b) The Commons Answer, 26 February 1673

Most Gracious Sovereign,

We, your Majesty's most humble and loyal subjects, the knights, citizens and burgesses in this present parliament assembled, do render to your sacred Majesty our most dutiful thanks, for that, to our unspeakable comfort, your Majesty hath been pleased so often to reiterate unto us those gracious promises and assurances of maintaining the religion now established, and the liberties and properties of your people, and we do not in the least measure doubt but that your Majesty had the same gracious intentions, in giving satisfaction to your subjects, by your answer to our last petition and address. Yet upon a serious consideration thereof we find that the said answer is not sufficient to clear the apprehensions that may justly remain in the minds of your people, by your Majesty's having claimed a power to suspend penal statutes in matters ecclesiastical, and which your Majesty does still seem to assert in the said Answer to be entrusted in the Crown, and never questioned in the reigns of any of your ancestors. Wherein we humbly conceive your Majesty hath been very much misinformed, since no such power was ever claimed or exercised by any of your Majesty's predecessors; and if it should be admitted might tend to the interrupting of the free course of the laws, and altering the legislative power, which hath always been acknowledged to reside in your Majesty, and your two Houses of Parliament.

We do therefore, with unanimous consent, become again most humble suitors unto your sacred Majesty, that you would be pleased to give us a full and satisfactory answer to our said petition and address; and that your Majesty would take such effectual order that the proceedings in this matter may not for the future be drawn into consequence or example. *Ibid.* 257

[On 7 March Charles cancelled the Declaration.]

115. Declaration of Indulgence, 1687

King James the Second his gracious declaration to all his loving subjects for liberty of conscience (4 April 1687)

It having pleased Almighty God not only to bring us to the imperial crown of these kingdoms through the greatest difficulties, but to preserve us by a more than ordinary providence upon the throne of our royal ancestors, there is nothing now that we so earnestly desire as to establish our government on such a foundation as may make our subjects happy, and unite them to us by inclination as well as duty. Which we think can be done by no means so effectually as by granting to them the free exercise of their religion for the time to come, and add that to the perfect enjoyment of their property, which has never been in any case invaded by us since our coming to the crown. Which being the two things men value most, shall ever be preserved in these kingdoms during our reign over them, as the truest methods of their peace and our glory.

We cannot but heartily wish, as it will easily be believed, that all the people of our dominions were members of the Catholic Church, yet we humbly thank Almighty God it is and hath of long time been our constant sense and opinion (which upon divers occasions we have declared), that conscience ought not to be constrained, nor people forced in matters of mere religion. It has ever been directly contrary to our inclination, as we think it is to the interest of government, which it destroys by spoiling trade, depopulating countries and discouraging strangers; and finally, that it never obtained the end for which it was employed. And in this we are the more confirmed by the reflections we have made upon the conduct of the four last reigns. For after all the frequent and pressing endeavours that were used in each of them to reduce this kingdom to an exact conformity in religion, it is visible the success has not answered the design, and that the difficulty is invincible. We therefore, out of our princely care and affection unto all our loving subjects, that they may live at ease and quiet, and for the increase of trade and encouragement of strangers, have thought fit by virtue of our royal prerogative to issue forth this our Declaration of Indulgence, making no doubt of the concurrence of our two houses of Parliament when we shall think it convenient for them to meet.

In the first place we do declare, that we will protect and maintain our archbishops, bishops and clergy, and all other our subjects of the Church of England in the free exercise of their religion as by law established, and in the quiet and full enjoyment of all their possessions, without any molestation or disturbance whatsoever.

We do likewise declare, that it is our royal will and pleasure that from henceforth the execution of all and all manner of penal laws in matters ecclesiastical, for not coming to church, or not receiving the sacrament, or for any other nonconformity to the religion established, or for or by reason of the exercise of religion in any manner whatsoever, be immediately suspended; and the further execution of the said penal laws and every of them is hereby suspended.

And to the end that by the liberty hereby granted the peace and security of the government in the practice thereof may not be endangered, we have thought fit, and do hereby straitly charge and command all our loving subjects, that as we do freely give them leave to meet and serve God after their own way and manner, be it in private houses or places purposely hired or built for that use, so that they take especial care, that nothing be preached or taught amongst them which may any ways tend to alienate the hearts of our people from us or our government, and that their meetings and assemblies be peaceably, openly and publicly held, and all persons freely admitted to them, and that they do signify and make known to some one or more of the next justices of the peace, what place or places they set apart for their uses.

And that all our subjects may enjoy such their religious assemblies with greater assurance and protection, we have thought it requisite, and do hereby command, that no disturbance of any kind be made or given unto them, under pain of our displeasure, and to be further proceeded against with the utmost severity.

And forasmuch as we are desirous to have the benefit of the service of all our loving subjects, which by the law of nature is inseparably annexed to and inherent in our royal person; and that none of our subjects may for the future be under any discouragement or disability (who are otherwise well inclined and fit to serve us) by reason of some oaths or tests that have been usually administered on such occasions, we do hereby further declare, that it is our royal will and pleasure that the oaths commonly called 'the oaths of supremacy and allegiance', and also the several tests and declarations mentioned in the Acts of Parliament made in the 25th and 30th years of the reign of our late royal brother, King Charles II, shall not at any time hereafter be required to be taken, declared or subscribed by any person or persons whatsoever who is or shall be employed in any office or place of trust either civil or military under us, or in our government. And we do further declare it to be our pleasure and intention from time to time hereafter to grant our royal dispensations under our Great Seal to all our loving subjects so to be employed, who shall not take the said oaths, or subscribe or declare the said tests or declarations in the above-mentioned Acts and every of them.

And to the end that all our loving subjects may receive and enjoy the full benefit and advantage of our gracious indulgence hereby intended, and may be acquitted and discharged from all pains, penalties, forfeitures and disabilities by them or any of them incurred or forfeited, or which they shall or may at any time hereafter be liable to, for or by reason of their nonconformity, or the exercise of their religion, and from all suits, troubles or disturbances for the same, we do hereby give our free and ample pardon unto all nonconformists, recusants and other our loving subjects for all crimes and things by them committed or done contrary to the penal laws formerly made relating to religion and the profession or exercise thereof; hereby declaring that this our royal pardon and indemnity shall be as good and effectual to all intents and purposes as if every individual person had been therein particularly named, or had particular pardons under our Great Seal, which we do likewise declare shall from time to time be granted unto any person or persons desiring the same, willing and requiring our judges, justices and other officers to take notice of and obey our royal will and pleasure herein before declared.

And although the freedom and assurance we have hereby given in relation to religion and property might be sufficient to remove from the minds of our loving subjects all fears and jealousies in relation to either, yet we have thought fit further to declare, that we will maintain them in all their properties and possessions, as well of church and abbey lands as in any other their lands and properties whatsoever.

Cardwell, Annals, II, 359–63

IV. COMMONS VERSUS LORDS

However, some of the fiercest parliamentary battles of this period were fought not between king and Parliament but between the two Houses.[1] Relations between Lords and Commons were strained right up to 1714 and beyond. The Lords, unexpectedly strengthened by the Interregnum, were in a position to challenge the Commons head-on for the first time since the separation of the houses, and the resistance of the Commons provoked a whole series of crises ending with the Peerage Bill of 1719.

The most important field of conflict was the least eventful. Throughout the reign of Charles II the Commons showed themselves unduly sensitive to any attempt on the part of the Lords to encroach on their sole right to initiate and amend money bills. In 1671 they resolved that the ancient rule forbidding the Lords to alter the rate of tax applied to excises and other new duties as well as to direct taxes (**117a**), and in 1678 they even objected to the Lords' altering the date for the disbandment of the army, because it was contained in a money bill (**117b**). Such disputes were so common that on this last occasion, in 1678, Anchitel Grey the diarist merely noted: 'The arguments in the House upon this vote were chiefly what had been used formerly upon like occasions.'[2] In fact, the Commons claimed very far-reaching powers, including the right to render any statute immune from amendment in the Upper House simply by tacking a financial clause to it. This right was rarely exercised, but when it was, in 1700 (the Irish Land Grants bill) and 1704 (the Occasional Conformity bill), a deadlock immediately ensued. Moreover, the Lords never accepted this principle until 1911, and in 1740 and again in 1763 no less an authority than Lord Chancellor Hardwicke categorically declared that the Lords still possessed the right to amend money bills.[3]

But in the reign of Charles II the most savage quarrels between the two Houses were provoked by the Lords' claim to act as a court of law. Their

[1] A. S. Turberville, 'The House of Lords under Charles II' (2 pts, *EHR*, XLIV (1929), 400, XLV (1930), 58) is mainly narrative, but it remains the only authority.
[2] Grey, *Debates*, VI, 110.
[3] P. C. Yorke, *Philip Yorke Earl of Hardwicke* (1913), I, 195, III, 383.

right to act as a court of first instance, often exercised in the later Middle Ages, had lapsed under the Tudors, but it was revived in 1626. In the succeeding parliaments they continued to entertain original pleas, and during the 1640's they were particularly active, replacing Star Chamber as an instrument for pursuing the enemies of the State and enforcing the press censorship. The Lords' undoubted powers to subpœna witnesses and put them under oath were useful in impeachment proceedings, and the Commons watched with complacency the use of such powers against the Levellers and other 'anti-social' elements; in the notorious case of the Quaker James Nayler in 1656 the Commons themselves used judicial powers which no one had supposed they possessed. However, after the Restoration the judicial activity of the Lords became more and more prominent, and one lawyer remarked in 1663: 'The jurisdiction of the Star Chamber is now transformed into the House of Lords, but somewhat in a nobler way.'[1]

The Commons' mounting alarm found a vent in the case of *Skinner v. The East India Company* (**116**). In 1666 Thomas Skinner, an 'interloper',[2] petitioned the king, protesting at the East India Company's seizure of his goods in Sumatra in 1659. The Privy Council tried to mediate and failed, and in January 1667 Charles referred the matter to the House of Lords, since it was doubtful whether the courts of Common Law had jurisdiction over crimes not committed within the realm or on the high seas. The judges denied this, but notwithstanding in October 1667 the Lords proceeded to the assessment of damages against the company, and its directors petitioned the House of Commons, querying the Lords' right to act at all, and pointing out that part of the damages would fall on Members of the Commons who were also members of the company.[3] Despite a two-month adjournment beyond Christmas, the dispute dragged on into the following May, 1668, when the Commons voted that the Lords had exceeded their jurisdiction, and were also guilty of a grave breach of privilege. The Lords passed a stinging counter-resolution (**116**). Parliament was prorogued until October 1669, but as soon as it met the case proceeded, and the Commons took notice of the fact that during the recess the Lords had imprisoned one of their own Members, Sir Samuel Barnardiston, deputy governor of the East India Company. This produced another fierce resolution from the Commons (**116**), and Charles ordered another prorogation until February 1670, when he prevailed with both Houses to abandon the case and expunge all references to it from their Journals.[4] Thus the issue was left drawn, but in fact the Lords made no further attempt to act as a court of first instance, except in the process of impeachment.

[1] Holdsworth, *History of English Law*, I, 367.
[2] A merchant infringing the monopoly of trade with the Indies granted to the East India Company in its charter.
[3] *ST*, VI, 721–2, printed in Costin and Watson, I, 157–8.　　[4] *CJ*, IX, 126, printed *ibid.* I, 161.

The Lords' right to act as a court of appeal, however, was another matter. In 1675 Thomas Shirley appealed to the Lords against a Chancery decree in favour of Sir John Fagg, M.P., and the Commons took this as a breach of privilege.[1] They denied the Lords' right to hear appeals from Chancery, and arrested four barristers who were appearing in another case pending (118). Both Houses were now in a fine frenzy. The Commons imprisoned Fagg for putting in an answer to Shirley's plea before the Lords, and they dismissed their own sergeant-at-arms when he released the four barristers at the request of the Gentleman Usher of the Black Rod. On 4 June the Lords resolved to proceed with no further business until they received satisfaction. *Shirley v. Fagg* easily survived a short prorogation, from June to October, but during the prorogation that followed, from November 1675 to February 1677, it and all its attendant disputes were quietly dropped. The appellate jurisdiction of the House of Lords was not called in question again.[2]

116. Skinner *v.* The East India Company, 1668–70

Commons, 2 May 1668

Resolved:

1. That the Lords' taking cognisance of the matter set forth and contained in the petition of Thomas Skinner, merchant, against the governor and company of merchants trading to the East Indies, concerning the taking away the petitioner's ship and goods, and assaulting his person, and their Lordships' overruling the plea of the said governor and company, the said cause coming before their House originally, only upon the complaint of the said Skinner, being a common plea, is not agreeable to the law of the land, and tending to deprive the subject of his right, ease and benefit due to him by the said laws.

2. That the Lords' taking cognisance of the right and title of the island in the petition mentioned, and giving damages thereupon against the said governor and company, is not warranted by the laws of this kingdom.

3. That the said Thomas Skinner, in commencing and prosecuting a suit by petition in the House of Lords against the Company of Merchants trading to the East Indies (wherein several Members of this House are parties concerned with the said company, in particular interests and estates), and in procuring judgement therein, with directions to be served upon the governor, being a Member of this House, ...is [guilty of] a breach of the privilege of this House.   *PH*, IV, 422–3

[1] For a good summary see Turberville, *op. cit.* XLV, 71 ff.
[2] A complete series of extracts from documents is printed in Costin and Watson, I, 167–79.

Lords, 7 May 1668

It was resolved, That the House of Commons entertaining the scandalous petition of the East India Company against the Lords' House of Parliament, and their proceedings, examinations and votes thereupon had and made, are a breach of the privileges of the House of Peers, and contrary to the fair correspondency which ought to be between the two Houses, and unexampled in former times, [and]

That the House of Lords taking cognisance of the cause of Thomas Skinner, merchant, a person highly oppressed and injured in East India by the governor and company of merchants of London trading thither, and overruling the plea of the said company, and adjudging five thousand pounds damages thereupon against the said governor and company, is agreeable to the laws of the land and well warranted by the law and custom of Parliament, and justified by many parliamentary precedents, ancient and modern.   HMC, 8th Report, pp. 172–3

[Immediately upon the adjournment the Lords sent for Sir Samuel Barnardiston, M.P., deputy governor of the East India Company, who had presented the company's petition, denying the jurisdiction of the Lords in this case. He was fined £300, but refused to pay, and was imprisoned until 10 August. As a result, next session the Commons passed the following resolutions.]

1. That it is an inherent right of every commoner of England to prepare and present petitions to the House of Commons in case of grievance, and the House of Commons to receive the same; in evidence whereof, it is one of the first works that is done by the Commons, to appoint a grand committee to receive petitions and informations of grievances.

2. That it is the undoubted right and privilege of the Commons to judge and determine concerning the nature and matter of such petitions, how far they are fit or unfit to be received; and that in no age they found any person presenting a grievance by way of petition to the House of Commons, and received by them, that was ever censured by the Lords, without complaint by the Commons.

3. That no court whatsoever hath power to judge or censure any petition presented to the House of Commons, and received by them, unless transmitted from thence, or the matter complained of by them; and that no suitors for justice in any inferior court in law or equity are therefore punishable criminally, though untrue, or suable by way of

action in any other court; but are only subject to a moderate fine or amercement by that court, unless in some cases specially provided by Act of Parliament, as appeals, or the like. In case men should be punishable in other courts for presenting petitions to the House of Commons, it may deter his Majesty's subjects from seeking redress of their grievances, and frustrate the principal end for which parliaments were ordained.

4. Whereas a petition from the East India Company was presented to the House by Sir Samuel Barnardiston and others, complaining of grievances therein, which the Lords have censured under the notion of a scandalous paper or libel, the said censure, and proceeding of the Lords against the said Sir Samuel, are contrary to and a subversion of the rights and privileges of the House of Commons, and liberties of the commons of England; and further, no petition, or any matter depending in the House of Commons, can be taken notice of by the Lords without breach of privilege, unless permitted by the House of Commons.

5. That the continuance upon record of the judgement given by the Lords, and complained of by the Commons in the last session of Parliament, in the case of Thomas Skinner and the East India Company, is prejudicial to the rights of the commons of England.   *PH*, IV, 423–3

117. Finance Bills

(*a*) [Commons, 13 April 1671.]

The House then proceeded to the reading the amendments and clauses sent from the Lords, to the bill for an imposition on foreign commodities, which were once read.

And the first amendments sent from the Lords being for changing the proportion of the impositions on white sugars from one penny per pound to halfpenny half-farthing, was read the second time, and debated.

Resolved, &c., *nemine contradicente*, that in all aids given to the King by the Commons the rate or tax ought not to be altered by the Lords.

[Conference, 20 April 1671.]

...Their Lordships had neither reason nor precedent offered by the Commons to back that resolution, but were told that this was a right so fundamentally settled in the Commons that they could not give reasons for it, for that would be a weakening of the Commons' right and privilege.

Yet the Lords in Parliament, upon full consideration thereof...are come to this resolution, *nemine contradicente*:

That the power exercised by the House of Peers in making the amendments and abatements in the bill...[in question], both as to the matter, measure and time concerning the rates and impositions on merchandise, is a fundamental, inherent and undoubted right of the House of Peers, from which they cannot depart.

Reasons

*   *   *   *   *   *

4ly, If this right should be denied, the Lords have not a negative voice allowed them in bills of this nature, for if the Lords, who have the power of treating, advising, giving counsel and applying remedies, cannot amend, abate or refuse a bill in part, by what consequence of reason can they enjoy a liberty to reject the whole? When the Commons shall think fit to question it, they may pretend the same grounds for it.

5ly, In any case of judicature, which is undoubtedly and indisputably the peculiar right and privilege of the House of Lords, if their Lordships send down a bill to the Commons for giving judgement in a legislative way they allow and acknowledge the same right in the Commons to amend, change and alter such bills as the Lords have exercised in this bill of impositions sent up by the Commons.

6ly, By this new maxim of the House of Commons a hard and ignoble choice is left to the Lords, either to refuse the Crown supplies when they are most necessary, or to consent to ways and proportions of aid which neither their own judgement or interest, nor the good of the government and people, can admit.

7ly, If positive assertion can introduce a right, what security have the Lords that the House of Commons shall not in other bills (pretended to be for the general good of the commons, whereof they will conceive themselves the fittest judges) claim the same peculiar privilege, in exclusion of any deliberation or alteration of the Lords, when they shall judge it necessary or expedient.

*   *   *   *   *   *

[Two days later Parliament was prorogued, and did not meet again until 4 February 1673, by which time the matter was apparently forgotten.]

CJ, IX, 235, 239

(*b*) [On 21 June 1678 the Lords took into consideration the Supply Bill for the disbandment of the army, and amended the clause which stated that the troops in England must be disbanded by 30 June. The Commons, without a leg to stand on, argued the point, but had to give way, especially since by that time 30 June was passed.[1] The Act was amended to read '30 July', three days more grace than the Lords had suggested,[2] but to save their face the Commons passed this Resolution.]

[Commons, 3 July 1678.]

Resolved, etc., That all aids and supplies, and aids to his Majesty in Parliament, are the sole gift of the Commons; and all bills for the granting of any such aids and supplies ought to begin with the Commons; and that it is the undoubted and sole right of the Commons to direct, limit and appoint in such bills the ends, purposes, considerations, conditions, limitations and qualifications of such grants, which ought not to be changed or altered by the House of Lords. *CJ*, IX, 509

118. Shirley *v.* Fagg, 1675

[Lords, 17 May 1675.]

Then the lord keeper...gave the House a report of the effect of the late conference; which was to communicate to their lordships, by Sir Richard Temple (who said he was appointed by the House of Commons to communicate to you), a resolve of that House, *videlicet*:

> Resolved, &c., that the appeal brought by Doctor Shirley in the House of Lords against Sir John Fagg, a Member of the House of Commons, and the proceeding thereupon, is a breach of the undoubted rights and privileges of the House of Commons, and therefore the Commons desire that there be no further proceedings in that case before their lordships.

The House took the matter of this conference into consideration, and after a serious debate made this declaration following:

> The Lords do order and declare, that it is the undoubted right of the Lords, in judicature, to receive and determine in time of Parliament appeals from inferior courts, though a member of either House be concerned therein, that there may be no failure of justice in the land; and from this right, and the exercise thereof, the Lords will not depart. *LJ*, XII, 694

[1] *LJ*, XIII, 257, 262, 265.
[2] For extracts from the Act, see no. **109**, p. 396 above.

CHAPTER 12

THE JUDICIARY, 1660-1688[1]

Even the modest legal reforms adopted during the Interregnum were abandoned at the Restoration. The use of law-French, for instance, was at once reimposed, and continued into the reign of George II. At first Charles II honoured his father's undertaking in 1641 to appoint judges 'during good behaviour', but this undertaking was never confirmed by statute, and after Clarendon's fall in 1667 the practice was resumed of issuing patents *durante bene placito*.[2] In 1673 the judges' opposition to the Declaration of Indulgence led to the first clear-cut dismissals for political reasons during this reign, and in February 1674, as a result, a bill was introduced in the Commons to regulate judges' salaries and inhibit their dismissal by the Crown. The interesting thing is that it ran into strong opposition from a number of backbenchers who were normally no friends of the monarchy. They voiced the fear that if judges were given complete security of tenure they would evolve into a separate species of political man, below the king but above the people. Examples of the arbitrary and tyrannical conduct of judges in recent years were not wanting, and the bill made no further progress.[3]

The conduct of the judges in the 1630's, of course, had undermined the public prestige they had enjoyed in the era of Coke, and the complaints continued without a break into the reign of Charles II. But the autocratic bad temper of many judges after the Restoration, particularly at assizes, was largely occasioned by the difficulty of handling ignorant and partisan juries, especially now that they could not be disciplined by Star Chamber. In 1667 Lord Chief Justice Keeling was summoned to the Bar of the House of Commons for bullying and harrying juries, and even disparaging Magna Carta (**119**). Though he disdained to make an apology the House took no action against him, but it did pass a resolution that the fining and imprisoning of juries for giving a verdict against the judge's summing-up was illegal. In 1670 this was upheld by King's Bench. Edward Bushel, a juryman at the London Court of Sessions, was imprisoned for refusing to bring in a verdict against the Quakers Penn and Mead. On a writ of *habeas corpus* into King's Bench Lord Chief Justice Vaughan found in favour of the prisoner, and declared that judges could not punish jurymen for their verdict unless there

---

[1] A. F. Havighurst, 'The Judiciary and Politics in the Reign of Charles II' (2 pts, *Law Quarterly Review*, LXVI (1950), 62, 229), is indispensable. Holdsworth also has an interesting review of Charles II's judges, in *History of English Law*, VI, 500 ff.

[2] But see p. 90 above.

[3] Grey, *Debates*, II, 415-20 (13 February 1674).

was evidence of criminal collusion. But it should be noticed that he was very far from asserting the modern doctrine of the jury's absolute impartiality; on the contrary, he argued from the common-sense medieval notion that the jury, drawn from the neighbourhood, knew more about the facts of the case and the parties concerned than the judge; and his idea of what constituted 'discreet and lawful assistance of the jury' is very far from our own (**120**).

Moreover, since juries could no longer be punished after the event it was all the more important now to hammer them into shape beforehand, and the reluctance of many juries to bring in verdicts against those prosecuted under the Conventicles Act was a further source of irritation to some judges.[1] The standards of a later age were reflected in the persons of lord chief justices like Matthew Hale and to some extent Francis North, but the manners of most of the judges, if not their abilities, left a great deal to be desired. As late as 1687 Justice Holloway of King's Bench could refer quite naturally and without equivocation to his 'menacing and threatening' an assize jury at Reading in an attempt to secure an acquittal (**125**). Meanwhile Scroggs, Pemberton and Jeffreys, the villains of the great political trials of the period 1678–85, behaved deplorably, but their manner in court, and particularly in cross-examination, arose not from natural ignorance but deliberate policy. It was their duty to obtain certain verdicts, despite the unreliability of a great deal of the Crown's evidence and the untrustworthiness of most of their juries. During the Exclusion Crisis they were particularly vulnerable, in the crossfire between king and Parliament. Lord Chief Justice Scroggs won the favour of the Commons by his ruthless handling of Edward Coleman and other 'Popish Plotters' in 1678,[2] but when he bowed to pressure from Whitehall, and summed up in favour of Wakeman and Marshal in July 1679, he risked an impeachment, which duly came when the next parliament assembled in 1680. Lord Chief Justice North and Sir George Jeffreys, then Recorder of London, narrowly escaped the same fate.

During these troubled years the king juggled with judicial appointments at will. Four judges were dismissed without explanation in April 1679, and new appointments were made with a view to conciliating the Opposition. This policy was abandoned in February 1680, when Sir Robert Atkins was abruptly removed from Common Pleas and Sir Francis Pemberton from King's Bench. In April 1681 Scroggs had to be pensioned off, and Pemberton replaced him as chief justice of King's Bench and presided over the 'revenge' trials that followed. In December 1682, however, Pemberton was transferred to Common Pleas and soon afterwards dismissed a second time in circum-

---

[1] See the Commons debate of 22 March 1671 (*ibid.* I, 406 ff.).

[2] 'Mr Speaker,' he said, 'you shall find me the same man, and nothing on my part shall be wanting. When a knife is at my throat I will pluck it away, and I shall not stand upon usual forms' (*ibid.* VI, 213).

stances which remain obscure. He was succeeded by Edmund Saunders, who died in September 1683 and was succeeded by Jeffreys.

Charles II was doubtful about Jeffreys, because of his unpopularity in the profession and his lack of legal learning.[1] But neither accusation has been satisfactorily proved, and if he differed from his contemporaries on the bench it was only in degree. The violence of his cross-examinations and the partiality of his summings-up are horrifying to those raised on modern criteria of judicial conduct, but in the seventeenth century, and particularly in treason trials, they were nothing out of the way. What doomed the victims of Charles II's tribunals was not so much the conduct of the judges as the convention which denied those accused of treason a copy of the indictment or the services of counsel except on points of law. The House of Commons in 1679 was horrified at the very idea of men accused of treason being given an outline of the evidence against them,[2] and though even Jeffreys regarded the convention as ridiculous he was not prepared to break it (122). When all has been said, however, Jeffreys at his worst was worse than any English judge before or since, and he can be seen at his worst in the trial of Dame Alice Lisle (123).

Jeffreys' conduct as chief justice earned him the lord chancellorship in 1685; but it is a mistake to assume that he was secure in James II's favour. Sir Edward Herbert, his successor as chief justice of King's Bench, was a persistent critic, and many top legal appointments in 1687 and 1688 were made against his advice; there were frequent rumours of his dismissal, which was apparently only prevented by the difficulty of finding a suitable successor. Another false assumption often made is that the bench under James II, because it was purged with a regularity and an extravagance hitherto unknown, was a subservient tool of the Crown. This is not supported by the evidence.

The loyalty and obedience of the Tory bench appointed in Charles II's last years ought to have satisfied any monarch, but they went the way of the Tory parliament of 1685, and for substantially the same reason—refusal to acknowledge the dispensing power. As soon as Parliament objected to the commissioning of Roman Catholic army officers in November 1685 it was prorogued, and the king sounded out the judges. Sir William Gregory, of the Exchequer, and Sir Cresswell Levinz were dismissed in February 1686, and in March a test case was laid on.[3] Sir Edward Hales's coachman accused his master of holding the king's commission without having complied with the Test Act, and he was given the verdict at Rochester assizes. Pleading a dispensation under the Great Seal, Hales then appealed to King's Bench, but

[1] S. W. Singer (ed.), *Diary and Correspondence of Henry Hyde, Earl of Clarendon*, I (1828), 82–3.
[2] Grey, *Debates*, VII, 106–7, 114–16 (14–15 April 1679).
[3] For this, and much of what follows, see A. F. Havighurst, 'James II and the Twelve Men in Scarlet', *Law Quarterly Review*, LXIX (1953), 522.

before the case came on, in June, James dismissed the chief justice of common pleas, Sir Thomas Jones, and the chief baron of Exchequer, Sir William Montague, together with two puisne judges, Charlton and Nevill. Lord Chief Justice Herbert was a convinced supporter of the dispensing power, but by a strained device the judges from the other two courts were also dragged in (124). All but one agreed with Herbert, and there is no real reason to doubt their honesty; though very few judges had ever acknowledged the king's suspending power many of them had always supported the dispensing power.

However, Sir Robert Sawyer, attorney-general, and Heneage Finch, solicitor-general, who had held office respectively since 1681 and 1679, and had led for the Crown in all the most notorious treason trials of the last five years, declined the invidious task of prosecuting Hales. Finch was dismissed in favour of Sir Thomas Powys, but Sawyer remained, despite his well-publicised refusal to draw up dispensations for Roman Catholics—even the king's natural son, Berwick. His survival for nearly two years is typical of the confusion in the judiciary and the legal profession at this time, and the only conceivable reason for it is that his obvious successor was Jeffreys' bête noire, William Williams. Williams had been Speaker in the Exclusion Parliaments of 1680 and 1681, and he had been defence counsel to many of his whig associates in the trials that followed, notably Edmund Fitzharris and Algernon Sydney. Jeffreys detested him, and so apparently did other judges,[1] but he was now an ardent royalist, and when Sawyer was at length dismissed in favour of the incompetent Powys in December 1687 he had to be offered the vacant solicitor-generalship.

Moreover, despite the purge of 1686, James continued to have difficulty with his judges, notably on the key question of desertion from the colours. 7 Hen. VII, c. 1. had made this a felony in certain circumstances, and this had been expanded and confirmed by 3 Hen. VIII, c. 5; but some held that the latter Act had been repealed under Mary I, and though in the 'Case of Soldiers', 1601, the judges had denied this, and confirmed that desertion was punishable at Common Law, the question was still wide open.[2] It became increasingly important with the steady growth of the army in this reign. Sir John Holt, Recorder of London, declined to convict a deserter brought before him early in 1687, but in April King's Bench was asked to grant execution against another deserter, condemned at Reading assizes, so that he could be shot before his regiment at Plymouth. Lord Chief Justice Herbert, supported by Sir Francis Wythens, ruled against the Crown (125).[3] Wythens was at once dismissed, with Holt, but as the chief supporter of the dis-

---

[1] See L. C. J. Wright's spiteful and apparently unprovoked remark during the trial of the seven bishops, no. 127, p. 444 below.

[2] Holdsworth, *History of English Law*, VI, 228 ff.

[3] Havighurst, *op. cit.* p. 534.

pensing power Herbert was too important to be sacrificed. Instead he was ordered to change places with Sir Robert Wright, chief justice of common pleas, who at once granted the Crown's application.

This should have had a chastening effect on Herbert, but he went ahead and voted, as a member of the Commission for Ecclesiastical Causes, against the condemnation of the Fellows of Magdalen College in December 1687.[1] But many of his fellow judges were no more reliable, and the prosecution of the Seven Bishops in 1688 went sadly awry. On 27 April James reissued his Declaration of Indulgence,[2] and on 4 May he ordered it to be read on two successive Sundays in all the churches of the Anglican communion, in London on 20 and 27 May and in the provinces on 3 and 10 June. On 18 May the archbishop of Canterbury and six of his bishops presented a petition to the king asking him to withdraw the order on the ground that the suspending power had never been recognised by Parliament (126). When the petition was published next day the bishops were charged with seditious libel.[3]

The trial had strong elements of the grotesque. Defence counsel included a former lord chief justice (Pemberton), another ex-judge (Levinz), and the former attorney- and solicitor-general (Sawyer and Finch). This and the eminence of the accused made the proceedings more decorous than usual, and the judges had to vent their spleen on the solicitor-general, who conducted the case for the Crown. His superior, Powys, was so incompetent that he had omitted to furnish proof that the bishops had ever submitted a petition to the king, and his case almost collapsed at the outset. Subsequently the lord chief justice allowed the pleading to degenerate into a discussion of the suspending power, though in his summing-up he insisted that it had nothing to do with the case. His colleagues Sir Richard Holloway and Sir John Powell then intervened to argue cogently against the suspending power, and in favour of acquittal, and the attempt of Sir Richard Alibone, a Catholic appointed the year before, to refute them was distinguished by energy rather than good sense (127). The jury returned a verdict of not guilty and the following day Holloway and Powell were dismissed. The doubts of three generations of judges concerning the suspending power were sustained, and it was demonstrated again that no judge could be permanently bought.

There was only one change in legal procedure between 1660 and 1688, but it was an important one. The Act abolishing the Court of Star Chamber in 1641[4] decreed that any man imprisoned by order of the king or the council was entitled to a writ of *habeas corpus* from King's Bench or Common Pleas,

---

[1] Havighurst, *op. cit.* pp. 536–7. Sir Thomas Jenner, a judge almost as notorious as Jeffreys, voted with him, which shows yet again that such men were not necessarily timeservers.

[2] No. 115 p. 410 above.

[3] See Roger Thomas, 'The Seven Bishops and Their Petition', *Journal of Ecclesiastical History*, XII (1961), 56.

[4] No. 61, p. 223 above.

and that upon return of the writ the jailer must certify the true cause of imprisonment.[1] But this did not cover commitment on the orders of a secretary of state, which was increasingly common. Moreover, there was doubt as to whether a judge could issue a writ in vacation, and which courts could issue it in term; jailers were often ordered to delay returning the writ; judges could delay issuing the writ, then postpone the hearing on its return; the king's prisoners were often carried from prison to prison, calling for the issue of a new writ each time, and sometimes they were taken to places like the Channel Islands, where the writ did not run. One of the articles in Clarendon's impeachment in 1667 accused him of imprisoning the king's subjects in 'remote islands, garrisons and other places',[2] and indeed many doubtful characters left over from the Interregnum, like John Lambert, were silenced in this way. (Nor was this anything new; Charles I had sent Prynne to Jersey, and Cromwell, Lilburne.)

A bill to make the issue of the writ obligatory was introduced in the Commons in 1668, but it sank in committee. In 1670 a bill to prevent the removal of prisoners from the jurisdiction of the English courts passed the Commons but was lost in the Lords.[3] In 1674 a similar bill was brought in again, and with it another designed to reform *habeas corpus* procedure; they were both lost on the prorogation.[4] Meanwhile Secretary Coventry was criticised in 1674 for having a man arrested on a verbal order, and in 1677 it was found that his colleague Williamson was issuing general warrants 'on suspicion of seditious practices'.[5] With this, and the mounting political tension, the need for legislative reform was obvious, but further bills in 1675 and 1677 failed. Finally, in the first Exclusion Parliament, in 1679, the previous bills were combined in the Habeas Corpus Amendment Act (121), which laid down a watertight procedure for the issue of the writ, set a time limit for its hearing, frustrated equivocation on the part of judges or jailers, and forbade the transportation of prisoners overseas. It passed the Lords, in mysterious circumstances, on the last day of the session.[6]

Undoubtedly the Act made it more difficult for the government to take up men on suspicion, and many of those implicated in the Rye House Plot or Monmouth's Rebellion owed their lives to it. James II's dislike testifies to its effectiveness, as does its suspension in 1689. But the infrequency of parliaments after 1679 meant that further reform must wait on the Revolution.

[1] Holdsworth, IX, 115 ff.
[2] Article IV, printed Browning, *English Historical Documents*, p. 193.
[3] It is calendared in *HMC, 8th Report*, p. 142. See also Holdsworth, *History of English Law*, IX, 117.
[4] For the debates on the second bill, see Grey, II, 365–7, 414, 433–5.
[5] *Ibid.* II, 424–5, IV, 261 ff.
[6] G. Davies and E. L. Klotz, 'The Habeas Corpus Act of 1679 in the House of Lords', *Huntington Library Quarterly*, III (1940), 469; Helen A. Nutting, 'The Most Wholesome Law', *American Historical Review*, LXV (1960), 527.

A man indicted for treason or felony was still not allowed the services of counsel except on points of law, and could not put his witnesses on oath. Even Jeffreys considered it a scandal that such a man could not have a copy of the indictment, either (**122**); but in this respect, if in no other, he was ahead of his time.[1]

119. Lord Chief Justice Keeling

[Commons, 16 October 1667.]

The Lord Chief Justice Keeling was complained of by some of the House for his severe and illegal fining and imprisoning juries....A committee was nominated and appointed to inquire into the matter and complaint and to make a report thereof to the House, to the intent that a course may be taken that judges may not at their wills and pleasures impose fines and imprison or affront either grand juries or petty juries for giving and adhering to their verdicts.

Milward, *Diary*, pp. 88–9

[11 December 1667.]

Sir Thomas Gower reports from the committee the following articles of accusation against the Lord Chief Justice Keeling:

1. That he imposed upon the consciences of the grand jury of Somersetshire, to find a verdict contrary to their judgements, and bound them to their good behaviour. Sir Hugh Wyndham...he reproached for being the head of a faction, for no other cause than finding a bill according to his conscience. He drew the verdict and made the jury find it. Sir Hugh said he was the King's servant and a Member of Parliament...; he told the grand jury they were his servants, and he would make the best in England stoop.

2. In an indictment for murder [at Devon assizes], which the jury found manslaughter because they found no malice prepense, he told them they must be ruled by him in matter of law, and forced them to find the bill murder. The man was executed accordingly, without reprieve, notwithstanding the address of the gentlemen of the bench to him.....

[1] In 1696 (7 & 8 Wm. III, c. 3, printed Costin and Watson, I, 80) those accused of treason were allowed a copy of the indictment and the services of counsel, who could summon witnesses on oath. In 1702 (1 Ann, st. 2, c. 9, § 3) those accused of felony were allowed to put their witnesses on oath, and in 1708 (7 Ann, c. 21, § 14) those accused of treason were allowed a list of the prosecution witnesses and the jury before the trial. It became customary for counsel to defend those indicted for felony, though the practice did not receive statutory approval until 1837 (Holdsworth, *History of English Law*, IX, 235).

3. One before him speaking of Magna Carta, he said, 'Magna Farta? what ado with this have we?'

[The committee recommended that he be impeached, but the House after some debate decided to hear him at the bar.]   Grey, *Debates*, I, 62–3

[12 December 1667.]

The Lord Chief Justice Keeling came to the bar. A chair was set for him,...but he stood....

As to the slight speaking of the Magna Carta, he affirmed that it being long since he did not remember,...but it might be possible, Magna Carta being often and ignorantly pressed upon him, that he did utter that indecent expression; but as he doth not remember neither can it reasonably be imagined that he should speak these words in any dishonour to that great charter, for it is evidently known to all men his great loyalty to his sovereign and laws....

The case in Devonshire was this. A weaver, having divers servants and apprentices, gave order to a servant and authority to oversee them and in his absence correct the younger prentices....A prentice boy... neglecting his work, this servant beat him about the head with a broomstick,...of which the boy died within two or three hours. The jury would find this manslaughter; he caused them to go out again and bring it in murder....'And though I was petitioned', said the chief justice, 'by Sir Thomas Clifford[1] for his reprieve, yet I confess I did not grant it, because I do acknowledge I am very strict and severe against highway robbers and in case of blood.'

The case in Somersetshire was this. The grand jury was of persons of great [wealth] and ability, [such] as Sir Hugh Wyndham and others; they brought in a bill of a man that was killed, *per infortuniam*.[2] The chief justice told them they ought to bring in the bill either *billa vera* or else *ignoramus*. 'I also told them', said he, 'they had...to examine anything that shall be brought before them by proofs; and if they find the proofs to be slight or not material, then to find it *ignoramus*, and if it be sufficiently proved, then to bring it in *billa vera*, and then to leave it to the trial of the court....

'Notwithstanding, the grand jury would not alter....I desired them better to consider of it that night, but at the next day they were of the

[1] Of Ugbrooke, a confidant of Charles II and his brother, and one of the coming men in the government.
[2] By misadventure. They were usurping the functions of an inquest jury.

same judgement, and told me they were resolved not to alter from it, whereupon I fined some of them £20 a man, bound them to their good behaviour, and to appear at the King's Bench bar the next term. Notwithstanding, I offered them to withdraw their fine and recognisance for the good behaviour if they would submit, which they refused, and the matter came to a hearing, and the judges with one consent said that I was in the right, and had done no more but what was just and lawful....'

I...am very confident that he made a very good and sufficient defence to everything charged upon him as to the point of integrity and justice,[1] but without doubt he had failed in point of passion and discretion.

After he was withdrawn it came to a debate of four hours at least. Many did aggravate, others did extenuate his failings. In the close the House passed two votes:

1. First, that the late proceedings and precedents in fining and imprisoning juries for giving in their verdict was illegal, and that a bill be brought in to prevent the like for the future.

2. Secondly, that there shall be no further prosecution or proceedings against the chief justice upon this charge.　Milward, *Diary*, pp. 166–70

120. Bushel's Case. King's Bench, 1670

[Edward Bushel, a member of the jury at the London sessions, had refused to convict two Quakers of holding an unlawful conventicle. He was imprisoned by the presiding magistrate for giving a verdict against a judge's direction in a matter of law, but he sued out a writ of *habeas corpus* in King's Bench.]

L. C. J. Vaughan.... If the meaning of these words, 'Finding against the direction of the court in matter of law', be that if the judge, having heard the evidence given in court (for he knows no other), shall tell the jury, 'Upon this evidence, the law is for the plaintiff, or for the defendant, and you are under the pain of fine and imprisonment to find accordingly', then the jury ought of duty to do so. Every man sees that the jury is but a troublesome delay, great charge, and of no use in determining right and wrong, and therefore the trials by them may be better abolished than continued—which were a strange, new-found conclusion, after a trial so celebrated for many hundreds of years.

For if the judge, from the evidence, shall by his own judgement first resolve upon any trial what the fact is, and so knowing the fact shall

---

[1] Four other similar cases were taken into consideration.

then resolve what the law is, and order the jury penally to find accordingly, what either necessary or convenient use can be fancied of juries, or to continue trials by them at all?

But if the jury be not obliged in all trials to follow such directions, if given, but only in some sort of trials (as, for instance, in trials for criminal matters upon indictments or appeals), why then the consequence will be, though not in all yet in criminal trials, the jury (as of no material use) ought to be either omitted or abolished, which were the greater mischief to the people than to abolish them in civil trials. And how the jury should in any other manner...find against the direction of the court in matter of law is really not conceivable.

True it is, if it fall out upon some special trial that the jury being ready to give their verdict, and before it is given the judge shall ask whether they find such a particular thing propounded by him, or whether they find the matter of fact to be such as a witness or witnesses have deposed; and the jury answer, they find the matter of fact to be so. If then the judge shall declare, the matter of fact being by you so found to be, the law is for the plaintiff, and you are to find accordingly for him; if notwithstanding they find for the defendant, this may be thought a finding in matter of law against the direction of the court, for in that case the jury first declare the fact, as it is found by themselves, to which fact the judge declares how the law is consequent.

And this is ordinary: when the jury find unexpectedly for the plaintiff or defendant the judge will ask, how do you find such a fact in particular? And upon their answer he will say, then it is for the defendant, though they found for the plaintiff, or *e contrario*, and thereupon they rectify their verdict. And in these cases the jury, and not the judge, resolve and find what the fact is. Wherefore always in discreet and lawful assistance of the jury the judge his direction is hypothetical and upon supposition, and not positive, and upon coercion....

It is true, if the jury were to have no other evidence for the fact but what is deposed in court the judge might know their evidence, and the fact from it, equally as they, and so direct what the law were in the case, though even then the judge and jury might honestly differ in the result from the evidence as well as two judges may, which often happens. But the evidence which the jury have of the fact is much other than that, for:

1. Being returned of the vicinage whence the cause of the action ariseth, the law supposeth them thence to have sufficient knowledge to

try the matter in issue (and so they must) though no evidence were given on either side in court; but to this evidence the judge is a stranger.

2. They may have evidence from their own personal knowledge, by which they may be assured, and sometimes are, that what is deposed in court is absolutely false; but to this the judge is a stranger....

*   *   *   *   *   *

7. To what end is the jury to be returned out of the vicinage whence the cause of the action ariseth? To what end must hundredors be of the jury, whom the law supposeth to have nearer knowledge of the fact that those of the vicinage in general?... To what end must they have such a certain freehold, and be *probi et legales homines*, and not of affinity with the parties concerned?... To what end must they undergo the heavy punishment of a villainous judgement, if after all this they implicitly must give a verdict by the dictates and authority of another man, under pains of fines and imprisonment, when sworn to do it according to the best of their own knowledge?...

*   *   *   *   *   *

The chief justice delivered the opinion of the court, and accordingly the prisoners were discharged.   *ST*, VI, 1006–12

121. The Habeas Corpus Amendment Act, 1679

31 Car. II, c. 2. *An Act for the better securing the liberty of the subject and for prevention of imprisonments beyond the seas.*

Whereas great delays have been used by sheriffs, gaolers and other officers to whose custody any of the King's subjects have been committed for criminal or supposed criminal matters in making returns of writs of *habeas corpus* to them directed,...contrary to their duty and the known law of the land, whereby many of the King's subjects have been and hereafter may be long detained in prison in such cases where by law they are bailable, to their great charge and vexation. For the prevention whereof...be it enacted...that whensoever any person or persons shall bring any *habeas corpus* directed unto any sheriff or sheriff's gaoler, minister or other persons whatsoever for any person in his or their custody...the said officer or officers...shall within three days after the service thereof as aforesaid (unless the commitment aforesaid was for treason or felony plainly and specially expressed in the warrant of commitment)...bring or cause to be brought the body of the party so committed ... before the lord chancellor, or lord keeper of the Great Seal of England for the time being, or the judges or barons of the said court from whence the said writ shall issue or...is made returnable,... and shall likewise then certify the true causes of his detainer or imprisonment...

[If the court was more than twenty miles from the prison the gaoler was allowed ten days, and if more than a hundred, twenty days.]

ii. And to the intent that no sheriff, gaoler or other officer may pretend ignorance of the import of any such writ, be it enacted...that all such writs shall be marked in this manner, *per statutum tricesimo primo Caroli Secundi regis*, and shall be signed by the person that awards the same.

And if any person or persons shall be or stand committed or detained as aforesaid for any crime, unless for treason or felony,...in the vacation time and out of term, it shall and may be lawful to and for the person or persons so committed...to appeal or complain to the lord chancellor or lord keeper or any of his Majesty's justices...; and the said lord chancellor...[etc.] are hereby authorised and required...to award and grant a *habeas corpus*...returnable immediate[ly] before... [him]. And upon service thereof...the officer...in whose custody the party is so committed or detained shall within the times respectively before limited bring such prisoner...before the said lord chancellor ...[etc.].... And thereupon within two days after the party shall be brought before them the said lord chancellor...[etc.] shall discharge the said prisoner from his imprisonment, taking his or their recognisance ...for his or their appearance in the court of King's Bench the term following, or at the next assizes, sessions or general gaol-delivery of and for such county, city or place where the commitment was...as the case shall require;...unless it shall appear...that the party so committed is detained...for such matters or offences for the which by the law the prisoner is not bailable.

* * * * * *

vi. Provided always...that if any person or persons shall be committed for high treason or felony..., [and] upon his prayer or petition in open court the first week of the term or the first day of the sessions of oyer and terminer or general gaol-delivery to be brought to his trial, shall not be indicted some time in the next term [or] sessions...after such commitments, it shall and may be lawful to and for the judges... to set at liberty the prisoner upon bail, unless it appear to...[them] upon oath that the witnesses for the King could not be produced the same term....And if any person or persons committed as aforesaid... shall not be indicted and tried the second term...after his commitment ...he shall be discharged from his imprisonment.

VII. Provided always that nothing in this Act shall extend to discharge out of prison any person charged in debt, or other action or with process in any civil cause....

VIII. Provided always...that if any person or persons, subjects of this realm, shall be committed to any prison or in custody of any officer or officers whatsoever for any criminal or supposed criminal matter, that the said person shall not be removed from the said prison and custody into the custody of any other officer or officers unless it be by *habeas corpus* or some other legal writ....

* * * * * *

X. And be it enacted...that a *habeas corpus*...may be directed and run into any county palatine, the Cinque Ports or other privileged places within the kingdom of England, dominion of Wales or town of Berwick-upon-Tweed, and the islands of Jersey or Guernsey, any law or usage to the contrary notwithstanding.

XI. And for preventing illegal imprisonments in prisons beyond the seas, be it further enacted...that no subject of this realm...shall or may be sent prisoner into Scotland, Ireland, Jersey, Guernsey, Tangier, or into any parts, garrisons, islands or places beyond the seas which are or at any time hereafter shall be within or without the dominions of his Majesty, his heirs or successors, and that every such imprisonment is hereby enacted and adjudged to be illegal....

* * * * * *

SR, v, 935–8

122. Rex *v.* Rosewall, King's Bench, 26 November 1684, for high treason

Mr Pollexfen. My lord, I have one word to move for myself, and the others that are appointed to be of counsel for Mr Rosewall. We think it our duty to apply ourselves to your lordship for this favour; that, to enable us the better to do our duty for the person for whom we are assigned, your lordship and the court would please to order that we may have a copy of the indictment. We do acknowledge that it is not a usual thing to have copies granted (though there be no express law that we know against it) in capital matters....

L.C.J. Jeffreys. Look you, if you speak to me privately, as to my own particular opinion, it is hard for me to say that there is any express resolution of the law in the matter; but the practice has always been to deny a copy of the indictment. And therefore if you ask me as a judge to have a copy of the indictment delivered to you in a case of high treason I must answer you, show me any precedents where it was done. For there are abundance of cases in the law which seem hard in themselves, but the law is so because the practice has been so, and we cannot alter the practice of the law without an Act of Parliament. I think it is a hard case that a man should have counsel to defend himself for a twopenny trespass, and his witness examined upon oath; but if he steal, commit murder or felony, nay, high treason, where life, estate, honour and all are concerned, he shall neither have counsel, nor his witnesses examined upon oath. But yet you know as well as I that the practice of the law is so; and the practice is the law.

Pollexfen. My lord, we heard the other day the indictment read..., but we desire such a copy as may enable us to argue as we ought to do, and as the court will expect from us, being assigned by the court.

L.C.J. ...It is hard, I confess, and so are many other things in the law; but I am wonderfully tender of making precedents, and therefore if it has not been practised I do not see how we can do it.　ST, x, 266–8

123. Rex *v*. Lisle, Winchester assizes, 27 August 1685, for high treason

[Dame Alice Lisle, the highly respectable and elderly widow of a regicide, was accused of high treason in that she had sheltered Hicks and Nelthorp, two nonconformist clergymen who were fugitives from Monmouth's army. Jeffreys was clearly intent on a conviction, but his main difficulty was to prove that Mrs Lisle knew who the men were and what they had been doing. He cross-examined Dunne, the agent who had brought them to her house, for several hours,[1] but got nowhere. After a brief interval he resumed, but Dunne eventually stood mute, despite a series of hysterical outbursts from

---

[1] He asked nearly 200 questions and made several short harangues, and Pollexfen, the prosecuting attorney, also joined in.

the bench. After a further interval for the examination of other witnesses Jeffreys had him back, and tried to persuade him to testify that over dinner that night Mrs Lisle had talked about the battle of Sedgemoor with her guests.]

L.C.J. I pity thee with all my soul, and pray to God Almighty for thee to forgive thee, and to the blessed Jesus to mediate for thee; and I pray for thee with as much earnestness as I would for my own soul; and I beg of thee once more, as thou regardest thy own eternal welfare, to tell all the truth. . . .

Dunne. My lord, I will tell all I know.

L.C.J. What discourse had you that night at the table in the room?

Dunne. I cannot tell what discourse truly, my lord, there was.

L.C.J. Was there nothing of coming from beyond seas, who came from thence, and how they came? Come, I would have it rather the effect of thy own ingenuity than lead thee by any questions that I can propound. Come, tell us, what was the discourse?

Dunne. I do not remember all the discourse.

L.C.J. Prithee, let me ask thee one question, and answer me it fairly. Didst thou hear Nelthorp's name named in the room? . . . I will assure you, Nelthorp told me all the story before I came out of town.[1]

Dunne. I think, my lord, he was called Nelthorp in the room, and there was some discourse about him.

L.C.J. Ay, there was unquestionably, and I know thou wert by, and that made me the more concerned to press upon thee the danger of forswearing thyself. . . .

Dunne. What does your lordship ask me?

L.C.J. Come, I will ask thee a plain question: was there no discourse there about the battle, and of their being in the army?

Dunne. There was some such discourse, my lord.

L.C.J. Ay, prithee now, tell us what that discourse was. . . .

Dunne. My lord, I will tell you, when I have recollected it, if you will give me time till tomorrow morning.

L.C.J. Nay, but we cannot stay so long. . . . Prithee, tell us what the discourse was.

Dunne. My lord, they did talk of fighting, but I cannot exactly tell what the discourse was.

---

[1] Nelthorp had been taken and was in prison. The point was, of course, that he was a notorious rebel of whom the prisoner might be expected to have heard.

L.C.J. And thou saidst thou didst eat and drink with them in the same room?

Dunne. I did so, my lord, I confess it....

L.C.J. ...Jesus God, that we should live to see such creatures among mankind, and among us, too, to the shame and reproach be it spoken of our nation and religion!...I pity thee with all my soul, and pray for thee, but it cannot but make all mankind to tremble and be filled with horror, that such a wretched creature should live upon the earth! Prithee be free, and tell us what discourse there was.

Dunne. My lord, they did talk of fighting, but I cannot remember what it was....

L.C.J. Well, I see thou wilt answer nothing ingenuously, therefore I will trouble myself no more with thee.

[Despite the unsatisfactory nature of these exchanges Jeffreys did not blush to tell the jury that the fact was proved, though his summing-up was padded out with a review of the history of this century, panegyrics on monarchy, and invectives against the Nonconformists and similar arch-rebels.]

L.C.J. ...Blessed God! What is the way that this devil of sedition comes to bewitch people to such a height, when Almighty God had so lately delivered us from the misery and confusion of a civil war? It is that way surely, we find it but too plain, which he had always found very successful, the practice of saintship, conscience, and that glorious name, religion. What religion can it be?...Good God! That we should live in such an age, when men call God to assist and protect them in a rebellion! For, not to reflect upon what was done in former times, it is late enough for us to remember, but not without horror, that men have been tied by all the bonds and contracts hell could invent in a combination and confederacy to murder both the late King and his present Majesty, and all this while this must be sanctified with the name of religion.[1]...Jesus God! that ever we should have such a generation of vipers amongst us, that can plunge themselves into the most horrid impieties, and yet think to escape confusion here, and purchase a crown of glory hereafter!

When we consider, gentlemen, the ringleader of this late rebellion, the centre of all our trouble, the arch-rebel and traitor Monmouth I mean, should arrive to such a height of impudence and villainy, as to bless God that he could with satisfaction reflect upon a two years' life

---

[1] The Rye House Plot.

very regularly spent. But how? In manifest adultery and uncleanness; nor can it be spoke or thought of without inexpressible horror.[1] . . .

Gentlemen, let us all join in hearty prayers to our God, the God of infinite mercy, that as he has yet once more delivered our sovereign, and us with him, out of the jaws of these lions and ravenous wolves, so he would still please to preserve him and us from the hands of all our enemies, and I pray God it may have that good effect upon all of us as to make us more careful and conscientious in our duty to him and his vice-regent, the King. . . .

But now, gentlemen, to come to the particular case before you; and the fact, upon the evidence, stands thus. It is very notorious this fellow Hicks was actually in this rebellion; . . . [it] is undeniably and unquestionably proved. That there are sufficient testimonies to satisfy you that this woman did receive and harbour him, is that which is left to your consideration; and for that the proofs lie thus. And truly I am sorry to have occasion for repeating the circumstances of the proof; I mean, the great art that has been used to conceal it, how difficult it was to come at it, what time has been spent in endeavouring to find out truth in a fellow [Dunne] that in defiance of all admonition, threats and persuasion would prevaricate and shuffle to conceal that truth—nay, lie and forswear himself to contradict it. . . . But, not to go backward and forward, as he has done in his evidence, . . . at least we are told that. . . they all supped together; there they fell into discourse; there Nelthorp's name was named, and they talked of being in the army, and of the fight; and so it is all come out, and makes a full and positive evidence. . . .

. . . Truth will come out, and I hope you will not be deceived by any specious pretences. Our forefathers have been deluded, but the deception, I hope, is now at an end. And I must needs say, if all these witnesses that have freely discovered their knowledge, joined to the truth that is at length drawn from that Dunne, be worthy of any credit, it is as plain a proof as can be given, and as evident as the sun at noonday.

Gentlemen, upon your consciences be it. The preservation of the government, the life of the King, the safety and honour of our religion, and the discharge of our consciences as loyal men, good Christians and faithful subjects, are at stake. . . . I charge you, therefore, as you will answer it at the bar of the last judgement, where you and we must all appear, deliver your verdict according to conscience and truth. . . .

[1] The reference is to Monmouth's scaffold speech, and his liaison with Lady Henrietta Wentworth.

Juryman. Pray, my lord, some of us desire to know of your lordship in point of law, whether it be the same thing, and equally treason, in receiving him before he was convicted of treason, as if it had been after.[1]

L.C.J. It is all the same. That certainly can be [in] no doubt.

Then the jury withdrew, and [they] staying out a while, the Lord Jeffreys expressed a great deal of impatience, and said, he wondered that in so plain a case they would go from the bar, and would have sent for them with an intimation that if they did not come quickly he would adjourn, and let them lie by it all night. But after about half an hour's stay the jury returned, and the foreman addressed himself to the court thus.

Foreman. My lord, we have one thing to beg of your lordship some directions in, before we can give our verdict in this case. We have some doubt upon us whether there be sufficient proof that she knew Hicks to have been in the army.

L.C.J. There is as full proof as proof can be; but you are judges of the proof. For my part, I thought there was no difficulty in it.

Foreman. My lord, we are in some doubt of it....

L.C.J. I cannot tell what would satisfy you. Did she not inquire of Dunne, whether Hicks had been in the army? And when he told her he did not know she did not say she would refuse him if he had been there, but ordered him to come by night..., and when he and Nelthorp came, discoursed with them about the battle and the army. Come, come, gentlemen, it is a plain proof.

Foreman. My lord, we do not remember that it was proved that she did ask any such questions when they were there.

L.C.J. Sure you do not remember anything that passed. Did not Dunne tell you there was such discourse, and she was by, and Nelthorp's name was named?...I wonder what it is you doubt of....

Then the jury laid their heads together for near a quarter of an hour, and at length agreed, and...delivered [a verdict of guilty].[2]

L.C.J. Gentlemen, I did not think I should have had any occasion to speak after your verdict, but finding some hesitancy and doubt among you, I cannot but say I wonder it should come about;

[1] This was the crux of the matter, and the chief legal reason given for reversing this judgement on a writ of error in the next reign.

[2] The Whig historians of the next generation (Oldmixon, Kennett, Ralph, etc.) all say that the jury at first returned a verdict of not guilty, and Jeffreys sent them back. But there is no contemporary evidence of this, and there were limits to what even Jeffreys could do.

for I think in my conscience the evidence was as full and plain as could be, and if I had been among you, and she had been my own mother, I should have found her guilty.   *ST*, XI, 354–9, 362–74[1]

124. Godden *v*. Hales, King's Bench, 16 June 1686

[Arthur Godden, Sir Edward Hales's coachman, brought a collusive action against him for holding a colonel's commission without complying with the Test Act. On 29 March Hales was convicted at Rochester assizes, but he pleaded a dispensation under the Great Seal and appealed to King's Bench, Lord Chief Justice Herbert presiding.]

L.C.J. This is a case of great consequence, but of as little difficulty as ever any case was that raised so great an expectation, for if the King cannot dispense with this statute he cannot dispense with any penal law whatsoever....

There is no law whatsoever but may be dispensed with by the supreme law-giver; as the laws of God may be dispensed with by God himself; as it appears by God's command to Abraham to offer up his son Isaac. So likewise the law of Man may be dispensed with by the legislator, for a law may either be too wide or too narrow, and there may be many cases which may be out of the conveniencies which did induce the law to be made; for it is impossible for the wisest law-maker to foresee all the cases that may be or are to be remedied, and therefore there must be a power somewhere, able to dispense with these laws. But as to the case of simony that is objected by the other side, that is against the laws of God, and a special offence, and therefore *malum in se*, which I do agree the King cannot dispense with....

The case of the sheriff is a much stronger case than this, and comes up to it in every particular, for that statute[2] doth disable the party to take and the King to grant; and there is also a clause in that statute which says that the patent shall be void notwithstanding any *non obstante* to the contrary,...and yet by the opinion of all the judges of England the King has a power of dispensing with that statute....

---

[1] Some doubts have been cast on the authenticity of this record, and they are discussed by Keeton, *Lord Chancellor Jeffreys*, pp. 314–15. However, most of the examination is in Jeffrey's usual style, and so was the summing up, which in any case must be taken as a whole and either entirely accepted or entirely dismissed. Keeton, who is one of Jeffreys' leading admirers, accepts *ST* as 'a reasonably accurate record' (*Trial for Treason*, pp. 104–5).

[2] 27 Hen. VIII, c. 24 (§ 2).

[However, on the strained plea that this doubt about the statute of sheriffs affected the whole administration of justice, Herbert adjourned the case to take the opinion of the judges of common pleas and the barons of the Exchequer. Of the other eleven judges all but one fully concurred with him, and on 21 June, when the hearing was resumed, he so reported.]

...We think we may very well declare the opinion of the court to be that the King may dispense in this case; and the judges go upon these grounds:

1. That the Kings of England are sovereign princes.
2. That the laws of England are the King's laws.
3. That therefore 'tis an inseparable prerogative in the Kings of England to dispense with penal laws in particular cases, and upon particular necessary reasons.
4. That of those reasons and those necessities the King himself is sole judge....
5. That this is not a trust invested in or granted to the King by the people, but the ancient remains of the sovereign power and prerogative of the Kings of England, which never yet was taken from them, nor can be. And therefore, such a dispensation appearing upon record to come time enough to save him from the forfeiture, judgement ought to be given for the defendant.

ST, XI, 1196–9

125. The deserter's case, 1687[1]

Upon Tuesday the 19th [April] a soldier that was for running away from his colours condemned at Reading [assizes] by Mr Justice Hollo-way was brought to the King's Bench bar. The counsel, Mr Attorney General, Sir Robert Sawyer, said that the soldier was condemned, and it was his Majesty's pleasure, though he was condemned in Berkshire, that he should be executed at Plymouth, where the regiment or company that he was of did now quarter. And he did therefore move that the conviction of the soldier and the judgement against him to die that were brought up with him might be filed in that court.

The court (i.e. my Lord Chief Justice Herbert) said, 'You would not have us file them before we hear them read?' So they were both read. The lord chief justice said: 'They shall be filed, or rather, taken into the care and custody of the court.' The counsel, Mr Attorney General,

[1] The defendant was so much a cipher that his name is uncertain; it is variously given as Beale or Dale.

moved that the court would award execution against the prisoner. The court...said, 'What have you more to urge?' 'Nothing at all.' 'Have you any precedents to strengthen your motion with?' He answered, 'No'. The chief justice said that he did think there had no question at all risen upon that Act[1] till of late days, [and] that the majority of his brethren had delivered their opinion that a soldier ought to be condemned to die upon that Act.[2] He had spent as much time as his leisure would admit him, and many serious thoughts upon it, for it was a great case, and concerned life, which if it were taken away by mistake there remains no remedy; but he could not reach or comprehend those reasons that induced his brethren to be of that opinion. His judgement was well known in that case, for he had declared it very publicly, and the more he thought of it the more he was confirmed therein, and he could never concur to award execution for a man to die upon an offence which the law did not condemn him for, as he did in his judgement and conscience verily believe it did not that man. But he was but one, and it belongs most properly to you, brother Holloway, to award execution who condemned him....

He said further, if this Act had reached the case he would have said it had been a very useful and very necessary Act. Now the peace cannot be preserved without an army, but the Act does not reach the case, and I can never concur to award execution against that man the law condemns not....

Mr Justice Wythens said he had and would serve the King in all things that he could possibly, and so would all that court he was sure, and desired the King's counsel...to acquaint his Majesty so with great earnestness, but hoped he should be excused in case of blood, for he could not concur to award execution against a person tried by another court.

The chief justice told him, 'Do not insist upon that reason, Brother, for it has nothing in it. If the law condemned him I would proceed, though I had not heard the trial.'

Mr Justice Holloway he gave the narrative of the trial, and said he would have had a Frenchman that was charged with the same crimes convicted that he thought a very cunning knave, and have had this man [ac]quitt[ed]; but the jury [ac]quitted the Frenchman and found

---

[1] Either 7 Hen. VII, c. 1 or 3 Hen. VIII, c. 5. See p. 423 above.

[2] Presumably a reference to the Case of Soldiers, 1601, in which the judges decided that by virtue of the above Acts desertion was a felony.

this, though indeed he had solicited and menaced the jury very much to find him guilty, for otherwise they had not. Although he went to his Majesty when he came to town out of his circuit, and gave him an account of the whole matter, and interceded with the King for his pardon,[1] but the King answered, he had done like a just judge in condemning him, and he would do like a just general in executing him. But he was so dejected and confounded in the court that he was like to sink down.

Then Mr Justice Powell he spoke [so] low that nobody could hear him, though the chief justice desired him twice to speak up, saying it was a very great case, and in a public court, and he desired that all that was said that day might be heard by all the court that were so well able to judge. But he did not speak up, thereupon the chief justice said, 'I will repeat so much of my brother's discourse as I plainly heard. He saith he thinks this court cannot award execution against the prisoner to die in any county but where he was condemned, and desired time to consult precedents.'

In the close the conviction and condemnation were not filed but taken into the custody of the court, and the prisoner to be safely kept until the court sent for him again....

The chief justice called his man Hyde, and sent him to Whitehall, it was supposed to inquire whether his Majesty was at leisure. His man came again, and the chief justice presently rose out of the court and went to Whitehall.   Dr Williams's Library, *Morrice Entring Book*, 2, ff. 98–100

126. The Petition of the Seven Bishops, 18 May 1688

To the King's Most Excellent Majesty:

> The humble petition of William, archbishop of Canterbury, and of divers of the suffragan bishops of that province, now present with him, in behalf of themselves, and others of their absent brethren, and of the clergy of their respective dioceses,

Humbly sheweth,

That the great averseness they find in themselves to the distributing and publishing in all their churches your Majesty's late Declaration for liberty of conscience proceeds neither from any want of duty and obedience to your Majesty (our holy mother the Church of England

---

[1] Presumably on the grounds that he was only seventeen, and had originally been pressed for short-term service against Monmouth in 1685.

being both in her principles and constant practice unquestionably loyal, and having to her great honour been more than once publicly acknowledged to be so by your gracious Majesty), nor yet from any want of due tenderness to Dissenters, in relation to whom they are willing to come to such a temper as shall be thought fit, when that matter shall be considered and settled in Parliament and Convocation; but among many other considerations from this especially, because that Declaration if founded upon such a dispensing power as hath been often declared illegal in Parliament, and particularly in the years 1662[-3], 1672[-3], and in the beginning of your Majesty's reign, and is a matter of so great moment and consequence to the whole nation, both in Church and State, that your petitioners cannot in prudence, honour or conscience so far make themselves parties to it as the distribution of it all over the nation, and the solemn publication of it once and again even in God's house, and in the time of his divine service, must amount to in common and reasonable construction. Your petitioners therefore most humbly and earnestly beseech your Majesty, that you will be graciously pleased not to insist upon their distributing and reading your Majesty's said Declaration.

And your petitioners shall ever pray, etc.

[*Signed.*] William Cantuar   William St Asaph
            Thomas Bath & Wells   Francis Ely
            John Chichester   Thomas Peterborough
            Jonathan Bristol.

Cardwell, *Annals*, II, 367–70

127. The Trial of the Seven Bishops, King's Bench, 29 June 1688

*   *   *   *   *   *

Mr Justice Holloway. Mr Solicitor, there is one thing I would fain be satisfied in: you say the bishops have no power to petition the King?

Solicitor General. Not out of Parliament, Sir.

Holloway. Pray give me leave, sir. Then, the King having made such a declaration of a general toleration and liberty of conscience, and afterwards he comes and requires the bishops to disperse this declaration, this, they say, they cannot do, because they apprehend it is contrary to law, and contrary to their function. What can they do, if they may not petition?

S.G. I'll tell you what they should have done, sir. If they were commanded to do anything against their conscience they should have acquiesced till the meeting of the Parliament. (*At which some people in the court hissed.*)

Attorney General. This is very fine indeed! I hope the court and the jury will take notice of this carriage.

S.G. My lord, it is one thing for a man to submit to his prince if the King lay a command upon him that he cannot obey, and another thing to affront him. If the King will impose upon a man what he cannot do, he must acquiesce; but shall he come and fly in the face of his prince? Shall he say it is illegal, and the prince acts against prudence, honour or conscience, and throw dirt in the King's face? Sure that is not permitted; that is libelling with a witness.

L.C.J. Truly, Mr Solicitor, I am of opinion that the bishops might petition the King, but this is not the right of way bringing it in. I am not of that mind that they cannot petition the King out of Parliament, but if they may petition, yet they ought to have done it after another manner. For if they may in this reflective way petition the King, I am sure it will make the government very precarious.

Mr Justice Powell. Mr Solicitor, it would have been too late to stay for a parliament, for it was to have been distributed by such a time.

S.G. They might have lain under it and submitted.

Powell. No, they would have run into contempt of the King's commands, without petitioning the King not to insist upon it; and if they had petitioned, and not have shown the reason why they could not obey, it would have been looked upon as a piece of sullenness, and that they would have been blamed for as much on the other side.

* * * * * *

L.C.J. [After a review of the prosecution's evidence, and proof of the delivery and publication of the petition.] Gentlemen, after this was proved, then the defendants came to their part; and these gentlemen that were of counsel for my lords let themselves into their defence by notable learned speeches, by telling you that my lords the bishops are guardians to the Church. They have read you a clause of a statute made in Queen Elizabeth's time,[1] by which they say my lords the bishops were under a curse if they did not take care of that law. Then they show you some records; one in Richard II's time which they could make little

---

[1] Act of Uniformity, 1559, § 4 printed *PCD*, pp. 17–18.

of, by reason their witness could not read it; but it was, in short, a liberty given to the King to dispense with the statute of provisors. Then they show you some journals of Parliament, first in the year 1662[-3], where the King, had granted an indulgence, and the House of Commons declared it was not fit to be done, unless it were by Act of Parliament,...and so likewise...in 1672[-3], which is all nothing but addresses and votes, or orders of the House, or discourses,...but these are not declarations in Parliament....A declaration in Parliament is a law, and that must be by the King, Lords and Commons....In all these things (as far as I can observe) nothing can be gathered out of them one way or the other; it is nothing but discourses. Sometimes this dispensing power[1] has been allowed, as in Richard II's time, and sometimes it has been denied; and the King did once waive it. Mr Solicitor tells you the reason, there was a lump of money in the case; but I wonder indeed to hear it come from him.

S.G. My lord, I never gave my vote for money, I assure you.

L.C.J. ...The truth of it is, the dispensing power is out of the case, it is only a word used in the petition. But truly, I will not take upon me to give my opinion in the question, to determine that now, for it is not before me. The only question before me is—and so it is before you, gentlemen, it being a question of fact—whether here be a certain proof of a publication? And then the next question is a question of law indeed, whether if there be a publication proved it be a libel...?

Now, gentlemen, anything that shall disturb the government, or make mischief and a stir among the people, is certainly within the case of *libellis famosis*, and I must in short give you my opinion, I do take it to be a libel. Now, this being a point of law, if my brothers have anything to say to it, I suppose they will deliver their opinions.

Holloway. Look you, gentlemen, it is not usual for any person to say anything after the chief justice has summed up the evidence; it is not according to the course of the court. But this is a case of an extraordinary nature, and there being a point of law in it it is very fit everybody should deliver their own opinion. The question is, whether this petition of my lords the bishops is a libel or no. Gentlemen, the end and intention of every action is to be considered, and likewise in this case we are to consider the nature of the offence that these noble persons are charged with; it is for delivering a petition which, according

---

[1] Here and throughout, the term 'dispensing power' was used to cover the power to suspend a statute as well as the power to dispense individuals from the provisions of a statute.

as they have made their defence, was with all the humility and decency that could be; so that if there was no ill intent, and they were not (as it is not, nor can be pretended they were) men of evil lives, or the like, to deliver a petition cannot be a fault, it being the right of every subject to petition. If you are satisfied there was an ill intention, of sedition or the like, you ought to find them guilty; but if there be nothing in the case that you find, but only that they did deliver a petition to save themselves harmless, and to free themselves from blame, by showing the reason of their disobedience to the King's command, which they apprehended to be a grievance to them, and which they could not in conscience give obedience to, I cannot think it is a libel. It is left to you, gentlemen, but that is my opinion.

L.C.J. Look you, by the way, brother, I did not ask you to sum up the evidence (for that is not usual), but only to deliver your opinion whether it be a libel or no.

Powell. Truly I cannot see, for my part, anything of sedition, or any other crime, fixed upon these reverend fathers, my lords the bishops. For, gentlemen, to make it a libel it must be false, it must be malicious, and it must tend to sedition. As to the falsehood, I see nothing that is offered by the King's counsel, nor anything as to malice; it was presented with all the humility and decency that became the King's subjects to approach their prince with....

Gentlemen, we must consider what they say is illegal in it. They say, they apprehend the declaration is illegal because it is founded upon a dispensing power which the King claims, to dispense with the laws concerning ecclesiastical affairs. Gentlemen, I do not remember in any case in all our law...that there is any such power in the King, and the case must turn upon that. In short, if there be no such dispensing power in the King, then that can be no libel which they presented to the King, which says that the declaration, being founded upon such a pretended power, is illegal....I can see no difference, nor know of one in law, between the King's power to dispense with laws ecclesiastical and his power to dispense with any other laws whatsoever. If this be once allowed of, there will need no Parliament; all the legislature will be in the King, which is a thing worth considering, and I leave the issue to God and your consciences.

Mr Justice Alibone.[1] ...I think in the first place, that no man can take upon him to write against the actual exercise of the government,

---

[1] Sir Richard Alibone, a Roman Catholic appointed in April 1687.

unless he have leave from the government, but he makes a libel, be what he writes true or false. For if once we come to impeach the government by way of argument it is the argument that makes it the government or not the government. . . .

Then I lay down this for my next position, that no private man can take upon him to write concerning the government at all, for what has any private man to do with the government if his interest be not stirred or shaken? It is the business of the government to manage matters relating to the government; it is the business of subjects to mind only their own properties and interests. . . .

I do agree that every man may petition the government or the King in a matter that relates to his own private interest, but to meddle with a matter that relates to the government, I do not think my lords the bishops had any power to do more than any others. When the House of Lords and Commons are in being, it is a proper way of applying to the King; there is all the openness in the world for those that are Members of Parliament to make what addresses they please to the government, for the rectifying, altering, regulating and making of what law they please, but if every man shall come and interpose his advice, I think there can never be an end of advising the government. I think there was an instance of this in King James's time, when by a solemn resolution it was declared to be a high misdemeanour, and next to treason, [to petition] the King to put the penal laws in execution.

Powell. Brother, I think you do mistake a little.

Alibone. Brother, I dare rely upon that I am right. It was so declared by all the judges.

S.G. The Puritans presented a petition to that purpose, and in it they said if it would not be granted they would come with a great number.[1]

Powell. Aye, there it is.

Alibone. I tell you, Mr Solicitor, the resolution of the judges is, that such a petition is next door to treason. . . .

Mr Pollexfen. They threatened, unless their request was granted, several thousands of the King's subjects would be discontented.

Powell. That is the reason of that judgement, I affirm it.

Alibone. But then I'll tell you, brother, again. . .for any man to raise a report that the King will or will not permit a toleration, if either of

---

[1] Though everyone is rather confused, the reference is clearly to the Northamptonshire Petition of 1605, see p. 127 above.

these be disagreeable to the people, whether he may or not, it is against law. For we are not to measure things from any truth they have in themselves, but from that aspect they have upon the government, for there may be every tittle of a libel true, and yet it may be a libel still. ... This is my opinion as to law in general. I will not debate the prerogatives of the King nor the privileges of the subject, but as this fact is, I think these venerable bishops did meddle with that which did not belong to them; they took upon them, in a petition, to contradict the actual exercise of the government, which I think no particular persons, or singular body, may do.

[This concluded the case. The jury stayed out all night and next morning about ten brought in a verdict of 'not guilty'.]

ST, xii, 416–17, 424–9

CHAPTER 13

THE CATHOLIC PROBLEM AND THE REVOLUTION

As Sir Henry Capel told the Commons in 1680, 'In the descent of four kings, still the parliaments have been troubled with Popery; laws have been made against it, and all fail.'[1] The legislation of Elizabeth alone barred Catholics from public office, the universities and the professions, mulcted them of £20 a month (or the income from two-thirds of their estates), and made Roman priests liable to the penalties of high treason simply for remaining in the kingdom.[2] To this James I added three statutes. The first, in 1606 (**128**), imposed on Catholics a new oath of allegiance, which remained in force until the Revolution; the second, in the same year, imposed severe restrictions on Catholic wives and their Protestant husbands,[3] and the third, in 1610, permitted the authorities to tender the new oath to anyone over the age of eighteen.[4]

But it was only rarely that any of this legislation was enthusiastically or efficiently enforced, and except during a brief period immediately after the discovery of the Gunpowder Plot in 1605 the Crown was uncooperative. As a result a sizeable minority of Catholics obstinately survived; their numbers have been estimated at 27,000, and these are merely the recusants convict, and heads of households into the bargain. A large allowance must be made for wives and dependants, and an even larger allowance for the 'church Papists', those conformist Catholics regarded with equal hostility by the English authorities and the Roman Church.[5] Moreover, a disproportionate number of these surviving recusants were nobility and gentry, a fact of which Parliament showed itself aware in 1606 when it authorised the government to refuse the recusancy fines, even if proffered, and proceed against the estates of wealthy Catholics (**128**).[6] Some historians have been

---

[1] Grey, *Debates*, VII, 360 (26 October 1680).

[2] Havran, *Catholics in Caroline England*, ch. 1, has a good summary. See also Elton, *Tudor Constitution*, pp. 410 ff.

[3] *TCD*, p. 94. [4] *Ibid.* p. 105.

[5] Magee, *English Recusants*, pp. 99, 104 ff. Usher (*Reconstruction*, I, 156–9) even suggests that there were as many as a million Catholics in 1603, nearly a quarter of the population.

[6] Aveling, *West Riding Recusants*, p. 191; Magee, *op. cit.* pp. 127–8, 138–49. Trimble's contention, in *The Catholic Laity in Elizabethan England*, that the recusant gentry and nobility were almost eliminated by 1603 is patently ridiculous, and it is even doubtful now whether the recusancy laws, except against priests, were enforced with any greater severity by Elizabeth than by James I. See Williams, *Bath and Rome*, pp. 6, 102 n. 16, and authorities there cited.

too ready to dismiss the obsession of seventeenth-century parliaments with the Catholic problem as mere brainsick fancy; such evidence as we have suggests that there was a problem, and there was a solid nucleus of possible support for the famous Popish Plot of 1640 or 1678.

On the other hand, James I and Charles I both found it impossible to prosecute a successful foreign policy in a Europe still dominated by Catholic powers while they were persecuting their own Catholic subjects. The resultant slackening in persecution[1] was always regarded with uneasiness by Parliament, and especially after the outbreak of the Thirty Years War. The Commons addressed a sharp memorial to James I on the subject in 1621,[2] but his son was no better, finding it difficult to evade the provisions of his marriage treaty with Henrietta Maria. The plausible assertion that he and Buckingham were 'soft' towards Roman Catholicism[3] did Charles I lasting harm, and in the 1630's his attempt to enforce the recusancy laws again, largely for financial motives, was offset by his wife's aggressive Catholicism, his many contacts with leading Roman ecclesiastics, and the large number of conversions which occurred at Whitehall.[4] This was the raw material out of which the parliamentary leaders fashioned the myth of a great Popish conspiracy.

As was to be expected, the Long Parliament's attitude to the Catholics was ferocious. Those who fought for the king lost all their estates, and were not allowed to proceed to composition like Protestant royalists; but even those who remained neutral lost two-thirds, and on top of this they had to pay double taxes.[5] Moreover, the better to identify and isolate the enemy, Parliament introduced a more detailed and specific oath of allegiance (**129**) which was a model for the Tests of 1673 and 1678. However, this animus was not shared by the leaders of the New Model Army, and the end of the Civil Wars ushered in a period of comparative relaxation which was encouraged by the complete overthrow of the Anglican establishment.[6] Cromwell was positively benevolent, and it is significant that persecution was not renewed until 1657, when the Protector attempted the first serious modification of army rule, and allied himself with a civilian parliament. The

[1] This is most evident in the execution of priests. 124 perished under Elizabeth, 19 under James I, only 2 between 1625 and 1640, and 21 between 1640 and 1646. Havran, *op. cit.* pp. 111–12; Mathew, *Catholicism in England*, p. 82.

[2] No. **14**, p. 43 above.

[3] See the resolutions of a Commons' subcommittee in 1629, no. **44**, p. 156 above.

[4] The picture presented by Havran is not entirely clear. The general conclusion must be that in certain areas there was an increased drive for enforcement, but this was limited in scope and the machinery available was not very efficient. Cf. Aveling, in *Catholic Record Society*, LIII (1961), 291 ff., and Barnes, *Somerset*, pp. 14–15.

[5] Nos. **78–9**, pp. 274–7 above.

[6] Again, the execution of priests is a useful indication; only two were executed between 1649 and 1660. More generally, see Hardacre, *Royalists during the Puritan Revolution*, pp. 55–9, 89, 117–18; Paul, *Lord Protector*, pp. 327–8, 332; Williams, *Bath and Rome*, p. 17.

Humble Petition and Advice excluded from Parliament not only recusants but the husbands, fathers and fathers-in-law of recusants,[1] and in June 1657 Parliament again redrafted the oath of allegiance and ordered the seizure of two-thirds of recusants' estates. Yet the edge of persecution was still blunted, and on the eve of the Restoration many of the leading Catholics were in negotiation with the usurping government.[2]

This proved fatal to the Catholic cause in 1660 and 1661. The Cavalier Parliament at once assumed the attitude of all its predecessors, while most of the royalists who returned from exile were convinced that the Catholics had betrayed their master's cause. In these circumstances hopes of toleration soon vanished, and the King's Declaration in December 1662,[3] in which he spoke of his and his father's great debt to the Catholics and his desire to ameliorate their sufferings, did him and them nothing but harm. Nevertheless, there is no evidence to suggest that the penal laws were executed with any new vigour in the 1660's, and some to suggest that they were not. The Protestant Dissenters, associated in the public mind with egalitarianism and anti-royalism, were the first target. In 1669 Charles II even ventured to issue orders forbidding the Act of 1581 to be enforced, and though Parliament obliged him to countermand these in 1671 it is significant that the list of recusants drawn up by the Exchequer on this occasion contained no noblemen and very few gentry.[4]

But the Declaration of Indulgence in March 1672[5] provoked a violent reaction, and in 1673 he was forced to cancel it and at the same time give his assent to the Test Act (130). The sting of this Act did not lie in the straight-forward anti-Catholic declaration imposed on all office-holders, but in the fact that they were now obliged to take the oaths of allegiance and supremacy in open court, and produce written evidence that they had taken the Anglican communion. The king's brother, the duke of York, and the lord treasurer, Lord Clifford, were forced to resign, and other Catholics had to perform the functions of their offices by deputy. However, the execution of the old penal laws continued to be lax and inefficient. On 14 November 1673 the Council again ordered them to be enforced, and in February 1675 Danby, anxious to identify his master more closely with the Protestant cause and bring in some more money at the same time, ordered the confiscation of two-thirds of all recusants' estates. But he found that the machinery had rusted in disuse, that a great deal of the money collected still stuck to the fingers of those collecting it, and it was difficult even to establish who were Catholics and who were not, since jury presentations commonly made no

[1] No. 96, p. 352 above.
[2] Hardacre, op. cit. pp. 119–20, 137–8.
[3] No. 112, p. 403 above.
[4] J. A. Williams, 'English Catholicism under Charles II', Recusant History, VII (1963), 123.
[5] No. 113, p. 407 above.

distinction between Protestant and Catholic recusants.[1] The census conducted by the Church of England in 1676 suggests that the number of Catholics had declined to 13,856 freeholders (as against more than 108,000 Protestant Dissenters and nearly 2½ million Anglicans).[2] But contemporaries regarded such figures with cynicism, and in 1677 the House of Lords decided to sacrifice the main principle at stake in return for accurate information. They sent down a bill 'for the preservation of the Protestant religion and the more effectual conviction and prosecution of Popish recusants', by which those Catholics who concealed their religion and were detected would be subject to the full weight of the penal laws, but those who registered themselves at Quarter Sessions would merely pay a shilling in the pound on their annual income.[3] Predictably, the Commons rejected it out of hand, with a sarcastic note by the Speaker that 'upon reading the said bill, and opening the substance thereof to the House, it appeared to be much different from the title.'[4] The known conversion of the heir to the throne, and the king's ambiguous relations with France, had deeply inflamed the prejudices of the nation, and this bid for toleration of a sort came too late. When educated men like Sir Peter Leicester were ready to believe that the Jesuits, by their influence on the Puritans, had caused the Great Rebellion, and were now the inspiration of the Protestant Dissenters,[5] the excesses of the Popish Plot scare are not at all surprising (131).

The myth of a Popish Plot to murder Charles II, put his Catholic brother on the throne and return the country to the Roman allegiance by force originated with Titus Oates and his associates in September 1678. The subsequent scare owed a great deal to the parallel discovery that Danby had been negotiating for a secret treaty with France, and to the determination of the Opposition in the Lords to force a dissolution of Parliament; but the basic popular appeal was always to religious prejudice and intolerance of the basest sort, and famous pamphlets like *An Appeal from the Country to the City* (133) helped to prolong a mood of hatred and hysteria in which twenty-four Catholics, seventeen of them priests, perished on the scaffold.[6] All the same, it is doubtful how far this affected the ordinary lay Catholic outside London, or even Whitehall. During the crisis parliaments sat for weeks rather than months, and they were so concerned with the succession question that they

---

[1] J. A. Williams, 'Some Sidelights on Recusancy Finance under Charles II', *Dublin Review*, Autumn 1959, p. 245. In March 1678 the Commons took note of the fact that Quakers were now being indicted as 'recusants' (*CJ*, IX, 455; Grey, *Debates*, V, 250).

[2] Browning, *English Historical Documents*, pp. 411 ff. But Magee argues that the Catholics still constituted 7–10% of the gentry (*English Recusants*, pp. 168–71).

[3] *LJ*, XIII, 48, 51; *HMC, 9th Report*, pt. 2, pp. 82–3.

[4] *CJ*, IX, 414; Grey, *Debates*, IV, 334–7.

[5] Cf. the statement of a Somerset grand jury in 1681: 'there is scarce a conventicle but there will be a Jesuit' (Williams, *Recusant History*, VII, 135).

[6] Mathew, *Catholicism in England*, pp. 106–9.

had little time for anything else; certainly they never meddled with the administration of the law as the Long Parliament tried to do.[1] In January 1679 an Order in Council threatened magistrates with instant dismissal if they did not enforce the penal laws to the hilt, but the government had no other powers of coercion, and what Danby at the height of his power had been unable to accomplish his harassed and precariously established successors certainly could not; indeed, an increase in persecution is not noticeable until the crisis had begun to die away in 1681.[2] In terms of positive legislation the only achievement of the Opposition was the second Test Act of 1678 (**132**), which finally drove the Catholic peers from the Lords.[3]

It was only natural that the parliaments of 1679 and 1680 should concentrate on the succession, and to many it was a serious weakness of the Test Act of 1673 that the king was the only office-holder exempt from it.[4] In 1679 the first Exclusion Parliament brought in a bill to exclude James, duke of York, from the succession, only to be prorogued and then dissolved before the bill went to the Lords. The next parliament, in 1680, brought in another Exclusion Bill (**134**), which did go to the Lords and was defeated there. A third parliament, at Oxford in 1681, brought in a third Exclusion Bill, but it was cut off by a snap dissolution.

The Exclusion Crisis has been little studied.[5] Undoubtedly Lord Shaftesbury and his associates in both Houses wanted further constitutional reforms involving the wholesale amendment of the Restoration Settlement, but the views of most of their supporters were narrow in the extreme and downright old-fashioned. Far from being a rehearsal for the Revolution of 1688, this crisis was regarded by most contemporaries, on both sides, as a repeat performance of 1641; after all, John Pym was the originator of the 'Popish Plot', and it was not difficult to identify the Exclusionists with the 'Men of 1641'. Capel protested in 1680, 'Parliament brought in the king without blood, but of late still we are told that the Church is in danger, and the actions of 1641 thrown amongst us';[6] but this is scarcely surprising when we realise that the comparison between 1679 and 1642 had already been quite explicitly put by the author of *An Appeal from the Country* (**133**). But this the bulk of the Commons gentry could not stand; hostility to Rome would carry them far, but not into civil war. Too many of them now believed implicitly in the

---

[1] In fact, they were more interested in relaxing the persecution of Protestant Dissenters. See H. Horwitz, 'Protestant Reconciliation in the Exclusion Crisis', *Journal of Ecclesiastical History*, XV (1964), 201.

[2] Williams, *Dublin Review*, pp. 251 ff., and *Recusant History*, VII, 136–7.

[3] Hitherto an occasional Catholic was found in the Commons, too. See, for instance, Grey, *Debates*, IV, 188.

[4] In 1677 the Lords had proposed a bill for this purpose. See *State Tracts*, I, 98 ff.; *HMC, 9th Report*, pt. 2, p. 81; *PH*, IV, 854.

[5] Except by J. R. Jones, whose *First Whigs* is indispensable.

[6] Grey, *Debates*, VII, 362.

absolutism of monarchy and the sanctity of non-resistance; the execution of Charles I had been too great a shock and was still too near.[1] In the end their reverence for divine right and hereditary succession triumphed over their emotional fear of Popery, especially when the less responsible elements in the Opposition ran the king's bastard son, the Duke of Monmouth, as a candidate for the succession, on the cynical grounds that a king with a weak title must rule weakly (**133**).[2] In November 1680 the Commons Opposition split on this issue, and the partisans of James's daughter Mary forced the adoption of an amendment to the Exclusion bill which stated that on Charles's death the crown should pass as though James were legally dead.[3] All Monmouth's supporters could secure was a passing reference to 'the heirs of his Majesty's body', and the gentry would not stomach an illegitimate heir. Under the stress of these internal contradictions the Exclusion movement fell to pieces. Indeed, so fierce was the reaction, intensified by the Rye House Plot of 1683, that the Anglican Church was moved to reaffirm its adherence to the principles of non-resistance with a vigour which proved embarrassing only a few years later (**135**).

All the same, when he dissolved the Oxford parliament in March 1681, Charles II felt obliged to order the execution of the penal laws yet again, and this time his words took effect.[4] The figures for the receipt of recusancy fines in the Exchequer leaped from £250 in 1680–1 to £5,444 in 1681–2 and £4,444 in 1682–3.[5] But the return of the duke of York from Scotland at Easter 1682 brought an immediate falling-off, to £2,000 in 1683–4 and £384 in 1684–5.[6] In July 1684 the Receivers were dismissed altogether, and in October, almost certainly on James's initiative, the 'cabinet council' discussed a suspension of the penal laws.[7]

Charles II was too canny to meddle with this, but on 27 February 1685, only three weeks after his accession, James II issued instructions that no proceedings were to be taken against Catholics who had been sufferers in the Great Rebellion, or were closely related to such sufferers, or who had testified to their loyalty to the Crown since then—a broad and inclusive definition. In March 1687 even this thin pretence was abandoned, and the penal laws were suspended altogether.[8]

---

[1] Sir Robert Filmer's remarkable *Patriarcha* was not published until 1680, but Sir Peter Leicester's remarks in 1677 (**131**) suggest that his theories were already well known.

[2] It must be stressed, however, that Monmouth's candidature was never part of the official Opposition platform. See O. W. Furley, 'Pamphlet Literature in the Exclusion Campaign', *Cambridge Historical Journal*, XIII (1957), 31 ff.

[3] § 6, no. **134** below. *CJ*, IX, 647, 648 (6 November).

[4] Browning, *English Historical Documents*, pp. 394–5 (9 April 1681).

[5] Williams, *Recusant History*, VII, 139. (The fines were handed in a year in arrears.)

[6] *Loc. cit.*

[7] North, *Lives of the Norths* I, 309; Barillon au Roi, 6/16 October 1684, PRO *Trans*.

[8] *CSPD*, *1685*, no. 243; *Calendars of Treasury Books*, VIII, 176, 1262.

There seems to have been little opposition to this aspect of James's policy, except from a few obstinate bigots; few seriously believed in the Popish Plot any longer, and many were thoroughly ashamed of the whole episode. In May 1685 Oates and Dangerfield, the principal informers, were convicted of perjury, and the king remarked to Sir John Reresby that now the plot was dead. Reresby replied, with some truth, that 'it was long since dead, and now it was buried'.[1]

But encroachment on the Test Act was quite another thing. In the summer and autumn of 1685 James extended to England a process already adopted in Ireland, of dispensing Catholic army officers from the test by letters patent under the Great Seal. Finding Parliament obdurately opposed, he turned to the judges, who gave a decision in favour of the dispensing power in the case of *Godden v. Hales*, 1686.[2]

But his policy was a complete failure. It was not to be expected that he would recruit many advisers or ministers of state from a class which had been excluded from the professions and the centres of higher education for three generations; what Catholics he was able to find willing to accept government office were substandard, and his cynical expectation that the lifting of the tests would produce a flood of converts was never realised.[3] Though Lord Bellasis was appointed first lord of the treasury in 1687, and Arundel of Wardour lord privy seal, the burden of administration and policy still fell on Protestants like Godolphin and Sunderland, on Scots Catholics like Melfort, or Irishmen like Tyrconnel. William Herbert, marquess of Powis, the premier Catholic peer, was not given office at all.

Indeed, as is well known, James only succeeded in splitting the Catholic community in England. The lay peers were in favour of a temporising policy, even after the announcement of the queen's pregnancy in 1687. They were steadily backed by Pope Innocent XI, and therefore by the papal nuncio and the secular clergy, led by Buonaventura Gifford and John Leyburn, who were appointed bishops *in partibus* in 1688. Opposed to them were the Scots and Irish ministers, particularly Tyrconnel and Castlemaine, and the Jesuits, led by the notorious Fr Edward Petre, who all advocated a 'forward' policy. This division reflected the divisions of Catholic Europe, and was in turn intensified by them. Louis XIV, at odds with the Pope, and detesting the Jansenist heresy, supported the Jesuits, while the king of Spain and his minister in London supported the Pope and the secular clergy. In these circumstances the creation of a Catholic nation was as far off as ever.

But James's attempts to win over the Protestant Dissenters were equally a failure.[4] In April 1687 he issued a Declaration of Indulgence suspending all

[1] Reresby, *Memoirs*, p. 365.   [2] No. **124**, p. 438 above.   [3] Kenyon, *Stuarts*, pp. 166–7.
[4] With some qualifications. See Kenyon, *Sunderland*, pp. 171–5, 186 ff., and J. R. Jones, 'James II's Whig Collaborators', *Historical Journal*, III (1960), 65.

the penal legislation against Protestants as well as Dissenters, as well as the Test Act.[1] But the vigorous campaign in the constituencies that followed during the winter of 1687–8 was not an apparent success, and in March 1688 the date for the summons of a new parliament had to be postponed from May to November. His decision to reissue his Declaration of Indulgence was in these circumstances a confession of failure. He was furious with the Church of England, on which he blamed all his troubles, and his order that the Declaration be read from the pulpits was an act of spite. He got what he deserved. Ninety per cent of the clergy refused to obey, and the acquittal of the seven bishops on charges of seditious libel was a resounding political defeat.[2] On the day of the acquittal, 30 June, the famous Invitation of the Seven was dispatched to William of Orange.[3]

William's Declaration in September 1688[4] made great play with the threat of Popery, and the Revolution was accompanied by a certain amount of public hysteria. Nevertheless, this brief and tragic reign worked to the advantage of the Catholics in the long run. It had been the contention of most English Protestants throughout this century that the Catholics were a powerful and malevolent minority working ceaselessly for the overthrow of the establishment in Church and State, and unless they were persecuted relentlessly and continuously they would simply engulf the reformed religion. But under James II the Catholics had their opportunity, and they did not take it. For three years the penal laws were suspended entirely; for two years the Test Act was evaded by dispensation or suspension; Catholic priests were free to operate in public, Jesuits and other regulars entered the country in large numbers, schools were opened and a great drive for converts began. Yet recusants did not emerge from hiding in large numbers, and remarkably few converts were made—amongst the nobility, for instance, only Peterborough, Yarmouth and Sunderland, and they recanted in 1689. As Macaulay remarks in another connection, 'It was hardly worth while to violate the most sacred obligations of law and of plighted faith for the purpose of making such converts as these.'[5] Even the famous assault on the Anglican church amounted to very little. The bishop of London was suspended, but the persistent rumours that James intended to appoint a Catholic priest to this see or to the vacant archbishopric of York came to nothing, and probably had no foundation at all.[6] In 1686 James did issue a dispensation for an Anglican clergyman to hold a benefice after his conversion to Rome, but this is an isolated example.[7] The notorious Jesuits attracted the usual

---

[1] No. 115, p. 410 above.   [2] See p. 424 above.

[3] Williams, *Eighteenth Century Constitution*, p. 8.   [4] *Ibid.* p. 10.   [5] *History*, I, 574.

[6] The institution in January 1688 of four Catholic sees independent of the Anglican hierarchy points to the same conclusion. See Hemphill, *Vicars Apostolic*, p. 16.

[7] John Massey, Josiah Bassett and Obadiah Walker, who were granted the same privilege, were heads of Oxford or Cambridge colleges.

hostility, but even they opened two magnificent schools in London, whose rules laid it down, 'There shall not be, either by masters or scholars, any tampering or meddling to persuade anyone from the profession of his religion.'[1] Similarly, the marked moderation displayed by the secular clergy, not to mention the Pope, redounded to the advantage of the Catholic laity.

So the reaction after the Revolution was mixed. A panic measure passed in May 1689 forbade recusants to come within ten miles of London,[2] but when the Lords in December discussed the enforcement of the penal laws the minority in favour of toleration was strong enough to block any action.[3] Catholics were obliged to pay double land-tax, but this seems to have been accepted in lieu of their liabilities under the Act of 1581.[4] In 1723 an additional aid of £100,000 in one year was levied on recusants, but after ten years only £63,000 had been collected, and the experiment was not repeated.[5] An Act of 1700[6] made Catholics incapable of inheriting or purchasing land, but the continued existence of a flourishing Catholic nobility and gentry testifies to its ineffectiveness. The last priest was executed in 1680, and nothing more is heard of Popish plots except during the brief hysteria of the Gordon Riots in 1780. The Catholic problem was no longer a political issue.

128. 3 Jac. I, c. 4: An Act for the better discovering and repressing of Popish recusants (1606)

Forasmuch as it is found by daily experience that many his Majesty's subjects that adhere in their hearts to the Popish religion, by the infection drawn from thence, and by the wicked and devilish counsel of Jesuits, seminaries and other like persons dangerous to the Church and State, are so far perverted in the point of their loyalties and due allegiance unto the King's Majesty and the Crown of England, as they are ready to entertain and execute any treasonable conspiracies and practices, as evidently appears by that more than barbarous and horrible attempt to have blown up with gunpowder the King, Queen, Prince, Lords and Commons in the House of Parliament assembled, tending to the utter subversion of the whole State, lately undertaken by the instigation of Jesuits and seminaries, and in advancement of their religion by their scholars taught and instructed by them to that purpose, which attempt

---

[1] Beales, *Education under Penalty*, pp. 250–4.   [2] Costin and Watson, I, 61.

[3] *House of Lords MSS.*, II, 385–8 (13, 19 December 1689).

[4] W. R. Ward, *The English Land Tax in the Eighteenth Century* (Oxford 1953), pp. 32–3; Aveling, *Catholicism in East Yorkshire*, pp. 49–50; J. A. Williams, 'The Problem of the Double Land Tax', *Dublin Review*, spring 1959, p. 32.

[5] Magee, *English Recusants*, pp. 176–7.

[6] Williams, *Eighteenth Century Constitution*, no. 204, p. 331.

by the only goodness of Almighty God was discovered and defeated; and where[as] divers persons Popishly affected do nevertheless, the better to cover and hide their false hearts, and with the more safety to attend the opportunity to execute their mischievous designs, repair sometimes to church to escape the penalties of the laws in that behalf provided; for the better discovery therefore of such persons and their evil affections to the King's Majesty and the State of this his realm, to the end that being known their evil purposes may be the better prevented; be it enacted...that every Popish recusant convicted or hereafter to be convicted which heretofore hath conformed him or herself, or which shall hereafter conform him or herself, and repair to church ...shall within the first year next after the end of this session of Parliament...or within the first year next after that he or she shall...conform his or herself, and after the first said year shall once in every year following at the least, receive the blessed sacrament of the Lord's Supper.... And if any recusant so conformed shall not receive the sacrament... accordingly, he or she shall...forfeit for the first year twenty pounds, and for the second year...forty pounds, and for every year after... threescore pounds, until he or she shall have received the said sacrament as is aforesaid....

*   *   *   *   *   *

[§ v re-enacted, with slight alterations, the provisions of 23 Eliz., c. 1 and 29 Eliz., c. 6,[1] which imposed a fine of £20 a month on recusants, and permitted the government to take the income from two-thirds of their estates in default.]

VI.   ...Now forasmuch as the said penalty of twenty pounds monthly is a greater burden unto men of small living than unto such as are of better ability..., who, rather than they will have two parts of their lands to be seized, will be ready always to pay the said twenty pounds..., and yet retain the residue of their living and inheritance in their own hands, being of great yearly value, which they do for the most part employ (as experience hath taught) to the maintenance of superstition and the Popish religion, and to the relief of Jesuits, seminaries, Popish priests and other dangerous persons to the State; therefore to the intent that hereafter the penalty...might be inflicted in better proportion upon men of great ability, be it enacted...that the King's Majesty, his heirs and successors, shall from and after the Feast of St Michael the

---

[1] Elton, *Tudor Constitution*, p. 432, and *PCD*, p. 88, respectively.

Archangel [29 September] next coming after the end of this session of Parliament, have full power and liberty to refuse the penalty of twenty pounds a month, though it be tendered..., and thereupon to seize and take to his own use...two parts in three parts to be divided as well of all the lands, tenements and hereditaments, leases and farms that at the time of such seizure shall be or afterwards shall come to any the said offenders..., or any other to his or her use, or in trust for him or her, or at his or her disposition, or whereby or wherewith, or in consideration whereof, such offender or his family or any of them shall be relieved, maintained or kept....

* * * * * *

VIII. And for the better trial how his Majesty's subjects stand affected in point of their loyalty and due obedience, be it also enacted...that from and after the end of this present session of Parliament it shall be lawful to and for any bishop in his diocese, or any two justices of the peace, whereof one of them to be of the quorum, within the limits of their jurisdiction out of sessions, to require any person of the age of eighteen years or above, being or which shall be convict or indicted of or for any recusancy, other than noblemen or noblewomen,...or any person passing in or through the county, shire or liberty, and unknown, except as is last before excepted, that being examined by them upon oath, shall confess or not deny himself or herself to be a recusant, or shall confess or not deny that he or she has not received the said sacrament twice within the year when last past, to take the oath hereafter following, upon the Holy Evangelist, which said bishop or two justices of peace shall certify in writing...at the next General or Quarter Sessions...the Christian name, surname and place of abode of every person which shall so take the oath, which certificate shall be there recorded by the clerk of the peace....

IX. ...The tenor of which said oath hereafter followeth:

I, A.B., do truly and sincerely acknowledge, profess, testify and declare in my conscience before God and the world, that our Sovereign Lord King James is lawful and rightful king of this realm and of all other his Majesty's dominions and countries, and that the Pope, neither of himself nor by any authority of the Church or See of Rome, or by any other means with any other, hath any power or authority to depose the King, or to dispose [of] any of his Majesty's kingdoms or dominions, or to authorise any foreign prince to invade or annoy him or his countries, or to discharge any of his subjects of their allegiance and obedience to his Majesty, or to give licence or leave to any of them to bear arms, raise tumult, or to offer any violence or hurt to his Majesty's royal person, state or government, or to any of his Majesty's subjects within his Majesty's dominions. Also I do swear from my heart that notwithstanding any declaration or sentence of excommunication or deprivation made or granted or to be made or granted by the Pope or his successors, or by any authority derived or pretended to be derived from him or his see, against the said king, his heirs or successors, or any absolution of the said subjects from their obedience, I will bear faith and true allegiance to his Majesty, his heirs and successors, and him or them will defend to the uttermost of my power against all conspiracies and attempts whatsoever which shall be made against his or their persons, their crown and dignity, by reason or colour or any such sentence or declaration or otherwise, and will do my best endeavour to disclose and make known unto his Majesty, his heirs and successors, all treasons and traitorous conspiracies which I shall know or hear of to be against him or any of them. And I do further swear, that I do from my heart abhor, detest and abjure as impious and heretical this damnable doctrine and position that princes which be excommunicated and deprived by the Pope may be deposed or murdered by their subjects or any other whatsoever. And I do believe and in my conscience am resolved, that neither the Pope nor any person whatsoever hath power to absolve me of this oath or any part thereof, which I acknowledge by good and full authority to be lawfully ministered unto me, and do renounce all pardons and dispensations to the contrary. And all these things I do plainly and sincerely acknowledge and swear, according to these express words by me spoken, and according to the plain and common sense and understanding of the same words, without any equivocation or mental evasion or secret reservation whatsoever. And I do make this recognition and acknowledgement heartily, willingly and truly, upon the true faith of a Christian. So help me God.

459

Unto which oath so taken, the said person shall subscribe his or her name or mark.

* * * * * *

SR, IV, 1071–7

129. The Sequestration Ordinance of 18 August 1643

For explanation and enlargement of a former ordinance lately made[1] ...Be it now declared and ordained that in the number of such delinquents and Papists who shall come within the compass of the said former ordinance...shall be reckoned and accounted...[those who have joined the King's army; those who have conveyed away their estates to escape taxation or sequestration; those concealing or sheltering delinquents; those hindering or molesting sequestrators]...or that have willingly harboured any Popish priests or Jesuits in their houses or dwellings since 29 November 1642, or that shall hereafter so harbour any; and all and every person or persons which at any time heretofore have been convicted of Popish recusancy, and so continue, or...that have been at mass at any time within one whole year before 26 March 1643, or shall hereafter be at mass; or whose children or grandchildren, or any of them living in house with them, or under their...tuition and government, shall be brought up in the Popish religion; and all such persons as, being of the age of twenty-one years or above, shall refuse to take the oath hereafter expressed, which oath any two or more of the said committees [*sc.* committeemen] for sequestration..., or any two justices of peace, or the mayor...of any city or town corporate, shall have power to administer....

The tenor of which oath followeth *in haec verba*, viz.,

> I, A.B., do abjure and renounce the Pope's supremacy and authority over the Catholic Church in general, and over myself in particular; and I do believe that there is not any transubstantiation in the sacrament of the Lord's Supper, or in the elements of bread and wine after consecration thereof by any person whatsoever; and I do also believe that there is not any Purgatory, or that the consecrated host, crucifixes or images ought to be worshipped, or that any worship is due unto any of them, and I also believe that salvation cannot be merited by works; and all doctrines in affirmation of the said points I do abjure and renounce, without any equivocation, mental

---

[1] No. **79**, p. 277 above.

reservation, or secret evasion whatsoever, taking the words by me spoken according to the common and usual meaning of them. So help me God.

[All refusing this oath] shall forfeit as Papists within this and the former ordinance.

*   *   *   *   *   *

Firth and Rait, I, 254–6

130. 25 Car. II, c. 2: An Act for preventing dangers which may happen from Popish recusants (1673)

For preventing dangers which may happen from Popish recusants, and quieting the minds of his Majesty's good subjects, be it enacted...that all and every person or persons, as well peers as commoners, that shall bear any office or offices, civil or military, or shall receive any pay, salary, fee or wages by reason of any patent of trust from or under his Majesty, or any of his Majesty's predecessors, or by his or their authority derived from him or them within the realm..., or shall be of the household or in the service or employment of his Majesty or of his royal highness the duke of York, who shall inhabit, reside or be within the city of London or Westminster or within thirty miles distant from the same on the first day of the Easter Term...1673..., all and every the said persons shall personally appear before the end of the said term, or of Trinity Term next following, in his Majesty's High Court of Chancery or in his Majesty's Court of King's Bench, and there in public and open court between the hours of nine of the clock and twelve...take the several oaths of supremacy and allegiance, which oath of allegiance is contained in a statute made in the third year of King James;[1]...and that all and every of the said respective persons and officers, not having taken the said oaths in the said respective courts as aforesaid, shall on or before the first day of August, 1673, at the Quarter Sessions for that county or place where he or they shall be, inhabit or reside on the twentieth day of May, take the said oaths in open court...; and the said respective officers aforesaid shall also receive the sacrament of the Lord's Supper according to the usage of the Church of England at or before the first day of August, 1673, in some parish church upon the Lord's Day, commonly called Sunday, immediately after the Divine Service and sermon....And every of the said persons

---

[1] No. 128 above.

in the respective court where he takes the said oaths shall first deliver a certificate of such his receiving the said sacrament as aforesaid under the hands of the respective minister and churchwarden, and shall then make proof of the truth thereof by two credible witnesses at the least upon oath, all which shall be inquired of and put upon record in the respective courts.

III. And be it further enacted...that all and every the person and persons aforesaid that do or shall neglect or refuse to take the said oaths and sacrament...shall be *ipso facto* adjudged incapable and disabled in law to all intents and purposes whatsoever to have, occupy or enjoy the said office or offices, employment or employments....

IV. And be it further enacted that all and every such person and persons that...after such neglect or refusal shall execute any of the said offices or employments..., being lawfully convicted..., shall be disabled from thenceforth to sue or use any action...in course of law, or to prosecute any suit in any court of equity, or to be guardian of any child, or executor or administrator of any person, or capable of any legacy, or deed of gifts, or to bear any office within this realm..., and shall forfeit the sum of five hundred pounds....

* * * * * *

VIII. And be it further enacted...that at the same time when the persons concerned in this Act shall take the aforesaid oaths of supremacy and allegiance, they shall likewise make and subscribe this Declaration under the same penalties and forfeitures as by this Act is appointed:

> I, A.B., do declare that I do believe that there is not any transubstantiation in the sacrament of the Lord's Supper, or in the elements of bread and wine, at or after the consecration thereof by any person whatsoever.

Of which subscription there shall be the like register kept as of the taking the oaths aforesaid.

* * * * * *

SR, v, 782–5

131. Sir Peter Leicester's charge to the grand jury at Nether Knotsford, Cheshire, 2 October 1677

The power, office and jurisdiction of justices of peace (saith the Lord Coke...) is such a form of subordinate government for the tranquillity and quiet of this realm as no part of the Christian world hath the like, if duly executed; here the streams of justice flow to every man's door. Indeed, the due administration of justice is the main pillar which supports a kingdom, for by justice is the throne established; and not only so, but it renders it also glorious and flourishing in the eyes of others, for justice exalts a nation.

Now administration of justice supposeth a law, whereby justice may be administered; punishment to the transgressors and protection to the innocent; for where there is no law there can be no transgression. And the law always supposeth a power to compel obedience thereunto..., the law hath in itself, or carries along with it, a forcing power; for otherwise it cannot be put in execution, and then it is all one, as if it were no law.

It is therefore the sovereign power which supporteth the laws, and that is our Sovereign Lord the King.... The laws have not their maintenance from the Parliament, as some of the late seditious pamphlets do falsely suggest to the people, but from the King; for it is he that makes judges and justices of peace and other officers, for the better execution of the laws; and the power of all the forces in this kingdom are [sic] in the King, as one of his most just and undoubted prerogatives, which we may read in the preamble of the statute of 12 Car. II, c. 6.[1] And therefore, having *jus gladii* only in himself, he is both the prime author and preserver of our laws—nay, it is no longer a law than the supreme power is pleased to allow it so, because he is uncontrollable in his actions, and hath no lawful superior on earth to control him.

And this power is given him from God, and therefore due to him *jure divino*; wherefore the King is called by the Apostle[2] Θεοῦ διάκονος, God's officer or minister, not the people's officer; neither doth he bear the sword in vain. And St Peter strictly chargeth us[3] to submit ourselves to all mankind in authority in regard of the Lord (for so the words in the original do properly signify and import)....

We see then the supreme power lodged in his Majesty *jure divino*, by the law of God. Let us now see how it is lodged in him *jure humano*, by the laws of our nation....

[And he embarks on a long review of English history, with special emphasis on the illegal encroachments of the bishop of Rome and the conspiracies fomented by his emissaries, culminating in Gunpowder Plot.]

[1] The Militia Act of 1661, no. **100**, p. 374 above.
[2] Paul, Rom. xiii. 4.   [3] I Pet. ii. 13.

And ever since have these engineers been continually hatching new devices for stirring up rebellions in our nation, and to disturb the peace of Israel. In the reign of King Charles I there was a sort of sectaries called Puritans, these were tickled in the ears by the Jesuits, that the ceremonies of our Church were Popish, and that our bishops intended to bring in Popery, which animated that party so far that they raised a rebellion against the King, having some principal men to head the faction, and countenanced by some members of the Parliament, A.D. 1640, which at last ended with an execrable murder of the said King under the specious show of a court of justice, and then [they] banished his children and set up Oliver Cromwell, called the Protector, 1655. All this we have seen acted with our own eyes.

And now at this present how many Jesuitical pamphlets are daily scattered among the people to ensnare weaker judgements, and to draw them on to raise a new rebellion? And how many kinds of sectaries have we now amongst us, and numerous parties of each sort? To wit, Presbyterians, Anabaptists, Independents, Quakers, and I know not what; all fed by the Jesuitical party now lurking in every corner of our kingdom, and following the humours and inclinations of the persons everywhere, as they find them to stand affected according to the several sects, purposely to make divisions amongst us, yet all agreeing in this, that they separate from the Church of England and betake themselves into private conventicles, each sect apart by themselves; and hence it was that the statute against seditious conventicles was enacted, 22 Car. II, 1670.[1] But now these sectaries grow so numerous that they build themselves meeting-houses for their own party almost everywhere, to the confronting of authority and the scandal of the true Protestant religion. . . .

And therefore, gentlemen, that I may draw to an end (for I hasten), what remains but the counterplotting of these engineers, who are continually undermining the peace both of our Church and State? I mean our old implacable enemies the Papists, with all their new enchanted crew of sectaries of all sorts, which will best be done by the putting of all the laws made against them into speedy execution, whereunto we ourselves, every justice of peace in his station, must make it his business strictly to find them out; for the country people are generally so rotten that they will not complain

_____
[1] No. 105, p. 383 above.

of them, though they see and know of these seditious meetings before their eyes daily.

* * * * * *

Chetham Society, 3rd ser., v (1953), 87–91

132. 30 Car. II, st. 2, c. 1: An Act for the more effectual preserving the King's person and government by disabling Papists from sitting in either House of Parliament (1678)

Forasmuch as divers good laws have been made for preventing the increase and danger of Popery in this kingdom, which have not had the desired effects by reason of the free access which Popish recusants have had to his Majesty's Court, and by reason of the liberty which of late some of the recusants have had or taken to sit and vote in Parliament; wherefore, and for the safety of his Majesty's royal person and government, be it enacted by the King's most excellent Majesty... that from and after... 1 December 1678 no person that now is or hereafter shall be a Peer of this realm or member of the House of Peers shall vote or make his proxy in the House of Peers, or sit there during any debate..., nor any person that now is or hereafter shall be a Member of the House of Commons shall vote in the House of Commons or sit there during any debate in the said House of Commons after their Speaker is chosen until such Peer or Member shall from time to time respectively and in manner following first take the several oaths of allegiance and supremacy, and make, subscribe and audibly repeat this declaration following:

> I, A.B., do solemnly and sincerely, in the presence of God, profess, testify and declare that I do believe that in the sacrament of the Lord's Supper there is not any transubstantiation of the elements of bread and wine into the body and blood of Christ at or after the consecration thereof by any person whatsoever; and that the invocation or adoration of the Virgin Mary or any other saint, and the sacrifice of the mass as they are now used in the Church of Rome, are superstitious and idolatrous. And I do solemnly, in the presence of God, profess, testify and declare that I do make this declaration and every part thereof in the plain and ordinary sense of the words read unto me, as they are commonly understood by English

Protestants, without any evasion, equivocation or mental reservation whatsoever, and without any dispensation already granted me for this purpose by the Pope or any other authority or person whatsoever, and without any hope of any such dispensation from any person or authority whatsoever, or without thinking that I am or can be acquitted before God or Man or absolved of this declaration or any part thereof, although the Pope, or any other person or persons or power whatsoever should dispense with or annul the same, or declare that it was null and void from the beginning.

Which said oaths and declaration shall be in this and every succeeding Parliament solemnly and publicly made and subscribed....

II. And be it further enacted that after the said first day of December every Peer of this realm..., and every Peer of the kingdom of Scotland or of the kingdom of Ireland, being of the age of one and twenty years and upwards, not having taken the said oaths and made and subscribed the said declaration, and every Member of the House of Commons... as aforesaid..., and every person now or hereafter convicted of Popish recusancy, who hereafter shall at any time...come advisedly into and remain in the presence of the King's Majesty or Queen's Majesty, or shall come into the Court, or house where they or any of them reside, ...shall incur and suffer all the pains, penalties, forfeitures and disabilities in this Act mentioned or contained....

* * * * * *

XI. Provided always that nothing in this Act contained shall extend to his royal Highness the duke of York. *SR*, v, 894–6

133. 'An Appeal from the country to the city, for the preservation of his Majesty's person, liberty, property and the Protestant religion' (late 1679)

...'Tis our humble request, that those who have most power amongst you would so far trouble themselves as to go to the top of your new-raised pyramid[1] and from thence take a survey of that magnificent pile of building whereof you are yet masters. In which posture...be

---

[1] The Fire Monument, completed in 1677. In 1681 the notorious inscription ascribing the fire to 'the treachery and malice of the Popish faction' was incised on its east side. This was erased under James II, restored under William III, and finally removed in 1830.

pleased to fancy to yourselves these following objects which you will infallibly see come to pass whenever Popery prevails.

First, imagine you see the whole town in a flame, occasioned this second time by the same Popish malice which set it on fire before. At the same instant, fancy that amongst the distracted crowd you behold troops of Papists ravishing your wives and daughters, dashing your little children's brains out against the walls, plundering your houses and cutting your own throats, by the name of heretic dogs. Then represent to yourselves the Tower playing off its cannon, and battering down your houses about your ears. Also, casting your eye towards Smithfield, imagine you see your father, or your mother, or some of your nearest and dearest relations, tied to a stake in the midst of flames, when with hands and eyes lifted up to heaven, they scream and cry out to that God for whose cause they die, which was a frequent spectacle the last time Popery reigned amongst us. Fancy you behold those beautiful churches, erected for the true worship of God, abused and turned into idolatrous temples, to the dishonour of Christ, and scandal of religion, the ministers of God's Holy Word torn in pieces before your eyes, and their very best friends not daring even to speak in their behalf. Your trading's bad, and in a manner lost already, but then the only commodity will be fire and sword, the only object, women running with their hair about their ears, men covered with blood, children sprawling under horses' feet, and only the walls of houses left standing; when those that survive this fatal day may sigh and cry, here once stood my house, there my friends', and here my kinsman's, but alas, that time is past! The only noise will then be, O my wife! O my husband! O my dearest children!...

...Without a miracle, our apparent ruin is at hand, the sword already hangs over our heads, and seems to be supported by no stronger force than that of a single hair, his Majesty's life. ...But, as your interests are united, so let your resolutions be the same; and the first hour wherein you hear of the King's untimely end, let no other noise be heard among you but that of arm, arm to revenge your sovereign's death both upon his murderers and their whole party, for that there is no such thing as an English Papist, who is not in the Plot, at least in his good wishes.... Think not to fare better than the rest by meddling less, for that conqueror's promises are never kept, especially coming from that sort of people, whose maxim it is, never to keep their words with heretics. Therefore, if ever a Popish successor comes amongst you, let his promises of keeping your religion and laws, or of his conversion, be never so plausible, credit them not, for if you do you will infallibly be deceived..., or if you think to bind and fetter him by the laws that will be no better than the wise men of Gotham hedging in the cuckoo; for when he (as all other Popish kings do) governs by an army, what will all your laws signify? You will not then have parliaments to appeal to; he and his Council will levy his arbitrary taxes, and his army shall gather them for him. Therefore you may much easier prevent the distemper at first, than remedy it when it has once got a head....

First then, that you may know who are your enemies at this time; they are young, beggarly officers, courtiers, over-hot churchmen and Papists. The young officer or soldier, his interest makes him wish for a standing army, not considering any further than his own pay and plunder, and, so help us, to ruin you that way. The courtier endeavours to advance taxes, oppress the people by vast and illegal impositions, when, looking upon his Prince but as his ox, he fattens him upon his neighbours' pasture, only for his own eating. Over-hot churchmen are bribed to wish well to Popery by the hopes (if not of a cardinal's cap) yet at least of a command over some abbey, priory, or other ecclesiastical preferment, whereof the Roman Church hath so great plenty. These are the men who exclaim against our parliaments' proceedings in relation to the Plot as too violent, calling these times by no other name but that of forty or forty-one, when to amuse as well his sacred Majesty as his good people, they again threaten us with another forty-eight; and all this is done to vindicate underhand the Catholic party, by throwing a suspicion on the fanatic. These are the gentlemen who so magnify the principles of Bishop Laud, and so much extol the writings of the same-spirited prelate, Dr Heylin, who hath made more Papists by his books than Christians by his sermons. These are those episcopal tantivies who make even the very scriptures pimp for the court, who out of Urim and Thummim can extort a sermon to prove the not paying of tithes and taxes to be the sin against the Holy Ghost, and had rather see the kingdom run down with blood than part with the least hem of a consecrated frock, which they themselves made holy....Lastly, the chief and most dangerous of your enemies are Papists, who to make sure of their own game allure all the three forementioned parties to their side, by the arguments aforesaid. Their design is to bring in Popery, which they can no ways effect but either by a Popish successor or by the French arms. The first of these we may ourselves prevent, and for the latter, if they conquer they will undoubtedly conquer for themselves, and not for him that brought them in. And if we ever should be reduced to that extremity, either to submit to the French or to our own Popish successor, every man that hath any brains or generoisty will soon find it his interest of the two rather to submit to a foreign power who hath not violated the laws of nature in fighting against his own subjects, and who will also be less revengeful, and more likely to let us enjoy our own religion and liberties, than any Popish successor will....

* * * * * *

Give me leave in the next place, gentlemen, to inform you wherein is your greatest danger, both in relation to your city and yourselves. First, then, as to your city, the chiefest danger whereunto, it is obvious, is that of fire, for wherever the Jesuit interest prevails, they will above all things desire the burning of London.... There is one eminent great Papist, who in the time of that fire pretended to secure many of the incendiaries, but secretly suffered them all to escape,...for a Popish king or a Popish successor cannot but rejoice in the flames of such a too powerful city. Secondly, the greatest danger...upon the King's untimely death will proceed from a confusion and want of some eminent and interested person whom you may trust to lead you against a French and Popish army; for which purpose no person is fitter than his Grace the duke of Monmouth, as well for quality, courage and conduct, as for that his life and fortune depends upon the same bottom with yours; he will stand by you, therefore ought you to stand by him. And remember the rule is, 'He who hath the worst title, ever makes the best king', as being constrained by a gracious government to supply what he wants in title, [so] instead of 'God and my Right', his motto may be, 'God and my People'.... *State Tracts*, I, 401–10

134. The Exclusion Bill, November 1680

Whereas James, duke of York, is notoriously known to have been perverted from the Protestant to the Popish religion, whereby not only great encouragement hath been given to the Popish party to enter into and carry on most devilish and horrid plots and conspiracies for the destruction of his Majesty's sacred person and government, and for the extirpation of the true Protestant religion, but also if the said duke should succeed to the imperial crown of this realm, nothing is more manifest than that a total change of religion within these kingdoms would ensue.

For the prevention whereof, be it therefore enacted by and with the advice and consent of the Lords spiritual and temporal and the Commons in this present parliament assembled, and by the authority of the same, that the said James, duke of York, shall be and is by authority of the present parliament excluded and made for ever incapable to inherit, possess or enjoy the imperial crown of this realm and of the kingdom of Ireland and the dominions and territories to them or either of them belonging, or to have, exercise or enjoy any dominion, power, jurisdiction or authority within the same...

[2.] And be it further enacted by the authority aforesaid that if the said James, duke of York, shall at any time hereafter challenge, claim, or attempt to possess or enjoy, or shall take upon him to use or exercise any dominion, power, authority or jurisdiction within the said kingdoms...as king or chief magistrate of the same, that then he, the said James, duke of York, for every such offence shall be deemed and adjudged guilty of high treason, and shall suffer the pains, penalties and forfeitures as in cases of high treason; and further, that if any person or persons whatsoever shall assist, aid, maintain, abet, or willingly adhere unto the said James, duke of York, in such his challenge, claim or attempt, or shall of themselves attempt or endeavour to put or bring the said James, duke of York, into the possession or exercise of any regal power, jurisdiction or authority within the kingdoms or dominions aforesaid, or shall by writing or preaching advisedly publish, maintain or declare that he hath any right, title or authority to exercise the office of king or chief magistrate..., that then every such person shall be deemed and adjudged guilty of high treason...

[3.] And be it further enacted...that if the said James, duke of York, shall at any time from and after the fifth day of November in the year of our Lord God 1680 return or come into or within any of the kingdoms or dominions aforesaid, that then he...shall be deemed and adjudged guilty of high treason....And further, that if any person or persons whatsoever shall be aiding or assisting unto such return of the said James, duke of York, that then every such person shall be deemed and adjudged guilty of high treason....

*   *   *   *   *   *

[5.] And be it further enacted and declared...that it shall and may be lawful to and for all magistrates, officers and other subjects whatsoever ...to apprehend and secure the said James, duke of York, and every other person offending in the premises, and with him or them in case of resistance to fight and him or them by force to subdue, for all which actings and for so doing they are and shall be by virtue of this Act saved harmless and indemnified.

[6.] Provided...that nothing in this Act contained shall be construed, deemed or adjudged to disable any person from inheriting or enjoying the imperial crown of the realms and dominions aforesaid..., but that in case the said James, duke of York, shall survive his now Majesty and the heirs of his Majesty's body, the said imperial crown shall descend to and be enjoyed by such person and persons successively during the lifetime of the said James, duke of York, as should have inherited and enjoyed the same in case the said James, duke of York, were naturally dead, anything in this Act contained to the contrary notwithstanding.

House of Lords MSS, 1678–1688, pp. 195–7

135. **The judgement and decree of the University of Oxford, passed in their Convocation, July 21, 1683, against certain pernicious books and damnable doctrines, destructive to the sacred persons of Princes, their State and government, and of all human society**

*   *   *   *   *   *

...To the honour of the holy and undivided Trinity, the preservation of Catholic truth in the Church, and that the King's Majesty may be secured from the attempts of open and bloody enemies, and the machinations of traitorous heretics and schismatics, we the vice-chancellor, doctors, proctors and masters, regent and not regent, met in Convocation in the accustomed manner, time and place, on Saturday the 21 of July in the year 1683, concerning certain propositions contained in divers books and writings published in English, and also in the Latin tongue, repugnant to the Holy Scriptures, decrees of Councils, writings of the Fathers, the faith and profession of the Primitive Church, and also destructive of the kingly government, the safety of his Majesty's person, the public peace, the laws of nature and bonds of human society; by our unanimous assent and consent have decreed and determined in manner and form following:

Proposition 1. All civil authority is derived originally from the people.

2. There is a mutual compact, tacit or express, between a prince and his subject, and that if he perform not his duty they are discharged from theirs.

3. That if lawful governors become tyrants, or govern otherwise than by the laws of God and man they ought to do, they forfeit the right they had unto their government.

> *Lex Rex.* Buchanan, *de Jure Regni, Vindiciae Contra Tyrannos.* Bellarmine, *De Conciliis, De Pontifice.* Milton. Goodwin. Baxter, *H.C.*[1]

4. The sovereignty of England is in the three Estates, viz., King, Lords and Commons. The King has but a coordinate power, and may be overruled by the other two.

> *Lex Rex.* Hunton, *Of a limited and mixed Monarchy.* Baxter, *H.C., Polit. Catech.*

* * * * * *

9. There lies no obligation upon Christians to passive obedience when the prince commands anything against the laws of our country; and the primitive Christians chose rather to die than resist because Christianity was not yet settled by the laws of the Empire.

> *Julian Apostate.*

10. Possession and strength give a right to govern, and success in a cause or endeavour proclaims it to be lawful and just; to pursue it is to comply with the will of God, because it is to follow the conduct of his providence.

> Hobbes. Owen's sermon before the Regicides, January 31, 1648[–9]. Baxter, Jenkin's Petition, October, 1651.

11. In the state of nature there is no difference between good and evil, right and wrong; the state of nature is a state of war, in which every man hath a right to all things.

12. The foundation of civil authority is this natural right, which is not given but left to the Supreme Magistrate upon men's entering into societies, and not only a foreign invader but a domestic rebel puts himself again into a state of nature, to be proceeded against not as a subject

---

[1] *Holy Commonwealth.* These citations have been transcribed as they stand.

but as an enemy; and consequently acquires by his rebellion the same right over the life of his prince as the prince for the most heinous crimes has over the life of his own subjects.

Hobbes, *De Cive, Leviathan.*

* * * * * *

26. King Charles the First was lawfully put to death, and his murderers were the blessed instruments of God's Glory in their generation.

Milton. Goodwin. Owen.

27. King Charles the First made war upon his Parliament; and in such case the King may not only be resisted, but he ceaseth to be King.

Baxter.

We decree, judge and declare all and every of these propositions to be false, seditious and impious; and most of them to be also heretical and blasphemous, infamous to Christian religion, and destructive of all government in Church and State.

We further decree that the books which contain the foresaid propositions and impious doctrines are fitted to deprive good manners, corrupt the minds of unwary men, stir up seditions and tumults, overthrow states and kingdoms, and lead to rebellion, murder of princes, and atheism itself. And therefore we interdict all members of the university from the reading the said books, under the penalties in the [university] statutes expressed. We also order the before-recited books to be publicly burnt by the hand of our marshal, in the court of our schools.

* * * * * *

Lastly, we command and strictly enjoin all and singular readers, tutors, catechists, and others to whom the care and trust of instruction of youth is committed, that they diligently instruct and ground their scholars in that most necessary doctrine, which in a manner is the badge and character of the Church of England, of submitting 'to every ordinance of Man for the Lord's sake, whether it be to the King as supreme, or unto governors, as unto them that are sent by him for the punishment of evildoers and for the praise of them that do well' [1 Pet. ii. 13–14], teaching that this submission and obedience is to be clear, absolute, and without exception of any state or order of men; also that all supplications, prayers, intercessions and giving of thanks be made

473

for all men, for the King and all that are in authority, that we may lead a quiet and peaceable life in all godliness and honesty, for this is good and acceptable in the sight of God our Saviour. And in especial manner that they press and oblige them humbly to offer their most ardent and daily prayers at the Throne of Grace for the preservation of our Sovereign Lord King Charles from the attempts of open violence and secret machinations of perfidious traitors; that he, the Defender of the Faith, being safe under the defence of the Most High, may continue his reign on earth till he exchange it for that of a late and happy immortality. *State Tracts*, II, 153–6

GOVERNMENT

BOOK IV

GOVERNMENT

CHAPTER 14

CENTRAL GOVERNMENT, 1603-1688

The organisation and method of central government changed little in this period, and constitutional historians must focus their attention on the slow development of the Cabinet out of the Privy Council. But in truth there is little that is wonderful about this, and the marvel would be if the cabinet had *not* developed. What made it unusual was the fact that its members continued to be drawn from one or the other of the Houses of Parliament, and the crucial decision not to abandon this practice was made some years after the Revolution, and then not necessarily with the convenience of the king's government in mind.

In 1598 the Privy Council[1] still numbered as few as twelve persons: the archbishop of Canterbury, the lord treasurer, the lord high admiral, the principal (or senior) secretary of state, the chancellor of exchequer, the lord chamberlain, the treasurer of the Household, the comptroller and lord high butler. Then the accidental destruction of the Council Registers for 1598–1613 leaves a gap, but it is known that in 1610 the size of the Council had increased to 20, and by 1617 it numbered 28, by 1623 35, and by 1625 40. In 1630 it still stood at 42.[2] It was generally felt that this inflation lowered the prestige of the individual councillor and made it more difficult to impose secrecy,[3] and the reasons for it are not at all clear. Of course, the Council still had to settle a great many disputes of a legal or quasi-legal nature, and sift petitions to the Crown, and this made it necessary to ensure a quorum at all times. The orders governing the sittings of Council issued on Charles I's accession and renewed in 1628[4] were largely concerned with this aspect of its activities, and it is possible that it was already losing its function as an advisory or policy-making body; very secret matters like the Spanish marriage negotiations were submitted to a group of nine councillors, and in 1621 and 1624 James I experimented with a Council of War which included several men who were not councillors at all.[5] In times of crisis policy was decided in small committees of Council, like the famous Scottish Committee of 1640, which comprised the king, Stafford, Laud, Juxon, Hamilton, Cottington, Vane, Windebank and the lord general, Northumberland (**136**). The parlia-

---

[1] In general see E. R. Turner, *Privy Council of England*, and for previous developments, Elton, *Tudor Constitution*, pp. 87 ff.
[2] *Idem.* 'The origin of the Cabinet Council', *EHR*, xxxviii (1923), 187.
[3] Willson, *Privy Councillors*, pp. 22–3.   [4] *APC, 1627–8*, pp. 331–2.
[5] E. H. Carlyle, 'Commitees of Council Under the Earlier Stuarts', *EHR*, xxi (1906), 673; *TCD*, pp. 380.

mentary opposition viewed such developments with alarm, and in the Nineteen Propositions in 1642 they demanded that the Council be reduced to a maximum of twenty-five and made responsible for all policy decisions.[1]

From the Restoration onwards there was a tendency for the Privy Council to grow even larger, and inevitably policy-making tended to devolve on a smaller group, the 'cabinet council', which was a committee of the Council proper. Its formal powers—of summons and interrogation, for instance—depended on its members' status as Councillors.[2] However, such developments were regarded with some disfavour, even by those most concerned in them, and in 1668 an attempt was made to revitalise the Privy Council by reforming its committees. Henceforward no matter was to be decided at Council until it had been before the appropriate committee, but conversely no topic was to be discussed at a committee unless it had been referred to it by the full Council (137). The Council Order introducing this reform also instituted standing committees on foreign affairs, trade, the navy and grievances.

From the first the Committee on Foreign Affairs was the senior committee, and it was the only one excepted from the rule forbidding committees to discuss matters not referred to them by Council. Nor was it confined to foreign policy; it was instructed to supervise the correspondence between the king's ministers and his justices of peace 'concerning the temper of the kingdom', and it dealt with other confidential matters as well. In November 1672, for instance, it advised the king on the nomination of a new Speaker, and in December it also discussed the dismissal of two judges.[3] However, its association in the public mind with the king's unpopular foreign policy caused it to be labelled a Popish junta, and early in the Exclusion crisis Charles and his advisers decided to kill two birds with one stone; they made a bid for popularity by abolishing the hated 'secret committee', and at the same time they tried to reduce the Council to manageable proportions.[4] On 21 April 1679 Charles dismissed the Privy Council en bloc and swore in another of thirty; fifteen office holders and fifteen others (ten noblemen and five commoners); and agreed to take no major decision without its advice—a reform remarkably like that demanded of Charles I in the Nineteen Propositions (140).

Nevertheless, only two days later the Committee on Foreign Affairs was revived in the transparent disguise of a 'Committee of Intelligence', consisting of the lord president, the lord chamberlain, the captain-general, the two secretaries of state, the first lord of the Treasury, Lord Halifax and Sir William Temple.[5] The only innovation was the inclusion of two men with-

---

[1] No. 67, p. 244 above.
[2] Sir William Anson, 'The Cabinet in the Seventeenth and Eighteenth Centuries', EHR, xxix (1914), 58. [3] Law Quarterly Review, LXVI (1950), 72–3 (Havighurst).
[4] Turner, 'The Privy Council of 1679', EHR, xxx (1915), 251 ff.
[5] Ibid. p. 265; G. Davies, 'Council and Cabinet, 1679–1688', EHR, xxxvii (1922), 55.

out office, Halifax and Temple (though Temple was still technically envoy to the Netherlands). The duties of this committee were not limited to foreign affairs, of course; it drafted some at least of the King's Messages to Parliament in the session October 1680 to January 1681, it probably discussed the summons or dissolution of Parliament, and it certainly discussed delicate matters like the execution of the penal laws against Catholics.[1] Meanwhile Charles's promise to consult the Privy Council at all times was soon forgotten, and there arose a small group of confidential ministers who acted as an informal quorum, to the disgust of those less favoured.[2]

These tendencies were accentuated under James II, perhaps because of the religious divisions his policy provoked,[3] and he tended to transact his business in smaller and smaller committees and with increasing informality. Torcy records that towards the end of 1687 he was taking important decisions in a camarilla consisting of himself, the earl of Sunderland and the Jesuit Edward Petre (141), and foreign ambassadors constantly referred to a 'Catholic Council' which had no constitutional or legal status and whose composition is unknown. The Privy Council still met to transact routine business, but the king regarded it with such contempt that on several occasions in 1688 he sat by himself with the clerks and issued Council Orders.[4]

However, James II was nothing if not natural; he behaved precisely as the mood took him, and his impatience with formalities and his tendency to take advice from a few were unusual only in that he—or perhaps other people—tried to give his practices some familiar or quasi-familiar constitutional form. Throughout this century, behind the formal apparatus of councils, cabinets, committees and camarillas lay the simple, usually quite easy, relationship between the king and one or two trusted ministers or advisers. The really important decisions were taken in complete privacy, without surviving records, and we are lucky to possess the earl of Danby's notes for what he obviously anticipated would be a difficult audience with Charles II in 1677 (139).[5] Sir Henry Vane's notes of the opinions

[1] See p. 453 above.
[2] See an interesting letter, 5 October 1681, from Sir Leoline Jenkins to his fellow secretary of state, Conway, printed Costin and Watson, I, 331. However, the assertions of the lord privy seal, the earl of Anglesey, need not be taken too seriously.
[3] In fact, this is not the whole story, for even such bodies as the Committee for Regulation contained a majority of Protestants to the end. There was something in James's character that made him impatient with large councils.
[4] This happened on 26 February, 4, 10, 18, 25 March, 8, 19, 22 April, 19, 20 May, 10 July, 26 August and 1 October 1688 (PRO, Privy Council Registers). Most of these 'meetings' were to issue orders for the regulation of corporations, but on 10 March he swore in a new lord-lieutenant of Sussex, on 26 August he dealt with East India Company business, and on 1 October he issued Dartmouth's sailing-orders.
[5] The most revealing account of confidential discussions of this nature is Halifax's notes of his conversations with William III in 1689 and 1690. See Williams, *Eighteenth Century Constitution*, pp. 60–4.

given at the Scottish Committee on 5 May 1640 are something of a rarity too (**136**).

Danby was usually given the informal title of 'chief minister', but in this century it was never clear whether it attached itself to any particular office or not. By the early eighteenth century the Treasury had established its primacy over the other departments of state,[1] but whether the head of the Treasury enjoyed automatic seniority over the other ministers and advisers of the king was another matter, and of course it was certainly not true of the period prior to 1667. No one would have called Lord Buckhurst (1603–8), the earl of Portland (1628–35) or the earl of Southampton (1660–7) chief ministers, yet they were all lord treasurers. The title was most often accorded after the Restoration to the minister responsible for Parliament, and especially for a refractory and cantankerous House of Commons. Amongst Danby's papers are a multitude of lists testifying to his close study of the Commons (**138**).

The secretary of state was emerging in the seventeenth century as the chief rival to the Treasurer, and the older, traditional officers were slipping behind —the last lord chancellor to be an effective chief minister was Clarendon (1660–7). But the secretaryship of state is a slippery office to discuss, and this reflects a certain contemporary instability; the volume of work expected of a Secretary after 1660 was probably greater than before, but it is difficult to demonstrate that the importance of the office increased as a result.[2] The great Secretaries of the later seventeenth century, such as Arlington (1662–74) and Sunderland (1683–8), probably had less influence than Robert Cecil (1603–1612); on the other hand in the 1670's two very efficient Secretaries, Williamson and Henry Coventry, were clearly subordinate to Danby. In the period from 1612 to 1642 those secretaries of state whose names are at all well known—Henry Vane, and perhaps Windebank and Conway—were essentially ministers of the second rank; nor does the office seem to have been a stepping-stone to anything higher. A Secretary who would make himself great was cursed by the duality of his office, and by the inflexible rule that the 'sitting' Secretary always moved up to the senior and more important Southern Department when a new Secretary was appointed. The establishment of a humble junior colleague who would not make a nuisance of himself, like Salisbury's Sir John Herbert ('Mr Secondary Herbert'), could be an inconvenience in these circumstances, as the earl of Sunderland found. In 1680 he chose Sir Leoline Jenkins, 'useful and firm', as his junior colleague; but in 1681 he was dismissed, and on his reappointment in 1683 he had to serve for more than a year as junior to the same Jenkins. On the other hand, the Treasury was put in commission for the first time in 1613, and after that

---

[1] See Baxter, *Development of the Treasury*.
[2] See in general, Evans, *Principal Secretaryship of State*.

the practice was common. Not until Walpole's time could anyone overcome the handicap of being a mere first commissioner.

All this is natural enough, again, and a wise king tried to avoid having any one chief minister. When James II dismissed the earl of Rochester from the Treasury in 1687 and put it into commission, he announced that henceforward none of the great offices of state, of lord treasurer, lord high admiral or captain-general, should be held by one man not of the blood royal. William III took the same view; his secretaries of state were allowed little initiative, and his Treasury Commission was reshuffled at frequent intervals. It is common to say in such circumstances that such and such a king 'acted as his own prime minister', but in fact he was merely behaving as a seventeenth-century monarch should. The times were not yet ripe for the emergence of a prime minister, just as they were not yet ripe for the emergence of a cabinet; and the cabinet council (so-called) was still summoned by the king, who also presided over it. It is even arguable that the presence of a chief minister with unquestioned authority, like Buckingham or Clarendon, suggests a serious weakness in the monarch concerned. In other cases—that of Danby, for instance, or Laud—this primacy was more imagined than real.

136. Committee of the Privy Council for Scots Affairs, 5 May 1640

No danger in undertaking this war, whether the Scots are to be reduced or no. To reduce them by force as the state of this kingdom stands. If his Majesty had not declared himself so soon, he would have declared himself for no war with Scotland, they would have given him plentifully. The city to be called immediately and quickened to lend £100,000. The shipping money to be put vigorously upon collection. These two ways will furnish your Majesty plentifully to go on with arms and war against Scotland. The manner of the war? Stopping of the trade of Scotland no prejudice, for they had the trade free with England for the cattle. A defensive war? Totally against it. Offensive war into the kingdom. His opinion, few months make an end of the war do you invade them.[1]

Lord Admiral. If no more money, then what proposed? How then to make an offensive war a difficulty. Whether to do nothing, and let them alone, or go on with a vigorous war?

Lord-lieutenant of Ireland. Go vigorously on or let them alone, no defensive war, loss of honour and reputation, the quiet of England will hold out long. You will languish as betwixt Saul and David, go on with

[1] This speech was probably by the lord general, Northumberland. See Wedgwood, *Strafford*, pp. 286–7.

an offensive war as you first designed, loosed and absolved from all rules of government, being reduced to extreme necessity, everything is to be done that power might admit, and that you are to do. They [having] in Ireland you may employ here to reduce this kingdom. Confident as anything under heaven, Scotland shall not hold out five months. One summer well employed will do it. Venture all I had, I would carry it or lose all. Whether a defensive war as impossible as an offensive, or whether to let them alone?

Lord Archbishop. Tried all ways and refused all ways, by the law of God you should have subsistence and ought to have it and lawfully to take it.

Lord Cottington. Leagues abroad they may make and will, and therefore the defence of this kingdom. The Lower House are weary both of King and Church, all ways shall be just to raise moneys by this unavoidable necessity, therefore to be used being lawful.

Lord-lieutenant of Ireland. Commission of array to be put in execution, they are to bring them to the borders. In reason of state you have power, when they are there, to use them at the King's pay. If any of the Lords can show you a better way let them do it.

Ob[jection]. Town full of nobility who will talk of it.

[Answer.] He will make them smart for it.

CSPD, 1640, pp. 112–13.[1]

137. The Council Reforms of 1668

[Privy Council minutes, 12 February 1668.]

Order for regulation and establishment of the Committees of the Privy Council. His Majesty upon the 31st of January last caused an Order to be read and passed[2] for establishing a future regulation of the committees of his Privy Council; and some additions being since held necessary to be made thereunto, the same were this day read and allowed of, as follows.

His Majesty having among other the important parts of his affairs taken into his princely consideration the way and method of managing matters at the Council Board, and reflecting that his councils would have

---

[1] These notes of Vane's were used against Strafford at his impeachment (see art. XXIII, p. 210 above), and they have often been questioned. But Gardiner, after a close examination, concluded that they were substantially genuine, (*History of England*, IX, 120 ff.).

[2] Merely a formal order setting up the four Standing Committees. See Turner, *Privy Council*, II, 266–7.

more reputation if they were put into a more settled and established course, has thought fit to appoint certain Standing Committees for several businesses, together with regular days and places for their assembling, in such sort as follows.

1. *Foreign Affairs.* The Committee of Foreign Affairs to consist of these persons following (besides his Royal Highness,[1] who is understood to be of all committees where he pleases to be), viz., Prince Rupert, lord keeper [Bridgeman], lord privy seal [Robartes], duke of Buckingham, duke of Albermarle, duke of Ormond, Lord Arlington and Mr Secretary Morrice; to which committee his Majesty doth also hereby refer the corresponding with justices of the peace, and other his Majesty's officers and ministers in the several counties of the kingdom, concerning the temper of the kingdom, etc. The constant day for this committee to meet to be every Monday, besides such other days wherein any extraordinary occasion shall oblige them to assemble; and the place of their meeting to be at the Lord Arlington's lodgings in Whitehall.

2. *Navy.* Such matters as concern the admiralty and navy, as also all military matters, fortifications, etc., so far as they are fit to be brought to the Council Board without intermeddling with what concerns the proper officers (unless it shall by them be so desired), his Majesty is pleased that they be under the consideration of the following committee, viz., Prince Rupert, duke of Albemarle, lord chamberlain, earl of Anglesey, earl of Carlisle, earl of Craven, Lord Arlington, Lord Berkeley, Lord Ashley, Mr Comptroller, Mr Vice Chamberlain, Mr Secretary Morrice, Sir William Coventry and Sir John Duncombe; the usual day of meeting to be Wednesday, and oftener as he that presides shall direct; and the place to be the Council Chamber, and hereof three or more of them to be a quorum.

3. *Trade.* A committee for the business of trade, under whose consideration is to come whatsoever concerns his Majesty's foreign plantations, as also what relates to his kingdoms of Scotland and Ireland, in such matters only relating to either of those kingdoms as properly belong to the cognisance of the Council Board, [and] the Isles of Jersey and Guernsey; which is to consist of the lord privy seal, duke of Buckingham, duke of Ormond, earl of Ossory, earl of Bridgewater, earl of Anglesey, earl of Lauderdale, Lord Arlington, Lord Holles, Lord Ashley, Mr Comptroller, Mr Vice Chamberlain, Mr Secretary Morrice, Sir William Coventry; the usual day of meeting to be every

---

[1] James, duke of York.

Thursday in the Council Chamber, and oftener as he that presides shall direct, and hereof three or more of them to be a quorum....

4. *Complaints and Grievances.* A committee to whom all petitions of complaint and grievance are to be referred, in which his Majesty hath thought fit hereby particularly to prescribe not to meddle with property, or what relates to *meum* and *tuum*. And to this committee his Majesty is pleased that all matters which concern acts of state, or of the Council, be referred; the persons to be the archbishop of Canterbury, lord keeper, lord privy seal, lord great chamberlain, lord chamberlain, earl of Bridgewater, earl of Anglesey, earl of Bath, earl of Carberry, Viscount Fitzhardinge, Lord Arlington, Lord Holles, Lord Ashley, Mr Secretary Morrice, Mr Chancellor of the duchy [of Lancaster] and Sir John Duncombe; the constant days to be Fridays in the Council Chamber.

And his Majesty's further meaning is that to these two last committees any of the Council may have liberty to come and vote, and that his two principal secretaries of state be ever understood to be of all committees....

And for the better carrying on of business at these several committees his Majesty thinks fit, and accordingly is pleased to appoint, that each of these committees be assigned to the particular care of some one person, who is constantly to attend it. In that of the navy and military matters his Royal Highness may preside if he so please, or else the lord general [Albemarle]; in foreign matters, the Lord Arlington; in matters of state and grievances, the lord keeper.

All things relating to the Treasury in England or Ireland [are] to be immediately referred to the Lords Commissioners of the Treasury, from whence it may come again to the Council Board, in case the matter be of such a nature as they cannot or would not willingly give their determination therein.

Besides which aforesaid committees, if there shall happen anything extraordinary, that requires advice of any mixed nature, other than what is before determined, his Majesty's meaning and intention is that particular Committees be in such cases appointed for them, as hath been hitherto accustomed,...and that as on the one side nothing is hereafter to be resolved in Council till the matter has been first examined and [shall] have received the opinion of some committee or other, so on the other hand that nothing be referred to any committee until it hath been first read at the board, except in foreign affairs....   PRO, PC 2/10, 176–7

138. Sir Richard Wiseman's report on the state of the House of Commons, to the Earl of Danby, 1676

Bedford

Sir Humphrey Winch is my particular friend and acquaintance, and I know him to have good inclinations for the service of the King, and he is one that I will use my endeavours withal to get to attend and be every day as I am myself for the King's service.

Sir John Napier, Mr [Paulet] St John, Sir William Beecher. These three gentlemen have of late voted ill. The first I will commit to the care of Colonel Whiteley, who I know can manage him. The second I can say little to at present. The third has formerly voted well, and I hope to be able to give such an account of him as may be trusted to as to the grounding a judgement upon his vote, which way it is like to go. In the meantime I hope the best.

*   *   *   *   *   *

Cambridge

Sir Thomas Chichele, Sir Charles Wheeler. I hope I have no need [to say] anything of these two gentlemen. I am sure I need not of the last to your Lordship,[1] and as to the first only this, [that his Majesty] would please to let him and other of his servants know that he expects from them all a diligent attendance and a faithful and honest discharge of their duty.

Sir Thomas Hatton. He voted ill last session, [but I will apply] to him, having good hopes of him....

Lord Allington. I have spoken to your Lordship of him formerly, and I hope your Lordship will think upon what I said.

Mr [Roger] Pepys is not able to attend; but if he we[re he wou]ld be against us, unless his cousin Pepys (the commissioner) prevail upon him.

*   *   *   *   *   *

Devonshire

Sir Coplestone Bampfield, Sir Courtney Poole. Sir Courtney Poole promised me to make sure of...Bampfield. I will put him in mind of it.

Sir James Smith, Mr [Thomas] Walker. Sir James Smith to take care of Mr Walker's attendance. [He will] be certainly honest.

---

[1] Wheeler was a staunch supporter and perhaps a personal friend of Danby's.

Sir Edward Seymour. He must be sent to by the King that he may attend.

Sir Gilbert Talbot, Sir Nicholas Slanning. He was absent most part if not all last sess[ion]. [Lord] Arundel should be sure to take care of him.

Mr [Peter] Prideaux, Sir John Powell, are known to your Lordship to be sure men.

Mr [William] Harbord, disserves the King and is put in secretary [to the lord-lieutenant].

Sir Henry Ford serves the King and is put out. Truly, my Lord, Sir Harry Ford must not be forgotten.

Sir John Maynard. He has sometimes done very well. I guess [he is] prepared to it when he has done so.

Sir John Roll, Sir Thomas Berry. These two gentlemen ought to be applied to. [The first] is accounted an honest gentleman. The last is a stranger to me. There are many honest [gentlemen] that can give your lordship information of them both.

Sir William Morris. I guess he will not come up.

Sir Arthur Harris. I know not.

Sir Francis Drake. Sir William Drake is dejected at his be[ing put out of the commission of the] Peace, as I am informed by a letter out of that county.

Mr Samuel Foote is a fierce mutineer.

Mr [William] Russell. My Lord Allington and Mr Nowell are [his brothers-in-law]. They might do some good with him.

Mr [Josiah] Child. I am loth to speak plain Engl[ish, but if] he were well observed he might be proved to be a capital offender.

Mr [Joseph] Maynard. He seldom or never goes right....

* * * * * *

Gloucester

Mr [John Grubham] Howe. Your Lordship knows who can influence him.

Sir Bainham Throgmorton. I cannot be very secure of this gentleman, for he will not do much out of honesty; but he may be secured other ways.

Mr [Henry] Norwood. I fear Mr Norwood would show tricks too, if he could get by [with] them.

Sir Henry Capel was a very ill man the last session, and spoiled *Sir Francis Russell* and some others; but I believe he will not be able to do it any more, for to my own knowledge both Sir Francis Russell and Sir Roland Berkely were out of countenance at it before they left the town. I have very good acquaintance with them both.

Serjeant [Evan] Seyes. My lord chancellor may work miracles upon Serjeant Seyes. He may please to try.

Mr Henry Powle. As to Mr Powle and Sir Thomas Meres, your lordship may have a better account of them before Michaelmas.

Mr [John] Georges. I think he is dead.

Hereford

Mr Thomas Price, Mr [Herbert] Westphaling, Mr [Humphrey] Cornwall, Sir John Barnaby, Sir Thomas Williams. I will make no doubt of these first four gentlemen, nor of the fifth, unless the doubtfulness of his election makes him sometimes leave the question, which ought not to be.

Sir John Kirle, Lord Scudamore. These two had better be absent than present. The first of them is generally absent.

Mr Reginald Graham went very ill, contrary to expectation, and I hear he does not repent of it. If I had got but half so much money as he hath done, and many others, by the Crown, I would not have done as he and they do, many of them.

Hertford

Sir Richard Franklin. To be in the care of Sir Christopher Musgrave.

Dr [Thomas] Arris. To be spoken to to attend and sit it out. . . .

Mr Samuel Grimston. My lord chancellor should conjure both father and son.

Mr [William] Hale is a discreet gentleman, governed too much by his uncle Garroway.

Sir Thomas Bide is past cure.

Huntingdon

Sir John Cotton. He is a very good man, and rarely misses in his vote, and then by mistake only. Some person (trusty) should always sit near him.

Sir Lionel Walden has been made to juggle and prevaricate in the King's service, but he will leave Sir Robert Carr for the time to come.

Mr [Robert] Aprice is corrupted by Captain Titus, but I hope to work a cure upon him.

Sir Nicholas Pedley is a very ill man hitherto, and I know not how to make him better.

*   *   *   *   *   *

Lincoln

Col. [William] Broxholme went very honestly last session notwithstanding the ill influences of Sir Robert Carr, and I believe he will be steady.

Mr [Peregrine] Bertie.[1]

Sir Robert Carr. Assuredly if the King please to turn off this gentleman it would be for his service, but if not that in the next place I wish he might be employed abroad....

Sir John Newton. I suspect he has been corrupted by Sir Robert Carr....

Sir William Thorold is very ancient and attends not.

Lord Castleton was absent last session, and I wish he might be this, unless I were better persuaded than as yet I am of him.

Mr [Henry] Monson. Mr Cheney must take care of this gentleman, and that most particularly, for he is very uncertain unless one be at his elbow.

Sir Philip Harcourt, Sir Anthony Irby. These two gentlemen I have little hopes of.

Sir Thomas Meres. I may possibly give a further account of him before Michaelmas. Col. Whiteley can do much with him, and has hinted to me something of that nature, as if Sir Thomas might be treated with.[2]

*   *   *   *   *   *

Browning, *Danby*, III, 97–100

139. Earl of Danby, 'Memorandums'[3] in June 1677 for the king

The necessity of having officers to assist me, having neither time to labour as I ought to do in his Majesty's other concerns, nor to think of improving his revenue; nor dare I trust that anything I would do for his service shall not be exposed to public knowledge.

[1] Danby's brother-in-law.
[2] This is unlikely, since Meres was one of the leaders of the 'Country Party', as was Powle (see under Gloucester above).   [3] In the sense of notes, for a subsequent audience.

That nothing is more necessary than to let the world see he will reward and punish, and that no longer time must be lost therein, for that people begin already to think he will do neither. That nothing can spoil his affairs at home but unsteadiness of resolution in those steps he has begun, and want of vigour to discountenance all such as pretend to others.

Note here the variety of opposition this must meet:

As the persuasive arguments of the dissenters,

Their conjunction with others,

The no possibility of convincing some, and the discouragement that gives.

Memorandum: Bishop Duresme [Durham], Colonel Norton, the Test. F. Munson, Coleman, Talbot.

Till he can fall into the humour of the people he can never be great nor rich, and while differences continue prerogative must suffer, unless he can live without Parliament.

That the condition of his revenue will not permit that.

As to foreign affairs, I cannot as a Councillor but consider them in the first place as they stand with the interest of England, and then I am for concerting the peace with the prince of Orange to his satisfaction, and making the alliance strict with him, by which many advantages may accrue to us, as the flag from Spain, great advantages in trade from them, etc. Whereas I know none from France.... I shall only boldly affirm that were the king of France in the place of the king of England his actions have shown he would not forgo so many of his greatest concerns both at home and abroad for ten times as many good words as we have received, especially when a peace made in favour of him shall maintain our ill humour here; and I could never see what useful help we can receive from him when the peace shall be made.

But against this also there will be strong opposition from mistaken opinions, and whilst the King will remain almost single in his opinion against all others in his kingdom it will also be necessary to show upon what foundations he will build or maintain himself....

Browning, Danby, II, 69–71

140. The king's speech in Council, 21 April 1679[1]

His Majesty gives you all thanks for your service to him here, and for all the good advices you have given him, which might have been more

---

[1] Delivered by the lord chancellor.

frequent if the great number of this Council had not made it unfit for the secrecy and dispatch that are necessary in many great affairs. This forced him to use a small number of you in a foreign committee, and sometimes the advice of some few of them (upon such occasions) for many years past. He is sorry for the ill success he has found in this course, and sensible of the ill posture of affairs from that, and some unhappy accidents which have raised great jealousies and dissatisfaction among his good subjects, and thereby left the Crown and government in a condition too weak for those dangers we have reason to fear both at home and abroad.

These his Majesty hopes may yet be prevented by a course of wise and steady counsels for the future.... To this end he has resolved to lay aside the use he may have hitherto made of any single ministry or private advices, or foreign committees for the general direction of his affairs, and to constitute such a Privy Council as may not only by its number be fit for the consultation and digestion of all business, both domestic and foreign, but also by the choice of them out of the several parts this State is composed of may be best informed in the true constitutions of it, and thereby the most able to counsel him in all the affairs and interests of this Crown and nation. And by the constant advice of such a Council his Majesty is resolved hereafter to govern his kingdoms, together with the frequent use of his Great Council of Parliament, which he takes to be the true ancient constitution of this State and government.

Now for the greater dignity of this Council his Majesty resolves their constant number shall be limited to that of thirty, and for their greater authority there shall be fifteen of his chief officers, who shall be Privy Councillors by their places; and for the other fifteen he will choose ten out of the several ranks of the nobility, and five commoners of the realm whose known abilities, interest and esteem in the nation shall render them without any supposition of either betraying or mistaking the true interests of the kingdom and consequently of advising him ill.

In the first place therefore, and to take care of the Church, his Majesty will have the archbishop of Canterbury and [the] bishop of London for the time being; and to inform him well in what concerns the laws, the lord chancellor and one of the lord chief justices; for the navy and stores...the [lord high] admiral and [the] master of the ordnance; for the Treasury, the [lord] treasurer and [the] chancellor of the Exchequer (or, whenever any of these charges are in commission, then the first commissioner to serve in their room). The rest of the fifteen shall be the lord privy seal, the master of the horse, [the] lord steward and lord chamberlain of his Household, the groom of the stole and the two secretaries of state. And these shall be all the offices of his kingdom to which the dignity of a Privy Councillor shall be annexed. The other (15) his Majesty has resolved, and hopes he has not chosen ill. His Majesty intends besides to have such princes of his blood as he shall at any time call to this board, being here in court, a president of the Council whenever he shall find it necessary, and the secretary for Scotland....But these, being uncertain, he reckons not of the constant number of thirty, which shall never be exceeded.

...His Majesty was also pleased to declare that he would have all his affairs here debated freely, of what kind soever they were, and therefore absolutely [in] secrecy. His Majesty was also pleased to declare that he would communicate this alteration of the Council unto both Houses of Parliament in a few words. *EHR*, xvii (1912), 684–5[1]

141. The Privy Council in 1687

[Memoir by the marquis de Torcy, October 1687.]

It is usually held once a week, and the King of England is present. When he has come to a decision in his privy chamber with the ministers he has summoned to him, he notifies it to the Council for form's sake, and they usually have it several days before it is published....Besides the Privy Council there is usually another held every Sunday in the King's presence. It is called the Cabinet Council. Despatches are read there, and they deliberate on the answers that should be sent. Those present at this Council are Prince George,[2] the lord chancellor, the earl of Sunderland,[3] Lord Arundel,[4] the earl of Middleton,[3] Lord Godolphin, the duke of Ormond,[5] Lord Dartmouth. Mr Bridgeman, the earl of Sunderland's first secretary, acts as secretary to this Council. The most important business is transacted in the privy chamber of the King of England, and he takes the most important decisions there with Lord Sunderland, Father Petre, or others whom he calls to him.

PRO, 31/3/174, 134

[1] From 'Inner and Outer Cabinet and Privy Council from William III to George II', by H. W. V. Temperley.
[2] Of Denmark, Princess Anne's husband.
[3] Secretaries of state.   [4] Lord privy seal.
[5] Lord steward. (The original has 'le comte d'Ormond'.)

CHAPTER 15

LOCAL GOVERNMENT, 1603–1688

The workhorse of local government continued to be the justice of the peace.[1] His duties were multifarious: as well as administering the criminal law in minor cases he executed an increasing number of economic, social and ecclesiastical statutes. He sought out and detained priests, and later Dissenting ministers, he destroyed 'massing stuff' and objects of superstition, he fixed wages, had vagabonds flogged, decided the paternity of bastards, held down the price of corn and other basic foodstuffs, protected the manufacture of favoured substances such as saltpetre, and so on and so forth. Moreover, he was the king's officer in every locality—usually the only one—charged with the exposition and defence of royal policy, and expected to provide the central government with an unceasing stream of information, especially in the field of 'security'. It is not surprising that an active royalist like Sir Peter Leicester delivered charges which read like political tracts.[2]

However, even if he was chosen by and for the central government, the justice was selected from amongst a limited number of men, and he was a native not only of the county but usually also of the division for which he sat. The centrifugal tendency of the Commission of the Peace, the danger that its members would come to regard themselves as representatives of the localities against the government, was always present, and the ministers of James I and Charles I made recurrent efforts to limit their duties and place them under stricter supervision.

The most convenient agents of supervision were the assize judges, who visited each county at least once a year. It became the custom for the lord chancellor, sometimes even the king, to address the judges before they departed on circuit,[3] and they were expected to repeat the relevant parts of this discourse to the justices of the peace at the assizes. Of course, this meant that duties not specifically mentioned by the judges tended to be neglected, but in 1631 Charles I's government decided to refine and regularise this procedure.

The stop in trade organised by the London merchants in 1629 and 1630, coupled with poor harvests and an outbreak of plague, caused widespread

---

[1] In general, see Webb, *English Local Government*, vol. I, bk. II, ch. I–IV, and *Northants Record Society*, I (1924), introduction (S. A. Peyton). There are also two first-class studies of English counties in the first half of this century, W. B. Willcox on Gloucestershire and Thomas G. Barnes on Somerset.

[2] See no. **131**, p. 462 above.

[3] See 'A Charge to the Judges of Assize 1627/8', ed. Thomas G. Barnes, *Huntington Library Quarterly*, XXIV (1961), 251.

destitution and distress. This gave Charles I and Laud the excuse to launch the most ambitious scheme for the supervision of local government in this century. For some time it had been evident that the Elizabethan poor-laws, especially in so far as they required the punishment of 'sturdy beggars' and the apprenticeship of orphans and paupers' sons to a trade, were being neglected or even ignored. Therefore in January 1631 Charles I issued a Book of Orders (142). Eight basic orders required the justices of peace to meet singly in each hundred once a month and receive the reports of the constables on the administration of the poor-laws and take a rough census of vagabonds and rogues in the district. A series of supplementary directions pointed to methods, statutory and otherwise, for enforcing the law in such cases. Justices were then to report to the sheriff, who would in turn report to the assize judges, and they to a special commission of the Privy Council set up for each county. This machinery was strengthened in 1632 by a proclamation ordering the landed nobility and gentry to repair to their country seats and stay there, busying themselves with local government and the welfare of their tenants (143). James I had issued similar proclamations, and so had Charles I in 1626,[1] but these had been short-term measures. The proclamation of 1632 was of indefinite duration and stringently enforced.[2]

The machinery set up by the commission of 1631 worked; the government saw to it that it did. But whether the poor-laws were more strictly enforced as a result is open to doubt.[3] In any case, it was all swept away in the Civil Wars, and the only innovation to survive at the Restoration was the monthly meeting of a single justice in petty sessions.

The Civil Wars hastened the devolution from local into provincial government—what the Webbs called 'the development of an extra-legal constitution'—which had been proceeding for some generations. The preface of the Book of Orders mentioned with some irritation the growing independence of the justices of peace, 'their power and authority in their several places, whereby they hold others under them in awe' (142). The only weapon that could be used against them was Star Chamber, and the failure to re-establish it in 1660 was crucial. During Charles II's reign the Privy Council occasionally summoned justices before it for questioning, but the practice was frowned on, not least by the House of Commons, and was apparently dropped. Dismissal from the commission was now the only weapon left to the government; it was practised on a large scale by Charles II from 1680 to 1683, by James II from 1686 to 1688, and by William III from 1696 to 1698; always with ambiguous results.

---

[1] *Foedera*, XVIII, 798 (23 November 1626).
[2] Stone, *Aristocracy*, pp. 397–8.
[3] Barnes, *Somerset*, ch. VII, suggests that there was some improvement in that county; but Jordan, taking a larger sample and analysing the returns, is sceptical (*Philanthropy in England*, pp. 134–5).

In the short term the Civil Wars enormously strengthened the county oligarchy. The County Committees, the Sequestration Committees, the Committees for the Assessment, for Plundered Ministers, and so on (usually identical in personnel) which the Long Parliament set up, gave this county oligarchy a formal shape, much wider powers than hitherto, and a substantial independence of the harassed central authority.[1] Indeed, so oppressive was this new oligarchy in some counties that it provoked a revolt from within.[2] Cromwell ran into the same difficulties as his royal predecessors, and the appointment of the major-generals in 1655 was a confession that in the sphere of security and counter-espionage at least the normal machinery of local government had broken down.[3]

The Restoration only brought a further relaxation of central authority. The Poor Law of 1662, the notorious Act of Settlement, divided the nation into the landed sheep and the landless goats. The latter could now be removed from the parish in which they were settled back to the parish of their birth, even if they were able and willing to find work, and according to one critic it 'made the most effectual and extensive invasion of the rights of Englishmen which had ever been attempted since the Conquest'.[4]

A similar distinction between the God-given race of landowners and the rest was made by the Game Act of 1671 (**144**), the most stringent and comprehensive of the famous Game Laws. It gave gamekeepers power to enter houses to search for guns, nets and sporting dogs, which those below the rank of esquire were not only forbidden to use but even to own; it gave a single justice—usually the landowner concerned—power to award summary punishment, and the decision of Quarter Sessions, staffed by neighbouring landowners, was final. Such blatant class legislation confirmed the social ascendancy of the squirearchy, but in the end their administration of the Game Laws, 'grossly partial, selfishly biased, and swayed by consideration of their own class interest even to the verge of corruption', wrecked the reputation of the rural justices and made an important contribution to their ultimate downfall.[5]

Charles II and James II would probably have cared little for this growing division between Court and Country if the country interest had not shown a tendency to coalesce into an obstructive force at Westminster, and if the country gentry did not control so many parliamentary boroughs. Increasing care was taken with elections, but without commensurate results, and the truth is that in the reign of Charles II the government really had no greater

---

[1] See p. 271 above, and authorities there cited.
[2] Everitt, *Committee of Kent*, pp. 46 ff.
[3] See p. 336 above.
[4] Quoted by Webb, *English Local Government*, VII (*English Poor History*, pt. I), 321. Extracts from the Act are printed in Browning, *Documents*, p. 464.
[5] Webb, *op. cit.* I (*Parish and County*), 597–9.

control over the composition of the House of Commons than in the reign of Henry VIII.[1]

One solution to this problem was to harness the mounting power of the nobility through the office of lord-lieutenant. Increasingly in the reign of Charles II the lord-lieutenant became the channel through which the patronage available to the Crown—magistracies, deputy lieutenancies, advantageous leases of Crown lands, governorships of forts and castles, and so on—was distributed in each county, and appropriate care was taken with his selection.[2] In the sixteenth century the duties of the lieutenant had been almost exclusively military; he had been responsible for raising, training and leading into battle the county militia; but he had been a district rather than a county officer, with no necessary connection with the shire to which he was appointed. Moreover, prior to 1642 many counties did not have a lieutenant at all. After 1660 he retained his military function, of course, but this tended to be overshadowed by his civilian duties; he was at once the king's spokesman in the county and the county's spokesman at court. Almost invariably he was a substantial landowner in the county to which he was appointed, and preferably a member of an old-established family. Removable only on grounds of lunacy or gross disloyalty, he, his deputy-lieutenants and the justices of the *quorum*[3] formed a remarkably well-organised and resistant core of local government. A man with the prestige of the duke of Norfolk was almost supreme in his dukedom, able, with a suitable show of consultation, to choose parliamentary candidates at will, and able, too, to give the leadership badly needed by the gentry in periods of national crisis (**145**).

Between 1680 and 1688 the Crown made a determined effort to regain its position in the localities, and this was not the least important cause of the Revolution. In the winter and spring of 1680 known adherents of the Exclusionist Opposition were dismissed from their magistracies in numbers unheard-of since 1661,[4] and this purge continued after the dissolution of the Oxford Parliament in 1681 and was extended to the lieutenancies and deputy-lieutenancies. The Corporation Act was stringently enforced, perhaps for the first time since 1664, and proceedings under writs of *quo warranto* were taken against the charters of many parliamentary corporations.[5] The confiscation

---

[1] Exceptions are more apparent than real. For instance, in 1685 the government made a great effort in a number of boroughs, but it owed its majority to the enthusiastic support of the upper classes more than anything. See R. H. George, 'Elections and Electioneering in 1685', *Transactions Royal Historical Society*, 4th ser., XIX (1936), 167. It is worth noticing that even in 1685 the government could not place its servants at will (*CSPD, 1685*, nos. 92, 381, 393, 410, 489, 520).

[2] A. Browning, 'Parties and Party Organisation in the Reign of Charles II', *Transactions Royal Historical Society*, 4th ser. XXX (1947), 21.

[3] Elton, *Tudor Constitution*, pp. 452–3, 456–7.

[4] Jones, *First Whigs*, p. 120.

[5] R. H. George, 'Notes on the Bill of Rights', *American Historical Review*, XLIII (1937), 670, and 'The Charters Granted to English Parliamentary Corporations in 1688', *EHR*, LV (1940), 47.

of London's charter in 1683 terrified many others into surrender, and the beneficial results were to be seen in the parliament of 1685.

James II, using similar techniques, made a determined bid to secure parliamentary support for his pro-Catholic policy. In October 1686 a select committee of Council was appointed to revise the magistracy, and over the next five months nearly half the justices of peace in England and Wales were replaced. A year later the lord-lieutenants were requested to put to the deputy-lieutenants and justices in their county the notorious Three Questions: would they live in amity with their neighbours, of whatever religious persuasion; if elected to Parliament, would they support the repeal of the Test Acts; or would they support the election of candidates so minded? Most of those who replied in the negative to the last two questions—as well as many lord-lieutenants who refused to put them at all—were dismissed, constituting a second purge of local government within a year.[1] At the same time the new charters issued since 1681 enabled the king to 'regulate' a large proportion of the parliamentary corporations by dismissing their members and officers.

But it is apparent that James's government was hampered at every turn by lack of information on the localities. This had been one of the primary difficulties of government throughout the century, and it is significant that under Charles II the Committee for Foreign Affairs, the most important government junta, was given the task of gathering and collating information from the provinces, mainly from assize judges or justices of peace.[2] It is true that James II's own purges, of the judiciary as well as the magistracy, had cut off many reliable sources of information, but to a great extent it was a problem he had inherited.[3] It is apparent, for instance, that no seventeenth-century government even possessed a record of the various parliamentary boroughs and their franchises; nor did the House of Commons. As a result in 1688 a determined effort was made for the first time in the modern era to secure this and similar information. In April 1688 agents were despatched from London to recruit support for the government in the localities and establish correspondents in each town and county who would disseminate government propaganda, verbal and printed. They were asked to report on the parliamentary franchise and the local leaders who got out the vote, the effectiveness of 'regulation', and the loyalty of the customs and excise officers. In August 1688, with an election in the offing, these agents were sent out again (146). Their reports arrived too late to benefit James, and they never seem to have been received into the government archives;[4] so after the Revolution govern-

<hr>

[1] Macaulay, *History*, I, 747 ff.; Kenyon, *Nobility in the Revolution*, pp. 7–8.
[2] See p. 478 above. [3] Kenyon, *Sunderland*, pp. 187 ff.
[4] Some disappeared, others remained in the possession of William Bridgeman, under-secretary to the Southern Department. These are now in the Bodleian Library, and were published by Sir George Duckett, q.v.

ments were in the same state of ignorance as their predecessors. On the other hand, though James's electoral activities and his interference in local government were sharply criticised in William's Declaration of 30 September 1688, the Bill of Rights contained no direct reference to them, and no legislation was passed to prevent a recurrence.[1] It was clearly felt that James's activities had been so unconventional and contrary to custom that they could be safely ignored.

142. The Book of Orders, 5 January 1631

Orders and Directions, together with a Commission for the better administration of justice and more perfect information of his Majesty, how and by whom the laws and statutes tending to the relief of the poor, the well-ordering and training up of youth in trades, and the reformation of disorders and disordered persons are executed throughout the kingdom. . . .

[The Commission.]

Charles, by the Grace of God. . . [etc.], to. . . [all the members of the Privy Council], Greeting.

Whereas divers good laws and statutes, most necessary for these times, have during the happy reign of Queen Elizabeth and of our late Father of blessed memory, and since our coming to the crown of England, been with great wisdom, piety and policy made and enacted in Parliament, as well for the charitable relief of aged and impotent poor people, not able by their labours to get their livings, and for the training up of youth in honest and profitable trades and mysteries, by putting them forth to be apprentices, as also for the setting to work of idle persons, who being of ability to work in some kind or other do nevertheless refuse to labour, and either wander up and down the city and country begging, or which is worse, maintain themselves by filching and stealing; and for the punishment of sundry rogues and vagabonds, and setting of them to work; and for the suppressing of that odious and loathsome sin of drunkenness, and the repressing of idleness, the root of so many evils, the due execution of which, and the like laws and statutes, would prevent and cut off many offences and crimes of high nature.

And whereas we are informed that the defect of the execution of the

---

[1] Williams, *Eighteenth Century Constitution*, nos. **2, 10**. However, the abortive Corporation Bill of 1690 was designed to protect the boroughs against 'regulation'.

said good and politics laws and constitutions in that behalf made proceedeth especially from the neglect of duty in some of our justices of the peace and other officers...to whom the care and trust of seeing the said laws be put in execution is...principally committed, which remissness and neglect of duty doth grow and arise from this: that by the most of the said laws there are little or no penalties or forfeiture at all inflicted upon the said justices...for not performing their duties in that behalf; or if any be, yet partly by reason of the smallness thereof, and partly by reason of their power and authority in their several places, whereby they hold others under them in awe, there are few or no complaints or informations made of the neglects and want of due execution of the offices of the said justices....And although the care and diligence of our judges and justices of assize be never so great, yet by reason of the shortness of the assizes and sessions in every county, and multiplicity of business, they neither have due information of the said neglects, nor in those times can take such exact courses as were requisite for redress of such general abuses and inconveniences so highly importing the public good of this our realm,...by reason whereof the said justices of peace...are now of late in most parts of this our kingdom grown secure in their said negligence, and the said politic and necessary laws and statutes laid aside or little regarded, as laws of small use or consequence....

Know ye therefore that we...have constituted, authorised and appointed you to be our Commissioners, and by these presents do... strictly require you,...either by examination upon oath, or by all and every such good and lawful means as to you...shall seem convenient and requisite from time to time henceforth, to make inquiries, and thereby to inform yourselves how all and every the laws and statutes now in force which any way concern the relief of impotent or poor people,...the punishment or setting to work of rogues and vagabonds, ...the repressing of drunkenness and idleness, the reforming of abuses committed in inns and alehouses,...the keeping of watches and wards duly, and how other public services for God, the King and the Commonwealth, are put into practice and executed....

* * * * * *

And we do further by these presents give full power and authority unto you, or any six or more of you, to call unto you for your assistance in the premises...all or any of our justices of assize,...and to give such directions and instructions...as well to our said justices of assize, oyer and terminer and gaol delivery for their several circuits, as also to our justices, mayors, bailiffs and other head officers within cities and boroughs, clerks of the assize and sessions, and other officers...as to you...shall seem meet and requisite and shall be agreeable to the laws and statutes of this our realm, for the better execution of the laws and statutes in the time to come....

And we do hereby further will and require you, that you...give unto us a particular and true information of the care and industry of our justices of the peace...as upon the said inquiry you shall find diligent in putting the said laws, statutes, orders and directions in execution;...and if contrariwise you shall find any of our said justices of peace...negligent and remiss in their...performance and execution of the the said laws and statutes committed to their charge, or the orders and directions given by you,...then our pleasure is that you do likewise certify the names of such as you shall find so remiss and negligent, that accordingly order may be taken for their removing and displacing out of the Commission of the Peace, as men unworthy of their said trust and places, as also deserving such further punishment in our court of Star Chamber or otherwise as may by law be inflicted upon them.

*　　*　　*　　*　　*　　*

[The Commissioners were authorised to appoint deputies in every county and borough.]

Orders

I

That the justices of peace of every shire within the realm do divide themselves, and allot amongst themselves what justices of the peace, and what hundreds, shall attend monthly at some certain places of the shire. And at this day and place the high constables, petty constables and churchwardens and overseers for the poor of those hundreds shall attend the said justices. And there inquiry shall be made and information taken by the justices how every of these officers in their several places have done their duties in execution of the laws mentioned in the commission annexed, and what persons have offended against any of the said laws.

499

II

Where neglect or defect is found in any of the said officers in making their presentments condign punishment [is] to be inflicted upon them by the justices according to law.

*   *   *   *   *   *

V

For encouragement to men that do inform and prosecute others for offending against these laws or any of them, liberty [is] to be left to the justices of peace…to reward the informer or prosecutor out of part of the money levied upon his or their presentments or information.

Though the statute[s] do not prescribe this, yet this is not against the law that gives the penalty to the poor, which penalty nor no part thereof would else come unto the poor but by this means.

VI

That the several justices of peace of every shire do once every three months certify and account in writing to the high sheriff of the county of their proceedings in this way.…

VII

That the high sheriff, within fourteen days after this account delivered, do send the same over to the justices of assize for that county, or to one of them, and the justice or justices that receive the same [are] to certify it in the beginning of every term next after to the lords commissioners.…

Directions

*   *   *   *   *   *

II

That stewards to lords and gentlemen, in keeping their leets twice a year, do specially inquire upon those articles that tend to the reformation and punishment of common offences and abuses: as of bakers and brewers, for breaking of assizes; of forestallers and regraters; against tradesmen of all sorts for selling with underweights or at excessive prices, or things unwholesome, or things made in deceit; of people, breakers of houses, common thieves and their receivers; haunters of taverns or alehouses; those that go in good clothes and fare well, and none knows whereof they live; those that be night walkers; builders of cottages and takers in of inmates; offences of victuallers, artificers, workmen and labourers.

* * * * * *

V

That the weekly taxations for relief of the poor...be in these times of scarcity raised to higher rates in every parish than in times tofore were used; and contributions had from other parishes to help the weaker parishes, especially from those places where depopulations have been....

* * * * * *

IX

If in any parish there be found any persons that live out of service, or that live idly and will not work for reasonable wages, or live to spend all they have at the alehouse, those persons to be brought by the high constables and petty constables to the justices at their meeting, there to be ordered and punished as shall be found fit.

X

That the correction houses in all counties may be made adjoining to the common prisons, and the gaoler to be made governor of them, that so he may employ to work prisoners committed for final causes, and so they may learn honestly by labour, and not live idly and miserably long in prison, whereby they are made worse when they come out than they were when they went in....

XI

That no man harbour rogues in their [sic] barns or out-housings; and the wandering persons with women and children [are] to give account to the constable or justice of peace where they were married, and where their children were christened; for these people live like savages, neither marry, nor bury nor christen, which licentious liberty makes so many delight to be rogues and wanderers.

* * * * * *

143. A proclamation commanding the gentry to keep their residence at their mansions in the country, and forbidding them to make their habitations in London and places adjoining, 20 June 1632

The King's most excellent Majesty hath observed that of late years a great number of the nobility and gentry, and abler sort of his people, with their families, have resorted to the cities of London and Westminster, and places adjoining, and there made their residence more than in former times, contrary to the ancient usage of the English nation, which hath occasioned divers inconveniences. For where[as] by their residence and abiding in the several counties where their means ariseth, they served the King in several places according to their degree and ranks, in aid of the government, whereby, and by their housekeeping in those parts, the realm was defended and the meaner sort of people were guided, directed and relieved; but by their residence in the said cities...they have not employment, but live without doing any service to his Majesty or his people, a great part of their money and substance is drawn from the several counties whence it ariseth, and is spent in the city in excess of apparel provided from foreign parts, to the enriching of other nations and unnecessary consumption of a great part of the treasure of this realm, and in other delights and expenses, even to the wasting of their estates, which is not issued into the parts whence it ariseth, nor are the people of them relieved therewith or by their hospitality, nor yet set on work, as they might and would be were it not for the absence of the principal men out of their counties, and the excessive use of foreign commodities. By this occasion also...the prices of all kind of victuals, both in the said cities and divers other places from whence those cities are served are exceedingly increased, and the several counties undefended, the poorer sort are unrelieved, and not guided or governed as they might be in case those persons of quality and respect resided among them.

* * * * * *

Therefore his Majesty doth straitly charge and command his lords, both spiritual and temporal, the lieutenants and deputy-lieutenants of counties, justices assigned for conservation of the peace, baronets, knights, esquires and gentlemen, and clerks having benefices with cure, or prebends or dignities in cathedral or collegiate churches, and all other his Majesty's subjects of the several parts of the realm that have mansion houses and places of residence in other parts, and are not of his Majesty's Council, or bound to daily attendance on his Highness, his dearest consort the Queen, or their children, that before the end of forty days next after the publishing of this proclamation...they with their families depart from the cities of London and Westminster, suburbs and liberties thereof, and places adjoining, and resort to the several counties where they usually resided, and there keep their habitations and hospitality, attend their services, and be ready for the defence and guidance of those parts, as their callings, degrees and abilities shall extend, upon such pains as are to be inflicted upon those that shall neglect the public service and defence of the realm, in contempt of his Majesty's royal command; and that as well those hereby commanded to return to their several counties as those which are already there do upon the same pains continue the residence of themselves and their families there....

And...his Majesty doth charge and command the lord mayor of the city of London, and the aldermen...and the justices...that every of them make special observation of all those that shall be disobedient to this our command, and from time to time present their names to some of our counsel learned, whom we do command to take due examination or notice of the qualities of their offences, and to cause prosecution to be had against them in our court of Star Chamber, or any other our courts of justice, as the case shall require....

Finally, his Majesty doth hereby declare, that it is his firm resolution to withstand this great and growing evil by all just ways, and by a constant severity towards the offenders in that behalf; for which cause his Majesty doth give this timely warning that none do hereafter presume to offend, nor put themselves to unnecessary charge in providing themselves to return in winter to the said cities and places adjacent, but that they conform themselves to this his royal commandment as they tender their duties to his Majesty, or the good and welfare of their counties and themselves. *Foedera*, XIX, 374–6

144. The Game Act, 1671

22 & 23 Car. II, c. 25: *An Act for the better preservation of the game and for securing warrens not enclosed and the several fishings of this realm*

Whereas divers disorderly persons, laying aside their lawful trades and employments, do betake themselves to the stealing, taking and

killing of conies,[1] hares, pheasants, partridges and other game intended
to be preserved by former laws, with guns, dogs, tramells,[2] lowbells,[3]
hays,[4] and other nets, snares, hare-pipes and other engines, to the great
damage of this realm, and prejudice of noblemen, gentlemen and lords
of manors and other owners of warrens; for remedy whereof be it
enacted...that all lords of manors or other royalties not under the
degree of esquire may from henceforth by writings under their hands
and seals authorise one or more gamekeeper or gamekeepers within
their respective manors or royalties, who...may take and seize all such
guns, bows, greyhounds, setting dogs, lurchers or other dogs to kill
hares or conies, ferrets, trammels, lowbells, hays or other nets, hare-
pipes, snares or other engines for the taking and killing of conies, hares,
pheasants, partridges or other game as within the precincts of such
respective manors shall be used by any person or persons who by this
Act are prohibited to keep or use the same. And moreover that the
said gamekeeper or gamekeepers...may in the daytime search the
houses, outhouses or other places of any such person or persons by this
Act prohibited to keep or use the same, as upon good ground shall be
suspected to have or keep in his or their custody any guns, bows...
[dogs, nets, etc., as above], and the same...to seize, detain and keep,
to and for the use of the lord of the manor..., or otherwise to cut in
pieces or destroy, as things by this Act prohibited to be kept by persons
of their degree.

II. And it is hereby enacted and declared that all and every person
and persons not having lands and tenements, or some other estate of
inheritance in his own or his wife's right, of the clear yearly value of
one hundred pounds *per annum* or for term of life, or having lease or
leases of ninety-nine years or for any longer term of the clear yearly
value of one hundred and fifty pounds, other than the son and heir
apparent of an esquire, or other person of higher degree, and the owners
and keepers of forests, parks, chases or warrens, being stocked with
deer or conies for their necessary use..., are hereby declared to be
persons by the laws of this realm not allowed to have or keep for themselves or any other person or persons any guns, bows...[dogs, nets,
etc., as above], but shall be and are hereby prohibited to have, keep or
use the same.

[1] Rabbits.
[2] A semi-permanent net, with side walls and a roof; for birds.
[3] A bell used to lure birds at night.   [4] A specialised kind of rabbit net.

[§§ III–IV made it an offence to take rabbits in or near warrens; for offences committed in the warren itself the punishment was treble damages and three months' imprisonment. §§ VI–VII made it an offence to fish protected rivers, weirs, fishponds, etc., and gave justices power to destroy the offenders' equipment.]

VIII. Provided always...that if any person or persons shall find him or themselves aggrieved by any judgement that shall happen to be given by any justice of the peace by virtue of this Act, it shall and may be lawful for such person or persons so aggrieved to appeal unto the justices of peace in their general Quarter Sessions....And such judgement, order or determination as by the said justices shall be made upon the said appeal shall be final to all intents and purposes whatsoever, if no title to land, royalty or fishery be therein concerned.

IX. Provided always...that neither this Act nor anything therein contained shall extend or be construed to extend to the taking away or abridging of any royalty or prerogative royal of his Majesty, nor to abridge, change or alter any part of the Forest Laws of this realm....

SR, v, 745–6

145. A duke in his dukedom

[Henry Howard, third duke of Norfolk in the second creation, had conformed to the Church of England in 1679, the rest of his great family remaining Catholic. He was already lord-lieutenant of Surrey and Berkshire in 1683, when he was also appointed to Norfolk in an attempt to reunite that county after the disastrous feuds of the 1670's.[1] His secretary, Francis Negus, wrote from London to Edward l'Estrange, clerk to the lieutenancy of Norfolk, a few days after the death of Charles II.]

[10 February 1685.]

Now that his Majesty hath declared he will call a parliament (and 'tis believed the beginning of May) my lord duke thinks it fit there should be early thoughts had thereof, and commands me to write to you that you do as soon as may be desire the deputy-lieutenants that they will speedily meet in their several divisions and consult the rest of the justices of the peace and militia officers and gentry, in order to the fixing on fit representatives, and more particularly for knights of the county, which being communicated at a general meeting they may so resolve on two persons as may carry it without opposition....When

[1] See J. R. Jones, 'The First Whig Party in Norfolk', *Durham University Journal*, XLVI (1953), 13, and R. W. Ketton-Cremer, 'The End of the Pastons', in *Norfolk Portraits* (London, 1944).

the gentry have met, they will please to let my lord duke hear from them. ...

His grace being well assured of Lord Townshend's interest, desires his lordship may be consulted, and his grace desires those near Sir John Holland will take him in at their meetings.

Norfolk Records Society, xxx (1961), 63

[Two days later Negus sent on a report of events in Surrey, obviously as a model for the Norfolk gentry.]

[12 February 1685.]

His grace desired them [the Surrey gentry] to agree amongst themselves to nominate persons that they thought fit to stand for knights, and when they had named three his grace desired they would let their names be written in so many pieces of papers as there were gentlemen who had voices, and that every one would mark two of this [*sic*] and then fold up the papers and put them in a hat, which being mingled together were opened and counted, and by that means the two that had most voices were resolved on, and everyone declared he would make his interest unanimous for those two, . . . which in all probability may be a means to prevent any contest, nor can anything be more fair, because my lord would by no means nominate who should stand, and his grace is to meet those of Berkshire tomorrow. ...

HMC, 11th Report, vii, 106

[L'Estrange's minutes, 26 February 1685.]

The deputy-lieutenants . . . being met at the Grand Jury Chamber in the Castle at Norwich with above 100 of the chief gentlemen from all parts of this county, his grace's letter was read, as follows:

London, 21 February 1685

Gentlemen,

I am very sorry my occasions will not permit me to be in Norfolk by the time you have appointed for a general meeting, . . . which I would by no means have deferred; for though I hope the King will find our county of Norfolk so unanimous that we shall have no opposition made to those that will be named, yet it is good in these cases to be as early as we can; and as I am very sure that you will think of none but such as have approved themselves fit for such a trust, you may be sure that I shall readily concur to whatever you among yourselves shall approve of....

After the reading of the aforesaid letter Sir Thomas Hare and Sir Jacob Astley were unanimously agreed upon...to be recommended to the county,...and accordingly a paper was subscribed by them all to serve Sir Thomas Hare and Sir Jacob Astley with their entire interests at the next election, an account whereof was given to his Grace by his deputy-lieutenants. *Norfolk Records Society*, xxx, 65–6

[Rather than accept James II's revision of the magistracy and the lieutenancy in 1688, the duke went to France; but he was not dismissed from his post, and he returned in time to take part in the Revolution.]

[Minutes, 3 December 1688.]

Pursuant to orders received from his grace, the deputy-lieutenants, militia officers and other gentlemen[1] were summoned to attend his grace at Lin Regis [King's Lynn] the 7th...December by 9 of the clock in the forenoon; who appeared accordingly and accompanied his grace into the market place, where the mayor of Lin, being attended by the aldermen and a great number of people, made this following speech to his grace:

My Lord,

The daily alarms we receive as well from foreign as domestic enemies give us just apprehensions of approaching dangers, which press us to apply with all earnestness to your grace as our great patron, in a humble confidence to succeed in our expectations that we may be put into such a posture by your grace's direction and conduct as may make us appear as zealous as any in the defence of the Protestant religion, the laws and ancient government of the kingdom, being the desire of many hundreds amongst us who most humbly challenge a right for your grace's protection.

[The duke replied.]

I am very much obliged to you and the rest of the body and those here present for your good opinion of me and the confidence you have that I will do what in me lies to support and defend your laws and liberties and the Protestant religion,

---

[1] Who had all paraded at Norwich on the 1st.

which I will never deceive you in. And since the coming of the prince of Orange has given us an opportunity to declare for the defence of them, I can only assure you that no man will venture his life more freely for the defence of the laws, liberty and Protestant religion than I will do....

The same day the duke issued orders for the militia horse and foot to move to Lynn. *Ibid.* pp. 94–5

[13 December 1688.]

His grace the duke of Norfolk having an account that the King was withdrawn from Whitehall, went away for London, and ordered summons[es] to be sent to his deputy-lieutenants and other gentlemen to attend at Norwich upon Saturday the 15th instant to be ready to receive such orders as should then be sent.

[15 December.]

His grace hearing that the Irish were coming towards Norfolk came back to Thetford, and ordered that his troop of militia horse which was then upon duty at Norwich should forthwith march to Thetford....

The same day towards night the following letter was received from his grace and communicated to the gentlemen at Norwich:

Gentlemen,

I suppose it is no news to you that the King is come back to London and that there is a very fair prospect of all things being settled by a Parliament....I am resolved to go for London, but being informed from thence that all people flock in great numbers thither upon this great occasion, I have deferred my journey till Monday morning [17th] to expect the company of such gentlemen whose own curiosity or the desire that the county of Norfolk may appear as numerous and in as handsome a posture as other counties will strive to do, will incline to keep me company, which though I might be thought to have some private interest in, and that I may take a great deal of pride to appear accompanied by so many worthy and honest gentlemen, who have never left me and whom I will never forsake, I assure you I would not move this if your own and your county's honour were not in my opinion concerned in it as much as...[mine]. *Ibid.* pp. 96–7

146. Instructions for those that shall go into Wales[1]

1. You shall make the King's Declaration[2] the chief subject of your discourse with such persons as you shall think fit to speak with. . . .

2. You must make it your principal care to settle the minds of people, especially of those that are designed for Members of Parliament, or such who do or are likely to come up to the King's measures in relation to the penal laws and tests, against all endeavours which may be made by the King's adversaries for diverting the effects of his good intentions. And it being very probable that when Parliament shall meet this will chiefly be endeavoured by some indirect means, as by attempting to make some difference between the King and his two Houses of Parliament, or either of them, or by starting somewhat which may be a dispute between the two Houses, you are particularly to forewarn and caution all persons who are likely to be Members against this artifice.

3. You are to assure those that are of the Church of England that his Majesty will maintain the same according to his word.

4. You are to engage all people of what persuasion soever to live friendly together, as becomes fellow subjects, disposing them to unite their endeavours to render effectual his Majesty's gracious intentions for their ease and advantage; and you are to tell them that his Majesty will favour them most as shall be of that peaceable disposition as to sacrifice all private animosities to the public good.

5. You are to remove as much as may be all fears and jealousies out of people's hearts, by telling them his Majesty designs only the universal happiness of all his people.

6. You are to make acquaintance with the leading, active and interested men in the county, or in the towns and corporations, who are inclinable to abrogate the penal laws for religion, and the tests, and engage them to improve their interest for effecting it.

7. You are to inform yourself (as privately as may be) whether the persons proposed to be chosen, by the list given you, be right-principled, and so disposed to part with the laws as [they] may be depended on.

8. You are to inform yourself whether the regulations made in the respective corporations have been of proper persons for his Majesty's service.

[1] The instructions for those going into England (Duckett, I, 194–7) are longer but less specific.
[2] For liberty of conscience, no. 115, p. 410 above.

9. You are to inform yourself who are the electors in the respective corporations and boroughs, and by what manner elections are made, who influences them, and who are fittest to be chosen in those places where none are yet proposed.

10. You are to inform yourself of the behaviour of the officers of the several branches of his Majesty's revenue in relation to elections, whether they promote his Majesty's interest as they ought to do, and further what in them lies the repeal of the penal laws and tests.

11. [You are] to acquaint yourselves with the preachers of the Dissenting congregations, and to encourage them to employ their interest for the abrogating those laws and tests, and if you find any of them dissatisfied, inquire who they correspond with in London and give them notice of it.

12. [You are] to inform yourself of some fit person in each corporation with whom a correspondence may be held for the knowledge of the true state of the same, and to whom books and pamphlets may be sent, to disperse them for the people's better information.

13. You are from time to time to advise with the Catholic gentlemen.

14. You are likewise to inform those you converse with that liberty of conscience hath been the cause of the Hollanders' great trade, riches and power, etc.

15. You shall take care to make all persons understand that the late proceedings against the bishops were necessary to support his Majesty's Declaration for liberty of conscience, which the King will always maintain, as likewise his prerogative on which it is founded.

16. That their disobedience and their petition were designed only to obstruct the meeting of Parliament, and to prevent the establishing of what they apprehend, etc., which is so far from discouraging his Majesty that he is more resolved than ever to pursue this great work, not doubting to effect it, whatsoever opposition he may meet with.

Duckett, Penal Laws, I, 197–9

BIBLIOGRAPHY

The following are books cited hitherto by a short title or the name of the author only. Among them are a few articles cited more than once in the footnotes.

Abbott, W. C. (ed.) *The Writings and Speeches of Oliver Cromwell*, 4 vols. Cambridge (Mass.), 1937–47.

Ashley, M. P. *Financial and Commercial Policy under the Cromwellian Protectorate.* Oxford, 1934.

Ashton, R. *The Crown and the Money Market, 1603–1640.* Oxford, 1960.

Aveling, H. *Post Reformation Catholicism in East Yorkshire, 1558–1790.* East Yorks Local History Society, 1960.

—— 'The Catholic Recusants of the West Riding of Yorkshire, 1558–1790', *Proceedings of the Leeds Philosophical and Literary Society*, vol. x, 1963.

Aylmer, G. E. *The King's Servants: the Civil Service of Charles I, 1625–1642.* London, 1961.

Babbage, S. B. *Puritanism and Richard Bancroft.* London, 1962.

Barnes, T. G. *Somerset, 1625–1640: a County's Government during the 'Personal Rule'.* Oxford, 1961.

Baxter, S. B. *The Development of the Treasury, 1660–1714.* London, 1957.

Beales, A. C. F. *Education under Penalty: English Catholic Education from the Reformation to the Fall of James II.* London, 1963.

Bell, H. E. *An Introduction to the History and Records of the Court of Wards and Liveries.* Cambridge, 1953.

Birdsall, P. '*Non obstante*—a Study of the Dispensing Power of English Kings', in *Essays in History and Political Theory in Honor of Charles Howard McIlwain.* Cambridge (Mass.), 1936.

Bosher, R. S. *The Making of the Restoration Settlement: the Influence of the Laudians, 1649–1662.* London, 1951.

Bowyer, R. *The Parliamentary Diary of Robert Bowyer, 1606–1607*, ed. D. H. Willson. Minneapolis, 1931.

Browning, A. *Thomas Osborne Earl of Danby*, 3 vols. Glasgow, 1944–51.

—— (ed.) *English Historical Documents, 1660–1714.* London, 1953.

Brunton, D. and Pennington, D. H. *Members of the Long Parliament.* London, 1954.

Burton, T. *Diary of Thomas Burton, Esq., Member in the Parliaments of Oliver and Richard Cromwell*, 4 vols. London, 1828.

Cardwell, E. (ed.) *Documentary Annals of the Reformed Church of England*, 2 vols. Oxford, 1844.

Cardwell, E. (ed.) *Synodalia: a Collection of Articles of Religion, Canons and Proceedings of Convocations in the Province of Canterbury*, 2 vols. Oxford, 1842.

Clarendon, Edward Hyde, Earl of. *History of the Rebellion and Civil Wars in England*, ed. W. D. Macray. 6 vols. Oxford, 1888.

Coke, Sir Edward. *The Reports of Sir Edward Coke*, ed. J. H. Thomas and J. F. Frazer, 13 pts. in 6 vols. London, 1826.

Commons, House of. *Commons Debates, 1621*, ed. W. Notestein, F. H. Relf and H. Simpson, 7 vols. New Haven, 1935.

—— *Debates in the House of Commons in 1625*, ed. S. R. Gardiner. Camden Society, 1873.

Costin, W. C. and Watson, J. S. (eds.) *The Law and Working of the Constitution: Documents, 1660–1914*, 2 vols. London, 1952.

Curtis, M. H. *Oxford and Cambridge in Transition, 1558–1642*. Oxford, 1959.

D'Ewes, Sir Simonds. *The Autobiography and Correspondence of Sir Simonds d'Ewes*, ed. J. O. Halliwell, 2 vols. London, 1845.

—— *The Journal of Sir Simonds d'Ewes from the Beginning of the Long Parliament to the Opening of the Trial of the Earl of Strafford*, ed. W. Notestein. New Haven, 1923.

—— *The Journal of Sir Simonds d'Ewes from the First Recess of the Long Parliament to the Withdrawal of King Charles from London*, ed. W. H. Coates. New Haven, 1942.

Dietz, F. C. *English Public Finance, 1558–1641*. London, 1932.

Duckett, Sir George (ed.) *Penal Laws and Test Act, 1687–1688*, 2 vols. London, 1882.

Elton, G. R. (ed.) *The Tudor Constitution: Documents and Commentary*. Cambridge, 1960.

Evans, F. M. G. *The Principal Secretary of State: a Survey of the Office from 1558 to 1680*. Manchester, 1923.

Everitt, A. M. *The County Committee of Kent in the Civil War*. Leicester, 1957.

—— *Suffolk and the Great Rebellion, 1640–1660*. Suffolk Records Society, 1960.

Every, G. *The High Church Party, 1688–1718*. London, 1956.

Filmer, Sir Robert. *Patriarcha and Other Political Works*, ed. P. Laslett. Oxford, 1949.

Finch, M. E. *The Wealth of Five Northamptonshire Families, 1540–1640*. Northants Record Society, 1956.

Firth, C. H. *Cromwell's Army*, 4th ed. London, 1962.

—— *The House of Lords during the Civil War*. London, 1910.

—— *The Last Years of the Protectorate*, 2 vols. London, 1909.

Firth, C. H. and Rait, R. S. (eds.) *Acts and Ordinances of the Interregnum, 1642–1660*, 3 vols. London, 1911.

Fisher, F. J. (ed.) *Essays in the Economic and Social History of Tudor and Stuart England in Honour of R. H. Tawney.* Cambridge, 1961.

Foedera, conventiones, literae et cuiuscunque generis acta publica, ed. T. Rymer and R. Sanderson, 20 vols. London, 1704–32.

Forster, J. *Sir John Eliot,* 2 vols. London, 1865.

Fuller, T. *The Church History of Britain,* ed. J. Nichols, 3 vols. London, 1868.

Gardiner, S. R. *History of England from the Accession of James I to the Outbreak of Civil War, 1603–1642,* 10 vols. London, 1883–4.

—— *History of the Great Civil War,* 4 vols. London, 1893.

—— *History of the Commonwealth and Protectorate,* 3 vols. London, 1894–1901.

—— (ed.) *Notes of the Debates in the House of Lords.* Camden Society, 1879.

—— *Parliamentary Debates in 1610.* Camden Society, 1862.

—— *Reports of Cases in the Courts of Star Chamber and High Commission.* Camden Society, 1886.

George, C. H. and K. *The Protestant Mind of the English Reformation, 1570–1640.* Princeton, 1961.

Godbolt, J. *Reports of Certain Cases Arising in the Several Courts of Record at Westminster.* London, 1652.

Grey, A. (ed.) *Debates of the House of Commons from the Year 1667 to the Year 1694,* 10 vols. London, 1769.

Haller, W. *The Rise of Puritanism.* New York, 1938.

—— *Liberty and Reformation in the Puritan Revolution.* New York, 1955.

Haller, W. and Davies, G. (eds.) *The Leveller Tracts 1647–1653.* New York, 1944.

Hardacre, P. H. *The Royalists during the Puritan Revolution.* The Hague, 1956.

Havighurst, A. F. 'The Judiciary and Politics in the reign of Charles II', *Law Quarterly Review,* LXVI (1950), 62, 229 (2 pts.).

—— 'James II and the Twelve Men in Scarlet', *ibid.* LXIX (1953), 522.

Havran, M. J. *The Catholics in Caroline England.* Stanford, 1962.

Hemphill, B. *The Early Vicars Apostolic of England.* London, 1954.

Hexter, J. H. *The Reign of King Pym.* Cambridge (Mass.), 1941.

Hill, C. *Economic Problems of the Church from Archbishop Whigift to the Long Parliament.* Oxford, 1956.

—— *Puritanism and Revolution.* London, 1958.

—— *Society and Puritanism in pre-Revolutionary England.* London, 1964.

Holdsworth, W. S. *A History of English law,* 14 vols. London, 1922–64.

Hughes, E. *Studies in Administration and Finance, 1558–1825.* Manchester, 1934.

Hulme, H. *The Life of Sir John Eliot, 1592–1632: Struggle for Parliamentary Freedom.* London, 1957.

Hurstfield, J. *The Queen's Wards.* London, 1958.

James I, King. *Works.* London, 1616.

Jones, J. R. *The First Whigs: the Politics of the Exclusion Crisis, 1678–1683.* London, 1961.

Jordan, W. K. *Philanthropy in England, 1480–1660.* London, 1959.

Judson, M. A. *The Crisis of the Constitution: an Essay in Constitutional and Political Thought in England, 1603–1645.* New Brunswick (N.J.), 1949.

Kearney, H. F. *The Eleven Years' Tyranny of Charles I.* Historical Association, London, 1962.

Keeler, M. F. *The Long Parliament, 1640–1641.* Philadelphia, 1954.

Keeton, G. W. *Lord Chancellor Jeffreys and the Stuart Cause.* London, 1965.

—— *Trial for Treason.* London, 1959.

Kennedy, W. *English Taxation, 1640–1799.* London, 1913.

Kenyon, J. P. *The Nobility in the Revolution of 1688.* Hull, 1963.

—— *Robert Spencer Earl of Sunderland.* London, 1958.

—— *The Stuarts.* London, 1958.

Laud, W. *Sermons,* ed. J. W. Hatherell. London, 1829.

—— *Works,* ed. W. Scott and J. Bliss, 7 vols. Oxford, 1847–60.

Lords, House of. *See* Gardiner *and* Relf.

Macaulay, T. B. *History of England from the Accession of James II,* 3 vols. (Everyman ed.). London, 1906.

Macpherson, C. B. *The Political Theory of Possessive Individualism.* Oxford, 1962.

Magee, B. *The English Recusants: a Study of the Post-Reformation Catholic Survival and the Operation of the Recusancy Laws.* London, 1938.

Maguire, M. H. 'The Attack of the Common Lawyers on the Oath *ex officio*', in *Essays in History and Political Theory in Honor of Charles Howard McIlwain.* Cambridge (Mass.), 1936.

Makower, F. *The Constitutional History and Constitution of the Church of England.* London, 1895.

Mathew, D. *Catholicism in England: the Portrait of a Minority.* London, 1955.

Miller, P. *Orthodoxy in Massachusetts, 1630–1650.* Cambridge (Mass.), 1933.

Milton, John, *Works,* 18 vols. New York, 1931–8.

Milward, J. *The Diary of John Milward,* ed. C. Robbins. Cambridge, 1938.

Mitchell, W. B. *The Rise of the Revolutionary Party in the English House of Commons, 1603–1629.* New York, 1957.

Moir, T. L. *The Addled Parliament of 1614.* Oxford, 1958.

New, J. F. H. *Anglican and Puritan: the Basis of Their Opposition, 1558–1640.* London, 1964.

North, R. *The Lives of Francis North, Baron Guilford, Sir Dudley North and Dr John North,* ed. A. Jessopp, 3 vols. London, 1890.

Nuttall, G. F. and Chadwick, O. (eds.) *From Uniformity to Unity, 1662–1962.* London, 1962.

Ogg, D. *England in the Reign of Charles II,* 2 vols, 2nd ed. Oxford, 1955.

Ogg, D. *England in the Reigns of James II and William III.* Oxford, 1955.

Paul, R. S. *The Lord Protector: Religion and Politics in the Life of Oliver Cromwell.* London, 1955.

Pennington, D. H. and Roots, I. A. (eds.) *The Committee at Stafford, 1643–1645: the Order Book of the Staffordshire County Committee.* Manchester, 1957.

Petyt, W. *Jus Parliamentarium: or the Ancient Power, Jurisdiction, Rights and Liberties of the Most High Court of Parliament.* London, 1739.

Pocock, J. G. *The Ancient Constitution and the Feudal Law.* Cambridge, 1957.

Relf, F. H. *The Petition of Right.* Minneapolis, 1917.

—— (ed.) *Notes of the Debates in the House of Lords...1621, 1625, 1628.* Camden Society, 1929.

Reresby, Sir John. *Memoirs*, ed. A. Browning. Glasgow, 1936.

Rushworth, J. (ed.), *Historical Collections of Private Passages of State*, 8 vols. London, 1659–1701.

Shaw, W. A. *A History of the English Church during the Civil Wars and under the Commonwealth*, 2 vols. London, 1900.

Solt, L. F. *Saints in Arms: Puritanism and Democracy in Cromwell's Army.* Stanford, 1959.

Somers Tracts. A Collection of Scarce and Valuable Tracts, ed. Sir Walter Scott, 13 vols. London, 1809–15.

Speeches and Passages of This Great and Happy Parliament. London, 1641.

State Tracts...a Collection of Several Treatises Relating to the Government... Now Published in a Body to Show the Necessity and Clear the Legality of the Late Revolution, 2 vols. London, 1693.

Stone, L. *The Crisis of the Aristocracy, 1558–1641.* Oxford, 1965.

Sykes, N. *From Sheldon to Secker: Aspects of English Church History, 1660–1768.* Cambridge, 1959.

Tanner, J. R. *Tudor Constitutional Documents*, 2nd ed. Cambridge, 1930.

Trevor-Roper, H. R. 'Oliver Cromwell and His Parliaments', in *Essays Presented to Sir Lewis Namier*, ed. R. Pares and A. J. P. Taylor. London, 1956.

—— 'Scotland and the Puritan Revolution', in *Historical Essays, 1600–1750.* eds. H. E. Bell and R. L. Ollard. London, 1963.

Trimble, W. R. *The Catholic Laity in Elizabethan England.* Cambridge (Mass.), 1964.

Turner, E. R. *The Cabinet Council of England in the Seventeenth and Eighteenth Centuries, 1622–1784*, 2 vols. Baltimore, 1930–2.

—— *The Privy Council of England in the Seventeenth and Eighteenth Centuries, 1603–1784*, 2 vols. Baltimore, 1927–8.

Usher, R. G. *The Reconstruction of the English Church*, 2 vols. New York, 1910.

Usher, R. G. *The Rise and Fall of High Commission*. Oxford, 1913.

Webb, S. and B. *English Local Government from the Revolution to the Municipal Reform Act*; vol. I, *The Parish and the County*; vols. II–III, *The Manor and the Borough*. London, 1924.

—— *English Poor Law History*, pt. I, *The Old Poor Law*. London, 1927.

Wedgwood, C. V. *The Great Rebellion: the King's Peace, 1637–1641*. London, 1955.

—— *The Great Rebellion: the King's War, 1641–1647*. London, 1958.

—— *Thomas Wentworth First Earl of Strafford, 1593–1641: A Revaluation*. London, 1961.

—— *The Trial of Charles I*. London, 1964.[1]

Weston, C. C. *English Constitutional Theory and the House of Lords, 1556–1832*. London, 1965.

Willcox, W. B. *Gloucestershire: A Study in Local Government, 1590–1640*. New Haven, 1940.

Williams, E. N. *The Eighteenth Century Constitution, 1688–1815: Documents and Commentary*. Cambridge, 1960.

Williams, J. A. *Bath and Rome: the Living Link*. Bath, 1963.

—— 'English Catholicism under Charles II', *Recusant History*, vol. VII, 1963.

—— 'Some Sidelights on Recusancy Finance under Charles II'. *Dublin Review*, autumn 1959.

Willson, D. H. *King James VI and I*. London, 1956.

—— *The Privy Councillors in the House of Commons, 1604–1629*. Minneapolis, 1940.

Woodhouse, A. S. P. (ed.) *Puritanism and Liberty, Being the Army Debates [1647–9]*, 2nd ed. London, 1950.

Wormald, B. H. G. *Clarendon: Politics, History and Religion*. Cambridge, 1951.

Wormuth, F. D. *The Royal Prerogative, 1603–1649*. Ithaca, New York, 1939.

Yule, G. *The Independents in the English Civil War*. Cambridge, 1958.

[1] Published in the U.S.A. under the title *A Coffin for King Charles*.

INDEX

Figures in bold type indicate document numbers